IN THE SHADOW OF REVOLUTION

123 - 131 ✓
169 - 179 ✓
49 - 65 ✓
179 - 181 ✓
33 - 48 ✓
131 - 139 ✓
181 - 206 ✓
213 - 218 ✓
243 - 251 ✓
219 - 234   15 — write about
235 - 240 ✓   this one
277 - 281 ✓   best rep
               of communism

324 - 330   6
367 - 390   23

In the Shadow of Revolution

□ *Life Stories of Russian Women*

FROM 1917 TO THE
SECOND WORLD WAR

EDITED BY
Sheila Fitzpatrick AND Yuri Slezkine

TRANSLATED BY YURI SLEZKINE

Princeton University Press, Princeton, New Jersey

Copyright © 2000 by Princeton University Press
Published by Princeton University Press, 41 William Street,
Princeton, New Jersey 08540
In the United Kingdom: Princeton University Press
Chichester, West Sussex

Library of Congress Cataloging-in-Publication Data

In the shadow of revolution : life stories of Russian women
from 1917 to the second world war / edited by Sheila Fritzpatrick
and Yuri Slezkine ; translated by Yuri Slezkine.
    p.   cm.
Includes bibliographical references and index.
ISBN 0-691-01948-7 (cl : acid-free paper) —
ISBN 0-691-01949-5 (pb : acid-free paper)
1. Women—Soviet Union—Biography
2. Soviet Union—History—1917–1936
3. Soviet Union—History—1925–1953
I. Fitzpatrick, Sheila   II. Slezkine, Yuri, 1956–
DK37.2 .I5 2000
947.084′082—dc21   99-054904

This book has been composed in Times Roman

The paper used in this publication
meets the minimum requirements of
ANSI/NISO Z39.48-1992 (R 1997)
(*Permanence of Paper*)

www.pup.princeton.edu

Printed in the United States of America

10 9 8 7 6 5 4 3 2 1

10 9 8 7 6 5
(pbk.)
ISBN-13: 978-0-691-01949-9 (pbk.)

ISBN-10: 0-691-01949-5 (pbk.)

CONTENTS

PREFACE   vii

ACKNOWLEDGMENTS   ix

INTRODUCTION   3

   Sheila Fitzpatrick, Lives and Times   3
   Yuri Slezkine, Lives as Tales   18

PART I. Civil War as a Way of Life (1917–1920)   31

   1. Ekaterina Olitskaia, *My Reminiscences* (1)   33
   2. Anna Litveiko, *In 1917*   49
   3. P. E. Melgunova-Stepanova, *Where Laughter Is Never Heard*   66
   4. Anna Andzhievskaia, *A Mother's Story*   73
   5. Zinaida Zhemchuzhnaia, *The Road to Exile*   82
   6. Nadezhda Krupskaia, *Autobiography*   111
   7. Tatiana Varsher, *Things Seen and Suffered*   113
   8. Zinaida Patrikeeva, *Cavalry Boy*   118
   9. Irina Elenevskaia, *Recollections*   123
   10. Sofia Volkonskaia, *The Way of Bitterness*   140

PART II. Toward "New Forms of Life" (The 1920s)   167

   11. Agrippina Korevanova, *My Life*   169
   12. Anonymous, *What Am I to Do?*   207
   13. Ekaterina Olitskaia, *My Reminiscences* (2)   209
   14. Paraskeva Ivanova, *Why I Do Not Belong in the Party*   213
   15. Maria Belskaia, *Arina's Children*   219
   16. Antonina Solovieva, *Sent by the Komsomol*   235
   17. Nenila Bazeleva et al., *Peasant Narratives* (1)   241
   18. Anna Balashova, *A Worker's Life*   243
   19. Valentina Bogdan, *Students in the First Five-Year Plan*   252
   20. Alla Kiparenko, *Building the City of Youth*   277
   21. Anna Iankovskaia, *A Belomor Confession*   282
   22. Lidia Libedinskaia, *The Green Lamp*   286

PART III. "Life Has Become Merrier" (The 1930s)   303

   23. Pasha Angelina, *The Most Important Thing*   305
   24. Efrosinia Kislova et al., *Peasant Narratives* (2)   322
   25. Fruma Treivas, *We Were Fighting for an Idea!* 324
   26. N. I. Slavnikova et al., *Speeches by Stakhanovites*   331
   27. Ulianova, *A Cross-Examination*   342

28. Anna Shchetinina, *A Sea Captain's Story*   350
29. Kh. Khuttonen, *Farewell to the Komsomol*   354
30. Anastasia Plotnikova, *Autobiography*   356
31. A. V. Vlasovskaia et al., *Speeches by Stakhanovites' Wives*   359
32. Inna Shikheeva-Gaister, *A Family Chronicle*   367
33. Evdokia Maslennikova, *The Story of My Life*   391
34. Valentina Bogdan, *Memoirs of an Engineer*   394
35. Frida Troib et al., *Engineers' Wives*   419
36. Ekaterina Olitskaia, *My Reminiscences* (3)   424

GLOSSARY   435

INDEX   437

PREFACE

THIS BOOK is a collection of life stories of Russian women in the first half of the twentieth century. The Russian Revolution of 1917 is the great event in whose shadow these women lived—most of them in the Soviet Union, under the regime established by the Bolsheviks in October 1917, but some of them as émigrés outside Russia. The women whose stories we have chosen had a wide range of experiences in the revolution and attitudes to the Soviet regime. Some were politically active, others less so, but the lives of all of them were deeply affected, for good or ill, by the political upheavals of the times.

It is characteristic of twentieth-century Russian women's autobiographies to take their structure not so much from private events like childbirth or marriage but from great public events: the revolution of 1917, the Civil War of 1918–20, the switch to the New Economic Policy in the 1920s, collectivization at the beginning of the 1930s, the Great Terror in 1937–38, the Second World War, starting for Soviet citizens in 1941. Our volume is divided into three parts corresponding to this conventional structure: the first presents stories of the revolution and Civil War, the second of the New Economic Policy (NEP) and collectivization, and the third focuses on Stalinist society of the 1930s, including the Great Terror.

The life stories the authors in this volume tell begin with the revolution (or, in some cases, a prerevolutionary childhood that throws the revolution and its aftermath into sharp relief) and end before the Second World War. Recognizing that all chronological limits are to some extent arbitrary, we chose this cut-off point because the Second World War, like the revolution, was a breakpoint in the lives of many Soviet women.

We have made our selection with a view to maximizing variety with regard to social background, occupation, and political conviction (but not ethnicity, because systematic representation of ethnic/national variety in the multinational Soviet Union would have required a separate volume). The women whose life stories we publish—most of them for the first time in English, some of them directly from newly opened Soviet archives—range from intellectuals of aristocratic birth to Soviet milkmaids, from housewives to engineers, and from Bolshevik activists to dedicated opponents of the Soviet regime. We have also sought to provide examples of the greatest possible range of autobiographical genres: literary memoirs, oral interview, personal dossier, public speech, letters to the editor, and so on. Sheila Fitzpatrick's introduction investigates the social history context of these women's lives, while Yuri Slezkine's discusses the structure of the autobiographical narratives.

Gender was a meaningful category for all our authors, from those who embraced the idea of revolutionary liberation (which sometimes meant dressing and behaving like men) to those who played the traditional role of housewives and helpmates. We made our selection with an eye to illuminating the variety

of meanings Russian women attached to gender and problems they experienced
in connection with it. The revolution promised "liberation" for women: this
meant different things to different people, in different contexts, and at different
times, with something like a conservative reaction to "liberationist" ideology,
symbolized by the reversal of the 1918 law permitting abortion, occurring in
the mid-1930s. We do not believe that there was any single "woman's experience" of the revolution, but rather that there was a range of women's experiences that can usefully be considered apart from those of men. These women
lived in the shadow of revolution, but their life stories—less familiar than
men's, and for that reason all the more valuable—illuminate its meaning.

TRANSLATION

The translator has attempted to preserve the style of the original texts, some of
which are highly formulaic, filled with awkward neologisms, and occasionally
ungrammatical. The excerpt by Sophia Volkonskaia was taken from her own
English translation of the Russian original.

TRANSLITERATION

We have used a modified form of the Library of Congress system, substituting
y for ii and yi endings, dropping the extra i in common names like Maria, and
substituting an i for the soft sign in names like Zinoviev. Diacritical marks are
used in citation of sources but not in the text.

ACKNOWLEDGMENTS

THE EDITORS wish to acknowledge with appreciation the following:

Tsentr dokumentatsii "Narodnyi Arkhiv" (Moscow), for permission to publish memoirs by Treivas and Belskaia;

Elena Iakobson, daughter of Z. Zhemchuzhnaia, and "Hermitage" publishers for permission to publish an extract from Z. Zhemchuzhnaia, *Puti izgnaniia*;

A. I. Dobkin, editor of *Zven'ia*, for permission to publish extracts from "60 let kolkhoznoi zhizni glazami krest'ian";

Valentina Bogdan, for permission to publish extracts from her two books of memoirs, *Studenty pervoi piatiletki* and *Mimikriia v SSSR*;

Possev-Verlag, for permission to publish extracts from E. Olitskaia's memoirs, *Moi vospominaniia*;

Inna Shikheeva-Gaister, for permission to publish extracts from her book, *Semeinaia khronika vremen kul'ta lichnosti*.

We also wish to thank Stephen Bittner for calling our attention to the Maslennikova autobiography; James Andrews, Peter Blitstein, Christopher Burton, Eleonor Gilburd, Brian Kassof, Ethan Pollock, Joshua Sanborn, Jarrod Tanny, and Lisa Walker for research assistance; Lisa Little, for help with the translation; and the Russian Studies Workshop at the University of Chicago, Eric Naiman, and Reginald E. Zelnik for useful criticism of drafts of the introduction.

Paperback cover illustrations, top to bottom, left to right:
V. A. Serov, "Portrait of M. Ia. Lvova," 1895. From I. E. Grabar', *Valentin Aleksandrovich Serov* (Moscow: Knebel, 1913). V. A. Serov, "Portrait of A. Ia. Simonovich," 1899. From N. Ia. Simonovich-Efimova, *Vospominaniia o Valentine Aleksandroviche Serove* (Leningrad: Khudozhniki RSFSR, 1964). G. G. Raizhskii, "A Delegate," 1927. From *50 let sovetskogo iskusstva* (Moscow: Sovetskii khudozhnik, 1967). I. E. Grabar, "Svetlana," 1933. From O. I. Podobedova, *Igor' Emmanuilovich Grabar'* (Moscow: Sovetskii khudozhnik, 1964). N. A. Kasatkin, "Time to Study (A Pioneer Girl with Books)," 1926. From *50 let sovetskogo iskusstva* (Moscow: Sovetskii khudozhnik, 1967). Iu. Pimenov, "Portrait of L. A. Eremina," 1935. From O. M. Beskin, *Iurii Pimenov* (Moscow: Sovetskii khudozhnik, 1960). Z. E. Serebriakova, "Self-portrait," 1924. From Z. I. Serebriakova, *Al'bom reproduktsii* (Moscow: Sovetskii khudozhnik, 1969). A. A. Plastov, "Ekaterina Andreevna Sharymova," 1964. From A. A. Plastov, *Reproduktsii* (Moscow: Sovetskii khudozhnik, 1972).

IN THE SHADOW OF REVOLUTION

☐ SHEILA FITZPATRICK

Lives and Times

WOMEN's autobiography (so recent scholarship tells us)[1] tends to focus on private rather than public matters, favor confession over testimony, show the authors in relation to a significant male Other such as a husband, and even question their right to tell an independent life story. But the life stories told by twentieth-century Russian women scarcely fit this mold. The typical autobiography[2] by a Russian woman in our period (1917–41) belongs to the genre of testimony—bearing witness to the times—not confession; it deals more with public matters than private, familial ones. If there is a preoccupying Other in these stories, it is more likely the state than a husband or father. Russian women often write of themselves as victims, though not usually on account of their gender: they (and their menfolk) are victims of Communism, Capitalism, or simply History. But a surprisingly large number portray themselves and their female relatives as strong women—not dependents but tough and savvy survivors, morally and even physically stronger than their men.[3]

These women seem to have few doubts about their ability to bear witness. Asked shortly after the revolution about how she viewed the new government, Tatiana Varsher, one of our memoirists, replies challengingly: "With the wide-open eyes of a historian." As it happens, Tatiana Varsher actually was a professional historian; but other women express similar sentiments. "I want to write about the way those [revolutionary] events were perceived and reflected in the humble and distant corner of Russia that was the Cossack town of Korenovskaia," writes Zinaida Zhemchuzhnaia; describing a Civil War battle in the town, she notes that "curiosity kept me outside." For other women, the urge to testify comes

---

[1] See, for example, Mary G. Mason, "The Other Voice: Autobiographies of Women Writers," in James Olney, ed., *Autobiography: Essays Theoretical and Critical* (Princeton, N.J.: Princeton Univ. Press, 1980); Shari Benstock, ed., *The Private Self: Theory and Practice of Women's Autobiographical Writings* (Chapel Hill: Univ. of North Carolina Press, 1988); Bella Brodzki and Celeste Schenck, eds., *Life/Lines: Theorizing Women's Autobiography* (Ithaca, N.Y.: Cornell Univ. Press, 1988); Shirley Neuman, ed., *Autobiography and Questions of Gender* (London: Cass, 1991).

[2] I use the term *autobiography* to cover the whole range of writing or speaking about lives, including memoirs, not in the specialized sense of self-exploration proposed by Karl Weintraub in "Autobiography and Historical Consciousness," *Critical Inquiry* (June 1975).

[3] On the "strong woman," see Vera Sandomirsky Dunham, "The Strong-Woman Motif," in Cyril E. Black, ed., *The Transformation of Russian Society: Aspects of Social Change since 1961* (Cambridge, Mass.: Harvard Univ. Press, 1960). On the tensions for women in the revolutionary era between the "masculine" pole of equality/independence and the "feminine" pole of supportiveness/nurturing/dependency, see Elizabeth Wood, *The Baba and the Comrade: Gender and Politics in Revolutionary Russia* (Bloomington: Indiana Univ. Press, 1997). For discussion of the interesting but exceptional case of Nadezhda Mandelstam, a strong and assertive character who presents herself as wife and helpmeet in her autobiography, see Beth Holmgren, *Women's Works in Stalin's Time: On Lidiia Chukovskaia and Nadezhda Mandelstam* (Bloomington: Indiana Univ. Press, 1993).

from a desire for justice or revenge: "I would very much like for my [story] to be published, if only because of all our suffering and undeserved torment," writes a peasant victim of collectivization, Maria Belskaia.

All this suggests that Russian women have thought about their lives in the twentieth century in very different ways from, say, American women. This denotes differences of culture and, above all, differences in twentieth-century experience. The penchant for testimony runs across the spectrum of Russian women's autobiography: émigré, Soviet, internal émigré, and post-Soviet.[4] Russian women (like Russian men) write about their lives in the context of the times because they perceive their times as remarkable, overshadowing private concerns, impossible to ignore. They had the misfortune, as the Chinese proverb has it, to live in exciting times, and that is reflected in the way they tell their lives; their autobiographies are often like war stories. They remember their lives and structure their narratives in terms of great public events—the revolution, the Civil War, collectivization, the Great Purges, and the Second World War—rather than the personal milestones of marriage, childbirth, divorce, and widowhood. One of our autobiographers, the Stakhanovite tractor-driver Pasha Angelina, mocks the American biographer who wanted to know the date of her wedding.

Despite the common thread of testimony, there is great variety in the way Russian women saw their lives and times. For one thing, some of the women wrote their memoirs as émigrés, and their perspective naturally differed from that of Soviet citizens. There were differences among the émigrés, too, notably between those who emigrated soon after the revolution and those who left the Soviet Union during the Second World War.[5] Of the Soviet life stories, some were composed for a Soviet public in a spirit of Soviet patriotism, others were written "for the drawer" or for unofficial (*samizdat*) circulation by alienated Soviet citizens, who might be called internal émigrés. The date of writing is often significant in Soviet memoirs. In the life story of Fruma Treivas, for example, the narrator frequently contrasts the way she understood things in the 1930s with the way she understands them now (in the 1990s). If she had recorded a life story in 1936 (or in 1926 or 1946), it would undoubtedly have been very different.[6]

It is important to understand the constraints that shaped the writing of Soviet memoirs. Those written for publication were all subject to censorship, the severity of which changed over time.[7] In the Stalin period, censorship was very severe:

[4] Of our selections, ten are from émigrés (Olitskaia [three], Melgunova-Stepanova, Zhemchuzhnaia, Varsher, Elenevskaia, Volkonskaia, and Bogdan [two]), and three are internal-émigré or post-Soviet (Belskaia, Treivas, and Shikheeva-Gaister). Of the twenty-one Soviet selections, ten are published memoirs, and the rest are oral life stories, letters, and curricula vitae written for official purposes.

[5] Volkonskaia, Melgunova-Stepanova, Varsher, Zhemchuzhina, and Elenevskaia are in the first group, Bogdan in the second.

[6] For a similar dual perspective, see Raisa Orlova, *Memoirs*, trans. Samuel Cioran (New York: Random House, 1983). See also the successive versions of the life story of an Uzbek woman discussed in Marianne Kamp, "Unveiling Uzbek Women: Liberation, Representation, and Discourse, 1906–1929," Ph.D. diss., University of Chicago, 1998, chap. 5.

[7] For an excellent discussion of censorship and internal censorship of Soviet memoirs, see Hiroaki Kuromiya's "Soviet Memoirs as a Historical Source," in S. Fitzpatrick and L. Viola, eds., *A Researcher's Guide to Sources on Soviet Social History in the 1930s* (Armonk, N.Y.: Sharpe, 1990).

topics like the Great Purges were taboo; disgraced revolutionary leaders like Trotsky were unmentionable. After Stalin's death in 1953, the Khrushchev thaw melted some of the ice, allowing the publication of Anna Litveiko's relatively unstereotyped account of a working girl's revolution, as well as Lidia Libedinskaia's memoir of youth in an intelligentsia family with aristocratic antecedents. Even during this period of relaxation, however, censorship still shaped the way people told their life stories: Libedinskaia could make only the most cursory reference to her father's disappearance in the Great Purges.[8]

Soviet ideological controls began to crumble during perestroika in the mid-1980s and then disappeared altogether with the collapse of the Soviet Union in 1991. This is not to say that autobiographies published in Russia in the 1990s were free from external influences, for what publishers and readers wanted at that time were the life stories of victims of the Soviet regime. Similar market constraints operated in the West in the prewar years, when Bolshevik atrocities were a basic feature of the genre of Russian émigré memoirs. In the 1970s, similarly, dissent and opposition (as in Olitskaia's memoir) were standard components in the popular Western publishing genre of Soviet dissident memoirs.[9]

Russian women told their life stories in many different genres, written and oral, and we have tried to give as broad a representation of their variety as possible. Among the important Soviet genres were revolutionary lives, workers' lives, and life stories of Stakhanovites—workers and peasants rewarded for outstanding production results. Lives of revolutionaries, drawing on a prerevolutionary tradition of exemplary lives, were particularly popular in the 1920s.[10] In the early 1930s a project called "History of Factories and Plants," sponsored by the writer Maxim Gorky, collected life stories of workers.[11] Participant accounts of revolution and Civil War emphasizing the heroism of the struggle were another major genre.[12]

Stakhanovites sometimes wrote their life stories, as in Pasha Angelina's case,[13] but more often recited short accounts of their lives at the public meetings where Stakhanovites' achievements were celebrated.[14] This was one common type of

---

[8] For evidence on the continuing constraints of the Khrushchev period, compare Eugenia Ginzburg's famous first volume of her autobiography, *Journey into the Whirlwind*, trans. Paul Stevenson and Max Hayward (San Diego: Harcourt Brace Jovanovich, 1967), which she initially hoped would be published in the Soviet Union, to her second volume, *Within the Whirlwind*, trans. Ian Boland (San Diego: Harcourt Brace Jovanovich, 1981), which was not written for Soviet publication.

[9] For a discussion of the specific characteristics of émigré and dissident memoirs, see Hiroaki Kuromiya, "Émigré and Dissident Memoir Literature," in Fitzpatrick and Viola, *Researcher's Guide*, 257–60.

[10] Krupskaia's autobiography is an example of this genre, along with many others in the volume of the "Granat" encyclopedia where it was published.

[11] See S. V. Zhuravlev, *Fenomen "Istorii fabrik i zavodov": Gor'kovskoe nachinanie v kontekste epokhi 1930'kh godov* (Moscow: IRI RAN, 1997). Balashova's life story is an example of the genre.

[12] Andzhievskaia and Patrikeeva's stories, both taken from a volume of participants' accounts of the Civil War from the late 1930s, are examples.

[13] Stories like Angelina's, Litveiko's, and Maslennikova's were usually written with the aid of a journalist (or sometimes simply ghostwritten), but this was rarely acknowledged. Shchetinina's life story is unusual in that it was published under the name of the interviewer, not the interviewee.

[14] Slavnikova et al. Less frequently, Stakhanovites' *wives* told their life stories in similar circumstances, for example, Vlasovskaia et al.

Soviet success story; another was the story of a woman of humble origins who rose to prominence after (as a result of) the revolution.[15] Both resemble the genre known in Latin America as *testimonios*, in which men and women from revolutionary liberation movements testify about their participation in the struggle, portraying themselves less as individuals than as representatives of a collective experience.[16]

The 1960s and 1970s saw a spate of Soviet publication of participant accounts of collectivization and the industrialization drive of the 1930s, often with a particular regional focus.[17] "Participants" in this context meant activists, often party and Komsomol members, and their stories were told in a spirit of celebration. Those who participated as victims—for example, peasants like Belskaia who were expropriated as kulaks during collectivization—had no public voice in Soviet times, and in the rare instances where their stories were recorded, they could not be published.[18] It was not until the post-Soviet 1990s that oral history, often victim-focused, flourished. A new People's Archive was established in Moscow to collect such documents; similar initiatives to collect personal documents and testimony sprang up all over Russia.[19]

All through the Soviet period, Soviet citizens had the habit of writing to newspapers and political leaders with appeals and complaints, and it was customary to include a short autobiographical statement in such letters.[20] Only in rare cases were such letters published,[21] but Soviet institutional and newspaper archives are full of them.[22] We drew on the archives for other interesting types of Soviet autobiography as well. One is the official autobiography that all Soviet citizens wrote for their personnel files.[23] Another—particularly interesting because of its specificity to Soviet-type political systems—is the public autobiographical statement made in a context of public interrogation, such as party purges, where the validity of the life story was liable to be challenged.[24]

[15] For example, Maslennikova.

[16] On *testimonios*, see Doris Sommer, "'Not Just a Personal Story': Women's *Testimonios* and the Plural Self," in Brodzki and Scheck, *Life/Lines*, 107–30.

[17] For example, Solovieva, Kiparenko.

[18] For example, Bazeleva et al., Kislova et al., whose stories were recorded by a Leningrad ethnomusicologist in the 1970s and 1980s but were published only in the 1990s.

[19] Treivas is an oral history from the People's Archive, which also contains successive versions of Belskaia's autobiography. Western scholars have also participated in the collection of oral history in the 1990s: see, for example, the valuable collection edited by Barbara A. Engel and Anastasia Posadskaya-Vanderbek, *A Revolution of Their Own: Voices of Women in Soviet History* (Boulder, Colo.: Westview, 1998). Another collection of oral histories from women, in this case longtime émigrés in England, is *Memories of Revolution: Russian Women Remember*, ed. Anna Horsbrugh-Porter (London: Routledge, 1993).

[20] On the genre of letters to authority, see Sheila Fitzpatrick, "Supplicants and Citizens: Public Letter-Writing in Soviet Russia in the 1930s," *Slavic Review* 55 (spring 1996): 1; for examples, see "From *Krest'ianskaia gazeta*'s Files: Life Story of a Peasant Striver," *Russian History* 24 (1997): 1–2; and *Pis'ma vo vlast', 1917–1927*, ed. A. Ia. Livshin and I. B. Orlov (Moscow: ROSSPEN, 1998).

[21] In such cases, for example, Anonymous and Ivanova in our volume, we have no way of knowing how heavily the letters were edited—or even whether they were genuine in the first place.

[22] Khuttonen is an example of an unpublished letter.

[23] Plotnikova's autobiography is in this category.

[24] For example, Ulianova, an autobiographical statement by a nominee for election during the Great Purges.

Central to a great many of our autobiographical accounts are, of course, the revolutions of 1917. The February Revolution is remembered as a joyful, carefree, bloodless event by memoirists from all sides of the political spectrum, from the liberal Zinaida Zhemchuzhnaia and the future Socialist Revolutionary Ekaterina Olitskaia to the young working-class Bolshevik Anna Litveiko. The October Revolution is dutifully foregrounded by our Soviet memoirists, but as Litveiko admits, "there was none of the pure devil-may-care joy of the kind that we had felt after the February Revolution. Then we had had nothing to worry about. . . . But now we were in power, and we were responsible for everything." Émigré memoirists do not usually accord October the status of an event: they remember, rather, a drift into chaos and brutality, culminating in the Civil War, in which their familiar world was destroyed.

The Civil War was a time of upheaval for almost everyone and chaotic movement and flight for many. Zhemchuzhnaia describes life in a southern town that was periodically taken and retaken by Red and White forces. Zinaida Patrikeeva and Anna Andzhievskaia fought for the Reds and relate these experiences in the heroic mode of Soviet Civil War participants' accounts. Anastasia Plotnikova, a soldier's wife of peasant background, fled from beleaguered Petrograd to Siberia, from whence she and her husband rather unexpectedly reemerged as Bolsheviks. Another soldier's wife, M. I. Nesgorova,[25] tells a laconic tale of hard times: "They took my children to an orphanage, but when my husband came back from the Red Army, we got them back." Ulianova, a young Jewish girl, went from the shtetl to working for the Cheka after the Reds took over the area. Inna Shikheeva-Gaister's parents and their siblings and Fruma Treivas and her brother all made their way out of the pale to Moscow and new opportunities.

Collectivization was a major milestone for a number of our narrators, but they had very different perceptions of it. For Pasha Angelina, collectivization was a fight between the poor peasants of the village—the Angelin family—and the kulaks; for Antonia Solovieva, a Komsomol collectivizer from the town, "gangs of kulak criminals" were the background against which collectivizers performed their heroic feats. But Valentina Bogdan's classmate committed suicide rather than continue as a collectivizer. Nenila Bazeleva and Maria Belskaia, victims of dekulakization, remembered it bitterly: "If you were a good farmer you got dekulakized—that is, you had everything taken away from you."

The terror of 1937–38 was a taboo subject in Soviet publishing during the Stalin period and for many years after, but in the late 1980s perestroika saw an outburst of memoirs by Gulag survivors and their relatives that continued in the 1990s. Inna Shikheeva-Gaister writes of her Communist parents' arrest and the subsequent fate of their children. Olitskaia, a rare Purges victim who was a genuine opponent of the regime, made her involuntary journey to Gulag in the same freight car as the writer Eugenia Ginzburg and offers a parallel account of it,[26] much less sympathetic to the Communist victims. For nonelite women, the Great Purges were both less important and differently perceived. M. K. Razina, an

---

[25] In Vlasovskaia et al.   [26] See Ginzburg, *Journey*, part 2.

agricultural laborer, was pleased by the downfall of local "kulak" bosses who had forced her out of the state farm.[27] In a conversation between a guard and a cleaning lady reported by Valentina Bogdan, the *Schadenfreude*, being disinterested, is even more striking. The subject is the arrest of the regional party boss, Evdokimov, and his wife's suicide:

> "Who is Evdokimov?
> "Don't you know? He was a member of the Provincial Executive Committee and our delegate to the Supreme Soviet. His wife was a big Communist, too."
> "Then she got what she deserved."

Testimony is so important in twentieth-century Russian women's autobiography that we had some difficulty finding instances of the confessional mode. Anna Iankovskaia's autobiographical statement on her redemption from a life of crime and Kh. Khuttonen's despairing statement on her resignation from the Komsomol fall into this category, as does Paraskeva Ivanova's dramatic letter to the editor on her seduction and induction into a life of promiscuity by a Communist superior. But it is Agrippina Korevanova's autobiography—a product of Gorky's project for publishing the lives of ordinary people—that is the real exception to the dominance of testimony.

> What made me want to write? I think there were two main reasons.
> First of all, my life was so sad that I kept thinking of suicide, and so I decided to describe all my sufferings, so that after my death people would discover my notebooks and find out what had made me want to kill myself.
> The second reason was my rage and horror at the unfairness of life; my protest against the oppression of women; and my hatred for a fat wallet. I wrote about all this in poor literary style but with great bitterness and passion. There was no practical use in it, of course, but at least it provided some relief.

Of course, personal life coexists with public life in almost all the autobiographical narratives in this volume. Zhemchuzhnaia tells us of her happiness when her husband, Boris, rejoins her and of her fears for her young daughter, yet the central purpose of her narrative is to tell about "the times we lived in," as is also true of Bogdan. Even Irina Elenevskaia, after writing a vivid evocation of a blissful childhood in the prerevolutionary part of her memoir, switches to a different vein of sociopolitical reportage in describing her Civil War experiences in Petrograd. Occasionally the personal intrudes vividly and almost destabilizes the testimonial character, as in Andzhievskaia's poignant account of the loss of her infant daughter. But more often, especially in Soviet narratives, personal information is minimized or omitted. Ulianova, recounting her life as a candidate for office, is confused and embarrassed by questions about her separation from her husband. The Stakhanovite Pasha Angelina does not even mention her (divorced?) husband, though her parents and siblings—all Soviet activists—and her three children are named. (The youngest was called Stalina.)

---

[27] In Slavnikova et al.

We encounter many self-presented "strong women" in these autobiographies. Princess Volkonskaia takes the lead, with her intrepid clandestine journey into civil-war Russia to rescue her imprisoned husband. But Zina Patrikeeva, the nurse who becomes a cavalryman, is a counterpart on the Red side, not to mention the dauntless Olitskaia, representing the anti-Bolshevik socialist underground. Anna Shchetinina, a Soviet sea captain, underlines her strength and independence by attributing to herself "male" characteristics—"I am a practical person with a mathematical mind, . . . not a romantic"—and comparing herself favorably as a fledgling ship's mate to her male counterpart, "a dandy and a weakling, [who] often made mistakes [and] used to wear a flower in his lapel." Bilia Misostish-khova, a feisty young Kabardian Stakhanovite, boasted of her mountain-climbing achievements and promised that "in parachute jumping I am also going to be ahead of the men."[28] As we will see, even housewives (wives of Stakhanovite workers) were likely to describe themselves as the source of strength in the family.

In addition to these first-person "strong women," numerous examples of such types are described in the third person in various narratives. The independent, work-oriented mother and the grandmother (or, in Shikheeva-Gaister's story, the devoted family servant), who is the rock on which the family stands, appear in both Gaister's and Libedinskaia's memoirs.[29] Belskaia's memoir was dedicated to her indomitable peasant mother, Arina. Varsher and Volkonskaia, both émigré memoirists, give us pen-portraits of nightmarish strong women—Bolsheviks who are at least as ruthless and pitiless as their male counterparts. A different kind of revolutionary strong woman, the sexually liberated one, is presented in Bogdan's portrayal of her college contemporary, Olga, willful, independent, free-spirited, and sexually adventurous. Olitskaia's version of the liberated woman has still a different slant: "I did not know anything about housework," she writes (apropos of a visit from her mother-in-law), "and hated bourgeois family life and every-thing it stood for."

This is not to deny that victimhood is an important theme of twentieth-century Russian women's autobiography. Paraskeva Ivanova's repentant story of life as a "liberated woman" presents herself as a victim of a man's exploitation. The peasant Efrosinia Kislova strikes a typical "victim" note,[30] beginning her story with the plaint, "I had more sorrows than anybody else." The folksongs Kislova sings for the interviewer seem to be mainly about suffering at the hands of men, but in her story, and that of other peasant interviewees, it is the *state* that is the victimizer: "The government got all the grain, and we got the ashes" (Kislova); "Then this government came along, and dekulakized us" (Bazeleva). In Bel-skaia's memoir, a veritable saga of a peasant family's victimization by the state, written under the influence of perestroika, this is developed into an indictment of

[28] In Slavnikova et al.

[29] A classic representation of these types is in Elena Bonner, *Mothers and Daughters*, trans. Anto-nina W. Bouis (New York: Knopf, 1993).

[30] Kislova, in Bazeleva et al. For more on the victim's plea, see Golfo Alexopoulos, "The Ritual Lament: A Narrative of Appeal in the 1920s and 1930s," *Russian History* 42 (1997): 1–2.

Stalin ("Our very 'great' thanks to him for such a 'happy childhood,'" she writes sarcastically). The memoirs of first-wave émigrés like Volkonskaia and Melgunova-Stepanova also tell a story of victimization by the Bolsheviks and the Soviet state; so do Great Purge victims like Shikheeva-Gaister, Treivas, and Olitskaia. Bogdan, a second-wave émigré, shifts key unexpectedly at the end of her memoirs to issue a comprehensive indictment of the Bolsheviks' victimization of the Soviet people.

There are other versions of the victimization story that indict other perpetrators—the tsarist government, capitalists and landowners, the Whites in the Civil War. The old regime is a standard target in Soviet autobiographies. Stakhanovite *testimonios* often compare their miserable, oppressed life in the past with present happiness, as in Razina's story[31]:

> I will tell you about my life and about how I used to live. . . . When I was eleven, I lost my mother and became an orphan. When I was twelve, I was given as a nanny to the village kulaks, and then, when I was fourteen, to the manor house, to look after their children. . . . I couldn't read or write. My life was very bad, and I didn't know that there was a different, better life.

There are, of course, women whose autobiographical narratives focus on victimization by men. Korevanova points the finger at her father, father-in-law, and husband, not to mention assorted male Soviet officials who mistreated her in later life. Some of this is put in a frame of prerevolutionary exploitation, but it is clear that for Korevanova exploitation is gendered. Even when she is assaulted by unknown assailants, she assumes the assailant was male and warns him that on her death "I will leave behind not one, not two *women* (my emphasis) loyal to the revolution, but perhaps hundreds." Litveiko describes her mother's victimization by a drunken husband and her own decision to throw her father out of the house— "my first independent act, and I was very proud of it" (though later she had wondered whether she had made her mother happier or unhappier). "Anonymous" casts herself as a victim of husbands who either abandon her or stifle her self-development by forbidding her to work.

Many of our memoirists had education and professional skills; most worked for pay outside the home throughout their lives. Educational experiences, from tsarist gymnasium to Soviet industrial academy, are part of almost all the life stories and are prominent in many. For the Soviet contingent, a typical experience was "promotion" (*vydvizhenie*) to higher education[32] as an adult, usually understood as opening the gates of opportunity that would have remained closed but for the revolution. Treivas, Ulianova, Maslennikova, Angelina, and a whole host of Shikheeva-Gaister's parents, aunts, and uncles experienced this. Our memoirists had a range of professions and occupations. Along with the standard occupations of teacher, nurse, factory worker, kolkhoznik, journalist, writer, propagandist, and

[31] In Slavnikova et al.

[32] In the 1920s and first half of the 1930s, affirmative action policies sent hundreds of thousands of workers, peasants, Communists, and non-Russians without full secondary education to rabfaks (workers' preparatory schools), party schools, engineering schools, and other higher educational institutions.

administrator, the group includes a sea captain (Shchetinina), an engineer (Bogdan), a tractor-driver (Angelina), an underground revolutionary in Soviet times (Olitskaia), and a professional thief (Iankovskaia).

Despite their education and skills, the upper-class and intelligentsia women in our sample are deferential to their husbands and report no significant conflicts within the family on the issue of work outside the home.[33] Such conflicts surely occurred,[34] but they were evidently judged too trivial for inclusion in life stories that are also testimony about "the times we lived in." Two elite housewives, Frida Troib and N. P. Ivanova, were rescued from boredom by the wives' volunteer movement, but they portray their husbands as welcoming the change. The working-class *vydvizhenka*, Evdokia Maslennikova, portrays her husband as a wise older mentor who encouraged her self-development: "If I am now an active Bolshevik, that's to a great extent thanks to him, his conversations with me, his friendly, comradely advice."

Family conflict, usually involving husbands' attempts to restrict or control their wives' activities outside the home, is reported much more frequently in lower-class women's life stories. Anna Balashova's marriage ran into trouble when she got involved in trade-union and party work at the factory; Korevanova reports that the same thing often happened when working-class wives joined her women's group. Peasant Stakhanovites told similar stories of how "backward" husbands tried to suppress their wives' growing consciousness. Gadiliaeva, a milkmaid from Bashkiria, represents her divorce from an unsatisfactory husband as part of the development process that led her to join the kolkhoz and become a Stakhanovite. For the Armenian peasant Budagian, the payment structure in the kolkhoz, rewarding those who worked harder, automatically solved these problems: "How can your husband exploit you when you make more money than he does? That usually shuts him up."[35]

The statements quoted above are from the *testimonios* of Stakhanovites. Women who testified as Stakhanovites' *wives* naturally struck a different note, representing the purpose of their lives as support for their husbands, and sometimes (surprisingly, in view of the general Soviet propaganda emphasis on women working) mentioning that the task was easier now that their husbands' increased earnings allowed them to quit the workforce. Many of these women, however, portray themselves as distinctly superior helpmeets, more cultured, motivated, and organized than their menfolk, who have to keep potential backsliding husbands up to the mark. Vlasovskaia was angry when her husband, who

---

[33] To the educated but deferential wives like Zhemchuzhnaia and Bogdan in our group may be added Libedinskaia, though this is not evident in the extract from her memoirs published here. Later in the memoir, in the sections covering the period after her marriage to Libedinsky in the early 1940s, she makes a striking switch in self-representation from the independent, albeit childish, actor of the first half of the memoir to a devoted helpmeet whose own life and work are totally subordinated to her husband's.

[34] See, for example, Galina Shtange's diary (in *Intimacy and Terror: Soviet Diaries of the 1930s*, ed. V. Garros, N. Korenevskaya, and T. Lahusen [New York: New Press, 1995]), in which her adult children resented her volunteer work, or N. V.'s letter about her husband's objections to her working outside the home in *Obshchestvennitsa*, no. 6 (1939): 46.

[35] From Slavnikova et al.

had "kind of let himself go," initially failed to become a Stakhanovite. Nesgorova noted her role in protecting her husband from drinking and "bad influences." Poliakova pushed her husband to become a Stakhanovite, forced him to listen to her reading aloud in the evenings, even when he wanted to go to bed, and tested him to see if he had stayed awake at the theater and movies. "I wanted him to be a cultured person," she said. "I didn't want him to lag behind other men."[36]

In Alla Kiparenko's story of pioneering life in the Far East, one of the Komsomol girls alarms her colleagues by marrying a hot-tempered ne'er-do-well who drinks and has a poor work record—but fortunately marriage to a superior woman straightens him out: "He tried his best to catch up with his wife, and soon his productivity results began to approach hers." Even Princess Volkonskaia's story, ostensibly one of total devotion to her husband, manages to convey a whiff of the same patronizing attitude to husbands as the Stakhanovite wives: in her memoirs Prince Peter, henpecked by his mother, passive, and apparently too refined to express (or feel?) any strong emotion, cuts a drab figure beside his dashing wife. Had he been a locomotive driver, like Vlasovskaia's husband, he, too, would have needed coaching in self-assertiveness.

Class—the difference between the noble Princess Volkonskaia and the proletarian Vlasovskaia—had enormous resonance in postrevolutionary Russian society. For most of our narrators, it seems to have been a matter of more vital interest and anxiety than gender, which is hardly surprising given its salience in creating dangers and opportunities for families and individuals. Nobles and other "former people" like Princess Volkonskaia were seen as class enemies of the revolution. Their estates and personal property were confiscated and they were forced to share their homes with strangers. They were liable to conscription for forced labor and house searches, and lived in fear of arrest.

As Marxists, the Bolsheviks thought class determined and therefore predicted political allegiance: proletarians were for the revolution, members of the bourgeoisie and other "alien" classes against it. They would not tolerate ambiguity; Zinaida Zhemchuzhina remarks on their adherence to a "rigid, preconceived pattern" that required all citizens to be identified by class and treated accordingly: "You were either a member of the bourgeoisie, who should be robbed and murdered, or a proletarian, who deserved all the good things in life." Hyperbole aside, life chances depended, in many formal and informal ways, on class. Lidia Libedinskaia describes how she was almost expelled from the Young Pioneers because of her "bad" class origins; Valentina Bogdan relates that one of her schoolmates was denied admission to college because his parents were disenfranchised as "class aliens." Elenevskaia describes how her apartment house in Petrograd in the early 1920s was divided by class, each household "identifying with either the 'bourgeoisie' or the 'toilers.'"

Of course, there was an obverse side to this discrimination: proletarians, in Zhemchuzhnaia's phrase, "deserved all the good things in life" and were beneficiaries of positive discrimination in all sorts of areas, from housing to education

[36] From Vlasovskaia et al.

and promotion. The young worker Anna Balashova and her mother were allocated good housing—"some people from the bourgeoisie used to live there, but they had run away." Bogdan, critical but not altogether unsympathetic, notes the varieties of a new social type among her fellow students, the working-class *vydvizhentsy* (there were apparently no *vydvizhenki* at Bogdan's engineering school at the end of the 1920s). Angelina, a peasant who became a famous Stakhanovite and Supreme Soviet deputy, reflects on her upward mobility and compares it with the lesser type available in capitalist societies. Inna Gaister's Jewish parents and their siblings left the pale and rose almost en masse into the new Soviet elite; so did Fruma Treivas and her brother, whose father was a kosher butcher, and Ulianova.

Although the Bolsheviks often treated class as a self-evident quantity, this was far from the case in the experience of many of our narrators.[37] Zhemchuzhnaia noted the contortions the Bolsheviks in Cossack lands had to go through to make local social groups fit into a Marxist framework (priests, teachers, and Cossacks were assigned to the bourgeoisie, non-Cossack peasants to the proletariat). She and Olitskaia both had the problem that their fathers, as noble landowners, were now seen as exploiters, whereas to their families they seemed enlightened men who had tried to help the peasants. Class was also a puzzle for the young Libedinskaia, whose grandmother was both noble (a "former person") and an enthusiast for the revolution. Praskovia Dorozhinskaia's father was expropriated as a kulak even though he had belonged to the local Committee of the Poor.[38] Olitskaia notes that "dekulakization" on her father's former estates during the Civil War was a farce: when Bolsheviks pressured the villagers to identify their kulaks, they simply "elected" someone unpopular or dispensable to that status.

The Bolsheviks' class cosmogony, and particularly its class-hatred component, appealed instinctively to the unhappy Korevanova, whose epiphany as a Bolshevik came when her heart "ached with hatred" for the Whites. Ten years later, Korevanova's women's brigade (with the exception of one "tender-hearted" member) evicted class enemies from their apartments in a mood of grim satisfaction: they were getting what they deserved! The young worker Anna Litveiko was not a natural hater, but she quickly mastered a pamphlet called *Spiders and Flies*, describing bosses as spiders who drank the blood of the workers by appropriating their labor, and recounted its content to her workmates "the way I used to tell them about Nat Pinkerton."[39]

Lidia Libedinskaia's father, a nobly born economist working for the Soviet regime as a "bourgeois specialist," continued to carry business cards identifying him as "Count Tolstoy." His quixotic reason was that "just as only a scoundrel would have been ashamed of his proletarian origin before the revolution, so it did not become a decent person to deny his gentry background after the revolution." But many of our narrators and the people they encountered *did* feel obliged to

---

[37] On this problem, see my "Ascribing Class: The Construction of Social Identity in Soviet Russia," *Journal of Modern History* 65 (1993): 4.

[38] Bazeleva et al.

[39] The Nat Pinkerton detective stories were very popular in Russia in the teens and twenties.

disguise their social class. Sometimes it was a literal disguise, as when Princess Volkonskaia, making her adventurous foray back into Soviet territory to rescue her husband, donned a scarf in order to look like a humble schoolteacher. But often the disguise was more complex—a new biography to suit a new identity or at least the blotting out of certain episodes in the past. Bogdan's landlady in her college days had to hide the fact that her late husband had fought for the Whites in the Civil War (making her the widow of a "counterrevolutionary"). Zhemchuzhnaia and her husband hid the same secret and felt themselves under the sword of Damocles. Ulianova and Anastasia Plotnikova narrowly escaped "unmasking" for dubious points in their life stories.

Something almost all our narrators have in common is that they implicitly accept a "two camps" view of the world: one is either pro-Soviet or anti-Soviet; indifference or agnosticism is not an option. Each camp is preoccupied with the other's privileges and power. Those on the Soviet side focus on the privileges—goods, housing, access to education and culture—that must be stripped from the old "bourgeoisie." Those on the other side see the Communists as the ones who are accumulating power and privilege. These contrasting perspectives come out particularly vividly in the way our narrators treat the transfer of goods and material possessions attendant upon the revolution. Those losing possessions suffer—but they generally try to emphasize the cultural/sentimental aspect of their loss rather than the material. Those gaining possessions rejoice—but many of them stress that they are not the kind of people who really care about material things.

Volkonskaia, one of many victims of revolutionary confiscations and house searches, admits to the extreme unpleasantness of seeing strangers handling her possessions, but retreats to philosophical detachment with the comment that "our sense of property has been developed in us for generations; the inverse process will probably take as long—if not longer." Zhemchuzhnaia's commentary on the confiscation of her personal property by the Bolsheviks during the Civil War is noticeably more bitter than Volkonskaia's; she was infuriated when the confiscators lectured her on her lack of "consciousness" in failing to sacrifice her possessions voluntarily. She called this her "Soviet baptism," for it was then that she learned that her life as well as her property had ceased to belong to her—"they had become the 'people's' and were transferred to the state." Describing the process of confiscation, both she and Olitskaia express their disdain for the personal greed of the confiscators—and these simple workers and soldiers, in their turn, are reported as showing astonishment at these "bourgeois" women's lack of covetousness and indifference to the valuables in their houses.

As the autobiographical narratives move into the 1930s, we start to see goods in new hands. There are inheritors who take a straightforward pleasure in their new identity as possessors of goods, notably the Stakhanovites, who proudly report on the crêpe-de-chine dresses and sewing machines they have received as rewards for their high productivity. Valentina Bogdan also reports with pleasure, albeit less naively stated, at her acquisition of a good apartment in a new building for Communist administrators, engineers, and Stakhanovites. (She is perhaps the only one of our memoirists who would not object too much to being called "bourgeois.") Bogdan's friend, Tania, also has good luck with housing in Leningrad:

> Our apartment not only came fully furnished, it actually had dishes, linen, dresses, and even playing cards! The previous owners must have been some kind of old-regime people: in their trunk we found some very old-fashioned dresses with spangles and lace, and lots of silverware—spoons, glass-holders, candlesticks, and so on. They had all been arrested and, I guess, sent to a camp, so we inherited the apartment the way they had left it on the day of their arrest.

Valentina is shocked by this, but Tania takes it in stride: "I never even think about it. They weren't arrested because of us, after all!"

"Nobody [in my family] ever owned anything," Krupskaia states in her autobiography. This pride in nonpossession was widespread among Bolsheviks, and it caused some complications as a new generation of Communists—spurred on, Trotsky tells us, by their wives[40]—assumed a privileged lifestyle. Treivas explains how, at the time, she and her husband did not perceive themselves as privileged, despite their access to special stores, the chauffeur-driven car for her husband, the good apartment. After all, her husband was "killing himself working long hours at an important job, all for the glory of the Motherland and Stalin"; he needed the car to drive him to work. His salary was limited by the "party maximum." Their furniture belonged to the state, not to them; each item bore a small metal plate with a number indicating this fact. They paid little attention to money and possessions.

Shikheeva-Gaister's father lived in similar elite conditions. But in this case there was some perception of a problem. One of the father's friends "did not approve of my father's eager acceptance of Stalin's little gifts, such as the beautiful apartment in the House of Government, the dacha, or the car that my mother did not mind using herself." Gaister defends her father against his friend's criticisms in similar terms to Treivas: he worked hard for his benefits; the furniture in the apartment was not fancy and belonged to the government; the only personal valuables were a grand piano and a refrigerator brought from America. "There was no cult of things in our household," Gaister reassures the reader.

As NOTED at the beginning of this essay, almost all our autobiographical narrators told their life stories as part of the story of their times. Sometimes this was an imperative of the genre: for example, the Soviet success stories ritually presented in public by Stakhanovites and *vydvizhenki* require the narrator to recount her life this way. My story is the story of the people, Angelina tells us. Maslennikova tells her story not because of its individuality—"there is nothing particularly remarkable about my biography"—but because of its representativeness. The stories of Great Purge victims and émigrés, though in many ways totally different from the

---

[40] Trotsky, *The Revolution Betrayed* (London: New Park, 1967), 102–3.

success stories, share this characteristic of reporting not so much "what happened to me" as "what happened to people like me, to my generation." It is not just "my story" but "stories like mine" (in Korevanova's phrase) that are important.

The almost total avoidance of the confessional genre suggests that living through civil upheavals may not be conducive to self-exploration. It is not just that the outside world demands attention but also that individual identity is destabilized. The revolution itself set out to produce "new Soviet men" (and women), meaning that old ones had to be discarded. The thief Anna Iankovskaia acquires a new self; the boyfriend of Olitskaia's working-class friend, Niura, takes the name Waldemar and calls her Nellie, explaining: "We are the masters of the country now, . . . so our names should be noble, too.'" Perhaps, to paraphrase Marx, the task of revolutionary autobiography is not to understand the self but to record its change.

Scholars have recently drawn attention to the importance of Soviet self-fashioning—learning to "speak Bolshevik," perfecting one's identity as a real Soviet citizen.[41] Many of our autobiographical narratives—notably those of the Stakhanovites and the *vydvizhenki*—are clearly practicing this art. During the Great Purges, the elderly mother of one of Bogdan's friends went so far in self-re-creation as to edit her old diaries to emphasize her loyal Soviet persona. As this last example suggests with particular force, the task of self-construction (-reconstruction) is very different from the task of self-exploration. Indeed, the two may be incompatible.

The binary scheme of "old life" and "new life," "then" and "now," is pervasive in Russian/Soviet twentieth-century autobiography. The breakpoint is the revolution (or some equivalent like emigration or collectivization), which cuts lives in half. "This is where I finish the story of my old life and begin the story of my new life," says A. M. Zinovieva, of the marriage to a worker in 1923 that freed her from slavery to a cruel mistress." "That is when the second half of my biography begins," Maslennikova explains of her move from the village to Moscow in 1921. Varsher, an émigré memoirist, supplies another perspective on revolutionary transformation in her story of the metamorphosis of Konkordia Gromova, a humble, kindly student, into comrade Natasha, a Bolshevik executioner.

Some lives are double rather than binary, for self-fashioning as a Soviet citizen implies that there is a non- or anti-Soviet self that is being denied.[42] These anti-selves are shadowy Doppelgänger that sometimes rise up and threaten to engulf the Soviet self, as in the case of Ulianova and Plotnikova. Even Soviet citizens unaware of a Doppelgänger may suddenly find themselves slipping into another identity, that of enemy of the people. "I turned out to be a terrorist," Olitskaia's

[41] See Stephen Kotkin, *Magnetic Mountain: Stalinism as a Civilization* (Berkeley: Univ. of California Press, 1995), chap. 5; and Jochen Hellbeck, "Fashioning the Stalinist Soul: The Diary of Stepan Podlubnyi (1931–1939)," *Jahrbücher für Geschichte Osteuropas* 44 (1996): 3.

[42] For elaboration of these points, see Sheila Fitzpatrick, "Lives under Fire: Autobiographical Narratives and their Challenges in Soviet Russia," in *De Russie et d'ailleurs. Feux croisés sur l'histoire. Pour Marc Ferro* (Paris: Institut des Études Slaves, 1995), and idem, "The Two Faces of Anastasia: Narratives and Counter-Narratives of Identity in Stalinist Everyday Life," in Eric Naiman and Christina Kiaer, eds., *Everyday Subjects: Formations of Identity in Early Soviet Culture* (forthcoming).

friend, Niura, tells her on the way to Gulag—not an admission of guilt, for Niura asserts her innocence, but a factual report on an involuntary change of identity.

Revolutions create "might have beens" for everyone who lives through them. But if one's life had gone differently, would one have been the same person? The "might have beens" make identity precarious: one may even feel, in the words of an old Russian woman interviewed in the 1990s, that one had lived "someone else's life,"[43] not the life one was born to live. Even Valentina Bogdan, whose sense of self seems rocklike, turns out to have had a kind of double life: the title of her first volume of memoirs, *Students of the First Five-Year Plan*, implies a Soviet life, while the title of her second volume tells us this was only *Mimicry in the USSR*, the imitation of a Soviet life. But how can the imitation life be distinguished from the real one? The most urgent task of autobiography, for many of those who live in troubled times, is to establish that the real Plotnikova is the proletarian, not the kulak's daughter; that the real Bogdan is the principled anti-Communist, not the privileged Soviet elite member. Self-understanding becomes irrelevant, even dangerous. Under such circumstances, the object of the autobiographical quest is not self-discovery in the normal sense, but rather the discovery of a *usable* self.

[43] Engel and Posadskaya, *Revolution*, 46 (Dubova interview).

□ YURI SLEZKINE

Lives as Tales

MOST SELECTIONS included in this volume are parts of larger narratives that range from self-consciously literary autobiographies to unrehearsed (but edited) interviews to fully scripted Stakhanovite speeches. All purport to represent the author's past while differing widely on what constitutes authorship or the past. Some are ghostwritten, some are pseudonymous, and some may be fabrications. A few were communicated by people who "lived in the past," yet others remembered by those who had caught up with the future. All, one way or another, are artfully arranged compositions. As G. K. Chesterton put it, "without such selection and completion, our life seems a tangle of unfinished tales, a heap of novels, all volume one."[1]

The texts most closely connected to the Russian literary canon are the émigré gentry memoirs. Fully extended, they comprise lives that begin with childhood, are interrupted by revolution, and end—or lose all coherence—at the time of emigration. The childhoods are all happy, and all the happy childhoods are more or less vivid reflections of Leo Tolstoy's vision of lost innocence.[2] The childhood's sacred center is the country estate, where the protagonist enjoys a special relationship with the sprawling house, the overgrown park, the lily-covered pond, the peasant nanny who is as innocent as the young author, and the peasant children who may or may not be as innocent. Nature equals *Narod* (Volk) equals Childhood, which also includes the pleasures of swimming, mushroom picking, drinking tea on the terrace at dusk, and "something as enduring, in retrospect, as the long table that on summer birthdays and name days used to be laid for afternoon chocolate out of doors, in an alley of birches, limes, and maples at its debouchment on the smooth-sanded space of the garden proper that separated the park and the house."[3] In the city, cluttered with eccentric tutors and stern school principals, the mystery of estate life reappears through the magic of Christmas and during protracted childhood illnesses.

In most émigré autobiographies, the age of innocence (common to the author and her country) lasts until a certain point during the Civil War, so that some

---

[1] Cf. G. K. Chesterton, *Charles Dickens, The Last of the Great Men* (New York: The Press of the Readers Club, 1942), 140.

[2] Andrew Baruch Wachtel, *The Battle for Childhood: Creation of a Russian Myth* (Stanford: Stanford University Press, 1990). Gentry girlhoods and gentry boyhoods might be experienced and recalled in different ways (see Mary F. Zirin, "Butterflies with Broken Wings?—Early Autobiographical Depictions of Girlhood in Russia," in Marianne Liljeström, Eila Mäntyasaari, and Arja Rosenholm, eds., *Gender Restructuring in Russian Studies*, Slavica Tamperensia, vol. 2 [Tampere: University of Tampere Press, 1993], 255–66), but to most postrevolutionary exiles they seemed equally Tolstoyan.

[3] Vladimir Nabokov, *Speak, Memory: An Autobiography Revisited* (New York: Putnam's, 1966), 171.

protagonists are well beyond chronological childhood when they first taste of the Tree of Knowledge. The Edenic continuity is maintained through repeated pilgrimages to the country estate, but also through the magical world revealed in books (discovered serendipitously in father's library); intense friendships formed at boarding schools (mythologized by Pushkin and feminized by Lidia Charskaia); first loves, kisses, and balls experienced in quick succession (though not necessarily in that order); and the easy camaraderie, passionate intellectual quest, and low-cost radicalism of earnest but carefree student days. Even matrimony and childbirth refuse to interfere with innocence or succumb to the quotidian.[4]

Tolstoy's "pseudo-autobiographical"[5] childhood ends with the death of the narrator's mother. Gentry émigrés' days of playfulness and serenity end with the rape of old Russia. The Bolshevik whirlwind that razes paradise takes the heroine through countless railway stations and makeshift shelters to a Sabbath of leering monsters—an inverted world of pompous plebeians, naked emperors, swaggering women, urban sailors, and tongue-tied orators. A key episode in most such memoirs is the solemn Soviet rally dedicated to an indeterminate date of allegedly global significance. No one means what he says, and no one could if he tried because the words make no sense. No one belongs, and even if someone did, no one would know because attendance is mandatory for all. NKSO greets VTsIK, VonKh salutes RKKI, and mechanical oracles keep "droning on and on, saying the same things over and over again," as Zinaida Zhemchuzhnaia puts it.

While reason sleeps, the heroine's main duty is to preserve the home or recreate it elsewhere (with the help of plywood partitions, "shrapnel" gruel, and a "bourgeois" stove). Her duty is to be with her children and her husband—especially with her husband. (The children may have their nanny or Grandma, after all; the husband, deprived of the Motherland, has only her as both his cause and support.) And so in 1919 Princess Sofia Volkonskaia returns to Russia from the safety of England to replicate the sacrifice of Princess Maria Volkonskaia, who in 1827 left her child behind in order to follow her Decembrist husband into Siberian exile. The twentieth-century princess knows what she is doing, and everyone around her, including her husband and his jailers, seems to know how to "read" her actions (largely because everyone around her has read N. A. Nekrasov's "Russian Women," which elevated Maria's martyrdom to epic proportions and transformed Maria herself into every Russian woman's ancestor).[6] Sofia does enjoy

[4] On the tradition of women's school reminiscences, see Toby W. Clyman and Judith Clyman, eds., *Russia through Women's Eyes: Autobiographies from Tsarist Russia* (New Haven: Yale University Press: 1996), 33–35.

[5] Wachtel's term, referring to "first-person retrospective narratives in which the author and the protagonist are not the same person." See Wachtel, *The Battle for Childhood*, 3.

[6] Note, in particular, the remarkable similarity between Sofia's memoir of her meeting with her husband in the Cheka prison and Nekrasov's description of Maria's meeting with her husband in the Peter and Paul Fortress. Maria wrote her own autobiography, modeled on Princess Natal'ia Dolgorukova's 1767 description of a similar self-imposed exile, but it was Nekrasov's version that became canonical. (Since Sofia Volkonskaia's first husband was Prince Dolgorukov, one wonders if it was not Fate itself that wrote the script.) See Clyman and Vowles, *Russia through Women's Eyes*, 15; and Catriona Kelly, *A History of Russian Women's Writing, 1820–1992* (Oxford: Clarendon, 1994), 49–50.

the descendant's advantage: she writes her own (ironic) tribute, acts in front of a prepared audience, and edits the final episode by saving her husband from prison rather than kneeling before him and kissing his fetters. But salvation proves illusory and unfulfilled martyrdom results in oblivion, as Sofia Volkonskaia renames her triumph *Vae Victis* ("Woe to the Vanquished").

One reason for the difference is the nature of the evil they face. Maria's nemesis—at least according to Nekrasov—was Nicholas I, "the vengeful coward." Sofia's tormentors are ubiquitous, making even an underground Siberian refuge an impossible dream. In émigré memoirs, the revolution is primarily about invasion—by neighbors, strangers, policemen, and lice. Homes are vandalized for the sheer pleasure of it, dismantled for fuel, or transformed into pagan shrines or "communal" (as in forced cohabitation) apartments. Accompanied by a cold wind and the smell of herring, the creatures of the night crawl in and take over, "making themselves at home among my things, eating off my china, sleeping in my bed, on my own sheets. . . ."[7] Gleefully but methodically, sailors, Latvians, Jews, and "nauseating" females desecrate whatever remains of the author's home (already turned into a prison by the "communal" neighbors), sully the relics of her lost innocence, and make it clear that her possessions and perhaps even her children belong to the "people" while she herself does not. Nor does she belong to herself: she is a "former person" (*byvshaia*) and a "deprived person" (*lishenka*), which means that she is no longer a person at all. Sofia Volkonskaia's attempts at cleansing herself only increase the pollution, not least because the foulest place of all is the bathhouse—a steam-filled country for decayed bodies without either clothes or souls, a cesspool for women without homes.

> Hideousness and deformity in every imaginable form and variety. . . . Underfed bodies, meager, pendant breasts, crooked legs, legs swollen with oedema, legs with big knots of varicose veins, like blue worms moving under the skin; big flat feet deformed by the ugly angles of inbent toes; backs covered with the bright dots of purulent boils, marked by the red lines of itching scabies; necks and shoulders powdered with the pink patches of syphilitic roseolas, innocently peeping out from under the thick gray coat of dirt and lice of many months' accumulation.[8]

The only alternative to nonliving among the ruins of Russia is death through emigration, which almost invariably involves the crossing of a river, a sea, or some other Styx substitute—death as an eternal void or death as an endless journey through a world of shadows where only memory speaks. "Money, ruin, pov-

---

[7] See Sofia Volkonskaia, below. For the paradigmatic Russian treatment of this theme, often including a fantasy of glorious retribution, see M. A. Bulgakov's *White Guard*, *Heart of a Dog*, and numerous early stories, especially "The Fire of the Khans" and "House No. 13." In *Master and Margarita* the judgment is delayed but equally unequivocal when the well-ensconced plebeian usurpers are confronted by their worst nightmare—the aristocracy from Hell.

[8] Cf. Nadya L. Peterson, "Dirty Women: Cultural Connotations of Cleanliness in Soviet Russia," in Helena Goscilo and Beth Holmgren, eds., *Russia—Women—Culture* (Bloomington: Indiana University Press, 1996): 177–205.

erty. . . . Giving gymnastics lessons, acting in a cinema studio, reading aloud to
an old banker, nursing in a clinic in Nice, driving a taxi in the streets of Paris. . . .
The bitter fruits of defeat."[9]

SOVIET RUSSIA was also ruled by memory. The revolution devoted much of its
energy to commemorating and memorializing itself, and the revolutionaries,
known as "participants," spent more and more time reminiscing (until they joined
their émigré counterparts in doing almost nothing else).

By the mid-1930s there were two Heroic Ages to remember: the age of revolution and civil war, known in memoir collections as "the unforgettable days" or
"the struggle for Soviet power," and the age of industrialization and collectivization, usually entitled "the building of socialism" or "the epoch of the first five-
year plans."[10] There were two main modes of remembering the two ages: a memoir specifically devoted to one's encounter with eternity ("How We Liberated
Rostov," "How I Saw Lenin," "How We Built the Cheliabinsk Tractor Plant") or
a more or less complete autobiography running through those events and struc-
tured in relation to them. There were two basic kinds of autobiographies: curricula
vitae that most Soviet employees produced for their personnel files, and published
life stories that served as official templates for particular editions of Soviet man
or woman (the two never becoming fully fused). And finally, there were two
principal types of authors: the elect (including Lenin's wife N. K. Krupskaia),
who possessed sacred knowledge from the very beginning or received it early in
life by virtue of an instinctive sensitivity to injustice or unusual susceptibility to
the printed word, and the masses, who had to undergo a dramatic—preferably
public—conversion experience.[11] The elect's subjectivity was objective (Krupskaia's is the only autobiography in the volume written in the third person); all the
others had to strive mightily for a similar transparency and to reaffirm their tenu-
ous hold on it through regular public self-narration.[12] The cause, the consequence,

[9] Dots in the original (by Sofia Volkonskaia). For a collection of oral reminiscences by England-
based émigrés, see Anna Horsburgh-Porter, ed., *Memories of Revolution: Russian Women Remember*
(London: Routledge, 1993).

[10] The third Heroic Age—that of the "Great Patriotic War"—is not a part of the revolution as
defined in this book. Here and elsewhere, our (and everybody else's) discussion of Soviet sacred
chronology owes a great deal to Katerina Clark's *The Soviet Novel: History as Ritual* (Chicago:
University of Chicago Press, 1981).

[11] On the role of innate moral knowledge and book learning in the autobiographies of prominent
revolutionaries, see Hilde Hoogenboom, "Vera Figner and Revolutionary Autobiographies: The
Influence of Gender on Genre," in Rosalind Marsh, ed., *Women in Russia and Ukraine* (Cambridge:
Cambridge University Press, 1996), 78–93. On the class consciousness of educated revolutionary
autobiographers (who spoke *for*, not *from* or *with* the people"), see Beth Holmgren, "For the Good
of the Cause: Russian Women's Autobiography in the Twentieth Century," in Toby W. Clyman and
Diana Greene, eds., *Women Writers in Russian Literature* (Westport, Conn.: Greenwood, 1994), 131;
and Richard Stites, *The Women's Liberation Movement in Russia: Feminism, Nihilism, and Bolshevism, 1860–1930* (Princeton, N.J.: Princeton University Press, 1990), 154.

[12] For early Soviet autobiographies, see Igal Halfin's "From Darkness to Light: Student Communist
Autobiography during NEP," *Jahrbücher für Geschichte Osteuropas* 45 (1997): 210–36. See also his
"Construction of the Workers' Intelligentsia: 'Proletarianism' of Soviet Universities in the 1920's,"
Ph.D. diss., Columbia University, 1995.

and the clearest sign of this quest's success was the coincidence of public good and private happiness—something that Krupskaia both epitomized (she was married to the cause) and put into question (her cause was her husband, whom "throughout her life, from 1894 on, she did everything in her power to help"). Indeed, virtually all the prominent female Bolsheviks were the wives and helpers of even more prominent male Bolsheviks or professional experts on the "question of women's equality" or—most frequently—wives and experts rolled into one. They seemed to have an easier time resolving the "individual/collective dialectic" than many other revolutionaries, such as, say, Pavel Korchagin from N. Ostrovsky's *How the Steel Was Tempered*, but their strategy was clearly not applicable to men and therefore suspect on the "women's equality" count. Perhaps more unsettling for the Bolsheviks, "the Krupskaia solution" appeared to be specific to the party elite, and therefore not applicable to most women either.

This difficulty becomes apparent late in the autobiography, however (and rather late in our period). The beginning of a standard account of a redeemed Soviet life tends to be fairly uncomplicated because it usually takes place where gentry émigré life comes to an end—in the dark. Before the revolution (in the part of the autobiography usually entitled "the struggle against autocracy" or "prison and exile"), the elect and their early converts live in a subterranean world of secret societies, illegal publications, and agents provocateurs, surfacing occasionally in order to participate in mass events that prefigure the revolutionary catharsis (the clairvoyance of these conscious revolutionaries is the mirror image of the crystal-clear memory of the émigré memoirists).[13] The conspirators' determination and fortitude are assured by female members, who demonstrate (in their own, as well as other people's recollections) a remarkable capacity and indeed eagerness for self-sacrifice reminiscent of the Siberian martyrdom of Decembrist wives.[14]

In most worker and peasant autobiographies, on the other hand, the primeval darkness is quite unrelieved, and so it appears, again similarly to the gentry émigré denouements, as either impenetrable (A. N. Vinogradova claims to have been born at the age of twenty-six) or infernal. On the basis of a different set of experiences, and shaped by the tradition of Cinderella tales, worker autobiographies, and especially Maxim Gorky's mythopoeic *Childhood* and *Among the People*, the allegedly universal age of innocence is transformed into a time of loneliness, bitterness, and abuse.[15] Female autobiographies, in particular, draw on a

[13] Upper-class revolutionary autobiographies may begin with a false happy childhood, distinguished by the outward trappings of innocence but poisoned by an early perception of evil and History (in the tradition of Alexander Herzen's *My Past and Thoughts*). Cf. Hoogenboom, "Vera Figner and Revolutionary Autobiographies," 80–81.

[14] In Beth Holmgren's words, "their narratives of committed oppositional self-sacrifice established an inspirational model for an entire generation; they could use autobiography as secular saint's life, a pilgrim's testimonial to the true faith" (Holmgren, "For the Good of the Cause," 129). See also Barbara Elpern Engel, *Mothers and Daughters: Women of the Intelligentsia in Nineteenth-Century Russia* (Cambridge: Cambridge University Press, 1983). esp. 141–42, 173, 181–83; and Beth Holmgren, *Women's Works in Stalin's Time: On Lidiia Chukovskaia and Nadezhda Mandelstam* (Bloomington: Indiana University Press, 1993), 11.

[15] See Wachtel, *The Battle for Childhood*, and Halfin, "From Darkness to Light," passim. For a discussion of the earliest Russian workers' autobiographies, beginning with Vasilii Gerasimov's

familiar repertoire of folk laments to evoke a ghastly world of cruel stepmothers, colicky infants, loveless matches, and heartless in-laws: the world of autocracy as peasant patriarchy.

The first (optional) breakthrough comes with the discovery of the pleasures of reading, in which the author indulges furtively by moon or candlelight, à la Gorky. Reading leads to understanding, understanding leads to writing, and writing defies death because transcribing one's life, according to Agrippina Korevanova, amounts to composing an endless suicide note.[16]

None of this is enough, however: the key moment and the structural center in all Soviet darkness-to-light life stories is the moment of final and more or less sudden illumination through conversion. The heroine attains consciousness "with her heart rather than her mind," as Pasha Angelina puts it.

> Our life was not yet happy in those days. We, the ordinary people, did not yet realize to what pinnacles of wealth and joy our government, with its collectivization and industrialization, would lead us. . . . The members of our kolkhoz may not yet have seen the fruits of the new life, but they believed in it firmly and irreversibly.[17]

This belief is instilled in "the ordinary people" by a Bolshevik evangelist who performs conversions by uttering incantations, working miracles, and mortifying the flesh. In Korevanova's case, it is a "living corpse" who walks out onto the theater stage to the loudest applause she has ever heard in her life.

> When it finally grew quiet, he said: "Comrades, I have risen from the dead!" There was more loud applause, and then he talked about how he had been in a White prison and how they had tortured him. He had been hurt so badly he could barely move. My heart ached with hatred for the Whites. Finally, I had found my path in life!"

The best time for conversion is the revolution—the "unforgettable days" of living a full life, of marching in step with History, of truly finding one's path. Indeed, "historical time" moves so fast that it appears to stop altogether—and thus becomes truly unforgettable.[18] To Anna Litveiko, the "October battles"

1881–82 *Life*, see Reginald E. Zelnik's "On the Eve: Life Histories and Identities of Some Revolutionary Workers, 1870–1905," in Lewis H. Siegelbaum and Ronald Grigor Suny, eds., *Making Workers Soviet: Power, Class, and Identity* (Ithaca, N.Y.: Cornell University Press, 1994): 27–65; and *Law and Disorder on the Narova River: The Kreenholm Strike of 1872* (Berkeley: University of California Press, 1995), esp. 223–95. See also Halfin, "From Darkness to Light," 227–29. For excellent discussions of the very influential but little-known genre of priests' autobiographies, see Gregory L. Freeze., ed., *Description of the Clergy in Rural Russia: The Memoir of a Nineteenth-Century Parish Priest* (Ithaca, N.Y.: Cornell University Press, 1985); and Laurie Manchester, "Secular Ascetics: The Mentality of Orthodox Clergymen's Sons in Late Imperial Russia," Ph.D. diss., Columbia University, 1995.

[16] See Agrippina Korevanova, below. For the role of reading in the making of a "conscious" Russian worker, see Zelnik, "On the Eve;" and Zelnik, trans. and ed., *A Radical Worker in Tsarist Russia: The Autobiography of Semen Ivanovich Kanatchikov* (Stanford: Stanford University Press, 1986).

[17] Cf. Halfin, "From Darkness to Light," 219–20.

[18] Cf. Clark, *The Soviet Novel*, 40.

appear as "one uninterrupted day, the happiest day in my life." Pre-1930s happiness is transitory, however, and "revolutionary ardor" (*revoliutsionnyi poryv*) is usually followed by the stern imposition of "revolutionary order." The erstwhile dreamers and lovers ("all of us were a little bit in love") turn into soldiers as Anna Litveiko, among others, conducts searches, confiscates property, expels "former people" from their homes, and finally departs for the front (where the pregnant A. Andzhievskaia, as a member of a revolutionary tribunal, is busy "liquidating scoundrels"). As far as Tatiana Varsher and Irina Elenevskaia are concerned, they have become executioners and "nauseating women." They have fallen into the "revolutionary routine" (*revoliutsionnye budni*).

The "unforgettable days" are not inimitable. They can be foreshadowed (as when Litveiko has "a feeling that something very big is about to happen, that things are changing irrevocably, and that I need to prepare myself"), and they can be staged over and over again. Indeed, they *must* be staged over and over again because that is the best way to secure new conversions and because conversions are never secure—and hence always in need of reenactment (including the act of writing an autobiography).[19] Parades, solemn processions, congresses, and awards ceremonies provide some of Soviet lives' most satisfying climaxes. For a Zhemchuzhnaia, they may be distilled representations of Bolshevik cretinism; for the Stakhanovites, they are moments of well-scripted and well-staged catharsis, sacred inarticulateness, and almost erotic rapture. "I was so excited," writes Korevanova of receiving an honorary diploma in November 1928, "that if Soviet Power had been just one person I would have thrown my arms around him and given him a big hug and I would have said: 'Oh, my dear! Thank you for not forgetting an old woman like me. You saw everything and you knew exactly what you were seeing. May you live and prosper, for the good of all working people!'"

Before long, it turns out that Soviet Power is, in fact, one person. Stalin sees everything and knows exactly what he is seeing. His life equals the revolution, which means that his *Short Course of the History of the Communist Party* is both his autobiography and the biography of every Soviet citizen.[20] To come into contact with him is to relive the revolution and replay one's own conversion. "I walked to the podium feeling completely numb. There was a lump in my throat, and I could not utter a sound. I just stood there silently, looking at Stalin."

It is as if Angelina, as well as Slavnikova, Budagian, and the Soviet Everywoman, were not sure how to express their love for him, how to give him that "big hug"—how to be women under socialism. They "just stand there looking at Stalin," who responds with riddles, the way an oracle should, and invokes the unforgettable days, which are equally enigmatic. On the one hand, there is the equality-as-maleness option. The cavalrywoman Zinaida Patrikeeva tries to

---

[19] Halfin, "From Darkness to Light," 220. See also Geoffrey Galt Harpham, "Conversion and the Language of Autobiography," in James Olney, ed., *Studies in Autobiography* (New York: Oxford University Press, 1988), 42–50.

[20] Brian Kassof, "Contemporary Stalinist Autobiography: The Impossible Genre" (unpublished manuscript; I am grateful to the author for sharing it with me), 18; Clark, *The Soviet Novel*, 44, 122–23; Halfin, "From Darkness to Light," 220.

"catch up with her comrades" by galloping as hard as she can and by converting her skirt into "something resembling pants"—until the Red Cavalry commander solemnly baptizes her "Zinovy." On the other hand, there is Andzhievskaia's version of the Krupskaia solution. "I was a loyal disciple of Andzhievsky [an "exhausted, pale" Bolshevik who "feels the suffering" of the masses]. We read Lenin together. We swore to live and to die for the proletarian revolution. Soon afterwards I became his wife." Neither option was ever endorsed by the party fully and without equivocation, and neither appears to be entirely without pitfalls.[21] Patrikeeva never becomes a cavalryman: she may be "the first one in an attack and the last one to retreat," but she always remains a boy or a sister of mercy, to be patronized accordingly.[22] Andzhievskaia never makes it to socialism: she metes out death sentences at the revolutionary tribunal "literally up to the last day" of her pregnancy, but her own revolution comes to an end with the death of her husband and child. (Similarly, the leading Bolshevik "women's organizer," K. N. Samoilova, portrayed by the émigré Tatiana Varsher as an ascetic dogooder-turned-executioner, is remembered by some of her comrades as the ultimate loyal wife who bore her husband's name and knew no peace until she died on the same spot and of the same disease as he had.)[23]

This dilemma became publicly painful during the NEP period, which tended to be passed over in Stalinist autobiographies but was quite lavish in the production of its own.[24] Most NEP-era memoirs focused on the "unforgettable days," but some also asked why "the revolutionary routine" had become so forgettable and what could be done to make it more revolutionary. Paraskeva Ivanova's autobiography (from comrade to prostitute) points to the dangers of the Patrikeeva option and ends with a vow to "purge herself of filth" with the help of her new Komsomol husband who understands her "as a human being."[25] Anonymous's life story (from comrade to housewife) warns about new Communist husbands and ends with the question: "Am I really destined to spend the rest of my life in the kitchen simply because I am the wife of an important official?"[26] Only Korevanova sol-

[21] See, in particular, Elizabeth A. Wood, *The Baba and the Comrade: Gender and Politics in Revolutionary Russia* (Bloomington: Indiana University Press, 1997), 52–60. For changing legal solutions, see Wendy Z. Goldman, *Women, the State, and Revolution: Soviet Family Policy and Social Life, 1917–1936* (Cambridge: Cambridge University Press, 1993).

[22] Patrikeeva is a literary descendant of the "Cavalry Maiden" Nadezhda Durova, whose 1836 autobiography describes her career in the Russian army during the Napoleonic wars. Durova is more self-conscious as an author, more self-reliant as a hero (she comes up with her own new name), and more self-reflective about her gender transgression (which she treats as a complete disguise resulting in a new male identity), but she, too, can only fool her audience (or take advantage of its acquiescence) for as long as she claims to be merely a boy. Or so she seems to suggest by subtracting seven years from her actual age in her autobiography. See Nadezhda Durova, *The Cavalry Maiden: Journals of a Russian Officer in the Napoleonic Wars* (translation, introduction, and notes by Mary Fleming Zirin) (Bloomington: Indiana University Press, 1989).

[23] S. F. Vinogradova, "Zhizn', otdannaia revoliutsii," in *Leningradki: Vospominaniia, ocherki, dokumenty* (Leningrad: Lenizdat, 1968), 120–38. See also Barbara Evans Clements, *Bolshevik Women* (Cambridge: Cambridge University Press, 1997), 74, 216, 225.

[24] V. S. Golubtsov, *Memuary kak istochnik po istorii sovetskogo obshchestva* (Moscow: MGU, 1970).

[25] Cf. Eric Naiman, *Sex in Public: The Incarnation of Early Soviet Ideology* (Princeton, N.J.: Princeton University Press, 1997).

[26] Cf. Wood, *The Baba and the Comrade*, 200–208.

diers on undeterred. Her 1938 autobiography can be expansive on the 1920s because her struggles—like those of N. Ostrovsky's Pavel Korchagin—have never subsided. She does not wear pants, does not marry a comrade, and does not notice either the NEP or the First Five-Year Plan. Her kerchief tied neatly in back, she combats ignorance, indifference, and accordion playing in the way the pre-revolutionary radical saints used to do—until, on the last page of her autobiography, all her dreams are fully realized.[27]

Dreams change as life unfolds, however. Korevanova's dreams evolve from "universal justice" to "freedom from pots and pans" to preparing fifteen female activists for work at the district party committee. Perhaps more to the point, she remains completely and bitterly alone even as her dreams change.

> Nature endowed me with a sound constitution and a good memory, but then sent me down a stern, cheerless, lonely path in life. I lost my family when I was very young; death took away my mother and then my brother and sister, and I have been alone ever since. Every step I ever took was accompanied by the hard struggle for existence. Whenever I found a family I could call my own, doom would strike again: that family would melt away and I would be alone again.

This is true of most autobiographical peasant childhoods, but in Korevanova's case it is true of the rest of her life as well. She finds her true family in the party, of course, but the party proves to be a stern patriarchal institution that sends her out to do female chores and rewards her with an occasional honorary diploma.[28] These diplomas are crucially important reminders that her sacrifice is not in vain, but they do little to relieve her loneliness or cure her sickness. Unable to form her own family—either as a sister of mercy or as a mother of homeless children—she seems out of place in the dream-come-true Soviet family of the 1930s.

The reason for everyone's complete contentment and Korevanova's relative obsolescence was the First Five-Year Plan of 1928–32. The autobiographers of the 1930s had a new revolution, a new "struggle for socialism," a new Age of Heroes to remember. Indeed, all autobiographers of the 1930s were heroes, which meant that only official heroes were allowed to write autobiographies and that, officially, all Soviet autobiographies of the 1930s "had a place for heroism" (*v zhizni vsegda est' mesto podvigu*). Some places were more conducive to heroism than others, and the best were the five-year-plan construction sites where the "children of October" could forge their own unforgettable days and their own "revolutionary ardor."

[27] A kerchief tied behind a women's head (rather than under the chin) was an important sign of the transition from a peasant to a proletarian identity. See Victoria E. Bonnell, "The Peasant Woman in Stalinist Political Art of the 1930s," *The American Historical Review* 98, no. 1 (1993): 60; and Elizabeth Waters, "The Female Form in Soviet Political Iconography, 1917–1932," in Barbara Evans Clements, Barbara Alpern Engel, and Christine D. Worobec, eds., *Russia's Women: Accommodation, Resistance, Transformation* (Berkeley: University of California Press, 1991), 234.

[28] On the revolutionary community as family, see Evans Clements, *Bolshevik Women*, 82–83. On the sex-based division of labor in such families, see Evans Clements, *Bolshevik Women*, 141; and Elpern Engel, *Mothers and Daughters*, 92, 173, 181–83.

The female memoirs of the second revolution resemble their male counterparts in emphasizing enthusiasm, togetherness, and the superhuman effort that conquers time, space, and the enemy. They remain uncertain on the "big hug" question, however. In A. V. Kiparenko's story of the construction of Komsomolsk, the first female volunteers are grudgingly allowed to join the first convoy to the site for two reasons: because "all that consciousness-raising on the subject of women's equality has not been in vain," and because there are certain advantages to having women aboard "that were understood by all the young people." Upon arrival, the women "keep up with the men in every way" while also cooking their meals, washing their "sweat-drenched shirts," curing them of scurvy, teaching them "genuine culture"—and all without ever missing a day on account of pregnancy. The story ends with the arrival of more than two thousand would-be brides who move into a dorm built especially for them and reemerge a few hours later "arm in arm with beaming young builders." The construction of a new life begins, appropriately enough, with matrimony.

If most industrialization narratives harken back to the exhilaration and eroticism of "revolutionary ardor," the memoirs of collectivization tend to rely on the Civil War tradition of the "cavalrywoman adventure" story. The heroine—whether a crusading outsider or a local activist—survives enemy conspiracies, ambushes, beatings, and assassination attempts to prevail (with the timely help of a party mentor) over a world of implacable kulaks, inert peasants, and insufficiently enlightened comrades. Angelina becomes a tractor driver who keeps beating out her male competition all the way to the Kremlin;[29] Solovieva wins her own equal-rights battle before she embarks on a class war in the countryside:

> There were three girls: Marusia, Sonia, and myself. Some of the boys were looking at us with mistrust and condescension, but we did not let it affect us. We were dressed the same way as the men—in camouflage fatigues. It made us look determined, and we carried ourselves with dignity.

Collectivization may have been "exactly what [the peasants] have been waiting for," as Angelina puts it, but in virtually all collectivization memoirs, a small group of activists is surrounded on all sides by hostility and incomprehension. Angelina's village is collectivized by the Angelin family, while Solovieva, like all reminiscing collectivizers, emphasizes the remoteness of her district and the ubiquity and lethal ferocity of kulak resistance (even if it comes in the shape of a single sand-filled bottle). Either way, the heroine must go to war because the second revolution must be a reenactment of the first one.

Wars require enemies (however poorly armed), and enemies have memories. The official recollection of the first revolution is inverted in émigré memoirs; the official story of the second one is countered by the oral laments and, after perestroika, the published autobiographies of collectivization's victims. In these

---

[29] A woman on a tractor was the central image in the iconography of collectivization. Generally, collectivization from within was represented as a largely female effort. See Bonnell, "The Peasant Woman," passim.

accounts (authored primarily by women) the second revolution turns out to have been a brutal massacre, expropriation turns out to have been robbery, and the lone crusaders against kulak terrorism and rural backwardness turn out to have been backed by the army and secret police.[30] Most important, rich peasants turn out to have been poor (or simply peasants), and this means that their suffering was, as Belskaia puts it, "undeserved." Or was it? These are not random victims, after all; they are, in Belskaia's words, "the most hard-working and industrious (*rabotiashchie i trudoliubivye*) of our peasants," "the true masters of the land and of the grain" who "earned their glory through their own efforts." They are true martyrs, in other words, because they suffer for the ancient peasant way of life—a way of life that serves as the foundation for any meaningful existence and is distinguished above all by a love of work ("hard-working" being the most common term of praise for a peasant in general, and for a peasant woman, in particular). The reason for their martyrdom is also "ancient": it is the envy of the less hard-working and less industrious, of "the loafers and jealous nobodies . . . abandoned by God and useless to the devil." Collectivization, in other words, is both an invasion by evil aliens (as in the émigré gentry narratives) and a triumph of jealous neighbors (as in the evil eye). Both are clearly useful to the devil.

The victims' narratives became public only about half a century after the events they described. Back in the second half of the 1930s the Stalin revolution was still being remembered by happy people as the most immediate cause of their happiness. Indeed, remembrance became the USSR's main preoccupation even as the journals specializing in old-Bolshevik memoirs (such as *Red Chronicle* and *Prison and Exile*) were being closed down and the old Bolsheviks themselves ("the participants") were being shot.[31] Time stood still. The future became the present, and there was nothing but the past to look forward to. The country's sacred center (the Lenin Mausoleum) was a tomb, and the country's sacred text (Stalin's *Short Course*) was a history book.[32] Most novels were biographies (histories of heroes), most public utterances were autobiographies, and all autobiographies were particular manifestations of Stalin's *Short Course*. "Our lives are so inextricably linked to the lives of our state and party," writes Angelina, that "the exciting biography of our country . . . is also the biography of each and every Soviet citizen." Indeed, the main official reason for purging, arresting, and shooting Soviet citizens was the fact that their biographies were not equal to the state and party. Because evil actions stemmed from deviant biographies, the state and party had to engage in massive biographical research while Soviet citizens had to keep editing their lives.[33] Prison interrogations, purge confessions (such as Ulianova's), "reforging" monologues (such as Iankovskaia's), personnel file auto-

[30] On the special role of women as the chroniclers of suffering in the Stalin era, see Holmgren, *Women's Works in Stalin's Time*, 1–11 and passim.

[31] Golubtsov, *Memuary*, 17; Kassof, "Contemporary," 18.

[32] Vladimir Paperno, *Kul'tura Dva* (Moscow: Novoe literaturnoe obozrenie, 1996), 45–46.

[33] Sheila Fitzpatrick, "Lives under Fire: Autobiographical Narratives and Their Challenges in Stalin's Russia," in *De Russie et d'ailleurs. Feux croisés sur l'histoire. Pour Marc Ferro* (Paris, 1995); Peter Holquist, " 'Information is the Alpha and Omega of Our Work': Bolshevik Surveillance in its Pan-European Context," *Journal of Modern History* 69, no. 3 (1997): 415–50.

biographies (such as Plotnikova's), denunciations, and even diaries were more or less self-conscious and more or less coerced attempts to reconcile the biography of the country with the biography of each and every Soviet citizen.[34]

Redemption was never final and sometimes impossible (especially as some acquired characteristics became inheritable toward the end of the 1930s), but a hard-earned purity meant absolute happiness—as Angelina, Slavnikova, and many others demonstrated over and over again. In Slavnikova's case, happiness was "some cream-colored shoes for 180 rubles, a crepe-de-chine dress for 200 rubles, and an overcoat for 700 rubles," but one could be even more adventurous. Angelina remembers her reaction to Stalin's report to the Eighteenth Party Congress in 1938:

> Referring to the state of our country, Iosif Vissarionovich used the most appropriate word possible: "prosperity." As he talked about the affluent, cultured life of Soviet people, I thought of the many recent events in our village that could illustrate his words. One collective farmer was building a brick house with a metal roof; another one had gone to Stalino to buy a motorcycle; a third one was planning a trip to a resort in Sochi; and a fourth one was all set on sending his daughter to a music school. The stars from the Moscow Art Theater had visited Staro-Beshevo, and new movies were being shown in our village club.

The source of such culture and prosperity was Stalin ("who works great miracles," as A. N. Vinogradova puts it), and its happiest and most grateful consumers were often represented as women. By the late 1930s female images on Soviet posters and paintings had become prominent and rather rotund, while the Soviet woman's dilemma had been neatly resolved according to a given woman's level of prosperity.[35] The already prosperous wives of high officials were to devote themselves to their husbands while engaging in charity work known as volunteerism (in what amounted to a revised version of the Krupskaia solution). Blue-collar women were to combine reproduction with production while aspiring to acquire the consumer sophistication and home-making expertise of their social betters. Only the peasant women were left to continue Patrikeeva's cavalry attack on prejudice for a while longer (except that now they were riding tractors).[36]

Their challenge was great, but so was their reward. Few public events in the second half of the 1930s were staged as dramatically, or were considered more emblematic of Soviet achievement, than the meetings of (male) party leaders with female Stakhanovites, most of them rural and many of them non-Russian. The leaders were at their most playful and jocose; the women were at their most

---

[34] See, in particular, Jochen Hellbeck, ed., *Tagebuch aus Moskau, 1931–1939* (by Stepan Podlubnyi) (Munich: Deutscher Taschenbuch Verlag, 1996); Jochen Hellbeck, "Fashioning the Stalinist Soul: The Diary of Stepan Podlubnyi (1931–1939)," *Jahrbücher für Geschichte Osteuropas*, no. 3 (1996): 344–73; "Writing the Self in the Time of Terror: The 1937 Diary of Aleksandr Afinogenov," in Laura Engelstein and Stefanie Sandler, eds., *Self and Story in Russian History* (Ithaca, N.Y.: Cornell University Press, in press); and Véronique Garros, Natalia Korenevskaya, and Thomas Lahusen, eds., *Intimacy and Terror: Soviet Diaries of the 1930s* (New York: The New Press, 1995).

[35] Bonnell, "The Peasant Woman," esp. 71–82.

[36] Sheila Fitzpatrick, *The Cultural Front: Power and Culture in Revolutionary Russia* (Ithaca, N.Y.: Cornell University Press, 1992), 231–35.

ingenuous, incoherent, and immature (even the forty-five-year-old A. N. Vinogradova claimed to be eighteen). They boasted and swooned disarmingly, provoking smiles among the leaders and "laughter in the audience," but they also provided the most intense expression of the fusion between state/party/Stalin and each and every Soviet citizen. They arrived as Stalin's brides; they left endowed with both consciousness and womanhood. "This year twenty-three women took pregnancy leave," reported Z. S. Budagian, "and I was asked to say a very special thank you to comrade Stalin on their behalf. [Applause.]"

Even heaven has its detractors, and so does the 1930s Soviet version of "prosperous living, fun, and happiness." Valentina Bogdan's memoir, published in emigration, is a remarkable story of a "First Five-Year Plan student," pioneering engineer, and privileged member of the Soviet professional elite who is also an Orthodox Christian and self-conscious Cossack. Her life has no childhood, happy or dark, no conversion experience, and no denouement by way of either death or immortality. It is a story of life-long emigration within the USSR, a life in search of a plot that would become popular in recollections of the "stagnation period" but remains rare in reference to Stalinism.

The most common and influential autobiographical mode of disowning the 1930s is the camp memoir. Written for the most part by the betrayed beneficiaries of the two revolutions, it reverses the official darkness-to-light journey and ends up with a plot that echoes the canonical gentry émigré narrative. First comes the age of innocence, complete with remote father and loyal peasant nanny (a refugee from collectivization). There is the estate, now known as the dacha, which lies at the very center of Arcadia and offers mushroom-picking, swimming, picnicking, twilight conversations, and the sound of a faraway train. There is Christmas, now known as New Year's, which brings midnight magic into familiar places. There are the joys of reading—mostly Russian classics but also Dickens, Thackeray, and Balzac. There are the intense first friendships and timid first loves, the endless arguments over the eternal questions, the long nights on southbound trains, and the first glimpse of the sea. And then *they* come and take it all away. "My parents' arrest marked the end of my childhood," writes Shikheeva-Gaister, "my happy and peaceful childhood." The "prosperous" homemakers and former revolutionaries who may or may not have invaded and searched Volkonskaia's home are now invaded and searched themselves, while their children, who have done so well at reenacting gentry childhoods, are now expelled from Stalin's and Tolstoy's paradise. What follows is a rapid descent into hell, but if most émigré narratives end at the gate or the first circle, the camp memoir is primarily about life in the underworld. The daughters go back to the place from which their mothers emerged—a place where all children are orphans, all women are widows, all food is rationed, and all apartments (and bathhouses) are communal. In a cattle car headed for a Siberian camp, they meet the long-time underground resident Ekaterina Olitskaia, a dispossessed gentry woman who never emigrated and an ascetic revolutionary who never triumphed. They have nothing to say to each other.

PART I

□ Civil War as a Way of Life

(1917–1920)

IN FEBRUARY (old style) 1917, in the midst of the First World War, the Romanov dynasty fell, giving way to a Provisional Government dominated first by liberals and then by moderate socialists who were unable to deal with the country's problems. As order and administration collapsed in the summer, peasants started seizing landowners' estates. In October the Bolsheviks, intransigent socialists whose refusal to cooperate was much resented by socialist competitors (Mensheviks and Social Revolutionaries, or SRs), gathered support in the armed forces and among the big-city working class and seized power in the name of the soviets, almost without resistance from Kerensky's government. The Bolsheviks, proclaiming themselves the "vanguard of the proletariat," understood politics as class war and dealt violently and intolerantly with opponents; as many memoirs in this section indicate, they had little support from Russia's traditionally radical intelligentsia (which they labeled "bourgeois," though many of its members actually came from the nobility).

Civil War broke out in 1918. The Bolsheviks ("Reds") held the center of the country and "White" armies gathered at various points on the periphery. Husbands and brothers (and even some of our women memoirists) went off to fight for the Whites or the Reds. Hunger took hold in the towns, and in the south many towns were captured and recaptured by competing forces. By the end of 1920 the Whites were essentially defeated, and many officers and supporters left the country with them. Once the Reds recaptured frontier territory, borders were closed and departure became difficult. Nevertheless, an estimated one million persons, many of them from the nobility and the intelligentsia, emigrated during the revolution and Civil War period.

The Bolsheviks (who officially changed the party's name to Communist in 1918) called their regime "soviet" and a "dictatorship of the proletariat." In fact, it was a one-party state in which opposition parties were harassed and in effect outlawed. The Cheka came into existence shortly after the October Revolution with the purpose of combating counterrevolution and sabotage. The Bolsheviks were not ashamed to admit that they practiced terror and expropriation against class enemies.

Life in the towns was miserable during the Civil War. Industry was at a near standstill, food was rationed and extremely scarce, livable housing was scarce, and local soviets had begun the practice of settling proletarian families into "bourgeois" apartments along with their original owners. Local authorities often prohibited private trade and closed markets, and black markets flourished. The enormous problems of running a country, as against making a revolution, came home to the new regime; its leaders' work experience ran more to underground organization and émigré political journalism than administration. In the spring of 1921 the regime abandoned the maximalist economic program of "War Communism," ceased requisitioning grain, and allowed markets to reopen. This so-called New Economic Policy brought a quick economic revival, though many Communists felt it as a retreat and a betrayal.

1 □ EKATERINA OLITSKAIA

My Reminiscences (1)

□ Ekaterina Olitskaia grew up on her parents' estate outside Kursk, in southern Russia. Her father, a one-time revolutionary, prisoner, political émigré, and Zurich-educated agronomer, was a gentleman farmer who tried to combine his admiration for the Russian peasant with his enthusiasm for scientific agriculture. Her mother, a wealthy aristocrat, was a medical doctor with a Swiss degree who never became certified in Russia because of the couple's banishment from large cities. Olitskaia was raised by her Russian nanny and French and German governesses before being sent to a school in Kursk, where she became a socialist. In the fall of 1916 she and her friend Olia were admitted to the Stebut Agricultural Institute for women in Petrograd.[1]

ON FEBRUARY 18[2] the workers of the Putilov plant went out on strike. The strike spread, and by February 22 almost all the large factories of Petrograd had joined in. Our institute was supposed to go on strike and stage a demonstration on the 23rd, but revolutionary events forced us to change our plans. On the morning of the 22nd we were still lying in bed when Olia's mother, who had gone out to buy some bread, came rushing in very excited. She told us that all the stores were closed, and the streetcars were not running. She had seen large crowds in the streets and heard shots being fired. Olia and I leaped out of bed, threw on our clothes, and, ignoring her mother's desperate pleas, ran out the door to go to our institute. The city was overflowing with people. Large crowds were gathering under revolutionary appeals that had been pasted on fences and walls. Some policemen were trying to disperse the crowds and tear down the appeals. The farther we went, the thicker the crowds became. We could not even reach the institute. The bridges were being cordoned off by the police, who had formed a thick human chain to hold back the people. Carried by the crowd in one direction and then another, we tried to make our way to another bridge. It, too, had been cordoned off. A large group of demonstrators was moving toward us down Kronverksky Avenue, a red banner floating in the wind over their heads, when,

From E. Olitskaia, *Moi vospominaniia* (Frankfurt/Main: Possev-Verlag, 1971), 64–138 (abridged). This memoir was written in the 1960s after the author's release from camp and exile. Before being published in Germany, the manuscript circulated in *samizdat* (illegally produced typescript copies) in the Soviet Union. For further selections from Olitskaia, see selections 13 and 36 in this volume.

[1] The name of St. Petersburg, Russia's capital, was changed to Petrograd upon the outbreak of war. In 1924, after Lenin's death, it was renamed Leningrad.

[2] Russia's calendar was changed early in 1918; the "old style" dates were thirteen days behind the "new style," meaning that the "February Revolution" actually took place in March (new style) and the "October Revolution" in November. Olitskaia is using old-style dates.

suddenly, a Cossack detachment emerged from a small alley not far from where we were.[3] In their black sheepskin hats and flowing black capes, they came riding straight at the demonstrators, with their whips raised high in the air. At that moment I ceased to exist—except for my eyes, which were glued to the Cossacks. "It's really going to happen! Right here in front of me, they're going to bring their whips down on the people's heads. They're going to trample them under the hooves of their horses . . ." The Cossack detachment cut into the crowd. The crowd parted and pressed up against the buildings on either side. Then I heard a loud "Hurrah!" Never before or since have I heard such a cheer. Restraining their horses and still holding their whips high in the air, the Cossacks rode through the middle of the crowd. The demonstrators greeted them with shouts of "Hurrah!" and tore their hats off their heads. Having passed through the crowd, the Cossacks disappeared. The demonstrators closed ranks and resumed their march in our direction. Frozen and silent in a paroxysm of fear, we did not understand right away what had just taken place before our eyes, but when it finally came home to us that the Cossacks had not brought down their whips and had refused to disperse the crowd, everyone went wild. Some people started crying, others hugged each other. "Hurrah!" we shouted at the demonstrators. Our crowd joined the demonstration, which kept growing and expanding. It must be the revolution! What else could it be? It's the revolution! It will prevail! Even the Cossacks are with the people!

On that first day of the insurrection Olia and I never did make it to our institute. All day long we just walked in the streets among the crowds, not knowing where we were going or why. We shouted greetings to the soldiers who had joined the people. We yelled "Never again!" in front of burning police stations. Somewhere in the distance we could hear shooting. On some streets the secret police were shooting at people from their attic hiding places. I was very happy. I was also quite lucky. During the entire February Revolution I never saw a single dead body, a single lynching. The February Revolution that I witnessed was bloodless.

At night in our room we had endless conversations about the struggle and the revolution.

"What would you do if you found out that a plainclothes policeman was hiding in our apartment? Would you inform on him?" my sister Ania kept asking.

I answered without hesitation: "Of course, but it would not be informing because it would be part of the struggle—in defense of the people's rights and in defense of the triumphant revolution."

I had no doubt that the revolution was going to triumph. As we watched the police and court archives going down in flames, I felt humbled by the majesty of the fire but a little upset about the destruction of the archives. Then someone explained to me that they were being burnt not only out of hatred but also as part of the revolutionary plan, in case we lost. So I tossed my head and laughed at the doubters.

[3] Cossacks—armed farmers organized into autonomous "armies" (eleven in all at the time of the revolution), which received grants of land in the imperial borderlands in exchange for military service. In the last decades of the Russian Empire, mounted Cossack units were often used to suppress strikes and demonstrations.

The next day Olia and I decided that nothing would deter us from reaching the institute. We did not want to watch the revolution; we wanted to make it. But what needed to be done? We had to get to the institute to receive our instructions. As we made our way from the Petrograd District to the Finland Station, we saw the same crowds of defiant people, the same barricades—many of them abandoned and no longer needed, and streetcars standing still or overturned. Something I hadn't seen before were the army trucks loaded with bread that had been brought in from the barracks. They stopped at bread lines and distributed bread among the women.

I was right. The Stebut Agricultural Institute for Women was buzzing with activity. Everyone was completely exhausted. A Georgian girl, whom I had met and liked at the beginning of the semester, said: "We need people at the medical post and the cafeteria," but the kitchen manager did not give us a chance to choose.

"Come with me. My girls are on their last legs. We need help."

Olia and I followed her into the cafeteria. It was empty. The tables were bare; there were no tablecloths. The floor was dirty and covered with cigarette butts. We were just starting to clean up, when Valia called out: "No time for that, Comrades! The fire in the oven is going out!"

While we were carrying wood and kindling for the oven, the cafeteria had filled up with soldiers and workers. They had stacked their guns against the wall and now sat rubbing their freezing hands, talking loudly, and laughing. We started running around with bowls full of hot cereal. From morning till night we handed them out to cold, hungry men. There was nothing else left to eat: only tea, cereal, and mustard in unlimited quantities.

Trucks full of people kept pulling up to our cafeteria. Each of them had a student from the Military Medical Academy in charge. In those early days medical students served as both officers and doctors.

"Feed these people, Comrades," they said to us. "And make sure it's hot. Whatever it is, it's got to be hot!"

The weather in Petrograd was clear and very cold. All the plants and factories were closed down. The blanket of smoke that always hung over the city had lifted. During the day the sky was incredibly blue; at night, with all the electricity cut off, it was very dark and the sky was covered with stars. For five days without a break we ladled out hot cereal, carried wood, and kept the fire going. The soldiers who came to eat told us about what was going on in the city. At first there were very few of us working in the cafeteria, but then more and more girls came, and I finally decided that they could do without me and asked the revolutionary committee of the institute to transfer me to another job.

"The Tauride Palace[4] has asked us for more people," I was told. "Get a pass and go present yourself before the military commander of the Tauride Palace."

PETROGRAD was seething with anticipation and excitement. The Tauride Palace was one of the main magnets for popular grievances, hopes, demands, and demonstrations. Happy and excited, Olia and I walked through the streets of Petro-

---

[4] Tauride Palace—location of the State Duma.

grad. I had not bothered to go to the Tauride Square before. The last Duma sessions had not interested us, but now we were inside its historic halls. The square was full of people. Right in front of the entrance, somebody was standing on a truck making a speech, as was the custom in those days. After standing over a hot stove for so long, Olia and I were totally enraptured by what we heard. Speakers followed one after another. At the other end of the square somebody else was speaking from another truck. Having squeezed our way through the crowd, we used our passes to report to the commander of the Tauride Palace. He put me at a desk in front of Kerensky's[5] office. I was supposed to check the passes and make sure that the citizens who were aimlessly wandering around the palace did not interfere with the work going on behind closed doors.

I got bored sitting at that desk. While in other halls the revolution was being debated and celebrated, speeches were being made, and bitter arguments were being conducted, there it was completely quiet. People with or without briefcases kept going by, and I could hear fragments of sentences, sometimes calm and sometimes agitated. I did not feel that I was really needed there, and when I was asked to accept special dishes intended for Kerensky—whose very name was pronounced with a kind of awe—I lost all patience. I was deaf to the argument that after long hours of intense work Kerensky needed a light, nutritional diet. Chuckling, the commander offered me another job: "There's work that's very important, but that nobody wants to do. On the ground floor there's a cafeteria where our troops are being fed. They need someone to slice the bread down there."

I sliced bread from morning till night, loaf after loaf, till my hands bled. Each night Olia and I would walk through the deserted streets to the Petrograd District. The city was under a curfew, but we had our passes so we didn't have to worry about the checkpoints. Still, life was crazy, and there were other causes for worry. Often, when we got home, Olia's mother would tell us how dangerous it was outside and how she and other pedestrians had had to crawl over some bridges on their hands and knees because of the shooting at street corners. We simply laughed as we pictured Anna Vasilievna crawling over a bridge on her hands and knees.

While some things were falling apart, others were being organized. Unions, committees, and associations were springing up everywhere. Even the thieves were organizing themselves: I once saw an announcement that at a certain time under a certain bridge, the pickpockets would be holding their organizational meeting. All over town rallies—planned and spontaneous—were taking place. People were making speeches from trucks, balconies, hilltops, and the bases of statues. All kinds of exciting news kept arriving: the Petrograd Revolution was being supported by Moscow; Rodzianko[6] had formed a government; Nicholas II had abdicated in favor of Michael;[7] Michael had also abdicated. New parties and

[5] A. F. Kerensky (1881–1970)—member of the Socialist Revolutionary Party, minister in the Provisional Government, prime minister from July to October 1917.

[6] M. V. Rodzianko (1859–1924)—last president of the State Duma.

[7] Grand Duke Mikhail Aleksandrovich (1878–1918), Tsar Nicholas II's brother.

local soviets of worker's representatives were being organized. New and ever more complicated issues were being raised. Passions were being inflamed. However, we inexperienced young people never imagined that there were any serious contradictions within the workers' movement since we just tended to agree with whomever had spoken last.

In late March or early April, when the first revolutionary storm had passed, our student organizations issued a new directive: "Return to your hometowns, Comrades; you are needed in the provinces." At the same time we started getting letters from home, asking us to come back. Our parents were worried about us. I was reluctant to leave Petrograd. As I was leaving my institute, I somehow sensed that I would never return. Shortly before our departure, after we had definitely decided to return to Kursk, my sister talked me into going to see our aunt, Marusia. On the way home we had an argument. Ania had never been interested in politics, had never belonged to any political movement, and had always tried to catch me in some inconsistency, carelessness, or insincerity.

"I'm not sure I know what I want—probably just to live in peace, without gunshots and fires," she was saying, "but I do know that you are not being honest with yourself. Just imagine that all your ideals come true and they take Father's land away. What would we live on? How would you pay your tuition?"

My sister had hit a raw nerve. I had often argued with my friend Raia about whether my father was an exploiter. I was absolutely certain that my father was not running his Sorochino estate for profit and that his goal was not to exploit the peasants but to help them and spread knowledge among them. In fact, the conditions under which they had to live and work only made his project more difficult. My father and I knew this, but from the outside, even for Ania, our father was an exploiter, and we were living off the exploitation of the peasants. This made me even more impatient for a revolutionary resolution to the agrarian question and for an end to the awkward situation in which our father and all of us found ourselves. "We'll live like thousands of people do. And Father will be working and making more money than ever, and he'll be a lot happier. I can understand when other people say these things, but when you, knowing what you do . . . You think we're living off the peasants and want to go on living like that." "It doesn't depend on me. It is not what I want at all, but it's the way it has always been and still remains, no matter what you say."

THE provinces were slow to join the revolution. The workers' movement had been decimated during the years of reaction. When we arrived, Kursk did not even have any party cells. They were gradually being resurrected, mostly by young people who clustered around two or three adults. I remember how we welcomed one of them, a peasant Socialist Revolutionary[8] named Pianykh, who had been freed by the revolution after twelve years of hard labor. This frail and kindly old man was our icon, but he could not become our leader. We needed a specific

---

[8] Socialist Revolutionary (SR) Party—a non-Marxist socialist party. The SR platform promised land to the peasants.

cause, and soon we found it. We were preparing a congress of student socialists in order to join forces in the name of the revolution. At the same time we were organizing general education schools for the workers. Workers streamed in; the City Duma donated a building; and students became the teachers. Armed with books, we lectured on Russian history, literature, political economy, and mathematics. We felt powerless to give the workers the knowledge they needed. They thanked us fervently, although we were really studying along with them. Often the students would enlighten their teachers just by posing timely questions. Strange as it may seem, the revolutionary editions of magazines and even newspapers rarely made it to Kursk that spring.

The railway station was about two versts[9] from the city. One could buy many newspapers there. The student union talked the City Duma into giving us one of the city's newspaper stands. There we sold the periodicals of all the socialist parties. The money to purchase the first order of newspapers and magazines was raised by collection among the citizens of Kursk. The stand was staffed by students, who worked for free, of course. We took turns going to the railway station, buying the periodicals, and delivering them to the stand. We worked shifts, and all profits were reinvested to expand our operation. Finally, the city was regularly receiving the press of all political persuasions. We carried the *People's Voice*, *New Life*, *People's Cause*, *Pravda*, and other socialist newspapers and magazines.

I will never forget the May Day celebrations in Kursk in 1917. They truly represented the sheer, boundless joy of a free people. The crowds savored the words, slogans, red banners, and revolutionary songs. Everyone was galvanized by the liberty, equality, and fraternity that had been achieved so quickly—or so we thought. In less than a month, life demonstrated to me and others that the struggle for the people's happiness, fraternity, and equality was just beginning.

Sometime in late May the Congress of Student Socialists of Kursk Province, which we had been preparing, finally took place. By then, party organizations in Kursk had gathered strength. The City Duma was divided into political factions. Both my mother and Raia's had joined the Social Democrats.[10] My sister, Dutia, who had also returned to Kursk, signed up with the Bolsheviks. I, along with several friends, became a Socialist Revolutionary. Joining a party was extremely easy, and people were joining in droves. Our student community also split into parties, and from the very beginning the congress was divided into factions. Even when we sat down at the table covered with a red cloth, we arranged ourselves according to party affiliation. It was clear that there could be no unity among student socialists. We had been able to join forces against the tsar, but a joint effort to build a new society was proving impossible. The students could not reach a common decision on a single issue: (1) immediate peace or war until

[9] Verst—Russian measurement equivalent to thirty-five hundred feet.

[10] The Russian Social Democratic (SD) Labor Party was divided into Menshevik and Bolshevik factions. The Mensheviks (here "Social Democrats") subscribed to the "orthodox" Marxist view that Russia must pass through the capitalist stage of development before reaching socialism. The Bolsheviks (future Communists) believed in an immediate socialist revolution led by a tightly organized "vanguard" party.

victory; (2) the earliest possible convocation of the Constituent Assembly or the immediate seizure of power by the soviets of workers' and soldiers' deputies; (3) the solution of the agrarian question by the Constituent Assembly[11] or the immediate revolutionary seizure of gentry lands by the peasants. We argued about all these issues and were unable to reach a consensus.

THE October coup[12] swept away the old leaders and brought in new ones. The Bolsheviks and Left SRs began running Kursk. Many young people found themselves in responsible positions. For instance, Matvei Rozhdestvensky, an eighteen-year-old law student, became the commissar of agriculture, while Munia Kogan, who was the same age, was appointed one of the editors of the only Kursk newspaper.

I could not find any SRs. They were either in prison or underground. Most members of the intelligentsia were boycotting the new regime. I could not accept what was going on. I was dismayed by the dissolution of the Constituent Assembly, the closing down of socialist newspapers, and the banning of the SR Party. I did not want to see my good friends, Matvei and Munia, and could barely stand my sister, Dutia.

In 1918 all industry, factories, plants, banks, houses, and trade were nationalized. It was a difficult time of ruin and disintegration, of total confusion both in the army and at workplaces. It was a lot easier to destroy than to create something new. Some people boycotted the new regime; others were not trusted; and still others wanted to build a new life but did not know how. Millions of petty entrepreneurs and artisans, both in town and in the villages, took advantage of the shortages and engaged in rampant speculation. The violent methods of War Communism[13] corrupted the leaders and infuriated the people.

Crude antireligious propaganda, the confiscation of church property, the mockery of popular beliefs, and the attendant moral collapse—all this I saw with my own eyes in Kursk. All this was, in one way or another, a part of my life.

The peasant unrest of the summer of 1918 was something I only heard about. I heard about the so-called struggle between the poor peasants and the kulaks, about the formation of the committees of the poor (the main power in the village), and about the raids on villages by worker detachments to confiscate the excess grain needed by the starving cities.

Peasants were being dekulakized.[14] Anyone who expressed discontent was a kulak. Peasant families that had never used hired labor were put down as kulaks. A household that had two cows, a cow and a calf, or a pair of horses was

---

[11] Constituent Assembly—the body which was to determine the constitutional future of Russia after the February Revolution. Elected in November 1917, it was dissolved by the Bolsheviks on its first meeting (in January 1918).

[12] That is, the Bolshevik Revolution of 1917.

[13] War Communism—a set of measures adopted by the Bolsheviks between 1918 and 1921, which involved strict administrative centralization; the nationalization of banking, transport, foreign trade, and large-scale industry; the expropriation of peasant produce; and the rationing of basic goods and services.

[14] The expropriation and deportation of "kulaks."

considered kulak. Villages that refused to give up excess grain or expose kulaks were raided by punitive detachments. So peasants had special meetings to decide who was going to be a kulak. I was astonished by all this, but the peasants explained: "We were ordered to uncover kulaks, so what else can we do?"

Village assemblies elected kulaks the way they used to elect elders. To spare the children, they usually chose childless bachelors.

Most workers in Russia had ties to their villages. When the general collapse reached the factories, the workers survived by manufacturing small objects such as lighters, which they sold at the market, or by going back to the village, where they alarmed the peasants even further with their stories about the disintegration of the economy.

Peasants couldn't buy anything: there were no sacks, no ropes, no axes, no matches. There was no soap in the stores; it had to be bought in back alleys or secretly at the market. According to the ridiculous rumors that were circulating, this soap was made from the bodies of little children who had been kidnapped and murdered for that purpose.

All the valuables confiscated from the rich townspeople, the village kulaks, and the churches were carried away and piled up somewhere. Some things ended up in the confiscators' pockets or disappeared later from warehouses. Who didn't take things in those days! Even Dutia brought home a couple of icons in metal mounting for our maid, Akulina. She claimed, of course, that nobody wanted those icons, but that did not change the facts.

Books, paintings, and albums from private collections were taken to public libraries, where they were dumped in cellars. Nobody recorded or catalogued them.

In libraries, undesirable books were being taken off the shelves according to special lists or following the orders of newly appointed librarians. The entire history of Russia found itself beyond the pale: Kliuchevsky, Platonov of course, Elpatievsky, Karamzin.[15] In the early years of the revolution only Pokrovsky was held in high regard.[16] Leo Tolstoy got into trouble for his religious and philosophical works, but in the heat of the battle *Anna Karenina*, *War and Peace*, and *Resurrection* were also swept off the shelves.

I felt completely alone in Kursk with my alarm and indignation. I could talk to Father and argue with Dutia until I was blue in the face, but that was it. The vicious gossip, the rumors, the whispers in dark alleys, the endless jokes and sarcastic criticisms made life unbearable. All non-Communist organizations were deep underground. I did not have any ties with them.

FINALLY, a friend of my parents who came down from Moscow to streamline the tanning industry, got me a job in the Kursk District Tanning Commission. All

[15] V. O. Kliuchevsky (1841–1911), S. F. Platonov (1860–1933), and N. M. Karamzin (1766–1826)—prominent Russian historians. S. Ia. Elpatievsky (1854–1933)—publicist, author of several memoirs.

[16] M. N. Pokrovsky (1868–1932)—Marxist historian, Bolshevik, Deputy Commissar of Enlightenment from 1918 to 1932.

Kursk tanneries had been nationalized and were, along with all the shoe factories in the province, run by the workers themselves. The commission was headed by a young worker by the name of Mukhin. He was a Bolshevik, of course, and was full of energy, but, alas, was also semiliterate.

Our friend got me a position in the department of statistics. I was very nervous because I was afraid I might not be up to the job. It turned out to be true. As soon as I came, I was given an abacus, which I had never used before, and sheets of paper with long columns of numbers. I did not know anybody in the office. Trembling with fear, I sat down at my desk, pulled the abacus closer, and started counting. All around me, people were walking and talking, and I could hear the rattling of typewriters. I never once raised my eyes. I even refused the cup of tea that the cleaning woman brought for me. Over and over again I added up the numbers, and each time I got a different result. The numbers had been typed very neatly and clearly, but the sum total remained a mystery to me. At the end of the day I went home in absolute despair. The next morning I did not want to go back, but my parents prevailed upon me.

At work I was in for a surprise. Mukhin had transferred me from the Department of Statistics to his own office as an assistant secretary. "You'll be my personal secretary," he said.

They brought in a tiny desk and put it in the director's office. Across from me, at a large desk, sat Secretary Logvinov. He and I were on our own. Mukhin was gone for most of the day. Logvinov gave me a register book and a pile of sheets with executive orders printed on them. "You'll be keeping the order book," he said.

There were quite a few orders. I worked hard for about three days, but when I had copied them all, there was nothing left for me to do. I would get one, maybe two, new orders a day, but my working day consisted of eight hours! When I asked Logvinov what I was supposed to do, he said: "Just sit there quietly. I don't have anything to do either."

"Why do you need an assistant then?" I asked.

"Director's orders," he grinned. "What's your problem, you're getting paid, aren't you?"

MUKHIN had a very young, pleasant wife, a simple worker in a shoe-repair shop. They had a little daughter. Every once in a while his wife would drop by our office, and we would chat. She was a simple, friendly, but uneducated woman. At first I did not pay any attention to Mukhin's kindness to me. Sometimes I thought he was showing off because he wanted to convert me politically.

Once, the wife of the chairman of the city executive committee came to see Mukhin. He fawned and fussed over her. "So this is how the Bolsheviks receive their bosses' wives," I thought. From a drawer in his desk Mukhin took out a piece of beautiful kid leather. Then he summoned a cobbler, who took her foot measurements right there in the office. "He's our best cobbler," said Mukhin. He motioned for the man to stay, and turned to me: "There's enough here for two pairs of shoes. Would you like to order the same kind for yourself?"

Of course I would. The cobbler measured my feet, too. Within a week our shoes were ready, and absolutely dream shoes they were, too. But when I modeled them for the other employees, it turned out that none of them had ever been able to get any leather, except perhaps by special permit, and, even then, black calfskin at best. There was a special ban on using kid leather to make shoes for the general population.

I began to get suspicious. Mukhin was not around. He was in Moscow on business. So the matter had to wait until his return. As soon as he got back, he put a little package on my desk.

"This is from Moscow. To go with your new shoes."

Inside the package were silk stockings, an incredible luxury in those days.

"How much do I owe you for the stockings and shoes?" I asked uncertainly. I was wondering whether I could afford them. I was making three or four hundred thousand rubles a month at the time.

"Oh come on!" he said. "It was no trouble at all. And anyway, the shoes don't have a price because you can't get kid leather like this in any store."

The blood rushed to my face. "So this is a present from a director to his secretary?! Who told you I would accept this kind of present from a director?! I absolutely insist on paying for the shoes." And I threw the stockings on his desk.

Red-faced and confused, Mukhin said, without looking up: "I'll ask for a bill."

I stormed out of the office. I was sure that I had lost my job. But when I came back the next morning, the only change was that my desk had been moved to the common room and placed by the partition. I had been formally transferred to the records department. I was very happy with my new job and with the fact that I was suddenly popular in the office. At home I waved my new shoes under my sister's nose and yelled: "See what your proletarian directors and chairmen's wives are up to! Bribes, theft, adultery—everything the way it used to be under the capitalists!"

I OBSERVED life around me with silent indignation. Instead of a bright world of peace and liberty I saw a world of violence and bitter fighting. People who had until recently freely expressed their hopes and ideas were becoming secretive. Instead of improving, the material situation was getting worse all the time. I still have a postcard issued by the Central Committee for Assistance to the Starving. It cost 1,250 rubles. One kind of injustice had been replaced by another. To curb peasant discontent, the authorities sent out Chinese and Latvian detachments. People told terrible stories about the atrocities they had committed. Who could we trust? What could we trust in?

The mumbling and whispering of the Philistines was repulsive to me, but free criticism did not exist. Even *Novaia zhizn'*, which was published by Gorky,[17] had been closed down. The tendentious Communist press was the only source of information available. We knew nothing about life in Russia. I had heard rumors

---

[17] Maxim Gorky (1868–1936)—a popular writer "from the people" sympathetic to the Social Democrats; had a close, if rocky, relationship with Lenin and later Stalin.

of an uprising in Yaroslavl, a mutiny in Kronstadt, a Czechoslovak struggle on the Volga, of Kolchak in Siberia, and of countless anarchist bands.[18]

The rumors concerning Kolchak and Yudenich[19] were followed by rumors of an offensive by General Denikin.[20] These were more persistent and more believable. Denikin's army was moving toward us, and moving incredibly fast.

The Communist press talked about the outrages perpetrated by the Whites, about their ties to foreign invaders, about the estate and factory owners who followed the Denikin army, about the return of the land and factories to the capitalists, and about atrocities, floggings, hangings, and anti-Jewish pogroms. All this I could believe, but they also said that the SRs and the SDs were supporting General Denikin and his army that consisted of White Guardists and old tsarist generals. This I absolutely refused to believe. Neither the SRs nor the SDs were capable of joining the tsarist generals.

The prospect of Denikin's army entering the city seemed all the more unsettling because my sister was a Communist. We had no doubt that Denikin's men were killing Communists and persecuting their families. If Kursk fell, my sister might be arrested and maybe even hanged. Anything was possible . . . Also, the persistent rumors of anti-Jewish pogroms perpetrated by the White Army meant that the families of my closest friends, Raia and Shura, were in real danger. But while nobody around me wanted Denikin to come, their disgust with the Communists kept growing. The closer the Denikin detachments got, the worse the terror became. The town was paralyzed with fear. Sometimes it seemed that they were doing this on purpose. On one of the last nights, twenty-four representatives of the Kursk bourgeoisie were arrested. They were not accused of anything in particular—they were simply taken hostage. Among the twenty-four was Korotkov—the same Korotkov who, as mayor, had helped us organize student rallies. All of them were taken to Orel. In Orel all twenty-four were shot.

Hostage-taking—the very notion made me think of barbarism. In those days everybody was drawing analogies between our revolution and the French Revolution. Some people were saying that the Great French Revolution had also known hostage-taking. At first I had not wanted to believe it, but then I had rummaged through my books and discovered that it was the terrible, cruel truth. So much the worse for the French Revolution.

KURSK was preparing to defend itself against Denikin. Everyone expected decisive battles to take place outside the city. People were not allowed to walk outside after dark. But at the very last moment it turned out that the defenders had been

[18] Armed Czech and Slovak POWs traveling to Vladivostok in an attempt to rejoin the First World War on the side of the Allies clashed repeatedly with Bolshevik forces. A. V. Kolchak (1873–1920)—admiral, leader of the White (anti-Bolshevik) forces in Siberia from 1918 to 1920.

[19] N. N. Iudenich (1862–1933)—tsarist general and leader of White forces in northeastern Russia from 1919 to 1920.

[20] A. A. Denikin (1872–1947)—tsarist general, commander-in-chief of the (White) Armed Forces of Southern Russia from February 1919 to April 1920.

betrayed and that all the cannons had been sabotaged. The city was surrounded. The troops were retreating; the Bolsheviks were running away. Meanwhile, the population knew nothing. At 3:00 P.M. a light carriage stopped by our front door. Out climbed the woman who had been running an orphanage in the building of the old Noblemen's Assembly. Helped by her husband, she pulled three large wicker baskets out of the carriage and asked my mother to keep them. She did not say what was inside the baskets. Nor did she tell us that the Bolsheviks were surrendering the town to the Whites.

My sister, who was a member of a special defense detachment, had not been home for two days. That night Ania and I were invited to a friend's wedding. Everything was very modest, simple, and fun. Because of the curfew, we celebrated all night long. In the morning the whole noisy crowd said good-bye to the newlyweds. Their house was at the edge of the city. The streets were empty and quiet. In this silence the sound of hooves striking the cobblestones rang loudly and clearly. A mounted detachment appeared from an alley and rode off toward the center of town. They were Denikin's men. On the shoulders of their gray coats glistened the long-forgotten officer's epaulets. Denikin's troops were marching solemnly into Kursk. They knew there would be no fighting and that they were expected by their people. The troops were followed by carts full of food: white bread, flour, and sugar. All these delicacies were being handed out to the population.

The city was tense, and so was our house. We had lived through the Bolsheviks. We knew what they were like, but nobody knew what Denikin's men would be like. The army was passing through the city, occupying the station and mounting guards along the railway track. Fearing anti-Jewish pogroms, my friend's family—the mother and children—moved into our house as soon as they heard about the arrival of the Whites. Only the father stayed behind. The best gynecologist in Kursk, he was a nonparty person of generally liberal views. His wife belonged to the far-left wing of the SDs. Many even considered her a Bolshevik, but she had never belonged to the Bolshevik Party. Because of my Communist sister our house was not very safe, but the fear of pogroms brought people anyway.

On the surface everything was peaceful. The Whites had not yet formed a civilian administration, but they were busy advertising themselves. Long-forgotten goods were being handed out from carts, and Soviet thousand-ruble notes with the word "trash" printed across them had been scattered all over the city. Office employees returned to work, but the managers were gone. No one knew what was going to happen to the various institutions. The Tanning Commission employees decided to save all the office property. Fearing looters, they decided that the employees should take everything home: one person would take the typewriter; another, the paper; and so on. I was supposed to hide the counting machine. We pledged to keep everything until life returned to normal. The city grew silent as people waited for what would happen next. Grand announcements by our new masters were posted on walls. People read them but kept their doubts to themselves. Everyone was skeptical of these new promises.

The peaceful flow of our life was interrupted by two events. Somebody told my mother that Dutia, armed, had been seen on the outskirts of the city when the Whites were already on their way in. She had been trying to get to the train station, but it had already been taken. My mother became alarmed. Meanwhile, because of the apparent calm in the city, my friend's mother had decided to go back home. It turned out, however, that the situation was not as calm as we had thought. Twice in the two days that had passed since the arrival of the Whites, soldiers had broken into their house and demanded ransom from their father because he was a Jew. He had given them the money, and they had left.

"Now," he said, "the worst is over. From now on I'm not giving them another cent."

But soon they heard the sound of rifle butts beating on their door again. Another group of soldiers demanded money. The father said that he had already paid twice and that he had nothing left. The soldiers ordered him to come with them. Without his coat or hat, he was led down the street by about six soldiers. Fortunately, a White officer appeared from around the corner. He questioned the soldiers about what was going on, cursed them rudely, apologized to the doctor, and escorted him home. He refused to come in: "Our men are also capable of outrages, I'm afraid. If anything happens again, please complain to headquarters."

Notices signed by the military commander were posted all over the city: "In case of rights violations on the part of the military, the population is urged to complain immediately to military headquarters and to the military commander of the city. Banditry and looting will be dealt with by the full force of the law, including execution. In case of searches, demand to be shown a warrant signed by the military commander of the city."

Reading these announcements, I suddenly remembered the baskets that had been brought into our house and stacked up in the front room. I was sure that our place would be searched. When I got back home, Mother was not there. I decided not to wait for her and started opening the baskets. Akulina helped me. The baskets were filled with linen taken from the Noblemen's Assembly: tablecloths and towels of the finest quality with the satin-stitched emblems of the Assembly. Imagine how we would have looked if the search had revealed all that! There was so much linen that I panicked: I had no time to burn it all and no place to hide it. I grabbed the scissors and started cutting off the emblems. Akulina stood over me and lamented: "Such fine work going to waste!" I threw all the cut-off pieces into the stove. When Mother came home, she did not reproach me. She, too, wondered why anybody would want to impose these baskets on us. Mother was in pretty bad shape at that time. She never said anything, but, looking at her face, I knew that she never stopped thinking about Dutia. Had she managed to escape? Had she been arrested? Was she alive?

On the fourth or fifth day of the White administration they came to search our place. Judging by the behavior of the people doing the search, Dutia had not been arrested. The soldiers were restrained, but thorough. We knew they would not find anything, but we did have somebody else's chests that had been in the house for almost three years. This is how it happened. We had taken in a lodger, an officer and his family. Shortly before the revolution the whole family had gone to visit some relatives and never returned. We had never heard from them since then, and their things were still where they had left them, untouched. We explained this to the search party. They decided to open the chests. We did not have the keys, of course, so they had to break the locks. In the very first chest they found arms, but the soldiers' suspicions abated quickly. In the other chests were some officer's things as well as sugar, grain, and flour. The food was rotten and covered with mold. One glance was enough to show that it had been there for a long time. Their commander announced: "The weapons will have to be confiscated. They are supposed to be turned in."

We did not mind. They listed the arms in their inventory and set them aside. I noticed, however, that our lodger's military boots had been placed in the same pile. They had not been listed in the inventory. I pulled them out.

"Don't touch anything!" yelled the officer who was in charge of the search.

"What do you mean, don't touch?" I said. "You haven't included these boots in the inventory." Mother was pulling at my sleeve, but I would not be stopped—I wanted to know if Denikin's men robbed people during searches.

"Would you like to leave with us?" snapped the officer.

"With or without you, but I'll certainly go to your headquarters and ask for an explanation," I answered.

The search was over. The soldiers left with the arms and the boots. I argued with Mother:

"Why do they post those notices? I'm going down to headquarters."

I was getting dressed when the bell rang. On the porch stood the officer who had just left. He handed me the boots.

"I'm sorry," he mumbled. "I shouldn't have taken them, but you know . . . my prestige with the men."

Prestige my foot! Just scared of headquarters, the thief!

THE Whites had occupied the city and all the surrounding area. They were moving quickly toward Orel and Tula. I still could not make up my mind. There were no SRs or SDs with them, of course. The posters did say "All power to the Constituent Assembly," but in the meantime . . . Actually, in the city itself there were no atrocities and no terror. Communists were being arrested. My mother was interrogated and then released. Suddenly Raia's mother was arrested. We were all very worried. Then later in the day an orderly came and brought a note from her asking for her robe, slippers, towel, and toothbrush. We calmed down. A week later she, too, came back. Everything seemed to be going smoothly, but my own life was not going anywhere. I mean, my public life. Everything was dominated by the military. We were on the front line.

A friend of mine had a neighbor, who taught German. Her husband, an SR, had been sentenced to death under the tsar but had managed to escape and, in 1905, had emigrated to England. We liked Olga Afanasyevna and were friendly with her son, Seva, who was two years older than we were. Seva was a student at the

Petrograd Polytechnic. During the war he had been drafted, had enrolled in a military school, and, upon completion, had been sent to the front as an officer. His mother had not heard from him since the revolution. Now she had received a letter from him. Seva wrote that he was in the White Army and that he would get a leave of absence to come see her. We were amazed that Seva, whom we had considered prorevolutionary, could be with the Whites. I could not wait for him to come, hoping that he might help me sort things out.

Seva did come, but, unfortunately, he could not sort things out for us. He told us that he had joined the Whites because the officers had had their epaulets torn off; because their officer's honor had been violated; and because he had been loyal to his oath.

"We joined the White Army because it stood for the Constituent Assembly; because any government should be legitimate; and because at the front we had had enough of the chaos and slackness that bordered on treason. We were suspected, distrusted, insulted, and sold off. Finally, we joined the White Army because we valued the honor of our arms."

None of these arguments convinced us. We wanted to know what the White Army would bring the people. Seva evaded our questions. He kept talking about the White Army's mission to liberate Russia and to guide it to the Constituent Assembly, which would decide the fate of the people. As an officer of the White Army, there was probably nothing else he could tell us. But it seemed to us that he was disappointed in the White movement and had only stayed out of inertia. When we asked him about the Jewish pogroms, atrocities, and floggings in the villages, his answers were vague: "The commanders are trying their best to put an end to it. A lot depends on the unit that enters a city."

He also talked about the heroism of the Russian officer corps. He was the first to tell me about the "psychological attacks," in which officer battalions, armed with nothing but riding crops, had marched against the Reds in closed formation. As the dead ones fell, the live ones had closed ranks. They had marched unarmed, singing and smiling, and the Red Army men had broken down.

But Seva also talked about drunkenness and corruption. He did not criticize the White Army. He simply described things, leaving me to draw my own conclusions. The White movement appeared to me to be rootless, disjointed, and doomed. There was no one idea that could inspire all its participants. Seva spent less than a week in Kursk and, apparently without much enthusiasm, left to join his unit at the front.

THE Whites were in Kursk for a very short time. The reorganized Bolshevik army forced them to retreat as quickly as they had come. Though during their stay in Kursk the Whites had not committed any atrocities, their departure was marked by a terrible tragedy. There was no fighting in the city, but there was panic. A lot of representatives of the bourgeoisie were leaving with Denikin. Loaded down with suitcases and bags, the fugitives were in a hurry to get out of the city. The prisoners who had been arrested by the Whites were neither evacuated nor released. When the Whites left, the last Cossack detachment broke into the prison and hacked the inmates to pieces. The news spread quickly, and many people went to the prison to identify the bodies. Without a word my mother went, too. She was brought back in a cab. We brought her inside and helped her lie down on the couch in the living room. Even then Mother did not say anything. Breathing heavily, with her heart beating quickly, she just lay there, wondering if the muti-lated woman's body she had seen was her daughter's. At that moment Dutia was hurrying home, afraid to think what the Whites might have done to her family. I was standing by the dining room window. Suddenly I saw my sister. She was wearing a trench coat and a sheepskin hat, and I did not recognize her at first.

"It's Dutia," I shouted and ran to open the door.

THE Bolsheviks celebrated their return with a horrendous campaign of terror. Actually, there was nobody left for them to persecute. Everyone who had been in any way connected with the Whites had left with them. But they suspected each and every one of us. There seemed to be no end to the searches and arrests.

ANOTHER May Day was approaching. Once again the city was preparing for the celebration. I stayed away from all public life in those days. I felt sad, depressed, and jealous, but I could not go against my conscience. In any case, the popular festival had been replaced by official, state-directed solemnities.

My younger brother's student friends told me with indignation that the Com-mittee on Popular Enlightenment had sent them the texts of the slogans that they were supposed to write on their banners. "If they'd at least offered to let us choose which banner we wanted to carry—if only for the sake of appearances! Not to mention that attendance is obligatory!"

On May 1 I stayed home during the demonstration. I didn't have a job, so nobody could force me to demonstrate under threat of being fired. In those days, all rallies, meetings, and demonstrations were compulsory.

How had the young people agreed among themselves? Who had given them the idea? In any case, every student had a narrow strip of red cloth in his pocket. On the square, when their column reached the tribune where the city authorities were standing, the students threw down the official banners, tied their mouths shut with the strips of red cloth, and passed by the tribune in total silence.

2 □ ANNA LITVEIKO

In 1917

□ Anna Osipovna Litveiko was born in 1899 (the same year as Olitskaia) into a family of factory workers. In 1918 she fought with the Red Army in Ukraine, and in 1919 she was chosen by the Komsomol Central Committee to perform a "special task" behind enemy lines in the Caucasus (she does not elaborate). After the Civil War she became a professional party propagandist. Like many Soviet workers' publications, Litveiko's memoir was ghostwritten ("rendered in literary form"). It was published in the youth journal *Iunost'* during the Khrushchev "Thaw."

WHEN THE February Revolution began, I was eighteen years old. My friend, Nadia, was nineteen, and Tania was seventeen. We all worked at the Elektrolampa Factory in Presnia.[1] In the first days of the revolution the factory was shut down, so we just ran around town from morning till night.

Everything seemed strange. I knew that the Cossacks were feared because they beat people with their whips. I also remembered how my father, in 1905, had returned home from the last barricade, all beaten up, his clothes torn and his pockets full of cartridges. We had buried the cartridges and then waited for the searches to begin and for the arrival of the Cossacks. But now the Cossacks were riding around wearing red ribbons and fraternizing with the people. The people would shout, "Long live the revolution!" and the Cossacks would smile and ride on.

We kept rushing around town as if carried by the wind.

Once we heard someone say: "Let's liberate the soldiers from the Spasskie Barracks!" We ran straight there. In front of the huge barracks gates stood an enormous crowd. A sentry with a rifle warned: "Don't come any closer, or I'll shoot!" The crowd kept pushing forward until the sentry was pressed right up against the gate, but he never fired a shot.

We tried to edge our way into the middle of the crowd, while shouting to the soldiers who were hanging out of the barracks windows: "Long live the revolution! Soldiers, come out!"

At first Nadia, Tania, and I were holding hands, but then Nadia was pulled off in another direction. As we got closer to the barracks, the crowd grew thicker. Those in the back kept pushing forward. The crowd pressed against the gates until the gates finally gave way. There was not a single officer in the yard. They had all

From Anna Litveiko, "V semnadtsatom," *Iunost'*, no. 3 (1957): 3–17.
[1] Krasnaia Presnia—an industrial district of Moscow.

gone off to hide, but the soldiers came running toward us, waving their caps and embracing total strangers. Then someone shouted: "They're tearing down the tsarist eagles in the Kremlin. Let's go over there!"

"Come on, girls!" shouted Nadia, and started pushing her way through the crowd.

Tania tried to stop us. "Let's wait and see what happens here."

But how could we wait? How could we miss something like that?

We ran clear across town to the Kremlin. Red Square was full of people. In those days iron double-headed eagles, symbols of Russian autocracy, hung over the square. Somebody said: "The tsar's been thrown out, but his eagles are still hanging there!" Someone else replied: "If you're so brave, why don't you climb up there and take them down."

"No problem!" Some fellows of about eighteen or twenty—probably factory boys—ran over and climbed up the towers, then fearlessly scaled the spires, tore off the iron eagles, and threw them down. The eagles must have been all rusted through: a single blow with a stick would knock them loose.

But somebody nearby was already reporting: "They're rounding up policemen!"

"Come on girls, let's go see what's happening!" pleaded Nadia again. We ran out the Kremlin gates and rushed through the traffic into the neighboring streets. There we saw a group of people leading a policeman. His hands were tied, and he was wearing a funny outfit that looked like a dress. Some woman was explaining to the crowd: "They caught this fatso in our shed. He was so scared he was trying to hide under a skirt. I bet he was a lot braver when he was beating other people!"

She kept running up to him and spitting in his face until she was pulled away. Meanwhile, three more policemen were being led toward us: one had been dragged out of a cellar; the other two had been hiding in attics. "Why waste time with them? Let's try them right here!" some people shouted.

There was a rally at the Bolshoi.[2] None of us had ever been to the Bolshoi before, but Nadia had always dreamed of seeing a real ballet. She loved everything beautiful and bright. She loved music and dancing.

That night the three of us stood in the parterre of the Bolshoi right next to the stage and clapped noisily for all the speakers.

Day after day passed in this way. The revolution seemed like a wonderful holiday. We were happy. We felt like adults for the first time. For the first time we felt completely free. We promised each other that we would always be together and that we would always be friends. We did not think about what we would do next. It seemed to us that all our dreams were already coming true.

IN the past, the three of us would often ask each other as we walked home from work: Are we really going to spend the rest of our lives languishing at the Elektrolampa factory?

---

[2] Bolshoi—an opera and ballet theater in Moscow.

The work was monotonous and boring. We were supposed to attach carbon wires to the glass stem of each lightbulb. The foreman used to walk between the tables. Sometimes he would stop beside a worker and start yelling and cursing, or he might tell a dirty joke or even pinch or hit the worker.

There were only women on our floor; the men worked downstairs. The girls would argue over boys and sometimes even fight. The three of us were disgusted by it all and decided to leave the factory, become nurses, and "go to the people," that is, work in the village.

None of us knew much about village life: we had all grown up in the city, in workers' families. Somehow we never thought of ourselves as the "people," never thought about the fact that there was not much farther we could "go." Nor did we know we were repeating formulas that had become obsolete. The only thing that really mattered was our desire to change our lives.

My father used to drink himself into a stupor on a regular basis. When drunk, he would chase my mother around with a knife; when sober, he would beg for forgiveness and feel sorry for himself. My mother had to do it all on her own: she took in washing from the neighbors, cleaned people's apartments, and chopped wood. Mother had eight children. Almost every year or two another would come along.

When I turned eleven, I started working; then my sister went to work, too. Things got a little better. Mother rented a three-room apartment in Pykhov Alley and sublet two of the rooms to students. She washed and mended their clothes and cooked for them.

One New Year's Eve my father got drunk and cut Mother on the shoulder and breast with a razor. When he had sobered up, my sister and I kicked him out of the house. It was my first independent act, and I was very proud of myself. We never asked for my mother's opinion, though, and I never knew if her life had improved as a result of this family revolution. She was quiet and never talked about her feelings, but later I realized that she had never stopped loving my father.

Our tenants were always arguing about politics. When they were out, we would sneak into their room and look at their books.

I used to read a lot. Nadia, Tania, and I worked at the same table at the factory. As soon as the foreman left the room, I would start telling my friends about what I had been reading: Gogol, Korolenko, Turgenev, Gorky, as well as *The Leuchtweiss Cave*[3] and Nat Pinkerton.[4] In other words, I used to read whatever I could get my hands on.

I also used to tell my friends about our tenants: what they were like and what they talked about. Actually, I was in love with one of them. He had big, dark, and, most important, kind eyes. He was very well-educated, polite, and quiet, and had

[3] This best-selling popular novel of the prewar period by V. A. Reder featured a well-born outlaw who defended the poor.

[4] Russian version of the serial detective stories featuring Nat Pinkerton were popular in Russia at this time.

a very special name: Donat. I think I liked him because he was so different from my father. It was probably from these students that I first heard about "going to the people," or leaving for the village.

AFTER the first revolutionary days had passed, the factory started operating again. For the first time we were supposed to elect a factory committee. I am not even sure why, but somehow I got elected.

In those days rallies were being held everywhere: on the shop floor, in the factory yard, near the zoo. The workers from Trekhgorka, Elektrolampa, and Tilman's used to walk by the zoo after their shifts. There was a kind of square there, and rallies started up spontaneously and raged day and night, from one shift to the next. People simply could not go home. There were rallies by the City Duma, too, where the Lenin Museum is now.

Speakers used to climb up on lampposts. Somebody would say: "We're defending the revolution! We must fight the war until we achieve victory!" Then he would be dragged down, and somebody in a faded trench coat would climb up and yell: "Have you ever been in the trenches? Have you ever tasted soldier's gruel? Have you ever been food for lice? Well I have, and now here I am, a cripple. What do I need victory for? Down with the war!"

I knew that there were Social Democrats and SRs. Our tenants were always one or the other. Only Donat had been neither. He used to say he was his own person.

Donat had been drafted and sent to the front right before the February Revolution. Perhaps he had already joined some party—but which one?

I knew that the SRs were promising "Land and Freedom." Quite recently, of course, my friends and I had been planning to "go to the people" and work in a village, but that was simply because we had wanted to go somewhere and do something. But actually I thought to myself: "What do I need land for? What would I do with it?" So I decided that I was probably for the Social Democrats.

Then suddenly it turned out that there were different kinds of Social Democrats. The Mensheviks would make speeches at rallies, and then the Bolsheviks would get up and speak. They talked about the Provisional Government,[5] the war, and land—and it all sounded pretty different depending on whom you were listening to.

The Bolsheviks said: "The Provisional Government is continuing the war and is not giving land to the peasants . . ." I had thought the revolution was over, and now it turned out that it was only just beginning.

The Mensheviks said: "The Provisional Government was created by the revolution, and we must support it if we want to support the revolution . . ." That also made sense. So who was right?

After a rally at the factory, two tables would usually be set up. At one you could sign up with the Bolsheviks, at the other, with the Mensheviks.

Where did I belong?

[5] The Provisional Government formally ruled Russia from the collapse of the old regime in the February Revolution to the Bolshevik seizure of power in October.

Nadia and Tania did not know either. Tania was completely confused, while Nadia was beginning to get tired of rallies: "It's the same thing over and over again. How about going to a dance for a change?"

What was I to do? I was dying to sign up with somebody.

A Menshevik by the name of Chatsky often spoke in our factory yard. He spoke well, without stumbling, but for some reason the workers called him Chattersky.

There were two Bolsheviks on our factory committee, Natasha Bogacheva and Fadeev. Natasha was known as a pretty tough customer. She was already over thirty, a mother and a soldier's wife, but she acted as if she had nothing to lose: a "no big deal, I'm not afraid of anything" kind of thing. I liked that. She was an energetic, loud woman. When words and ideas failed her, she would persuade people by screaming, putting on pressure, or through the sheer force of her indomitable and courageous personality. Nor was she averse to using strong language.

Fadeev was quieter, more thoughtful, and probably more serious. I liked him, too.

At our factory all the Bolsheviks were workers, whereas the Mensheviks who came to talk to us tended to be intellectuals. I decided that it made sense to stick to my own kind. But then I was told that it was often the other way around—that the Mensheviks were the workers, and the Bolsheviks the intellectuals. How could I figure it all out?

Once after a rally I waited for Fadeev, and we walked home together. "What is the difference between the Bolsheviks and the Mensheviks?" I asked him. This is how he explained it to me: "You see, the tsar has been kicked out, but the burzhuis[6] have stayed and grabbed all the power. The Bolsheviks are the ones who want to fight the bourgeoisie to the end. The Mensheviks are neither one thing nor another."

I wanted to fight to the end. "Neither one thing nor another" did not appeal to me at all. If it was to the end, then I was going to sign up with the Bolsheviks.

Tania hesitated. She still was not sure; she preferred to wait. Tania was slow; she could never make up her mind. Nadia told me: "There's more to life than just meetings . . . ."

I got offended. I was certainly not going to force anyone. Had they forgotten how we used to say: "We'll always be together"?

After the shop floor meeting I went over to the Bolshevik table and signed up. Natasha Bogacheva said: "I'll take you down to the district committee."

There were no written recommendations in those days. Natasha simply said that she would vouch for me, and Fadeev said that I would not let them down. So they accepted me and I became a Bolshevik. That was in March.

Now, as soon as work was over, I always ran straight to the district committee. Everything was very informal. After work, rank-and-file party members would come to the committee, talk about the mood at their factories, and receive

[6] Burzhui—derogatory Russian slang for "bourgeois."

assignments. Often, having agreed on what needed to be done, we would sing revolutionary songs. Except for the secretary, there were no professional committee members in those days. There was no technical personnel, either. We did everything ourselves.

I started getting assignments, too. There was a special book, called *Spiders and Flies*. It was all laid out very clearly. The bosses were the spiders. They drank our blood and appropriated the unpaid labor of the workers.

I would tell all this to the girls in our shop the way I used to tell them about Nat Pinkerton. I also added what I had heard at the district committee: that the bosses were still ordering us around and that only the Bolsheviks could change things.

Tania listened in silence, but occasionally she would shake her head and say: "How do you know? Each person looks after himself."

In those days people argued everywhere: on the shop floor, in the courtyard, in the streets, at home. If two people disagreed, a crowd would immediately gather around them—so interested were people in the main issues of the day: the policy of the Provisional Government, the war, and the land.

I already knew the Bolshevik point of view on all these things and tried to get a word in at every opportunity. That is what we had been told to do at the district committee: to fight for people's hearts whenever possible.

These discussions continued at home. Behind the partition our students argued all the time. We had only two students left. One was a Bolshevik; the other was from an intelligentsia family and was sensitive and extremely nice, but to my great disappointment, did not trust the Bolsheviks. He used to say: "Violence breeds more injustice. Bolshevism is barbarism."

Meanwhile, I argued with my sister Maria. She was in love with an SR whom she had met at work, and kept repeating: "Land and freedom—that's what the people need. Land for the peasants and freedom for everybody. The Bolsheviks want a dictatorship of the working class. What kind of freedom can you have under a dictatorship?"

I tried to reason with her: "If we, the workers, take over power, we'll build a good life for all working people, but if you allow freedom for the bourgeoisie, there won't be any freedom for the people."

Maria would not listen, and I used to get angry: "Oh, stop repeating somebody else's words! As if you weren't a worker yourself, for goodness sake! What are you afraid of?"

Maria would also get angry. We simply could not agree. Then our little sister, Katiushka (whom I had not even noticed during our arguments) said that she was on my side.

As for our mother, neither Maria nor I could do anything with her. Mother was a fair and honest person. She also wanted our lives to change, of course, but dealing with party differences was something else . . . "This is too far over my head," she used to say. "You're educated, so you figure it out. I've got enough troubles of my own."

At the factory we kept stopping work to go to endless rallies. At one rally the

Bolsheviks proposed an eight-hour working day. The management had no choice but to agree.

There were other reasons for the gatherings. The foremen at our factory were very rude. One of the worst was a German by the name of Müller. One day he hit a woman who was working with a soldering iron, and her hand got burned. The Bolsheviks decided to go to war over this. All work stopped when the emergency whistle sounded. Everybody poured into the yard. Natasha opened the meeting on behalf of the factory committee and said that we would be discussing the behavior of foreman Müller. Müller was standing right there, looking nervous and scared. We had never seen him like that before.

At the meeting it was decided to cart Müller out of the factory yard in a wheelbarrow. Immediately a large wheelbarrow was brought in, and, accompanied by the jeering and laughter of the assembled workers, the foreman was loaded into it, wheeled to the factory gates, and dumped outside.

It was considered a great dishonor. After this Müller would never be able to work at the factory again.

After Müller had been dispatched, Fadeev took the floor and said: "See how much power we, the workers, have. When we are united, we can solve any problem. When we seize all the power, we'll solve even bigger problems. We'll run the whole state."

The next day the management also apologized to the factory committee and promised that there would be no more violence toward the workers.

That night Tania stopped by our place to ask for some embroidery thread, but that was just an excuse. Before leaving, she paused awkwardly and said, sort of as an afterthought: "It looks like the Bolsheviks really are on our side . . ."

"It looks like!" She still isn't sure! So I told her: "You keep thinking while there's so much work to be done, and you still can't decide!"

THE four youngest party members in our district were Mikhail Dugachev, Anatoly Popov, Serezha Bystrov, and I.

In May we formed a group. It was Mikhail Dugachev's idea. I remember him saying: "The working youth is yearning for revolutionary struggle but cannot always find the right way. We must attract them to the district committee. They can start as volunteers and then eventually they'll want to join the party themselves."

We decided that we would all talk with young people at work.

This is how the Presnia Union of Working Youth got started.

During the lunch break I gathered all the girls on our shop floor together. I told them about the Bolshevik Party and about its goals. I also improvised about how we would study together and about the concerts and parties we would have. I was not really sure what we were going to do in the Union, but I knew that I had to make it sound attractive to the girls. To be honest, I mentioned one more thing: that there would be boys from other factories in our Union. I do not know what made the strongest impression, but many of the girls agreed to join the Union.

Only Nadia disappointed me. "I got invited to a dance tonight," she said. "Why don't you come with me instead." But Tania came up to me and asked: "Can I come with you to the district committee?"

EVENTUALLY our Union had everything: its own district committee, membership cards, a treasurer, and fees. We wondered what else we could do.

Finally we decided that we had better familiarize ourselves with the teachings of Karl Marx. But where should we begin? Misha Dugachev suggested: "Let's study the Erfurt Program[7] and how Engels criticized it." We started reading the Erfurt Program aloud. I think only two people in our group understood any of it: Misha Dugachev and Anatoly Popov.

Anatoly was a gymnasium [high school] student. He was the son of the writer Serafimovich. He was the most educated person in our Union, perhaps even more educated than Dugachev himself. Anatoly had read Marx and Engels and had studied the history of philosophy, including some utopian socialists who, it turned out, had lived before Marx and Engels.

So we started reading the Erfurt Program and continued on and on, without a break. After each reading Anatoly Popov would explain some point; Dugachev would question something he had said; and we would all sit there trying valiantly to listen, afraid to admit to ourselves that, no matter how hard Misha and Anatoly tried, we could not understand anything at all. Couldn't they tell?

It was terribly frustrating!

One thing we had in abundance was perseverance. We might not be able to understand, but we went on listening anyway. Misha and Anatoly would finish their argument, and Anatoly would resume reading. We would try not to fall asleep and not to talk. It would be very quiet in the room. All of a sudden somebody behind me would start fidgeting and sighing. I would look back and see Petia Vorobiev shoving Vasia Ustinov and whispering: "Do you understand any of this?"

Ustinov would brush him off: "Let me listen."

Petia would insist: "I know you don't understand anything."

Petia was the most restless and impatient of us all. I would try to hush him up: "We can't hear."

"You don't understand anything either. Quit pretending and trying to act like a professor!"

Then suddenly something would happen to Petia's mischievous face: his forehead would pucker and disappear under his bangs, his nose would become short and upturned, and his mouth would fall open in a droopy senile gape.

Unable to stand it any longer, Vasia Ustinov and I would burst out laughing.

Misha Dugachev would frown: "We're trying to do serious work, and you're acting like children."

So again we would sit and listen to the Erfurt Program.

---

[7] Erfurt Program—1891 Program of the German Social Democratic Party, coauthored by Karl Kautsky and Friedrich Engels.

Finally we, too, had to admit that there was not much sense in these studies. At first Dugachev exploded: "Why have you been misleading us and yourselves?" But later both he and Anatoly admitted that they had made a mistake. Thus ended our study of the Erfurt program.

WE began staging literary evenings for the young people of the district. We read Gorky's *Song of the Stormy Petrel* and *Mother*,[8] as well as Nekrasov.[9] At these evenings we also talked about what the new Provisional Government was like, and why the Mensheviks and the SRs wanted to continue the war.

Usually about fifty people would come, but I still felt bad because Nadia was not with us. We had to make it fun. We had to attract all the young people.

We started going on long walks in the country on Sundays. I remember sitting on the edge of the bank high over the Moscow River, listening to Kolachev's stories about the underground work of the Bolsheviks that was being carried out during the period of reaction.

The things we talked about on those hikes! For example, what life would be like after the Bolsheviks took over. We thought that communism would begin as soon as the soviets assumed power. Money was not even mentioned; it was clear to us that money would disappear right away.

What would it be like to live under communism?

Anatoly Popov imagined enormous public buildings that would include huge cafeterias, laundromats, day care centers, and kindergartens, that would free families from all household chores. The only kind of property we would allow would be books and clothes.

On clothing, however, our opinions were divided: some of us rejected this form of property as well. And, anyway, how were the members of the new society supposed to dress?

Finally we agreed that under communism everything was going to be beautiful—both spiritually (there would be no more greed or envy) and externally (all clothing would be light—in weight and color).

But what should a Bolshevik look like in the meantime, before the final victory had been won?

In those days I was nicknamed the "gymnasium student." I did dress like one: on holidays I wore a black silk ribbon in my hair. I made my own clothes—sometimes from imitation satin but usually from printed cotton fabric—which I tried to make as attractive as possible.

In the Gorodskoi District, where the headquarters of all the district unions of working youth were located, there was a girl whose name I would rather not mention. She was totally devoted to the cause and never thought about anything but the cause. She did not care at all about her appearance. Her skirt was held together by a safety pin, her stockings were always twisted, and her hair was

---

[8] Maxim Gorki's *Song of the Stormy Petrel* (1901) and *Mother* (1907) are works of fiction that prophesied revolution and were later canonized as founding works of "socialist realism."

[9] Nikolai Nekrasov (1821–1877)—a famous Russian poet, admired by radical intellectuals for his "civic-minded" works protesting social injustice.

short and unkempt. She did not care about anything as long as the soviets achieved power.

"That girl is a true revolutionary," I thought, but while I respected her, I could not part with my own ribbon or braids. Did that mean that I was not a true Bolshevik? But I was prepared to give my life for the revolution!

That summer all of us were a little bit in love, but our views on family were strict and uncompromising. Bolsheviks had no right to start one until the final victory of the revolution. We felt the same way during the Civil War. After a while some "apostates," as we called them, started appearing in our midst, but they felt guilty about not being true to our convictions and kept their marriages secret as long as they could. (Weddings were completely out of the question!)

EVERYTHING changed the day we found out about the massacre of the July demonstrators in Petrograd.[10] The district committee doors were no longer open to everybody. During our meetings the doors were closed, and not everybody was admitted. Lists of names and other committee documents were hidden in workers' apartments.

Not so long ago we had spent a merry February running around town and welcoming the revolution. Now we learned that the right-wing parties were back in government and that Lenin had gone underground.

Two or three weeks later we were sitting on the steps of the district committee porch. It was getting dark. Kolachev was standing in front of us with a notebook in his hands, saying that the Sixth Congress of the Bolshevik Party had just finished its work, that there was no longer any point in talking with the Provisional Government, that power would have to be taken by force, and that we needed to prepare ourselves for military insurrection.

Because of the need for secrecy, only the activists were allowed to hear the report on the party congress.

That night I had a feeling that something very big was about to happen, that things were changing irrevocably, and that I needed to prepare myself . . . I had a certain sense of foreboding and apprehension, but at the same time I knew for sure that this was the only way. There was no alternative. Everything about that night seemed solemn and momentous: the day of reckoning was approaching.

Kolachev told us: "There are people in the party who are not sure that we need to take power now, who think we should wait for the world revolution." I did not understand. What was there to be unsure about?

WE knew the uprising was coming and that there would be fighting. One would have thought that everything else could wait. And yet Tania and I enrolled in the Prechistenka workers' education course. In fact, not just Tania and I, but also Vasia Ustinov, Serezha Iakovlev, Sasha Sokolov, and Fedia Kucherov. I cannot explain why we did this at such a strange time. It was like a kind of thirst; we felt we simply could not put off anything.

---

[10] Refers to the killing of several hundred Bolshevik-led protesters by army units loyal to the Provisional Government on July 3–5, 1917.

Every night, as we walked home to Presnia from Prechistenka, we would exchange a dozen French words and try to remember the tributaries of the Volga and Enisei rivers. As if that were not enough, we would usually take the long route through Red Square, stopping by the old Execution Block and the Minin and Pozharsky monument, to test one another: Who were Minin and Pozharsky? When did they live? Who was executed on that spot?[11]

What would Red Square look like after our victory? Would we tear down the Execution Block or keep it as a monument? Tania and I thought we should demolish it and then forget about it. "Let's plant flowers and trees all over Moscow," I would say. Although we had not conquered it yet, we already considered it completely our own.

FINALLY the day we had been waiting for arrived. In my mind, the week of the October battles felt like one uninterrupted day—the happiest day of my life.

That morning as I was walking to work I saw crowds of people and abandoned streetcars. The night before we had heard about some important events in Petrograd. Now it was our turn!

I started running.

At the factory committee Natasha Bogacheva and Fadeev were reading appeals. One was from the Bolshevik Military Revolutionary Committee, urging people to take part in the uprising; the other, from the Committee of Public Safety,[12] appealed for calm and the continuation of work.

Natasha came to a quick decision: "Hand over that 'Safety' one. I'll tear it into little pieces so that nobody else has to read such nonsense." Fadeev stopped her, carefully folded the appeal from the Committee of Public Safety, and put it in his desk drawer. Having done that, he went to the factory gates to post the appeal from the Military Revolutionary Committee.

Natasha quickly informed me: "Last night they met with the soldiers. The soldiers are with us. Go tell the people." She was in a hurry: "I've got to sound the whistle. As soon as you hear it, make sure every single person in your shop leaves the building!"

The factory was shut down. There was a rally in the yard. People were saying that the Provisional Government had been deposed; that in Petrograd the soviets had seized power and the Bolsheviks had issued a decree on land and peace; that here in Moscow the Bolsheviks had already taken the Kremlin, the telephone and telegraph exchange, and the governor's residence; and that all the Presnia factories had gone out on strike.

I also spoke: "We must rise up! There is no—and can be no—other way!"

After the rally we went down to the district committee. In the courtyard Fedia Shinogin was forming a military detachment, which included squads from different factories. There were not enough arms. Petia Vorobiev demanded a rifle.

---

[11] Kuzma Minin and Prince Dmitry Pozharsky—leaders of Russian resistance to Polish and Swedish occupation during the "Time of Troubles" of 1598–1613.

[12] The Committee of Public Safety was set up in October by opponents of the Soviet's Military Revolutionary Committee.

Complaining bitterly, he went in to see Kolachev. Misha Dugachev, Anatoly Popov, and Zharov went to the Kremlin to get more arms. The soldiers of the Fifty-sixth Regiment who were quartered there were sympathetic to the revolution and had promised to give the districts some arms.

Natasha Bogacheva and I were told to go to the district soviet and take the soviet stamp away from the chairman, a Menshevik. Another worker came with us.

Everything went a lot more smoothly than we had expected. Natasha went straight to the point: "The Bolsheviks have taken power." (This was an exaggeration in the case of Moscow, but Natasha had warned us on the way: "Don't parlay with the Menshevik, or he'll drown us in words.") "Hand over the stamp, Citizen Chairman!"

The chairman of the soviet was a lawyer, so he started talking about legality. "Who are you? Who gave you this power? Why are you acting illegally?"

We realized right away that he was just trying to keep up appearances. He must have known about the events in Petrograd.

To be honest, in our Presnia soviet there were still more SRs and Mensheviks than Bolsheviks, but at that point I felt that I could not only take away their stamp—I could do anything. There was no stopping me. He was talking about rights, but I knew that we were the ones in the right.

Finally the chairman said with irritation: "If you think you have the right to do it then go ahead and take the stamp. The secretary has it." And with that he left immediately.

Natasha Bogacheva and the other worker stayed in the soviet building while I went back to the district committee.

In the evening all the district committee officers left for the Trekhgorka cafeteria, saying that the Military Revolutionary Committee of the Presnia district would be located there. We young people were left behind: Vasia Ustinov, Shura Sokolov, Serezha Iakovlev, Fedia Kucherov, Tania, and myself. "Guard the committee and be prepared," they told us.

What were we supposed to be prepared for? And how could we be prepared? We had only two rifles, and only one of those was working. So we just sat there, listening. The sound of gunfire was coming from somewhere, probably downtown. Some people were already involved in action, and here we were, on the sidelines.

So we decided there was no point in waiting and that we should go get arms for ourselves. We did not have any instructions, but not far away, at the end of the Predtechensky Alley, was a district militia post. We gave the rifles to Vasia Ustinov and Shura Sokolov, who went on ahead while the rest of us followed.

The militia men were sitting around a table, armed. There were more of them than us, but they looked as if they had already been scared by something before we even arrived.

Vasia Ustinov began in the same way Natasha had in the soviet: "The Bolsheviks have taken power. Surrender your weapons."

We surrounded the table where they were sitting. They were armed and we were not, but we acted as if this were the way it was supposed to be.

"Put all your weapons on the table, or you'll be searched!" ordered Vasia.

They put their revolvers down: "That's fine with us. We were just told we had to sit here."

We let them go home and divided their weapons among us.

We went back feeling like heroes. If we could pull this off, we could do anything. Back in the district committee, we spent the whole night taking our weapons apart and teaching each other how to use them. In the morning we went to the Trekhgorka cafeteria, to the Military Revolutionary Committee.

No one showered us with praise: there were other, more urgent things to be done. People were saying that the district did not have enough weapons; that Zharov, Dugachev, and Popov had not returned from the Kremlin and that something funny was going on there—the cadets had surrounded the Kremlin and were not letting anybody in or out; that Shinogin had taken all the armed workers to the city soviet; and that it was not clear whether the soldiers were going to support us.

In the center, fighting had already broken out. Some workers came to the district committee and said that cadet detachments had been seen in our district. In other words, everything turned out to be a lot more difficult than we had imagined the night before, after our first victory.

It was decided to send a delegation to the Khodynka barracks to try to talk the soldiers into taking part in the uprising. Before leaving with the delegation, Kolachev said that somebody must be sent to the Moscow Soviet to get in touch with the Shinogin detachment and ask them to come back if they could.

I saw that Tania wanted to go and said: "Send Rybakova and me. We look so inoffensive, nobody will ever suspect us."

We really did look inoffensive. I had on a bright hand-knitted scarf and a hat of the same color that Mother had recently made for me; in other words, an ordinary girl's outfit. It was strange to think that, looking like that, I had already been to the soviet to take away their stamp and to the militia post to get weapons. Tania was wearing a simple gray shawl.

We walked across Kudrinskaia Square, down Nikitskaia, and then through side streets. Cadets were standing on street corners and in doorways. Across the street were armed soldiers. The shooting had already started.

Somebody yelled from behind a door: "Girls, have you lost your minds? Take cover quickly! Can't you hear the shooting?"

You should have seen my Tania! She just kept on walking as if nothing were happening. How could I be afraid if Tania was not? At cadet checkpoints we would say something about our sick mother and a doctor. They just shrugged: "Go on through, girls, but make it snappy. You're underfoot here!"

The Soviet was in the same place that it is now, on Skobelev Square. Some cadets had surrounded the square; others were hiding on the top floors of the nearby buildings and shooting at the soviet building. The Red guardsmen were firing back with rifles and machine guns.

The Soviet building was filled with detachments of workers; from here they were sent to guard the post office and the telegraph exchange. Communications people were running up and down the corridors. The Military Revolutionary Committee continued working right there, too.

We kept asking: "Have you seen the Presnia detachment?" Some answered: "They're down in the alley," while others said: "They're up on the roof!"

Someone with a red armband called us over and led us up to the second-floor hall, where wounded Red guardsmen were lying on the floor. "Give us a hand here."

Finally we felt needed. A young nurse gave us some rolls of bandage and told us what to do. Tania and I started bandaging the wounded. For the first time in my life I saw wounds and blood.

We could not leave the wounded, but I kept worrying: after all we had been given a different assignment! We had to find Shinogin.

All of a sudden there was a loud noise. Shattered glass fell all over the floor, and someone started moaning. Someone else shouted: "We're being shot at from an armored car!"

Everyone rushed down to the street. We did, too. Outside, everybody was shooting at an armored car that was standing right in front of the building. There was so much shooting that I was totally confused. I had my Smith & Wesson in my hand. I was dying to shoot at the armored car, but what should I aim at? I was not going to shoot just for the sake of shooting. I wanted to do it right. While I was trying to decide where to aim, the armored car fired one last round and quickly disappeared.

Right in front of us, a man was lying on the ground. Tania and I ran to him and tried to help him get up. He was not able to.

We started dragging him. I had not realized that wounded people were so heavy. The two of us could barely move him.

I asked him: "Did you get to shoot?"

He looked surprised: "Of course."

I was terribly jealous of that man. He might never be able to walk again, but he had managed to shoot. He had not gotten confused and missed his chance.

"Well, I didn't," I admitted to him.

"Don't worry, you will," he smiled.

We were back in the hall helping the nurse when we heard: "What are you girls doing here?"

I turned around and there was Fedia Shinogin, with a rifle slung over his shoulder and a revolver resting on his hip. Behind him I could see Vasia Ustinov and other familiar faces from Tilman's, Trekhgorka, and Elektrolampa. I had thought that they were Presnia's best hope, but here they were while the district was left defenseless.

It turned out they had just come back from guard duty. Some of them had, in fact, been down in the alley while others were up on the roof.

Fedia told us to wait while he went to the Military Revolutionary Committee to find out what we should do.

The nurse managed to get some hot water, mugs, tea, sugar, and bread. We helped her feed the wounded and give them tea.

The wounded seemed to me to be a special breed of people. If you were wounded, you were a hero. If they asked me for something, I could not run fast enough.

Fedia returned. The members of the Revolutionary Committee had told us to go back to the district and had promised help.

We headed back before dawn, walking singly or in pairs. Only when we got to Presnia did Shinogin order us to walk in formation.

The Trekhgorka cafeteria was seething with excitement. A large crowd was there. Weapons were being handed out. You could hear the clicking of rifle safeties being released.

THE next day a Bolshevik officer named Zlatoverov came over from the Military Revolutionary Committee to take charge of military operations in the district (the committee had kept its promise). His first order was to move our committee closer to the action: from Trekhgorka to Kudrinskaia Square.

We chose the fire station next to the square and moved over there in the evening. We walked down Bolshaia Presnia, keeping to the middle of the street, away from the sidewalks: most of the shots came from doorways. People were using gates, carts, and logs to build barricades.

The next morning two cannons were brought over from Khodynka and placed at the entrance to the zoo. They were used to fire on the center of the city. Then one of them was moved to Kudrinskaia Square. There was another one by the Gorbaty Bridge.

In the middle of the day the soldiers from Khodynka arrived. Before they came, the barricades had been manned by armed workers.

There was fighting in the streets.

Tania and I were told to organize a medical post. We did not know much about medicine, but the city committee had sent us a nurse. She told us what to do. The first thing we needed to do was to obtain cotton, bandages, and stretchers. How were we to accomplish that? We did not even need to ask. We already knew. We just went to private pharmacies and said: "Give us this, that, and the other." Wary pharmacists would bring us large packages of cotton and rolls of bandages. We gave them receipts, even though nobody demanded them. They must have thrown them away the minute we left.

We set up our post in the committee building and also demanded a separate room for our wounded at the local hospital. We did not trust the hospital doctors and nurses, so we sent my little sister there as our commissar.

In addition to working at the medical post, Tania and I continued our reconnaissance work. We would walk down Nikitskaia to the Manège, note where cadet units were being assembled, and then walk back to the Military Revolutionary Committee.

We saw Fedia Shinogin's unit by the Nikitskie Gates: they were building a barricade. Fedia was surrounded by boys, who were dragging logs and sacks, scouting the nearby alleys, and waiting for more orders. Whenever shooting began, they would scatter like sparrows, hiding in doorways and cellars until it ceased, then crawl back out and again surround Shinogin.

There was a lot of fighting around the Nikitskie Gates. One shell hit a pharmacy where our men were holed up. Bottles of alcohol caught fire. The cadets surrounded the burning building and would not let anyone leave. A lot of our men died in there.

The battles around the Nikitskie Gates and Novinsky Boulevard were the last ones in our district. On Novinsky Boulevard there were no barricades. People were shooting from behind trees, hitching posts, and benches, running from one tree to the next. I remember seeing a file of cadets among the trees. Our guys shot at them with the cannon that stood on Kudrinskaia Square. The cadets scattered, but then resumed their formation and started firing back.

At one point I saw a man in a trench coat lying face down in the street next to the boulevard. There was still shooting going on, so I decided to move him into a doorway first, and then bandage him and send for the stretchers.

He was heavy, and the shooting would not stop. I was talking to him, but he did not respond. I bent down and turned his head face up: his eyes were immobile and seemed to be made of very pale blue glass. He had a reddish mustache stained with tobacco and a simple peasant face, not very young (in those days people thirty years old seemed old to me). He probably had a wife and children in a village somewhere. They must still be there, living their lives, never knowing what happened.

I had never seen a dead person up close before.

I felt terrible because there was nothing I could do.

Afterward, when the fighting had ended, we buried the martyrs of the revolution. The coffins draped in red cloth were carried from Presnia to Red Square. There was no band and no flowers, just the song, "You've Sacrificed Yourselves." Enormous mass graves were dug by the Kremlin Wall and the coffins were put in one after another.

I kept seeing the face of that man as I walked in our column.

FINALLY the Committee of Public Safety capitulated. We had seized power!

But there was none of the pure devil-may-care joy of the kind we had felt after the February Revolution. Then we had had nothing to worry about. The revolution had taken place, and everything was wonderful. But now we were in power, and we were responsible for everything. There was a lot of concern. We were in charge now, but life was getting worse, not better. The shopkeepers were conspiring against us: closing down their shops and kiosks and hiding their merchandise. It was late fall, but you could buy neither food nor fuel.

We had seized power. To keep it, we had to make things work.

Tania and I were told to go to the lumber yard and distribute everything we could find among the population. This was the very first assignment we received from the Soviet government. We glanced at each other: "Do we truly look like government representatives?"

In the yard we found an old bookkeeper and told him: "Open up right away. We have a written order." The old man looked confused and went to get the owner. The owner started arguing, but we showed him the order demanding requisition. What was left to argue about? We opened the gates, and, out of nowhere, an endless line of people formed. The owner disappeared, but the old bookkeeper told us that he needed to fill out receipts to keep his records straight. We told him that was okay.

The wood was being given away for free. Tania and I supervised the proceedings, walking up and down the line and listening to what people had to say. There was a lot of discontent. People were cursing the Bolsheviks for closing down the shops. We explained to them: "It's the owners who are closing down the shops. See, the Bolsheviks want the people to have everything."

OUR next assignment was to evacuate two large residential buildings in Predtechensky Alley and have workers move in. The slogan was "Peace for the huts, war on the palaces!" It was important to demonstrate to the people right away what the revolution would bring to the huts.

Both buildings belonged to the same owner, probably a very rich man—the buildings were built of stone. We never saw the owner. The renters were pretty rich, too.

We would enter their apartments and say: "This building is being nationalized. You have twenty-four hours to move out." Some obeyed immediately while others cursed us—the Bolsheviks in general or Soviet rule. Tania and I were not shy anymore. We did not need to look at each other for reassurance: "Do we truly look like government representatives?" There was no time for doubt or uncertainty.

Shopkeepers were forced to open their shops, but the shops were empty. Meanwhile stockpiles of food big enough to feed one family for ten years were rotting in their homes. Tania and I had to go on searches and go through other people's chests, cellars, and hideaways, and drag out sackfuls of sugar, grain, flour, and sometimes even weapons. We did not mind. "How come they're hiding all this when people are starving?" Some people welcomed us with saccharine smiles: "Feel free to look around. We have nothing to hide." Leaving was often a very different story. We drew up inventories of what had been confiscated and made them sign. Let them see that we were taking it for the state.

In those days all sorts of anarchists and just plain bandits were claiming to be Bolsheviks, and the real Bolsheviks were blamed for what they did. The anarchists filled a mansion on Povarskaia with valuables and weapons. Later we had to clean out the place.

The boys from our Union were being made guards or militia men.

Achieving revolutionary order was now the most important task.

3 □ P. E. Melgunova-Stepanova

Where Laughter Is Never Heard

□ The daughter of a well-known Moscow physician, P. E. Melgunova-Stepanova was a student activist (at the Bestuzhev Women's Institute of Higher Learning), a rural teacher, a published historian, and a socialist intellectual. She and her husband, the prominent historian and "People's Socialist" leader S. P. Melgunov ("M" in the memoir), were among the founders of the Anti-Bolshevik Alliance for the Rebirth of Russia. In 1920 Melgunov was tried as a counterrevolutionary and sentenced to death, but the sentence was commuted to ten years in prison. In 1922 the couple was expelled from Russia.

IT WAS February 17, 1920.

The shrill sound of the doorbell startled us. I went to open the door. In the doorway stood a tall blonde in a sealskin coat, a woolen shawl covering her head.

"I'm looking for M."

"He is not receiving anyone. Can I help you?"

"It's about a book . . ."

He came out to talk to her . . . The door banged, and she was gone.

"She's a Latvian Cheka agent."[1]

"Let's escape through the back door while we still have time!"

"No, I'm too tired of all this. Let them come. I can't live like this anymore."

We were again interrupted by the sound of the bell.

"There are a couple more things I need to tell him," said the agent breathlessly as she walked quickly past me into the hallway.

"He's the one, Citizen," she said, turning to the fair-haired Latvian commissar who had followed her inside.

"All right, you can go now," he said.

Still she lingered.

"Oh, right!" he said, as he pulled out a "squint" (Soviet thousand-ruble bills were named after Lenin, who had a squint) and handed it to her.

"Is that all?" she asked angrily.

"It's more than enough," he snapped and, mumbling something about cab fare, turned his back on her.

"Where's the telephone?" He rushed out to make a call.

"I've got him . . . Yeah, I'm waiting . . . for the soldiers . . . Right." We could hear the agitation in his voice.

From P. E. Mel'gunova-Stepanova, *Gde ne slyshno smekha* . . . (Paris: n.p., 1928), 24–36 (abridged).

[1] Cheka—the Extraordinary Commission for Combating Counter-Revolution, Sabotage, and Speculation. The name of the Soviet secret police from 1918 to 1922.

"They'll be here soon. Everybody sit down." He put his revolver down on the desk and leaned back in the armchair. We were sitting at the table. The samovar was still boiling. The Latvian kept looking around nervously. The slightest movement made him prick up his ears. Minutes dragged by endlessly and seemed like hours. The commissar was completely focused on the sounds coming from the street and kept growing more impatient and less alert. His anxiety was so great that he did not notice our silent "conversations."

The bell rang, feebly. Must be somebody to see us. What terrible timing! The Latvian rushed to the door.

"Yes, he's here," we could hear him say, "come on in!"

Looking fearfully over his shoulder and carrying a small pile of books under his arm, Sh entered the room.

"I just stopped by for a second, to pick up some books," he mumbled.

"All right, all right, we know what kind of books you mean. We know everything!" The commissar raised his voice threateningly. "You're not going anywhere until we have this all cleared up."

"Please, let me call the State Publishing House. I've just come from a meeting there. They'll explain everything. Really, please."

"Sit down and shut up. Telephone calls aren't allowed."

Looking depressed and pale, Sh lowered himself into an armchair and stared at us with horror.

Next, we heard a short, imperious ring. The Latvian leaped up. We could hear heavy footsteps and the thumping of rifle butts. A small door that led into the corridor opened: on the doorstep, striking a theatrical pose, his hand on a revolver stuck in his belt, a red cavalry cap on his head, stood a dark-haired man of average height flanked by soldiers carrying rifles. For a moment there was complete silence.

"Citizen, please follow me into the study. Comrade Commissar, you stay here with the others." Then he turned abruptly and left the room.

They spent less than half an hour in the study. We could hear the soldiers' footsteps in the hallway, some isolated words, and the sound of drawers being pulled out . . . Finally they came back.

"Pack his bag," I was told by the armed man, who turned out to be a plenipotentiary from the Special Section. He graciously allowed me to put in some pencils, paper, and a book (which were all confiscated immediately upon my arrival in prison), and never showed any impatience as he sat there observing us closely.

"Where should I make inquiries in case of a misunderstanding?"

"You can ask me."

"What is your name?"

"Agranov."[2] This comedian—whom we would come to know only too well—was putting on quite a self-assured performance.

We said good-bye, convinced that our separation would not last long. We never

[2] Ia. S. Agranov (1893–1938)—leading official of the Soviet secret police from 1923 until his execution in 1938.

dreamed that we would not see each other again until the day M was sentenced to be shot, six months later.

Most of the soldiers who had filled the hallway left with them. Only the Latvian commissar and two armed guards stayed behind to conduct a new search and to arrest all our visitors.

THE Latvian immediately got down to business, beginning with a painstaking search of our room.

The soldiers quietly made their way from the door to the couch and, with a questioning glance at the commissar, sat down and made themselves comfortable. The commissar was going methodically through our desk, not missing a thing and occasionally setting aside on the bed some old letters that he found suspicious. I tried to argue, pointing out how old they were, but it was no use.

"Who is this?" asked the Latvian, taking a portrait from the desk drawer.

"My brother."

"Where is he now?"

"In Rome."

He put it in the pile of things to be confiscated.

I couldn't contain myself. "What do you need that for? I told you he lived in Rome."

"A White . . . We'll find him there! We'll find him anywhere!" he exclaimed with pride.

Then came some handmade diagrams of Müller's exercises, with the number of repetitions for each one: 5 and 5, and so forth.

"What is this?"

"Calisthenics."

"Calisthenics . . . We know all about your calisthenics . . . This is a code. We'll have to decipher it. We understand these things. You can't pull the wool over my eyes."

On and on it went, in the same vein: notes with abbreviated words, a ribbon with faded letters from the 1905 election,[3] postcards in foreign languages. Everything seemed suspicious to him, and every explanation provoked a ridiculous outburst of shouts and threats. It was better to keep silent. The pile of "evidence" on the bed continued to grow. His pedantic perusal of every scrap from beginning to end kept the diligent but not-too-literate commissar behind the desk for many hours. He began to grow tired and nervous. The soldiers were snoring peacefully on the couch, their rifles in their hands. Sh kept pestering the commissar until he was allowed to go into the next room and lie down on a mattress.

During the course of the night the room had become very cold.

"Light the stove," ordered the commissar.

"We are not allowed to do it before eight o'clock. All the tenants are supposed to light fires at the same time to make sure there is no smoke inside."

Outside a cold dawn was just beginning to break.

---

[3] 1905 election—the first election to the State Duma.

The Latvian dozed off over a new pile of letters.

"Asleep, eh?" mumbled one of the soldiers, waking up and looking at his boss with a touch of contempt when the latter emitted a loud snore. While the commissar slept, we sat there in a kind of stupor . . . The dead silence finally woke him up. He started to his feet, swept up all the letters, and added them to the "evidence"—"Let the others figure it out!"

The morning brought some animation. It had gotten so cold I could hear my teeth chattering. We lit the stove, using piles of *Sibirskaia gazeta*, which we had hurriedly stuffed under the bed when they showed up. The stove did not work well, and soon the room was completely filled with smoke. Sh, who suffered from an eye ailment, cried and begged the commissar to let him lean out the window, which the Latvian insisted on keeping closed.

"Go into the next room if you want some air."

The smoke kept getting thicker.

"You're doing this on purpose!" The commissar rushed toward me just as I was trying to squeeze in another newspaper. When he had pulled it out, he went berserk.

"What is this you are trying to burn? Where did you get it?"

"From the garbage bin."

He grabbed at a batch that was already engulfed in flames, but drew back, his fingers burned. Then, apparently recalling that he had seen me getting the paper from under the bed, he crawled over there to check. I had not yet managed to burn them all.

This newspaper episode was interrupted by the bell. Our former concierge had come to do the dishes and put the samovar on.

The soldier let her in without a word. After she finished her work, she started walking toward the door.

"Where do you think you're going?"

"I'm all done, sir. It's time for me to go home."

"Go ask the commissar. I can't let you go."

"Tell your soldier to let me go," she said, entering the bedroom.

"Have you lost your mind? We are not letting anybody out of here."

"But I live here. I'm the concierge," said the old woman, still not understanding.

"I already said that you can't leave!" he screamed.

All at once she realized what was happening. Crying, she threw herself at his feet.

"My son is sick in bed. I need to feed him. Let me go, for God's sake."

"Get away from me, you old hag!" yelled the Latvian, rudely pushing her away. "Shut up, or I'll lock you in a cold room." (There were lots of "cold rooms." The house had no central heating.) "Just keep your mouth shut," and he stomped his foot angrily.

Frightened and choking back sobs, she sat hunched over in the corner.

Meanwhile the search continued. They had not even finished half of the room yet.

"I'm going to go through the whole apartment in the same way," announced the commissar, as if he could hear our thoughts.

"At this rate even a week won't be enough."

"One week, two weeks—we'll take a whole month if we need to. We know what we're doing. We'll turn up every shred of evidence."

A desperate moan came from the corner where the concierge was sitting. Her son was in bed with pneumonia.

The bell rang again.

The commissar turned to me and said, "Open the door."

Without opening the door, I shouted loudly, "Go away! It's a trap!"

No sooner had I uttered the words than the Latvian, beside himself with fury, shoved me out of the way and dashed from the apartment. One of our neighbors was running up the stairs. The commissar grabbed him by the collar and, after overcoming considerable resistance, dragged him into our apartment.

"How dare you warn him?" he roared at me, but before I had a chance to say anything he turned to the neighbor: "What did you come for?"

"To get some coal. My coal is stored in their kitchen."

"Take everything out of your pockets."

The neighbor emptied the contents of his pockets onto the desk where, after a thorough examination, they remained. "Sit down."

The neighbor sat down by the wall, drew the trench coat he wore as a robe closer around his shoulders and tried to smooth down his uncombed hair.

Less than ten minutes later another ring made the commissar jump up and run to the door. The neighbor's wife, disheveled and agitated, ran into the room and, with the words "I want to be with you," threw her arms around him.

"Who told you he was here and that this was a roundup?"

"The concierge's husband. I went down to find out . . ." She realized what she was saying and fell silent.

The commissar, who was searching through the wardrobe, discovered some money in a drawer.

"Put it away," he said, handing me the package.

Our neighbor could not contain himself: "How come this citizen gets her money back, and I don't?"

"Because this citizen is free, and you are under arrest."

The man practically jumped out of his skin.

The commissar started to take the bed apart.

"We've done our share of searches," he boasted. "One time I found diamonds in a bed like this."

Having finished with the bed, he took apart the lamp, unscrewing every little piece. Next came the chest.

The smoke was irritating our eyes.

The Latvian was getting more and more nervous. Finally he picked up the phone and dialed, but got no response.

"Still home in bed, the sons of bitches," he cursed. "A person might be getting sick—perhaps even with typhoid fever—and they don't even give a damn."

He kept running over to the phone. Hungry and furious, he still did not dare drink our tea, apparently for fear of being poisoned. At about ten in the morning he gave up and sent one of the soldiers out to get him some breakfast. "He'll get something for you, too," he mumbled in our direction and went back to reading the letters. About an hour later the soldier came back. He had brought some white bread, cheese, and other snacks—a sumptuous breakfast by the standards of those days. Calmly relishing his meal, the commissar ate every bit down to the last crumb while his men looked on hungrily.

Vera Nikolaevna, the concierge, made some hot cereal for us. There was enough to go around, and we also gave some to the soldiers, who looked as if they were about to faint.

"We've been doing searches for three nights without a break," said the older of the two soldiers when the commissar left the room.

There was something repulsive about the younger soldier, but the older one seemed simpler. I had been watching them closely. The pile of "material evidence" on the bed continued to grow, and something had to be done.

Finally, an opportunity arose that could not be missed. The commissar was standing by the telephone; the younger soldier was leaning against the door frame and dozing off; the "prisoners" were snoozing in their chairs; and only the older one was left by the stove. The risk was great, but I had no choice, and a pack of letters flew from the bed into the stove. No, I was not imagining things: the soldier grunted approvingly and turned away when I looked at him . . .

The commissar came back. With renewed energy, he went back to knocking on the floor and the walls, feeling the wallpaper, scrutinizing the heater and the vents, and then reading on and on. Our prospects did not look bright. The search of the first room had been going on for more than sixteen hours, and there were seven rooms in the apartment! When would it ever end? Perhaps the cold would drive away the obstinate Latvian: hadn't he said that he thought he was getting sick?

At around three the bell rang.

"Who is it? What do they want?"

The Latvian went to open the door, and then we heard violent cursing, the sound of running feet on the stairs, the noise of a struggle, and loud protests, until finally the commissar reemerged dragging our old concierge by the collar.

"Just you wait . . . telling everybody, warning everybody! I'll have you put away!" he screamed at the top of his voice, still cursing violently.

"You got no right to arrest me," persisted the old man. "I came for my wife. My son is sick. I ran down to the station, and the commissar himself told me: 'Just go on up there; they got no right to arrest you.'"

"Got no right?" mimicked the Latvian. "Just spend a little time in jail and you and your commissar will find out what my rights are."

The concierge looked frightened and changed his tone: "Let us go, for God's sake, Mr. Commissar, Sir. We have nothing to do with this. We'll pray for you . . ."

The two old people looked up at the fair-haired commissar with tears in their eyes.

"Shut up and quit pestering me. I told you to sit down, so do it, or you'll come with me when I leave."

Finally he was promised a replacement. He cheered up, put down some letters he had been reading, and was going to add a few to the pile on the bed when he noticed that some were missing.

"You took them! You burned them!" he began.

"What should I do with the chests?" interrupted the soldier who had been sent to check the storage shelf in the kitchen.

The Latvian ran to the kitchen. "Break all the locks," I heard him yell.

The locks were broken, and a cloud of dust rose over a pile of moth-eaten clothes.

"Those belong to a former tenant."

"Where is he?"

"He moved away."

"To the East, I bet?"

"No, I think to Petrograd."

And again the stupid remark: "We'll find him wherever he is! We'll find them all!"

There were storage shelves in the hall, too.

"Climb up there," said the commissar to the older soldier, "see what you can find. . ."

"Two suitcases."

"Open them!"

"They're empty."

"What else?"

"A cot."

"What else?"

A quick, barely perceptible glance in my direction.

"Nothing, nothing at all."

"Get down."

I could not help looking at him again: in the closet stood a large box containing a heavy silver tea set. The soldier had thanked us for the cereal.

4 □ ANNA ANDZHIEVSKAIA

A Mother's Story

□ The series Women in the Civil War, from which this piece was taken, is part of a larger project, *The Civil War in the USSR: Sketches and Reminiscences by Participants*. Some entries were sent in by authors; others are transcribed and edited interviews. The volume is an early example of the genre of celebration of heroic events in Soviet history through the memoirs of participants. The action takes place in the North Caucasus near Russia's southern border.

IN FEBRUARY 1917 there was a workers' rally in the city of Piatigorsk. Representatives from all the parties were expected to speak. A group of us girls, who worked at various Piatigorsk resorts, made our way toward the stage. Even though we were only eighteen to twenty years old, we were "terribly serious young girls": we liked to read books and were not interested in idle chatter.

The stage was crowded with speakers. The SRs and Mensheviks were sermonizing about fighting the war to the end. Then an exhausted, pale soldier in a hospital gown began speaking. He was the first to throw the slogan "Down with the war!" in the faces of the SRs and Mensheviks. No sooner had he finished his rousing speech than shouts of "Bolshevik demagogue!" were heard all around.

At that time I found his manner of speaking somewhat forced: his extraordinary fervor and enthusiasm seemed artificial and his revolutionary ardor, theatrical.

Right after the rally I met Comrade Andzhievsky. I told him quite frankly what I thought of his speech. He was amazed at my reaction and responded: "If you had lived through as much as I have, you would know how sincere I was."

Comrade Andzhievsky's passionate speeches, his firm stand against the war, and his growing influence among the soldiers began to worry the military authorities.

A decision was made to send Andzhievsky back to the front as soon as possible. But when the soldiers found out about this, they declared: "Whoever takes Comrade Andzhievsky away from us is going to regret it."

The commanding officers of Regiment 113 decided to stage a new election to the regiment committee, of which Andzhievsky was the chairman.

However, Andzhievsky was reelected. Then a decision was made to disband the Bolshevik-influenced regiment and send the men home. This measure had a good chance of succeeding: the authorities knew that the soldiers were sick of the

From *Zhenshchina v grazhdanskoi voine. Epizody bor'by na Severnom Kavkaze i Ukraine v 1917–1920 gg.* (Moscow: OGIZ, 1938), 54–63 (abridged).

war and would gladly throw down their rifles and head for home. This was "a stab in the back of the revolution," as we put it in those days. Without a disciplined, close-knit, Bolshevik-dominated organization, the struggle for revolutionary slogans was unthinkable. All the soldiers with Bolshevik sympathies understood this, and so, of course, did Andzhievsky. Finally, a general rally for Regiment 113 was convened. The commanders put forward their enticing proposal to let the soldiers go home. It was a frightening moment. The soldiers hesitated. Many were ready to accept the plan. Shouts of approval were already coming from all sides.

Then, mustering all his strength and will, Andzhievsky addressed the soldiers. He told them that the officers' proposal was a provocation. He argued that the soldiers should stay. "If the achievements of the revolution, which you paid for with your own blood, are not dear to you, then go ahead and throw down your rifles . . ."

The words of Andzhievsky touched every heart, as if they were burning coals.

In the end, the regiment refused to disband. After the rally, which took place behind the railway station in the town square of the Konstantinogorskaia suburb, the soldiers made a seat for Andzhievsky with their rifles and carried him triumphantly all the way down the main street to the other side of town.

The secret of Andzhievsky's popularity consisted in his ability to empathize with the interests of the masses—to be able to sense and feel their suffering in a deep and direct way. Tirelessly, he propagandized and talked to the workers. I was a loyal disciple of Andzhievsky. We read Lenin together. We swore to live and die for the proletarian revolution. Soon afterward I became his wife.

At the end of October the soviets in Petrograd took power. I remember how Andzhievsky and a group of comrades brought this news to a meeting of the City Duma. In the evening we left the Duma and rushed to Regiment 113 to call a rally. The soldiers greeted the long-awaited news of the downfall of the hated Provisional Government with shouts of joy and triumph.

By the time we got back to the Duma the SRs had already formed a "Committee of Salvation." The next day the newspapers published long articles written by the Menshevik Lunin and the Right SR[1] Leonid Orlov, articles directed against Andzhievsky and me.

At that time I was working in the very den of the Mensheviks, the Union of Commercial Employees. At an extraordinary meeting of the union, the Mensheviks and SRs were going to approve an anti-Bolshevik resolution condemning the takeover. By then, however, I had already formed a women's section that supported the Bolsheviks. We were all young girls. Andzhievsky taught us how we should act and how we should counter the efforts of the Mensheviks who dominated the unions.

At one of the meetings, when the Mensheviks were trying to push their resolution through, I got up and declared: "Everything the Mensheviks are saying is a lie! The coup is not a usurpation but a legitimate takeover of power because only

---

[1] After the Bolshevik seizure of power in October the SR Party split, the majority ("Right SRs") opposing the Bolsheviks and a minority ("Left SRs") supporting them.

the workers can be the genuine defenders of the workers' cause. Whoever votes for the Menshevik resolution, votes for the bourgeoisie!" My women's group supported me, and, having disrupted the voting, we left the meeting.

The next day the newspaper published an article in which some Menshevik sounded the alarm, saying that the Bolshevik policies were beginning to penetrate the unions, where they had found support not only among men but also among women. He mentioned me by name and said that I had been undermining the decisions of the unions.

The next day, when we came to the union to pay our dues, we were met with hostility. The people there refused to shake hands with us or accept our dues and then told us that we had been expelled from the union. Before leaving, we said: "Soon our union will become Bolshevik!"

Our women's Bolshevik group intensified its agitation work. I remember how we distributed Bolshevik newspapers and leaflets, listened to what the masses were saying, exposed slander, and explained Bolshevik policies.

At the beginning of 1918 the Piatigorsk Soviet approved a resolution on the takeover of all power by the soviets. A Bolshevik executive committee, headed by Andzhievsky, was formed. Bolshevik influence was already great. The huge three-story building by the marketplace—the former Seferov Hotel to which the Bolshevik soviet now moved—was always packed with people. They came there with all kinds of problems.

That was the beginning of the bitter struggle with the counterrevolution, which tried to undermine soviet power in every way.

THE situation in the rear was probably just as dangerous as the one at the front. We had a lot of trouble with one of the unit commanders, a certain Nizheviasov. At first people trusted him, but when he and his men came back from the front loaded with samovars, gramophones, and other things, the attitude toward them changed. Special meetings devoted to this case were held both at the party and the executive committees. Comrades from the Bolshevik committee were sent out to Nizheviasov's men, but even they could not improve the situation. The corruption had gone too far.

We started getting anonymous letters about Nizheviasov's brutalities and plundering. Girls who had been raped and murdered were found on Goriachaia Mountain. More and more often Nizheviasov refused to obey the executive committee. Furthermore, it was discovered that he had made up a list of the members of the party and executive committee who were "to be eliminated." We decided to take decisive measures against Nizheviasov.

We informed Vladikavkaz of our decision. Andzhievsky and I went to Kislovodsk. In Kislovodsk Andzhievsky reported to the party committee on the Nizheviasov affair. After that the committee urgently mobilized party and union members and issued a leaflet declaring Nizheviasov a traitor to the revolution.

I stayed in Kislovodsk, while Andzhievsky continued on.

The next day he went back to Piatigorsk, but before he got there Nizheviasov had already been disarmed and executed by the chairman of the Sovnarkom of the

Terek Republic, Comrade Buachidze, who had arrived in an armored car from Vladikavkaz.[2]

The party committee sent several Communists to Moscow to see Comrade Lenin. Andzhievsky was very excited after his meeting with Vladimir Ilich.[3] Lenin had listened attentively and asked several questions: "What's the food situation there? What measures are being taken to form soviets? How is the party committee working? How are the relations with the mountain population?"[4] Having listened to the answers, Lenin gave specific instructions on how to proceed, emphasizing specifically the food question and the importance of relations with the peoples of the Caucasus.

The Terek front of the civil war needed new reinforcements. The Shkuro offensive had to be stopped.[5] In early August 1918 Andzhievsky and I went to the front near Essentuki. Our unit had a group of about twenty medics in it. I was part of that group.

We left Piatigorsk in the morning. It was a clear day. Everybody was in a bright, cheerful mood. We marched along, singing revolutionary songs. The singing was frequently interrupted by laughter and jokes. On the way, the nurses taught us how to wrap a bandage and give first aid. When we arrived, the men spread out across the field.

A reconnaissance party reported that the Whites were already approaching. Our men took cover in the undergrowth. Soon the fighting began. We could not see the enemy—they were hidden behind the bushes.

Toward evening the fighting grew more intense. We heard that our advance detachment was running out of ammunition. The cart drivers who carried the ammunition refused to go to the front line. "The carts won't make it through the swamps," they said. I reproached the comrades: "You could each carry a few boxes." I grabbed one of the boxes, but the comrades protested because I was pretty far along in my pregnancy. My example spurred on the drivers, and the ammunition was delivered.

The fighting continued all night. Very early on, Comrade Anisimov, the commander of the unit, was killed. Andzhievsky took over as commander.

As a result of the fighting that lasted several days, Shkuro was pushed back to Beslan.

We were full of anxiety. The mobilization of Communists continued. Workers' detachments were being formed. Night after night we would sit in the committee room, waiting for the arrival of Communist detachments from Mineralnye vody, Georgievsk, and Zheleznovodsk. Andzhievsky always went out to meet them on the road behind Mt. Mashuk.

In those days the committee was almost constantly in session. I suggested that

---

[2] Sovnarkom—the Council of People's Commissars of the Terek Soviet Republic, an autonomous part of the Russian Federation between March 1918 and February 1918. Vladikavkaz was its capital.

[3] That is, Lenin (Ilich was Lenin's patronymic).

[4] Mountain population—the non-Russian peoples of the North Caucuses were collectively known to Russians as "mountaineers."

[5] A. G. Shkuro (1887–1947)—Kuban Cossack leader who commanded White detachments in the North Caucasus in 1918–19.

we organize a Communist sewing shop and a mess hall for the fighters. We commandeered sewing machines from the local stores. Women Communists and Communists' wives sewed the fighters' uniforms and linen. It was very difficult to get thread and material.

In late August, when Ilin's unit arrived, we had more trouble. It was one of those spontaneously formed units that acted independently, without obeying the high command. We had to liquidate that scoundrel, too.

But this was nothing compared to the Sorokin affair.

In October 1918 Sorokin withdrew the Eleventh Army to Piatigorsk, leaving a gap at the front. Typhus was rampant in the town, and the arriving units immediately became infected. There were not enough beds to go around. The People's House, the executive committee, and other institutions were packed with sick people from the front. In those difficult days of the revolution Sorokin showed his true nature. Reports of drunken orgies at his headquarters reached the party committee and the central executive committee of the North Caucasus. Sorokin and his men would get drunk and carouse around town with a band of musicians. They would break into the People's House or a restaurant, smash the dishes, raise all kinds of hell, and then refuse to pay. On numerous occasions, Sorokin was called to order by comrade Rubin and other members of the executive committee to whom he was directly responsible.

It was a terrible blow for all of us when Sorokin brutally massacred the members of the executive committee—comrades Abram Rubin, Semen Dunaevsky, Boris Rozhansky, Mikhail Vlasov, and Viktor Krainy and his sixteen-year-old brother, Abram Krainy. Only after the elimination of Sorokin—this enemy of the revolution—could we embark on the reorganization of our units.

In the following months the front line continued to draw closer and closer. There was not enough food to feed the population. The town was decimated by typhus. The sick lay in corridors, on floors, and even on the ground in courtyards. The epidemic had spread to the civilian population. The fight against it was made more difficult by the lack of medications, food, and medical personnel.

The situation at the front continued to deteriorate. About two weeks before we abandoned Piatigorsk we lost our communication with the center through Sviatoi Krest. Information from the front was contradictory. Our situation was unclear. Reports from the Stavropol front said that the Whites were approaching. The counterrevolutionary Cossacks were restless and the kulaks began rioting.

We remained in Piatigorsk until the very end, waiting for reinforcements and hoping that the White circle would be broken and that we would be able to get in touch with the center. Finally it became clear to us that there was only one way out: a retreat to Vladikavkaz past the Cossack settlements.

Before we left Piatigorsk I had been working as a people's juror in a revolutionary tribunal. I was far along in my pregnancy, but I kept going to the tribunal literally up to the last day. The case had to do with some counterfeiters. When the contractions started, I ran home.

I went into labor that same day. I had a baby girl.

Then the retreat began. My baby and I were put in a carriage. It was around January 5 or 6. Andzhievsky's sister and my sixteen-year-old little brother, Vania, were with us. Andzhievsky, with the members of the executive committee and the Communist detachment, was the last to leave Piatigorsk. Several comrades were left behind to set up an underground network.

Andzhievsky caught up with us in Zolskaia, and we continued on our way.

Our retreat must have presented a horrible sight. An army of typhus victims made up the rear. Wrapped in blankets, they kept staggering and falling as they walked. Many would fall down and never get up again. Some would come up to our carriage and demand that we get out, but, seeing a sick woman with a tiny baby, would then leave in silence. Hundreds of people moaned and cried as they ran, afraid of falling into the hands of the White bandits. They knew they were walking to their death, but the knowledge that they would die among comrades and friends gave them strength and comfort. People in gray uniforms and blankets lay scattered on the snow. Upon reaching the next settlement, the comrades begged the Cossacks for carts to go and pick up the fallen.

We never stayed long in the Cossack settlements because the Whites were right behind us. Finally we reached Prokhladnaia. We stayed in a poor Cossack's hut. In such huts people usually received us well and shared everything they had with us. This time the hostess lit the stove and then ran to the neighbors to ask for a basin. She warmed up the water and bathed my baby herself. As she was bathing her, she kept crying and saying: "Poor child, where are you going, what's going to happen to you?" Andzhievsky tried to comfort us. He said: "That's okay, she'll be all the stronger for it!"

The next morning we got on a train and went to Vladikavkaz. Soon after we arrived the Whites surrounded the city. The problem of evacuation arose. They put me and my baby on the train that was carrying soviet documents and valuables. Traveling with us were my little brother and Andzhievsky's sister, Nadezhda, who had come down with typhus. The station of Beslan informed us by telegraph: "The line to Grozny is open. Send the train on." We left Vladikavkaz on January 12, at seven in the evening. One armored car was in front, and the other was at the end of the train. In Beslan the train stopped.

"Why are we standing still?"

"Nobody knows."

The station master said that the line was closed.

Later we found out that the first armored car had been derailed by bandits. At night we could hear artillery fire in the distance. "Get up, Comrades," I said, "or the Whites are going to capture us without firing a shot."

Suddenly a piece of shrapnel hit our car. It came in through the only window that was still intact. Pieces of glass and wood flew in all directions. Everybody jumped up and ran out of the car. I handed the baby to my brother: "Go to the station. I'll get Nadia and the sick comrade out of here." Not having heard a single word I said, my brother ran off with the Red Army men to Nazran.

I took Nadezhda to the station. I had to drag her along the ground because I did not have the strength to lift her. Then I ran back for the sick comrade.

Having left them in a room at the station, I rushed off to look for my baby. I walked all over the station building. The rooms were full of people sick with typhus. They lay in filthy puddles of their own feces. Some of them were already dead. I kept asking if anybody had seen a boy with a baby, but nobody answered.

Then I rushed out onto the platform and immediately ran into an officer. He took out his saber and started waving it and yelling at me: "Who are you? Where did you come from?"

"I'm a passenger."

He grabbed my arm and started interrogating me in a threatening tone of voice: "What are you doing here?"

"I'm looking for my baby! Let me go!"

He did not believe me and would not let me go. I was only twenty-one at the time. I had long braids and did not look like a mother.

"What baby? What a bunch of nonsense!" said the officer as he dragged me into the station building. He pushed me into the room where the telegraph operators were working and told them: "Watch her, she's crazy." Then he locked the door and left.

On the desk the telegraph machines were rattling wildly—apparently someone was trying to get in touch with the station—but the operators were standing by the window looking out. Not realizing who they were, I said: "Comrades, go answer and tell Vladikavkaz that the Whites are already in Beslan and that our train has been stopped."

"We are not comrades," they said. "Keep quiet, or we'll make you quiet!" One of them grabbed a rifle.

Then I realized they were traitors. What was I to do? I got the revolver Andzhievsky had given me and prepared it in case I had to commit suicide.

I suffered terribly. I couldn't quit thinking about my baby.

The fighting ended. The Whites had forgotten about me. Through the window I could see them standing in formation in front of the station building. Their commander thanked the management of the station. From his words I realized that we had been betrayed. It turned out that, the day before, the White reconnaissance party had come to Beslan and agreed with the management to have our train detained until their men arrived.

The Whites went on to Vladikavkaz. Before leaving, they shot several switchmen and guards whom the management had identified as Bolsheviks.

That night, having been left alone in the wire room, I sneaked out through the window and once again started searching for my baby. But there was nobody around. So they had been killed! Both Vania and my little girl!

I wandered around all night, looking for children among the corpses that lay everywhere. I looked at them all. In a wooden box by one of the cars I found the body of a newborn baby. "Maybe my little girl is also lying somewhere out in a field, frozen," I thought with a shudder.

The next day I got a bad case of mastitis. I was delirious with pain and fever. In my nightmares, I kept seeing my baby lying in the snow. She was crying, but I was afraid to touch her because I thought that my hands were on fire. I tried to give her my breast to feed her without touching her with my hands. It was horrible!

I did not find my little girl. The only thing that gave me comfort were the rumors that Vladikavkaz was holding out and would not surrender. I tried to help. I found the place where the Whites had laid their field telephone wires and cut them.

WE were all following the fate of Vladikavkaz with great anxiety. We could see the burning native settlements that the Whites had set on fire. With a group of comrades, I made my way back to Vladikavkaz. Soon afterward, Shkuro took the city. Vladikavkaz was full of officers. Then the arrests began.

One morning I heard the clinking of spurs in the corridor, then a knock on the door. The woman I was staying with had gone to the market, and I was there alone. Suddenly a whole crowd of officers broke into the room, shouting: "Hands up!"

Having found nothing, they took me under guard to their counterespionage unit. There they started interrogating me, but I refused to talk. "Just you wait, we'll make you talk," the executioners said.

They put me in a cell for those sentenced to die. During the interrogations, they subjected me to such mental torture that I kept losing consciousness. All the while, they were trying to find out where Andzhievsky was. Then, hoping that Andzhievsky would come to see me, the Whites let me go home. At that time, I received reliable information that Andzhievsky had retreated to Tiflis with everybody else.

Over and over again, the Whites would break into my room at midnight and begin searching. Those searches drove me crazy. Every day I had to show up at the counterespionage unit. One day, after I arrived, one of the clerks—he must have been one of ours—came up to me and said quietly: "Leave the city immediately, or they'll hang you."

I moved to Tiflis, and then to Baku, where I found Andzhievsky in hiding. There were constant searches. We kept moving from one place to another. On August 17 Andzhievsky persuaded me to go to the movies with him.

I really did not want to go. I was very depressed and didn't feel like seeing anything or talking. Andzhievsky, on the other hand, was very agitated and was talking a lot.

When we came out of the theater and crossed the street, there was a car waiting behind the corner and about twenty British policemen, dressed in Scottish kilts.[6] They rushed toward us and grabbed Grigory. I started screaming loudly, hoping to get help from passers-by, but Andzhievsky said: "Ania, calm down. We're in public."

"You don't understand what's going on," I answered.

"I understand perfectly well, but you must pull yourself together." There were,

---

[6] British forces occupied Baku from July 25 to September 14, 1918, on the invitation of the non-Bolshevik majority of the Baku City Soviet.

indeed, people all around, but they stayed at a distance, obviously afraid to do anything. We were pushed into the car and taken to British headquarters.

They took off my clothes, unbraided my hair, and cut off the heels of my shoes: they were looking for diamonds. I was searched by the Kabardian Prince Kubatiev from Kislovodsk. I do not remember much. I was ill and had a fever. Otherwise I would probably have lost my mind.

Andzhievsky was immediately put on the steamer *Kruger* and taken to Petrovsk. In Petrovsk he was subjected to gross humiliation. He was led around town in chains, with a placard on his back that read "Thief, murderer, robber."

In Piatigorsk he was put in a cell full of water. He was kept in chains all the time. Then he was tried and sentenced to be hanged.

On August 31 he was hanged. The Whites were in a hurry to finish him off. He was a very dangerous enemy.

After his execution I was released. When I got home and heard about Andzhievsky's death, I collapsed. I lost the use of my arm, leg, and half my face.

As soon as I began to get better, I asked the party committee to send me to the front. They sent me to Derbent, where I stayed until the Soviet troops arrived.

In 1920 some comrades and I went to Piatigorsk. Once again I tried to find my little girl. I was told that my younger brother was alive and was living in Stavropol, where he was working in the Komsomol organization. Vania found out that I was in Piatigorsk and came down to tell me about my baby.

. . . Having jumped out of the train in Beslan, he ran toward Nazran. There he met an Ingush woman who had a newborn baby of her own. She fed my little girl and gave her a bath. Vania took the baby and continued walking. Some nurse persuaded him to give the baby to her. She told him that she was going to Vladikavkaz and that she would bring the baby to me. Later Vania found out that the nurse had taken the baby back to the same Ingush woman and left her there.

I decided to go see the Ingush woman. The party committee gave me the money for the trip. When I got there, I saw a baby in her arms and ran toward her. I thought that the girl looked like Andzhievsky. But the Ingush woman said that it was her baby and that my baby had gotten sick and died on August 31. That was the day Andzhievsky had died.

I decided that the Ingush woman was lying to me, and I offered her money. But she shook her head and said: "The mullah wanted to buy your girl; he offered me a lamb and some chickens, but I didn't give her to him. I wouldn't give her to anybody."

"What do you mean, you wouldn't? I'm her mother!"

"No, I am her mother. I nursed her. She's my daughter. We made her a Muslim. We called her Mardzhan. Allah will reward us all for that; we'll all be in heaven— we and you and your husband."

She showed me my little girl's diapers and a blanket. Then she took me to a little grave. I cried at the grave of that child, not knowing whether it was mine or somebody else's.

5 □ Zinaida Zhemchuzhnaia

The Road to Exile

□ Zinaida Zhemchuzhnaia (née Volkova) was born in 1887 in a small town in the Urals, where her father worked as the head physician in a large French-owned factory. When she was ten years old, both her parents died, and she was sent to the Nicholas I Orphanage for Noble Girls located in Moscow. After graduating, she went on to study the natural sciences at the University of Geneva and the Moscow Women's Institute of Higher Learning. At the beginning of World War I, her husband Boris (real name: Alexander) was drafted into the army as a doctor, and Zhemchuzhnaia and her baby daughter, Lena, moved to the Cossack settlement of Korenovskaia in the Kuban region, where she had been offered a teaching position in a new five-year high school (gymnasium).

WHEN THE NEWS of Nicholas II's abdication and the formation of the Provisional Government reached us, it caught us completely unawares. Only very gradually, as we kept reading the exultant speeches of the politicians, the triumphant articles in the newspapers, and the descriptions of the rallies and demonstrations by the exhilarated crowds, did we begin to comprehend the significance of the unfolding events and to feel ourselves a part of the universal celebration. For the first time ever I regretted the fact that I was in the middle of nowhere, far from Moscow, at this historic moment.

I will not attempt a general assessment of the political transformation that was taking place at that time—this has been done by numerous politicians and eyewitnesses. I only want to write about the way those events were perceived and reflected in the humble and distant corner of Russia that was the Cossack town of Korenovskaia.

The feeling of joy was accompanied by a sense of responsibility. We represented the town's intelligentsia, and thus had a duty to inform the population of the changes that had taken place and to mark those changes in an appropriate fashion. I believe that not only we, but all the members of the provincial Russian intelligentsia felt totally unprepared for this task. We were not used to dealing with the masses or speaking in public. We all shuddered at the thought of having to make a speech before a large audience. And yet we could not be silent; we had an obligation to take the initiative into our hands.

One evening the principal convened a meeting of all the local intelligentsia: the teachers, the policeman, the Cossack elder, and a few merchants. Everyone was

From Z. Zhemchuzhnaia, *Puti izgnaniia* (Tenafly, N.J.: Hermitage, 1987), 93–164 (abridged).

eager for our town to take part in the general celebration. We decided to call a
meeting the next day in the schoolyard. The question of who would address the
people provoked a long argument. Nobody wanted to do it. Finally one of the
teachers volunteered. It was decided that the principal would open the meeting,
followed by the elder, who would speak to the Cossacks in Ukrainian. Next would
come the teacher, and then, hopefully, someone might volunteer. The priest proposed to celebrate mass on the square in front of the new church, while the music
teacher offered to compose a cantata and have his choir learn it. The school was
closed for three days to give us time to construct a monument and make flags and
banners. I told my SR colleague, Petr Nikolaevich, about the meeting and was
glad I did, because he contributed more than anybody to the success of the meeting. Petr Nikolaevich took the floor after the formal speeches of the principal, the
elder, and the teacher, whose presentation was informative, but dry. Even more
than his words, it was his enthusiasm and his dark, burning eyes that created the
excitement and fervor the event was lacking.

We were happy the meeting had been a success. Petr Nikolaevich was full
of hope. We pictured the future of free Russia as an endless triumphal procession. We grew dizzy as we imagined the heights of achievement and development that our country, freed from arbitrariness and bureaucratic constraints, could
attain. What made us especially happy, however, was that the revolution had
been bloodless and that power was in the hands of respected, enlightened leaders.
After the meeting we no longer felt isolated; we had joined the common flow of
our country's life. The mass was even more successful. An arch adorned with
ribbons, branches, and flowers had been erected on the square. A red cloth was
draped over the podium. The students from all the local schools stood around
the square in their white uniforms, with red flags and colorful banners covered with slogans. Behind them in a solid ring stood the townspeople in brightly
colored clothes. The colorful atmosphere was further enhanced by the intense
blueness of the sky and the snowy whiteness of orchards in bloom. The clear
young voices singing the cantata sounded in unison with the songs of the
larks and the smell of the steppe, and rose to the skies in one common prayer
of joyous gratitude. There was no place for dark forebodings on that beatific
spring day.

Even though most of the exams had been canceled, we insisted on holding the
final exams for the graduating class. This gave us yet another reason to rejoice
when we saw the fruits of our labor—the transformation of wild and unruly Cossack children into educated young men and women.

We were only waiting for an end to the war. It seemed senseless to kill and be
killed when everyone was so happy. I was hoping that Boris would come home
soon and that we would never have to part again.

The Cossacks, especially the older people, were wary of the political changes.
They had no reason to be dissatisfied with the government. They had always been
a privileged estate and were used to fighting for "the Faith, the Tsar, and the
Fatherland." Now the tsar was gone, and it was not at all clear what would take

his place. And they were also against allowing non-Cossacks to own land, something the latter were hoping for.

In July I let Lena's nanny go home to her village for a visit, and Lena and I went to Liubomir.

Uncle Paul was alarmed by the twist the peasants had put on the political changes. He would gather them together and talk to them, trying to explain the meaning of what was going on. They would always listen, but the conclusion was always the same: all land belonged to the peasants. They had heard rumors that the government had issued an order giving the land to the peasants but that it was being concealed by the landowners. City agitators turned up and were listened to with rapt attention because they were saying the things the masses wanted to hear. "If they don't give you the land, take it away by force!" "Rob and burn out the landowners!" "Don't obey the draft!" "Peace now!" "All power to the people!"

"What on earth has happened to these people," complained the cook. "They're out of their minds, using words you can't understand: protalians, sploiters."[1] "They're drinking your blood," they say. "What blood?" I ask. "Take me," I says, "I grew up in the big house—they found me a husband, treated my children well, taught them how to read and write." Then they just say, "You're not politically awares. Pretty soon we'll be living in that house, playing on them pianos."

My friend's aunts were offended by this kind of talk because they thought they had no reason to feel guilty and because they had always considered the peasants their friends, always helped them and treated their diseases—and now all of a sudden it turned out that they were exploiters. They were especially offended for Uncle Paul, who had, in fact, devoted his whole life to the peasants' interests before becoming an "enemy of the people."

In Pisarevka, where migrant workers were being hired for the summer, the mood was even more somber. On one faraway estate the warden's house had been burned down. Field overseers were refusing to work, fearing for their lives. The manor house at Pisarevka was being guarded by soldiers who had been provided by the governor at the request of the aristocratic landowner. This latter circumstance greatly annoyed V.M., the manager:

"It's like teasing a bull with a red cloth," he said when he arrived in Liubomir. "The peasants are being difficult enough as it is; not our own—the outsiders are causing all the trouble. I need to bring the harvest in and dig out the beets, but after that I'm leaving. I told the owner a year ago that this was going to be my last year. To tell you the truth, I don't have any desire to risk my life for his interests."

He had brought over some of the proclamations that were being handed out to the peasants. It was the same old stuff. "Rob the robbers!" "Down with the landowners!" "Down with the war!"

"It's all well and good for the politicians in the capital to issue decrees about freedom. They don't know the peasant. I'd just like to see them in our shoes."

"What do you think will happen now?" asked Aunt Liza.

[1] That is, "proletarians," "exploiters."

"What will happen is that they are going to rob, and burn, and kill until they slide down to the very bottom."

Uncle Paul disagreed, saying that the government would take whatever measures were necessary and would not allow this to happen.

Without answering, V.M. went out into the garden, where Lena was skipping wildly back and forth.

"Is that your daughter?" he asked me. "She's beautiful. Does she look like her father?"

"Very much so."

"At first I felt bad when I heard that you had married, but I always knew I wasn't your type. Anyway, make sure you don't stay around here too long," he added in a hushed voice. "God knows how things will turn out. I also advised Paul to take all his valuables and leave, the way many landowners have done. But they don't believe that anything will happen to them."

"But what about you?" I asked. "You are in an even more dangerous position. What's the point of waiting until the harvest is in if you believe that everything will be stolen anyway?"

"It may be pointless, but I have to stay here until the end of the harvest. I don't want to look like a coward."

THE October takeover,[2] like the February one, took place in the capitals, so we found out about it from the newspapers. Then some of the Cossacks started coming home from the front line. The army was falling apart. The war was ending of its own accord. We heard of some cases of officers being lynched. But nothing disturbed the peace of our town.

At the end of November Boris arrived without warning. It had become impossible to stay at the front. That night we all gathered at the principal's and listened with horror and disgust to Boris's stories about the mindless terror being perpetrated by the soldiers, about the humiliation and the violence, about the killing of officers. The army's disintegration was complete. Incited by the new government, frenzied mobs of soldiers joined frenzied mobs of peasants to demand their own brand of freedom. Death to the landowners and the bourgeoisie! Rob the robbers! All power to the people!

AFTER three months of calm the wave of Bolshevism finally reached us. A Cossack checkpoint set up at Tikhoretskaia was instructed not to let the Bolsheviks into the Kuban region,[3] but the Cossacks had not yet learned to shoot at their own people and offered no resistance. The Kuban government, the Council, and those officers who feared reprisals retreated beyond the Kuban. So did all the Cossacks who did not want to remain under the Soviets. Boris also left with them. I tried to keep him, tried to convince him of the senselessness of running away from a power that had already been established, that sooner or later we would have to

---

[2] That is, the Bolshevik Revolution.

[3] Kuban—region of southern Russia with a large Cossack population.

obey. But Boris thought that individual officers who stayed behind were in greater danger than those who were organized in a group. Later I learned just how right he had been.

The rich merchants had closed down their stores and left town. The Baronovs had offered me and another teacher half their house, and we had foolishly agreed and moved in.

On March 4 the first Red Army units entered the town. They were dusty, dirty, and shabby, and had cartridge belts draped across their chests, rifles slung over their shoulders, and revolvers resting on their hips.

Despite all these weapons, they looked rather pathetic. In fact, they looked more like a gang of robbers to whom the new government had promised encouragement and support in place of the knout. Most of them were drunk because the first thing they always did was to loot the wine cellars.

At five o'clock a rally was convened in front of the town hall. The commissar, who was completely drunk, caught sight of the priest in the crowd. He told him to come closer and then, without saying a word, pulled out his revolver and killed him right on the spot. The crowd gasped. That kindly old priest was beloved by the townspeople. Shocked by such an unexpected event, they just stood there, listening to the commissar whose tongue would not obey him as he struggled with words like "the vangar of the revolution," "religion is the hopium of the people," and, by way of conclusion, "proletarians of all countries, unite!" Silent and shaken, the spectators dispersed. With one shot the commissar had quenched the flickering hope that the Moscow government was a true and just power. The Cossacks, brought up on respect for authority, were prepared to recognize the new government and give up many of their privileges if the government was a just one. After the brutal murder of the priest there were no more illusions. The Bolsheviks had shown their true face.

We sat in the teachers' lounge for a long time, afraid to leave. Every one of us saw himself as a potential victim on the bloody altar of the revolution. It was frightening, terribly frightening. I was trembling inside—and could not stop trembling the whole time the Bolsheviks were in town. Only then did I realize what a mistake we had made by moving into the town's best house.

The next morning they started looting the remaining shops. Bosenko, who had been trying to ingratiate himself with the local non-Cossacks and had donned a large red bow, saw his house and shop hacked to pieces, and his daughter raped. The commissar and his entourage came to our school as well, but seeing that we were busy in our classrooms, they left without saying anything.

Having taken care of the bourgeoisie, they moved on to the Cossacks. Under the pretext of searching for weapons, they broke into people's homes and took away their animals and grain. Every Cossack had weapons, of course, but few were caught. Those who did get caught were shot on the spot. Most had had time to bury their rifles in the steppe. The confiscated grain was dumped on the edge of town, where it rotted in the sun and rain. It was the pointlessness of this robbery that upset the hard-working Cossacks the most.

The revolution was supposed to follow a rigid, preconceived pattern. First, each society had to be divided into classes. You were either a member of the bourgeoisie, who should be robbed and murdered, or you were a proletarian, who deserved all the good things in life. In Russia the gentry were being killed, but what about the Kuban, where there were no gentry? So priests, teachers, and pretty much anyone who was neatly dressed became part of the bourgeoisie. You could not get rich off the Cossacks, however, so they, too, were included in the bourgeoisie. The local non-Cossacks became proletarians, even though there were many prosperous merchants and peasants among them who did not fit the profile. And finally, there were the local poor, mostly drunkards and loafers, who joined the Red Army men and took part in their robberies and beatings. In this town of about thirty thousand, there were no more than three thousand non-Cossacks, of whom only a few could be called poor, and yet it was these very people who were now in charge of Korenovskaia. It was the same in the rest of Russia, where a quarter of a million Bolsheviks and their supporters had seized power over 200 million people.

A drunken cobbler was made chairman of the town soviet. He convened meetings and held forth in the most solemn fashion, having learned a few highfalutin words from the Bolsheviks. His speeches were equally incomprehensible to him and to his listeners, mostly non-Cossack women who cracked sunflower seeds between their teeth and gossiped loudly. Meanwhile, the Cossacks sat gloomily at home. Every so often, yet another one would dig up his rifle and disappear in the middle of the night, to join the others across the river.

Having finished with the Korenovskaia Cossacks, the Red Army men left to install Soviet power on neighboring farmsteads.

One of my students told me that a teacher had been hanged on Borovik's farm. I did not believe him, but, unfortunately, the rumor turned out to be true. Borovik came to see me and said that my friend Petr Nikolaevich had been trying to get into Korenovskaia because he was worried about me. He did not have a pass. He was stopped and arrested by a Red mounted patrol. Some eager farmhand volunteered the information that he had criticized Bolsheviks at a rally. So they hanged him. Before leaving the farm, he had asked Borovik to give me his money and personal effects. I refused, asking Borovik to keep them. The only thing I took was his notebook, which I hid away and did not open for many years.

My instinct for self-preservation kept telling me that some things were better left unexamined and that I needed to shut them out of my mind and heart and to wipe them from my memory. Otherwise one would not survive or would go insane. I did not want to keep anything that would remind me of Petr Nikolaevich. I never talked about him. But somewhere in the back of my mind I preserved an unsullied image of him.

The present was frightening, but the future might be even more frightening. I had to shut my eyes and try as hard as I could to concentrate on simple, mundane things. And to go on living. We were in the hands of armed madmen. They were like rabid dogs, and we had to hide and try not to attract their attention.

I needed all the self-possession I could muster when a gang of soldiers and local hoodlums appeared on our doorstep. There could be no doubt about the purpose of their visit. I sent Lena and her nanny out the back way and then went to open the front door.

"How can I help you, Comrades?"

"We're here to arrest you," said one of them, who was a little older than the rest.

"Show me your warrant."

After two weeks of looting, the commissar had started giving them arrest warrants. These did not have any warrants.

"Who needs a warrant?" said somebody in the crowd. "It's clear enough. You hobnobbed with officers, and now you're hiding arms."

I remained calm. "You can conduct a search. If you find arms, you can arrest me."

They liked that idea because rumors of valuables hidden by the Baronovs had been circulating for a long time. They talked among themselves and then a whole crowd of them started toward the door. I stood in the entrance.

"Only Red Army men may enter to conduct the search. I won't allow anyone else to go in."

The teenaged hoodlums were impressed by my schoolmarmish tone. They grumbled and hung around a while longer, but then they left. Four soldiers entered the house. First they went through our things: books, dresses, linen—nothing interesting there. Then they came to the part of the house that was locked and demanded the key. I did not have it. They broke down the door with the butts of their rifles. The huge hall and living room were filled to the ceiling with various goods: bolts of cloth, household utensils, clothing, and sacks of sugar, grain, and flour. How funny that was! They were supposed to go inform their commissar, but instead their hands moved with feverish speed as one thing after another disappeared into their huge pockets. They stopped only when they could not squeeze anything else into their pockets or under their shirts.

"You're really something, little lady," the oldest one told me. "Imagine living next to all this stuff and not even using it." He handed me a bag of sugar. "That's the bourgeoisie for you," said another with admiration.

Happy and excited, the Red Army men had completely forgotten about their intention to arrest me as they went off to report their discovery to their commissar.

TROOPS kept arriving both from the north and from Ekaterinodar, which the Bolsheviks had taken without a fight and renamed Krasnodar.[4] Our school was taken over to house soldiers, and classes came to a halt. The Reds who had arrived from the north under the command of a former hospital orderly named Sorokin were somewhat better disciplined and more like a real army. Or perhaps there was nothing left to loot, and they believed that Soviet power had already been in-

[4] *Krasnyi* means "red" in Russian.

stalled. There were rumors floating around that some other army was coming from the north and that there would be a battle around Korenovskaia.

We did not receive any newspapers or any other communication from the rest of Russia, so we did not know that Kornilov and his men had reached the Don.[5] There they had been joined by some of the Cossack units and by the officers who had managed to escape from their soldiers. The united Volunteer Army, led by three former commanders-in-chief—Kornilov, Alekseev,[6] and Denikin[7]—was moving toward Ekaterinodar in order to join up with the Kuban units.

By the evening of March 16 Korenovskaia had been turned into a military camp. I heard that there were as many as twenty thousand soldiers in the town. Early the next morning the artillery barrage began. The troops were moved to the other side of the Beisuzhok, about three or four versts[8] outside of town. In front of the town hall carts were being loaded with stolen goods and military documents. The non-Cossacks who had made common cause with the Bolsheviks were leaving town, loaded down with bags and children. On the previous night we had been told that civilians were in no danger and that the enemy would be destroyed outside the town limits by superior forces, but those assurances had not inspired much confidence.

Machine-gun fire could be heard quite clearly; shells flew overhead, and several exploded at the far end of town. Many of the residents were hiding in our school basement. I sent Lena and her nanny there, too, but did not go myself. Curiosity kept me outside. I had never seen war at close range before. Any war is organized murder, but international wars at least follow some rules. There are certain campaign plans and troop deployments, and the enemy wounded are picked up and treated. But the civil war had no rules of any kind. It was every man for himself; every battle became a matter of individual life and death. No one took prisoners. The wounded were finished off on the spot. For Kornilov's men not to win meant to perish: they had nowhere to retreat, no reinforcements, no rear. They had to fight their way like a hunted animal through a pack of hounds. Everyone was a hero, everyone performed amazing feats of bravery because there was no alternative to being a hero. Every man tried to sell his life at the highest possible price. They attacked fearlessly and fought to the last breath because they knew they could expect no mercy. Their daring, their furious charge, and their will to win and thus survive finally broke the Reds. The Reds had a well-supplied rear, occupied territories, stockpiles of ammunition, and numerical superiority, but they had no will to win and no willingness to die, now that their wildest dreams had come true. And so their twenty-thousand-strong army could not withstand the onslaught of three thousand men.

[5] L. G. Kornilov (1870–1918)—tsarist general, commander-in-chief of the Provisional Government's forces in July–August 1917, and first commander of the (White) Volunteer Army.

[6] M. V. Alekseev (1857–1918)—tsarist general, chief of staff of the Russian Imperial Army from 1915 to 1917, and one of the organizers of the Volunteer Army.

[7] A. A. Denikin (1872–1947)—tsarist general, commander-in-chief of the (White) Armed Forces of Southern Russia from February 1919 to April 1920.

[8] Verst—Russian measurement equivalent to thirty-five hundred feet.

A battle is a purely animal act. All things human—the mind and the emotions—get turned off. What is left are the primitive instincts of aggression and self-preservation.

Like a stampeding herd of cows being pursued by predators, the Reds came rushing down the street. As they ran they dropped their guns and kicked off their heavy boots. Some became so winded they collapsed and were trampled by those running behind, who were in turn trampled by horses. Carts were overturned. The air was filled with the sounds of heavy breathing, snorting, crying, and shouting.

The cavalry of the victors came flying in on the heels of these panicked men. Why pursue them, one would think, when victory was certain and the enemy was on the run? But the pursuers looked even more terrible than the pursued. In the ecstasy of battle, with wild roving eyes, and mouths opened in a frenzied "hurrah," they looked like dreadful demons, even more animal-like than the animals they were hunting. They were firing shots, slashing with their sabers, and trampling the enemy under the hooves of their horses.

It was as if a hurricane were passing through the town, leaving behind the bodies of the dead and the wounded, and were immediately dispatched with a shot or a blow with a rifle butt.

It was all over in about two hours. The residents emerged from their cellars and started picking up the bodies. Kornilov's men took possession of the town.

The school was commandeered by an officers' company, and a company of cadets was moved into the empty half of our house. I looked on with apprehension as several dozen strapping young men entered our yard, but no sooner had they come in than they lay down on the floor and, fully clothed, fell asleep. Fatigued to the point of total exhaustion, they slept for at least fifteen hours. Finally they began to wake up and go wash themselves. We put the samovar on for them, but we did not have any bread or sugar. Dinner was brought from the field kitchen, and they shared it with us. Most of them were just boys, between eighteen and twenty years old. They should have been in school or just about to start their adult life, and yet each one had a bitter story to tell: of looted homes and estates, of destroyed families, of murdered parents or relatives, of friends tortured before their eyes. They were all united by a desire for vengeance, a hatred for their oppressors.

During the day there was a rally in front of the town hall. General Alekseev urged the Cossacks to join them. But the Cossacks, who had willingly provided them with room and board, stopped short of joining. These were all strangers: strange generals, a strange army. "Their own people" were across the Kuban, and they were waiting to join up with them. After the rally there was a parade of sorts: rank after straight rank of tall, handsome young men—warrior-barbarians—marched by. Dressed differently, they could be Roman legionnaires, so much had their psyches been altered by war.

They were the children of intelligentsia parents. They had been raised in the spirit of Christian morality, gone to school, and danced at balls. But nothing from their past had anything to do with the present. All their past had been discarded as unnecessary and even harmful under the present circumstances; it had been shed the way a snake sheds its skin. Kindness, pity, compassion, and justice had been abandoned, to be replaced by cruelty, hatred, and anger. "An eye for an eye," "a tooth for a tooth"—or even two for each one. Apparently, constant danger and the proximity of death result in a sort of selection, in the preservation of only those things that are absolutely necessary for survival: one's reflexes and instincts. The mind is replaced by discipline. Their commanders did all their thinking for them. Only the strategic genius of a Kornilov or Alekseev could help them escape from their hopeless situation.

Having banished their former moral values and their memories of the past to the farthest recesses of their souls, they were transformed into magnificent barbarians trained to withstand all sorts of privations: hunger, cold, and sleeplessness. They fell asleep the moment their bodies assumed a horizontal position; they could even sleep in the saddle; and they could swim across ice-cold rivers. They exceeded the Reds—those benighted peasants—in cruelty. Just how hardened must an educated person become to be able to finish off the wounded? As far as they were concerned, the Bolsheviks were not human—they were just "Red scum." And so they kept on killing—killing and enjoying the killing.

On the night of the second day, Kornilov's men quietly left town, retreating not to Platnirovskaia, where the Reds were expecting them, but to Ust-Labinskaia.

The next morning, the Red troops, having regrouped and been strengthened by reinforcements, began shelling the town, not realizing that Kornilov's men had already left. When there was no response, scouts were sent out, and soon afterward the "brave" troops entered the town, to the accompaniment of music and songs. Now it was the Reds' turn to be quartered in the school and in our house. The arrests and searches began again. We, too, were searched. As I was watching, one of the soldiers took my watch off my desk and put it into his pocket. What could I say? All the ones who had come from the south were wearing rings and wristwatches. They did not want to fight anymore. The soldiers could not help admiring the tactical skills of the Whites. A whole army—with its artillery, its wounded, and a large train—had simply vanished, melted away. The units that had been sent out in pursuit could not find it.

"Those are some generals!" said one soldier admiringly as he put the samovar on in our kitchen. "They're the real thing, not like ours. They just disappeared right out from under our noses."

"Let them go," shrugged another one. "They are done for, anyway. No point shedding our proletarian blood for no good reason."

Soon the troops moved on. We went to see what had happened to our school. Heaven help us! The hurricane that had ravaged the town had passed through here as well. When we came in the door, we saw a filthy floor almost a foot deep in dirt; greasy walls covered with obscene graffiti; desks and benches that had been chopped up for firewood; books from which all the pages had been torn out to make cigarettes; maps lying in pieces and paintings torn off the walls . . . My lab had become a pile of broken glass, with little puddles of brightly colored reagents here and there. The microscope and all the instruments were gone. Everything I had collected over the years with such love and care had been destroyed. We did not know if it was the Whites or the Reds who had wreaked such havoc. Most likely both. The officers probably never stopped to think that this was a school where children came to study. For them it was a temporary shelter that they could easily convert into a barracks. When life is measured in days, one does not think about the future or worry about other people's interests. But the breaking of the vials and test tubes was obviously an act of Red vandalism, of cruel, senseless amusement.

In my eyes, our school stood as a symbol of the whole of Russia—violated, humiliated, swept up by the storm of universal destruction.

But life had to go on. We wiped away our tears, called on some student volunteers, and started cleaning.

My constant fear for Boris's life was now mixed with a new fear: can the war have made a barbarian out of him, too? My only hope was that, as a doctor, he was supposed to treat people, not kill them.

We lived on rumors. The Cossacks were in constant touch with "their own people across the Kuban." It was from them we found out that Kornilov's men had joined up with the Kuban Cossacks and that a battle over Ekaterinodar was imminent.

On April 9 we began hearing artillery fire. Several days of total uncertainty followed. According to rumors, the city had been taken and the Reds were on the run. Indeed, more and more retreating units kept passing through our town. The Cossacks cheered up and started preparing to welcome their troops. There was no doubt that after the fall of Ekaterinodar the Reds would not be able to remain in the Kuban.

On April 13 we heard that Kornilov had been killed by a grenade on a farm where he had his headquarters, and that the White Army had retreated. The flow of Red Army troops turned south again.

The retreat of the White Army was a terrible blow to the Cossacks. Many of them returned home with stories of huge casualties, a shortage of ammunition, and the hopeless position of the Whites.

I had to abandon all hope of seeing Boris any time soon. I was consumed by fear and uncertainty. What if he was one of the casualties? This torture of uncertainty lasted for many months.

The real war reached Korenovskaia in July 1918, when the White Army, supplied with new ammunition and reinforced by the Don Cossacks who had rebelled against the Bolsheviks, launched another offensive in the Kuban. Once again Korenovskaia was chosen by the Reds to be the battlefield. This time they set up their defenses at the far end of town, so that the shells flew over our heads. The school housed the Red headquarters, and our yard served as a hospital. Many of the town residents were hiding in a large basement where a Greek merchant kept his grain. The basement was an excellent illustration of the "life goes on" concept. Over the course of three days people settled in and made themselves comfortable. Piles of grain served as couches, tables, and beds. At night, when the shooting subsided, people would go out to get food, stoves, and blankets. Friendships were formed. The children played. Even social distinctions were observed: we were given the best corner, so that nobody would step over us. Shells were bursting overhead, but the conversation about children, prices, and all the rest went on unabated, with momentary pauses when there were loud explosions.

In our corner the literature teacher started reciting Pushkin, and gradually more and more listeners came to join us. After dark some people went out in an attempt to discover what was going on. But nobody knew anything. The force of the explosions was our only indication of where the main fighting was taking place.

I was consumed with worry about Boris. He might be somewhere out there, among the attackers, and I trembled at the sound of every shell, praying silently: "Please pass him by." The lack of sleep and fresh air made me dizzy.

I was amazed by the adaptability of human beings. People were eating, talking, and sleeping as if they had always lived in this basement. Meanwhile, above us other people were killing each other. Nobody talked about it and it seemed as if nobody was thinking about it.

By the end of the third day we heard new sounds: the rattling of machine guns and the high-pitched whining of bullets.

"They're coming!"

"Who's coming?" asked some frightened voices.

But nobody knew.

Somebody opened the door to the basement. And suddenly it seemed as if we had been thrust onto the crest of a wave. The sounds of exploding shells, machine-gun fire, shouting, and the tramping of men and horses were fused into a deafening cacophony. A ferocious "Hurrah!" swept over our heads. Several minutes later all was quiet. The wave had rolled over us.

The town had been taken. Like timid shadows, looking over our shoulders, we crawled up the ladder. The streets were empty, quiet, and dark. Holding Lena in my arms and keeping close to the fences, I made my way to our house. There were horses snorting quietly in our yard, but inside the house all was quiet: everyone was asleep. I recognized this ability to fall asleep within seconds and, having taken a closer look, could make out the epaulets of the officers.

I had only one concern—to try to find out whatever I could about Boris. All morning I stood at the railway station, hoping to see some Kuban units. I could not help marveling at how fickle military fortune was. Not so long ago the defeated, desperate, disheveled, and almost unarmed troops had been fleeing from Krasnodar. And now here was an endless flow of train cars filled with men, horses, artillery pieces, shells, and food. Everyone was well-dressed and certain of victory. Both in town and at the railway station the atmosphere was one of calm professionalism. These were all newly formed units of the Volunteer Army. No longer did they have the cohesion, the daring, and the cruel grit that had distinguished Kornilov's magnificent barbarians.

Boris arrived in the evening. When he embraced me, I felt an enormous weight lift off my shoulders; I felt as light as if I had grown wings. What a terrible burden of fear and uncertainty I had been carrying all these months!

It was late, but when my colleagues learned of his arrival, they all came over. Everyone wanted to be reassured that this was the end, that the Bolsheviks would not be allowed to return. Boris was quite certain of that. Sitting beside him on the couch and feeling his arm around me, I was happy, even though the things he was talking about should have provoked horror and revulsion. All negative emotions had been temporarily erased from my soul, and I was smiling happily as I listened to him talk about the difficult marches, the starvation, the cold, and the constant danger. It all seemed like a scary fairy tale; the reality was that he was here, beside me, and that we would never have to part again.

I made the bed for him, but I did not want to go to sleep—I was not willing to surrender even a tiny portion of my happiness to oblivion. I was filled with such acute tenderness, with such gratitude to him for being alive. I was afraid to even close my eyes. What if I opened them and he was no longer there by my side? I was afraid to move, afraid I might frighten my happiness away.

In the early morning it did get chased away by the sound of artillery fire. I quietly got up and opened the window. There could be no doubt: they were shooting from the direction of Diadkovskaia. I had still not decided whether to wake Boris up, when a neighbor knocked on our door.

"The Bolsheviks are advancing. Wake him up, fast."

Boris woke up instantly at the sound of the word *Bolsheviks*. Listening to the approaching gunfire, he began to get dressed. In the street more and more people could be seen running toward the railway station.

"I'll go to the station and find out what's going on. If it's really the Bolsheviks, I'll come back for you. Now that I have been seen here, you won't be safe any more.

Then he left. With a heavy heart, I watched his tall figure disappear in the crowd. The station was about three versts away; he would not be back for another hour. Would he be back? Once again, that terrible weight dropped down on my shoulders and pressed me to the ground.

I went over to the school. I could watch from the second floor and perhaps spot Boris in the crowd a little earlier. In the direction of Ekaterinodar some figures were running across the railway tracks and drawing up in formation. In the streets the panic was growing. It seemed that the whole population of the town was running this time. Carts and wagons were blocking the way. All around them were huge crowds of women, children, adults, and the chaos of sacks and suitcases. They were all trying to move, bumping into one another, falling down, getting into one another's way. Down in the schoolyard, the wounded began to move, too. They must have been abandoned to their fate. Crawling, on all fours, or on crutches, the armless and legless human stumps gasped and moaned as they made their way laboriously up the street. And not one single person in that mindless human herd helped them; not one dropped a sack or offered them a spot on a cart. As they brushed past, people simply cursed them for slowing them down.

Finally I saw Boris running against the current and rushed out to meet him.

"We have to run," he shouted when he saw me. "There's no time to waste. The

Reds have already cut us off from the north and are now circling round from the south. Our troops left during the night.

We were running through a sea of carts, sacks, and people. We were being shoved and cursed as Boris used his powerful shoulders to cut a path for us.

"Boris, let's turn off into a side street. I know a shortcut, and it won't be as crowded there."

It was not easy to get out of the current. By myself, I would surely have been crushed. Once out of the crowd, it became easier to run, but I felt that my strength was running out and that my heart was about to stop beating.

"I can't go on, Boris. You run. You must get away. I'll stay behind."

Without saying a word or slowing his pace, Boris picked me up in his arms and continued running. At the station we were surrounded by even worse panic, even worse confusion. The frightened herd of refugees were throwing down the things they had brought there with such difficulty. Recoiling from the shots, they kept rushing in different directions, fighting and squeezing to get on a freight train that was already overflowing with people. Further down the track I could see the figures of Red Army men, shooting at the station. Every so often somebody from our side would respond.

I did not see any way of getting on. Angry, threatening bodies were blocking the way.

"Where do you think you're going? Can't you see there ain't any more room?" A huge fellow had stretched out his arms, blocking the entrance.

Without saying a word, Boris grabbed him by the collar, threw him down on the platform, and pushed me inside. The fellow wanted to start a fight, but the crowd did not back him up, so he went off, muttering to himself.

Boris went to get some intelligence. Bullets were whizzing by more and more often. I kept watching for Boris. The people inside the car were getting nervous: "Why aren't we moving? The Bolsheviks are almost here. They'll slaughter us all."

Then everyone's eyes turned to Boris, who was running in our direction.

"When are we leaving, Mr. Officer?"

"Here I am, Boris, here!" I shouted, thinking that he had not noticed me. But he ran past us.

"Officers, report!" I heard his powerful voice call out.

About a dozen officers jumped from different cars.

"That bastard of a station manager has put people on a train with no engineer. We've got an engineer, but he's from another train and refuses to drive this one. We need to move the passengers. Position yourselves at the doors and shoot anyone who does not obey orders. The passengers were already jumping onto the platform, pushing and shoving one another. Somebody screamed: "The wounded are being crushed!"

"Clear the way! The wounded come first!" shouted Boris, advancing toward the crowd and threatening with his revolver. The wounded were allowed to get off and then onto the other train.

"Form into lines. Anyone not in a line will not be allowed through," ordered the officers.

Relieved that there was someone they could obey, the people meekly formed lines and filed quickly into the cars.

Boris turned to me: "Run to the locomotive."

"Officers, to the locomotive!" ordered Boris, when everyone had climbed in.

The engineer was being guarded by two officers holding revolvers in their hands.

"Move it," ordered Boris.

Screeching and puffing, the locomotive reluctantly crept forward.

"Faster!" shouted Boris, pointing his revolver at the engineer.

The engineer accelerated.

"There are some logs over the tracks. We won't get through," he muttered.

"If we don't get through, I'll put a bullet through your head," was the answer.

We were approaching the Bolsheviks who were blocking the way.

"Full speed ahead!" ordered Boris.

We were being shot at from both sides of the track. Machine guns hammered hurriedly, hysterically. The bullets cracked against the side of the train like a bunch of nuts, shattering a window.

"Get down!" Boris shouted to me.

Groaning and wheezing, the old engine strained as hard as it could. The barking of the machine guns grew quieter, until it faded in the distance.

"We made it!" the engineer called out, turning toward us and grinning broadly. "Praise the Lord!" And, forgetting his Bolshevik sympathies, he fervently crossed himself.

The road ahead was clear. The officers could not help laughing when I got up from the floor, all covered with soot and dirt, "You just got your baptism by fire."

Several minutes later we reached the Platnirovka Station. The peace and quiet that reigned there seemed eerie. The red station building, the rows of Lombardy poplars, the white acacia hedges along the tracks, the white huts surrounded by fruit trees—everything looked familiar: peaceful, quiet, and somnolent. The people there, who had not experienced war, were friendly and kind. The wounded were fed and made snug in their cars. The refugees scattered through the town, looking for their friends. Some lay down and went to sleep right there by the tracks. The station manager invited Boris and me into his quarters, where I got washed up and put on his wife's dress, which was too loose for me. At night they put a rug out in the yard for us. Boris went right to sleep, but I lay gazing up at the star-filled Kuban sky, thanking fate for keeping us alive—and together.

We were surrounded on a small stretch of land between the Platnirovka and Dvinskaia stations—a handful of fighters with almost no ammunition. Sorokin's strong army was advancing from Korenovskaia. There was no hope of reinforcements; we had to stand firm.

Early the next morning the population of Platnirovka went out to dig trenches. Armed Cossacks joined the soldiers and took up positions in the trenches: every man counted. The Reds had been shelling the village since dawn. At first the station manager's wife and I hid or lay down on the floor whenever we heard a loud explosion, but then we stopped—mostly because we were impressed by the way the Cossack women just went on with their regular activities: feeding the animals, carrying water, washing clothes. The Red artillery men must have been fairly inexperienced because out of the dozens of shells that were fired, not a single one landed in the village.

In order not to be afraid, I needed to find something to do so I could pretend that nothing out of the ordinary was happening. I began helping to care for the wounded and in the cooking. I also forced myself to sit and calmly sip my tea when shells whizzed by overhead. By the end of the third day I no longer noticed them.

I also got used to our refugee status. I had only one change of clothing, which I would wash every evening and then put back on in the morning. It was strange to remember how many suitcases filled with unnecessary things we used to take on our trips.

I understood that only death could stop the flow of life. People were endowed with an incredible ability to adapt. Life had gone on in the basement during the shelling, and it now went on in this village—according to the same daily rhythm that could not be altered. Children still demanded attention and animals needed to be fed. The fighters also needed to be fed, and their clothes, washed. The Cossack women dodged bullets as they carried food to the trenches, and then made their way back with the empty dishes.

At the first light of dawn, Boris would take his rifle and go off to the trenches with everybody else. He was both a soldier and a doctor. The wounded were bandaged and given first aid in the trenches, and then carried to the train at night. Boris was assisted by two orderlies who stayed with the wounded during the day. Boris could have stayed with them as well, of course, but I knew it was easier for him to be in the trenches—there was no time to think there.

With the setting of the sun the shooting would stop, and the exhausted people would lay down on the ground and fall asleep.

Boris and I slept on a cart by the railway tracks. The carts had been prepared for the wounded in case we had to retreat but could not use the train.

Boris used to fall asleep immediately, but I could not sleep at all. I would lie there listening to the silence: the contented whispering of the Lombardy poplars; the perfunctory barking of the village dogs; the peaceful snorting of the never-unsaddled horses as they chewed their hay. Everyone was sleeping so blissfully, so tranquilly, as if they had not spent the whole day killing one another.

I could feel my head spinning from the insomnia, weakness, and constant stress. As I looked up at the sky, I felt I was drowning in its velvet infinity, swinging in its starry swings, and hearing its lullaby of heavenly rhythms. I was almost happy. Once again, Boris had been returned to me; I could feel his shoulder under my head, his breath on my cheek. And even if I died with him tomorrow—was that not happiness? Was it not happiness to stop living among people who had lost their wisdom and compassion, forgotten truth and virtue, and were now drowning in blood?

The quiet was once broken by loud cursing and the frenzied scream: "Talk, you Red scum!" This was followed by the crack of a whip, the sound of blows, and a pathetic, almost inhuman, doglike squealing. In one of the cars not far from us a prisoner was being interrogated. A few minutes went by, and then I heard a shot. They had killed him . . .

Where does all this cruelty come from? And how could people living in the same country and united by a common history, common religion, and common interests, suddenly, over the course of a few months, become mortal enemies, hating one another with such passion?

The people—whom our writers had taught us to love; "God's vessels"; the people in whose name dreamers such as the Decembrists,[9] Sofia Perovskaia,[10] and Kaliaev[11] had sacrificed themselves—these same people had turned out to be robbers and murderers. As the folk song went, "I will have some fun, oh some fun; I will use my knife, oh my knife."

They had killed an old priest, hanged a teacher, and, if the Bolsheviks caught us now, would not dozens of greedy hands reach for us to tear us apart?

The officers, in their stead, had also shed the mask of civilization. Oh how thin and fragile it had turned out to be, revealing the savage nature underneath: to kill or be killed . . .

Suddenly a terrible scream cut through the silence. It was immediately echoed by hundreds of other voices. With screams of primitive, savage terror, people began running like animals driven by instinct. The wounded were throwing themselves out of the train and crawling into the bushes.

This was hysteria, akin to the "scream" in my boarding school, when hundreds of girls would suddenly start running around the halls screaming for no apparent reason.

Fortunately, there are people who can control their instincts.

"Halt!" Boris shouted at the top of his voice, standing on the cart. "Halt or I'll shoot!"

Other voices joined in: "What's the matter? What's going on? Where are the Bolsheviks?"

Shots fired into the air finally stopped the mob. People stood there looking bewildered, as if they had just awakened. Who had been the first to scream? Why had they done it? No one knew. Within several minutes everybody was asleep again.

My whole body was paralyzed with fear, and, as I lay next to my sleepy husband, it took me a long time to get over the shock.

Panic is remarkable for its immediacy. The mind is not yet functioning, but instinct is already telling you: run, escape! Panic works like an electrical shock; it overloads your nervous system.

[9] Decembrists—military officers who staged an unsuccessful liberal-constitutionalist coup against autocracy in December 1825.

[10] S. L. Perovskaia (1854–1881)—revolutionary terrorist executed for her role in the assassination of Tsar Alexander II in 1881.

[11] I. P. Kaliaev (1877–1905)—member of the Socialist Revolutionary Party, hanged for assassinating the governor-general of Moscow in 1905.

As I trembled nervously and pressed myself against Boris's warm body, I felt proud of him. He was one of the few people who could keep his presence of mind in times of danger or assume control in times of confusion. The war had made him cruel, but he had not become a barbarian.

By the end of the third day we had almost run out of ammunition. More exhausted and gloomier than usual, the men went to sleep. Suddenly, right before dawn, I heard a bird singing, then another, and finally a whole chorus joined in. I listened, spellbound. Since the fighting had started, I had never once heard birds singing. Frightened by the shells, they had flown away. I could not help waking Boris: "Listen to the birds!" Boris listened and then heaved a deep and joyful sigh: "That means that the Bolsheviks have left." Indeed, the shells that had awakened us every morning could no longer be heard.

THEY were supposed to restore rail communications with Tikhoretskaia, but Boris and I, worried about Lena, decided that we could get there faster by cart. Korenovskaia was only seven versts away, but the journey took us three hours. The road had practically disappeared, and we had to go across the steppe.

The air was hot, muggy, and filled with the repulsive odor of dead horses that were scattered around the steppe, swollen and splayed. As we drew closer to town, the sound of shelling got louder.

"They're advancing again," Boris sighed. "We'd better go straight to the station."

"Let's stop by the house for just a minute and at least get a peek at Lena," I begged.

"It's an extra half hour. Enough to cut the place off," answered Boris, but turned toward the town anyway.

No sooner had I kissed Lena, washed, and changed, than we had to move on. Oh, how I wanted to stay, lie down on the soft bed, and sleep, sleep . . . But Boris urged me on, and I overcame my momentary weakness.

We stopped by the railway station.

"There's only one military train," said Boris when he got back, "and they won't let you on."

"I'll stay behind, Boris. You go by yourself. I still have time to get home."

Without answering, Boris turned the cart onto the road that ran along the tracks.

"Let's try to get to Vyselki. There may be other trains there."

We drove out of town and entered the steppe. The steppe was still and quiet, but it was not the usual, peaceful stillness of early evening. It was full of sinister foreboding. The sky was burning in the sunset, as if splattered with blood. The reflections of that blood stained the earth and the roadside hedges.

Several horsemen appeared from behind a hill. Boris turned the cart into the bushes. We hid and listened to the approaching sound of hooves. One sentence was carried by the wind: "Got a light, Comrade?" It was a Bolshevik patrol. My heart was beating so loudly, I thought the Bolsheviks would hear it.

They rode by without stopping.

"Damn," cursed Boris. "I thought we'd be able to spend the night at the farm, but I guess the Bolsheviks are there, too. We'd better turn back."

We turned off the road. It was getting dark fast. The steppe was frightening on a night like this: full of shadows, ghosts, melancholy, and fear. It transformed the trees into horsemen, and the sound of the wind, into the clattering of hooves.

Finally we could see the flickering of the station lights in the distance. We approached the tracks.

"Get out," ordered Boris. "We'll leave the cart here. One way or another, we've got to get on that train."

We crept along the tracks. Boris tried the doors of each car. They were all locked. Finally one door gave way under the pressure from his powerful shoulder. Boris lifted me up, pushed me in, and closed the door.

"Who's there?" somebody called.

"It's okay. I'm checking the cars," I heard Boris's calm voice reply. I found myself alone in total darkness. Holding on to the wall, I groped my way to the corner and sat down. I could hear the snorting and shuffling of horses. I was not afraid of horses; I was afraid of people. What will they do if they find me? I thought. Will they throw me out or will they kill me? They may decide that I am a spy. Or maybe, like that time in Korenovskaia, I am sitting in a train without a locomotive and the Bolsheviks will find me. Boris may not remember what car I am in and may not be able to find me.

Finally the train shuddered and started moving. After a few minutes it stopped again. For a long time we did not move. Exhausted and tense, I gradually fell into a kind of lethargic state of apathy and impassivity. Then suddenly somebody opened the door. I pressed myself into the corner. But he did not come in—just threw in some hay for the horses. I crawled under the horses to get some of the hay for my corner.

The train started moving again. I felt better with the horses around. There was something very cozy in the sound of their peaceful snorting and chewing.

Little by little the light started coming in through the cracks. The train stopped. Somebody outside was fussing with the lock. I hid behind the horses.

"Where are you?" asked Boris's voice.

"Oh, thank God!" I exclaimed, rushing toward him. "Where are we?"

"At the Vyselki Station. Korenovskaia is in the hands of the comrades again. So is the farm where we were going to spend the night. They'll attack here this morning."

As if to prove him right, the usual gasping, rattling, grumbling music started up again. Boris helped me climb out of the car. The embankment was already covered with sleeping bodies. No sooner had they arrived than they fell asleep . . .

Suddenly pieces of glass and wood went flying up into the air. One shell had hit the station building, another, the last car.

"They're beginning to get the hang of it, the bastards," came a lazy voice from among the bodies stretched out along the embankment.

Then something buzzed, whirred, and clicked before hitting a wall and then a tree, and finally pouring down like hail.

"Lie down in that ditch and don't get up until I come back," said Boris and left.

I pressed myself against the bottom of the ditch, trying to flatten myself entirely and merge with the earth.

The regularity of the ta-ta-ta and slap-slap terrified me. I found the machine guns much scarier than the shells. They seemed to spray everything, leaving no place to hide.

It was only then that, sighing and scratching themselves, the bodies on the embankment started to get up, find their horses, and harness them to the carts.

I was afraid to climb out and take a better look, so I waited for Boris, alone and frightened.

"Get up and run to the colonel's cart, see it over there?" said Boris, appearing at the edge of the ditch. "He wasn't happy about it, but he promised to take you."

"What about you?"

"I'll walk with the retreating units. Run, fast!"

I ran crouching, falling down, and hiding behind trees. The angry, sleepy-looking colonel gave me an unfriendly look but did not object when I climbed into the cart. It was even scarier there, with bullets flying everywhere and absolutely no cover. I could hardly keep myself from asking why we were not moving. Finally the colonel said to the young officer who was sitting in the box:

"Okay, let's go, but make it nice and slow."

The officer obviously shared my impatience and started off quickly.

"I said make it nice and slow!" repeated the colonel coldly. And so on we went, at a measured pace, amid machine-gun and artillery fire, people, horses, and carts.

"Nothing like a retreat to collect a crowd. When the time comes to attack, they all disappear." muttered the colonel. "Got caught napping and lost a railway station."

TIKHORETSKAIA, a large junction halfway between Rostov and Ekaterinodar, had been transformed into a large supply center and was filled with military men. There were staff headquarters, chancelleries, offices, intrigues—everything an army's rear is supposed to have.

I had to sleep lying fully dressed on a hard floor in a room with five officers. They all slept like logs, while I tossed and turned, afraid to get up. Oh, how fondly I now recalled those nights we had spent in a cart under the star-studded skies of the Platnirovskaia station!

On the seventh day, communication with Korenovskaia was finally restored, and we could return by train.

OUR town had suffered a great deal. The town hall had been destroyed by artillery fire; around the town square stood blackened stumps and the shells of former buildings. The yards and streets were filled with piles of things that had been ruined—pieces of furniture, shards of broken dishes. The small shops and warehouses had been totally ravaged. The Cossacks, who had been hiding from the Reds in the steppe, came back to find themselves ruined—their fields trampled, their horses taken away, their animals slaughtered, and their houses destroyed. The comrades had clearly had some fun before leaving.

But life's demands are so powerful that two weeks after the departure of the Reds (they seemed to have disappeared without a trace) the familiar routine had begun to reestablish itself. New pots and chickens and pigs appeared, new carts squeaked along, and the Cossacks went out to plow and sow—to water with their own sweat the blood-drenched soil of their beloved steppe.

The Sorokin Army had pulled back, and the Kuban was returning to its peaceful, familiar way of life.

Boris was transferred to Ekaterinodar, and, without much regret, I left Korenovskaia.

The once quiet and provincial Ekaterinodar had become a large metropolis. All those who had managed to save themselves were headed for the Kuban. Many were trying to leave the country through Novorossiisk. Night and day, the streets were filled with rich industrialists, diplomats, government bureaucrats, lawyers, politicians, and stylishly dressed women. But the majority were military men, representing—the way it looked to me—all the units that had ever existed in Russia: the uhlans, dragoons, hussars, cavalry guards ... Helmets, shakos, feathers, clinking stirrups, sabers, broadswords ... It was amazing how many military men were in the rear, rather than at the front. Huge shop windows glittered with perfume, powder, chocolate, silk, and lace. Jewelry stores exhibited rare family jewels brought from all over Russia and exchanged, with the help of obliging Armenians, for rapidly depreciating currency.

In the evenings the city fairly buzzed with activity, overrun by colorful waves of humanity. Lit-up billboards advertised various forms of entertainment, and the sound of music—mixed with that of thousands of voices—streamed out of cafes and restaurants. Famous and not-so-famous performers from the capitals came touring. Novitskaia sang her beautiful Russian songs.[12] Vertinsky was becoming fashionable.[13] In his harlequin suit, he would half-whisper, half-sing his songs, charming the ladies. New movie theaters were popping up everywhere. Vera Kholodnaia, Mozzhukhin, Polonsky, and Maksimov were the idols of the public.[14]

The general impression was that of a feast during the time of the plague. But in early 1919 the plague was still far off. The newspapers were full of stories about the successes of the Don Cossacks and the Volunteers; the joyous welcome they had received from the population; and, most important, the imminent arrival of the Allies, who had already sent special missions to acquaint themselves with the situation and had promised immediate help. There was no doubt in the minds of

---

[12] The author probably refers to N. V. Plevitskaia (1884–1941), a popular folk singer who emigrated with the Denikin Army, to become the voice of White émigré nostalgia in Paris. She died in a French prison, having been sentenced to fifteen years for helping her husband, General N. Skoblin, kidnap the head of the émigré Russian Military Union to the USSR.

[13] Aleksandr Vertinsky (1889–1957)—singer and songwriter famous for mannered, melancholy "ariettes." Left Russia after the civil war but returned in 1943.

[14] Vera Kholodnaia, Ivan Mozzhukhin, Vitold Polonsky, and Vladimir Maksimov—the biggest Russian movie stars of the silent era.

the illustrious refugees that they would soon be back in their houses and on their estates, enjoying their usual carefree existence. In the meantime, they condescended to the discomforts of provincial living and treated the local Cossacks with patronizing arrogance. Most tried to worm their way into the staff of the Volunteer Army as supply officers, advisers, and so on, hatching various intrigues and embroiling the command in politics. Speculators and self-seekers inflated the rear of the army, while honest and noble warriors fought at the front, risking their lives and suffering from cold and hunger. While the Cossacks sat in the trenches in desperate need of warm clothing and boots, the hangers-on in the rear strutted around in their smartly tailored Circassian coats, field jackets, and riding breeches. They drank wine, boasted of their heroic feats, and talked, and talked, and talked . . .

FINALLY we witnessed the great retreat. It was the third face of war I had seen. The first had been Kornilov's magnificent barbarians. The second had been the efficient military professionals of the second Kuban March, who had defeated Sorokin's army.

Now I saw the third face—tens of thousands of healthy, well-armed people abandoning the front. The formerly cohesive military units turned into an undisciplined, disorganized mob, each individual concerned only with his own personal salvation. Having lost all power of resistance, they simply went with the flow. Head to head, shoulder to shoulder, cart to cart, the terrible flood poured over the city, submerged Krasnaia Street, and streamed into back alleys. Beyond the city the brooks that were the streets and alleys merged into one powerful stream. Too wide for the roads, it spilled over into the fields. Horses became mired up to their bellies in the thick black mud and had to stop, exhausted. There was no time to pause, and the wave just rolled over them. The river bank for miles around had become one huge encampment. Every inch of the bridge and every spot on the ferries had to be fought for. Many of the horsemen tried to swim across, but the muddy waters of the Kuban are wide and swift, and not all of them reached the other shore.

The army units were followed by carts with refugees, an endless Gypsy camp of women, children, and baggage. Dirty tarps protected the carts from the sun and the rain. Food was cooked in pots over braziers, and clothes were hung around to dry. Trash and excrement were thrown out into the streets. There was a line of camels pulling Kalmyk wagons filled with men in bright robes and women in dirty, but colorful outfits.

How many hundreds of versts had they crossed, caught up in the elemental inertia of flight? Never washing, never changing their clothes, and only occasionally stretching their limbs when the road became too jammed to move. Meek, indifferent, accustomed to everything, they were but a small part of the flood. As if ancient, Scythian Rus had come to life . . .

The dull din of the refugee flood lasted seven days. The Kuban government and other offices were prepared to evacuate and were just waiting for an opportunity to join the general retreat. The Cossacks were not going to Novorossiisk with the

Volunteers, but to Georgia instead. They were hoping that the Georgians would live up to the terms of the Paris Treaty, for which the unfortunate Kalabukhov had paid with his life, and allow them to enter Georgia.[15]

I implored Boris to stay, arguing that this was the end; that there was no going back; that this might be our final farewell; and that this was his last chance to join Soviet life. But he was absolutely convinced that individuals were in greater danger than groups. "If we make it into Georgia," he said, "I will find a way to get you and Lena out, too."

The Kuban units were the last to leave, when the flood of refugees had already thinned out. Boris was on his horse, accompanying the field hospital.

It was hard, so very hard for me to say good-bye to him, but my alarm became truly desperate when, about two hours after his departure, I heard artillery fire.

"Mistress," Lena's nanny ran in, out of breath, "the Bolsheviks are in town."

EKATERINODAR, having once again become Krasnodar, was transformed as if by magic. The gigantic broom of the refugees had swept away all the chancelleries, offices, bright uniforms, and well-dressed women. The birds of passage had flown over the sea. The cafes, cabarets, theaters, and studios were closed down. The shop windows were bare. Not only chocolate, jewelry, and perfume but even the basic necessities had disappeared. The farmer's markets, where a few weeks before you could hardly move among the carts overflowing with food, were pictures of gaping emptiness. Women in scarves and men in caps walked hurriedly through the streets. It was obvious that only necessity could have driven them outside. In front of the few grocery stores that were open by order of the authorities stood long lines of people holding their newly received ration cards. The streets were never swept and were covered with sunflower-seed shells. Very quickly, Krasnodar acquired that bleak, gray look typical of a Soviet town.

The new bosses were refashioning our lives according to the Soviet stereotype. Housing, neighborhood, and district committees were established and were charged with monitoring the private lives of the citizens. Buildings were commandeered for the countless offices with unintelligible names: NKSO, NTO, NKP, and so forth. In order to furnish them, the commissars—in a perfectly businesslike manner—raided private apartments and took away carpets and furniture.

Before leaving, Boris had nailed several pieces of shoe leather to the underside of the table to keep them safe from searches. However, it was precisely this table that the commissar took a liking to. Hard as I tried to talk him into taking another, much better table, the original one was taken away. I could only hope that they would not turn it upside down and discover the hidden leather, or I would pay dearly for "concealing the people's property."

Essentially, all our property became the people's. Citizens had their houses,

---

[15] Georgia declared independence from Russia after the Bolshevik Revolution and was occupied by Soviet forces in 1921. In 1919 A. I. Kalabukhov, a proponent of Kuban autonomy, signed a treaty of friendship between the Kuban leadership and the Medzhilis, the government of the Chechen and Ingush, who had been fighting against the Volunteer Army for several months. By order of General Wrangel, Kalabukhov was court-martialed for treason and subsequently hanged.

carpets, and personal belongings—especially jewelry—taken away from them. At night, timid shadows, looking over their shoulders, would slip out and bury money and jewelry in their yards and gardens. Before the Whites had departed, I had gone to an Armenian shop and exchanged some gold and diamonds for cash, which I put in a metal box and buried in my garden. But I still had some things left and, on one particularly dark night, I went out into the yard to bury them in a hole I had dug in advance. Imagine my horror when I raised my head and saw a tall, white figure watching me from behind the fence.

"So you're digging, eh?" a hoarse voice asked me.

Caught red-handed, I did not know what to say.

"Don't be afraid. I'm digging, too."

Relieved, we both finished our work.

Every yard and every house contained some treasure. Soon the Reds figured this out and started tearing up the walls and floorboards during their searches.

In addition to their regular robberies, they proclaimed a citywide "search day." Having divided the city into districts, special "troikas" conducted simultaneous searches.

I was visited by two men and a woman. The woman had the nose of a hound. She rummaged in every corner, found all the things I had tried to hide, and after every find would reproach me for "concealing the people's property." At the last moment before the search began I had taken off my rings, bracelet, and gold watch, climbed onto a chair, and hidden them in the lamp shade. The woman found those, too. They took every loose piece of cloth, every spool of thread. The carpets had been taken earlier, as part of the compulsory requisitioning. All the charming things that Boris had brought from Paris were taken away. Finally, happy with their rich loot and having filled two carts, they exited, leaving me only those things that I was entitled to according to their "list": two sheets per bed, two pillow cases, two changes of underwear, one coat for each season, and so on. Their pillaging of my things had been conducted in the full conviction of their righteousness and my criminality, with threats and accusations about my lack of "consciousness."

Thus I received my Soviet baptism. My life and property were no longer mine. They had become the "people's" and were transferred to the state, which could dispose of them as it saw fit.

BORIS returned in May. Their march had ended in failure: Georgia had not allowed the Kuban Army into its territory. The conditions of the march had been extraordinarily difficult: they had traveled over mountain ranges and through passes where there was no food for their horses, through poor Circassian villages unable to feed them—without rest for the exhausted men and horses. Behind them, the Reds were moving swiftly along the convenient Black Sea highway, so that reaching Georgia before they did became a matter of life and death. When the Kuban men arrived in Adler, the negotiations started. The Georgians refused to fulfill the conditions of the treaty and closed the border. It was an attempt at self-preservation: an invasion by the Reds was inevitable.

There was no way out: behind them were the Bolsheviks; to the left were the mountains; to the right, the sea. Some units boarded the steamer *Beshtau* and left for the Crimea. But most stayed behind and surrendered to the Reds when they arrived. The Reds did not know what to do with so many prisoners, so they sent them north to evacuation points. Boris was assigned to the Krasnodar military hospital as a doctor. In this way he entered Soviet life.

KRASNODAR was celebrating the anniversary of the Great October Revolution. The dirty, gray city was decorated with flags. Carpets, confiscated from the population, were hanging from windows and balconies. On all the squares triumphal arches had been erected. The housing committees had "suggested" that all the residents attend the rallies and participate in the demonstrations. Not daring to disobey, the sullen and resentful citizens trudged toward the squares, with the regulation red ribbon on their chests.

Students from all the city schools were carrying red flags and banners as they converged on Catherine Square.

The speakers who had been sent down from the "center" quickly rattled off the obligatory speeches and were followed by local party organizers, who slowly formed their tongues around words that were like heavy stones. One could almost see the difficulty with which they formed their thoughts. Since no one had anything new to say, they just kept droning on and on, saying the same things over and over again, boring everyone to death. I did not even have the heart to restrain my students, who were beginning to get fidgety. Looking at the gray sky and the sullen faces, I remembered the bright sunny day, the solemn mass in the square in Korenovskaia, the joyous voices of the children mingling with the songs of the larks in the fields, and the happiness undiluted by foreboding that had filled our hearts.

How naive we were . . .

BORIS kept trying to get a transfer to Moscow, and finally he got one in 1921.

We arrived in Moscow.

And what a sight it was! The city resembled a hungry, shabby, dirty beggar. The houses, frozen stiff and topped by their dead chimneys, looked sullen. The noble townhouses that used to hide from curious eyes behind tall fences now stood exposed: every board and branch had been used for fuel. Snowdrifts covered the yards and the unswept sidewalks. Here and there stood gutted buildings that had been bombed, never finished, or simply ruined by neglect. They were dying a slow, lingering death, being taken apart log by log, brick by brick. The wind swept through vacant lots, piling up the snowdrifts. All the best buildings had been taken over by institutions: RKIRKK, MOSNKP, VONKh, NKSO, and so on, ad infinitum . . . A crowd of ragged Soviet employees from one of these tongue twisters would move in, rip the curtains off the windows, and tear up the upholstery. They would burn the furniture, portraits, and letters in the stove, stain the parquet floors with mud, and, having made that building totally unlivable, move on to another one. Only the faded tatters of old flags and banners would still flutter in the wind.

The inhabitants were worthy of their city. Exhausted and sullen, unshaven Soviets—in their soldier's trench coats, sheepskin coats, or women's fur coats tied with rope; in their worn-out shoes, someone else's galoshes, or awkward felt boots; in their homemade mittens and with their backpacks and sacks—ran up and down the streets pulling children's sleds. Streetcars rattled by with bodies hanging down from the steps like clusters of grapes. At streetcar stops passengers waited for countless hours, shoving and cursing one another. The tall, dark figures of women wrapped up in the most peculiar ways stood freezing in lines in front of grocery stores, waiting for the pathetic pittance of yet another ration.

Moscow was in the first phase of the Internationale: the old world had been completely destroyed. The "new" one had not yet begun. The first part of the program was being fulfilled: the Soviets were being trained by hunger and cold; leveled to the universal brotherhood of destitute and obedient citizens in a socialist state.[16]

Boris was attached to Narkomsobes (the Social Welfare Department), and we managed to get a room in the employee dormitory. A five-story townhouse in Merzliakovsky Alley, meant to hold five families, contained several hundred residents. Large rooms were divided by plywood partitions into small cells known as "apartments."

Our floor had five hundred people instead of five. We were considered lucky to get even this modest shelter in the grotesquely overcrowded city. Any kind of privacy was completely out of the question: everything that went on behind the partition could be heard in our "apartment." There were two half-baths, one of which was being used as a room, and one bathroom, which was used for storage. The bathtub did not function, but sometimes served as a bed for visitors. We all washed under the same tap, which constantly froze and barely dripped, so that everybody tried to get up early and line up in front of the sink. Our room had a high ceiling and large windows, so it was as cold inside as outside. Our first priority was to obtain a "bourgeoise," that is, a small iron stove. While the children and I sat on our bags in our winter coats, Boris went to the Smolensky Market and came back with a stove. He put a metal sheet on the floor, set the stove on top of it, and then connected the pipes and fitted them through a hole in the window. The paper we had wrapped our things in could serve as fuel, but hard as he tried, the fire just would not catch. The wind drove the smoke back down the pipe, and it soon became impossible to breathe. Fortunately, our neighbor smelled the smoke, knocked on our door, and showed us "the trick." It soon warmed up, and we could take off our coats.

We started fixing up our new apartment. By putting the wardrobe and the chest-of-drawers in the middle, we created a dining room and a children's room. By covering our beds with carpets, we turned them into couches. Then we put our

---

[16] Internationale—the anthem of the international socialist movement and the Soviet state anthem between 1918 and 1943; includes the lines: "The world of violence we will destroy / Down to its core, and then / Our new world we will build up, / He who has been naught, he shall be all."

pictures and tapestry on the walls, and made bookcases out of boxes. If not for the plebeian stove, the room would have looked quite presentable. But one could not complain about the stove. It was at the very center of our lives: we ate, warmed ourselves, and took baths in a wooden bowl in front of it. I used the same water for the laundry, and then dried the clothes on a line that I hung over the stove. The problem was that the "bourgeoise" was a very demanding little goddess. Her insatiable belly kept claiming new victims. Paper, cardboard, and boxes disappeared quickly; to be left without fuel meant to freeze. Boris used one of the remaining boxes to make a kind of sled, which he used to take with him when he went to work. He would bring unneeded books and papers from his office, pick up sticks along the way, and occasionally be lucky enough to run across a surviving piece of a fence. At night we would cover ourselves with all the blankets, jackets, and coats we had. By morning the room would be completely frozen. Next to problem number one, the cold, was problem number two, hunger. Boris had two jobs—one during the day and one at night, so his rations were quite good by the standards of the time: consisting mostly of "shrapnel" cereal which was practically impossible to make soft no matter how long you cooked it; rusty herring; frozen potatoes; and sometimes flour mixed with bran. I received special milk ration cards for the children and had to stand in line to get the milk. I also had to stand in line to buy bread. There was no fat of any kind, so I had to go to the Smolensky Market and trade for it with some of our clothes and plates.

The Smolensky Market presented a strange sight. There was no place for former rich people and gentry landowners in the socialist society. They were not entitled to ration cards but were generously given the right to either die or find a way to feed themselves. The only way was to sell things. These human shadows condemned to extinction stood or sat in long lines, shoulder to shoulder. Exhausted women with proud profiles and men with noble chins covered with stubble passed whole days stomping their feet and rubbing their hands in an attempt to stay warm.

I stood beside a tall, erect old woman. She was holding pieces of lace and colored ribbons in her hands, which were partially covered by worn-out kid gloves; an embroidered napkin was hanging over her arm; and a velvet cape with chinchillas was suspended from her shoulders. By her feet were an incomplete tea set, a silver goblet, a large comb with diamonds, high-heeled satin slippers, a dog's collar . . . Oh, if only things could talk!

Speculators, the direct link between the "aristocracy" and the "people" strolled to and fro. It was their job to convince some woman at the market that colored ribbons or a hand mirror were just the thing for her, and exchange them for some millet or potatoes. They made a good profit.

I traded a silver spoon for two bottles of hempseed oil. Unable to meet the eyes of the tall old lady, I poured some oil into her goblet. She did not even thank me, only her lips trembled.

Chased by the cold wind, I hurried home. It was faster to walk than to wait for the streetcar. The happy owner of precious "fats," I looked forward to making a "real" dinner: fried potatoes to go with the herring and some bran cakes.

We shared a common kitchen—a large room with a large stove in the middle. As there was no fuel, everybody used primus stoves. Like all other common facilities, the kitchen was extraordinarily dirty. The walls and the ceiling were covered with soot and spiderwebs; the dim window hardly let any light in. Ten stoves were hissing and whistling, spewing soot and producing a foul smell. A dozen housewives were laboring over the same menu: shrapnel, herring, potatoes . . . Envious eyes were looking at my cakes and my glass of hempseed oil.

"I traded for it at Smolensky today," I explained to one of my neighbors.

"What for?"

"A silver spoon."

"Not too bad."

"As long as you have something to trade," said another housewife dryly. "You're new here, but we traded everything away a long time ago."

Whether we wanted to or not, we knew everything about one another: who came, who went, who had had a fight, who had moved in with whom, who had gotten separated, who got a large ration, and who got a small one . . . We were all very different—from a cleaning lady to a professor's wife, but we all had the same interests: what to eat and how to get fuel. Hunger and cold were not conducive to tranquillity and equanimity, and conflicts over trifles flared up all the time. Somebody had stirred her cereal with somebody else's spoon by mistake, or somebody had accused somebody else of pouring some of her soup out. There was also political hostility. The wives of Communists received better rations and were better dressed. They were envied and distrusted, and were often the target of caustic remarks by non-Party women. They paid back in the same coin.

Fortunately, most of our immediate neighbors were male clerical workers, but ten women and as many children made our lives unpleasant enough.

Every once in a while we held apartment meetings, at which we determined the needs of individual tenants. This information was duly reported to the building committee, which distributed the rooms and set the prices for "living space," electricity, and water according to one's salary, so that the same room could cost either five or fifty rubles.

Toward the end of the first year we managed to get the room next to ours, which had a real wall. Finally we could talk without being heard by our neighbors.

ONE night we were awakened by a loud knock on the door. Boris opened it. Two GPU[17] agents with search warrants entered the room. My heart sank: somebody must have informed on us . . . They looked at our documents, books, and all the papers in the desk; went through the chest-of-drawers; threw the dresses out of the wardrobe. "Stand up, Citizen," said one of them to me. I stood wrapped in a blanket while he looked under the mattress and under the bed. Having finished with our room, he went to the next one.

"There are children sleeping in there," I said.

---

[17] GPU—State Political Directorate, the name of the Soviet secret police from 1922 to 1923, when it was renamed OGPU: Unified State Political Directorate.

Paying no attention to me, they turned everything upside down in there, too. Then they went out to talk on the phone that stood in the hall. I was sure that they were going to tell Boris to get dressed and follow them. But having finished their conversation, they left without closing the door behind them, and we heard them knock on another door. Had they left for good or would they be back? Would they arrest Boris? Tormented by doubt and uncertainty, we lay in bed listening to the imperious knocks as they moved from one door to the next. Finally we heard the front door bang. They had left.

Figures in robes and nightgowns gathered in the hall. Nobody knew the reason for the search, but everyone felt like a potential victim, everyone was afraid of what might happen next. Powerless and defenseless, these Soviets trembled before the omnipotent GPU. In the morning we discovered that a search had been conducted in all the apartments of the building, as well as in many other buildings. No one knew why.

After that night I never stopped fearing for Boris's life. Up until then he had managed to hide his counterrevolutionary past and his membership in the Volunteer Army, but given how pervasive the system of informing and eavesdropping was, sooner or later it had to come out.

  ☐ Soon afterward Boris was appointed head physician of the Chinese Eastern Railway Hospital in Harbin, Manchuria. During the temporary takeover of the railway administration by China in 1929 Boris chose to remain at the hospital rather than return to Moscow, and he was stripped of his Soviet citizenship. After the Japanese invasion the Zhemchuzhnaia family left Harbin. In 1939 they emigrated to Australia, where Boris worked as a physiotherapist and later a doctor. Zinaida died in 1961, the year she finished her autobiography.

6 □ NADEZHDA KRUPSKAIA

Autobiography

□ Nadezhda Konstantinovna Krupskaia (1869–1939), the wife of V. I. Lenin, wrote this autobiography for a volume of the "Granat" encyclopedia devoted to Soviet revolutionary leaders and public figures. Krupskaia's contribution is notable for its formality (most other contributors chose to submit longer first-person narratives, such as Krupskaia herself wrote on other occasions). Krupskaia's field of expertise was educational theory, and in the 1920s she held a high position in the People's Commissariat (Ministry) of Enlightenment. No favorite of Stalin's, she suffered various humiliations in the 1930s while continuing to occupy prominent, if increasingly less meaningful, positions in the Soviet government hierarchy until her death.

NADEZHDA Konstantinovna Krupskaia was born in 1869 in Petersburg. Her parents were of gentry background, but both became orphans at a young age and were educated at the government's expense: her mother at an institute and her father at a military school. After graduating, her mother went to work as a governess and her father went on to the Military Academy and then into service. Neither one ever owned any real estate or other property. Both had been attracted by revolutionary ideas in their youth, so K saw revolutionaries of all kinds from a very early age. Her father acted on his revolutionary convictions, was brought to trial, and was ultimately acquitted. Throughout their lives, K's parents were obliged to move from town to town as her father kept receiving new assignments. K was fourteen when her father died. After that, K and her mother made their living by renting out rooms, copying, tutoring, and doing other odd jobs. K attended Obolenskaia's gymnasium. After graduating from the gymnasium with a gold medal, she became a Tolstoyan for a while.[1] From 1891 to 1896 she taught on Sundays and at night in a school for workers (outside the Neva Gate). At that time she became a Marxist and started conducting propaganda among the workers. She was one of the founders of the Union for the Liberation of the Working Class.[2] During the strikes of 1896 she was arrested and exiled for three years to the village of Shushenskoe, Minusinsk District, where she married Vladimir Ilich Ulianov,[3] with whom she had previously worked in Petersburg, at the Union of Liberation.

From N. K. Krupskaia, autobiographical entry in *Deiateli SSSR i revoliutsionnogo dvizheniia Rossii: Entsiklopedicheskii slovar' Granat* (Moscow: Sovetskaia entsiklopediia, 1998; reprint of Moscow: Granat, 1927–29), 236–37.

[1] Tolstoyans—followers of Lev Tolstoy's teachings on nonviolence, simplicity, and moral self-improvement.

[2] Organization of Marxist intellectuals founded in St. Petersburg in 1895.

[3] V. I. Lenin's real name.

She spent her last year of exile in Ufa, where she also engaged in revolutionary underground work. In 1901 she was granted an overseas passport. Upon her arrival in Munich in the spring of 1901, she became first the secretary of *Iskra*,[4] then a member of the Overseas League of Russian Social Democrats, and finally, after the Third Party Congress, the secretary of the overseas divisions of the Central Committee and TsO.[5] In late 1905 she returned to Russia and began working as the secretary of the Central Committee. After she went abroad again in early 1908, she was tried in absentia on three counts of Article 102 violations.[6] While abroad, she worked as the secretary of various Bolshevik organizations while also studying foreign pedagogical literature and educational institutions, contributing articles to *Free Education*, and working on a book entitled *Popular Education in a Workers' Democracy*. After returning to Russia she worked for a while in the Central Committee Secretariat but was soon elected to the Vyborg District Duma, where she headed the section on education, while also taking part in the revolutionary movement. After the October takeover she became a member of the Council of the Peoples' Commissariat of Education in charge of extracurricular programs, and later the chair of the Political and Scientific Section of GUS.[7] At the same time she was assisting the Women's Department, the Komsomol, and the Young Pioneers while also contributing to various newspapers and magazines. Throughout her life, from 1894 on, she always did everything in her power to help Vladimir Ilich Lenin in his work.

[4] *Iskra*—émigré periodical of Russian Social Democrats.

[5] Central organ, that is, *Iskra*.

[6] Article 102 of the Criminal Code of 1903 dealt with political crimes.

[7] GUS—the advisory committee of scholars at the People's Commissariat of Enlightenment (Gosudarstvennyi uchenyi sovet).

7 □ TATIANA VARSHER

Things Seen and Suffered

□ A graduate of the Bestuzhev Women's Institute of Higher Learning, Tatiana Varsher was a professor of ancient history at the Petrograd Pedagogical (formerly Teacher's) Institute and, during War Communism, a "cultural enlightenment" lecturer in various schools and Soviet institutions. Her fiancé was executed by the Cheka. In 1921 she emigrated to Latvia and published this memoir a few years later.

"IF A WOMAN is worthy of a place on the scaffold, then give her a place in Parliament," proclaimed a popular feminist slogan. The Bolsheviks went much farther along the road to women's equality: not only did they give women their "place in Parliament," as well as some of the highest positions in the republic—they also gave them the job of executioner. I was sent to the Bestuzhev Institute right after high school.[1] At that time, according to the rules, all first-year students had to live in the dormitory. Among my roommates was Konkordia Nikolaevna Gromova. It was hard to imagine a greater contrast: on the one hand, a sixteen-year-old girl, a typical product of the Moscow professorial milieu who had seen nothing of life or people; on the other, the daughter of a village priest from Irkutsk Province who had spent several years working as a teacher among the peasants. Konkordia told me many interesting things: how she had saved up her ten-kopek coins to be able to make the trip to Petersburg; how desperately poor she was; and how she had traveled part of the way to Petersburg with the so-called silver convoy, which transported state gold and silver reserves. For some reason, of the many things she told me I was particularly struck by the story of how her father, the priest, had accompanied her to the nearest town—I do not remember if she was going off to work or already coming to the institute—and of how he had wanted to buy her some belts she could use to fasten her suitcase. It turned out that they cost one ruble, twenty-five kopeks, a piece. The old man had broken down and cried: "They're asking a ruble and a quarter for those belts, but you know we don't have that kind of money, Connie my dear. So you'll just have to go ahead and tie up your bag with string."

Even such common Bestuzhev entertainment as trips to the Aleksandrinsky Theater at thirty-two kopeks a seat was beyond her means. I remember trying to offer her tickets. "No," she would say, "don't tempt me, or I won't have enough

From T. Varsher, *Vidennoe i perezhitoe* (Berlin: Trud, 1923), 10–139 (abridged).

[1] Bestuzhev Courses—the St. Petersburg Women's Institute of Higher Learning. Founded by Professor K. N. Bestuzhev-Riumin in 1878, this was the most famous of the women's universities allowed to open in the second half of the 1870s (the others were at Kazan, Moscow, and Kiev). All but the one in St. Petersburg were closed by 1890 because of student radicalism.

left for postage: a stamp to Siberia costs ten kopeks these days." She was not able to work as a tutor: her education was not sufficient for the purpose and she spoke some kind of quaint Siberian dialect.

The next year we were allowed to leave the dormitory, but Konkordia and I continued to see each other every day: we were both elected secretaries of the mutual aid society. Konkordia was always trying to use some of the students' money for prisoners. Twice a week, loaded down with provisions, she would set out for the pretrial detention center. She was the one who introduced me to the illegal Red Cross organization. Her other concern was for sick people. If some student was seriously ill, there was no better nurse than Konkordia . She also loved children. I can still picture her: tall and awkward, in her long black dress— or "cassock," as I used to call it—tied with a leather belt above her waist, standing by our huge samovar and pouring out tea for the children who had come to the Christmas party at the institute. During the summer she was never idle: she would tour the areas that were suffering after a bad harvest and work in soup kitchens.

When the student riots began, many of us were expelled and later readmitted, but Konkordia never returned to the institute. She went to Paris. There she lived in a commune with other poor students, moving from one damp attic to another.

When she returned to Russia, Konkordia began editing an underground news-paper. She was arrested and exiled on several occasions, but she never stopped her work. Then she went underground, and I lost track of her.

One summer I was invited as a tutor to the aristocratic V household, in Tambov Province. The Vs had a guest: a Quaker who had been interested in Russia since the 1891 famine, who loved the country and had traveled everywhere. When he found out I had attended the Bestuzhev Institute, he grew extremely agitated: "I knew one of your fellow students quite well. I had never met anybody like her before. She was an example of absolute self-sacrifice. Oh, how that woman worked! How driven she was! She had a strange name." He produced his note-book and read: "Konkordia Nikolaevna Gromova."

In the summer of 1921 I read in *Pravda* that a "Comrade Natasha," mar-ried name Samoilova, had died of cholera during a propaganda trip down the Volga . . . Next to the story was a portrait of Konkordia Nikolaevna Gromova. The articles about her were written in that style of folksy sentimentality, so typical of the Bolsheviks. One such article recounted how hard Comrade Natasha had once worked on a "day of voluntary labor" and how everyone had tried to dis-suade her by telling her it was not her job to carry heavy logs around, and how she had refused to leave, saying, "I must work for the common cause. The pen won't fall out of my hand if I spend some time carrying logs." There was going to be a meeting in her honor, but I did not go. I thought it could not really be her and, in any case, a meeting organized by the Bolsheviks would be an insult to her memory.

Some time later, two of my former students came knocking at my door in the middle of the night. They had managed to escape from the Ekaterinoslav Cheka. Using fake IDs, they had spent a whole month traveling to Petersburg. They told me all about the horrors they had seen in the south. "It's hard to understand," I said, "how someone as good as Konkordia Gromova could get mixed up in all this filth."—"If you mean Konkordia Gromova or Comrade Natasha, you must be joking!" Talking both at once, they launched into a tale of how Konkordia Gromova had signed death sentences by the hundreds, organized punitive raids, and condemned whole villages to pillage and plunder.

"Listen," I asked, "were there any priests among the people she sent to the other world?"

"Of course. Many priests were executed. Why do you ask?"

I did not answer. I did not want to tell them that I had recalled an elderly village Father who had cried as he was saying farewell to his daughter: "They're asking a ruble and a quarter for those belts, but you know we don't have that kind of money, Connie my dear. So you'll just have to go ahead and tie up your bag with string."[2]

I FOUND out the hard way that, in order not to be late for my lectures, I needed an extra hour in the morning—"in case of emergency," as our precinct policeman used to say. The most common emergency was "the power's gone." The streetcar would suddenly stop; some passengers would wait, but the more impatient ones would get off, leaving some free seats behind. Taking advantage of this circumstance, I would sit down, take a book out of my briefcase, and start reading. A half an hour, perhaps an hour later, the streetcar would start moving again . . .

Last Wednesday my "extra hour" came in very handy. I had been in the streetcar for about twenty minutes when it suddenly stopped. Six Red Army men, three at each end, got in and said: "Everybody out!"—"What do you mean, 'Everybody out?'"—"Very simple: everybody has to get out to break up a barge on the Fontanka."—"I can't. I have to go give a lecture."—"What lecture, just do as you're told and get off the damned streetcar." I showed them my professor's ID. "We don't need no papers. Just get out. Can't you understand plain Russian? You've got hands, don't you? So get moving and go work on that barge . . . Just look at this fine lady with her fancy briefcase . . . Thinks she can impress us!" I got off the streetcar. A woman next to me was crying. She had been visiting her children's godmother at the other end of town and was now taking a head of cabbage home to them. "I have three little ones locked up at home waiting for me; they haven't had a single thing to eat since last night." Elementary decency required that I intercede on behalf of the unfortunate woman, but I could see that she was better off without my help. I and my plush coat only got on their nerves. The crowd kept growing. The cursing and swearing was getting louder. "I'll break your skull,"

---

[2] Konkordia (K. N.) Samoilova (Gromova) was one of the most prominent Bolshevik leaders in charge of work among women. After her husband, A. A. Samoilov, died of cholera in Astrakhan in 1918, she suffered what her Soviet biographer calls "a nervous breakdown." Upon her release from the hospital she turned down an offer to become the head of the All-Union Women's Department and soon became the chief political officer of a "propaganda ship" on the Volga. In the spring of 1921 she died of cholera in Astrakhan and was buried beside her husband. See S. F. Vinogradova, "Zhizn', otdannaia revoliutsii," in *Leningradki: Vospominaniia, ocherki, dokumenty* (Leningrad: Lenizdat, 1968), 120–38; see also Barbara Evans Clements, *Bolshevik Women* (Cambridge: Cambridge University Press, 1997), 216, 225.

screamed one of the soldiers. "Go ahead and break it; that's how you do every-thing, the devil take you!" I took advantage of the confusion and started running. I could hear the time-honored familiar phrases: "Get her! Catch her! Out of the way!" . . . I lost one of my galoshes, picked it up, and remembered through some animal instinct that, two buildings down, there was an unlocked front door, so I ran in and knocked at the first door, holding my briefcase and one of my galoshes in my hands . . . I explained what had happened, and they let me in: they turned out to be nice people, but what if they had been Chekists? Through the window I could see my fellow passengers being led to their "labor duty." Happily the woman with the cabbage was not among them. After about ten minutes I thanked my hosts, walked several blocks, "hung" onto a streetcar, and arrived fifteen min-utes before the lecture was to begin.

The next time the journey was uneventful, and I arrived exactly an hour before the lecture. "Please stop by the secretary's office," said the doorkeeper. "Another questionnaire?"—"Yes, Ma'am, in four copies. Also your last year's difference: one pound of bread, no less." Wonderful things, these "differences." Every once in a while they would realize that our salary could not last more than three days on the "subsistence minimum" and would come up with a complex calculation of what the "difference" amounted to. It would arrive a year later, after the ruble had fallen by another 400 percent. My last difference—I don't remember the exact amount although I had to sign for it on three separate forms—had been enough to buy a toothbrush.

Oh, how sick I was of these forms! "Fill out this form, T.S.,[3] but for God's sake don't write anything weird," begged the secretary. This was because the last time, under the question, "How do you view the present situation?" I had written our Moscow dishwasher's favorite curse: "Let the devil make his home in my womb if I understand anything." Who needed these forms "in four copies" was beyond me. One teacher I knew always answered the question, "What is your party affil-iation?" with the phrase, "Whichever way the wind is blowing."

This time there were some new questions: "When did you complete your edu-cation?" I wrote: "Graduated on such and such a date; education incomplete; hope it will remain so until the day I die." "How do you view the present gov-ernment?"—"With the wide-open eyes of a historian." "Did you finish grade school?" I wrote proudly: "Yes!"

"What am I going to do with you? Now tell me, why did you have to put an exclamation mark? You turn your back for one second, and she's sure to do something irresponsible . . ."

WHILE I was still at the institute, I had an unexpected visitor at home. They brought in a Chinese man and put him up in my dining room. He was supposed to move out in three days. That was a fine prospect: to live under the same roof with the "yellow peril." Sh wrote a note to some friend of his at the Commissariat of Enlightenment. I didn't feel like going down there, but could I really share my

---

[3] T.S. stands for Varsher's name and patronymic, a polite form of address in Russian.

apartment with a Chinaman? So I went. I was met by the doorkeeper. He seemed elated: "I am always so pleased to see one of my old customers!" A sign was hanging on the wall that said: "Please do not insult the employees by tipping them." Just try not insulting them! I insulted the doorkeeper with three rubles and asked him to help me find the right person. I left with a piece of paper: owing to the number of films in my possession, my apartment was not subject to a living space reduction. It had not been a pleasant thing to do, but at least the yellow peril had passed me by.

SOMEBODY showed me the text of Kollontai's[4] speech to the sailors: "Up to now our institutes have not been producing either wives or lovers for you. We will provide you with both wives and lovers." At the first opportunity I will make sure to ask the esteemed Aleksandra Mikhailovna how one is supposed to understand this: will each sailor receive a wife and a lover or will one sailor get the former and another, the latter. "What would you like, a wife or a lover?"—"I'll go for a wife, you know how it is—can't get by without a wife." "And you, Comrade?"— "I want a lover; I don't need no wife." Is Aleksandra Mikhailovna planning on training these future wives and lovers herself? Together or separately? At what age will the specialization begin? The curriculum should, of course, be different. Some will have to be taught how to cook and mend socks while others are taught how to sing and dance . . . Is that the idea? I really should ask Aleksandra Mikhailovna all about it.

THE writer S's former cook died in his apartment. He spent five days trying to get permission to bury her. The corpse lay in the kitchen while S, who slept in the servants' quarters because he could not keep the other rooms warm, cooked his meals and ate right next to it. Human beings are not like pigs—they can get used to anything.

[4] Aleksandra Mikhailovna Kollontai (1872–1952)—prominent Bolshevik theorist of women's liberation and head of the Central Committee's Women's' Department from 1919 to 1922.

8 □ ZINAIDA PATRIKEEVA

Cavalry Boy

□ In the summer of 1918 the nineteen-year-old Zinaida Patrikeeva fled
from German-occupied Nikolaev, where she had worked in a tobacco
factory, to Ekaterinoslav (today's Dnepropetrovsk), where she found
a job at the Rupaner Candy Factory. Before long, however, the war
caught up with her. See also the introduction to Andzhievskaia,
above.

PETLIURA'S men[1] approached the Dnieper and bombarded Ekaterinoslav with
heavy artillery shells.

Most of the working population hid in cellars; the bravest ones took up arms.
The Rupaner factory was closed down because all the workers had run away.

The artillery barrage grew more intense with every hour. Their fire was directed
at the working class suburbs. Everything around us was roaring and smoking and
groaning . . . Panic-stricken, we ran this way and that, trying to escape the exploding shells. There were fifteen of us.

I do not remember how we made it to the suburb of Zhuravlenskaia and crossed
over the railway tracks. There the barrage was not as heavy. At one point, we
came to a deep ravine. The men—all fourteen of them—ran all the way down and
then climbed up the other side, leaving me behind. I hung over the precipice,
unable to pull myself up. I cried and shouted as loud as I could, but the men did
not hear me and kept on running. My grip was getting weaker and weaker—
another moment and I would fall to the bottom . . . Fortunately, there was a hut
nearby where an old peasant lived. He had heard my screams and hurried to
my rescue. "Oh, my dear," he said, his voice trembling, "the Whites have just
shot my son. Give me your hand, I'll help you." He pulled me out and pointed into
the distance: "Your friends went that way. Run fast, or you'll be killed, too."
He gave me a loaf of bread and went back to his hut, and I started running
along the railway tracks. In the next village I finally caught up with my comrades. They had begun to worry about me and were very happy to see me safe and
sound.

WE continued on our way, all fifteen of us from the candy factory. Somewhere the
guys had managed to get a few guns.

"There is no going back for any of us now," said our leader. "Behind us is

From *Zhenshchina v grazhdanskoi voine. Epizody bor'by na Severnom Kavkaze i Ukraine v 1917–
1920 gg.* (Moscow: OGIZ, 1938), 234–46.
[1] S. V. Petliura (1879–1926)—Ukrainian nationalist leader during the civil war.

death; ahead is the unknown. So let's go search for a better life. This is what it means to be alive. We'll form a fighting unit. We'll arm ourselves and go to the next village. More people will join us there. Then we'll head straight east and join the Bolsheviks." We all agreed.

Tired and hungry, we reached the next village and asked the peasants for something to eat. They asked us: "Are you for the Bolsheviks or the Whites?"—"We are for the Bolsheviks, and we are running away from the Whites."

Then they gave us some cabbage and potatoes. The peasants did not have any bread. We walked like this for many days, obtaining food in the villages. The peasants often stopped me: "What are you doing with them, young lady?" and would invite me to stay with them. But I would refuse and continue eastward with my detachment.

Meanwhile, in Ekaterinoslav one government followed another. The bandit and cutthroat Makhno[2] also appeared on the scene. The Whites were all over the place, both behind and in front of us. Several times we had to break through enemy lines.

At one point we met up with another partisan group like ours. We joined forces and continued on toward the Donbass. They were also from Ekaterinoslav. Their leader was an old Bolshevik, a foreman from the Rupaner factory. He treated me as if I were his own daughter. Seeing that I could stand any privation and was not afraid of partisan life, he started giving me serious assignments. Every time we would approach a village, the commander would send me in first: "Go and find out who's there. But be very careful." So I would enter the village, find out everything we needed to know, and come back with a report.

We were lucky and managed to get some horses from the peasants. Our group became a cavalry detachment. There were about 150 of us: in each of the villages we had passed through, more peasants had joined up. I also got a horse, although I did not know how to ride. At first it was difficult to get used to the saddle, and my legs hurt all the time. But even though I did not know how to ride, I never fell off my horse. The fighters liked me because I tried not to lag behind the men and was turning into a real cavalrywoman.

At that time I was still wearing a skirt—the wide peasant kind. I must have looked strange to the peasants—they were not used to seeing women fighters. Some of them would laugh at me, while others said: "Don't go with them, or you'll be killed. Stay here with us. That's a man's job, not a woman's." I never answered. I would just spur on my horse and gallop ahead, to catch up with my comrades.

We were looking for Budenny.[3] Rumors about him had been flying over the steppes, like the wind. People said that he was for the workers and the poor, and was forming a cavalry army to fight Denikin.

I still remember how we managed to get away from the Whites on the Don steppes; how we made it all the way to the North Caucasus; and how we then

[2] Nestor Makhno (1889–1934)—Ukrainian peasant anarchist leader.
[3] Semen Mikhailovich Budenny (1883–1973)—Bolshevik cavalry commander.

searched around Platovskaia, Budenny's native village, until we finally found Semen Mikhailovich [Budenny] and joined his detachment.

AT that time Budenny's men were not yet very well organized. We wore non-descript clothing and rode all kinds of horses. Everything we had, our clothing and food, we got from the enemy.

In my unit I was the only woman—an expert on tobacco making, textiles, and candy.

I was given the worst horse, a really awful old mare. Whenever my unit galloped ahead, I would always trail behind. It made me feel very bad. Semen Mikhailovich saw this and began reproaching the men:

"What, you think that just because she's a woman you can give her the worst mare? Don't think of her as a woman—think of her as your comrade-in-arms." He called me up to him:

"What's your name?"

"Zina."

"Starting from today her name is Zinovy. And give her a good, fast horse so she can ride in front, not behind."

Right then and there they brought me a wonderful horse—black, tall, fast, and well-saddled. I mounted my new horse and became not Zina, but the fighter Zinovy. I cut my wide skirt up the middle, sewed on some buttons, and made something resembling pants, an outfit convenient for riding a horse. I was also given a greatcoat, a tall sheepskin hat, and boots. After that I looked like a cavalry boy, a fighter during battle and a sister of mercy afterward.

MOUNTED on strong horses, our Eleventh Division was approaching the White bastion, Rostov.

It was a somber, cloudy day. Opposite us stood the Georgievsky Regiment, which consisted entirely of officers who had been decorated with the Cross of St. George.[4] What a bunch of murderers they were!

When we clashed, they offered fierce resistance. Then we dismounted, drew our sabers, and attacked those sons of the gentry on foot.

Revolver in hand, I cut through a crowd of officers and fired all seven bullets, killing several people. One frightened officer raised his hands over his head. I ran up to him and tore off his epaulets and his cross. The edges of the Cross of St. George were covered with enamel, and in the middle, on a golden field, was an image of St. George, his horse trampling the dragon.

I do not know what that dragon was supposed to stand for. Maybe the Whites wanted to trample us in the same way, but it turned out the other way around.

At Rostov we captured many rifles and artillery pieces. It was a glorious victory!

I was given a Maxim machine gun. I attached it to my saddle and always carried it with me. As soon as the fighting began, I would dismount and shower those White bastards with bullets.

---

[4] Cross of St. George—prestigious medal awarded by the tsar for bravery in battle.

My comrades taught me how to shoot. I became quite good at the art of shooting a rifle, a revolver, and a pistol.

During the taking of Rostov, Kliment Efremovich Voroshilov[5] had command of the entire front, and with him at the front line was Semen Mikhailovich.

We entered Rostov on January 8, 1920.

The Whites were caught by surprise. Officers were strolling down the streets and getting drunk in bars. We swept down on them suddenly, like eagles.

How happy I was! My horse was adorned with officers' epaulets—I had torn them off, as many as I could, and tied them to the tail and mane of my horse. Other Budenny fighters had done the same. Our fighting horses looked pretty funny, all covered with gold and silver epaulets.

The food we got in Rostov was excellent. The population greeted us with joy. The woman at whose place I was staying—a local worker—kept asking me:

"Are there many of you? How long are you going to stay in Rostov? . . . Don't let the Whites come back; we've had enough of them."

I told her: "We're going to drive them all the way to the Black and Azov Seas."

"Are your parents alive?" the woman asked later.

"I am an orphan, and I don't remember my parents," I told her. "But don't bother feeling sorry for me. This march is hard, but things are going to get better."

The woman liked my words.

THIS is what was printed in the newspaper *Red Cavalryman* on June 19, 1920:

A NURSE HEROINE

During a cavalry attack near the village of Chervonnoe, when our left flank was being pressed by the enemy, a sister of mercy from the Sixty-first Cavalry Regiment, Zinaida Patrikeeva, rode forward and galloped all by herself toward the Polish column, shouting "Forward!"

Her courage and heroism inspired the whole regiment, which promptly took the offensive. The situation was saved. But nurse Zinaida had gone too far behind enemy lines and soon found herself near an enemy column that was retreating in panic. Right then and there, totally unarmed, she took a soldier prisoner.

Comrade Patrikeeva is a member of the Communist Party and is always at the front. Her behavior has earned her the love and respect of her Red Army comrades. She is always the first one in an attack and the last one to retreat.

When Wrangel[6] was finally driven into the Black Sea and the civil war was over, we had a Red Army congress in Ekaterinoslav. The congress was a solemn and happy occasion. Comrade Voroshilov made a long speech in which he thanked the cavalrymen on behalf of the party.

[5] K. E. Voroshilov (1881–1969)—Bolshevik military leader during the civil war, later a member of the Politburo of the Central Committee (1926–60), the People's Commissar of Military and Naval Affairs (1925–34), and Defense (1934–40).

[6] Baron P. N. Wrangel (1878–1928)—White general, commander-in-chief of the Armed Forces of Southern Russia from April 1920 to November 1920.

It was then that I received the Order of the Red Banner. Comrade Budenny himself pinned it on my chest.

"Well, Zinovy," said Budenny, "keep this order as a symbol of our victories." And he kissed me.

Then Comrade Voroshilov pointed to me and said:

"Here is our heroine! Along with us, in the saddle, she overcame all difficulties and achieved victory. She took part in the great marches of the heroic First Mounted Army."

He still remembers me.

If I had been a good speaker I would have addressed Kliment Efremovich [Voroshilov], Semen Mikhailovich [Budenny], and all those present with the following speech:

"Several years ago I, Zinaida Patrikeeva, came to this city as a poor orphan, hungry, in rags, and exhausted with suffering. It was here I embarked on my path of struggle. Now, in this same city, I am experiencing the happiest, most joyful moment of my life."

9 □ IRINA ELENEVSKAIA

Recollections

□ Irina Elenevskaia was born in St. Petersburg in 1897. Her mother was the daughter of a prominent orientalist, V. D. Smirnov. Her father, a Baltic German and a graduate of Dorpat (Tartu) University, worked in the Ministry of Foreign Affairs.

THE MOST important person in my early childhood was my nanny. She took over taking care of me from my wet nurse when I was a year old, and we were inseparable until she was replaced by my governesses. She was over fifty: she had raised my mother and vowed she would raise my mother's children as well. I was an only child, though, so all Nanny's affections were bestowed on me, her last and favorite charge.

Nanny was a typical representative of that class of Russian nannies, remarkable for their extraordinary loyalty to their charges, and looked on by the latter as true family members. She was said to have been the illegitimate daughter of a Polish priest and a serf girl. Perhaps it was her father's blood that endowed Nanny with the nobility and tact so rare in common people. Even though she took her meals with the servants in the kitchen and, when I had grown up, began sharing a room with one of the maids, she managed to keep her distance from them. She carried herself with great dignity and strictly followed her principles. She believed, for example, that it was not right for her to sit at the same table with her masters, so when my mother—if we were home alone—asked her to have tea with her and chat about things, she would always take her large tea cup to the snack table that stood by the wall, and talk across the room. Only on her name day, August 4, when she used to treat us to her cookies and her marvelous raspberry and black-currant tarts, would she sit down by the samovar.

Nanny fussed over me endlessly, with no thought for her own comfort. I was a nervous child and had trouble going to sleep. Nanny would sit beside me knitting stockings and drinking tea by the light of the icon candle, and no amount of persuasion on my mother's part could convince her to turn on the lamp.

Nanny and I usually got up early, around seven, and, in order not to wake up my parents who slept in the next room, we would walk down to the guest room at the other end of the apartment. It was there that Nanny did her reading, sounding out the obituary headings from *Novoe vremia*. I would often drop my toys and watch her pointing to each letter, naming it, and then slowly forming the syllables. By the age of three I had learned to read by myself: the names of the deceased had been my first ABCs.

From Irina Elenevskaia, *Vospominaniia* (Stockholm: n.p., 1968), 8–113 (abridged).

When I ate, Nanny used to stand behind my chair, showing me how to use a spoon—and later a knife and fork—and how to drink red wine mixed with water from a silver glass. I called that drink "wine tea."

After breakfast we would often go for a walk in the Summer Garden—in the winter with a sled, and in the spring and fall with a little bucket, shovel, and balls of various sizes. In the garden I would meet other children and often get so carried away playing that Nanny used to have a really hard time getting me to leave when it was time to go home.

Nanny and I lived in our own little world, totally separate from the world of grown-ups. My only time away from Nanny was an occasional Sunday when my mother had managed to talk Nanny into going to visit her godchild. Reluctantly, Nanny would put on her brown Easter dress, lace bonnet, gold brooch and earrings, and, grumbling that "even on a Sunday a person was not allowed to stay at home," she would leave me in the care of the maid. Three or four hours later she would come back, quickly change, and our life would return to its normal rhythm.

There were two times during the year, however, when my world overlapped with the grown-up world and when I felt close to my parents: during Christmas and Easter.

Perhaps because my father was a Lutheran, or maybe because Christmas, with its tree, candy, and presents, was closer to a child's psyche, my memories of Christmas are especially vivid.

My parents always bought a Christmas tree on the twenty-first or twenty-second of December. It was always huge—tall enough to reach the ceiling—and would be brought into the drawing room when I was not around. All the drawing room doors would be tightly shut, and I would be told that Grandfather Frost was making the tree grow; that the height of the tree depended on my behavior; and that if I peeked in, it would stop growing.

On the twenty-third of December my father always went to the Gostinyi Dvor Department Store and bought boxfuls of Christmas fruit and candy: red-cheeked Crimean apples, fragrant tangerines, various kinds of nuts, Turkish Delight, fruit jelly, gingerbread cookies, candy in bright wrappings—it would be impossible to name them all. Large bowls would be set out on the table in the pantry, and, under my mother's supervision, I used to fill them with the candy intended for the servants. It goes without saying that I always saved the prettiest apples and cookies for Nanny.

On the evening of the twenty-third, as I lay asleep after a long conversation with Nanny about the next day's Christmas tree, some young employees from the Ministry of Foreign Affairs, where my father worked, would come over to help decorate the tree. There was always a gold star at the very top, a charming cherub underneath, and, practically hidden behind the branches, Grandfather Frost with his moss hat, long beard, and cane.

I would spend Christmas Eve in a kind of daze, waiting impatiently for the evening. Finally it would come. Nanny would help me put on my white lacy dress and blue sash, tie a ribbon the same color as the sash to my freshly curled ringlets, and then, holding on to Nanny's hand, I would approach the drawing room door. The door would swing open and, to the sounds of the tune called "You've Been Caught, Little Bird," which my mother always played on the piano with great bravura, I would walk through the door and freeze at the sight of the magnificent tree, brilliant with lights. Under the tree were always countless presents, but, to my parents' disappointment, they never fascinated me as much as the tree itself. I was always mesmerized by the flickering of the many candles and their reflections in the glass balls, the variety of decorations, the smell of resin, and the soft tinkling of tiny bells. All that magnificence was so different from the way our drawing room normally looked that my imagination would soar.

My parents led an active social life. On Fridays my mother always received visitors. Between four and seven in the evening a tea table would be set up in her elegant boudoir, and her lady friends, numerous employees from my father's ministry department, and other diplomats would come to see her. Sometimes I was introduced to the visitors, and those cheerful young people would play noisy games with me—probably in an attempt to please the beautiful young hostess. Once, when we were playing hide-and-seek, young Prince Gagarin delighted me by climbing into the dirty linen basket, which stood in the corner of the big bathroom. Such naughtiness earned him a stern reprimand from my mother.

In addition to the Friday tea parties were the dinner receptions, and on Saturdays my parents would order a private box at the Mikhailovsky Theater, where a French company was playing.

On Wednesdays my father usually came to dinner accompanied by his colleague, Baron Lev Richardovich Rosen, who was an excellent cello player. Later, when he became secretary of our mission at the Bavarian Court, he was often asked by the king, who greatly admired his talent, to give small private concerts at the court. There is no doubt in my mind that had social prejudice not made a musical career impossible for him, he would have become a world celebrity.

My father was quite a good violinist and my mother played the piano beautifully, so that the music I heard as a child was of extremely high quality. When I grew a little older, I often asked to be allowed to leave my bedroom door slightly ajar and would go to sleep to the sounds of the wonderful trios coming from the living room.

While they did not spend much time with me, my parents always tried to give me the best possible education and the most refined upbringing, as well as providing me with an opportunity to be with other children, whose company I, as an only child, sorely missed.

I was not yet four years old when my parents employed a French woman, whose task was to make sure that I spoke French with an impeccable accent. Mademoiselle would come every day at ten, spend two hours playing with me, and then have breakfast with us. Her arrival always provoked the most serious apprehension on Nanny's part. She was afraid that the "infidel" might tire out the child or, God forbid, lay a hand on her. Therefore she declared to my mother that she simply must be present at our meetings, so every day, when the French woman arrived, she would solemnly take up her position on a large trunk in the corner of the room and watch us the whole time. Before long, however, she was persuaded that her charge was in no danger, and some time later, when the two of them were living in the country house together, she became very attached to Mademoiselle—as did everyone else in our house.

When I turned seven, my parents decided it was time I started taking dancing lessons, in order to learn to move gracefully, to curtsy when greeting adults, as well as to meet children my own age. It just so happened that Anna Doremidontovna Kh., who several years earlier had gotten a divorce from her husband, the millionaire Maksimovich, who was much older than she, and had recently married a young engineer, had decided to start dancing lessons for her five-year-old son by her first marriage, Penny (his real name was Evgraf), and had asked my mother to send me along. Altogether, there were six couples between the ages of five and eight. Our instructor was the choreographer Oblakov, who had been a soloist at the Mariinsky Theater.[1]

I adored those dance lessons because they enabled me to be around children my own age. Little Penny became very attached to me, and they started inviting me over on Sundays. He had all kinds of toys: electric trains, special tops, tin soldiers. For some reason I particularly remember a little excavator with tiny buckets that could actually scoop up fine sand.

WHEN I was six or seven we began spending our summers at my godmother's Zavetnoe estate in Finland.

It was such a pleasure to go to my dear Zavetnoe, where I enjoyed much more freedom than in the city. Moreover, the manager of the estate, Vasily, had four children, two of them boys my age, Lesha and Vania, and in their company I surveyed my domain. Later I tutored them in Russian and arithmetic.

My life in Zavetnoe was like one long holiday. The Fräulein (who had replaced Mademoiselle for the summer months) and I would get up at eight thirty, get dressed, and go to the terrace where morning tea was served. My godmother, who would have finished her morning walk in the park with her dog, Vogul, would be sitting on her couch behind a big table. On the table, arranged in the most appetizing fashion, would be delicious homemade rolls, toast, butter, honey, cream, and milk. The doors leading to the park were always wide open, letting in the fragrance of flowers and the chirping of birds.

Having finished our tea, the Fräulein and I would go for a walk in the park or make flower arrangements for all the rooms: partly from cultivated flowers, partly from wild flowers. Several dozen peasant women were always working in the park, to keep the paths, which totaled about five versts, in good order. Sometimes I helped sweep the paths or weed the flower beds.

Lunch was always served at noon, and as the Golovins constantly had visitors,

---

[1] Mariinsky Theater—opera and ballet theater in St. Petersburg.

no fewer than eight or ten people would come to the table. After breakfast the grown-ups would drink coffee and talk on the terrace, while the Fräulein and I would go to our room upstairs and spend time embroidering and reading until three o'clock, when it would be time to swim in the lake. Oh how wonderful the fragrant tea with jam and cookies would taste after a cold swim!

The time between afternoon tea and dinner would be devoted to long walks outside the estate, in exceptionally picturesque surroundings. Sometimes we would have the horses harnessed and go for a ride.

In the evenings we would play tennis or go boating.

Weekends brought great excitement to our pastoral existence. On Friday evenings the Golovin men and my father would arrive from Petersburg. A victoria drawn by trotters would be sent to fetch young Golovin and my father. My uncle preferred to drive his own droshky hitched to a fast Finnish horse. Sometimes Uncle brought his best friend, Lev Sergeevich Nekhliudov, a bohemian reputed to be "ugly to the point of being handsome" but loved by everyone for his gentle manner and extraordinary wit.

I would run to meet the carriages at the gate, at the end of the main alley, and be lifted up onto the carriage seat.

On Saturday mornings the men would pursue their favorite activities: the elder Golovin[2] would go fishing in his boat; his son, in a sports suit, would trim bushes and talk to the gardener; and my father would go for a walk in the park, and, sometimes, to my great joy, take me with him.

The weekends always passed very quickly; on Sundays, after dinner, the horses would be brought, and the men would be taken back to the station.

The culmination of the summer was always July 15, Vladimir Evgenievich Golovin's name day. The preparations were usually started long in advance. Vasily, the gardener, would grow particularly sweet melons in his greenhouse, preserve the choicest wild strawberries, decorate the terrace with exotic plants, and, right before the name day, make long festoons of grasses and flowers to hang in all the main rooms.

The butcher, who made the rounds of all the local estates and summer houses twice a week, would supply the veal and lamb. The whole house would be cleaned, floors waxed and doorknobs polished. Invitations would be sent out to all the neighbors whose acquaintance we kept.

The weather in mid-July was usually excellent, thus contributing to the generally festive mood. Finally the guests would arrive; some for afternoon tea and chocolate, others for dinner, to which only the closest friends had been invited. The ice-cream would be accompanied by champagne, in which large strawberries were floating.

After dinner the young people would scatter around the park and the garden, while the older ones sat down at card tables in front of the terrace and played by the light of candles covered with silk shades.

---

[2] Vladimir Evgenievich Golovin, the author's great uncle, was a well-known Petersburg divorce attorney.

My mother would often sit down at the piano in the study, and through the open windows one could hear the sounds of Chopin, or perhaps even Gypsy romances.

MEANWHILE, the time for me to start school was approaching, and all sorts of preparations had to be made.

After extensive discussions, my parents had decided to send me to Tagantseva's private gymnasium, which was considered a good academic school, famous for its excellent faculty and extensive curriculum. Anticipating my admission, my parents started looking for an apartment near the school, so that I could receive hot meals from home. I had had a serious intestinal illness when I was only a year old and had suffered from a delicate stomach ever since, so the question of nutrition was very important.

When I turned seven, we rented an apartment on Soliany Alley, five minutes away from Mokhovaia Street, where Tagantseva's gymnasium was located. We lived in that apartment until the revolution, and all my memories of youth are associated with it. Even now, in the twilight of my life, I only need to close my eyes to picture the sunlight streaming in through the windows of that charming apartment, fitted out with such exceptional taste. I was particularly fond of my own room and of my mother's boudoir, with its tapestry furniture.

House Number 7 on Soliany Alley belonged to a Lithuanian landowner by the name of Ivan Boleslavovich Zhuk and contained two apartments, each consisting of twelve rooms.

Visitors were greeted at the front door by an old doorman in livery—the always conscientious Adam Vikentievich. From the lobby, where in winter a fire was always crackling in the fireplace, a fairly wide, warm stairway led to a landing where a knight stood in full armor, holding a torch in his hand. I greatly admired that knight and was very proud of him.

In the fall of 1906 I was enrolled in the first grade at Tagantseva's gymnasium.

Our gymnasium occupied two floors in a large building on Mokhovaia Street. On the first floor were the first two grades and the exercise room, which served as a playroom during recess. On the second floor were all the other classrooms, from the third through the eighth grade; the gym; the assembly hall; the dining room; the teachers' common room, and, adjoining it, the apartment of the principal, Liubov Stepanovna Tagantseva.

Beginning with the second grade, each grade consisted of two sections of about twenty to twenty-five students. This enabled the teachers to maintain individual contact with each student, to observe and mold developing personalities.

The seriousness with which the teachers approached their pedagogical tasks was demonstrated by the fact that, at the end of each academic year, Liubov Stepanovna would always summon the mothers and talk to each one separately about her daughter's negative traits, to make sure they were corrected.

The school day always began with prayers. All the students and teachers headed by Liubov Stepanovna would gather in the assembly hall. A choir composed of the older girls would sing "Our Father," and one of the eighth-graders would read from the New Testament and say a prayer.

Small breaks between the classes lasted ten minutes; the lunch recess was forty-five minutes long. Students could bring their own sandwiches or buy a hot lunch at the gymnasium; those who lived nearby, like me, had hot meals brought in from home.

In the first grade, when there had been forty-three of us, we had just been feeling one another out. "Real friendship" began to flourish in the second grade, when we were separated into sections. It was then that I experienced both the joy of early attachments and the cruelty that is so stark in children, who do not know how to hide, or, at any rate, control, their likes and dislikes.

In the second grade we had a new student, Natasha Anichkova, who immediately became the target of all the teasing, bullying, and dirty tricks. For some reason the girls in her section took a disliking to her, although she was very gentle and kind and was always willing to share with other students the candy that was ever present in her pockets. Perhaps it was that very deference and desire to please that provoked the sadistic instincts of some of her peers. Whatever the reason, Natasha cried bitterly every day when she went home and asked her parents to take her out of the gymnasium.

Natasha was an only child, and her parents adored her. Her great uncle was General Mily Milievich Anichkov, whose wife, Elizaveta Petrovna, was my godmother's close friend. My parents had met the Anichkovs at the Golovins and had started frequenting their receptions. Once Natasha's mother asked my mother if I would seek her daughter out and perhaps even befriend her.

The role of protector of the "insulted and injured" appealed to me, and I started talking to Natasha during recess, even though friendship "across sections" was unusual. A lively child who frequently initiated games and other activities and was not shy in front of the teachers, I had gained considerable popularity among my fellow students, so my demonstrative preference for Natasha made an impression. She was left alone after that and eventually became well-liked.

Perhaps the girls would have changed their attitude toward Natasha even without my interference, but she considered me her savior and became attached to me in the "gymnasium way"—to the point of infatuation.

MY parents did not invite any young men to our house until I was sixteen years old, but my sixteenth birthday was celebrated with a ball so grand that everyone who came remembered it for a long time afterward.

Since we had sent out more than a hundred invitations, the apartment had to be prepared at least a day in advance. In my father's study, which adjoined the ballroom, a table with cool drinks was set up; my own room was turned into a card parlor for the older guests; and in the dining room was a long table for refreshments in the middle of which stood a tall vase with such beautiful flowers that the guests gasped when they saw them. The flowers spilled out luxuriously, like a colored fountain. My uncle had ordered them from Nice. There were flowers everywhere, but, with the exception of the ones on the dining-room table, all the flowers were white—as if all the guests had conspired to send white flowers to the sixteen-year-old birthday girl. I remember one particularly beautiful basket that took up a corner of my mother's boudoir. Filled with white lilacs, roses, and lilies of the valley, it was a present from Uncle Lesha (A. F. Shebunin, the first husband of my mother's older sister), who had sent the flowers from Crete, where he was consul general.

The young ladies had been asked to wear white dresses; before the cotillion they were handed bouquets of fresh white carnations and lilies of the valley, while the young men had white carnations attached to their lapels.

For the first time in my life I put on a long gown made of Brussels lace and had my long unruly hair arranged by a French hairdresser. My "coming out" was a great success.

IN addition to the balls, I attended parties at the Naval Academy, the Faculty of Jurisprudence, and the Lycée. The Jurisprudence party, held during my last winter as a gymnasium student, was the most successful. It started, as usual, with an operetta, in which all the female parts were played by the law students themselves. That season they put on "The Discovery of America," a charming thing. I absolutely refused to believe that the graceful prima donna was a young man, until I was introduced to him after the show.

The operetta was followed by a dance, which lasted until five in the morning, with a break for dinner in the magnificently decorated halls and classrooms. I had my dinner in an assembly hall that had been transformed into a Japanese garden complete with blooming cherry trees and arched bridges over streams made of tinted glass. Later, whenever I heard the opera *Madame Butterfly*, I always thought of that dinner at the Faculty of Jurisprudence.

Among the popular winter activities was skating—a graceful sport that I never quite mastered because of my poor sense of balance. The inner courtyard of the State Bank used to be converted into a skating rink for senior employees, and most of my friends went there regularly.

That winter flew by in a whirl; then came spring, final exams, and the last farewell to the gymnasium.

I had important decisions to make concerning my future education: the gymnasium had made us so hungry for knowledge that few of us wanted to go on living at home "making calls" until we got married. My friend, Ania, who had a talent for teaching, had applied to the history department of the Pedagogical Institute, but I was torn. I liked the law, but women were not allowed to serve as attorneys or work in the courtroom, so a legal education would have been purely academic, without the possibility of any practical application. A teaching career did not appeal to me at all, so in the end I decided to follow my parents' advice and study architecture. I had the necessary background: a gift for mathematics, a talent for drawing, and a great love of the fine arts. The Bagaeva Architecture School, to which I applied, emphasized the artistic aspects of architecture, leaving the technical side to the civil engineers.

The students were an extremely diverse group as far as age and social position were concerned. Whereas at the Tagantseva Gymnasium there had been only Petersburgers—the daughters of high government officials, military officers, attorneys, and government jurists—at the Bagaeva school one could meet natives of Siberia, southern Russia, and Moscow, including some married students who were much older than I.

I would like to point out one other peculiarity of the Bagaeva school: unlike what was going on at the university, in technical colleges, and at the Women's Higher Learning Institute, politics played no role whatsoever. Unfortunately, in those days most Russian students from the high school level on felt themselves quite capable of solving all the problems of the state without the benefit of special education, experience, or a knowledge of the people.

THE winter of 1914–15 passed quickly, and at the end of May, when I had finished my final exams, we moved to our estate. In rural Finland there were no signs of war. The Finns were not being drafted, and both on our estate and in the neighboring villages, the work in the fields proceeded as usual—as did our family life.

IN October we were cut off from Petersburg by the Bolshevik coup, and in January 1918 the Finnish civil war began.[3]

After Finland declared independence we no longer considered it a part of our country, and my mother and I stopped going to ladies' meetings, where gifts for the White soldiers were being knitted, sewn, and then secretly sent off. In theory we were, of course, on the side of the Finnish Whites, but after six months in Vyborg we realized that although the Finns felt nothing but hatred for the Russian Red soldiers, they also had no particular sympathy for the Russian Whites, seeing them as an alien and undesirable element.

The only exception were the Finns who had lived in Russia before the revolution, and especially those who had served in the Russian army, but during our stay in Vyborg we met only one such person, and, in any case, at such a time of violent political and national upheaval, few people had the courage to express their sentiments publicly.

Despite our friends' dire warnings, my mother and I decided to return to Petersburg. My mother was going to receive my father's life insurance, which was going to be honored, apparently, even though the Bolsheviks were in power. Besides, she wanted to be reunited with her cousin, Golovin, and, if the political situation remained hopeless, to help him sell off all our valuables and go abroad. As for me, I wanted to complete my education.

WE arrived in Petersburg at dusk and thus did not see the humiliation of our beautiful city on that first day. My uncle did not come to the station to meet us so as not to draw attention to us "returnees" from White Finland.

---

[3] After the October Revolution, the Finnish parliament declared independence from Russia. In the civil war that followed, the Whites, supported by Germany and led by the former tsarist general Baron Mannerheim, prevailed over the Reds backed by the Bolsheviks. The Treaty of Brest-Litovsk (March 3, 1918) confirmed Finland's independence.

All the more joyful, then, were our embraces in the hall of his apartment. My uncle opened the door himself even though his maid, the gray-eyed, brisk Sasha, was still working for him.

My uncle's apartment had not changed. The heavy curtains protected it from the revolutionary streets, the dim streetlamps, and the boarded-up market outside. My uncle's apartment was on Gagarinskaia Street, right across from the market.

My uncle had had to transfer from the Ministry of Commerce and Industry to the Administration of the Petersburg Port because his friendship with the deputy minister, Sergei Petrovich Veselago, could have hurt him.[4]

My uncle was pessimistic about the future course of the revolution and immediately agreed to my mother's suggestion that we sell everything and go abroad.

On that first night I expressed a desire to stay in Petersburg and continue my education. But the next morning, when I went out to take my favorite stroll down Gagarinskaia, Sergievskaia, Liteiny, and Mokhovaia, I realized I would not be able to remain in Petersburg. The sight of the dilapidated streets, the boarded-up windows, and the traces of bullets on the walls; the smell of the herring being sold on every corner; and, even worse, the ubiquitous groups of insolent undisciplined soldiers and the sad figures of "former people,"[5] timidly holding out matchboxes for sale, shoelaces, and so forth—it all depressed me terribly and I could feel my throat tightening with indignation. The odor of herring and the pathetic, frightened look in the eyes of those people followed me all the way home and came to represent, in my mind, the demise of the majestic city of art and beauty that had been my beloved native town. From that point on, I was just as anxious to escape as I had been earlier to return.

First, we needed to obtain ration cards for my mother and me. Women who were not employed could receive ration cards only as "housewives with no help," but there were two of us, and, besides, my uncle did not want to let his maid go because she had all kinds of "underground" connections that we could use to obtain food. Sasha was also an experienced cook, whereas my mother and I knew absolutely nothing about cooking.

My mother was the first to get a job: the head of the port administration, who liked my uncle, hired her as a secretary.

I was helped by a woman named Anert, who had graduated from the Bagaeva school before the revolution. She had heard I was in town and, moved by a feeling of professional solidarity with a "promising" female architect, came to see me and offered me a job as assistant to the engineer responsible for repairing the city slaughterhouse. "The work is not creative," she told me, "but the ration is good for both meat and vegetables, and that's very important. For this reason I would advise you to accept the position. Meanwhile, I will keep you in mind, and if something more interesting turns up, I'll let you know."

I was supposed to start work on September 15. On September 12 there was an election meeting in our building.

---

[4] The author's uncle, Evgeny Vladimirovich Golovin, had severed relations with his father (and stopped working as his assistant) when the latter married a provincial actress.

[5] "Former people"—prerevolutionary elites.

Housing committees consisted of a chair, a secretary, and one member. They had been introduced, on the one hand, in order to protect the tenants from the landlords, who were supposedly engaged in exploitative practices such as charging excessive rent or failing to conduct necessary repairs, and, on the other hand, to carry out various police decrees. In fact, the landlords were in a difficult position: they often received no rent because they had not made any repairs, but how could they possibly make repairs if all the necessary materials had disappeared?

The meeting took place in the apartment of the seamstress Zhuravleva, who lived in the courtyard wing. The building where Uncle rented his apartment consisted of two wings: one, facing the street, was inhabited by the "bourgeois element," and the other, facing the courtyard, housed all sorts of artisans and petty traders. The meeting reflected this division, with everyone present identifying with either the "bourgeoisie" or the "toilers."

The meeting was chaired by a man named Pashkov, a landowner who lived in the "bourgeois" wing but sported a Tolstoyan outfit: a Russian peasant shirt worn over pants tucked into tall boots. He seemed to know all the inhabitants of the courtyard wing and was obviously trying to ingratiate himself with them by attacking the landlord, Prince Volkonsky, and by talking about the need for the tenants to unite. Our family found him extremely unappealing.

When it came to a vote, Pashkov was elected chair, and he thanked the meeting for the honor. To my complete amazement, however, he went on to propose my candidacy for the position of secretary. Having exchanged looks with my mother and uncle, I agreed to run and was elected by a unanimous vote.

I was guided by the following considerations. All furniture sales had to be approved by the housing committee, which meant that I, as a member, could easily obtain all the permissions we required in order to sell my uncle's property. Furthermore, the secretary was responsible for assigning various duties around the building, so I could lighten the load for my family and some elderly tenants.

I was not surprised by the support I received from the "bourgeois" wing, but my popularity among the proletarians was unexpected. I probably owed it to the seamstress Zhuravleva, who used to make dresses for me; the herring salesman Koniazhkin, who would later play an important role in the sale of my uncle's property; and the mechanic Ivanov, who used to happily fix our meat grinder, which was used to grind all kinds of things and therefore kept breaking.

My mother, uncle, and I never went anywhere outside of work. We used to arrive home around six o'clock, and after our meager dinner would not have the energy or the desire to go out. At first I wanted to continue my studies by attending evening classes at the Fine Arts Academy since the Bagaeva school had closed down: Bagaeva had died and the school had been passed on to the authorities, who had not yet done anything with it. But the Fine Arts Academy was on Vasilievsky Island, almost as far from Gagarinskaia Street as the slaughterhouse. The streets were badly lit, and every day there were muggings and robberies, in which passers-by were stripped of their clothes. Besides, the whole purpose of our existence was to sell off my uncle's things and escape to Finland at the first opportunity, so we regarded our life in Petersburg as simply a necessary evil.

To conserve our strength and save fuel we would climb into bed early and read. I was rereading the French novels—Paul Bourget, Anatole France, and so forth—that my uncle had in large quantities. As I savored the descriptions of the life of the French aristocracy and upper middle class in the late nineteenth and early twentieth centuries, I would forget the sad and ugly reality of my own existence. In a Petersburg, completely deformed, strewn with empty sunflower seed shells, redolent with the smell of herring and salted fish, and enveloped in a damp November twilight, it was such a joy to read about sunlit Paris and its colorful life.

Sometimes I would be wrenched from this wonderful world by the sharp sound of the doorbell and an invitation to witness a search in one of the apartments in our building. Somebody from the housing committee had to be present at all searches, which usually took place after eleven at night; so when Pashkov was out of town and the mechanic Ivanov, another committee member, was on the night shift, I had no choice but to attend.

It was an extremely unpleasant duty and, had it not been for the considerations I described above, I would have resigned from the committee.

The searches were usually conducted by local militiamen—mostly sailors ("the pride and joy of the revolution") and one or two women of the lowest sort whose job was to search the women's bedrooms. I was nauseated by their impudent sailor faces, their rudeness, and the filthy jokes they made at the expense of the "bourgeois elements" whose apartments they were searching.

At the end of September we parted with Uncle's maid, who had gotten married, and, since I returned home from work an hour before my mother and uncle, the task of cooking our minimal dinner fell to me. Matches were strictly rationed, so I could not afford to use more than one to light the stove. Since this meant that lighting the stove was the most critical part of the dinner preparation, I was happy when my friend, Nikolai Boginsky, was there to help. He was the youngest of three brothers and had not been drafted until 1915. He had gone through the war without being injured and, after the Bolshevik takeover, he had been demobilized and returned to the Institute of Communications. In Petersburg he had gotten in touch with my uncle and, after my mother and I returned from Vyborg, had started visiting us. He usually stopped by on his way home from the institute, just when I was beginning to cook dinner. My mother facetiously called us "the cook and her friend the fireman," and we ourselves often laughed at the circumstances of our meetings. Instead of mother's cozy boudoir, with its tapestry chairs and fire burning brightly in the fireplace, there we were in my uncle's small kitchen grinding oats, frying frozen potatoes in castor oil, and making—right on top of the stove—pancakes out of ground potato peel mixed with fried oats. They say necessity is the mother of invention . . .

My mother's joke about the cook and the fireman proved prophetic. Without realizing it, I had captured the heart of the herring salesman Aleksandr Ivanovich Koniazhkin, who had made a fortune speculating in herring and other foodstuffs and who lived in the courtyard wing of our building. According to our former maid, Sasha, this upstart had one day announced the following: "I'd sure love to invite your young mistress to the theater and get an entire box for her, but I am afraid that tall gentleman in uniform who often comes to visit her would give me a thrashing."

When Sasha told me of this conquest, I decided to exploit the tender feelings of my new admirer by getting him involved in the sale of my uncle's things. Coming back from work I would often see Koniazhkin by our front door and tell him, among other things: "My uncle is selling some excellent suits. Would you like to come over this evening to take a look?" And poor Aleksandr Ivanovich would dutifully come and never leave without buying something. His last purchase was a Renaissance buffet, a collector's item that he bought for tens of thousands of "Duma" rubles. What on earth was he going to do with it?

As secretary of the housing committee, I tried to assign the older people to gate duty during daytime hours. Although my mother, who was only forty-three years old, could not be included in their number, I naturally gave her the best slots. Once when I came home from work during her shift, I witnessed the following scene. My mother was sitting in a folding chair, wearing a large lace hat and holding a French novel. Opposite her, sitting on top of an old hitching post and resting his chin on his walking stick, was a young man of about thirty in a nice suit. He turned out to be a former lawyer and a son of Mrs. General Anichkov by her first husband. He had brought a message from his mother and, since my own mother could not leave her post, their meeting had to take place under such peculiar circumstances.

It is interesting to note in this regard that in those cruel days the most basic concepts of right and wrong were changing. In relation to the people of your own circle the old principles were still in force, but when it came to the hated Bolshevik regime, anything was allowed. For example, Mrs. General Anichkov, the wife of a former court official, told us with great pride that she had managed to take a few logs from a pile of firewood that belonged to some Soviet institution. In other words, she had managed to steal.

FINALLY, the day of our long-planned escape to Finland had arrived. It was March 16, 1920, and the weather was beautiful: the snow-covered streets of Petersburg glistened in the bright sun; water from melting ice streamed down the sidewalks; and sparkling icicles broke off from the roofs.

We got up at seven as usual, but when we had had our fried-oat coffee and millet cereal we did not leave for work. Instead, we packed some sacks with clothes, basic toiletries, and extra shoes and then waited for our guide—a pretty, fair-haired Finnish woman. She was supposed to take us to a border village, where some Finnish smugglers were going to lead us across into Finland.

Our train was supposed to leave at four o'clock in the afternoon, but we set off before one because we were going to have to walk all the way from the Petersburg District to the Finland Station, stopping on the way to pick up another lady who was going to escape with us.

When we knocked on her kitchen door and she came out on the porch, we were shocked by her appearance: she was deathly pale, and her eyes were glazed over. "You'll have to go without me," she said, sobbing. "I can't go with you, I'm too

scared . . ." She did not finish her sentence, but we understood that she was thinking of the growing number of executions of people who had been captured while
trying to cross the Finnish border.

We did not attempt to change her mind but quietly said our farewells and
continued on to the railway station.

On the way we saw two dead horses, or rather skeletons of horses, because all
the soft parts had been cut out by starving citizens. The winter of 1920 had been
an especially hungry one, and people were eating anything they could find. They
were not even afraid to buy meat from the Chinese vendors who came to their
houses, although according to some sinister rumors it was human flesh—from
people who had been shot by the Bolsheviks.

After a long hike we arrived at the Finland Station. How many times had we
come here on clear winter days in order to travel to my uncle's estate on the
Karelian Isthmus to spend Christmas there! We would arrive at the station in cars
or in sleighs, all excited and looking forward to a stay in a beautiful country
house. And now here we were, weak from malnutrition, bent under the weight of
our bulky sacks, wearing felt boots and wrapped in woolen shawls in order to look
even more like the "sack people," who traveled to the countryside to trade clothing for food.

Finally our train arrived. Most of the passengers were soldiers returning to their
border posts after a leave, Finnish peasant women in headscarves who had been
selling watered-down milk and potatoes, and a few other nondescript-looking
people.

We sat down next to the door. In case of a militia raid we had some passes that
my uncle had printed at work, stating that we were employees of the Petersburg
Port Administration authorized to go to Shuvalovo to purchase food.

After a fairly long wait the train began to let off steam and finally started
moving. Suburban houses and sooty factory walls were followed by small summer houses and sad-looking woods.

The air in the car was heavy with the smell of cheap tobacco, wet felt boots, and
unwashed bodies. In order not to draw the attention of other passengers to our
"bourgeois" accents, we remained silent the whole way. The train moved slowly,
stopping at every station, so that we did not arrive in Shuvalovo till after five.
Most passengers had gotten off before then, and the only other people on the
platform were a few Finnish women and two or three soldiers.

The sun was beginning to set, casting long shadows on the snow-covered road.
Obeying a sign from our guide, we let everybody else walk ahead and then started
uphill on the country road, greedily inhaling the clear cold air as we walked.
When we were the only ones left on the road, our guide explained to us that it was
about two versts to her cottage and that when we got there we would have to be
very quiet because some Red Army men were quartered in another part of the
house and we would have to try to slip in unnoticed.

The purple March twilight had fallen when we walked through a doorway and
into a large room in our guide's house. The wooden table was covered with all

sorts of delicacies: black bread, salt pork, milk, eggs, and so on. The dinner preceding the night march was part of the deal: one hundred thousand Duma rubles per person.

After a hearty dinner we went into the next room, most of which was taken up by a wide bed, and we—all three of us—lay down on it to await the arrival of "the boys," as our guide kept calling them, who were supposed to pick us up at around eleven.

In spite of our physical exhaustion, we were too nervous to sleep. Lying on the bed, we listened to the sounds coming from outside. After the clock struck ten the part of the house that was occupied by the Red Army men grew quiet. The minutes went by very slowly.

The clock behind the wall struck eleven, then eleven thirty, and finally twelve. My uncle opened the door to the next room, where our guide and her mother were sitting, and, in a whisper, asked them if there was any problem. Our guide asked us to wait a little longer, saying that they were sometimes late. But when the clock struck one we could no longer stand it, and we all went into the next room. We had begun to suspect a trap, but our guide looked so upset and miserable that we were immediately reassured. Still, we insisted that she take us to meet the smugglers. We simply could not wait until dawn. In the morning the Red Army men were supposed to come into the house to get their food, and we would be in mortal danger.

After long negotiations we finally persuaded her to take us. It was after two o'clock when we went out the back door into the garden. Beyond the garden was a small clearing and the dark wall of the forest. The moon was shining brightly. We ran across the clearing as fast as we could. A fairly wide road with deep ruts made by skis led deep into the forest. It was obviously well-traveled because the snow was packed down, and it was easy to walk.

Having walked for about a verst and a half we came to another clearing, where a horrifying sight presented itself to us: two pairs of skis and broken ski poles were scattered around, and in some places the snow was beaten down and covered with puddles of scarlet blood. It was clear that shortly before our arrival a violent struggle had taken place there. "They got the boys," exclaimed our guide, clasping her hands. "That's why they didn't come." "This is most unfortunate," said my uncle. "There is no other choice but for you to take us to the border."

The guide nodded silently and started looking around as if trying to remember something. There were three different trails leading farther into the woods. The guide took the one that, judging by the ski tracks, the smugglers had used to get here.

As we went deeper into the forest, it was becoming harder and harder to walk. Although we all had felt boots on, the snow frequently gave way under our feet and we would sink up to our hips, weighted down by our sacks.

The eastern part of the sky was getting lighter, heralding the approach of sunrise. Suddenly we heard men's voices and the clinking of guns. The guide motioned for us to lie down in the snow behind some bushes. The voices were drawing nearer. We could clearly hear: "Well, Comrades, enough is enough. I don't guess we'll catch anybody tonight. It's going to be light soon, and those folks are afraid to cross the border during the day."

It must have been a Bolshevik ski patrol. We were lying in the snow trying not to breathe or look at one another.

When the voices died out in the distance, we got to our feet. "It's not much farther," said our guide softly and led the way down the trail. But soon she stopped and started looking around in confusion. When we caught up with her, we saw that the trail had disappeared. We were surrounded by the forest on all sides. "I took the wrong road," said the guide in a tone of despair.

Having discussed our position, we decided that walking away from the rising sun should take us to the border.

It had become even harder to walk, because now we were going through virgin snow, constantly sinking through and stumbling over tree stumps hidden under the snow. My mother was losing her strength. She stopped often to catch her breath and put some snow in her mouth. The guide took her sack, and she continued her slow movement through the snow.

The sun came up and rose higher and higher. We could hear the birds singing. The guide was now walking several dozen steps ahead of us. Her red skirt looked like a flame flickering among the tree trunks. Suddenly she stopped, peered into the distance and ran back toward us. "The border! The border!" she shouted, almost breathless. "That's the Sestra River at the foot of the hill!"

In an instant our fatigue was gone, and we practically ran forward. About a hundred steps farther, we found ourselves on the tall bank of a narrow river. It was still covered with ice, but in places we could see some sinister cracks. Could this little river stop us when we were so close to our destination? We had no choice. We shook hands with our guide, climbed down, and stepped onto the ice. The ice cracked but did not break. Oblivious to everything, we ran across and turned back only when we reached the opposite bank. Back where we had come from, our guide was sitting under a slender birch tree, waving to us. We waved back and started walking away. Soon we came to a fairly well-traveled road, which was probably used to transport logs. We walked past a curve in the road until we could no longer be seen from the river. Feeling safer, we sat down on some tree stumps to rest.

We were still resting when far in the distance we saw two figures walking in our direction. When they came nearer, we saw they were wearing military uniforms. We exchanged glances and saw the same question in one another's eyes: "What if they are Reds?" But there was nothing we could do. They had seen us and were walking straight toward us. We got up and went to meet them. When we were several steps away, they crossed their rifles and, pointing toward the river, said "*pois*," which means "away" in Finnish. We tried to explain through gestures that we had just come from there and that we wanted to stay in Finland, but they just kept repeating "*pois*."

At that point a peasant on a sled emerged from the forest and, noticing our little group, turned toward us. Having exchanged a few words in Finnish with the soldiers, he addressed us in Russian: "You must be refugees, but a decree was issued the other day that said no more refugees without visas would be allowed into Finland. There are too many of them, and we can't feed them all."

"Well, the law is the law," said my uncle. "In that case the soldiers might as well shoot us here and now because the very same fate awaits us if we go back. I can see no point in covering dozens of miles for that."

☐ In Finland Irina Elenevskaia married a White Army officer and, after a stint as a pianist in a movie theater in Björneborg (Pori), became a secretary at the Swiss Consulate in Åbo (Turku), Helsinki, and finally, in 1944, Stockholm. In both Finland and Sweden, she was a very active member of the Russian émigré community.

10 □ Sofia Volkonskaia

The Way of Bitterness

□ Princess Sofia Volkonskaia (née Countess Bobrinskaia; Princess Dolgorukova by her first marriage) belonged to one of the oldest and wealthiest Russian aristocratic families. Her father had been minister of agriculture in the tsarist government, and her second husband, Prince Petr Petrovich (Pierre) Volkonsky, had served as a Russian diplomat in London, Berlin, and Vienna. Before the revolution, S. A. Volkonskaia had worked as a surgeon in a St. Petersburg hospital. Her return to Soviet Russia, where her husband was in prison, was a remarkable reenactment of one of the most celebrated episodes in Russian history: the 1827 decision by Princess Maria Volkonskaia to join her husband, the Decembrist Sergei Volkonsky, in Siberian exile.

MAY 1919. A muddy little river, a few armed soldiers. A bridge—the borderline between Russia and Finland. I stand there hesitating, uncertain. The same old doubts assail me. . . . I am still on Russian soil, there is still time to turn back. Only a few steps across the bridge; but how hard it is to take them. They mean so much.

However, time is up. My decision is made. I cannot miss the chance that has been given me; one is not twice offered the opportunity of leaving Soviet Russia unmolested.

Only a few steps. . . . There. . . . It is done. I am over. The Rubicon is crossed. I am now in Finland. Russia is behind me—Soviet Russia. I am in a free country, among normal people. I ought to feel happy. But my heart is heavy: Pierre, my husband, has remained on the other side.

PEACEFUL sunny days at Bath. Every morning the old Princess would go into the town and drink a glass of mineral water; later in the afternoon we would all drive far into the country, while the evenings were mostly taken up by a game of Patience. To the eye of an outside observer no existence could be calmer or nearer the ideal state of animal placidity. But under the surface all was turmoil, at any rate as far as I was concerned. Day after day passed bringing me no news from Pierre, and my impatience, my anxiety, my fears grew with every hour. To add to my torment, vague rumors of a most disquieting nature reached us even at Bath,

From Princess Peter Wolkonsky, *The Way of Bitterness* (London: Methuen, 1931). This is the author's English version (with some editorial changes of transliteration, spelling, and punctuation) from S. A. Volkonskaia, *Gore pobezhdennym. Vae victis* (Paris: Oreste Zeluk, n.d.), 1–210 (abridged).

whilst the short communications of the Press were getting more and more alarming. A new wave of terrorism had swept over Russia: wholesale arrests, mass executions of the bourgeoisie were reported. . . . It was simply maddening! How I longed for the smallest sign—just a single line—to tell me they were safe in the little white house on the Furstadskaia!

NATURALLY they all said I was mad; at that time the idea of anyone returning to Russia was in itself absurd. First of all, argued my friends, I should never be able to get through; the frontier was closed and all communications with Russia had ceased. And even supposing the impossible—supposing I should succeed in getting to Petrograd—what help would I be able to offer? My presence would probably prove to be only one more burden in circumstances already difficult enough, one more source of worry and anxiety. They were probably right. I did not know. Perhaps I should really be unable to get into Russia; perhaps I could really be of no practical help. . . . Perhaps. . . . Still I could not—I simply could not—stay here any longer. I would go to Finland; there I would be at least nearer to the Russian frontier; from there it would be easier to learn something about events in Petrograd. I might even try and get in touch with Pierre. . . . Then I could decide what to do next.

IT is extraordinary to what an extent one's whole appearance can be altered by a simple shawl thrown over the head. I did not of course look like a real peasant woman, but I could have easily been taken for some local schoolmistress, or even the daughter of a village priest. No other disguise was required.

Early the next morning I was on my feet. The thought of those forty-two versts before me worked better than any alarm clock. Forty-two versts!

To make things worse, a decree had just been issued forbidding the inhabitants of Petrograd to appear in the streets after eight in the evening; soldiers patrolled the town demanding your documents. And if you had no documents?

I began by resting every five versts, then every two, then after each verst. The bag over my shoulders grew heavier and heavier, my feet got covered with blisters, and every muscle of my body ached. Would I be able to do it? From time to time I met some other troops on their way to Gatchina; my fears had been in vain—they never even looked at me, never thought of stopping me or of asking me a question. . . .

The versts grew longer and longer (the relativity of space!); my pace grew slower and slower. Like a pack-mule I followed the given path, without thought or feeling, the one dull idea throbbing through my brain—to reach Petrograd. An immense lassitude filled my being, enveloped me more and more with every step. . . .

Quite unexpectedly a voice sounded from behind: "Hey, Mother, where are you going?"

Immediately I was wide awake. All trace of fatigue had been absorbed as by a vacuum-cleaner. My heart missed a beat; I dared not turn round and confront my unknown interlocutor. Was I caught already? Another second and I heaved a sigh of relief. Neither the Red Army nor the Cheka were after me. It was a simple peasant woman, saying good-naturedly: "Aren't we going the same way?" I felt ready to kiss the old, dirty-looking creature. If only she were not so inquisitive. What need had she to know both the place whence I came and my destination? Of what interest could the details of my hastily invented life be to her, a perfect stranger? She did not look like a secret agent, yet it was with definite relief that I parted from her at the next crossroads. Poor innocent soul! How far we are sometimes from guessing the emotions that some seemingly insignificant act of ours will evoke in another's breast!

The sun was on the decline; a cold wind swept through the air; the road before me was still long. What was I to do? It was much too cold to pass the night out of doors; too cold and also too dangerous. I decided to try and get shelter somewhere. I knocked at the first door I came to.

"Won't you let me in for the night? I will pay you well."

They hardly listened.

"Go on, go on, *Matushka*.[1] It's a bad time for letting strangers in the house," and the door was slammed in my face. It was the same at the next house and the next. I gave it up.

There was a moment when I felt near to despair. It seemed that no will-power could ever make me conquer those last ten versts. Still my feet kept on going. . . .

Several carts overtook me on the road; each time a momentary gleam of hope would flicker up, only to die at once; no pleading gesture, no entreaty for a lift elicited the smallest sign of sympathy on the stony faces of those drivers.

I kept on moving. The only alternative was to lie down and die in the ditch by the roadside. Slower and slower I advanced; slower and slower and more and more painfully. At last, something like two versts from the capital, the gods took pity on me. A huge carriage overtook me, one of those black and yellow *lineikas*[2] that used to belong to the Court Administration and that had been confiscated by some Soviet institution. Having just passed me, it stopped. It was not my doing— I would never have dared to ask for help from any Soviet officials; simply some piece of harness had got loose. I went up to them:

"Won't you give me a lift, comrades?"

The faces looked far from encouraging. It was clearly a case for stratagem. In my pocket I had several boxes of foreign cigarettes of a good Turkish brand; I handed them round. Only a superman could have resisted the temptation of a good smoke after months of that abject stuff they call "Soviet *makhorka*."

A few smiles appeared on the grim faces, typical ersatz smiles. Cigarettes might be expensive in Soviet Russia, but human sympathy could at least be bought cheaply.

"What about that lift?"

---

[1] Matushka—little mother. [author's note]
[2] Lineika—long open carriage with two lengthwise seats facing each other.

"Oh, well, you may come with us as far as the city gates, but no farther."

I had hoped for more; the gates of the capital stood out before me as a dangerous obstacle on my way.

Surely some kind of control had been established there; I feared nothing as much as the request to present my papers. In the company of the Soviet officials I could have slipped past the guards unnoticed.

However, better accept what was offered; so with great alacrity I climbed onto the box, next to "Comrade Coachman." What a pleasure it was to stretch my legs! At a moment's notice I could invent no more plausible tale to satisfy the coachman's curiosity than the visit to an imaginary aunt in Gatchina, who had suddenly been taken ill about a fortnight ago. I had even the cheek to add some details about my "aunt's" illness. When the White Army had occupied Gatchina, I had found my retreat cut off. The story sounded quite probable.

"You have been through pretty hard times, I see," sympathized Comrade Coachman.

"You have no idea!" (There at last I was able to put in a word of truth!)

Bravely I embarked on a fantastic recital of the horrors of the White occupation (would the *reservatio mentalis* I made at that moment suffice to clear me in the eyes of the friends I was so basely calumniating?). I was ready to accuse even my own family with the worst atrocities if by doing so I could keep up the coachman's interest in my tale. The Narva Gates loomed before us in the dusk. A few more lies—and we were through. A sigh of relief escaped me. At the same moment the carriage stopped.

"Whoa, whoa," shouted the coachman, "time you got down, Comrade. I never noticed that we had passed the gates."

"Many thanks for the lift."

How my feet hurt! How my whole body ached! I looked at my watch: already past eight. The danger of being in the streets increased every minute. I could not attempt to reach the Furstadskaia that night, it was much too far; besides, I could hardly turn up at my mother-in-law's so late in the evening. A happy thought struck me. I would pass the night at the big hospital where until last spring I had worked as a doctor in one of the surgical wards. If I hurried I could be there in ten minutes. The streets were deserted, but here and there was some solitary figure on its way home. It was getting colder and colder. I hurried on, along the Zabalkansky, then down the Zagorodny. I should have to make my entry into the hospital as inconspicuous as possible; better then avoid the front entrance and try and slip in unnoticed in the back. . . . A nasty shock: the gates were already closed for the night. Only the small door under the porch was open, but I could see the watchman standing idly in the courtyard. What was I to do? Under cover of darkness I crept up to the door and stood waiting. Several minutes passed. Would he never move? Suddenly, with a loud yawn, the man turned his back and started lazily on his rounds of the hospital buildings. The door remained open. One swift movement and I was inside. The next moment I was hurrying up the long, empty courtyard, past the women's wards, past the ward for infectious diseases, past the urological barracks. How often I had made this same round last winter when on night duty; how well I knew every corner.

There at last was the tiny door leading to the surgical wards, next to it the window of the doctor's room. A pity the blind was down—I could not see which of the doctors was on duty. I hoped it was one of the surgeons; the staff was so large, there were many doctors whom I hardly knew, but I would naturally only have to give my name to be recognized.

I threw a cautious look round; all was quiet, no one seemed to have observed me. A moment to open the door, to slip through the dark corridor, then past the chief entrance, the big staircase, and the night porter, dozing peacefully in his arm-chair. Another short passage, and I was at the door of the doctor's room.

"What do you want? Strangers are not admitted in here." It was a lady-doctor from the medical department with whom I was only slightly acquainted. I began by declaring my identity, explained to her that I belonged to the younger surgeons. My name was, of course, familiar to her. "But where have you come from? At such a time and in such a state?" True, I had quite forgotten the shawl on my head, my dirty shoes, the bag over my shoulders.

"From London." (I have always been unable to resist the pleasure of cheap effect.)

"What?"

I offered her the few English biscuits left in my bag. If she had any doubts, that convinced her. Not all the money in the world could have bought such biscuits in the Petrograd of those days. Later somebody told me that my lady-colleague had taken one biscuit home to show it to her family, and treasured it for many weeks as a reminder of a happier world.

It caused me great suffering to get the shoes off my swollen, bleeding feet. I was in a state of complete bodily exhaustion, and every single little muscle throbbed with pain. Lying down on the hard, narrow couch in the study of the head doctor, brought me a feeling of sensuous delight of such intensity as I have rarely experienced. My last conscious thought was of what awaited me on the morrow.

There are limits to physical weariness, after which no psychological worries will keep you awake. I had reached my goal, but it had not been easy. I don't believe I could do it now. I am not even sure I would try.

NEXT morning. . . . I was up with the lark. . . . In other circumstances it would have probably meant bed for three days at least, but it is a well-known fact that even a serious wound will go unheeded in the ardor of battle. The hardest part lay in getting on my shoes. It made me think of [Hans Christian] Andersen's tale about the mermaid whose every step toward her fairy prince meant agony as though treading on sharp swords. In her days, as now, there were neither trams nor cabs.

How strange it felt being in Petrograd once more. I hardly noticed my surroundings; I could think of one thing only—what awaited me in our little white house?

The Furstadskaia. Old houses have the air of true aristocrats; whatever the passions raging within them, their faces remain calm and expressionless. Our houses had been deprived of their owners, the furniture inside had been ruined, the walls decorated by gross inscriptions. But outwardly they remained the same. Nothing seemed changed in the aspect of the white house: the windows were unbroken, the paint was still on the walls. Only the window-panes looked dirty, the door handle seemed dull and unpolished, and a slight, hardly perceptible air of neglect lay over everything. And there, with his back to me, fiddling at the gates, stood the old butler, who had been with the family for over forty years.

"Good morning, Ivan Adamovich."

"_____?"

"Don't you recognize me?"

"Your Highness!"

"How's the Prince?"

The words were spoken. Now, in a moment, I would know. With one word I had staked everything. Everything: the present and the future, the happiness, the very meaning of life. What would it be? Heads or tails, red or black? Somewhere the invisible croupier had cried out: "Rien ne va plus."[3] My heart stopped beating. What would it be: life or death?

How long he took to answer. Was he afraid of telling me? "Well? . . ."

The old man threw a cautious look round, came a step nearer, then in a low voice: "Petr Petrovich is in Moscow. . . ."

"Then he's alive? . . . The whole world was suddenly flooded with light, a loud roar filled my ears, the houses opposite seemed to sway. . . . He's alive!

"What's the matter? Your Highness! Do you feel ill?"

"No, no, it is over. Tell me all you know quickly."

Pierre, it appeared, was in the Ivanovsky prison camp in Moscow.[4] He had been in prison all the time, ever since the day of his arrest in the middle of June. First they had taken him to the Shpalernaia prison in Petrograd, then later he had been transferred to Moscow. News came seldom, in the form of postcards, that he was now and then allowed to send home. The last one had come about a week ago; it only said that he was in good health, little more; he did not complain. (As if one could complain on a postcard! As if Pierre would complain even were it possible!)

"And the old Princess, how is she?"

My mother-in-law was in Petrograd. When the house had been seized by the Red soldiers she had been left a small building at the back of the house and had lived there ever since. For a few weeks the house had been taken as head-quarters for the Red Bashkir Brigade.[5] Everything in the house had been broken, spoilt, or stolen; the books in the library used for cigarette paper, the furniture mostly

[3] Call in roulette ending the placing of bets.

[4] Ivanovsky—the official name was "Ivan Camp of Forced Labor." [author's note]

[5] Bashkir—a Turkic-speaking, predominantly Muslim ethnic group from the Southern Urals region of Russia.

burnt as fuel, the pictures cut and slashed. (Piercing the eyes of family portraits with bayonets has always been a favorite pastime of the Red warriors.) The first-comers had done most of the damage; the present occupants, the Bashkirs, behaved in a quieter way.

The old bitter feeling of resentment arose in me. So that was all Mother-in-law had achieved by refusing to go abroad: her house, all her belongings taken from her, and Pierre put in prison.

The old butler was in no hurry; there was a great deal to tell. I interrupted him.

"Is the Princess up? Do you think she will receive me?"

"One moment, your Highness."

He was soon back.

"This way please."

Mother-in-law was still in bed.

"Sophy! Toi! Est-ce possible?"[6]

Her deafness was even more pronounced than before; conversation was rendered extremely difficult. She showed me the latest postcard from Pierre: a few sentences of perfect French, inquiring after her health, evincing anxiety for her well-being. . . . Hardly a word about himself. What a typical Pierre letter!

Mother-in-law complained of the many hardships she had to endure: the scarcity of food, the high prices of fuel. . . .

"Et que comptes-tu faire? As-tu de l'argent?[7]

"Pas beaucoup. Mais il faut avant tout que je trouve où loger."[8]

It was a broad hint; difficult to misunderstand. The absence of identity paper put me in a very precarious position; it would, moreover, gravely imperil the life of anyone who offered to shelter me. A very serious danger at all times, it was doubly so at the present moment, as the city was still under martial law. The government never bluffed in questions of that kind: when it was said you'd be shot, it meant just that. Did Mother-in-law know all this? Did she understand?

"Je t'aurais naturellement offert de te loger chez moi; mais imagine-toi quelle malchance—la lampe dans la salle à manger est cassée depuis deux jours. Tu ne peux pourtant pas rester dans l'obscurité!"[9]

"Evidemment."[10]

No, she had no idea of what it all meant. A helpless old lady, cut off from all real contact with the outside world—how could she realize my desperate situation?

"Il faut, malheureusement, que je vous quitte."[11]

Outwardly I was calm; it would not do to let her read in my face the hopeless thought that kept hammering through my brain: Where am I to go now?

[6] Sophy! Could it really be you?
[7] "And what do you think of doing? Have you money?" [author's note]
[8] "Not much. But first I must find somewhere to live." [author's note]
[9] "Naturally I would have offered you a room here; but think what bad luck, for the last two days the lamp in the dining-room has been broken. You can't possibly remain in the dark." [author's note]
[10] "Of course." [author's note]
[11] "I am afraid I must go now." [author's note]

"Reviens me voir bien vite."[12]

"Dès que je pourrai."[13]

WHENEVER someone says in my presence that all human beings are nothing but dry, hard-hearted egoists I have a ready answer: Marianna.[14] She owed me nothing. I was neither a relative nor a very intimate friend. We had met at the same parties, had dined at the same table, had more than once passed the night together dancing or listening to the Gypsies. She probably counted such friends by the dozen. When I decided to go and see her on that November morning I had no intention of asking her to shelter me; you do not ask people—no, not even good friends—to risk everything, including their lives, for the pleasure of doing you a good turn. I was going to ask her for advice, for certain useful information. Nothing more.

Her room was on the ground floor. That made it easier. I could knock at her window from the street. . . .

A sleepy, bewildered face appeared behind the curtain.

"Sophy! You crazy being! Where, in heaven's name, have you dropped from?"

A moment later I was sitting on her bed, telling my story. Quite frankly I told her all my difficulties.

"Naturally, you are going to stay here with me. You will sleep on the couch—not very comfortable, but as there's nothing else, you'll have to rough it."

"But, Marianna, do you understand? I have got no identity papers, no permits. Should a search party come tonight, you will have to share my fate. Think of it."

"Nonsense! We'll go and see Gorky[15] together. I know him fairly well, and am quite sure he will not refuse you his help. He'll be able to arrange everything. As to the flat, it is quite simple: we've got no *dvornik*[16] to the house, so for the present nobody will know you are here. Later on we will put things right with the house committee, with which I am on the best of terms."

"Are you sure?"

No great effort was needed to persuade me.

At a time of vast social upheavals the usual standards of life undergo a severe change; heroism becomes an everyday occurrence, and the man who yesterday would have refused to lend his friend a sovereign will now, with hardly any hesitation, give up his life for him.

THE three or four days that elapsed while waiting for my papers to be ready were spent in frantic activity. It is a well-known fact that virtue always bears its own punishment, and I was now expiating that softness of heart that had made me give

---

[12] "Come and see me again soon." [author's note]

[13] "As soon as I can manage." [author's note]

[14] Countess Marianna Erikovna Zarkenau, daughter by first marriage of Princess Palei, the wife of the grand duke Paul. [author's note]

[15] The writer Maxim Gorky, who had good connections with Bolshevik leaders, was famous for his interventions in defense of endangered intellectuals and aristocrats during the civil war years.

[16] Doorkeeper. [author's note]

so many hasty promises to friends abroad. The absence of any means of transport was my chief difficulty; the trams ran most irregularly and were always crowded to the last inch. Cabmen had not yet ventured out into the streets; the few that were to be seen demanded such high fares as the reward of their courage that only the most sincere Communists could afford them. Besides, cabmen, being an institution invented by the *bourgeoisie*, were considered undesirable in a Communist state. The species soon died out, only to flourish anew two years later when the clever move called the introduction of the NEP[17] ruined Communism but saved the Communists; theory was sacrificed that individual power might be retained.

In the meantime nothing remained to the inhabitants of the capital but to go on foot. Even short distances seem to spread out indefinitely when measured by one's own footsteps. I sincerely pity the citizens of London if some future Communist revolution in England does away with all means of transport. London is so much larger than Petrograd.

I would have shown greater intelligence had I looked after my own affairs instead of giving up so much time to visiting places and people whom I often did not even know. One or two broken promises would not have made any great difference to me on the day of the Last Judgment.

But how could I, for instance, forgo to visit the mother of a well-known "White" general, who for many months had been unable to send her even a single word of greeting? How omit to take her his message, to let her know that he was abroad, alive and well, his only worry being for her safety? I remember so well the look of distrust, even of fear, with which the poor old lady opened the door and listened to my tale. A perfect stranger saying she had come from him, had seen him, had even talked to him not so very long ago . . . and the fleeting thought so clearly mirrored in her eyes: "How do I know? She may be an *agent provocateur* from the Cheka." . . . And then, later, when she had at last been convinced and no longer distrusted me, the change that came over her whole being, the radiance that illuminated her face at the joyful tidings I had brought her, the words of gratitude, the questions with which she overwhelmed me, while she furtively wiped away the tears that kept falling softly from her eyes.

At another place in answer to my knock (the doorbells had for the most part ceased to work), the door was opened not by the young lady I was seeking but by a fierce-looking sailor.

"What do you want?"

"Tell me, please, who is living here now?"

Of course I mentioned no names. *Nomina odiosa sunt.* Here, names were dangerous. It was a favorite trick of the Cheka, when it put someone into prison, to make a kind of trap out of the arrested person's rooms; all those who called were sent to join their friend in prison. No exception was made for the doctor calling on his sick patient, nor a neighbor coming to borrow a handful of salt—all explanations would in due course be given to the prison authorities. Sometimes this little game went on for weeks. One had to be very cautious when inquiring for an absent friend. This time my doubts were soon at an end.

---

[17] New Economic Policy, introduced in 1921.

"Have you no eyes?" shouted the sailor angrily. "Didn't you see the board outside stating that this is a sailor's club in the name of Comrade Lenin? If every idiot imagines she may disturb people for nothing. . . ."

But I listened no more. A hasty few strides had taken me down the stairs and into the street as the angry bang of the door resounded loudly through the house. I have never learnt what happened to the lady I wanted to see. Had she left town, was she dead, or in prison? To this day I have not the slightest idea.

MEANWHILE, with the help of Gorky, I had obtained permission to travel to Moscow. The certificate stated that I was being sent to Moscow on an official mission in the quality of a music instructress; a number of signatures and seals gave the paper an imposing aspect, and procured me the right of traveling first-class, with that minimum of comfort which was denied to ordinary mortals. . . .

The secret irony of my situation lay in my complete lack of any musical training. The wrecked nerves of half a dozen music-mistresses had been unable to endow me with an ear for rhythm. Luckily, nobody asked me to display my musical talents, and the document led me safely past all control officers and barriers. May God grant Gorky a happy and serene old age! Next day I was in Moscow.

I WAS now in quite a different situation from that in which I had been when I first reached Petrograd. All my papers, certificates, permits were in order; once more I felt like a human being. It is no exaggeration to say that in those days the absence of necessary documents made you an outcast. Not only were you in constant danger of arrest and prison, but every step was surrounded with difficulties; you would be equally unable to find either a meal or a roof, for no one (unless a devoted and fearless friend like Marianna) would let you in for the night; and after eight o'clock you would be arrested for being in the streets. Now, at least, I could without trembling pass the "militia-man"[18] posted at the corner of the street. It is on purpose that I use the word "militia"; a Chekist would always remain an object of fear, to me as to everybody else.

At Moscow I went straight from the station to the Sheremetevsky Alley; I had been told Prince Serge Volkonsky was living there.[19] Serge was a first cousin of Pierre's, a writer of a certain renown, a fervent admirer of Dalcroze's system of rhythmical gymnastics,[20] and formerly the director of the Imperial Theatres. I knew him but slightly; I do not think we had met more than three or four times in all. I knew that my arrival could hardly be welcome. The small flat already held five people; I was the sixth. None of the others had ever even seen me; unasked, unexpected, I dropped into their midst. One cold November afternoon I rang at their door.

---

[18] The revolution had abolished police; a great number had been killed, others had fled; the militia formed in its place was naturally much inferior. [author's note]

[19] S. M. Volkonsky (1869–1937)—historian, theater critic, and philosopher, author of a well-known memoir, *Moi vospominaniia* (1923–24); emigrated from Russia in December 1921.

[20] After Émile Jaques-Dalcroze, a Swiss composer and teacher.

"I am the wife of Pierre and have just arrived in Moscow to try and rescue him from prison. I've nowhere to live. Will you take me in?"

"Naturally."

They gave me one of their rooms; it was neither agreeable nor convenient for them, but they did it without a moment's hesitation. I hated being a nuisance but I had no choice; there was nothing else to do. Hostels did not exist, there were no apartments or rooms to let; all restaurants had been closed, all shops abolished. You were not allowed to buy either a piece of bread or a pair of stockings—not even a button. . . . Mad days, life upside down. The realm of topsy-turvydom. A nightmare fantasy of Wells[21] come true. Even now we sometimes ask ourselves: Can it really have been?

THE meeting took place in a small courtyard, under the supervision of an armed guard. The prisoners were led out in groups of about twenty, to meet a corresponding number of visitors. In a few seconds the yard was overcrowded. The air resounded with a loud murmur of voices; there was a great deal of jolting and pushing each other out of the way as each one hurried to find his friends among the crowd.

At the first glance I hardly recognized him: the thin face, the long hair, the small beard he had let grow—it felt like looking at a stranger. . . . He had not yet caught sight of me. . . . Did he not know me to be miles away, somewhere in England? "Hullo!" He turned round, a perplexed expression on his face. Our eyes met. A momentary doubt, then he understood; stretched out his arms: *"But it is absurd!"*[22]

What can one say to each other, after six months of separation, during a mere quarter of an hour, standing on the snow among a noisy crowd, surrounded by eavesdropping strangers, followed incessantly by the suspicious gaze of the prison guards. . . . What can one say? Detached words, broken sentences, a few short questions. We understood each other without speaking. One look, one touch of the hand, and all was said. The sound of a harsh voice broke the spell.

"Time is up, citizens. Visitors are requested to leave at once." Hurried embraces, confusion; couples torn asunder, pushed roughly towards the door. All the things I ought to have discussed with Pierre, all the important matters we were to have talked over, come rushing into my mind. All the many questions I wanted to ask him. "Hurry up, you there! Haven't you heard the command?" One had to obey.

"Good-bye, God bless you darling."

"Till next Sunday."

MY unexpected appearance in the prisoner's camp had not passed unnoticed; the whole prison was impressed. It hardly ever happened that someone of his own

---

[21] H. G. Wells (1866–1946), prolific British author whose works include *The Time Machine* (1895) and *The War of the Worlds* (1898).

[22] Italicized text is in English in the Russian version of the book.

accord returned to Soviet Russia. But that a wife should come back from abroad in order to rescue her husband—such a fact had never yet occurred.

A curious incident happened to me a day or two later. I had decided to apply to Commissar Medvedev, chief administrator of all Moscow prisons and ask him for an extra interview with my husband. Whilst waiting in Medvedev's anteroom I entered into conversation with my neighbor, a simple-looking peasant woman. It so happened that the woman had only that same morning been released from the Ivanovsky prison camp. Why it was called "camp" I never discovered. A former monastery turned hastily into a prison, it had nothing at all of a camp about it.

I was naturally much interested, for there were quite a number of details I was eager to learn concerning prison life—the amount and quality of the food, the way the prisoners were treated, etc. The woman proved talkative.

"Just imagine," said she, "what happened the other day: they've got a prince, there at the camp, and—would you believe it?—his wife came back to him from abroad! What do you say to that!"

"Impossible!"

She got angry with me for my alleged doubts.

"Some of our people even saw her!". . . .

There is a kind of peculiar pleasure in listening anonymously to a story about oneself, especially if one is made to play the part of heroine. It has all the charm of eavesdropping, unpoisoned by the fear of detection. I was preparing to draw her on, and to enjoy the situation to the full, when the door opened and I was called away. The commissar being absent, it was his lady secretary who received the applicants. I never thought one human heart could harbor so much malice.

"Why do you ask for an extra interview?"

"I have not seen my husband for half a year."

"So-so,[23] a former prince. . . . A bit of prison life will do him, and such as he, no end of good."

"?_____"

"In old times you certainly never thought of those you were bleeding to death behind prison bars. You persecuted and oppressed the people whilst you yourself wallowed in luxury and idleness."

"I assure you I never persecuted anybody."

"Now you will learn yourself how it feels having to bow your head and beg for mercy. You need not expect any indulgence from me!"

A veritable she-devil! A Communist ogress! Well, at least I knew where I stood. She would never grant my request—I might as well return the way I came. As luck would have it, at the same moment the commissar made his appearance. Of quiet demeanor, with a pale, ascetic face and a clever look in his big black eyes, he presented a complete contrast to his secretary. On hearing my plea he at once ordered the necessary permit to be issued. Later on I had to apply to him several times and always met with the same quiet courtesy, the same absence of all useless words. If only all Bolsheviks were like him! The revelation of his true

---

[23] The original Russian expression, *tak-tak*, means "I see."

character came to me much later: the soft voice, the charming manners were but a mask covering the ruthlessness of Torquemada,[24] a ferocity equaling that of Ghenghis Khan.[25] The sobs of a mother, the prayers of a wife had never been able to touch him, never once had his hand trembled when signing a death warrant. Even those in the Cheka feared him. . . . No, better a hundred jeering secretaries than this one man with the face of an ascetic and the soul of an executioner.

WE lived through the winter of 1920 in Moscow. Only those who have experienced it will understand. As to the others—no description will ever give them an adequate idea.

Yes, of course, we suffered from hunger. In a lesser degree than many others: we had a meal every day, sometimes even twice a day. And yet . . . without meat, without butter or sugar or white flour or fresh vegetables . . . frozen potatoes and millet cooked in water (the kind of grain Europeans give their poultry). Nothing else, day after day. Whatever one did, the thought of food never left one; it was constantly there, somewhere at the back of one's mind. It became an obsession and, like all fixed ideas, upset one's whole mental balance.

From time to time, after dark, strange people with bags behind their backs knocked stealthily at the kitchen door: the one offered flour, the other had a sack of potatoes, or perhaps even a bit of butter. They bargained in whispers, threw cautious glances all round them before leaving the house. . . . Bread traffic was for some reason a special feature of the Moscow University; it was carried on by the numerous attendants in the underground passages of the huge building. You had to wait till evening, then slip quietly along the deserted streets, knock at the stipulated door. . . . A little later you would hurry home by the shortest way, the newly bought loaf hidden under your coat, and the smell of the heavy, damp, black bread irresistibly teasing your tormented senses. Every shadow made you start: you were committing an illegal act punishable by law.

Food was our constant preoccupation; the one all-absorbing topic of every conversation: where, for how much, of what quality. . . . An operation was being performed in one of the town hospitals; the peritoneum had been cut open, the bowels laid out. Someone in the room mentioned the price of butter. The surgeon took it up, the assistant-surgeon replied. The operation went on; the hands of the surgeon ran automatically along the bowels, the assistant mechanically caught the squirting blood vessels, the nurse presented the instruments—while the all-important discussion of butter went on uninterrupted. I have not invented the story. I myself was present. I was the assistant.

We also suffered from cold. Here again we were better off than many others: the temperature in our rooms never dropped below four or five degrees (Réaumur);[26] in the morning we did not have to break the ice in the jug before taking a wash; not even during the severest frosts.

---

[24] Thomas Torquemada (1420–1498)—Ecclesiastic, leader of the Spanish Inquisition.

[25] Ghengis Khan (usually now rendered Genghiz or Jenghiz Khan)—thirteenth-century Mongol military leader and empire builder whose conquests included Russian lands.

[26] 4 degrees Réaumur = 37 degrees Fahrenheit.

We never took off our fur coats; we sat in them by day and slept in them by night. Reading was difficult; the hands that held the book kept freezing, whilst with gloves on you could not turn the pages. Sewing was even harder, for the fingers were numb with cold and refused to manipulate the needle. There was nothing left but to forgather miserably round the small kitchen stove and evoke for the hundredth time the memories of happier days. But it often happened that even the kitchen stove was cold.

The only housemaid had left several weeks ago. No one but Communists could afford the luxury of a servant: we had to do all the work ourselves. Hard work. We took turns in cooking the dinner, in heating the stove, in washing up. One of the hardest tasks consisted in bringing the big, heavy logs of wood up the stairs, all the way from the garage, and sawing them into small pieces. When during the fourth year of my medical training we learnt to perform amputations on corpses, the professor used to say: "the technique is quite simple; saw the bone in the same way as you saw a log of wood." Possibly, the other girls knew how to saw wood. For myself the experience was reversed; when my saw got stuck in one of those big frozen logs, I tried to think of the operating table: the same movement as when sawing through the tibia.

Worse was to come. As a result of the great frost, all water pipes burst in the insufficiently heated houses. For many weeks we were obliged to fetch the water from the next-door courtyard. It was no joking matter; there was always a long queue standing before the pump—at all hours of the day, but especially long close to lunch- and dinnertime; quite like the Paris underground *aux heures d'affluence*.[27] One's hands and toes grew stiff with cold. . . . At last you found yourself at the pump, your pail overflowing with icy water, your last pair of boots getting soaked through and through while you stood in the large pool that spread all round the pump. Then came the return journey with the heavy pail full of water, up the narrow, dark staircase covered with a slippery coat of ice, the inevitable result of overflowing water. The same thing had to be repeated twice, sometimes three times a day. But what right had we to complain? We lived on the second floor. . . . What about those who lived on the fifth?

It became every day more and more difficult to keep oneself clean. The gray horror—lice—found their way into every house. Time and again did I happen to discover one in my clothes; the first time I was sick with disgust and nearly burst out crying. For long I struggled, revolted against the inevitable; tried all the measures I had heard of. I rubbed my whole body with a stuff the smell of which would have turned the stomach of a whale; for many weeks I wore a small bag containing some unknown charm on a string round my neck; camphor oil, naphthaline—there was nothing I left untried. I even went the length of washing every morning, however great the cold, and of changing my underwear as often as my means permitted. . . . It was all of no avail. Both science and superstition proved powerless against the foe. So I gave up the useless struggle and accepted my fate

[27] At peak hours (Fr.).

with the meekness of Ghandi.[28] One can get accustomed even to vermin on one's body. True, I cannot boast of having ever reached the same degree of philosophical resignation as those who passed the time by betting whether the quantity of insects gathered in a sweep of the hand would prove an even or uneven number. They say the game was a very popular one—especially amongst prisoners. . . . The harder grew the general conditions of life, the greater became the scourge of dirt, lice, and epidemics. Even Lenin got alarmed. For a few weeks the streets were covered with enormous picture placards: "Is the louse going to conquer Communism?" And the passers-by sent up a silent prayer to Heaven that the monsters would destroy each other.

FROM time to time numbers of the former *bourgeois* class were called upon to work for the community. These tasks had nothing to do with the duty of keeping clean the part of the street and pavement opposite their own house, which fell to the lot of all the inhabitants of the city. Once or twice a week all the lodgers, with the exception of the very old and feeble, were turned out into the street and supplied with crowbars, shovels, brooms, etc. We did our work conscientiously: broke up the ice, shoveled the snow into big heaps, swept the pavement. Nobody thought of complaining; the work had to be done and we were quite ready to do our part.

The forced labor for the *bourgeoisie* was a very different thing. One day I received a summons—an order, under severe penalty, to present myself at eight o'clock next morning at the meeting place in a former police station.

I started at half-past seven. It was a dreary December morning, dark and cold; the snow was falling in big, heavy flakes, and I had had no breakfast. The room in the police station was unheated. We were about forty: young girls, ladies in old-fashioned hats, some in evening shoes and darned silk stockings; old gentlemen in worn overcoats, with pale faces and dull eyes. . . . A motley crowd. . . .

We had to wait for more than half an hour: shivering, sleepy, miserable. At last they made their appearance: well-fed, brutal, self-satisfied. First they counted us and marked the names of those absent. Then a column was formed, the order given, the march started. Across the whole town. Like prisoners, surrounded by an armed guard we were conveyed to the Riazansky station, situated at the other end of Moscow—a good hour's march. We were exhausted when we reached our destination. There they divided us into groups, and each group was given a separate task. It fell to my lot, with five or six others, to clean the snow from an empty space behind the station. They gave us big, heavy wooden shovels. The soldiers of our guard seated themselves round, lighted their cigarettes, and prepared to enjoy the show. It was quite evident that the task given us was a useless and unnecessary one; that its only point lay in humiliating us, the formerly privileged, in making us feel more keenly the cruel hand of today's masters and our own helplessness. The soldiers encouraged us mockingly in our work, laughing loudly

---

[28] Mahatma Gandhi (note spelling) (1869–1948), leader of the Indian independence movement, advocate of nonviolent disobedience.

at their own silly jokes. "Eh, you citizenness! You needn't be afraid of a bit of snow. High time you learn to do something with your hands. Hurry up!" The girl turned a wan face towards her tormentors. The heavy shovel with its load of snow seemed quite above the forces of that slender figure and the tiny delicate hands. She was going to say something when her foot in its ridiculous high-heeled shoe slipped, gave way, and landed her on all fours, up to the waist in the snow. Loud guffaws greeted her misadventure: "That's a good one. Worthy of the circus! Skirts just a bit higher please! Ho! ho! ho!" Not a hand stretched out to help her. . . . A little farther on an old man, even more poorly dressed than the rest, stood leaning against the wall. The pouches under the eyes, the gray pallor of the skin, all spoke of some serious disease. "Hello, Grandpa! What do you imagine you're here for? All your life long you have rested, now it is your turn to work while we look on." The leering faces were full of low vindictiveness. What a joy to be able to order about those one had always had to obey! There is no sight so ugly as the human beast in its moments of triumph.

In most situations in life many different emotions are combined. Here there was only one feeling, on their side as well as on ours: the feeling of hatred, in its purest and most intense form. "*In statu nascendi*," say the chemists.[29]

At dusk they dismissed us. By way of reward, each of us got a pound of the usual damp, clammy black bread, baked with bits of straw and even tree bark in it. Silently we made our way home, exhausted physically, morally humiliated and degraded. Thus did the victorious proletariat build up a new world.

Two or three weeks later we got another summons. Every apartment in the house was to send forth two of its members to clean lavatories and water-closets in various communal and government buildings. Which of us would go? . . . I refused. Let them put me in prison, let them shoot me, or do anything they liked— I was not going to submit. . . .

"And if no one goes?"

"I do not know and I do not care. I tell you, whatever happens, nobody is going to force me to clean other peoples' W.C.s." . . .

I stayed at home. And nothing happened. At the appointed hour the required number of workers made their appearance . Trotsky is supposed to have said: "Put up a notice that on such a day a general flogging is going to take place, and all the *bourgeois* will obediently form a queue."

WORST of all, perhaps, were the night searches. On ordinary days the electric current was cut off in the whole town at about nine p.m. If the light kept on burning in a certain district after that hour it meant that the Cheka intended visiting one of the houses. The people dared not go to bed, and sat trembling in fearful anticipation, listening to the sound of the rare motor-cars that passed in the street below; at once all conversation ceased, all thoughts were fixed on the one question—would it stop at the door, or would it pass on? No one but Chekists used a

---

[29] Literally, in a state of being born (Lat.); used in chemistry for an atom or molecule emerging from a chemical reaction in a state of abnormal reactivity.

motor-car by night. They usually arrived about two in the morning: a loud knocking at the door, loud, impatient voices on the landing, heavy footsteps, the thud of rifles, and the irruption of a dozen or so Red soldiers, unceremoniously taking possession of the whole flat. Then hour after hour of the search: everything turned upside down, drawers forced open, their contents spread out on the table or thrown onto the floor, every single thing minutely examined. . . . Strange hands rummaging among your dresses, crumpling up your linen; enemy eyes reading your correspondence; all your most intimate belongings looked over, discussed by a hostile crowd. . . . The first gray light of dawn showing up a picture of utter confusion and desolation. And lastly the most critical moment of all: the departure. Would anybody be arrested? It has all been depicted many times. All who lived in Russia during those years know the suspense of those terrible nights. Nobody escaped. Even today I hate the sound of a motor-car stopping at my door late in the evening.

We were lucky. They visited us twice that winter, but departed without making any arrests.

Many years later I was staying with some friends in Paris. I had gone to bed early and was asleep when my hostess, just back from the theatre, knocked at my door. In one second I was out of bed: "What's the matter? Have they come for a search?" . . . A kind of conditional reflex that takes a long time to disappear.

A NEW misery was in store for us; it came in the form of a notice from the "house committee" telling us to be ready to receive two new lodgers into our flat. We were, it appeared, occupying more space than was allotted to us according to Soviet law. Recriminations were of no avail. The couple thus forced on us—a young man and his wife—seemed quite nice, but . . . they were Communists. Even before their arrival there was none too much space in that flat. The Communists living in the next room were like the famous pea under the mattress that keeps one from sleeping all night; like the bit of dust in one's eye that after hours of vain rubbing feels like that beam which, according to tradition, one ought to remark only when it is in the eye of one's neighbor. Nothing could be more disagreeable than this living in close contact (having to cook our dinners on the same stove, to use the same bathroom devoid of hot water, etc.), with people who considered themselves a priori and in principle as our foes. Nothing could be more irritating than the feeling of being, even at home, under the constant eye of the enemy. "Take care," "Shut the door," "Do not talk so loud; the Communists may hear you." Pin-pricks? Yes, of course. But in that nightmare life of ours every pin-prick took the proportion of a serious wound.

I WAS beginning to despair. All ways had been tried, all protection sought, all connections appealed to. All of no avail. Pierre was in prison and the chances of his being set free seemed to grow less and less with every day. The Cheka having refused to obey the decision of the Central Executive Committee, the case was to all appearances lost. Nothing remained but to wait for a universal revolution with general pardon to all political prisoners; pending which I could see but one last move to be made.

At that time a peace treaty had just been signed between Soviet Russia and Estonia, according to which the subjects of both countries were to be allowed to return unmolested to their native land. Several generations of the Volkonsky family had owned land near Reval,[30] and all the members of the family, as belonging to the nobility of the former province of Estonia, had full right to consider themselves Estonian nationals. If the Soviet Government gave us permission to return to Reval—and there could be no official reason for refusing it—then Pierre would automatically be released. My brother-in-law would be able to conduct all the Estonian part of the transaction from [his family estate of] Fall. The chief drawback to this plan consisted in the length of time that would inevitably elapse before any result was attained. That meant weeks and weeks more of prison for Pierre. And there was always the possibility of failure in the end.

ONE day I was returning from prison in a very black mood, when in the street I met Count Paul X.

"How are you getting on?" he asked.

"Badly, very badly."

"And Pierre?"

"In prison."

"Have you been to see Boguslavsky?"

"No, I've never heard of him before."

Paul explained, talking as usual in his quick, exuberant way, excitedly gesticulating. Boguslavsky, said he, is a very mysterious personage, an old "sea-dog," who has many connections with the Cheka, is even said to be a personal friend of the all-powerful Dzerzhinsky;[31] at the same time Boguslavsky never refuses his help to the victims of the Soviet régime and has already saved many of them from prison. Paul was going to see him in the immediate future; if he wished, he could talk to him about Pierre.

"Be a dear and do it! I'll be grateful to you all my life if only you get Pierre out of prison."

He jotted down the chief points of the case.

"I cannot, of course, promise you anything. But I will do my best."

AND then, quite unexpectedly, the impossible happened. On Wednesday, the 25th of February, I had brought my parcel of provisions to the prison gates. After delivering it into the hands of the guard, I stood waiting for the usual "return parcel."

Suddenly, from behind the gates came the voice of Pierre: "I am free!"

"What? What are you saying?"

[30] Today's Tallinn.
[31] F. E. Dzerzhinsky (1877–1926)—a prominent Bolshevik leader, head of the Soviet secret police (Cheka and OGPU) from 1917 to 1923.

"Yes, I have already been notified."

"Then why don't you come out at once?"

"There is no hurry. I've got my things to pack; then I want to take leave of my companions. Come back here at two and bring with you the little sledge for my box."

I cannot to this day understand how a man who had been in prison (and what a prison!) for nearly nine months did not take the first opportunity to leave the prison gates behind him: and especially under Bolshevik rule, when every moment a change might have taken place, the order have been revoked and liberty refused. This small detail reflects the whole character of Pierre. It was one of the things that astonished me most in the course of the whole Revolution.

PIERRE was now free. To begin with—home and a bath.

AFTER a short rest—he had really earned it with his nine months in a Soviet prison—Pierre went to see and thank all those who in one way or another tried to help him regain his freedom. One of his first visits was to Boguslavsky. Pierre had hardly opened his mouth when the latter interrupted him:

"Do not thank anyone. You own your freedom entirely to your wife."

"How is that?"

In answer Boguslavsky told Pierre how he had obtained his release. When Count Paul X had asked him to help us, Boguslavsky appealed to Dzerzhinsky.

"Felix Eduardovich,"[32] said he, "have you ever read Nekrasov?"

"I know, I know," interrupted Dzerzhinsky. "You want to speak of 'Russian Women' and of the Princess Volkonskaia,"[33] and he immediately signed an order for Pierre's release.

That is what Boguslavsky told Pierre. It is, all modesty apart, a most remarkable story; probably a true one—there was no reason why Boguslavsky should have invented it. We do not, as a rule, credit Chekists with such gentlemanly feelings; we hardly picture them otherwise than as complete villains, incapable of any human emotions. Is it possible that even a Dzerzhinsky had his moments of weakness?

We will probably never learn the answer. Boguslavsky has since been shot and Dzerzhinsky died of heart-failure.

When at present I sometimes nag Pierre with a trifling question which he is unwilling to grant (and is there a wife who never exasperates her own husband?), he exclaims: "This is moral blackmail. She has saved me out of a Bolshevik prison and knows that I cannot refuse her anything!"

Our money flew with a speed that would have undoubtedly beaten all the records in the world. . . . The sheets were all gone, and I kept awake at nights wondering whether death from starvation would overtake us next week or the week

---

[32] In fact, Dzerzhinsky's patronymic was Edmundovich.

[33] "Russian Women," a classical poem by Nekrasov which tells the story of Princess Volkonskaia, wife of the Decembrist or partaker in the conspiracy of December 1825, who followed her husband to Siberia. [author's note]

after. Rescue came in an unexpected form: Aniuta Obolensky[34] had in some way discovered that the Board of the Soviet Library Committee included a few very kind gentlemen. They were ready, if asked, to effect a fictitious requisition of your library, and help you get it out of your confiscated house. You thus acquired the possibility of selling your own books, for by some unexplained whim of the authorities a few bookshops in Petrograd had been left open. It would have been fruitless to look for logic in the behavior of our new masters, but we could sometimes profit by its absence.

Aniuta's information proved correct. I will not attempt to describe my feelings when Pierre and myself, acting as assistants to a bright little Jew from the Library Committee, entered my lovely flat on the English Quay. I am not what is usually called a sentimentalist. But to witness my own rooms occupied by strangers, to see uncouth sailors making themselves at home among my own things, eating off my china, sleeping in my bed, on my own sheets . . . no, I never thought it would be quite as unpleasant. Our sense of property has been developed in us for generations; the inverse process will probably take as long—if not longer.

I've got to acknowledge that the intruders had kept my flat in seemingly good order. I had heard a great deal of the way proletarians used our homes: the underwear hung up to dry on a string across the drawing-room, the traces of dirty boots on the Aubusson carpets, the silk hangings cut up to make a skirt, books torn into cigarette paper. . . . I came prepared for the worst, and was agreeably surprised at the care the sailors had taken of my belongings. The carpets had been cleaned, most things stood in their old places; big photographs of my daughter adorned the tables. The new owners, naturally, ignorant of our true identities, were visibly displeased at our taking away the books, but the order was official, the signature correct, our certificates were regular. So they had to comply. I hoped I would be able at the same time to gain access to my writing-table and extract all letters, papers, and souvenirs most dear to me. But I failed. The door of my study was locked, the key, so they assured us, had been taken away by one of their absent comrades; as to the papers, they had all been destroyed. It may have been true. I dared not insist for fear of arousing suspicion; our situation, if discovered, would have been disagreeable to say the least of it. The funny part of it was that the sailors imagined themselves to be defending the interests of the absent owner against us—the representatives of the Soviets! . . . Life abounds in little jokes of this kind. A pity the public is for the most part utterly unappreciative. It requires a greater detachment of mind than most of us posses to enjoy the jokes life plays at our expense.

I felt my throat contract and a mist float before my eyes as the door of the flat closed behind us. Shall I ever again see the English Quay, my rooms looking out on to the Neva, the corner where we so often sat in the gathering twilight, watching the lights appear one by one on the other side, the graceful outlines of

[34] A. Obolensky—daughter of Prince Aleksei Obolensky, former procurator of the Holy Synod. [author's note]

the Imperial yachts standing out clearly against the evening sky, and the black shadows of the big, heavy barges gliding silently down the river? Or will the years to come still find me here, in this tiny house in a dirty little street on the outskirts of Paris, with no other view but the ever-drunken old coal-merchant opposite, and workmen drinking their apéritifs in the pub at the corner? . . .

ONE of the privations that made me suffer most was the impossibility of having a bath. Some (even most) people seemed to regard it in the light of a minor inconvenience. I did not know whether to admire them for their indifference to physical discomfort or despise them for feeling no need for bodily cleanliness: another example of the inconvenience of too careful upbringing, which only tends to develop an extra capacity for suffering and renders one more vulnerable than the mass of humanity to the blows of fate. After a month or two of nothing but a small tub and cold water I felt ready for even a communal bath. The usual public baths had long since been abolished, but I learnt somehow of the existence of a special bania[35] attached to the Alexander Theatre, where all artists and theatre workers could get a wash free. With the help of some friends I obtained a ticket entitling me to one wash in the bania.

It was my first visit to a communal bath, and I sincerely hope it will be my last. How to describe it? A medium-sized room, the air heavy with steam and the exhalations of human bodies; a crowd of naked women standing in various postures on the slimy, bespitten wooden floor; some nondescript bloodstained rags and cast-off bandages lying in an untidy heap in a corner. . . . The room filled with the noise of angry words and protests for a place near the hot water tap or vacant seat on one of the benches. . . . Hideousness and deformity in every imaginable form and variety. . . . Underfed bodies, meagre, pendant breasts, crooked legs, legs swollen with oedema, legs with big knots of varicose veins, like blue worms moving under the skin; big flat feet deformed by the ugly angles of inbent toes; backs covered with the bright dots of purulent boils, marked by the red lines of itching scabies; necks and shoulders powdered with the pink patches of syphilitic roseolas, innocently peeping out from under the thick gray coat of dirt and lice of many months' accumulation. . . . If hell exists, it surely resembles that bathing-room of the Alexander Theatre.

THE day came. The day of our departure. Some friends had kindly unearthed a motor-car to convey Mother-in-law and her luggage to the station. The old butler, also a native of Estonia, was going by the same train with his wife and daughter. Pierre and I had also been given a car—a big car belonging to the Commissariat of the Navy and obtained through some friends of Larisa Reisner,[36] the mistress of the famous sailor Raskolnikov,[37] who was commander of the Soviet fleet. The two sailors on the front seat gave the car a distinctly military appearance; those

[35] Bania—bathhouse.
[36] L. M. Reisner (1895–1926)—Bolshevik legislator, writer, and guerrilla commander.
[37] F. F. Raskolnikov (1892–1939)—deputy president of the Kronstadt soviet in 1917, later a Soviet arts administrator and diplomat.

who saw us probably pitied us for being under arrest. In Soviet Russia appearances are more deceptive than anywhere else.

We arrived at the station many hours before the train was due to leave: necessity, not Eisenbahnfieber.[38] On one of the side platforms stood a long train made up of trucks: that was our train. The platform was swarming with people, all heavily loaded, shouting, pushing, dragging their various belongings. There is no sight so desolate and so ugly as that of a train of repatriates from Soviet Russia. All the accumulated rubbish of years, the useless things that had been lying unheeded in some dark corner of the house, some dusty attic, or moldy cellar were now pulled into the open, shamelessly displayed to the light of the sun. Objects strange and unexpected met the eye: a broken parrot-cage next to a bicycle without wheels; an armless Pierrot seated on what was left of a rich fur coat; basins that had lost their enamel coatings; a chair without a back; an umbrella without a handle. . . . As to the persons to whom these things belonged, the less said about them the better. Three years of Bolshevism had been enough to turn these once normal people into the caricatures of human beings, terrorized, degraded, and warped both physically and mentally, that are called "Soviet citizens." Foreigners who witnessed the arrival of such a train at Narva no longer asked how it was possible for a country of a hundred and forty million people to bear the yoke of a handful of Communists. They had understood. And that, notwithstanding the fact that the repatriates were the happiest, not to say the only happy, people in Russia; they had won a bigger prize than the Calcutta Sweep—permission to leave the country. Never in all my life have I seen such fierce envy as that which burned in the eyes of the friends to whom I said good-bye before going abroad. Had it been possible to escape from the Soviets with the help of a self-inflicted wound in the hand, the way a few cowardly soldiers eluded the trenches during the war, all Russia would be today without fingers. Alas! freedom could be bought only by the sacrifice of one's head.

We were now faced with the problem of getting Mother-in-law into the train. No stretchers were to be had, so we helped her into her armchair, carried her to the train, and then with the help of a dozen strong men succeeded in lifting the heavy chair into the cattle-truck in which we had been given places. On the floor at one end of the truck we placed an air mattress, covered it with blankets, surrounded it with cushions, and laid down our invalid. After a great deal of rearranging of the cushions we succeeded in making her fairly comfortable. It was, in any case, the best we could do. The removal had badly taxed her strength. Her emaciated face, with its yellow-tinted skin and great pouches beneath the eyes looking out from under a heavy black hat, her thin body wrapped in a dark fur coat, the trembling hands and vague questioning glances, were terrible to behold. In those days people were used to many a sad and gruesome sight, but on seeing her the passers-by shuddered and hastily averted their eyes. . . .

We were not the only passengers in the truck. Besides the butler and his family there were also three or four strangers. Our luggage occupied but little space: a

---

[38] Railway fever (Ger.).

small box, two or three suit-cases with some worn-out linen and a few old dresses—that was all.

Hour after hour of waiting. No one knew at what time the train would start. Pierre kept pacing nervously up and down the platform. Nerves are catching; stories of people detained at the very last minute kept running through my mind. In which column of the great book of statistics would we be inscribed? Of those that had succeeded or of those that had failed? Only on the other side of the frontier would we be in safety.

Evening came and still nothing happened. It grew dark, a fine drizzling rain began to fall. We sat silently, in a state of dull somnolence, with neither thought nor feeling, only waiting, waiting. . . . Would the end never come?

Someone ran down the platform, a command rang out, then a shrill whistle and the train started: first slowly, then quicker and quicker. We were moving. Could it really be true?

There is many a slip between the city and the frontier. Were our sufferings still too light to balance the scales of Justice? Hadn't we yet earned out freedom? Or had the devil been granted permission to take us through one last ordeal?

About four or five miles from the town the train slowed down and then stopped altogether. What was the matter? Complete darkness reigned outside; it was pouring with rain. We could see nothing—nothing but a deep ditch at our feet and the vague outlines of untilled fields beyond.

The figure of a man with a lantern in his hand came running along the train; he was shouting something. As he came nearer we could distinguish the words: "The last ten trucks are not going any farther. All passengers are requested to take their places higher up." At first we did not understand. It took us some time to grasp the terrible fact that our truck was the last but one.

It was more than a calamity—it was disaster. The other trucks were all full, and it would have been no easy task to find places for us and for our luggage. Still, it could have been done, had it not been for the one insurmountable obstacle—my mother-in-law. To transport her from one truck to another without a stretcher, or even an armchair, was simply impossible. To jump from the high truck down into the darkness, the rain, the deep ditch below us, to pass the whole length of the train and to climb high up into another truck, was no easy task even for a young and healthy being. As for Mother-in-law, who could hardly move without help, the whole thing was absolutely out of the question. What then? If we remained in the car, we would be taken back to Petrograd—a Petrograd with nowhere to go, with our rooms already occupied by newcomers, with nothing to eat, no money to live on, with Mother-in-law in our hands and the prospects of a new departure uncertain. It was too awful even to contemplate. It was the end of everything.

In all our life together I have never seen Pierre so upset as at that moment. He forgot the rain, forgot his hat, jumped off the car and ran in search of the train commandant. The latter proved to be an amiable Estonian gentleman who would have been glad to help us but was quite powerless to do so. The engine, it appeared, was not sufficiently powerful; the train would either remain stuck where it was or else some of the trucks would have to be left behind. . . . Pierre was frantic. He argued, prayed, begged the Estonian in the name of his own mother. . . . Despair rendered him eloquent. The man could not resist him. He ran off, consulted someone, got the necessary permission and came back to tell Pierre that our car would be attached to the train. Pierre returned to us drenched to the skin, the water running down his face, his whole body trembling with excitement. But the battle had been won.

The manoeuvring began. Our car was moved up and down, first one way, then the other. We strained our eyes, peering into the darkness, trying to guess the meaning of each separate jolt; our brains were paralyzed with the sickening fear of being left behind. Mother-in-law had caught the general excitement: "Petia, Petia, que se passe-t-il? Qu'est ce que vous regardez tous les deux?"[39] Vainly we tried to soothe her.

One last movement of the truck: backwards . . . forwards . . . the clash of iron as we joined another car. . . . Now we were being attached to it, now the train was moving once more . . . moving in the right direction. Was it only another manoeuvre?

For some time now the train had been traveling steadily in the direction of Iamburg. But our nerves were still quivering; every lessening of speed seemed to announce a stop, to be followed by the dreaded journey backwards; every whistle seemed to portend disaster. . . .

On the second day we reached the frontier. With every hour the tension grew more strained. Nerves were stretched to breaking point. Mother-in-law was restless. Every few minutes she would call:

"Petia! Petia!"

"Que veux-tu, Maman?"

"Combien de degrés y-a-t-il dehors?"

"Je ne sais pas, il fait assez frais."

"Il n'y a pas de thermomètre à la fenêtre?"

"Mais non, voyons, Maman, tu sais bien que nous sommes dans un wagon de marchandises."[40]

The words were drowned in the noise of the wheels, and had to be shouted at the top of the voice. For a few minutes she would be quiet, then it would begin all over again:

"Petia, Petia, viens ici."[41] . . .

His patience was boundless; whatever his occupation, whether he was lying down or had just taken up a book, in a moment he was at her side. "Tu m'as appelé, Maman?"[42]

---

[39] Petia, Petia, what's going on? What are you two looking at?

[40] —Petia! Petia!—What do you want, Mother?—What's the temperature outside?—I don't know. It's fairly cool.—Isn't there a thermometer by the window?—I'm afraid not, Mother, you know we are in a freight car.

[41] Petia, Petia, come here.

[42] Did you call me, Mother?

She was very old, very ill and feeble, and, as often happens in such cases, very exacting.

We had still the frontier before us—the last and probably the most terrible obstacle of all; customs examination of luggage and of people, inspection of papers and documents. We had all heard of people turned back from the frontier because of some trifling irregularity, a small infraction of the rules. Some of them, as we knew, had been led straight to prison.

The personal examination included cutting open of coat linings, searching in the hair and beneath the dress. I was asked to take off my boots. A woman next to me was sobbing wildly; the precious stone she had hidden in the heel of her shoe had been discovered and taken from her; her own fate was still uncertain.

Mother-in-law had been allowed to remain in the truck: even the Chekists were impressed at the sight of her. The woman they sent in to search her did her work in a most perfunctory way; even she lacked courage to lay hands on such an invalid. Later we learnt that all the while Mother-in-law had kept three gold coins secreted on her person. All her life she had been in the habit of giving a certain sum of money to the priest on the celebration day of the chapel at Fall. Nothing, not even a revolution, would keep her from performing the traditional gesture. She probably never realized, never even stopped to think of the terrible danger that would have threatened all of us, and herself above all, had her ruse been discovered.

The search was ended, our papers examined. Everything went off smoothly. We had been allowed to pass. There followed a long period of waiting. Never, never in all my life had the minutes passed so slowly. It was many times worse than waiting for the results of a school examination, worse than waiting for a late sweetheart, or for the pangs of childbirth to come to an end. Every second was an eternity. Would the train never start? . . . Should we be allowed to cross over to the other side?

We could neither read, nor talk, nor even think. The man in the dock, on trial for his life, waiting for the verdict, will be unable to tell you what are his thoughts while the jury consider their decision. There are probably no coherent thoughts in his head; all ideas are drowned in the one tense expectation, the one terrible question: yes or no? Yes or no—will they let us go?

Every torture comes to an end. A whistle, a small jolt. The train starts—slowly, slowly, nearer and nearer to the frontier. . . .

A small muddy river. A few armed soldiers. A bridge. . . . I look at Pierre; but he is not looking at me. His glance is directed back, from where we had come, back—into Russia. . . . Now he makes the sign of the cross. We are in Estonia.

I fall on my knees, my face in my hands. Sobs are stifling me. . . . From the corner come the trembling sounds of an old voice:

"Petia! Petia! Sommes-nous arrivés?"[43]

---

[43] Petia, Petia, are we there yet?

AFTERWORD

"Well, and what next?" someone may inquire. Next? Next came our life in Europe, great expectations and even greater disappointments. . . . My own carelessness, other people's meanness. . . . Money, ruin, poverty. . . . Giving gymnastic lessons, acting in a cinema studio, reading aloud to an old banker, nursing in a clinic in Nice, driving a taxi in the streets of Paris. . . .

The bitter fruits of defeat.

PART II

□ Toward "New Forms of Life"
(THE 1920s)

FOR MANY people, especially the young, revolution meant liberation—emancipation from the stuffy conventions of "bourgeois morality" and the oppressive bondage of the family, freedom from housework for women, the right and duty to challenge philistine conventions of all sorts, including realism in the arts. But in real life there were problems: the legislation of the early revolutionary years permitting divorce and abortion and attempting to redress gender inequalities could mean something very different from liberation in practice. People started to complain that Communist men, preaching the new morality, were exploiting women even more than their bourgeois predecessors had done.

Of course, many people were untouched by the rhetoric of emancipation and were simply concerned about living normal lives. This was easier during the New Economic Policy than it had been during the civil war. The government left the peasants largely alone for most of the 1920s, despite the Bolsheviks' perpetual fear that "kulaks"—prosperous peasants, in Marxist definition exploiters of the poor—would stage a comeback. The intelligentsia also had an easier time, establishing a precarious modus vivendi with the regime. The towns were no longer hungry, though unemployment was high and members of the old privileged classes (the "bourgeoisie") continued to bear a stigma.

Within the Communist Party, there was a general sense of unfinished revolutionary business. Lenin's illness and death in 1924 brought a major leadership struggle in which Stalin was the ultimate winner and Trotsky the loser. Despite (or because of) this, the party's stance against internal "factions" hardened, and by the late 1920s the GPU (forerunner to the NKVD and KGB) was being used against party oppositionists. The great policy issues of the 1920s were whether "kulak" power in the countryside ought to be curtailed, and how to finance the coming industrialization drive—an ambitious task which the Bolsheviks thought crucial to revolutionary (which came to mean national) survival and the achievement of socialism.

The First Five-Year Plan (1929–32), embodied the Soviet industrialization project, focusing on metallurgy, machine building, and
mining, and the development of unindustrialized regions of the
country. Many Communists and young enthusiasts saw it in a heroic
light ("There are no fortresses Bolsheviks cannot storm," said
Stalin), but it sent urban and rural living standards plummeting.
With the transition to central economic planning, the state closed
down private businesses and trade and took over distribution, inaugurating a period of rationing and intense shortages of food and
consumer goods. In a boisterous Cultural Revolution at the end of
the 1920s, the loyalty of the intelligentsia ("bourgeois specialists")
came under suspicion; hundreds of thousands of workers and Communists were sent to higher education or promoted directly to mana-
gerial jobs under a crash program to create a "new Soviet intelligentsia" (meaning a new professional and administrative elite).
Religion and the church also came under heavy attack at this time,
and discrimination against "class enemies" (via disenfranchisement,
dismissal from jobs, eviction from housing, and deprivation of rations) rose to new heights.

The most important, and ultimately most damaging, of the social-
transformation initiatives of the First Five-Year Plan period was the
collectivization of peasant agriculture, carried out against the will of
most peasants by an army of urban Communists, Komsomols, and
volunteers. Along with all-out collectivization went dekulakization,
that is, the expropriation and deportation to remote regions of the
country of several million peasants judged to be "kulaks." Collectivization was meant to solve both the kulak problem and the problem of financing industrialization. In fact, it produced a disastrous
famine in major grain-growing regions in 1932–33, provoking mass
flight from the countryside to towns, where housing remained
grossly overstrained throughout the 1930s. The growth of Gulag,
the labor camp system, was also a product of the coercive policies
of the early 1930s.

11 ☐ AGRIPPINA KOREVANOVA

My Life

☐ Korevanova's *My Life*, written in the mid-1930s, was hailed by Soviet critics as an authentic, inspirational life story of an ordinary
woman worker who overcame adversity and rose from the people to
become a member of the prestigious Union of Writers. According to
the original editorial introduction, "A. Korevanova's example will
demonstrate to the new generation that it took the Great October
Socialist Revolution to emancipate women fully . . . The more the
young women of the USSR learn about their mothers' horrible past,
the greater will be their love and appreciation for their wonderful
socialist motherland, and the more resolutely they will fight against
the vestiges of that monstrous past in order to be worthy of the era in
which they live." Korevanova (1870–1937) died one year after she
finished writing her life story.

NATURE endowed me with a sound constitution and good memory, but then sent
me down a stern, cheerless, lonely path in life. I lost my family when I was very
young; death took away my mother and then my brother and sister, and I have
been alone ever since. Every step I ever took was accompanied by the hard struggle for existence. Whenever I found a family I could call my own, doom would
strike again: that family would melt away and I would be alone again.

Such has been my life. Straining with all my might, I made my way along
winding and confused trails, over ditches and potholes, until I emerged on this
straight and bright road of ours. I would like to share my story with our young
people, who have never experienced anything like it, and never will. It is only
from stories like mine that they can learn about the way things used to be. After
they learn about it, they will appreciate even more the life they have today—the
life they are creating anew . . .

I WAS born in 1869, in Revda, into a family of workers. My family was techni-
cally free, but the spirit of serfdom and slavery still lived on. Everyone kept
waiting for something, fearing something, depending on someone.

This stifling atmosphere poisoned my childhood, made my first steps shaky
and uncertain, and haunted me for the rest of my life.

There were four men in our family, and they all worked at the same factory. My
father was a blacksmith. He could read, and so could his middle brother Egor,
although with difficulty. Both could barely write.

All four of the women, as well as a fifth one who appeared later, were illiterate.
There were three children: the two of us and Uncle Egor's son.

From Agrippina Korevanova, *Moia zhizn'* (Moscow: Sovetskii pisatel', 1938), 10–341 (abridged).

My grandfather had been a serf worker at the Demidov plant, where he worked for his master for five kopeks in paper money and one pud of rye bread a month. That was as much as he ever made. When emancipation came[1] he was too old to be hired, so he had to take up cobbling.

In his old age Grandfather turned taciturn and fanatically religious. He lived by himself in the rear hut and spent his free time copying out the church canons with a goose quill.

My grandmother, also a former serf, had no special skills and had done manual work for her mistress. She was illiterate but very sharp. She lived with her children, apart from my grandfather.

My father, Gavrila Fedorovich, was as religious and hard-working as my grandfather. In his free time he used to escape from the family to work on something. As a little girl, I loved to watch him work, though I never dared approach him. I remember how happy he was when he finished a model of some kind of machine. He sent the model off somewhere and then waited anxiously for a reply. Instead, he got into trouble because of his invention and was interrogated several times. The model ended up in our shed, where the kids used to play on it, pretending it was a boat with oars.

Several years later I heard my father say angrily to Uncle Egor: "They've come up with a new machine, which is an exact copy of mine. Those scoundrels robbed me!"

After his failure with the machine, my father decided to plant some millet. He bought two sacks of seeds somewhere, but nothing ever came of that, either. For several years the seeds stood in the shed next to his machine. Then some of them were stolen by the kids, and the rest were eaten by the chickens.

Soon after I was born, our household began to fall apart. Aunt Fedosia was married off, and my father was drafted into the army. He could not claim an exemption because Uncle Egor was not much younger than he was.

There was a lot of grief, a lot of tears. They were taking him away for twenty-five years! My grandmother and uncles decided to do everything possible to save my married father from the draft. Uncle Egor volunteered to go in his place. They went down to the recruiting station together, but Egor was rejected because of something to do with his chest.

I do not know who told my grandmother to try to find a substitute. They managed to find one, but to pay him they had to sell their cow, their horse, and their clothes. Even that was not enough, however, so they had to borrow some cash against the house. On top of everything else, my father's substitute began using his position for all it was worth. Quite often he would show up at the door and shout:

"Bring on the food, Gavrila Fedorovich, or else I won't go soldiering for you!"

Those were very hard times for my father. He worked day and night. One part of the house was taken apart and the shed was sold, but he could still not make up for the loss. Our family sank into poverty.

---

[1] That is, the emancipation of the Russian serfs in 1861.

Around the same time, my older sister and grandfather died; Uncle Lavrenty was drafted into the army, and his wife left to follow after him; and Egor, my father's middle brother, began loafing around. There were frequent arguments and fights, and my father was often blamed:

"We have all been ruined because of you."

My mother was also from a serf family. She was born and raised in the village of Krasnoiar, where everyone was a charcoal burner. They burned charcoal in huge piles for the plants of their master, Demidov.

My mother was orphaned as a young girl and was working for her uncle when my grandmother and father first saw her. They liked her, even though she was three years older than my father and had no dowry at all. My grandmother and father were not after a dowry, though—they wanted a good person. So my father got married.

When I turned seven my father started teaching me to read. He wrote out the whole alphabet himself and taught me the Church Slavonic names of all the letters. It took me only one day to learn them all. Next he moved on to syllables and finally to two-syllable words. The rest I could do on my own. I had a good memory and was improving quickly.

WHEN I was nine my mother gave birth to a boy. Her labor was difficult. My father ran off to get the midwife, but she said that she was tired after a long day's work and promised to come the next morning—as if one could wait on something like that until she was rested. My mother suffered all night, and by morning she was dead. At about seven the midwife came, glanced quickly at my mother's body, and having seen the baby from a distance, asked no questions, but simply turned around and left.

My mother was buried. There were four of us children left. I was nine; my brother was six; my sister was three; and now there was also the baby.

We were poor, so we did not have enough money to hire help. My father was thirty-three years old. Soon he found himself a wife—a young woman of twenty, named Maria Prokhorovna. In those days a twenty-year-old woman was considered an old maid. The wedding was scheduled for two weeks later, but on that day the baby died, so the wedding had to be postponed. My three-year-old sister was taken in by Uncle Egor. There were two of us left.

In July my brother came down with smallpox. He was sick for a very long time; I was small and inexperienced, and my stepmother did not care. Soon my sister got smallpox, too. My grandmother and aunt, who had taken her in, were looking after her. She was sick for about a week and then died, but my brother suffered so long that both his eyes were burned by the smallpox. I was by his side twenty-four hours a day. My stepmother never lifted a finger to help.

He died in mid-July, and I was all alone.

MY father bought a little calendar for five kopeks. I was not allowed to read during the day, and at night we did not keep a fire going. So late at night, when everybody was asleep, I would sit by the window and read by moonlight. In the

evening it was the custom in our house to light a fire in the stove and lie down for
a nap. We called it our "dusktime nap." As soon as I could get free from the new
baby, I would grab the calendar and rush to the stove. The fire in the stove always
burned unevenly, but I was afraid to open the door and had to use whatever light
I could get from the little holes in the door.

Sometimes I would see letters that were not in the Slavonic alphabet. Actually,
they were the same letters but they looked quite different in printed form. Whenever I managed to figure out a letter, I would feel like screaming for joy. If my
father was already up, I would run to him and show him the new letter and ask
him what it was called. At first he was very patient and affectionate with me, but
then he became aloof.

"I'm busy," he would say in response to all my questions.

At some point I realized that he was only like this when my stepmother was
around, and I stopped pestering him when she was there. But the moment she
would go out the door, I would snuggle up to him. "My poor, poor little girl,"
he would say, and I could see the tears in his eyes. "Our Mama's gone!" Then I
would start crying, too.

Suddenly I would hear the angry voice of my stepmother: "What are you
whimpering about? What's the matter with you?"

"She misses her mother," my father would say, coming to my defense.

"What is there to miss? And how about you, you old fool, why don't you go
ahead and cry, too?"

I would feel sorry for my father, knowing how difficult it must be for him to
listen to such things, and cry even harder—for both of us.

"Shut up!" my stepmother would yell. "And you," she would turn to my father,
"what did you get married for if you were so happy sitting around hugging your
little daughter?"

Soon after that my stepmother had another baby, and then another. Just as one
would grow up a bit, another one—or sometimes two—would come along. I
never had a moment's rest from babysitting until my wedding day.

AMONG the children who used to come over to our place was a boy named Vasia.
He did not have a father. His mother worked as a hired laborer, and his brother
was married and lived apart. Vasia lived with his mother in a tiny, tumble-down
shack. They were very poor and often went hungry, but Vasia was always cheerful and optimistic.

I liked him a lot, even though his face had been scarred by smallpox. His
laughing gray eyes used to make me smile, if only through my tears. He played
the accordion and was a good dancer.

While we were still in our teens, my father used to like Vasia for his good
nature and intelligence, and would often help him out. He even used to say—
jokingly, of course:

"He may be poor but he's honest! Good health brings wealth. With a young
fellow like that you'd be in good hands. And I could use some help . . ."

In other words, Vasia was almost like a son to him—a future son-in-law, so we did not try very hard to hide our feelings for each other.

Even my stepmother seemed pleased in her way:

"With a boy like that she wouldn't need any dowry—she could go just as she is!"

So everything seemed to be going our way when disaster struck.

Aunt Marina, who had come to live with us to help me out with the kids, told my stepmother about our relationship. We were forbidden to see each other. By then, what had been a very close friendship had grown into first love.

We started seeing each other secretly. I would go out to the garden, for example, and he would be waiting on the hill by the chapel. He would wave his handkerchief, and I would pick up the buckets and run down to the river. We could not stand and talk for a long time, so I would carry the water back and forth while he waited. I would tell him about my situation, and he would try to comfort me:

"Just wait one more year. I'll make some money and we'll get married!"

Eventually my aunt discovered us, and my stepmother got madder than ever:

"Just look at who she's gone and hooked herself up with: a beggar and a ragamuffin! You don't really think that I'd want to be related to somebody like that, do you? I'll beat this love of yours right out of you!"

Vasia and I continued to see each other—not in the open anymore but behind the school building, which was also on the river bank.

Once we were sitting on the porch talking.

"I can't find a job anywhere," said Vasia. "I am going to go live with my uncle in the city. As soon as I find something there, I'll come back for you."

I told him: "While you're going back and forth, they'll marry me off. My aunt keeps telling people that I have a good dowry, even though I don't have anything at all!"

"Okay then," said Vasia, "tomorrow I'll go see a man I know. If he hires me, I won't go anywhere. You prepare everything for the wedding, and I'll ask the man for the money."

No sooner had he said these words than my aunt appeared from around the corner and started screaming at him:

"You bum! Scarecrow! Thief! You'd better stop trying to sweet talk her! She's not for the likes of you, and don't you forget it!"

I ran home and just sat there, in the kitchen, waiting for what was going to happen next.

When my aunt got home, she started telling me how bad I was and threatening:

"Just you wait! I am going to tell your mother everything!"

I was so hurt and angry that all the blood rushed to my face at once.

"You dirty sneak! How much longer are you going to be spying on me? I'm not a child anymore. What do you want from me? I wish you'd go to the devil!"

My aunt was astonished. I had always been so quiet and meek, and suddenly this . . .

"Just you wait! When your parents get back, they'll show you 'the devil.' Just you wait!"

I was getting ready to start sweeping, but suddenly I felt so terribly hurt that I just let the broom fall to the floor.

"Go ahead and snitch if you like, but you won't have me to beat up on anymore!"

Beside myself with grief, I grabbed a piece of rope and ran to the shed, where I threw it over a beam and started making a noose . . .

My aunt realized what was happening and ran after me. She snatched the rope and tried to get it away from me, but I held on. I kept trying to put it over my head, but she was tugging on it with all her might and telling me that God would punish me.

I cried frantically:

"Let me be, you viper!"

The doors of the shed were open, and through them I could see the cemetery. Suddenly I remembered my mother and grew weak. I fell to the ground and started sobbing. My aunt took the rope off my neck and said:

"For God's sake, forgive me! I won't ever do it again! Let's go back to the house. The kids are all alone, and your mother will be back soon."

"You go! I won't go in there while I still have breath in my body!"

She got really scared and pleaded with me for a long time. Then she took me by the hand and led me, sobbing, back into the house.

I do not know what she told my parents. All I know is that I had never been beaten so badly in my life. My father kept dragging me around by the hair and kicking me with his boots. My stepmother ran after him screaming:

"Let her have it! The bitch! The whore!"

I kept crying and begging my father to stop, but he would not listen. He beat me to the point where I could not even cry anymore. I thought I was going to die . . .

I WAS seventeen, and suitors kept appearing one after the other. As soon as I would get rid of one, another would come knocking at the door.

Once, in the middle of September, when I was out cleaning the yard, a man and a woman came by. They watched me work for a while and then asked if my father was at home. I said that he had not come back yet.

"That's okay, we'll be back to see you!"

I thought: "Why do they want to see me? I'm not sick, am I?"

When my father came home, I told him about the visit.

"They must be parents trying to make a match," he said. "Don't worry, they'll be back!"

Sure enough, just as we were sitting down to eat, the couple returned. Panic-stricken, I snatched up my sewing and ran upstairs. Several minutes later my aunt came in with a hot samovar and said:

"Help me set the table. Our guests will be taking their tea in here."

When everything was ready and I was about to leave the room, my father walked in with the guests. The man came right up to me and said:

"Why are you leaving? Come sit with us. We'll chat a little bit."

"I don't have time. There's some urgent work I have to do," I said evasively. "You go ahead, I'll be back as soon as I can."

A few minutes later my aunt showed up.

"What do you think you're doing? Why are you being so stubborn? They've come to offer you a good match, and here you are sulking!"

I got angry:

"Why don't you all just leave me alone? I'm not going to get married, no matter what!"

"Do you know who their son is?"

"Yes, and I don't like him. I hate him!"

They made me come to tea. I had been to the bathhouse that day and was wearing a scarf tied under my chin. The guest said:

"Don't you want to take off your scarf so we can get a better look at you?"

Angrily, I ripped the scarf off my head. The guest seemed to bore into me with his eyes . . .

When my father and stepmother went out to say good-bye to the guests, I cleaned up really fast, went to bed (or rather, to the rug in a dark corner that served as my bed), and started thinking:

"Vasia has already made five rubles. As soon as he makes another ten, we'll go away together and get married. If my stepmother won't give me anything, that's fine with me: the first holiday, I'll put on my good dress and go to the church to pray. Vasia will come, too, and we will get married."

Full of these dreams, I fell asleep. The next morning I worked as usual, and at night my father came home.

"Do you know Arkashka, the son of Efim Korevanov?" he asked about last night's guest.

"Yes."

"Well," said my father slowly, "I have arranged for you to marry him."

I had been stirring the embers in the stove. When I heard these words, the poker fell out of my hands, and a red-hot ember flew out of the stove. Without thinking, I grabbed it with my bare hands and threw it back in.

I ran out into the yard and stood in the garden for a while. Then I went into the bathhouse and sat down on a bench. No tears came; my head was spinning. I rested my head in my hands, and just sat there without moving. I don't know how long I was there. At some point my aunt came in and touched me on the shoulder. With a shudder, I looked up at her and started crying. Without saying a word, she left. Finally I walked out of the bathhouse and looked up at the hill, hoping to see Vasia.

He was not there!

Back in the house, I found my father in the kitchen.

"Papa," I begged, "Don't make me marry him . . . I don't like him at all."

"Why don't you like him? He's a handsome fellow and a good cobbler: he makes ladies' shoes and sells them for fifteen kopeks a pair. And his family has money!"

"I don't need their money, Daddy! I don't love their son!"

"What do you mean by love? Get married first, and then start thinking about love. You'll be fine—they live well. Your husband will have his own shop, and you'll be your own mistress, not some miserable maid. If you marry a poor man, you'll have to work, too."

"I'd rather work than marry him!"

"That's enough," said my father, "Don't be a fool. It's done."

"Papa, please don't make me marry him!" Sobbing, I threw myself at his feet.

"Stop blubbering! I told you it was done! If you refuse, I'll kick you out of the house with nothing! Not even a passport!"

VASIA was away, looking for a job. The preparations for the wedding were in full swing, but I continued to wait and hope. "If only Vasia would come back!" I thought. "Let my father turn me out! In the worst case, I'll tell the priest that I'm being married against my will, and he won't marry us!" Meanwhile, my fiancé kept coming by almost every day. I thought he was so repulsive I could not even look at him.

There was no word from Vasia, so I decided to run away. I put a few things in a little bundle and went out into the garden.

When I saw the church, I stretched out my arms, and cried:

"Mother of God, protect me! Tell me what to do!"

Then I saw the cemetery where my mother was buried. I fell to the ground and sobbed even louder:

"Oh Mama! Dearest Mama! If you were alive, they wouldn't be doing this to me! Oh my own dear Mama!"

They heard me inside the house, and my aunt came out. Hard-hearted as she was, she couldn't resist my tears and, sitting down beside me, started crying herself:

"Don't cry, dear Grusha,[2] don't cry, or you'll get sick, God forbid!"

"I wish I would get sick and die!" I said through my tears.

"There's nothing you can do, such is a woman's lot," she said and led me back into the house.

I kept trying to run away, but my beloved seemed to have vanished into thin air. I wanted to tell the priest that I was being married against my will, but it was all arranged in such a way that the priest never asked me if I was willing."

Farewell, joyless maidenhood!

MY father-in-law ruled his family with an iron hand. He was a grouch and a bully. My husband had also been forced to marry against his will. One day he told me the whole story:

"My father ordered me to marry, but I didn't want to. At first he tried to convince me, but then he started threatening that he'd kick me out of the house. He even beat me."

---

[2] Diminutive for Agrippina.

That Christmas we went over to my father's house. As we were walking home, I noticed that my husband was a little tipsy. When we got home, we found my father-in-law asleep on the floor of our room. He had never slept in our room before. My husband pretended to be completely drunk and collapsed onto the bed.

Not suspecting anything, I started to undress. Suddenly, my father-in-law reached up and grabbed hold of my blouse. I got away, but he jumped up and started running after me around the room. I had no place to go. First I hid behind the table; then I climbed up on the bed, crawled under the blanket, and just lay there shivering. I could see that my husband was watching his father, but he never said a word. Thinking that his son was drunk, the old man started dragging me off the bed. Finally, my husband could not stand it anymore.

"Dad, what are you up to?"

The old man, furious at his failure, ran downstairs and woke everybody up. Cursing at the top of his lungs and throwing my things out into the yard, he started to scream hysterically:

"I want her out of here! To hell with her! The bitch! She dragged me around by my beard!"

His daughter, my husband's sister, cried:

"What have you done? Go apologize, or you'll be in bad trouble!"

My husband was silent. I kept shivering.

She grabbed me by the hand and dragged me off the bed. I got dressed and followed her down the stairs.

My father-in-law was sitting on his bed with a mean smirk on his face.

"Tell him you're sorry!" shouted my husband's sister, giving me a hard push in the back.

I fell down on my knees at the old man's feet.

"Please forgive her!" With both hands, she pushed my head down and said while also bowing down herself: "Pardon her!"

I felt completely numb: no tears, no words, no thoughts of any kind. Finally I got up quietly and went back to my room. There I got undressed and climbed into bed. Then I started to cry. Did my husband hear me crying? I think so, but he kept quiet. I went to sleep determined to drown myself.

After that my life turned into a nightmare. Almost every day I was beaten and told to follow the example of the other daughter-in-law. Afterward our neighbors told me that she had won the old man's good graces by showing him "respect."

It is hard to remember now at what point I first started writing. I think it was the year my father-in-law died. I had done some writing before then as well, but not very seriously. I would jot something down on a piece of paper and then lose it. But this time I bought myself a notebook. When I finished it, I started a new one, and so it went.

What made me want to write? I think there were two main reasons.

First of all, my life was so sad that I kept thinking of suicide, and so I decided to describe all my sufferings, so that after my death people would discover my notebooks and find out what had made me want to kill myself.

The second reason was my rage and horror at the unfairness of life; my protest against the oppression of women; my sympathy for the poor; and my hatred for a fat wallet. I wrote about all this in poor literary style but with great bitterness and passion. There was no practical use in it, of course, but at least it provided some relief. I never thought of publishing it. I would just write about somebody and then read it to my husband. We would laugh over it, and that would be the end of it. My husband knew about my notebooks, but neither he nor the old man gave me any trouble over them: in fact, they were even proud that their woman was so educated.

Finally (although this does not really count as a reason), it happened once that having looked through all my notebooks, I put them together and really liked the fact that they resembled a book. For the first time, I had the frightening yet thrilling thought: "What if all this got printed in a real book—a book that people could read?" It made my head spin just to think of it, and I resumed my work with even greater ardor.

In 1902 there was a terrible typhoid epidemic. People were dying like flies. In the middle of July my husband got sick and died.

After he died I also came down with typhoid. I was all alone, and had to stay in bed. The only people I saw were my husband's creditors who kept coming in to steal things.

When I could finally get up, I looked around—and saw nothing but the bare walls. Everything had been stolen. Somebody had even taken our horse.

One lame cow was my only inheritance. There were also some sheep, but I had to sell them shortly afterward.

While I was sick, my father, under the pretext that I was dying, had attempted to become the guardian of all my property.

When I recovered a bit, one of the elders came by and said:

"You owe us a hundred rubles. You've got to pay up, do you hear?"

"Okay."

I sold something else and gave the money to the elder. I had nothing left. I lived in my house until the fall, when I was thrown out because of my debts. I am not going to describe what happened next; I do not even want to think about how people from all over descended on me and snatched up every little thing I had. Finally I just left it all, grabbed my lame cow, and set off for Ekaterinburg.

Whatever was not sold was taken by my father. My stepmother went through my chest and took all the most valuable things, including my manuscript. When I asked her: "Where's my notebook?" she answered gleefully: "I burned it in the stove." I felt like crying.

Sometime later, I ran into my father at the market. He seemed very happy to see me. He grabbed my hand and started crying.

"Grusha, dear! Is it really you? I had already prayed for the repose of your soul!"

"I don't have a father!" I said and pulled my hand away.

"What do you mean, Grusha? I am your father!"

"If I am your daughter, why did you treat me the way you did?"

"It was the devil's work . . ."

But I still loved my father, and we soon became reconciled again.

IT is hard to believe all the different jobs I had! I was a construction worker, a stevedore, a dishwasher, a baker, and a maid. Finally I became a nurse.

MARCH 1, 1917. The hospital was full of people. The patients were agitated, demanding access to newspapers, relatives, and friends. The management wouldn't allow it. The POWs had been placed under special supervision.

One of the nurses came in with incredible news:

"The tsar has abdicated!"

How? Why? What was going to happen? What should we do?

MARCH 10, 1917. Almost everyone had left and gone into town. I also decided to go. When I got to the gate I saw our supervisor standing there with his whole family. He looked at me but, amazingly enough, said nothing. He did not even ask me who had stayed behind in the ward. He had never let me leave before without questioning me first.

I felt like I was running on wooden legs, and it seemed to me that I could almost see the main street right through the brick buildings that were standing in the way. When I finally arrived, I could hear the music playing and I saw a huge cloud—black underneath and red on top—floating over the street. It was all the red banners and flags that were being held up by hundreds and thousands of people. It was hard to believe that there were so many people in our city. I peered excitedly at the banners, trying to read and understand the words inscribed on them.

Some troops marched solemnly by, in step. Every soldier had a red flower on his chest. Even their bayonets had blossomed with tiny red flowers. The soldiers were followed by workers and office employees carrying flags—and still more flags. Oh, how many flags there were!

Books were being sold on the sidewalk. I moved closer to take a look: *What Is a Republic? What Are Soviets? The Revolutionary Dictionary.*

Suddenly I caught sight of an odd group of people, mostly women. How pathetic they looked, how timid and poor! There was a little priest with them, too— the only one in all that crowd.

"They must be refugees," I thought. "There are so many of them in Ekaterinburg."

After them came a huge column with a very large, heavy flag. How much power was in that flag, how confident the standard-bearer's stride! He was a tall, broad-shouldered man in a slightly faded blouse . . . I could even see the knotty blue veins sticking out on his hand against the brown flagpole.

That column was like a hurricane. Whole groups of people kept rushing to join it.

"It's the Soviets! The Soviets!"

But what was written on the flag? The wind kept tearing at the cloth, and I could not make out the words, but I could feel my new copy of *What Are Soviets?* in my hand. I would know before long.

. . . After I had fed the patients, we started in on the books. We read until midnight . . .

March 11. All the hospital employees were running around with red ribbons on. There was a lot of loud talking and laughing. The supervisor did not even come by today. I saw him in the office and, oh, how obsequious he was! He even asked me:

"Did you see the procession yesterday?"

In the evening, once again, we read the books I had bought on the sidewalk. The patients split into two groups: those who were for the soviets and those who wanted the Constituent Assembly. I was very confused: if both were against the tsar and for popular rule, then what was the difference? I needed to do more reading. I needed to go into town . . . Two different parties could not be for the same thing.

JULY 8. In our hospital everybody was under the supervisor's influence and no-body knew for sure which party was on our side . . .

I was surprised that no one came down from the city to explain things to us. Over and over again, we would huddle together in some corner and whisper to one another:

"What number are you going to vote for?"

"Number Six. What about you?"

"Number Six? You've got to be kidding! That's all the rich folks . . . I was thinking about Number Five."

"Didn't the supervisor say Number Six?"

"Who cares what he said? Think about yourself, not the supervisor . . . He's on Number Six. You don't really want to vote for him, do you? I'm certainly not going to vote for Number Six. If not Five, then something else, but definitely not Six!"

We were wandering around in the dark. Some people did end up voting for Number Six, but most went for Number Two, the SRs. Ten of us voted for Number Five, the Bolsheviks, although, to be honest, none of us knew who the Bolsheviks were or what they wanted. The only thing we knew was that the Bolsheviks were for the poor people.

SOMEBODY—I can't remember who—told me that there was going to be a meeting of the League for Women's Equality on Zlatoustovskaia Street. I had never heard of a women's league before, so I went. There were a lot of people there. On the stage were two intelligentsia ladies: one sat at a desk writing something while the other one talked. I listened for a while and said to myself: "I know all this stuff. I've read about it in books!" She was talking about the way the wives and daughters of the boyars used to live in the old days—how they were kept locked up, and so forth.

She was followed by a woman who looked like a worker. Some women who knew her started whispering:

"That's Mashka Zavialova! I wonder what she's going to say!"

Mashka did not mince words:

"Comrades! What are we doing sitting here listening to stories about the daughters and wives of the boyars.[3] What do we need it for? We need to be fighting for our rights and for the improvement of the position of our women!"

The crowd grew agitated. People started buzzing around like bees in a hive: some were for Mashka, others were against her. Mashka finished up with:

"Comrade women! What are we doing at this meeting? This meeting is not for us!"

After that, all those who agreed with Mashka left the room. I left, too.

I went straight to the revolutionary committee and asked in a loud voice:

"How do I sign up?"

They all looked up at me in surprise. "Let them look if they want," I thought.

They pointed out the comrade that I needed to talk to. He seemed almost like a living corpse, he was so skinny and emaciated. He asked me where I lived, what I did for a living, and why I wanted to join the party. I told him everything. He listened carefully and said:

"It all sounds good. We'll take you in as a sympathizer! Come by in a couple of weeks, and we'll give you a card."

Two weeks later I went back to get my card, but the sign was no longer there.

"Where is the revolutionary committee?"

"They've moved."

So I went to their new location. There I was told that all the lists had been lost during the move. Without any fuss, they took down all the information again and postdated the application.

"Come to the city meeting at the theater on August 25."

On the evening of the 25th I took a seat high up in the gallery, so that I could see and hear everything really well. First they discussed current business, and then turned over the floor to the comrade who had interviewed me at the revolutionary committee. I had never heard louder applause in all my life. When it finally grew quiet, he said:

"Comrades, I have risen from the dead!"

There was more loud applause, and then he talked about how he had been in a White prison and how they had tortured him. He had been hurt so badly he could barely move. My heart ached with hatred for the Whites.

Finally, I had found my path in life!

WHAT a coincidence! The 1921 celebration of the triumph of the proletariat and Easter happened to fall on the same day.

At ten in the morning we received our packed lunches and began preparing for our march to the city. At twelve we left the hospital, carrying our banners and

[3] Boyars—noble Russian families dating to medieval times.

singing songs, but the singing never really took off. We kept starting new songs but, for some reason, we never finished any of them. In Red Square we formed into columns. There was a children's column ahead of us. The boys were all wearing red shirts and blue slacks, and the girls had on red dresses and shawls. Then a special bus arrived to take the children to May First Square. We followed behind them. I did not get to see the demonstration because I had to go to the Workers' Palace to greet the heroes of labor.

In the great hall stood seven long tables; the walls were covered with wreaths and red posters; in the middle of the hall was a red banner with the names of the heroes written on it in gold lettering—four hundred of them in all. The tables were covered with white tablecloths, and every participant was given a little piece of cloth instead of a paper napkin. The dinner consisted of three courses: soup, pork chops, and an apple compote. There was lemonade, too. Then came tea with sweet cake and meat pies. We female Communists served the guests and ate with them, too. After dinner we were all given tickets to the theater to see a play by Lunacharsky.[4]

"Don't bite off more than you can chew," as the saying goes. Sometimes I feel I already have too big a mouthful, but what can I do if I am so hungry, and it's good for me as well? I know, for example, that I cannot write well, but I want to write. I am dying to write. Can't you hear me?! I am shouting for everyone to hear: "Help me! Teach me!" I do not know how to write, but I want to write—I want it so badly that sometimes my eyes close from exhaustion, my head falls down onto the pillow; and still my hand reaches out for a pen and a piece of paper. Every day three separate voices argue within me. The first one shouts: I want to write! The second one says: I can't! And the third one whispers: You need to sleep! You need to rest! But the strongest of all is the one that shouts: I want to write! I want to write!

I need help, so that my thoughts do not disappear in vain as they did in the past but instead will be able to take on the right shape and maybe even do some good. Is it possible that such a passionate desire will result in nothing?

In December 1921 I was transferred to the children's home (that was what they started calling the city orphanage).

Those were very difficult days. During that one month, we had to "process" more than two thousand children.

Just to think that fourteen provinces would be hit by a bad harvest all in the same year! . . . Hunger drove the peasants to the south in search of food. They fled there, leaving their homes, families, and children behind . . . Many of them got sick on the way—from malnutrition, overcrowding, and typhoid lice. Many of them died. Their children became orphans. Where could a child go? To a children's home, of course!

---

[4] A. V. Lunacharsky (1875–1933)—prominent Bolshevik writer and intellectual, first People's Commissar of Enlightenment (1918–29).

There was no work. The adults had nothing to eat, and here was a place where children were being fed.

Women would get together and whisper:

"I heard they don't accept children who have parents."

"But we won't tell them that we're their mothers. We'll say that these are homeless children, and that will be the end of it! Don't worry, they'll take them in and feed them."

According to our lists, all the children in the children's home were orphans, but every once in a while some child would come up and say:

"Aunt Dasha, let me go home!"

"What do you mean? Where would you go? You don't have any parents."

"Yes, I do! Let me go!"

The teacher would tell him that he couldn't leave, but the boy would run away anyway and then come back.

"Where have you been?"

"Nowhere!" the child would say stubbornly. All attempts to get any information out of him would be in vain—he just would not talk.

The years 1921 and 1922 were fraught with bad harvests and hunger in the Urals. We at the children's home experienced food shortages, too. The children received only three-quarters of a pound of bread a day. That was not enough, of course. All they could think about was getting more to eat.

"Today Aunt Mania gave me a loaf of bread this big for tea!"

"And I only got a tiny little piece. I didn't get to eat the loaf."

"Hey guys! It's only eleven o'clock! A whole half hour to go before we get to eat!"

Whenever we entered the rooms, we would see potato peels all over the stove: that meant the children had been frying and eating them. We tried everything we could to prevent them from doing this, but it was impossible to be everywhere at once! They would sneak into the kitchen and either beg or steal some potato peels and then fry them. You would throw them away, and then—lo and behold—there would be more than ever on the stove.

We would tell them: "Children, it's bad for you!" But they would reply: "No, it's not. It's potatoes. We ate grass before and we're still alive."

Others would shout: "Give us more bread, and then we won't eat potato peels!"

Even so, they were better off with us than at home. We did not have enough bread, but still, it was bread after all, not grass, and we supplemented it with soup and cereal.

The children often talked about what they had had to eat before. "While Mother was alive, we at least had weeds to eat, but after she died, there weren't even any weeds. I was ready to chew on pebbles!"

Little by little the food situation began to improve. The children stopped frying potato peels, but the fights over bread and potatoes continued. Still, it was nothing like that winter.

The clothes the children wore were not good, but at least they were not rags. They were old, but mended and clean, and some kids even got brand new clothes.

Now, about bathing: when the first children arrived at our children's home, it was hard to believe how dirty they were. Meanwhile, we did not have either bathtubs or a bathhouse, and there wasn't even any place to heat up water. The rooms were very cold. There was no wood, and the stoves did not work: all the smoke ended up in the rooms. We found some iron stoves, but what could we do about the wood?

So we would gather wood chips or take our horse to the forest. The horse was hungry, too. There was no fodder, and she did not have the strength to carry any kind of load.

The children did not have any warm clothes or shoes. How could they go out in the cold? Finally, we had a stroke of luck. Once, while I was rummaging in the closet, I found an ancient sheepskin coat, all torn and dirty. We spent two days cleaning, combing, and mending it. After that the kids had something to wear when they went out to get wood. They would wear it during the day, and then we would mend it at night—it was so threadbare. It was covered with patches of all possible shapes and colors—but even so, it was a real winter coat!

There was an old shed that had belonged to somebody else next to our home. The children removed one log after another until there was nothing left. In the rare cases when we were given some wood, it was of no use: the wood was damp and did not burn.

Whenever we did manage to start a fire, we would bring a bucket of water and heat it up on top of the stove. Then we would put the horse trough next to it, and our bath tub would be ready.

We spent many a sleepless night sewing sleeves onto shirts and fixing pants and coats. The same was true for shoes. We would find a torn felt boot and cut out the sole, but there would normally not be enough for a whole sole. So we would tie several pieces together with a cord, and the sole would be ready.

The director of our home spent whole days running around town trying to find one thing or another. Whenever he was promised something, he would run back all excited, the tails of his trench coat flapping in the breeze. We knew what that meant. If he was running at full steam, the news must be good, and we would wait for him like children waiting for their father to come home. He would start shouting from the door: "I managed to get something again!"

There was an empty building in our courtyard, and our director obtained permission to use it as a bathhouse. First, the building needed to be repaired and restructured. But where were we to get the bricks, wood, or workers? So once again our director had to run around town knocking on various doors.

Finally we had a bathhouse of our own. It was open almost every day. The children were divided into groups, with each group bathing once every two weeks.

We combated dirt with all the means at our disposal, but because of overcrowding there was a lot of lice. Typhus, trachoma, and other epidemics broke out.

Doctor Paramonova spent whole days in our home. We hired a nurse. Two of the teachers, Nemeshaeva and Maltseva, caught typhus and died. Nor was I spared myself. On February 22 I came down with typhus and hovered between life and death for a long time. Nobody believed I would survive. Only in the summer did the epidemics begin to subside.

I NEEDED to interview one family in town and two more out by the Verkhisetsky factory. On the way back I stopped by the office of the district Department of Education to hand in my report. I was told to go see the secretary. When I entered, he said:

"We're sending you to the village of Poldnevaia to work in the local reading hut!"[5]

I was speechless. I just stood there as if I had been struck by lightning.

"Why are you looking at me like that? It's going to be a lot easier for you. Here you have a hard job, but over there it will only be books. Anyway, we need a permanent employee there, and you're the only one we can send! . . ."

I simply could not understand: "What's going on? How can this be? Are they getting rid of me? What about the children?. . . The commune is not ready yet. What will happen to the kids when they reach the end of their terms? Where will they go? Will they just leave, each going his own way? . . . "You can't do this! I'm not going anywhere! I don't know a thing about village work, and the commune is not ready yet!"

"Well, they'll just have to finish without you!"

"I'm not going! Let me finish my work with the commune, and then we'll see! . . ."

"What do you mean you aren't going? . . . The party organization is sending you!" said the secretary and looked at me severely. "It will be easier for you . . . We'll visit you there . . . Go ahead and get the paperwork from Kosheleva. It's all been decided anyway!"

Without saying a word I went out into the corridor. For a long time I just stood there looking out the window. Then, still in a daze, I walked into Kosheleva's office. I did not speak. My brain was working feverishly: "Should I refuse? . . . But they'll send me anyway! . . . It's the party cell! Oh, dear! . . . What should I do with the kids? What will happen to the girls when they hear that I'm leaving? . . ."

Kosheleva finished writing and, with a guilty look, handed me the papers. Without saying anything, I went out into the street. After a while, I remembered the papers and stopped to look at them, but my eyes were clouded over. With great difficulty I read about my new appointment.

The anger grew inside of me. Why? Why are they depriving me of my favorite work? Who's behind all this? Could it be the new director, with whom I didn't get along?

---

[5] Reading huts (*izby-chital'ni*) were established in many villages to help in the campaign to end illiteracy.

Thinking these thoughts I had been walking around town without noticing where I was going. Suddenly I looked up and found myself in the square. I had passed my house a long time ago. As I walked back and was approaching the gate, the pain I was feeling grew even worse. If any of the children saw me now, they would know right away that something was wrong. They would start asking questions. "What am I to do? Should I tell them? No . . . I don't think I should . . . I must prepare them first. . . . But if I don't, they'll find out anyway! . . ."

I sneaked into my room and lay down on my bed. Normally I would go into the girls' room first and see what they were doing, but this time I didn't.

I said to myself: "Let me calm down first, and then I'll go." Suddenly the door opened slowly and a girl's head appeared. She saw me and cried out "It's Auntie Grusha! She's back . . . How did you come in? . . . We didn't see you! . . ."

The other girls came running and started talking all at once.

I was lying in my bed, watching them: "My dear little sparrows!"

Then I said: "Girls, I'm very tired. Go to your room. I'll get some rest, and then I'll come in to see you."

I did not sleep at all that night. The next day I went around like a sleepwalker. The girls noticed it. "Auntie, why do you look so sad?"

Their worried looks and questions nearly broke my heart, but I continued to lie: "I'm not feeling very well."

Soon I began to pack. The girls noticed.

"Auntie, why are you packing your things? Are you leaving?"

"Where are you going? Why?"

"I'd like to rest up in my apartment in town. I'll spend some time there, and when I get well, I'll come back."

The girls did not believe me. They started crying and asking me questions. Fortunately, there were no teachers around. I had to calm them down and at the same time try to fight my own feelings. We decided I would spend no more than two months in my new apartment.

"We'll come to see you off!"

"Okay, girls! Go to bed, and when the time comes, I'll wake you up."

Somehow I got rid of them. I sat there not knowing what to do. The tears were pouring down my cheeks. Then I turned away from the window. Oh, well! I knew I had to leave immediately. I grabbed my bag. I was going to leave the building but . . . my feet carried me to the girls' room . . . They were already asleep.

It is impossible to describe how I felt.

I wanted to kiss them all—my sweet girls, my dear ones, my daughters . . .

I cannot remember running out of the house, crossing the courtyard, and walking through the gate—I cannot remember anything at all! When I finally came to, I was already far from the house. I buttoned up my coat, put my bag on my shoulder, and began to walk more slowly. My thoughts, however, grew ever more painful.

People may not believe me, but that is how it was.

People may tell me: "But those were not your children!"

No, they were not! But as I do not have any children, they do not have a mother. They are just as homeless as I am!

In Ekaterinburg I was told to go to the village of Kosulino as a reading hut employee.

Both the executive committee and the village soviet showed a great deal of understanding and tried to comply with all my requests. The population was friendly toward me. In other words, things got off to a great start.

I had not heard anything about a visit from the secretary of the district party committee, so when I saw him in my reading room I was surprised: "What was he doing here?"

He explained the reason for his visit:

"You need to start a party cell! That's why I am here."

After a short meeting we formed a six-person cell. I was elected secretary. We were nervous about our future work. We were all new in the party; two from the Lenin Levy,[6] with only one year of party experience, and three candidate members. Nobody knew anything about party work. I came up with a plan of activities according to district committee instructions, and we set out to implement it as best we could.

As a way to begin our work among women, we decided to have Red Get-togethers.

On the first day, I sat waiting. At about eleven o'clock the women started coming in. Some had brought their spinning, some their knitting, and others their children. As they were coming in they joked:

"The guests have arrived. What are you serving?"

"Is the samovar ready? We are here to drink some tea!"

I welcomed them warmly:

"Please come in. There is enough room for everybody. To tell you the truth, I didn't think of the samovar, but I do have some nice things for you here!"

"Actually, it would be great to have a samovar," I thought to myself. I had not worked much in villages and did not know the customs very well, and so it had not occurred to me.

The first time, only the women who lived nearby came. We talked for a while about this and that, and then somehow the conversation turned to the question of contagious diseases: who had caught what, when, and how. At that very moment someone brought in the papers. One of the women noticed the headline, "Protect the village!" and asked me to read the article.

According to the story, a priest in a certain village had syphilis, and by kissing the cross the whole village had caught it from him.

[6] Lenin Levy—massive effort to increase Communist Party membership upon Lenin's death in January 1924.

"Where did this sickness come from?" the people wondered.

Finally, it was all cleared up. The priest was taken away, and the church was closed down because everything there had been contaminated, from the cross to the communion plate and spoon to the handkerchief used to wipe the lips of those who took communion.

No sooner had I stopped reading than the room was filled with noise. The women said with revulsion:

"See, a thing like that would never even occur to us women. We kiss the cross and go to communion. We even take our children with us because we think it is something sacred, and then lo and behold, a thing like this happens. Come to think of it, you really never know what kind of priest you are going to get!"

It was a fine April morning. The bountiful sun began sending its precious rays to the earth: "Live on, Earth!"

With the sunrise all the birds, big and small, started going about their daily activities. The starling whistled with great dedication as he jumped from one twig to another behind the bird-cherry leaves. The roosters, awakened by the starling's song, rose slowly to their feet, flapped their wings, and confounded the starling with their loud "cock-a-doodle-doos." The trees and bushes also began to stir. All this promised a fine day—the kind that is known in the Urals as a "bee day."

The men and their horses appeared in the street, the metal parts of the harnesses tinkling as they went toward the field. Next came the ringing voices of the women who were going to fetch water. They all gathered around the spring dying for a chat, but there was nothing to talk about. All the previous day's news had been discussed, and nothing new had happened during the night. Suddenly they were joined by another woman. She was full of self-importance, for she was bringing some news.

"Have you heard the news?"

"What news?" the women asked anxiously.

"Paraskeva's daughter had her baby."

"Really? When?"

"Last night. It's a boy."

This caused a great commotion and a lot of curiosity. How were they going to baptize him: in church or the new way?

"The Soviet way, I guess, because the grandparents are nonbelievers. The grandmother is a women's delegate, and the grandfather is something or other in the reading hut. One of their sons is in the Komsomol, and the other one is a Pioneer—the whole family are Communists."

"And that woman from the reading hut won't let them go to the church. She'll talk them out of it."

I heard about this conversation from a women's delegate who was at the spring. I told her:

"He's already been here and told me that they'd had a son and that they wanted to Octobrize[7] him. We agreed to have it done on the seventh. I'm writing the invitations right now. Could you help me?"

On April 7 the representatives of the district party committee and the patron factories arrived.[8] We adorned the stage and gave the parents the best seats, so they could be seen from far away. The room was full. Everybody was curious to see what the new, Soviet "baptism" was going to be like.

I opened the proceedings. The presidium was very large. All the city guests were there, as well as the representatives from the village organizations, the parents, and the delegates who had been chosen by the participants.

I made a speech about the new forms of domestic life. The crowd listened attentively. Then the parents were asked what they wished to name the child. The parents said Vladimir, after Vladimir Ilich Lenin. We set it down accordingly. A representative of our patrons pinned a red star to the baby's clothes, presented him with a blanket, a warm shirt, and stockings, and put a cap on him. His mother received ten meters of calico.

After that the Komsomol secretary took the floor and declared that by the decision of the local cell the newborn Vladimir had been, as of that day, inducted into the Octobrist organization.[9] He went on to congratulate the parents.

The district party committee offered their own gift—a book on the history of the party. Many other people congratulated the parents on the birth of their son. Then the Octobrism was over. At the end the members of the village drama society presented a play called *A Woman's Benefit*.

The Octobrism was like a big holiday. People talked about it for a long time afterward. Some were impressed by the fact that the Soviet "baptism" had turned out to be so much fun. Others envied the mother and the baby for getting so many presents and for being honored in such a way.

IN October, by decision of the district Department of Education, I was relieved of my responsibilities in Kosulino.

When I asked for a reason they told me: "You've organized their work. Now it's time for you to go someplace else.

I really did not want to leave Kosulino. I had gotten used to the people and to my work there.

WHEN I arrived at the education department, they asked me: "Where do you want to go?"

I replied: "I don't want a ready-made position. Give me a village where nothing has been done yet."

The department head was only too happy to hear that. He suggested Tavatiu or Mikhailovsk. I would have gone to Tavatiu but I am afraid of water, and to get

[7] Octobrize—to perform a Soviet "baptism."
[8] Many villages had so-called patrons (*shefy*) in the city, who were supposed to provide political, ideological, and economic guidance and supervision.
[9] Octobrist organization—Communist organization for children seven to nine years of age.

there you needed to cross a lake. So I decided to go to the Mikhailovsk District. I was given a pass.

The Mikhailovsk district party committee appointed me head of the reading hut in the village of Tashkinovo, thirty-five versts from Mikhailovsk.

This village was the most isolated place in the district. Most of the population were members of religious sects. In other words, it was an old, prerevolutionary village.

Agitation against me began on the very first day. The woman who guarded the reading hut told the other women: "She's here to deceive our women. Don't have anything to do with her. Who needs her, the old hag! Her place is on top of the stove, but here she is, meddling in the library, scaring the young folks away."

What surprised me was that there had been a reading hut manager there before, but no traces of any work were to be seen. There was no paperwork, either. There were two little notebooks, but I could not decipher them.

I met the chairman of the village soviet, who was also the head of the party cell. "It's very cold in the reading hut," I complained. "You could catch a cold. Is there any way to heat it up? There's no light, either, and the reading hut is used mainly at night! . . ."

"You can't use the stove—it smokes, and we don't have an iron stove. So you'll just have to make do. As for a lamp, we can give you one."

The chairman got us some kerosene from the soviet warehouse. He was okay, a nice man, but the caretaker of the reading hut was a terrible nuisance.

Once, after a party meeting, I decided to stay and work, but the warden came and took away the lamp. "This lamp belongs to the soviet," she said. "You can't use it!"

Then an inspector from the district party committee came out and really gave me hell. He said that I was not doing anything and that nothing at all had been accomplished, and he even wrote in the visitors' book that my work was no good at all. "What is going on?" I thought. "It's only my eighth day here, after all!"

We organized the October celebrations as best we could. One of the party members gave a talk on how the October Revolution had taken place and what it had given to the peasants.

After the talk we showed some film strips and then a short play called *The Trial of the Worker Potekhin Who Subjected His Wife to Beating*. More than two hundred people were present, half of them women. There was a discussion after the play. At first the women were shy and kept silent, but when the men started talking, the women, too, demanded to be heard.

Asked whether the trial was fair and whether the accused had received sufficient punishment, the women said no, he had not, while the men said he should have been acquitted altogether. At the end of the evening the kids started playing games, and everybody stayed until late at night.

They finally thought about us. The Mikhailovsk district executive committee sent us an iron stove, ten pounds of kerosene, paper, notebooks, pencils, and envelopes. We still needed a bookcase, an index card holder, a shelf for the book exhibit, stools, benches, and a ceiling lamp.

A village club manager and head of the agricultural club were elected. Then a school for the liquidation of illiteracy was opened. Thirty-three people signed up. A local branch of the "Down with Illiteracy" society was started. Besides the agricultural club there were clubs devoted to cooperatives, politics, soviet construction, the study of nature, production, military training, and medicine. Twenty-four youngsters signed up for the military training club. At the end of the very first meeting they received their first lesson: marching in step. They marched a long way from the village and came back singing. The peasants looked out their windows or came out of their houses, marveling:

"Just look at them—it's as if there were just one man walking!"

"It sure is better this way—at least they aren't drunk and fighting."

And did they ever drink! It was always some kind of holiday, so there was constant drinking in one village or another. One night some drunkard drove his sled into a fence. His horse got its head hurt, and he himself flew out of the sled, lost his hat, and was dragged through the snow for a long time. It was lucky that our peasants caught the horse, put the drunk owner into the sled, and sent the horse down the road again—where to, no one knew.

And how those women drank and "fooled around"—it was shameful to watch! I started talking to the men about their drinking—about how it hurt the economy. I counted the amount of money lost over Christmas and came up with the huge sum of more than two thousand rubles.

I told them: "That's enough to buy a tractor! And that is only this community of forty-eight houses! The other villages are all doing the same!"

The men told me: "We understand, but we want to have fun, too. When summer comes, there won't be any time to have fun. And besides, our homebrew is so cheap: one pud of flour makes sixteen bottles!

WE invited people to become members of the cooperative. Nobody came. "We can do without cooperation," they said. "We had a cooperative before. We gave five rubles each, but those guys spent it all on vodka and on building houses for themselves, and the cooperative went broke."

It was a good cause, and it was a shame that it had been so badly mismanaged. The chairman was a good person, but he had been too trustful. Nobody had helped him. Sverdlovsk was far away, and the local party cell had been totally inactive.

We organized a conference dedicated to the memory of our writer from the Urals, Mamin-Sibiriak. We asked those participants who had books by Mamin-Sibiriak to bring them to the reading hut so that others could read them, too.

Then I went to Sverdlovsk[10] for a medical checkup. I was pronounced disabled, unfit for work. What was I to do? My work was just beginning, and now I had to stop! What a shame! If I quit now, all the new activities would stop. No, come what may, I had to stay on till summer.

---

[10] Earlier in the memoir, Korevanova refers to this Urals city by its prerevolutionary name, Eka-terinburg.

I learned that my landlady was going to host a women's get-together and de-cided to take advantage of it in order to start my work among women. Having first discussed it with the landlady on the night before the party, I had hung up some posters and a newspaper on the walls of her room and had brought in the book *A Woman's Gain*. When the women arrived, I asked if they wanted me to read to them. They all agreed willingly, sat me down in the middle, and listened very carefully. They liked the book and began talking about their own husbands. They all agreed that women should get involved in soviet and volunteer work. "If there had been a woman to watch over our cooperative, it might not have gone broke. There's got to be a woman in the soviet, too, or we'll never get out from under our husbands' thumbs!"

Without their realizing it, I steered the conversation toward the necessity of creating a women's section. The boldest among them said: "Go ahead and an-nounce a women's meeting. We'll all be there."

To drive the point home I offered to read the little book *The Rights of the Peasant Woman* and *Some Advice for Mothers*, a supplement to *Krest'ianskaia gazeta* [a newspaper for peasants]. They listened, and then the discussion resumed.

"See what kind of new law we've got—it takes care of women, too! And we didn't even know about it!"

"Do your husbands subscribe to the newspaper?" I asked them.

"Yes, they do."

"Have they ever read this booklet or any of these articles to you?"

"They certainly haven't," said the women. "They don't read or show them to us. They probably tore them all up to make cigarettes."

Finally, when I had read to them the laws on marriage, divorce, the rights of mothers and their children, the right of peasant women to own land, and assis-tance to women, they became really excited.

"You've got to study," I said, and told them about the school for the liquidation of illiteracy.

"We don't have time to study," the women answered. "We've got to weave and work around the house."

Then I showed them the poster "The Use of Machines in Agriculture" and explained to them that if you use machines you have more free time. Once again, we discussed the problem of illiteracy and compared the position of a literate woman to that of an illiterate one.

"That's right! If we could read like the men, we could do a lot on our own. But nobody explains anything to us or talks to us, and here we are, still living in the past."

There was a great deal of talking and arguing. At the end, everyone was very pleased. They asked me when they could come back for advice. Taking advantage of this mood, I suggested that they join the "Down with Illiteracy" society. Five women signed up and paid their membership dues right away. Looking at these women I, too, became very excited and forgot all about my illness.

Thus, slowly but surely, I began to fulfill my plan. Soon afterward there was the first meeting of the club for the study of natural sciences. Twelve people signed up, most of them poor peasants. They defined the goals of the club, decided to meet once a week, and elected the teacher as manager. It was hard to say how things would go, but I was happy that there was still time to get something done before the spring season.

Then a group of first-graders were brought to see the reading hut. They were so little, but each one had a notebook and asked questions—and in such a serious, businesslike manner! I was so moved I almost cried.

The times we had lived to see! Even a small child could see into the future and demand what he was entitled to. I thought about my own childhood and how I had learned to read. In those days we were not taught anything—in fact, they would beat us if they saw a book in our hands. And you never even thought of asking questions, or they would "show" you—and it would hurt, too. As for me, all the schooling I ever got was sitting at home and rocking a cradle.

IT never rains but it pours. Two people came from Sverdlovsk at the same time: the chairman of the regional political education department (he was also the inspector of reading huts) and the inspector of the regional military commissariat.

The political education inspector asked me a few questions but never even looked at my files, hard as I tried to show them to him: he was in a hurry to see the young woman teacher. He did not leave any instructions and did not tell me what I had done right or what I had done wrong, but wrote down in the inspection book that I had failed at my work. Why? What were my mistakes? How was I to correct them? There was no way of knowing.

Oh, these ladies' men! They drive around and pretend to be working, but actually they are just wasting money! The military instructor was smarter: he had his tea at the teacher's first, and then came to the reading hut and demanded to see the file of the military training club.

Next, the agronomist Sokolov came out from the district center. I asked him to take part in a question-and-answer session in the reading hut. A lot of people came and bombarded the agronomist with questions. In short, the event was a success.

When I issued an appeal to start a subscription to buy a medicine chest, the first ones to respond were the local forest rangers. The peasants started signing up, too, although slowly. When we had collected almost thirty rubles, I consulted the chairman of the village soviet and decided not to wait but to go ahead and order the medicine chest and then to continue the subscription.

Finally, the long-awaited medicine chest arrived. At the time, about twenty men were at the village soviet: it was the day the mail always came, and they were waiting for letters. Usually the mailman would take his horse to the stable first and then go to the village soviet to distribute the mail. This time, when the mailman appeared on the street with a box in his hands, everyone became very excited and started shouting: "Look, it's the medicine chest, the medicine chest!"

Some of them shouted "Hurray," some started applauding, and others ran toward the mailman. They took the box from him, ran into the building, and set the box on the table.

"Open it! We need to open it!" they shouted.

"How?"

There were no tools in the room. I shouted: "We must pay for it first, and then we can open it!"

It was hopeless. A huge knife appeared out of nowhere, and the lid fell to the floor with a loud bang. The wrappings flew out. They all held their breath in anticipation, and I was afraid they might break something.

"Take it easy, Comrades, or you'll break something!"

It turned out that there was another box inside the first one.

Finally the second box was opened, the lid put aside, and various bottles, vials, packages, and boxes neatly arranged on the table. The men were so fascinated by the whole thing that they forgot their reason for being there. Meanwhile, the mailman was sitting and smiling approvingly.

The news of the arrival of the medicine chest spread throughout the village. People started saying:

"Now we don't need to travel thirty-five versts. Now we have a doctor of our own!"

"Let's see how well it's going to treat us."

While waiting for the chest I had prepared a special register in which to enter the names of the patients and the medicine they received. After the chest arrived, I wrote to the district doctor asking for his help and for instructions on how to organize things, but he never replied. Then I drew up a schedule of health education classes, but that, too, remained only a project. I fell seriously ill.

On May 1 there was a solemn meeting at the school dedicated to literature. The kids made speeches about the significance of May 1. Then there was a play for children and a poetry recitation. The parents were there to admire their children. After the play the children were treated to sunflower seeds, nuts, and candy, while the chairman addressed them with a speech. Then the members of the military club staged their own performance and did it with such style that everyone present was greatly impressed. I could not be there because of my illness, but I was told later that the peasants had been saying among themselves:

"This was all the library woman's idea. If not for her, we wouldn't have had any of this!"

At night the Komsomol members celebrated the Komsomol Easter.[11] They walked around the village carrying paper lanterns and singing songs. It was very pretty and everybody was in an excellent mood.

During the preparations for the May 1 celebration I caught such a bad cold that I could not say a word without coughing. I was completely exhausted. I submitted my resignation and received instructions to hand over my responsibilities. I felt

---

[11] An antireligious festival.

bad leaving my work: things had really begun to pick up. But there was nothing I could do—I simply did not have any strength left.

DURING the first month of my retirement I was not truly aware that I had left everything behind: I felt ill and had the impression I was on vacation. However, the second month showed just how impossible my new situation was. All my money had run out. I had no place to live and had to stay with friends: days with one, nights with another. Suddenly I felt that life had been taken away from me. It seemed I had fallen into a hole, that I had lost myself and there were no live human beings around. I recalled various episodes of my life—my work, my joys and disappointments—but soon they, too, became dimmer, and I began to slide into a total void. I compared myself to a person who has fallen overboard. It seemed that the ship of my life had abandoned me and sailed into eternity. At times I came close to losing my mind.

In this mood I wrote to Tashkinovo, asking how things were and what the fate of my innovations had been. In their reply they told me bitterly that the work of the reading hut had practically come to a halt because the man who had replaced me was not fit for the job. This news made me even sadder. Finally, I decided to drop everything and go live with my adopted son Andrei, who worked at the Staroutkinskaia factory. I stayed there from the end of 1926 to the middle of 1928. I was so used to permanent work that the meaningless routine of domestic chores depressed me. I could not stand it for very long. When I had no patience left I wrote to a comrade in the city to send me money for the road.

In Sverdlovsk a wonderful surprise awaited me.

On November 24, 1928, I received an invitation to a conference of nonparty women,[12] convened by the city soviet. One of the points on the agenda was the honoring of heroes of labor. Suddenly I heard my name. It was followed by loud applause. I was so surprised I did not know what to do.

"Go up on the stage! Go on!" people around me were shouting.

I do not remember how I crossed the hall or how I climbed up onto the stage. When the audience saw me, they started clapping even louder.

When I received the honorary diploma, it trembled in my hand. I looked at it, but the letters were jumping around, and I could not form them into words. My heart was full of both joy and sadness at the same time. I was happy because my dear Soviet Power had not forgotten my many years of hard work and had singled me out, even though I had already left the ranks. I was so excited that if Soviet Power had been just one person I would have thrown my arms around him and given him a big hug and I would have said: "Oh, my dear! Thank you for not forgetting an old woman like me. You saw everything and you knew exactly what you were seeing. May you live and prosper, for the good of all working people!"

---

[12] For organizational purposes, "nonparty people" (i.e., those who were not members of the Communist Party) were often differentiated from "party people" (Communists).

But I was also sad because I had been born too late, wasted too much energy, and not done enough, and because now, just when the work of socialist construction was proceeding at full steam around me, I had become a disabled person, a sick woman. If only I had been born some twenty years later! How much more work I would have been able to do!

Here is a copy of that diploma with which I never part:

Dear Comrade,

On the tenth anniversary of the First Congress of Female Workers and Peasants the regional section of female workers and the Presidium of the city soviet single out for mention your persistent and constant work in the struggle for the consolidation of the achievements of the October Revolution, the consolidation of the new forms of domestic life, and the emancipation of female workers and peasants.

During the civil war you did not spare any effort to strengthen the rear or to help the fighters at the front. In the difficult conditions of economic ruin and famine you participated in the organization of nurseries, kindergartens, public cafeterias, and schools. You fought against epidemics, homelessness, ignorance, and illiteracy. By carrying out your responsibilities in a conscientious manner and participating actively in social life under the direction of the Communist Party, you earned a place in the front line of the working class.

Ahead of us we have the enormous challenges and difficulties of socialist construction, which can be overcome only with the active participation of millions of female workers and peasants. The successful realization of our program of construction is unthinkable without the cultural improvement of the masses, without a cultural revolution. It is necessary to overcome such vestiges of the past as illiteracy, drunkenness, homelessness, and religious superstition.

Through the soviets, we must improve the lives of female workers and peasants, raise their cultural level, and strengthen the defense capability of the Soviet Union.

In honoring you, the regional section of female workers and the Presidium of the city soviet honor one representative of the thousands of female volunteer workers forged by the October Revolution, and hope that you will continue to work cheerfully and tirelessly to consolidate the achievements of October!

Regional Section of Female Workers and Peasants
Presidium of the City Soviet
11/24/1928

At the first meeting of the new board of my residential cooperative we divided up our responsibilities. One member of the board was appointed head of the cultural work commission, while another, a woman, was to organize work among women. Neither one ever did anything. When they were asked at one board meeting to report on their work, the head of the women's commission announced:

"I haven't done anything and do not intend to!"

"Why not?"

She refused to explain why.

The cultural commission did not lift a finger either, using vacations, and so on, as an excuse. Meanwhile, the board was utterly engrossed in "current business." They just sat there all day long shuffling paper, like mice. Every once in a while a hand would appear, click the beads on an abacus, and then disappear again. There were no human faces to be seen.

My mood had changed completely. I was back at work. Once again, I was needed. And most important—it was spring and there was sunshine again. One evening I was standing by the window admiring the sunset when I heard someone enter my room. I turned around and saw one of the employees of our board, a young woman. She said hello and asked me what I was looking at.

"I'm admiring the way spring is struggling with winter and remembering our early years."

"I also saw something interesting while I was on my way here. It was muddy, and there were these two kids, a boy and a girl of about sixteen. She had shoes on, but he was wearing felt boots. They needed to cross the road. So the boy climbed on the girl's back, and she carried him across. He was holding onto her neck, with his legs wrapped around her. It looked so funny that the people passing by could not help smiling. I looked at them and thought: 'That boy probably doesn't have anything to wear except felt boots.' How many failings we still have! When are we going to overcome them? Look at our children's parks: spring is coming, it's time to open them, but whichever way you look, there's something missing. We got some tables and benches from the parents, and the cooperative will provide the flower beds and the snack bar, but one can't even begin without money—and I don't know where to get it. So I've come to ask for your advice. The city soviet suggested that we collect recyclable trash, but I can't do it by myself, I need people.

"Call a party cell meeting, and we'll talk about it," I told her.

The next day the party cell elected a financial commission and charged it with finding ways to procure the needed funds.

The commission consisted of three people, including myself. We decided to start collecting trash immediately. We would first put it into piles in the court-yards, and then find a horse and go pick up all the trash and turn it in.

The members of the commission informed their neighbors of the decision, and a gigantic cleaning operation began. People searched in their closets and sheds, and rummaged through old junk. In this way we also helped the housewives get rid of all kinds of unneeded rubbish, for which they were only too grateful.

Next to the offices of the board was an unoccupied room. We took it over temporarily and worked there for two days without a break, sifting through the trash, sorting it out, and washing all the bottles, dishes, and vials. After that, we borrowed a horse from one of the members of the cooperative, took the trash in, and received thirty-eight rubles and a few kopeks.

The women were very happy,

"Now we can open the playground!"

"Comrades!" I said. "We need to clean the park, cart in some sand, and find a supervisor, some counselors, and a caretaker."

"We'll get the park done tomorrow. We'll all come!"

"You'll be the supervisor, and then you can find the others yourself."

Several days later our park was filled with sounds—not those of the wind or a storm but the clear sounds of children's voices and of new children's songs.

The trees lowered their branches and listened to the new sounds with surprise. They had heard many things during their long lives: they had heard the moans and cries of serfs being flogged; they had heard the prayers of people asking God for death to deliver them from a hard life and oppression; they had heard the idle chatter of housewives sitting around the hissing samovar, around a table loaded with sweets, while a hungry child was begging in vain under their windows; and they had heard lovers whispering on a spring night, as they dreamed of their future happiness. Who knows what else these old lindens had heard! But not once in their long lives had they heard anything similar to what they were hearing right now! So how could they help being surprised?

The children's voices rang out from morning till night. The little ones puttered about cheerfully like sparrows, chasing one another on their unsteady legs, stumbling and crying, only to laugh again a minute later. And they sang: "Spring has come to make us happy!"

The playground required new funds every day, but they were not forthcoming. The board kept promising us money but never came up with any, and the parents did not always pay their dues. Meanwhile, the personnel had to be paid. As the head of the financial commission, I had to think of something. So we decided to start a lottery—the kind that would not cost us anything . . . We instructed two activists to go around and ask all the members of the cooperative for something for the lottery. Most people thought it was a good idea. The drawing ceremony was a lot of fun, and we made a very good profit.

Thus, little by little, I got involved in work once more. It cheered me up and gave me strength. I felt alive again. I knew that this work would not do anything for me personally—I was still retired and living in a cold room—but volunteer work gave me so much pleasure that I did not notice my troubles and was content to know I was alive again. I was needed! I spent my days at the party offices or running around town on errands, and at night I planned what I was going to do the next day. Sometimes I would get so carried away that I could not go to sleep. To take my mind off things, I would go to bed with the book *Popular Astronomy*, open the window and study the stars, comparing what the book said with what I could see in the sky. In this way, I was able to go to sleep.

I had other things to do, too. One local historian asked me to write down all the folk songs, fairy tales, and proverbs that I could remember. I used to do it at night: whenever I remembered something I would write it down without getting up, and then in the morning I would recopy my notes.

My work in the cooperative was not in vain. Soon a group of women activists formed around me. We started having meetings—in the summer in the garden, and when it got cold, in a big room next to the board office. At our meetings we read and discussed various things. As women are unable to talk one at a time, the room was always filled with noise, shouting, and laughter. Although the board office was next door, they did not pay any attention to us, and none of the members ever stopped by to see what all the noise was about.

Our meetings were a sort of club for self-improvement. I divided all the participants into ten groups, with each group dedicated to the study of one particular issue.

Soon the news of our meetings reached the provincial administration of cooperative housing, and I was elected head of the cultural commission. I was also entrusted with work among the women in our cooperative.

In this way I became the official organizer of women's activities. I was very happy with this assignment and set to work immediately. I had gotten two of my activists elected to the board of the cooperative, had found several speakers for the women's meetings, and had planned a whole series of other activities when suddenly I was struck by a terrible misfortune.

Our enemies saw that women had begun to rise up. They did not like it, so they decided to destroy me.

On the night of October 22, 1929, I was walking down a dark alley on my way to a meeting. It was a deserted place with no lights, and the houses stood there like black rocks, nearly indistinguishable from one another. As I was walking, I kept looking at the roofs, trying not to miss the house where the meeting was supposed to be. Finally, I reached the door and turned the knob. It was locked. I stopped to think: "Where could the entrance be then?" At that moment a well-dressed man with a briefcase came running up the stairs. I turned around and went into the courtyard, thinking there might be another entrance. All of a sudden, I felt as if I had fallen into a deep dark hole . . .

The next thing I knew I was standing by the dispensary, unable to understand what I was doing there and why I was feeling so weak and shaken up. I saw a bus and wanted to get in, but then decided against it: "No, I guess I'd better walk. The bus may make me feel even worse." The bus left, and I set off slowly. As I was crossing the street, I saw a woman I knew, a teacher from the children's home where I had once worked. After she recognized me, she asked in a frightened voice:

"What's the matter with you?"

"I don't know. I'm not feeling well."

"What do you mean 'not feeling well'? You're all bandaged up! What's wrong with you? Did somebody beat you up?"

I tried to touch my head, but I could not raise my arm. My left leg was stiff, too.

The woman took my arm and walked me home. There she helped me get undressed and then went for the doctor. The doctor examined my arm and legs. My head scarf was covered with blood.

"Someone must have hit you from behind. Your arm and both your legs are injured."

The next day some comrades came to see me. They said they had found me lying on the sidewalk, unconscious, and had called an ambulance. The people at the dispensary had stitched up the cuts on my head and put on a bandage, but why they had let me leave by myself in such a state was hard to understand. Apparently, someone had attacked me from behind in the courtyard, hit me on the head, and then thrown me out on the street, where I was later found by my comrades.

I was confined to my bed until mid-January, but when I got up and began to move around, I wrote about what had happened in a wall newspaper.[13]

Toward New Forms of Domestic Life
An Answer to an Inquiry

Whoever you are, you have made an inquiry by attacking me, and I am responding in this wall newspaper, and not only in this one. You wanted to take my life, but I do not value my life. It does not belong to me—it belongs to my party and the revolution. I will say more: do not think that I will disappear and that it will all end there. No, it will not! I am not alone. If I am gone, hundreds of women will take my place. Maybe even more. You wanted to frighten others, but you have failed. I am back, and I am not afraid of you. I have done volunteer work before, but now I will do even more. I will work for as long as I have the strength to work. I have not tried to find you, and I am not going to now—you yourself will find the place that you deserve. But I will say one thing: it is ridiculous to try and take away the life of an old woman who does not have long to live anyway. Ridiculous, indeed! It was not an old man who attacked me. It was a young man who attacked an old woman from behind. You must have a bad conscience. You must be a coward! I will leave behind not one, not two women loyal to the revolution, but perhaps hundreds! And just as many sons, all of them Communists! Long live the Communist Party! Down with all the oppositionists! Down with the whole gang, including the priests!

In my absence all cultural work had stopped completely. There was nobody to take my place. In January 1930 the provincial administration demanded a report on the work being done among the population and on the formation of the local branch of the "Down with Illiteracy" society. The board panicked, but it was too late: there were no records of any work among the population. They called a meeting but did not tell me about it because they knew I was sick.

I could not resist it, so—bad leg, bandaged head, and all—I dragged myself to the meeting. On the very next day I resumed my work. In spite of my illness, I had to go to board meetings every day. It was very hard, but I turned in the 1929 report on time.

The arrival of fall disturbed our women's anthill, stirring it up and starting a lot of fervent activity. The women simply would not sit at home with their children anymore.

From various corners of our cooperative, women came streaming in like rivers

---

[13] Wall newspapers were posted in many Soviet institutions and contained articles written by employees.

into a lake. You could hear the buzzing of their voices—they might be laughing or having an argument.

"Well, Comrades, do we need sewing classes or not?" asked the chairperson, banging the table with a ruler.

"Yes, we do!" shouted the women.

"At least we'll learn how to make shirts for our children."

"But who's going to teach us?"

"We'll find somebody!"

One woman raised her hand: "Comrades, we all need political training. Without it we are like newborn kittens. We don't understand anything."

"Of course we do! We'll ask the provincial administration to send us a lecturer."

"We need freedom from pots and pans! We need a cafeteria and a laundry!"

"In the summer we've got to open a children's playground and a laundry. We're sick of washing men's pants. Every time my husband goes anywhere on business, he comes back so dirty I never stop washing his clothes. I've got too many kids to bother with his pants."

"Everyone has problems. This one is sick of washing her husband's pants!" laughed the other women.

"We really do need to open a cafeteria. We'd use less wood that way, and have less work to do at home."

"I, for one, am against a communal kitchen. With our salaries you won't be able to feed your family in a cafeteria. At home you can cook something, and they'll at least get full."

"Can I have the floor?"

"Go right ahead."

"Comrades, I hear that some of you are against communal meals. Let me tell you something: no matter how long we hold on to the old ways, life itself will force us to switch to communal meals. Therefore we should all do it, and the sooner the better. I suggest that we elect a committee for the organization of a communal kitchen."

Voices were heard:

"That's right!"

"Comrades, nominate your candidates."

We nominated a committee and had it approved.

"Comrades, the meeting is hereby declared adjourned . . ."

"Wait, wait a second!" cried one woman waving her arms wildly. She rushed to the middle of the room and started talking very fast:

"I suggest we organize a reception for the wounded fighters of the Far Eastern Special Army. They are passing through our town. We must start a collection to buy them presents."

"Good idea!"

"That's right! Let's do it!"

The women all started talking at the same time and walking around. Money poured onto the table.

"When you give them the presents, tell them it's from the housewives!"

"Then they'll start driving you crazy with their pants! You'll have to open a special laundry for men's pants! Ha-ha-ha!"

Over the course of the next few days the women collected twenty-six rubles, bought food and tobacco, put it in a box, and handed the box to the Red Army men. The men accepted it with pleasure and thanked the women for their attention.

Everything seemed to be going very well but the more the cooperative expanded, the more money it owed. The chairman rushed around like a man possessed. The board deliberated, looked for solutions, and "took measures." An instruction issued in one corner of the room would get blocked in another.

The Urals provincial administration of cooperative housing pressured the chairmen, threatened them with exposure, and convened numerous meetings with chairmen, cultural commissions, and groups of activists, but things continued to go badly.

In all this commotion we, the women, were completely forgotten.

We carried on our activities in our cells and on children's playgrounds, demanding that the board comply with our resolutions concerning communal meals, laundry, and so on. But all that required money, and the board did not have any.

In September the city soviet issued a resolution "On the Eviction of Non-Toiling Members[14] of Residential Cooperatives."

That's when the fervent activity really began! To inspect our cooperative, five brigades consisting of both men and women were formed. In addition, the women had concerns of their own: before winter we absolutely had to open a kindergarten and find an appropriate building for it. During the day the women would work on the kindergarten idea, and at night they would expose non-toiling residents.

On their return they would tell me all about what had happened that day:

"Wherever we go, we get yelled at, and sometimes they even threaten to kick us out, but we carry on anyway."

"Sometimes you know in advance who you're dealing with. You go in and they produce such documents that you're at a loss to figure out where on earth they managed to get them."

"Three of us come to this house where we already know that the former owner lives. They used to own two houses and a tannery. We're suggesting that she vacate the premises, when one member of our brigade starts defending her, saying that it was the husband who had been a capitalist but that the wife herself was poor. After that we go to see a former priest's wife, and this tenderhearted friend of ours begins to defend her, too: 'Where is she going to go? Why pry into people's souls?'"

"Whoever let her join the brigade?"

---

[14] These were persons deprived of voting rights as class aliens. The eviction campaign was part of the intensified class discrimination that was the urban counterpart of dekulakization.

"I don't know. But she sure gets in the way. If we're going to let tears bother us, we won't evict anybody."

Although I was not a member of any brigade, I was kept well informed of their work.

My health was improving very slowly. My legs and head continued to bother me. I wrote to the provincial administration that because of my illness I could not continue as head of the cultural commission.

The newly elected head took a look at the files and said:

"Hey, it's almost all women!"

"Who else is able to work for us?"

"I didn't expect this."

He never showed up again. Who wants to bother with women? After him there were several more heads, but none of them stayed. All of them ran away because there was a lot of work and no pay. So I continued to do all the work myself, although it was hard for me . . .

Our women's group worked itself to utter exhaustion, but the board replied with empty promises to all our demands. The chairman showed up less and less often, and, when he did, it was obvious he had been drinking. Once he arrived all bandaged up. It turned out that he had had a party; a fight had broken out, and he had gotten his skull cracked. Everyone said:

"There's a fine chairman for you, a good example for us all!"

"With a chairman like that we'll end up with a reprimand, instead of an honorary diploma."

We tried as hard as we could, but at the Urals provincial administration we were told:

"Things are not going well in your area."

To this the women activists replied bitterly:

"Give us a different chairman. With this one we'll never get out of debt."

The chairman was summoned to the provincial administration to explain himself. After that, instead of working on improving his attitude, he began to take revenge on the women's group.

We did everything possible to open a communal kitchen, laundry, and kindergarten. We found a stone building for the kitchen, just right in every respect except that it did not have running water. That would have been easy to correct: the piping was on the same street and all that was needed was to lay more pipes across the yard, but no matter how many times we asked the board, nothing was ever done.

Here is another example.

The provincial administration told us that we could send several activists to attend special courses: one would become a librarian; two, liquidators of illiteracy; and another five, preschool teachers.

The chairman withheld this information from us and selected the candidates personally, without consulting anybody. In the process he deliberately mixed everything up, so that an illiterate woman would have become a librarian, and people who already had preschool teaching certificates would have been sent to attend the same courses again. Of course they all declined, and the vacancies remained unfilled.

In spite of all this, with almost no help from the board, the women's group opened the first communal kitchen in our cooperative on May 15.

As I said before, we did manage to open a communal kitchen, but the laundry and kindergarten ideas never got off the ground—all because of the negative attitude on the part of the board. We found a building for the laundry, but the board never bothered to get official title to it. As for the kindergarten, we found a nice, large wooden house. The doctor from the city examined it and found that it met all the necessary requirements, but suddenly we ran into another difficulty: the tenants of the house flatly refused to move out. The matter ended up in court, where it got stuck because the board did nothing to speed things up.

Next, we decided that we badly needed a resort of our own. We found a suitable country estate not far from town. On it were two houses, one with two stories, set in a beautiful location next to a lake teeming with fish. The houses could be used for the children and the adult vacationers, and the barns, to keep animals and poultry in. There was also a vegetable garden. We sent a delegation to inspect the estate. They came back ecstatic:

"It's a treasure!"

"Just think how the children will enjoy it!"

"As soon as we get a vacation, we're going to go straight there with our fishing rods and treat ourselves to some fresh fish soup," said the men. "And, well . . . perhaps some vodka to go with it! Doesn't sound too bad!"

"Good for you, girls! A great idea! Only how are you going to push it through?"

"Don't you worry," said the women firmly.

Then the bureaucratic runaround began. At the board subcommittee meeting, I said that our activists wanted to have a resort of their own and that a special delegation had already been to see the location and approved it wholeheartedly. The chairman asked with obvious envy:

"Where is this estate anyway?"

I answered that what mattered was not where it was but whether it was basically okay to have one.

"So you don't want to tell me where it is," interrupted the chairman and started arguing against buying the estate:

"Cooperatives don't have the right to own houses; they can only lease them."

Someone disagreed:

"What do you mean they don't have the right? Who told you that? Don't you try to weasel out of it. You're just embarrassed because the women thought of it before you did!"

The argument grew heated. It was clear that the chairman kept arguing only because he wanted the estate for himself. Finally, it was decided that the matter would be discussed at the general board meeting. All the activists were there and, hard as the chairman tried to resist, the meeting resolved to buy the estate. We reached an agreement with the owner and signed a contract with him. The only thing left was to have the contract approved and pay the money—and the estate would be ours.

That's what we thought, but the chairman thought otherwise. He did sign the contract but then "forgot" all about it. We waited for a long time and then began to insist:

"Why aren't you doing the rest of it? Where's the contract?"

At first the chairman would not answer, and then he disappeared altogether. The cultural work in the cooperative flourished, but the financial situation remained unsatisfactory. It was impossible to pay all the debts, hard as the activists and the board tried. It was at that time that we received a resolution stating that large residential cooperatives were to be divided into smaller ones and transferred to the jurisdiction of the district administration of cooperative housing. The local boards began to disband.

After the disappearance of the chairman the work of our board came to a complete halt. We needed a new chairman. A special meeting was called. The women activists declared:

"We should elect a woman!"

"We're sick and tired of having drunkards as chairmen."

"Women know more about the local conditions, and they can easily learn the rest."

"So who do you want to elect?"

"Borisova."

Borisova did not have a chance to accomplish anything. All she got to do was to terminate all the board's activities and blush because of someone else's mistakes. Finally, she had to liquidate the cooperative.

On August 31 the women activists assembled in the garden. Everyone sat down under the trees. The stern eye of the camera was slowly moving in our direction. An angry voice said:

"Don't move!"

And a minute later:

"That's it!"

That was our last meeting. The fighting Chernyshevsky cooperative was no more.

In 1916 I had written in my diary: "Everybody has a dream to live for, only I have no dreams left." Soon after that I, too, found my dreams. For a while I dreamed of universal justice. Years passed, and I found another dream: "When will I see housewives become free working women? Will I ever see it?"

At my advanced age each new beginning causes me to worry: "Will I be able to bring this project to conclusion?"

Now I can finally see that my dream has come true. I am surrounded by the women I gathered together so painstakingly six years ago. Today I cannot help smiling when I remember how awkward and timid were their first steps in volunteer work! They were semiliterate or completely illiterate. I used to worry that they might lose their way; that domestic tasks might distract them from their work; that taunts such as "you must be going to all those meetings because you have nothing else to do" might influence them! I used to feel bad when they did not get along. Some of them had serious problems with their husbands, who threatened them with divorce. Sometimes we would let in a wolf in sheep's clothing. There were times when those we subjected to criticism would lash out at us. Indeed, we had serious struggles in our own midst: after two different purges, our ranks have grown thinner but more cohesive.

On December 23, 1933, at a citywide conference of female shock workers,[15] I had to part with fifteen of my activists who had been transferred to the party district committee. I had nothing to be ashamed of.

Later, when I would ask the committee how my women were working, the reply would always be: "They are working well, thank you." Many of them have received commendations for active work.

When they remember the past they laugh at the timid and abused women they used to be. Now they are cheerful and content, and some have expressed a desire to join the party. Is this not worth living and working for?

[15] *Shock worker*—a term broadly used to describe outstanding workers in the factory or kolkhoz; derived from the term *shock work*, the name of a campaign launched during the First Five-Year Plan (1928–31) to increase industrial output through formalized competition among work brigades.

12 □ ANONYMOUS

What Am I to Do?

□ This entry comes from a collection of letters to the editor, compiled
by the journalist Lev Sosnovsky with the purpose of "directing the
searchlight at something we call the modern family." "The new family," according to Sosnovsky, "has not yet fully emerged from under
the rubble of the old one, and it is women, as well as children, who
are paying the heaviest price."

I AM WRITING to you because I am in despair; because I can see no way out. I am
asking you to sort this out for me and tell me the truth, whatever it is. Perhaps I
am wrong or perhaps this is the way things are supposed to be and they cannot be
otherwise. Finally, it may be that I am hysterical or abnormal, for sometimes it
seems to me that I have lost my mind.

I am the wife of a prominent provincial administrator—a party member and a
revolutionary.

I have gone through all the stages of our modern life. I divorced my first husband with whom I had lived for eleven years, and then, four years ago, met my
new husband who, in turn, also divorced his wife. He has two children who live
with their mother and get half his salary every month. I have a daughter from my
first marriage who lives with me. We lost sight of her father—also a Communist—a long time ago, so that my daughter is supported exclusively by me. In
fact, this is the way it has always been. Let me explain.

I got married in 1909, when I was not quite sixteen years old. I was a child then,
straight out of the gymnasium. I turned sixteen in September 1909 and had my
daughter in March. From the day she was born I had to support both of us. My
husband and I did not get along, and although we did not get divorced, we were
like complete strangers. I left for Petersburg and lived there with my little one
until the revolution broke out. I did not get any help from anyone and had to work
extremely hard to make ends meet. I was also going to school because I could not
reconcile myself to the fact that my life was already over. I kept thinking: my little
girl will grow up, and her father will be able to help. It was all a fantasy, however.
My daughter was sick a lot of the time. In quiet desperation, I had to concentrate
on everyday problems and think only of how I could support my daughter. When
the war began, things got even worse. My husband was sent to the front. There
was nothing to eat in the capital. My child was fading away before my very eyes.
So it was just when the revolution was breaking out, when life itself was calling

From L. Sosnovskii, ed., *Bol'nye voprosy (zhenshchina, sem'ia i deti)* (Leningrad: Priboi, 1926),
29–37 (abridged).

on me to join the revolution, that, for fear of losing my child, I had to leave the city and move south. I settled in a large city in the south.

With no money or friends, surrounded by strangers, I struggled to support the two of us. I had to work day and night, taking whatever job was offered and feeling that life was passing me by. I lived in terrible anguish. I kept dreaming of the time when my girl would grow up to be big and strong. All the while I was in the midst of the revolution. Regimes kept changing. Finally, Soviet power was firmly established.

Always working in one Soviet institution or another, I lived through hunger and the horror of having a hungry child. In early 1921 my husband tracked us down only to say that he wanted a divorce, for he had found somebody else who was right for him. It hardly seemed to matter. We were complete strangers by then.

That same year I started going out with a man whom I had met at work. He was a party member, tough and energetic—irreplaceable during the time of War Communism. A lot of pretty words were said (I did not know then that reality would be quite different). I dreamed about my future work, about the party. I thought: here is a man who will help me. It took his wife a long time to get used to the idea that he was leaving. I had to go through some very hard times because of him. He loved his children but had to leave them with their mother.

In other words, for two years I had to witness some truly heartbreaking scenes. I continued to work, but he was becoming more and more unhappy about it. "It's about time you quit," he would say. "I'm tired, and I want my wife to be at home all the time," and so on. As for volunteer or party work, he would not even hear of it. I was not a party member, but I thought that I would be able to join before long. So, little by little, I was forced to abandon everything. I even had to stop going to meetings because it annoyed him. When I complained about it, I would always hear that he was tired and upset, that it was hard having his old family in the same town, and so forth. As soon as we left, a new life would begin.

Finally, the long-awaited day came. We were going to leave. My husband had been transferred to one of the large southern provinces. Now he is an important official. Both the party and the executive committee value his opinion. He is firm. He is dependable. He is a Communist. But what about my life? The moment we arrived, my husband said: "Don't you even think about working. There are enough unemployed workers here without you." I felt completely lost. I did not know what to do. If we had still been in the town we had just left, I would have found work myself. People knew me there. But here I was a total stranger. Where could I go? I tried to go to a few places, but the answer was always the same: "You're N.N.'s wife—can't he support you? Look at all these unemployed people!" As if, by sitting at home, I could feed the unemployed.

After fifteen years of work, am I really destined to spend the rest of my life in the kitchen simply because I am the wife of an important official?

13 □ Ekaterina Olitskaia

My Reminiscences (2)

□ Arrested in 1924 (at the age of twenty-five) for printing an underground Socialist Revolutionary newspaper, Olitskaia was sent to the Solovki camp, where she met her husband and fellow SR, Shura, and then into exile in Chimkent, Kazakhstan, where her daughter, Musia, was born.

THE JOURNEY to our place of exile was long and expensive, but the desire for a meeting proved stronger than the obstacles. We were expecting guests: Shura's mother and my sister.

Shura's mother, Maria Mikhailovna, arrived first. We had never met, and I was very nervous. From what Shura had told me, I knew that his mother came from a family of railway workers and was an excellent housewife who thought that a woman's main responsibility in life was her family. I did not know anything about housework and hated bourgeois family life and everything it stood for. In the Chimkent exile community we were the only family, and our house served as a magnet for our single comrades. So, like it or not, I had to do housework, but I did a pretty poor job of it.

Right before Shura's mother arrived, we managed to move to a new place. We were overjoyed: at least she would be spared the sight of our dugout.

While Shura went to the train station to meet his mother, I did my best to prepare a proper welcome. I washed the floor, straightened up the whole apartment, and washed all the dishes until they sparkled. I dressed up myself and put a nice dress on our little Musia. As luck would have it, on that very day my tooth had started hurting. It had not bothered me from the time we were transported down from Solovki, but now it really made me miserable. I waited impatiently. Finally, I heard the sound of the wheels. I ran out with Musia in my arms. Shura was helping his mother climb out of the cart. I was not sure how to act around her. I knew that she really liked his first wife who, even though she had remarried, would often come by with her son.

"Katia, this is my mother."

Shura was beaming as he stood by his mother. Next to him stood a tall, thin, earnest woman. Her white voile dress set off her dark complexion. Her brown eyes with dark circles under them, just like Shura's, calmly scrutinized me.

Although not particularly warm or friendly, the first encounter passed off fairly smoothly. We took our guest inside. She carefully examined her surroundings. It seemed to me that even with Musia she was somewhat cold. I offered Maria

From E. Olitskaia, *Moi vospominaniia* (Frankfurt/Main: Possev-Verlag, 1971). For other excerpts from Olitskaia, see selections 1 and 36 in this volume.

Mikhailovna various dishes I had prepared, but all she would accept was a cup of tea with preserves. Shura and his mother could not take their eyes off each other. Shura kept stroking her hand and occasionally raised it to his lips. Every once in a while he would ask her a question, or she would tell him something about their Moscow relatives: about Tsilia, about Shura's little son . . . Maria Mikhailovna had nothing but praise for the boy.

I felt that Musia and I were not wanted and went out into the yard with her. But I could not stay there long. My tooth was aching so badly that I decided to go and see the dentist. I called Shura out and told him what I was going to do. Then I left.

When I got back I was feeling great. I found Shura and Maria Mikhailovna engrossed in conversation. Shura was pacing around the room. When I came in they fell silent. Musia was not with them. When I asked where she was, Shura suddenly realized that he had become so involved in conversation with his mother that he had completely forgotten about her.

I went out to look for Musia. I thought she was at our landlady's. She was already a year old, and she frequently played with the landlady's little girls. But neither Musia nor the landlady's daughters were anywhere to be seen. I looked all over the yard and the garden, and then ran out into the street. The longer I searched, the more worried I became and the angrier I got at Shura and his mother. To forget about a child!

The children were nowhere to be found, and no one had seen them. I ran over to our friends, the Malkins, a Social Democrat family that lived nearby. Malkin had been joined in exile by his wife and son. His little boy was around five and often played with Musia. Malkin was in the garden tutoring one of his local students. He told me that no one else was home, that his wife had gone off to the market. Not knowing what to do next I rushed home to get Shura involved in the search. At the corner I ran into Malkin's wife. A nice, friendly woman, she offered her help and asked me to wait a minute while she took her purchases inside. When she opened the door to her house, she cried out;

"Katia! Here they are!"

My Musia was lying on the floor in the middle of the room, and the Malkin boy and the landlady's daughter were covering her with a blanket and telling her it was time to go to sleep.

Relieved, I picked her up and ran home.

I laughed as I told Shura and Maria Mikhailovna about what Musia had been up to. Feeling guilty, Shura put her in his lap. Maria Mikhailovna was just shaking her head. For some reason I got the impression that something had happened between Shura and his mother and that they were upset about something.

I did everything I could to make things go smoothly, but nothing seemed to work. Nothing we did seemed to please Maria Mikhailovna. She was offended because we had moved Shura's cot out into the hall where he then slept. She did not like the fact that Shura made his own bed, that he carried water and sometimes washed the floor, that he helped wring out the laundry, and that he carried the baby when we went out. She did not like the fact that Musia had not been baptized. There was nothing she liked.

I learned all this two weeks after her arrival. It was on Musia's birthday. The whole exile community came over to celebrate with us. Besides our usual SR friends, there were the Social Democrats, the Anarchists, and the Zionists— around forty people in all. We had set out the food on tablecloths in the garden in front of the house. We put the samovar, which we had borrowed from the land-lady, on a little bench. The guests all brought their own cups, plates, and glasses. We all sat or lay down on the ground wherever we could. The birthday girl was sound asleep.

I poured out the first cups of tea. After that the guests helped themselves to more tea or whatever food they wanted. Maria Mikhailovna tried to make up for my poor efforts as a hostess, but she was pulled away from the samovar with laughter and joking. Maria Mikhailovna did not like that at all. She went inside the house, and, after the guests left, the displeasure that had been building up in her for two weeks came pouring out.

She was going to leave the very next day, Maria Mikhailovna announced. She was not going to spend another day in the house with me. At first I could not understand any of the reproaches being heaped on me. Completely stunned, Shura and I said nothing. But when Maria Mikhailovna said that she did not want to live in the same house with an unbaptized child, whom she did not consider her grand-child, Shura said:

"Well, Mother, then you'd better leave," and walked out of the room.

Maria Mikhailovna turned her back to me and began to cry. I was sitting by Musia's cot. We did not say another word to each other. After awhile, I went out to where Shura was. He was lying there with his head buried in his pillow.

"Shura, I don't understand what's going on. Why didn't you say anything be-fore? Why didn't you warn me? Surely we could have . . ."

"Don't worry about it," he said before I could finish. "That's not really the problem."

He hugged me, and with his arm still around my shoulders we walked out of the house and made our way through the town and out onto the steppe.

"On the very first day," Shura began, "as soon my mother arrived, I asked her how long she was planning to stay with us, and she said that she might actually stay for good. After all, I am her only child, and she could not live with her brother forever. But the problem, Katia, is that my mother does not want to live the way I do. She saw that Tsilia and my son could not keep me, so she thought that perhaps a second marriage, a second family, a second child . . . In other words, she was hoping that you would become her accomplice, that the two of you would be able to keep me from following the wrong path. But when she got here and realized that this was not going to happen, she was devastated. I told her that same day that our life was uncertain but that neither one of us would ever consider changing it. "You mean you are going to abandon a second wife and child?" she asked me. I answered: "If I do not abandon her for the revolution, she will abandon me." As soon as I said it I knew I should not have. I thought . . . I was hoping she would understand, that she would reconcile herself to it. I believe even now that sooner or later she will understand.

When we returned, Maria Mikhailovna had already gotten into bed.

The next morning we got up as if nothing had happened. Neither we nor Maria Mikhailovna said anything about the conversation we had had. Life went on as it had before, if anything, more peacefully and smoothly.

About two weeks later. Maria Mikhailovna started getting ready to leave. She began saying that she missed Moscow and her relatives. She constantly talked about how good life was in Moscow, how easy it was to get things, how well-dressed people were nowadays, how successful and well-off some of Shura's old friends had become.

SOON after Maria Mikhailovna left, my sister, Ania, arrived. Of course, my sister's visit was quite different. We never talked about our plans for the future, although she could probably guess what some of them were. A few times she tried to argue with us and to describe the various achievements of the Soviet state. While not denying that we lived under despotism, she claimed that if our side had won, we would act exactly the same way. But generally we avoided talking about politics, especially because she was not all that interested. It simply made her feel bad that we had chosen to live this way, that we could not be like other people.

My sister loved the caravans, the nomads' tents, the Uzbek crafts and customs. She even claimed to have seen a mirage from the window of our room that looked out onto the bare, burned-out steppe. She became great friends with one of our comrades, Valentin Kocharovsky. They used to walk together in the evenings, and even though I was tied down by Musia, they managed to get me to join them on some of their excursions to the Old City and the Sacred Grove with its holy birds and other exotic things.

We enjoyed Ania's presence, but her departure did not leave us feeling empty. We felt so good together, just the two of us. Musia did not count yet. She took up a lot of our energy. She complicated our life while also enriching it.

14 □ PARASKEVA IVANOVA

Why I Do Not Belong in the Party

□ Ivanova's letter, sent to a Soviet newspaper and published in a volume on "painful questions" of family, women's role, and private life
(see also Anonymous, selection 12 in this volume), offers a description of her experiences of sexual "liberation" as a young Communist
in the 1920s. The popular association of the revolution and free love
bothered the Bolshevik leaders, partly because of the messy private
lives of which this is an example, but it was not until the mid-1930s
that the Soviet regime firmly turned its back on "liberationist" ideology, outlawing abortion, condemning promiscuity, and exalting the
family values that most young Communists of the 1920s thought the
revolution had swept away forever.

IN 1920, as a young girl who barely understood the great goal of the struggle for
the October Revolution [of 1917], I joined the Komsomol in Primorsk. I was a
student at a trade union school at the time. The Komsomol instilled in me the
passionate desire to become not a deadweight but a valuable cog in the Great
Proletarian Machine for the construction of the future. At Red Army rallies and
city council meetings (we youngsters managed to sneak in even when we were
not supposed to), impassioned speeches were being made on how it was necessary to set to work without delay, while the situation was right. As a result, my
friends and I simply could not stand the idea of remaining in school for a long
time and waiting to become useful in some distant future. We left the trade union
school. We wanted to learn fast so we could start working right away. Give us
work, give us a real challenge, and that is all there is to it! We besieged the district
committee of the Komsomol: can you send us somewhere?—Yes, we can. In a
nearby town there's a six-week course on socialist education. Then I'm off! I'll
return as a specialist and turn things around in Primorsk. The classrooms were full
of enthusiastic young people like me: just give us an assignment. The most active
among us got together and started writing to the party: to the provincial committee, district committee, and town committee. Then there was a speech and a meeting, and I became a candidate member of the Communist Party of Ukraine.

Me, a candidate member of the party! Oh, now I would live for the party and
with the party! Six weeks of feverish activity—and then the prospect of real work.

I ended up in one of the worst bandit-ridden districts and went straight to the
party district committee. Can you use me? And they could, right away! A candi-

Letter from Paraskeva Ivanova in L. Sosnovsky, ed., *Bol'nye voprosy (zhenshchina, sem'ia i deti)*
(Leningrad: Priboi, 1926), 13–28 (abridged).

date for only two weeks, I became the head of the district women's section and then also the instructor of the party and the Komsomol district committees.

I was excited and ready to go. I was full of the ardent desire to do whatever I could to be useful. But I lacked practical skills. I did not understand the way things were done. I was young and inexperienced. But what did it matter? For I had firmly resolved to renounce everything personal and give all of myself to the party—irreversibly and without hesitation. I knew I had to rid myself of all the elements of the old ways that still lived within me and study, study as hard as I could to learn from the old Bolsheviks in order to become, if not better than them, as good as them . . .

At that time Comrade Ganov was the district secretary and by far the most experienced and mature of all the comrades—a real Bolshevik. It is easy to imagine how I regarded him. It seemed to me that you just could not get any better than our secretary. I did not just respect him—no, I held him in absolute, pure Komsomol awe.

As a real Bolshevik, Comrade Ganov could not help noticing my childlike adoration for him (he even called me "child") and, out of a sense of parental responsibility, took it upon himself to teach me a thing or two. And did he ever . . .

He asked me in, but instead of giving me clear instructions, remarked sarcastically: "You intellectuals, when will you ever learn anything?" A little chuckle; an assignment given in a condescending tone of voice. I could hardly fulfill that assignment. About 80 percent remained undone.

Another serious matter, and I was in Ganov's office again. "You're in the wrong business, Comrade! If you can't do it by yourself, read the instructions, try to understand, and then do whatever you want!" I was devastated. So I was of no use to anybody. So I was unable to do my job.

When the next case came up, I entered Ganov's office no longer with hope but with fear. "May I come in?"—"Please do, have a seat." I sat down and waited. He let everybody go home. He was chuckling and rubbing his hands. Then he got up from his chair, came over to me, and, instead of talking about business, started kissing and hugging me (he had a wife who was a teacher and also kept house). I was taken aback. The secretary grinned. "Are you too shy or something? Aren't you used to it? Or are you one of those gymnasium girls? With your bourgeois morality? There's no place for bourgeois morality in the party. The party has thrown it out the window." I got away from him and ran as fast as my legs would carry me to the women's department. My head was spinning and my thoughts were all confused. Could this be the "new forms of everyday life"?

That same night I got another lesson in the new forms of life. Comrade Artiun was walking home with me after our shift at the party committee. Suddenly he grabbed me. He did not embrace me, but squeezed me like a bear and clamped onto my lips like a leech. That wild beast pressed against my lips so hard that my teeth hurt.

The lesson did not end there. When I broke away, screaming, I could hear: "Another one playing the bourgeois lady!" I could not sleep that night—I kept thinking about the new forms of everyday life. Didn't I myself read *Kommunarka*[1] and try to convince other women of the correctness of the new way of life?

After that, I began to suffer from an inner conflict. The lessons of the "new communist way of life" seemed too new and ludicrous to me. My "bourgeois" body just could not stomach it. But the seed had been planted, and, once given the right climate, beautiful shoots soon began to appear.

One evening Comrade Ganov asked me in a patronizing tone of voice if I would stay after the party meeting. After everyone had gone, he took my arm and, chucking me under the chin, said: "Well, little girl, let's go out and have a talk." I went with him. When Comrade Ganov brought me to the mass graves and started talking about those who had died for Communism and so on, I was a captive audience; I trusted his every word. For here was a real Communist talking to me, not the secretary who had treated me with scorn. The man I saw before me now was a good, honest Communist. I was filled with gratitude. He had finally realized that I passionately wanted to be a real Bolshevik, to gain the kind of experience he possessed.

Meanwhile, the secretary had switched from fighters for Communism to the new way of life, and from the new way of life to beautiful eyes. After that he started kissing and hugging me and then suddenly said: "I love you." I was totally amazed. I felt a lump in my throat. Isn't he a Communist? What is he going to do to me? But isn't he married—with a family? Or maybe I'm wrong, and he's right? He's smarter than I am—and older. I told him what I was thinking. But Comrade Ganov gave me another lecture. "A family? Communists don't have families, and never will. What is a family? It's obsolete, completely obsolete. No, we're cultured people. We know that there used to be families. There were families under the Romanovs,[2] too"—and so on, and so forth. "And anyway, I love you—and you only. That's not my fault, is it? As for your obstinacy and hesitations, it's all bourgeois attitudes. It is not the Communist way. In fact, it's the influence of the gymnasium. If you love me, you must give yourself to me, especially because I love you and can't live without you."

I wanted to believe him. I was desperate to believe that he really loved me. But in the end my old "bourgeois" and peasant values proved too strong. "First leave your wife and then . . ."

I had several such lessons, and finally my new teacher completed my education. I began to understand quite clearly that my behavior had been bourgeois and that I had been influenced by my parents, ignorant peasants.

I began thinking of my parents as some kind of antedeluvian monsters. Comrade Ganov took care of the rest. He had his part down perfectly. I remember how I once came into his office to receive some practical advice on my work in the women's department. Comrade Ganov gave me his advice like a true Bolshevik and a father: taking me by the chin, kissing me, and calling me "a little devil," he

---

[1] *Kommunarka Ukrainy* (*Komunarka Ukraini*)—a journal published in the 1920s by the women's department of the Ukrainian Communist Party.

[2] The ruling dynasty in Russia until February 1917.

described the beauty of sunshine, fields, and my eyes, and, finally, told me to be at the party committee office at eight, so we could go to the field and "have a talk."

My work in the Komsomol and the women's department was going just fine. I was a brilliant student. From that point on, it was one long downward slide . . .

I proved myself a worthy student of such a skillful teacher. Whenever the secretary was away, or I myself was on various business trips, I would practice the new way of life and the new morality with Cheka men, policemen, "Komsomolers," and party members—on peasant carts, military carts, or wherever possible . . .

By the time I was sent by the party to work in the countryside, I had learned the new forms of everyday life so well that I made considerable progress propagating it among the unenlightened village youth—demonstrating by personal example how to practice the new way of life. The results exceeded all expectations, in large measure because I was supported by the district party committee, and in particular by Comrade Ganov, who visited me several times in order to give me "practical advice."

Several Komsomol members left their wives and started courting me. Another one beat up his wife. Even the chairman of the township party committee, himself a party candidate, began to show interest in the new way of life. He was a businesslike fellow who would not stop at anything in order to please his heart's desire—me, that is. He wanted to marry me and almost left his illiterate wife.

I was no longer a bourgeois lady, however. I had become a worthy Communist activist. Under Ganov's brilliant guidance, I had rid myself completely of the last traces of the old bourgeois morality. Ganov's new way of life defined marriage as a bourgeois institution and a vestige of the past. Accordingly, I handed the unfaithful spouse back to his poor wife, having first sapped him of a great deal of his strength—physical, diplomatic, and sexual . . .

Needless to say, learning the "Communist way of life" according to Ganov was not easy. My personality was split in two, and when Ganov was not around, "the other" part of me insisted that my "God" was a filthy and dishonest man who never spoke a word of truth.

In the town of N, Ganov continued to honor me with his attentions, and he gave me several more practical lessons in his hotel room. He even staged a melodramatic scene, in which he expressed a desire to unite his life with mine and tie himself down by having a baby. "Don't worry about the baby, I'll help," he said and left town for three months. When he came back I told him angrily that I had had an abortion (I hadn't really). There followed a show of grief and suffering: "I really wanted a baby . . ."

In 1924 I went to work in the youth department of a club for proletarian students. I liked my work. Komsomol life had a beneficial effect on me. I got to know a young miner, a Komsomol member. He was a good fellow, open and pure. His love for me was also pure. His idea of the new way of life was Lenin's, not Ganov's. There was one problem, however. Ganov's system had taken deep root inside of me. Despite the fact that I respected that Komsomol boy as a human being and a comrade—the first to treat me as a human being and not as a prostitute (such thoughts were tormenting me terribly), I still was not able to tell him the whole truth, even though I wanted to tell him all about myself. I was sure he would understand and would not laugh at me. Yes, I had learned Ganov's lessons well—so well, in fact, that even when I was already in love with that boy, I continued doing the same old thing and covering it up with base lies.

In the fall of 1924 Ganov himself arrived in town and almost destroyed everything. Once again, there were visits to the London hotel and orgies lasting all night. Then he managed to convince me that he would live with me, for which purpose he found two other girls and suggested we form a commune. "You find an apartment, and I'll pay the rent, maintenance, heating, and so on." The three of us rushed to look for an apartment. It was only when somebody mentioned in my presence that Ganov's wife was coming the next day to put an end to her husband's lies that I came to my senses and realized I had been fooled once again. After that, I seemed able to free myself of Ganov's influence. Still, there was something of Ganov in the way I viewed my relationship with the Komsomol boy. I kept wondering: why is this guy so nervous; why is he trying to prove something to me? What's the matter? Shouldn't he be satisfied with the certain number of hours I give him regularly?

We had such a hard time understanding each other that it took us a whole year of living together and working on my problem before we could agree on what the Komsomol way of life was all about . . .

Now, having rejected the emptiness and corrupting harmfulness of Ganov's rules, I face the question of how to start building anew. Where to begin?

As early as last fall I applied to become a full party member, with Ganov as my first reference. Now, however, I have decided not to send it and to leave the party altogether. The party does not need me the way I am, and my attitude toward the party is different from that of Ganov's. First, I will purge myself completely of Ganov's filth, and then, with a clear conscience, I will join the party—not as a prostitute but as a Leninist.

Now I have a comrade, my young Komsomol husband, who was the first person to understand me as a human being. With his help I will be able to find the correct road. Now, as I leave the party, I will not hesitate to expose my life and myself as a Communist—without blushing and without self-pity. I am not afraid of what others might say. What is shame? What is public opinion? It is a silent and ugly struggle: dirty on the inside, glamorous on the outside. As I leave the party, I say to all women Communists like myself:

Comrades, take a look at yourselves! Can it be that you, too, are victims of the "new way of life"? Stop now before it is too late. And you, the Komsomol girl I introduced to Ganov at his insistence, throw him out! Let me be an example to you. I am ill and must leave the party. I need prolonged, serious treatment. As for you, honest Communists, go and fight the Ganovs to make sure that our women Communists—your daughters—do not end up like me. Do not keep silent; do not ignore what may seem only a trifle now. Our whole life consists of little things. Such "educators" should be kicked right out of the party. They do not belong there. The party should not resemble the backstage of some cheap theater, where the most revolting, filthy scenes take place. I am sick and must leave the ranks in order to look around and understand, truly understand, where we are now, so that later (I am still young!) I can join Lenin's—not Ganov's—struggle with renewed energy!

>Candidate member of the Communist Party of Ukraine,
>Card No . . .
>Paraskeva Ivanova

15 □ Maria Belskaia

Arina's Children

□ Maria Karpovna Belskaia (née Nedobitkova), b. 1925, originally
wrote her story as a response to a letter published in 1987 in the
pro-perestroika magazine *Ogonek* by Ia. Gamaiun, a party member
since 1929, who argued that although collectivization may have been
a bad thing, time had healed all wounds, and hence excessive
glasnost was harmful. Ogonek did not publish Belskaia's letter, but
expanded versions were published in the Narodnyi arkhiv volume
cited above, as well as in M. K. Bel'skaia, *Deti Ariny* (Barnaul,
1991). Various versions of this manuscript and other materials relat-
ing to Belskaia's life are lodged in the Narodnyi arkhiv in Moscow.[1]

Our father, Karp Dmitrievich Nedobitkov, a peasant, returned home to his native
village after spending three years at the front in the First World War. His wife had
died while he was away, leaving four children.

A soldier's trenchcoat was the only thing he brought from the war—not counting a warm hood and a large enamel mug. That was all the wealth a peasant
soldier had. He needed to start rebuilding his life. So having found a good match
in a grass widow ten years his junior (although with a boy of her own), he decided
to strike out for the Altai [in Siberia] in search of free and fertile land.

Upon arrival, the entire family—which included his father (our grandfather,
Dmitry) and his two brothers, Arkhip and Nikolai, with their own families—
moved into an abandoned hut. Then they began thinking about building their own
houses.

The rich Altaian forests and free expanses made this possible. Anybody who
had the strength and skill, as well as the desire and ability to use them, was busy
building.

Still, it was not easy building that house, simple peasant hut though it was. My
father was a good carpenter, and my mother was hard-working, quick, and agile
enough to make their neighbors jealous, but I still remember how she used to cry
when she would talk about those days:

God knows, I've never had much luck! When I was little and lived with Father,
we were dirt poor. Our family was huge, and there weren't enough shoes and
clothes for everybody, so we had to keep hiring ourselves out. And what about
that house that your dad and I built? He didn't lay a single log without me. I

From *Zhenskaia sud'ba v Rossii. Dokumenty i vospominaniia*, ed. B. S. Ilizarov, comp. T. M.
Goriaeva (Moscow: Rossiia Molodaia, 1994); text prepared by L. P. Fomicheva, 42–59.
[1] Tsentr dokumentatsii "Narodnyi arkhiv" (TsDNA), f. 433 (lichnyi fond M. I. Bel'skoi-
Nedobitkovoi).

was right by his side the whole time. I mixed the mud myself and daubed those walls till my fingers bled. That's what that house cost us: a lot of blood, sweat, and tears.

One way or another they finished the hut, and our family moved in. They helped Uncle Arkhip build his house, too. Uncle Nikolay stayed in the old house.

Our family kept growing. My father had already had four kids of his own and my mother had brought her five-year-old boy with her, and then there were the six of us she had had by my father. That made thirteen in all.

How she dealt with such a crowd I cannot imagine. We were a hard-working family. My father and mother liked to breed cattle and fowl, and they knew how to look after them. We had three cows, two small horses, about five sheep, and some pigs, chickens, and geese. We plowed, sowed, spun, and wove everything ourselves, and all by hand. We never had any machines; we never even laid eyes on anything like that. All our clothes were coarse homespun. My mother made them herself, and often there was not enough cloth to go around.

Then came the revolution, and power started changing hands in the Altai. My father, his brother, Arkhip, and his good friend, Filipp Ivanovich Kolesnikov, joined a partisan unit called the "Red Mountain Eagles."

In one of the battles in the forest with the White Cossacks, Filipp Ivanovich was badly wounded, and he remained a cripple for the rest of his life. The bullet went through his right cheek, crushed his jaw, and damaged his tongue. It was a miracle he survived. To hide his deformity, Filipp Ivanovich wore a thick black beard. His speech was halting and slurred. Our two families were very close, and we truly loved and respected each other. My father would sometimes refuse to sit down at the dinner table if his friend was not there with him. My brothers and Filipp Ivanovich's boys were also inseparable. He had nine of them. They were even poorer than we were. They also had a little house, but there was nothing in it except a stove, a sleeping platform, and some benches.

But was ours really all that different?! There was the wide Russian stove we all loved so much and the warm platform under the ceiling where the kids slept winter and summer. There were the wide benches along the walls, the sturdy wooden table, two little benches, and three stools. That was all the furniture we had. Our common mattress was a saddlecloth made from sheep's wool, and my mother had made pillows from chicken and goose feathers. In one corner was a little cupboard that my father had made, with wooden spoons, bowls, pans, and a poker; on a shelf in front of the stove my mother kept flour; and in another corner, under the bench, was a large kneading trough. That was all the "kulak" wealth we had. I don't think this is how real kulaks would have lived. I can remember that there were not enough shoes to go around when we started school. You would just have to sit at home and wait for one of the others to return from school, and then put on his shoes as fast as you could and run all the way, trying not to be late.

I remember how my father once made boots for my oldest brother, Ivan—but only because he was about to get married. Otherwise, in the summer the whole family went barefoot, and in the winter we did the best we could with one pair of shoes for about every four of us. That shows what kind of kulaks we were.

That's how our family lived and grew. Then collectivization started. My father and mother were among the very first to join the kolkhoz. They turned over whatever they were supposed to—the cattle and the horses—and started working in the kolkhoz.

My father became the best hunter in the kolkhoz, and my mother, the first shock worker. Nobody worked harder than she did. No other family had as many labor days as we did.[2] That's when some people started envying us and wishing us ill—people, like Bugarikha, who pretended to be activists but really only liked to talk, not work.

We lived better in the kolkhoz than we had before. We had a cow, a horse, and some chickens, geese, pigs, and sheep. My father used to bring home a lot of furs, which could be traded in for calico, sugar, or anything else our family needed. We kids started wearing calico dresses and shirts, and I even got my first pair of soft leather shoes, which, however, I used to wear mostly on my hands. I remember caressing them and taking them to bed with me. That's how much I liked my new shoes.

But that was much later. The first terrible misfortune that struck our family took place before I was even born. Our Ivan (the Bolshevik) and two other young men were arrested, tried before a troika, and all sentenced to be shot. This is what happened.

Our Ivan, as the first village Komsomol member, and his friends, Guskov and Loganty Zuev, who were much older than he was, received an order from their superiors to carry out nationalization in the village. So our Ivan and the other two went to the house of a rich woman named Matiushikha, and started bullying her—in a joking kind of way. "Hey, granny! Show us what you've got hidden in these trunks! And what's in those jars in the pantry? Could it be honey, by any chance? Let's see where you've sewn up all your gold . . . Hey, if you keep whining and getting in the way like that, we're going to tie you up in a sack and throw you in the river . . ."

They paid dearly for that little joke. The guys, having searched her house, made a list of some of the stuff—a jar of honey and a few other little things—and then went back to the village soviet. Meanwhile, Matiushikha, having been egged on by somebody (she would never have come up with the idea herself), ran off to town and found the right people to complain to. She told them her story, embellishing it with all sorts of details that had nothing to do with those zealous "Komsomolers," and she had them punished all right: all three heroes were seized, taken away, and sentenced to be shot. It was 1924. Our Ivan was already married and had a daughter, Shurka. That was a time of awful confusion in the villages. You never knew what might get you into trouble. All our women started wailing. Anisia, Ivan's wife, kept sobbing, always with the same refrain: "Papa-a-a! Save our Vania . . . He's a fool. He didn't know what he was doing . . ."

Our father went into town. Having gone from one office to another, he ended up in the office of the chief prosecutor, who turned out to be an old friend of his,

---

[2] Labor days—Collective farmers were paid on the basis of the "labor day," a unit of measurement reflecting both time worked and the nature of work performed.

a Latvian rifleman he had met in the trenches on the German front and then again in the Riga barracks. The man heard my father out and promised to help. Sure enough: Ivan's death sentence was commuted to five years in prison. Guskov and Zuev were shot.

But let me go back to the first year of collectivization and describe what happened to the peasants—not the kulaks but the most hard-working and industrious of our peasants, the true salt of the earth.

The villagers were restless and depressed. Several families were being deported, including the family of my father's brother-in-law by his first marriage, Fedosei Rodionov. Just like Father, Fedosei had a new hut he had built himself, and although he had taken part in the partisan movement, he was still listed as a kulak. He had a large family of seven—all hard-working, honest people who had never lived off anybody's labor . . .

You could hear wailing and crying all over the village. Everyone walked to the outskirts to say farewell to relatives or just good neighbors. The deportees were the most hard-working men we had and would have been very useful in the kolkhoz. And why were they being deported? Because they had been building, plowing, and sowing with their own bare hands, never exploiting anybody? Our Pokrovka was a large village, and those who were not too lazy to work and look after their families lived well. All the power in that God-forsaken backwoods of ours was given to a bunch of self-seeking extremists, who ruined the village and scattered the villagers. Some people left on their own, others were exiled, while still others were arrested as enemies of the people.

They were going to deport our uncle Arkhip, too. And do you know why? All because he had built a house for himself and kept some cattle; because his shirt was wet with sweat; and because his family loved to work and never hired any help. One day Uncle Arkhip gathered all his children together, harnessed a couple of horses, loaded his belongings into some carts, and left our village forever. And that is how he saved himself from deportation and from unjust dekulakization.

Before leaving, he invited our father to go with him, but our father only laughed: "There's no reason in the world to dekulakize me. I fought for Soviet power and have my partisan card to prove it. You did, too. So why abandon the only home you've got? Nobody's going to touch us. There's no reason to."— "They'll find a reason if they try. How come you've got a new house and your own cattle? Why are you making a new gate? The other day a man from Charysh told me: 'If they don't take your geese, chickens, and houses away from you, you'll never understand what Soviet power is all about.' That's what he told me. And here you are, trying to live a nice life . . . So go get your kids, grease the wheels of your cart, and let's get out of here while we can."

Uncle Arkhip and his family left their native village—abandoning their house completely even though nobody had ordered them to—and ended up at a sheepherding state farm not far from Minusinsk. His children were able to get an education, though. Anisia, his oldest daughter, became a teacher; Katia, the youngest, a doctor; and Evsei, a veterinarian. Semen worked on the farm. During the

Patriotic War[3] he was sent to the front and died a hero's death at Stalingrad. Ivan became an award-winning collective farmer and a Hero of Socialist Labor. Such "kulaks" earned their glory through their own efforts, while the loafers and jealous nobodies died like dumb animals, abandoned by God and useless to the devil. All they had ever done was to eat people alive through envy and run errands for the enemies of the people, thinking all the while that they were following the correct party line.

Once Uncle Arkhip came down to Pokrovka with his famous son, Ivan the hero, and asked for his house back. But he was told: "Owing to the long period of inoccupancy, Arkhip Danilovich, your house has reverted to the state." So the words of that man from Charysh had come true after all: "If they don't take anything away from you, you'll never understand what Soviet power is all about."

That's what it was like in those days . . . Now is the time to try and figure out whose fault it was. Everybody suffered—children and grown-ups . . . Even if their parents were guilty of something, why did the children have to suffer so? But what were they guilty of? Just because one clever fool decided to immortalize himself in history, the peasants—the hard-working farmers, the true masters of the land and of the grain—had to suffer, and their old people, women, and children had to suffer along with them.

The same was true for our family. Together and separately, we starved, walked barefoot in the snow, came down with typhoid and malaria, went blind from exhaustion, suffered from whooping cough and tuberculosis, and went mad. None of us got any education; all our talents have gone to waste . . . Our childhood was poisoned and taken away from us; we did not have a happy youth; in fact, we did not have normal human lives at all. We were despised, distrusted, and kept out of all sorts of places. And what was it all for?

Now, this Stalinism is being talked about openly, if not yet with complete courage and determination. Who was entrusted with power? What was our great Stalin thinking of? Our very "great" thanks to him for such a "happy childhood."[4] We will never forget it; time itself will be powerless to erase it from our memory.

That's the way it was. We lived in the kolkhoz, tried as hard as we could, and were highly regarded by the authorities.

Our kolkhoz chairman was a wonderful man named Piankov, a young Communist, a real leader, and an honest, efficient administrator. He appreciated good work and treated working people with kindness and respect. He was friendly and down-to-earth, and always fair. Toward idlers and loafers, however, he was demanding and ruthless. He really got the kolkhoz working: the harvests never rotted in the fields, and all the members regularly received bread according to their labor days. We lived well, and there was enough of everything. Our family had a great life. We always had big loaves of fresh wheat bread at home. We also had milk, sour cream, butter, and our own meat. For almost every holiday, Mother

[3] The Soviet name for the Second World War.
[4] "Thank you, Comrade Stalin, for our happy childhood" was a standard formula of the 1930s.

sewed new dresses for us (out of calico, though). I, for one, had three new dresses: two warm flannel ones and one made out of sateen. I also had new black stockings knitted from the wool of our sheep. Shoes were the only thing our family almost never had—I guess we felt we did not really need them. We made everything ourselves, except for the salt, matches, and kerosene that Mother would buy for a few pennies at our village store.

In this way they lived, worked, and raised us children. The last ones to be born were Frosia, in 1929, and little Ira, in 1932. Mother did not have any more children. Some hard and terrible times were in store for our family.

First, we heard an alarming rumor: "Piankov's going to be fired." Indeed, the normally kind and cheerful chairman seemed gloomy and preoccupied, and would not look my father in the eye. He seemed to be avoiding Mother, too. We did not know the reason for this and continued to work hard. Mother continued to be the best worker in the kolkhoz.

Soon we heard that Piankov had been summoned to the city, and then later his whole family left our village. According to rumor, Piankov had been ordered to dekulakize our father, expel him from the kolkhoz, kick him out of his house, and confiscate all his property. He had banged his fist on the table indignantly as he tried to reason with them: "You want me to expel a family like that from the kolkhoz? How dare you?! They're the best we've got! She is our leading shock worker, and he's the best hunter and carpenter in the kolkhoz. This is something I will never do . . . Even if it means I have to . . . here, take this . . .," and Piankov threw his party card on the party secretary's desk. "If we have to expel people like that and drive them out of their own home, I no longer want to be a Communist. You'll just have to find yourself another chairman. Just look at that family . . one kid smaller than the next . . . and you want me to throw them out of their house. Why? What are your reasons?"

It did not take them long to find their reasons. Shortly afterward a new chairman by the name of Chizhik arrived in the kolkhoz. The whole village seemed to be holding its breath. As if before a terrible storm, people sat quietly, thinking to themselves: "What's going to happen now? What is this new chairman like? They say there'll be more dekulakizing . . . Rumor has it that this time it will be Karp Dmitrievich . . . We'll just have to wait and see."

At that time we had as a tenant an old schoolteacher—one of the Don Cossacks who had been exiled from the Don for being untrustworthy. He used to keep servants. He had been exiled to our remote region along with his pregnant maid, who was young enough to be his daughter. To hide the fact that she was his maid, Danila Andreevich (that was his name) had gotten her pregnant and then claimed she was his wife, not his maid.

Once, when his young wife was about to have her baby, Danila Andreevich and our father went into town together on some kolkhoz business. While there they had an argument, and they came back the worst of enemies. Danila did not even want to remain in our house and started packing his things. It turned out that they had disagreed about Soviet power: what it meant for the peasants, and who had suffered from it and why. Our father had, of course, argued along his usual line:

how he had been a partisan and fought the Cossacks who were defending the old regime. After that Danila had nothing but hatred for our father and our whole family.

The new chairman, Chizhik, often talked to the teacher in the village soviet or even in his own house. Chizhik was also a Don Cossack. Meanwhile, there was yet another Don Cossack, Churik, who kept issuing instructions from his high position on the provincial party committee. In this way, they conspired and plotted against people like us.

The chairman started picking on my parents to the point where it became persecution. Our Dema, who was already a teenager, was working at our village dairy factory (if you could call it that). He was a good worker. He was honest, disciplined, and conscientious. He never lied and was kind and affectionate, but he was also tough when he had to be. We, his younger brothers and sisters, loved and respected him very much.

One day Dema came home early and was very upset. He had been fired from the factory at the chairman's insistence: "A kulak's son cannot be trusted to work in a factory." The next thing we knew, our mother and father had both been expelled from the kolkhoz. In my mother's case the excuse was that she had not shown up for work for several days. This is how it happened.

Once, all the women from the kolkhoz were sent to float logs down the Charysh River. After about two weeks of standing in icy cold water and pushing giant logs toward the bank, Mother had gotten sick. Her whole body was covered with sores and huge boils. In her armpits she had enormous boils that hung down like dog teats. During the night she would scream, unable to move. I remember it all clearly. We would stoke up the bath house and have her sit in the dry heat. Then we would put a big wooden barrel in there and fill it with all sorts of herbs, some oats, and manure. Next we would pour in hot water, and then, when she could stand it, Mother would climb in. After that we would crank up the heat in the bath house, and she would sit there in the hot steam, sweating. Eventually she started to feel better, but she still could not work. There were no doctors in the village, so we all treated ourselves the best we could, using old country remedies.

While Mother was suffering from the boils and fever, the other women—especially the party activists like Nastasia Semenovna Bugareva, Akulina Egorovna Kosheleva, and a few others from among our new chairman's cheerleaders—also stayed home, absolutely refusing to go to work. "Are we mules or something? Look at Karp's woman: malingering and cooling her heels at home for more than a week now ... We also have kids to look after. We can stay home, too."

Even now, Mother gets angry at herself when she remembers those days: "What a fool I was! I should have gone down to the village soviet, pulled up my shirt, and shown them what kind of malingerer I was. I should have let them see what I had hanging from my armpits. They acted like they couldn't find their way to the sheds and the threshing floor without me. The same people who used to tell me not to drive myself and everyone else so hard were now blaming me for not taking them by the hand and leading them to work."

In any case, she did not go down to the village soviet until she was told she had been expelled. What could she do? Chizhik refused to talk to her and never even lifted his eyes from his desk. It was just: "You've been expelled, and that's that. We can do whatever we want to you."

Mother came home in tears: "How are we going to live now?" Soon afterward my father was expelled, too. They said he had been hunting for too long instead of building a kolkhoz stable. They had found their reasons all right.

And so we became a despised and persecuted family. There was no longer a place for us in our own village or in our own house. They started taxing us as nonmembers, constantly demanding all sorts of arrears. When we had nothing left to give, they came to confiscate our property. We began to go hungry. They did not give us a single crumb as payment for our labor days; everything had been deducted as tax arrears.

The first time they came to make their list, they put down Father's old sheep-skin coat (it happened to be hanging on the wall), the table, the two benches, the stools, the pots, and the oven forks. In the barn they put down our last cow. The geese and chickens had already been confiscated and taken to town. It was only then that Mother finally gathered up her dowry shawls, two towels she had embroidered herself, two skirts, and a dress and, having first tied them into a little bundle, took them one night to the barn behind the bath house and buried them in manure. As for the pillows, the saddlecloth, and the blanket—they were all confiscated.

I don't remember exactly when, but eventually an auction was held in our yard. The villagers got all our "wealth" for almost nothing. My brother Dema stood on the porch looking sadly at what was going on. The rest of us gathered by the wall of the house, crying and sniffling.

Dema had his boots on—the ones Father had made for him as the oldest son. He was a young man of fifteen, after all, who had already started going to dances and dating girls. Anyway, a village soviet representative walked up to him with a kind of smirk, pulled the boots off his feet, and added them to the pile. They were sold right away, of course, for next to nothing. It had started snowing, and the ground was already frozen in places. Dema unwrapped his foot bindings and walked, barefoot, down the porch steps and out of the yard. We were all sobbing.

For a few days we lived in our house, happy not to have been kicked out. Then one day, as I was sitting on a bench drinking salted water to kill the hunger, Mother came in crying. She was followed by a village soviet representative with a briefcase under his arm. We knew what that meant: he was there to take possession of our house. I turned white and tottered, and the clay mug fell out of my weak little hand. I was six years old at the time. The mug broke, and I fell off the bench and lost consciousness.

After he had finished writing, the representative said sternly: "You've got twenty-four hours. You have to be out of here by tomorrow evening. The village soviet is going to be moving in here with all the documents and the seal. We need this place to work in. Is that clear?" And he turned around and left.

Mother started crying. We did, too. But we were still hoping. We thought, "They can't really kick us out of our own house and into the street, can they? Where would we go? Who would let us in?"

Indeed, no one did offer to put us up. Everybody was scared of that terrible chairman, Chizhik, of being next on the list.

It was the last day we ever spent in our family nest. Early the next morning they brought over a squeaky old bookcase and a desk to match. Also two or three chairs, three old folders, and an inkwell with dried-up ink. It was still warm in the hut: Mother had started a fire in the stove at dawn. We crawled into a corner on top of the stove and watched fearfully as the things were being brought in. The smell of home was gone, replaced by an alien odor made up of strong tobacco, ancient dust, old papers, and, I guess, mice.

A cold blizzard was swirling around outside, and the frost had painted patterns on our dear old windows. We were being given menacing, hate-filled looks. "What do you think you're doing up there? Can't you see this is the village soviet now? You can't stay here all night. Get out of here!"

Frightened, we squeezed farther and farther into the corner, as if that could save us. Mother was out trying to find someone who would take us in. Father was no longer with us: he had been put in jail for supposedly driving two kolkhoz horses to Airit-Tura and selling them there.

Later, having come back with bad news, Mother stood in front of the stove trying to warm her red, frozen hands. Sobbing, she implored them: "Please, take pity on us. I've been everywhere; nobody will even let us sleep under a bench."

But they refused to even listen.

And what about the village soviet—do you think that it did not have any place to go? You've got to be kidding! It already occupied the best house in the whole village: the solid, bright, cheerful house of another former partisan, Anisim Gerasimovich Zuev. It used to be clean and freshly painted, but now it was covered with spit and filled with smoke. They just needed an excuse to kick us out of our house, and so they had decided to move.

Mother kept warming her hands in front of the stove while we lay trembling up in our corner. Our big brother, Dema, was no longer living at home; he had left to stay with the Kolesnikovs. Eremei and Trofim had climbed up on the bed and fallen asleep. Sima[5] had run off to Uncle Nikolai's place and was living there most of the time. Only the three of us—me, Frosia, and one-year-old little Ira— were up on the stove. Mother kept crying and asking them to let us stay . . .

It was getting dark; the eerie, cold blizzard winds were making the window rattle. We had not eaten in two days. Finally, the representatives and two other soviet employees nodded to each other, and then walked up to the stove and began pulling us down one by one. We started screaming, but that made them even angrier, and without a moment's hesitation they threw us all out into the cold entryway, and then out onto the porch. We were barefoot and had only our shirts on.

---

[5] One of Maria's two older half-brothers.

Having gotten rid of us, they started dragging the sleeping Trofim and Eremei off the bed. They jerked Trofim so hard that he fell on the floor and started crying, still half asleep and not understanding what was going on. We were shivering in the cold and crying when Mother and our two brothers came out, and we all went to Uncle Nikolai's. We had no place else to go. I think they had threatened him, "If you let them in, the same thing will happen to you." But he just kept cursing and said: "You mean, they just threw these kids out like puppies? So they could freeze to death? I say, let them do what they will, but blood is thicker than water."

We lived at Uncle Nikolai's for a short while, but when the sun grew warmer and spring seemed near, we decided to leave. He had a large family of his own, and we did not want to be in the way.

Next to our house was an old shack where we had lived while our house was being built. After we had moved into our house, it had served as a temporary shelter for those who had no place to live, and then as a shed for the kolkhoz calves. Now it came in handy again. It had no stove or porch, and the roof leaked badly. So we decided to fix it. On sunny days Mother and all us kids would go down to the river, break the ice which was already dark and caved in, and, standing up to the waist in icy cold water, dig out the sand and mud. Then we would carry it back to the shack in order to build a stove. We did build one—a nice stove that could get hot enough to bake bread or potatoes in. But of course we did not have anything to bake. I do not know how we survived. Mother secretly dug out her little bundle and, creeping along and looking over her shoulder, went from door to door trading the things for food: potatoes, bran, maybe a piece of bread. Sometimes we went around begging. We had heard nothing from our father.

When spring came, they kicked us out of the shack and put the kolkhoz calves in there. That was when our wanderings began. First, Mother found shelter at the house of a crippled old lady who lived at the very edge of the village. I do not know if she let us in out of the goodness of her heart or in exchange for something. In the spring we tilled her garden, and the kids took her cow out to pasture, so she would sometimes give us milk to drink. We slept in one tiny room, and when it got warmer, moved outside to a wooden deck that we shared with her cow. We kids were so hungry that one night we took turns sucking milk straight from the cow's udder. When your stomach is empty and you are dizzy with hunger, lying beside a cow with a full udder is torture.

The old lady threw us out, and we moved to the house of Dunka, whose nickname was the priest-woman.[6] We slept on the floor, next to her dying brother, who kept coughing and spitting out the bloody shreds of his diseased lungs. The priest-woman decided to rob us. She took some of our clothes and my brothers' old boots and hid them under the house. They were all we had left. Mother had been guarding them like the crown jewels because we were preparing to leave the village. Everyone was avoiding us as if we were lepers; nobody would talk to us, fearing that the same thing might happen to them.

---

[6] The Russian word *popikha* is a rather unflattering-sounding neologism denoting a woman who acts like a priest.

During the winter our Dema had joined some grown men who were on their way to a town called Ridder to see if they could find jobs in a mine. Now Mother decided to go there, too. It was a long way, five hundred kilometers by the long road—unless you wanted to climb the Altai Mountains. After the priest-woman's attempt to steal our "property," we moved to an abandoned house that stared out at the world from the black eye sockets of its empty windows. We got rid of the cobwebs, swept and washed the floor, and settled in. During the first night we were almost eaten alive by bedbugs. There were so many of them that we all jumped up in the middle of the night and started sweeping them out with a broom. But we had no place else to go . . . Then Mother thought of getting some wormwood and placing it around us at night. That stopped the invasion for a while, but the bedbugs turned out to be very smart. They would crawl up to the ceiling and then fall on top of us.

When it got dark Mother and some of the kids would go to the old threshing floor looking for last year's grain. Sometimes they would get caught and have whatever they had managed to scrape up taken from them. Our eight hundred labor days were not good enough even to pick up last year's waste.

One way or another, Mother collected about three to four kilograms of grain, took them to the mill, and asked a miller she knew to trade them for flour. She had to keep pleading until he finally agreed and gave her about three or four kilos of the most coarse-ground flour he had. Still, we were happy. Mother wrapped the flour in a little bundle and put it away for the trip.

Then summer came, the warm month of June. We often went into the mountains to gather wild onions, garlic, rhubarb, and other herbs. We would bring home whole sackfuls, boil them, and eat them with a little salt. That was what we got to eat. Also, sometimes my brothers would catch some fish in the river, and that would keep us going for a while.

Finally, one bright sunny morning we left our native village. Nobody saw us off. Nobody needed us. We took one last look at our dear old house, formed a single file, and, crying and with our shoulders sagging, set off on our journey. At the time, Eremei was twelve years old; Sima, eleven; Trofim, eight; I was six; Frosia was three; and little Ira, one. Mother was carrying her on her back, in an old shawl attached to her shoulders. We followed her one by one. Little Ira could not walk yet because she had a crippled leg. As a kolkhoz worker, Mother had ridden horses, carried heavy bags, and a couple of times, when her stomach was already swollen, had fallen off a horse. The baby's leg had gotten damaged, and little Ira was born with one foot turned inward . . .

With no food or warm shelter, we walked along, sleeping in abandoned sheds and haystacks. In the mountains we walked barefoot in the snow. Every once in a while Mother would sit down under a haystack, pull up her blouse, and, like little goslings, we would crawl under her blouse and press our red frozen feet against her warm body. Sometimes we would pee on each other's numb feet, to warm them just a little bit. We also slept in people's bathhouses, but sometimes we were not allowed in there either. Our legs grew swollen from hunger. We were starving, but there was nothing to eat. We knocked on people's windows and begged in Christ's name for a piece of bread or a potato. While we still had flour, Mother would mix it with cherry blossoms or hawthorn and boil it in our little pot, and we would be happy that we still had something like bread. But then the flour ran out, and we had to live on whatever good people could give us. In those hungry days, there were not many good people around . . .

Meanwhile, cruel, heartless, well-fed people used to laugh at us, set their dogs on us, and drive us from their villages. But we just kept on walking.

Little Ira used to cry: "Bread! Give me some bread! I'm hungry!" And we would look at her and cry ourselves, and try to distract her . . . And then one of us would go into a village and beg for some food for a hungry little girl.

Finally we arrived in Ridder, where Dema was staying with relatives. He was a mere boy himself, working as an apprentice in a lumber yard, his shirt all mended and patched. He picked up little Ira and burst into tears. He was getting five or six hundred grams of bread on his ration card, and now seven of us had appeared on his doorstep. That was 1933, during the time of bread rationing.

There had been no news of our father. And we still had no place to live: the people with whom Dema was staying had five children in a one-room house. We moved into some barracks, where we slept on bunks. Autumn came, and winter was not far behind. We had nothing to eat and nothing to wear. We did not know to whom we could turn for help. We did not want to approach the authorities because we were afraid they would say: "It serves you right, you kulaks." We had no papers of any kind, not even birth certificates. Soon all the kids started pleading with Mother: "Let's go home . . . Let's go back to our Pokrovka . . . Maybe Daddy's been let out . . . Maybe they'll give us our house back . . ." Eremei would say: "I'll catch rabbits in the winter; we'll survive somehow." And Trofim would say: "I'll catch fish in the river . . ."

We missed our Pokrovka terribly. We were desperate to return home. We were all sure that our father would be released from prison since he was not guilty of anything. Those two horses had been found; it turned out that they had run off to join another herd and had ended up in an Altaian sovkhoz.

We talked and talked, until we finally decided to go back home. It was fall. The ground had started to freeze, and in the morning the grass was covered with thick white frost. It was too cold to sleep under haystacks. We made it to Malaia Ubinka, the village where Mother had been born and where our grandmother still lived. She was hungry herself. Grandfather Nazar had just died of hunger and dysentery. Nobody was particularly happy to see us: Grandmother Aksinia and her youngest son, Izot, were barely alive themselves. We stayed with them for about a week. They had some potatoes, and we got to eat a little bit. Not very much, though: we were emaciated, and our legs were swollen from hunger and bruised after the long journey. But time would not stand still, and we were not wanted there anyway, so early one morning we threw our little sacks over our shoulders and set off down the road. Four hundred kilometers to go. Would we make it? Would we get back alive?

It was still warm, dry, and sunny. It was early September 1933.

We had walked about two or three kilometers. You could still see the village down below. The morning fog was rising slowly from the sleepy Ubinka River. We had no strength left in us. Little Ira was crying on Mother's back. Suddenly Frosia, who had just caught up with the rest of us, hobbling painfully on her swollen feet, sat down in the middle of the dusty road and said: "I can't walk anymore . . . I am not going anywhere, I am staying here." We all started crying and rushed toward her. A hungry three-year-old child with swollen little feet . . . How much longer could she walk? What could we do? God help us! None of was strong enough to carry her, so we decided to send her back to grandmother Aksinia. That was better than having to leave her with strangers in a strange village. We told her how to walk back and how to find Grandmother, and then sent her on her way. My brother, Eremei, took her by the hand and led her part of the way. When he came back, wiping away tears with his fists, we all collapsed on the road and started sobbing. There she went, our dear little Frosia, waddling downhill, stumbling on her little feet, until she disappeared from sight . . . We cried some more, and went on our way. "Surely some good people are bound to take pity on her . . ."

At night we stayed with the same good people who had invited us in before, when we were walking to Ridder. Mother told them of her grief, and they said: "Leave the two little ones in an orphanage somewhere. You'll be walking through Zmeevo. There's an orphanage there. You must leave them there, or you will die yourself and kill your children. When you recover, you can come back and get them."

Mother did as they told her. As for me, I could not wait to be left in an orphanage somewhere. I simply could not go on walking anymore, and I was starving. I kept begging her: "Please leave me in an orphanage! I can't take this anymore, we'll all die on the road."

Finally we arrived in Zmeevo. Mother left little Ira and me on the porch of an orphanage. When they saw someone come get us, Mother and the other kids went on their way. They were in a hurry to get home before the snows began. They assumed we had been taken in, but they were mistaken. For a whole month little Ira and I camped out by the wall of a two-storied wooden house where the local officials worked. They wrote down our names and where we were from. I lied, of course, telling them that my parents had died of hunger and disease, and naming some nonexistent place. Instead of sending us to the orphanage, they kept trying to check out who we were and whether we were really orphans. Mother had warned me: "Maria, dear, don't tell them Father's name, or they'll find out that we have been dekulakized and refuse to take you in. Give them my maiden name, 'Klinovitsky.'"

My illiterate mother knew what she was talking about. Without that warning, little Ira and I would have perished alone in a strange town, under the wall of the local soviet.

I cannot even begin to describe what we went through during that month. We sat under the wall day and night. Some passers-by would take pity on us and give us a piece of bread, a potato, even a kopeck. I did not know what to do with the coins: we had rarely used money in our family, and I didn't know how to buy things. Sometimes, in order to feed little Ira, who never stopped crying, I would overcome my embarrassment and stagger down the street begging. Little Ira still couldn't walk, so she would crawl up to passers-by, grab them by the ankles, and scream wildly through her tears: "Give me some bread, give me some brea-a-a-ad!"

What was that baby guilty of? Or me, for that matter? I was only six years old at the time. I was all swollen from hunger and could not walk anymore. I kept thinking: "What will happen to little Ira when I die? Where will they put her?" That was all I could think of. I did not want to go on living. I didn't want to suffer and starve like a homeless dog. There were people living all around us, but we were like untouchable lepers.

Finally, we were allowed into the orphanage. Oh, how happy we were! They liked little Ira and me there, and we loved them, too, with all our hearts. We were in that orphanage from October 1933 through April 1934.

Mother and the rest of the kids barely made it back to Pokrovka. There was no question of getting our house back, but our father had, indeed, been released. Some kind soul in prison had written to the right people about our father's case. There was no case, as it turned out . . . Having spent eight months in jail, our father had returned to his village—only to find his family gone and his house confiscated.

Anyway, there he was at his son Epifan's place, mending his shoes and getting ready to go look for us, when all of a sudden, Mother showed up. Oh, the tears that were shed! Mother had only the three oldest kids with her. She told him where and how she had lost their other children.

My father went to the kolkhoz to ask for some bread in payment for all those labor days he had put in. But the guard, Abram Abramovich, took him to the granary and said: "Look, Mitich . . . Not a single grain left, not even next year's. How we are going to sow in the spring, nobody knows."

So Chizhik had managed to ruin our kolkhoz and devastate the village. Out of about a hundred solidly built houses, only ten or fifteen were left. Our village, as we knew it, was gone.

Having rested a little, the family set off for the third time, back to Ridder. Along the way they picked up Frosia, whom they could barely recognize. Uncle Izot, himself sick and hungry, had been sending her out barefoot in the snow to run errands for him, and once he had whipped her so hard across the face that she had become blind in one eye. So now little Ira and I were the only ones still missing. Mother was worried sick about us, not daring to hope that she would find us alive. She kept wanting to come back and get us, but Father talked her out of it "Wait, Arina," he said. "Let's get on our feet first, find a place to live, get work, and then you can go and get them. What can we do for them now? We don't even know what to do for ourselves. If they are in that orphanage, God willing, they must be alive. Just be patient for a while longer. Then we'll go and get them."

All winter long Mother and the kids worked at a warehouse sorting vegetables.

They were paid in potatoes. That was a big help. Father got a job at the same lumber yard where Dema worked. Dema was living in a dorm. As for Sima, Mother found her a job as a nanny, and she never lived with us again. She got through the fifth grade in night school and for her good and honest work was inducted into the Komsomol and later elected to the city council as a deputy to the First Convocation of 1938.

Mother was driving herself crazy thinking about little Ira and me. In the early spring, no longer able to stand it, she set off for Zmeevo. The trip was three hundred kilometers. After about a week of nonstop walking, Mother reached our orphanage. It was April 7, my birthday. Crying with happiness, she told us about everything and took us back with her.

We found a place to live, but the landlady knew that no one else would rent to us, so she tyrannized us terribly, especially the little ones. She would order us to till her garden or dig a huge moat to prevent the cows from entering the garden or whitewash her hut. Mother—helped by the kids, of course—did everything without saying a word. Eventually, however, her strength and patience gave out, and when it came to that moat, she simply refused. "Let's go, kids, and dig a little hole for ourselves instead," she said. "Then nobody will be able to bully us." And that's exactly what we did—just left that place, never to return again, found some shovels, and started making a dugout.

We dug a hole of about three by five square meters, lined it with straw, and, when night came, went to sleep in our new "home." Then it started raining. We had lots of straw underneath, but the rain kept coming down from above. I had one of my malaria fevers, and all the others who were cold kept trying to cuddle up to me to get warm.

That is how we started our new life together. We were always hungry. There was not enough money for bread. Instead of bread, Mother would buy burned bread crust at the market, for three rubles a bucket. Once, when I had a fever, I looked at Mother with hungry eyes and said: "Mama, all I want is a little piece of bread." But I survived and got well again.

And then we got lucky. Mother found out from a neighbor that there was a special allowance for large families like ours. I cannot describe how happy we were when we received two thousand rubles (in old money) for seven kids. Father immediately bought a cow and a horse (and so became a "kulak" again), because without milk we were all suffering from night blindness and had grown so thin you could almost see through us.

My brothers were still little and were not allowed to work, but they lied about their age and eventually found jobs in construction. They both became mason's apprentices.

Then new construction began, and our dugout had to be torn down. A special commission came, measured everything, and paid us seven hundred rubles for it. So we borrowed two hundred more from uncle Kasian and bought ourselves a tiny little hut for nine hundred rubles. It was a real wooden hut, though, with a little fence, a small garden, and even a clean, wooden outhouse. We were so happy!

After that we started living well. This was in 1937–39. There was enough bread for everybody, and we had our own vegetables and milk. What else could we want?

Then came the Great Patriotic War. I quit school and went to work in a factory. I was fourteen years old.

In the fall of 1941 we were notified of Ivan's death. "Died a hero's death defending Leningrad." Trofim was wounded twice but fought all the way from Stalingrad to Sofia. There, while helping the Bulgarian partisans, he caught a cold and came down with a bad case of pleurisy. He was treated at a military hospital in Sochi and then brought home on a special hospital train. Three months later he died in Father's arms.

After the war we managed to add another little room to our house. Frosia got married and had a baby girl, but soon afterward was diagnosed with acute tuberculosis.

Sima [Frosia's daughter] had a wonderful voice and could draw very well, too, but she never developed her talents. I also had a good voice—I even sang in the Piatnitsky Choir for a short time, but I did not have the proper training.[7]

All my brothers are dead now.[8] So is little Ira. She became a seamstress, married an invalid of the Great Patriotic War (he had only one leg), and had two boys. But her husband drank a lot, and they got divorced. She took it hard, cried a lot, and spent some time in a psychiatric hospital. One day she disappeared and was later found dead on the bank of the Irtysh.

At the end of this confession of mine, I would like to say: if there is any justice in this world, will it never prevail? I would very much like for my letter to be published, if only because of all our suffering and undeserved torment. Is it not clear now just what kind of kulaks and enemies of the people we were?

Let my letter become a vivid illustration of the cruel time of Stalinist excesses.

---

[7] Belskaia won her place in the prestigious folk choir by auditioning in Moscow after the war: as she told a newspaper interviewer in 1990, "they gave me a salary of eight hundred rubles. I became rich and happy" (TsDNA, f. 270: cutting from *Rudnyi Altai*, February 9, 1990, 4). After five or six years, however, she resigned from the choir in anger at not being included in the choir's foreign tour because of her dubious social origins. Her lack of education did not interfere with her career in the Piatnitsky Choir, but it prevented her fulfilling other aspirations, for example, entering the Conservatory as a student and winning a place at the Studio of the Moscow Arts Theater.

[8] Ivan and Trofim were war casualties; Eremei, sentenced as a teenager on a charge of stealing, died of tuberculosis in a labor camp in 1943. Maria's two sisters, Ksenia and Frosia, were still alive c. 1990 (Frosia having recovered by a seeming miracle from her serious bout with tuberculosis), as was her mother, Arina. Her father died in 1954 at the age of seventy (TsDA, f. 270: "Nasha sem'ia Nedobitkovykh" [ms. by M. K. Belskaia-Nedobitkova, c. 1990]).

16 □ ANTONINA SOLOVIEVA

Sent by the Komsomol

□ In the 1960s it became popular in the Soviet Union to make local collections of memoirs of surviving participants in past heroic events such as the civil war and collectivization. This memoir of a young, urban, female Komsomol member from the Urals who took part in the collectivization campaign of the 1930s is typical of the genre, which shows conflict in black-and-white terms and demonizes the kulak as a "class enemy."

IN 1930 Komsomol members started going to the countryside to help the Communists. Dozens of young people were released from work in factories and offices and sent out to villages.

I had the honor of being one of them. I represented the Komsomol organization of the Voevodin Factory in Sverdlovsk. I remember how my factory friends accompanied me to the station. It was late fall. There was a cold wind blowing that went right through my old worn-out coat, and it was drizzling. My friends remained by my side until the very last moment.

"So, Tonia, don't let us down. It's a huge assignment, and it won't be easy," our Komsomol secretary, Misha Kolmakov, said.

As our train approached the small station, a few tiny gray huts flashed by the window, followed by a tall mountain covered with dry, faded grass.

The train came to a stop with a sudden jolt, and somebody's knapsack fell from an upper bunk.

"What are you waiting for? We've arrived!" said the man from the top bunk as he jumped down and headed for the door. At last we managed to get off the train. On a small yellow building was a large sign that read: Votkinsk.

At the district Komsomol committee we were greeted in a restrained but friendly manner. I was not alone. Six other people sent by the Urals Provincial Komsomol Committee had come to register the day before: Vasily Soloviev, a young metal worker from the Pervouralsky Pipe Plant; Mikhail Vodovozov, a lathe operator from Neviansk; Marusia Kashina from Nizhny Tagil; and three Komsomol members from Sarapul. The district secretary, Zakhvatkin, told us:

"For the time being, you'll be working in local organizations. Later, as the need arises, we will send you out to the surrounding villages. The situation there is very difficult."

From A. Solov'eva, "Po putevke Komsomola," in *Ot pokoleniia k pokoleniiu* (Sverdlovsk: Sredne-Ural'skoe knizhnoe izdatel'stvo, 1964), 235–43.

I remember that Vasia Soloviev was sent to the factory Komsomol committee, and Misha Vodovozov, to the local branch of the Society for the Assistance to the Army and Aviation. I became a recreation coordinator at the local club, and Marusia Kashina, an instructor at the district soviet. In other words, there was enough work to go around.

There I was, far from home. I missed noisy Sverdlovsk, my factory, the production brigade, and my friends, but I had no time to feel sorry for myself.

We did not remain in town for long. One cold day in January 1931 we were summoned to the district Komsomol committee. Everybody looked solemn and determined. There were three girls: Marusia, Sonia, and myself. Some of the boys were looking at us with mistrust and condescension, but we did not let it affect us. We were dressed the same way as the men—in camouflage fatigues. It made us look determined, and we carried ourselves with dignity.

Across the room were two young fellows in fatigues: one with dark Gypsy eyes, wearing a Red Army cap; the other light-haired, with a strong-willed decisive face, lightly scarred by smallpox. They were talking to each other in low tones and looking in our direction every once in a while. I realized they were talking about us. The light-haired one, Alesha Zakurdaev, worked for the district committee, but who was the dark one? He looked ferocious. I asked Sonia about him in a whisper. She looked over at the boys and said:

"You're right, he is truly ferocious—toward the class enemy, that is. That's Fedia Mashonkin, the scourge of the kulaks!"

Marusia and I looked at Fedia with awe. At that moment Zakhvatkin, his assistant Zhenia Bogatyrev, and two Communists from the party committee entered the room. The Communist Ermakov stood up, revealing his giant frame, and said softly:

"Comrade Komsomol members, we have assembled you here today because you, along with us Communists, will be going out to the countryside to help the collective farms and village soviets get ready for the spring sowing season. The situation in the villages is alarming. As you know, the country is counting on kolkhoz grain, while kulak scoundrels are hiding and spoiling the seeds and disorganizing the peasants. Your task is to engage in mass agitational work among the village youth from the unaffiliated middle stratum[1] and to find out where the kulaks are hiding the grain and who is wrecking the agricultural machinery. On top of everything else, owing to the intimidation on the part of the kulaks and their henchmen, many of the poor households have not yet joined the collective farms. This means that you will need to talk to these people and explain party policies and collectivization to them. This is your task."

This was a huge task; were we up to it? We really knew nothing about these things; we did not know how to begin. Zhenia Bogatyrev said, however, as if reading our thoughts:

---

[1] Peasants were officially divided into three groups based, in theory, on their wealth: the rich peasants, or "kulaks," who were considered implacably hostile to the regime; the middle peasants, who wavered between a pro- and antiregime position; and the poor peasants, who were considered to be the basis for regime support in the village.

"Do not allow yourselves to think that you don't know anything about this. Don't spread yourselves too thin—just do whatever you consider the most important thing. It will all become clearer when you get there. Also, your senior comrades from the party will be there to help and support you.

The objectives seemed clear enough, but we had so many questions that we stayed at the district committee late into the night.

WE got to our villages however we could. Some went by train and then on foot; some got a ride on a cart that was returning home from market; others walked the whole way. It was quite a trip. Most of our people were poorly dressed, and many wore army boots—not the kind of thing you would want to wear in the winter. So we ran as fast as we could, always hoping to make it to the next village.

There was no time to lose. After presenting their papers at the village soviet, the arriving Komsomol members would be sent to some collective farm or individual household—to the hardest possible spot. The objective was to talk individual peasants into joining the collective farm; to make sure that the collective farm was ready to begin sowing; and, most important, to find out where and by whom state grain was being hidden. Usually, our first task was to organize a group of activists (preferably from among the village youth), gain their trust, and start a frank conversation. We were quite successful, I must say. We would spend long evenings around a small table with a weakly flickering kerosene lamp at some collective farm headquarters or by a burning stove in some poor peasant's hut. Some of us would even join the peasant girls at their evening get-togethers. Usually the boys would come, too, and sing quiet songs. Whenever we found out about such get-togethers, we would show up unannounced.

One of our Komsomol activists, Kostia Lutkov, was particularly good at this. He acted completely natural, joking around, laughing a lot, and improvising funny rhymes. The men respected him, and the girls admired him. Sooner or later the subject of the kolkhoz would come up. Some of those who came to the get-togethers were under the kulaks' influence, but Kostia would listen patiently until everyone had spoken and then join the conversation as if he were one of them. Once a local field hand, Mitia Varlamov, asked Kostia for some tobacco. Kostia offered him some and said: "Just look at yourself, kid: your coat is all torn; you're wearing bast shoes; and your pants are made of sackcloth. Now, in the collective farm you could make some money, receive your grain ration, and even buy cologne for your evening get-togethers."

Mitia Varlamov, who was eighteen years old, looked at Kostia and asked shyly: "I can't really make that much in the kolkhoz, can I?"

"Just think about it," said Kostia, "All the land will be collectivized, so the kolkhoz will have plenty of it; all the horses will be in the same stable in the large collective farm yard; and all the machines—harvesting, sowing, and threshing—will stand next to each other in the same collective farm yard. With all that land and all those horses and machines—if you just work hard, you will be well-fed and well-dressed."

Mitia still did not get it. "But if you take all the machines away from the rich people, what are the field hands going to work on?" he asked.

"They aren't going to work for the rich people anymore," said Kostia. "In any case, most of them are already in the collective farm. The point is for you to work for yourself, not for the rich."

"And not just any old way, but on a machine," dark-eyed Nastia joined in. "Have you seen the red threshing machine they took away from Stepan last week?"

"I sure have," Mitia drawled. "Two years ago I spent the better part of the fall season threshing on that machine. Got paid peanuts for it, too." The kid looked hurt and turned away.

"That's what we're talking about," said Nastia, with a sly glance in Kostia's direction. "Just sign up, and nobody will cheat you anymore. You'll get what you earn."

The young people would leave the get-together feeling transformed, and Kostia would add new names to his list of youngsters who wished to build a new collective farm future.

It was through these young collective farm members that we were able to find out who was hiding grain and wrecking collective farm property. This information would be transmitted secretly, "through the grapevine." We would not know where the information had originated but would always check it out and, sure enough, often it would turn out to be correct.

The courageous Komsomol member Fedia Mashonkin was a real terror for the kulaks. He and some fearless Komsomol friends of his used to get on their horses and show up in some remote village late at night. They would talk to the local Komsomol representatives; get all the information they could from them on kulaks, hidden grain, suspects, and so on; and by the next morning the confiscated grain would be stored in the collective farm yard.

The Komsomol member Alesha Zakurdaev frequently visited the countryside on special party assignments. Once he uncovered a whole gang of kulak criminals. More than once he was shot at or ambushed, but he never abandoned his post. He fought bravely against the kulaks, reported them to the state and party organs, and helped the Communists arrest them and confiscate their property, which had been acquired dishonestly through the efforts of others.

Once I was in the village of Kelchino. The village soviet had received a report that the kulak Gerasim had a lot of hidden grain. The chair of the soviet found some activists from among the poor peasants, and we went to Gerasim's place to confiscate the grain. As soon as we opened the gate, the rocks started flying and we heard a rifle shot. We were forced to leave. We could not reach Votkinsk by telephone because the connection was very bad, so I took a horse from the soviet and rode there myself. I returned the same night accompanied by the armed Communists, Goroshnikov and Dudin, and the Komsomol members, Misha Vodovozov and Sonia. We had been riding along in silence, but when we reached the village, Sonia said:

"I know this Gerasim. He is very religious. We can use it to our advantage."

"Why do we care?" protested Goroshnikov.

"I'll dress up as a nun and ask him to let me in for the night. I know how to pray. Then in the morning I'll open the gate for you."

"It's too risky," said Misha Vodovozov. Dudin agreed.

We had no alternative, however, and time would not wait. The Communist Goroshnikov agreed to the plan. Sonia left her horse with us and disappeared into the dark. We stopped by the huts of our activists and made sure that Gerasim's house was being closely watched. Everyone was worried about Sonia. Finally the dim light of a kerosene lamp appeared in the little window, and we could see two moving shadows.

. . . At dawn we entered Gerasim's house without encountering any resistance. Gerasim himself was fast asleep, his sawn-off shotgun under his pillow, while a nun in bast shoes was praying with great feeling in front of the icon. Gerasim was arrested, as was Sonia, for her own safety. It was necessary to protect the identity of the brave Komsomol girl. Unfortunately, I have not been able to remember her last name.

But things did not always go so smoothly. The enemy tried to retaliate whenever opportunity afforded.

Once we were taking inventory of the confiscated property of a kulak. There were four of us: Liza Korobeinikova, a former field hand and Kelchino's first Komsomol member; Sasha Kosachev, the head of the reading hut; Cherepanov, a party member and the representative of the district executive committee; and I. We were sitting at a table drawing up lists of confiscated property items. A kerosene lamp with a metal shade hung over the table.

Suddenly we heard the sound of the window breaking, and then the lamp burst into little pieces and went out. A heavy object fell onto the table. Cherepanov ordered us to sit on the floor between the windows, and then he lit a match. On the table lay a half-pint bottle filled with river sand—another kulak weapon used not infrequently to kill people.

Two days later I learned from Liza who had thrown the bottle and who the intended victim had been. It turned out that the Kosachevo kulaks were out to get Sasha. I decided to go to Kosachevo immediately—to conduct an on-the-spot investigation and to inform the appropriate authorities of the attack. Unfortunately, the chairman of the village soviet would not let me go. Then later, in 1932, I discovered that the Kosachevo kulaks had been planning to drown me in the Kama River.

In the Svetliansky soviet, Valentin Piankov, the head of the reading hut, unmasked the local kulak, Andrei Kilin, in the district newspaper. Kilin was duly arrested by the state organs [i.e., police]. Some time later the enemy got back at Valia. They beat him up, and the Komsomol member, Piankov, had to spend a long time in the hospital.

The enemy also got rid of the brave and strong-willed Komsomol member, Marusia Kashina, who had been sent to Sharkan on a special assignment. For a long time nobody knew what had happened to her. Her disappearance was mysterious, and some people thought she had just gone home. It was not until the summer of 1931 that Marusia's fatigues, with her bloody identity papers in the jacket pocket, were found on a forest path outside Sharkan.

The work that had been conducted by Komsomol members in the countryside was later summarized at a caucus meeting of the district activists. The delegates made brief presentations about what had been accomplished. In fact, a great deal had been accomplished. We had exposed numerous plots and tricks used by the kulak elements. We had learned how to deal with them.

Many of the speakers talked about the danger of sabotage during the approaching sowing campaign. The Votkinsk Communists had resolved to have the first furrow plowed everywhere on the same day—Easter Day. Our activists had been informed of this, and there was no fear that any of the Votkinsk Komsomol members would remain on the sidelines. Every single one of us was going to join in the effort. The first furrow was to be known as the "red furrow."

Soon after the meeting the Komsomol organization of our factory embarked on active preparations for the expedition. Once again, Komsomol militants were going out to every collective farm, every village soviet. The "red furrows," plowed with their participation, helped to carry out the sowing campaign of 1931. The enemy plot to sabotage collective farm sowing did not succeed. Collectivization in the district proceeded at an even greater pace.

17 □ NENILA BAZELEVA ET AL.

Peasant Narratives (1)

□ The following oral narratives by peasant women were recorded in Pskov Province in the 1970s and 1980s by the musicologist E. N. Razumovskaia and her students from the College of Music at the Leningrad Conservatory. Such uncensored histories could not be published in the Brezhnev period.

NENILA PLATONOVNA BAZELEVA (B. 1890)
Recorded in 1988 in Safonovo Village, Kuninsky District

I was my mother and father's only daughter, so I wasn't young when I got married (I'd already turned twenty-five). I did not leave home—he had to move in. I didn't get to do the picking: they chose him for me, and I got married. My fiancé lived across the road from us on a farm (in those days everybody lived on farms). We got engaged and he left for the [First World] War. He spent three years as a prisoner, working for some landowner over there. When they let him come home again, we got married. We lived together for a little while—for a year—and then he had to go off to war again. In those days we had a war almost every other year: he would be home for a year and then gone for another year. Afterward our life got much better: we had our own firewood, a plowed field, and a good, broken-in stallion. But then this government came along, and dekulakized us. Do you even know what that means—to be "dekulakized"? If you were a good farmer you got dekulakized—that is, you had everything taken away from you. They took everything away from us—everything down to the last crumb, including the house. Just the kids and myself were left. My husband was taken away in a black raven.[1] We had ten children. Five of them died while my husband was gone.

PRASKOVIA KONSTANTINOVNA DOROZHINSKAIA (B. 1914)
Recorded in 1977 in Lysaia Gora Village, Usviatsky District

I grew up in Meliukhi, in a poor family. There were eleven of us. I started doing work around the house when I was about six. My father did not drink. At night he used to make yokes to sell at the market. We kids didn't go to school or to dances. We didn't have the time—nor did we have anything to wear. Dad was on the Committee of the Poor.[2] Those representatives of the poor never worked and ate

From E. N. Razumovskaia, ed., "60 let kolkhoznoi zhizni glazami krest'ian," in *Zven'ia: Istoricheskii al'manakh* I (Moscow: Progress Feniks Ateneum, 1991), 120–23, 125.

[1] Black raven—police van.

[2] During the civil war, the Bolsheviks encouraged the formation of peasant Committees of the Poor, which they saw as the Soviet regime's allies in the countryside.

only the chaff—even when there was lots of work and you could live well. We never had to eat the chaff—because we always worked like dogs. Dad never had anyone working for him. We did everything ourselves. In 1929 Dad was de-kulakized. Even though he had been on the Committee of the Poor, someone had complained that he was rich. The agents came at night, looking for weapons. While they were dekulakizing us, Dad got so upset that he became paralyzed. In 1937 the "black raven" kept making its rounds. All those who got denounced were taken away.

18 □ ANNA BALASHOVA

A Worker's Life

□ This entry is taken from a collection of autobiographies by the workers from the Trekhgorka Textile Factory in Moscow, compiled by the Survey and Biography Commission of the Institute of Party History at the Communist Academy (History of the Proletariat Section). The purpose of the project was, in the editor's words, "to present lifelike portraits of workers, devoid of clichés, posturing, and affectation." The subjects had to be "shock workers and *vydvizhenki* [promotion beneficiaries]." The autobiographies were written down by the historians M. K. Rozhkova and F. A. Kogan, and organized according to a specially prepared questionnaire.

MY MOTHER was born in a village. Her father was a blacksmith. He worked in somebody else's forge in another village. They were poor—with no house of their own, nor any land, nor a cow, nor a horse. They lived on my grandfather's salary, but he spent almost everything on drinking. When my mother turned sixteen, she went to Moscow and found a job in a seamstress's shop. She then met a man, who worked in a shop where they made church-plate, and married him. I was born soon afterward, in 1904. I do not remember my father because he died when I was two years old. My mother got very sick, and I was brought up by a childless old couple, who lived in the same apartment with us. At first they took me in temporarily, while my mother was sick, but then they got used to me and did not want to let me go.

They did odd jobs for a living. The old woman washed clothes and scrubbed floors. When I was three years old we moved to another room near Tver Road, on Second Iamskoe Pole Street, by the Duks Factory. That's how I started living apart from my mother. She would often come visit me during holidays.

We rented three rooms in a two-storied house but lived in only one of them and rented out the other two. In bad years we would rent out our room as well and move into the kitchen. You might say that our whole income came from those rooms. We cooked for our tenants and cleaned their rooms, and they paid for that separately. I do not know how much our tenants paid. They were all workers from the Duks Factory.

We lived the way all poor people do: when we had money we ate vegetable soup with meat or mushrooms, and then some buckwheat porridge as a second course; when we did not, we were glad to have some bread and tea.

From O. N. Chaadaeva, ed., *Rabotnitsa na sotsialisticheskoi stroike: Sbornik avtobiografii rabotnits* (Moscow: Partiinoe izd-vo, 1932), 103–14 (abridged).

The old people were very kind. The old woman really loved me and would never eat anything without giving me a bite, and the old man would sometimes bring me a piece of candy or an apple. I loved them both, especially the old woman.

When I was eight they sent me to a three-year parish school. Most of the students were cart drivers' children. The cart drivers all lived on Second Iamskoe Pole Street, and the school was next to the local church. The church had been built with their donations, so their children had a special place of honor in the school. Everybody knew that one girl, for example, was the daughter of a rich cart driver who owned a house and many horses, and so on. The rich ones were treated better than the poor ones. The teachers paid more attention to them and tutored them separately—for an extra fee, of course.

In my first year I was a good student, but then I quit studying. Nobody made sure I did my homework; nobody asked me anything or ever helped me. At home nobody knew how to read or write. I did not get credit for my second year and had to start over, but I did not feel bad about it: I was not the only one.

My conduct in school was not very good, but I did not act up too much because I was afraid of the teacher. I used to jump from one desk to another. I could not wait to finish and start making money.

One summer I worked at a tobacco factory, gluing together cigarette packs. All the kids from our building would take their sacks and go down to the factory, where they would give us the packs and everything we needed for gluing. We would take it all home, sit down in the courtyard or in somebody's doorway, and work. When we were all friends we would work together and then share the money equally, but when we had fights we would break up into small groups. We were paid per thousand packs; I do not remember how much. We made about two rubles over the summer. But we did not work every day.

The next summer I worked in a shop where they made all kinds of labels for cans and bottles. We children worked full-time—from eight in the morning till five-thirty in the evening, with a half-hour lunch break. Over the whole summer, I remember, I made enough money to buy shoes and galoshes: about six rubles, fifty kopeks.

I liked working in the summer. I was making my own money, just like a grown-up. I never wanted to quit working and go play with other children. I really wanted to work, so I could make money and acquire something.

One time they wanted to fire me from the label shop because I did not do my work right. The label sheets had to be held together with needles so that all one hundred labels matched exactly. Once I did not match them exactly, and the boss wanted to fire me. I was afraid of losing my wages, and I begged him: "It will never happen again. I'll do better next time." So he agreed to keep me there. It was profitable for him to hire children. Adults were paid more. At the end of the summer I got my wages.

I read whatever came my way. I did not read serious books; they were boring. I remember when I was in school, they used to talk about war.

My mother and Anna Sergeevna—the old woman—remembered how in 1905 the shells were flying around and you could not walk outside, and how a lot of people got hurt. My mother told me that it was because the discontented workers were fighting against their bosses—some kind of strike—and the police were trying to put it down. Of course the bosses had the money, the police, and the gendarmes, and what did the workers have? They fought with their bare hands. Some dead workers were put on a cart and taken to the police station. My mother went there to see for herself. My mother felt sorry for the workers.

I was puzzled. Why was it that some people were born to rule over other people? Why was there a tsar? Why were some people poor while others were born rich and could do whatever they wanted? Maybe this was the way it should be. It did not occur to me that you could do something so there would be no rich or poor any more.

I used to ask: what is better, a war or a strike? When I heard that strikes could take place in Moscow but wars were far away, I decided that wars were better.

At that time things were getting worse in Moscow. There were shortages of various goods, but it did not affect us very much because we never bought any goods anyway; we had nothing to buy them with.

In 1916 I graduated from the parish school. My mother came over and said: "Go on and study some more. I've been illiterate all my life, lived in poverty, and never had any luck. You should get an education so you can get an office job."

I entered the fourth grade of the city school; there were four grades in all. I was a good student. Then the February Revolution [of 1917] came along, and there were no classes for a while. Our teacher was very happy about the revolution and told us it was very good that the tsar had gotten thrown out; she also told us various bad things about tsarism. I only remember what she said about the liberation of the peasants: "When the peasants were liberated, it wasn't because of the tsar's kindness but because the peasants were rioting and the tsar had to give them freedom or they would have toppled the tsar."

I did not understand very much, nor did the other children; we just felt that something was going on and hoped for the best. Our teacher told us, "Life will change now."

When I finished the city school, they sent us poor children out to vegetable gardens to do summer work. The gardens were very far away, near Petrovsko-Razumovskoe. We had to go to the assembly point on Aleksandrovskaia Street first, and then out to the gardens. The gardens belonged to the city, and for some reason the manager was a priest. He wore his cassock, and sometimes his wife or daughter would come to watch over us.

They would just sit there under their parasols while we sweated and sweltered in the heat. The worst part was the weeding, when we kept cutting our hands on pieces of glass. We were supposed to be there at eight o'clock, so we had to leave home early, and then we would work until sunset—all day on our feet without any hot food.

After we had been working for two weeks, they announced that we would be paid half what they had promised because the state was poor and could not afford to pay more. We agreed because some money was better than no money at all. I worked there all summer long.

By this point my mother's younger brother, who had been living with her in the kitchen of the seamstress's shop, had grown up. He started making more money and decided to rent a room and live there with my mother and my grandmother from the village. They found a basement room on Bolshaia Kislovskaia Street.

Around that time there were meetings going on everywhere; workers from the Duks, Gabai, and other factories were constantly getting together in the fields around town. There were SRs, Bolsheviks, Mensheviks—all kinds of people. They all defended their own point of view. I understood that there was no stable power and that people were fighting for that power. It seemed to me that the SRs were connected with the peasants and that they defended the peasants above all. As for the Mensheviks, I do not know what they wanted. Everybody was preparing for the elections to the Constituent Assembly. Number 1 on the ballot were the bourgeoisie—the enemy.

Of our tenants, both workers from Duks, one was a Bolshevik and one an SR. Whenever they stayed home there would be no end to the arguing. No sooner would they get up in the morning than the Bolshevik would start yelling (the partitions were wooden and did not reach the ceiling, so you could hear everything): "Hey you, hick, the Bolsheviks are going to win anyway," and then he would argue about why and when.

I, of course, was a great fan of Number 5, the Bolsheviks. We children also used to go to those meetings in the fields and would also argue a lot. My friends and I would shout, "Vote for Number 5!" and those whose parents were SRs would shout for Number 3.

My friend Niurka Liubilkina and I were the noisiest. They also had a Bolshevik among their tenants, and her father was at the front. I was for Number 5.

Whenever our Bolshevik tenant would come home, he would always tell us what was being planned. They were not sure whose side the soldiers would be on. He told us that the Bolsheviks had gone to the barracks but could not enter because there was very strict order there.

When I graduated from the city school, my mother and uncle decided that I should continue with my studies. It was too early for me to start working: where could I go at the age of thirteen? In the fall of 1917 I started attending the high school near the zoo.

Soon the battles for soviet power began. I did not see any of the battles myself; I only heard the shots. In our neighborhood nothing was going on. We children played in the street as usual.

When things quieted down, I rushed over to my mother's place to find out if she was still alive. With great difficulty Anna Sergeevna and I made it as far as the zoo, but then were stopped by people with guns. The same thing happened by the Triumphal Arch. By taking side streets we made it to Nikitskie Gates. There were guards there, too, but we managed to get through. Many of the houses were damaged, and you could still hear shooting. I knew that the Whites and Bolsheviks were fighting for power.

Finally we arrived at my mother's. She told us they had not slept all night because the fighting was very close. Directly across from them was the Economic Society where the cadets had barricaded themselves, and the same thing was going on near the Vozdvizhene Church.

When it was all over we went back to school. The teachers asked us to write about our experiences. Most of the children wrote, "We were afraid the Bolsheviks would come," but my friend and I wrote, "We were afraid the cadets would come." During every break we would write on the board, "Comrades, vote for Number 5!" The others kept erasing it and writing, "Vote for Number 1!" Soon the teachers quit teaching—they did not want to work under the Bolsheviks. They told us to go to another school where we would be taught by "old teachers" for money. A lot of the students left, but I stayed behind. We got new teachers. They were students and military men, and some of them were volunteers who had never taught before. There were a few old teachers, but not from our school. One teacher told us why he had come to teach us. He had seen children carrying placards that read, "We want to be literate!" and he had understood their desire and come to help.

Soon they divided us into districts, and my friend and I were transferred to the Miusskaia Trade School because it was closer. When we arrived, we saw that we were the only girls. We did not like that, so we left. We returned to our old school but discipline was bad and there were no classes, so in 1918 I dropped out for good.

Around that time the old man—Vasily Ivanovich—died. Death came easily. He had been weak for a while but continued to be active, and then he spent a few days in bed and died peacefully.

The old woman became very sick. Those were hungry times. There was nothing to eat, and Anna Sergeevna and I moved in with my mother. My mother was also sick a lot. I started looking for a job. I did my mother's labor duty, cleaning snow and ice off the tracks on the Aleksandrovskaia Railroad. Then some ladies who lived in our building paid me to do their duty for them. At the railroad I was paid in cash and given a food ration.

In 1919 I got a job as a courier in the transportation division of the State Economic Council.[1] I was too young for other kinds of work. I liked to be a courier because it was easy work. I do not remember how much I was making—it seemed like a lot of rubles, but with my whole monthly salary I could not buy more than two or two and a half pounds of bread at the market. I worked as a courier for three and a half years, but then there was a layoff and I was among those who got laid off.

At that time my mother was very sick, and I had to take care of her. She could not move, so I had to feed her.

We did not live in the basement anymore. In 1920 we had moved to a room upstairs in the same building. Some people from the bourgeoisie had lived there

---

[1] State Economic Councils—local institutions subordinated to the Supreme Council of National Economy (1918–32).

before, but they had run away from the Soviet regime and the district housing committee had given their room to us. It was a good, large room.

I was unemployed for about a year. It was difficult to find a job: a lot of people were being laid off, and I had no skills. Finally, I became an apprentice in a private textile shop. They treated me well—I learned faster than the other apprentices. There were fifteen of us in all. Nobody could exploit us—the union made sure of that (we had all become members of the textile union). The union took good care of us. The boss was very scared of the union. For a while he made us apprentices clean the shop, but the union told him that he had to pay us double wages and that in the future he should hire a special worker to do the cleaning. I worked there for a year, and then the shop closed down.

I became unemployed again. I received unemployment compensation and took in work from a textile shop.

Six months later I enrolled in a textile union course for the training of skilled weavers. There were several Komsomol members in our class, and my friend and I also wanted to join. We discussed it a lot, but I just did not have the courage. What if they asked: "What have you been doing up to now? What kind of volunteer work have you done?" Since we had not done any, they would not accept us. I must say that before that time I had never been interested in social issues and had never truly gotten involved in them. But I had always been for the Soviet government. I decided to wait a while before joining the Komsomol. I thought I would work at a factory, prove myself there, and then I would be accepted.

I finished the course in 1924 and was hired as a weaver at the Trekhgorka Textile Factory.

At first I only had one machine, of course, but within three months I already had two, as a relief weaver. I worked very well, and after one year (very quickly for those days) I was assigned two machines of my own. I liked my work right away. Factory life brings people together, and soon I became friends with the weavers who had helped me when I first started.

I never missed work and always tried hard, so the foreman's assistants and even the foreman himself treated me well. Soon I was asked to become the collector of union fees. I enjoyed it and did it willingly and carefully.

I felt that I was more developed and better educated than most of the weavers so I considered it my duty to share my knowledge with them and to explain to them the actions of the Soviet government. Soon I became known as the "Communist."

Shortly afterward I was elected a shop union representative, and then, in 1926, a union activist. I was sent to the factory's night school of the trade union movement. At first I was placed in the beginning group because I was unfamiliar with union work, but later I was transferred to the advanced group. I liked the school. I came to understand the structure not only of the union organizations but of the party organizations as well. We studied every aspect of union work: labor safety, the functions of workers' and peasants' control, the goals of the trade union movement in the USSR and abroad, the history of the movement, and so on. It was all very exciting: I felt I was growing politically. When I arrived at the factory, I hadn't known how the state allocated its resources or how much, in addition to salaries, it spent on the workers' standard of living, such as resorts and sanatoriums. Now I understood the policies of the Soviet government.

In 1925 I got married. My husband, Aleksei, worked as a shift manager and telephone operator in the Kremlin transportation unit. Our good life did not last very long. After six months he realized I was not submissive enough. He wanted his wife to stay home with him: he had a lot of free time because he used to work for twenty-four hours and then rest for three days. But I was busy at work all the time. I worked different shifts. We were always fighting; we could not get along.

In 1927 I was elected a women's representative. I worked very hard. I was well known in our shop and in the party committee. In the shop they saw me as a person who could explain things, and they kept coming to me with different questions: why did they get this much in wages and not that much, and so on. When we switched over to the intensive work schedule, we needed to explain that the aim of this new intensive schedule was to lower the cost of our goods, and to convince them to join. We did convince them in the end. The first ones to sign up for the new schedule were the Communists and some nonparty people, but before long all the weavers from the fourth floor, where I worked, had joined in. Of these, half resolved that each worker would operate four machines at once, and it was a great success. I explained everything to them.

Everybody thought I was a party member. Once, when our Communists were having their military training, I was with them. Somebody said: "Have you joined the party? It's about time."

I was embarrassed and decided to join. I had thought a lot about it and had discussed it with my husband. He said, "They'll make you work a lot," and talked me out of it.

But this time he was not around. He was at a resort in the Crimea. I wrote to him that I was applying to join the party. His reply was "diplomatic": "It's not for women," he wrote. Basically he was not happy with the amount of volunteer work I was doing. At first he just knew he had an obedient wife who would spend all her free time at home waiting for him. On Sundays I used to beg him to stay home with me and cry over his neglect, saying I could not even tell whether I was married or single, but then, after I got involved in volunteer work, I no longer cared what my husband did. He had his life; I had mine. My eyes had been opened to a different kind of life, different social interests.

I stopped worrying about what my husband thought of me; I worried about whether this or that government campaign was going to succeed at our factory. At first I was often nervous, afraid I would not be able to do the work I had been assigned. I tried very hard and wanted to do the best I could.

Soon after I became a candidate party member, I was elected to the supervisory board of Osoaviakhim,[2] then a delegate to the provincial trade union congress, and then a member of the board of the factory club.

[2] Osoaviakhim—a voluntary society supporting aviation and civil defense.

When my child was born, and while I was still in the hospital, my husband left me for good, taking quite a few of my personal things with him. He did not even leave me a note. I sued him twice, to get my things back. He had even taken the table. The court made him return my things and pay alimony.

So I started living on my own, but my spirits were high. Aleksei came over a couple of times; he obviously was having doubts. He would have stayed if I had asked him, but I didn't.

While I was still nursing, my volunteer work had to be limited to the shop. It was at that time that socialist competitions and shock work came along. At a general meeting it was decided that we would compete with the Tver Proletarka Factory, and various pledges were made. In order to keep up, every weaver had to improve her work. We shop Communists were the first to challenge one another to a socialist competition. The nonparty weavers followed suit. At first the workers did not take it seriously. But when results began to be posted regularly and prizes awarded to the best workers, they began competing in earnest, everyone trying to achieve the best results possible.

I also received prizes. The unit I worked in was always the best.

Since I worked better than the other women's representatives, I was soon appointed to the party committee to be the women's representative for the whole factory. After that, I became the head of the organizational section of the party committee. I knew I was not politically ready for this work and did not feel confident, but I received good guidance and help from the committee secretary and the head of the culture and propaganda section. They had pledged to educate me and make a party functionary out of me. They helped me and taught me very well.

In October 1930 I attended a six-month course of party training in Zvenigorod. The course was based on independent study: we read on our own and then took part in study seminars. I received good political training there. Before then I was unfamiliar with the history of the party, with economics, and with the theory of Soviet work. I had read newspapers only rarely, having difficulty figuring things out, but after the course I could understand everything. The best part is that I became thoroughly acquainted with various deviations within the party and learned what they were all about.

In 1927, after I had already become a candidate party member, the party was waging its battle against the Trotskyites.[3] The Trotskyites were wrong. In our factory they were saying that the party policy on workers' wages was incorrect and that the workers were not being paid enough. They also argued against the intensive schedule—in other words, they posed as defenders of the working class.

I did not like the Trotskyites because I felt they were self-seekers, but I did not know much about them at the time. It was only during the course that I learned everything about the history of Trotskyism.

After the course was over I returned to my workbench. As I said, our unit worked very well and was the leader in plan fulfillment. So we decided to form

[3] Supporters of the Left Opposition in the Communist Party, led by Trotsky.

a commune and intensify our work even more. There were not enough workers, and some machines were idle, so we took them over as well. I was elected leader of the commune. We were all registered as one worker and shared the salary equally. At first things went well, and we worked with enthusiasm. But here's what happened. Skilled workers were paid no more than unskilled workers, even though those who were skilled worked much more and spent more energy than if they worked by themselves. As a result many workers lost interest in their work, and a month and a half later the commune fell apart.

In the fall I became a student at the Trade Academy, and in late September 1931 I was made foreman of the quality control department.

Before my arrival there had been talk in the department about making it a self-financing unit. Everyone said, "We are all for it," and seemed to think it already existed, but no formal contract had ever been signed. When I came, I asked them: "Does the unit exist or not? If it does, there has to be a contract." We then signed a contract with management, and the self-financing unit became a reality. For three months now it has been overfulfilling its plan.

In December 1931, when the factory overfulfilled its plan, three women from my unit applied to join the party. Another one applied on the anniversary of Lenin's death.[4] They were all old women with great experience and were among our best shock workers.

At the latest all-factory party conference I was elected a member of the party committee. I continue to work as a factory women's representative.

Among women, cases of absenteeism and bad discipline are less frequent than among men. Women participate more in socialist competition and in shock work. They are better workers. We have achieved a great deal thanks to the work of our women's representatives. We prepare all campaigns, shock work, and socialist competition with our activists, and then among the female masses. Recently we had a meeting for the new arrivals, most of whom were fresh from the village. We pay particular attention to the new cadres of women workers. They are the most backward politically. We have been successful at reeducating them. Within a short time many of them apply to join the party.

Recently we had a meeting for the oldest women workers that was dedicated to the anniversary of Lenin's death. About forty people attended. Six of them applied to join the party before the meeting was over.

Our next task is to organize the election of women's representatives. In recent months our activists have been scattered around too much because of the restructuring of shift work. We need to reorganize them.

Work among women is not easy, but it is an important, necessary, and interesting aspect of party work. I give it everything I've got.

[4] Lenin died in January 1924.

19 □ VALENTINA BOGDAN

Students in the First Five-Year Plan

□ Valentina Alekseevna Bogdan was born in the Cossack town of Kropotkin, in the Kuban region. Her father, the son of a priest, was a train
engineer. Her mother was from a Cossack family. For extracts from
the sequel to *Students in the First Five-Year Plan*, see selection 34 in
this volume. These two works, which comprise her memoirs, were
written for a Russian emigré audience. As of this writing, she was
living in England.

IT WAS 1929. A whole hour remained before the beginning of the exams, but the
lobby and corridors of the Krasnodar Institute of Food Industry were filled with
would-be students. Like most of the other girls from the provinces, Tania, Lida,
and I could not stand still. We knew there were four times as many applicants as
there were openings—a good reason to be nervous! Only a few people strolled
calmly back and forth, as though they were there to give, rather than take, the
exams. We envied them.

Finally we were allowed inside, and our first exam—Russian language—
began. The essay topics were written in chalk on the blackboard. Each person was
handed a sheet of paper with his or her last name on it, as well as the institute's
stamp. We could choose one of four topics. The topics were easy, practically the
same ones we had been given during our high school finals: Rise in the Standard
of Living of the Workers of the Russian Federation as a Result of the Fulfillment
of the First Five-Year Plan; Griboedov's Characters in Contemporary Society;[1]
Women in Revolutionary Fiction; Invisible Tears in the Works of Gogol.

I picked the second topic and wrote enthusiastically. I knew *Woe from Wit*
practically by heart, and Chatsky, the unmasker of vices, was one of my all-time
heroes. I had even tried to act like him for a while, until my mother put a stop to it.

"Which one did you choose?" I asked Tania outside after we had finished.

"The first one."

"Tania! How could you? I'm sure more than half the applicants picked that one.
You'll see."

"So what? A lot of people pick each topic. There are only four topics, and look
at this crowd. At least I knew what to write. Didn't we spend a whole year in
school analyzing and memorizing the five-year plan? When I started writing,
those figures came pouring out of my brain: so many meters of cloth, so many
pairs of shoes . . . I could write a whole poem when I think about how tractors and

From Valentina Bogdan, *Studenty pervoi piatiletki* (Buenos Aires: Nasha strana, 1973), 9–229
(abridged).
[1] A. S. Griboedov (1795–1829)—Russian playwright, author of the popular satirical play *Woe from
Wit*.

combine harvesters are going to make the peasant's life easier. I could have kept on writing, but I was afraid the professor would get bored and lower my grade . . . So I stressed the impact of the plan on the future of our Kropotkin. I did such a good job that I'll bet the entire admissions committee will want to move there. It will be a paradise once the plan has been fulfilled."

After a while Lida also came out.

"Did you pick the first topic?" I asked.

"What do you think? All that memorizing came in handy, but I am worried about my grammar. I kept thinking about it the whole time I was writing. I tried to stick to short sentences without any commas, just periods."

WHAT with all the nervousness and excitement, the exams were over before we knew it. Tania and I did fine, but Lida kept having problems and eventually got so depressed that it became almost impossible to cheer her up. We were told that the results would not be announced for another two weeks and that each applicant would receive a written notice from the admissions committee.

Before leaving for home we decided to take one last look at the institute. It was getting dark, but the building that was so dear to our hearts stood out clearly among the small private houses and against the evening sky. We stood there a long time gazing at the entrance. Before that moment the expression "a temple of science" had always seemed pretentious to me, but now this building did appear imposing, severe, and somehow spiritual—truly a temple! More than anything in the world, we wanted to enter it and join the elect. I said half-jokingly: "Girls, let's pray to the institute, asking it to admit us." We waited until nobody was around and then raised our arms and said loudly, in unison:

"Admit us within your walls! Admit us! Admit us!"

Shortly afterward we returned to Kropotkin, and the endless days of waiting began. Finally, the letter arrived. I looked inside, and shouting, "Admitted! I've been admitted!" I ran to the kitchen, where Mother was baking. Mother crossed herself. "Thank God! I told you everything would be fine. Now you need to start getting ready, preparing your dresses, your sheets . . ."

Soon Tania came running in. She looked happy. Obviously she was bringing good news.

"Here it is, finally!" She showed me her postcard. "I know you got yours, too: the mailman told me. Isn't it wonderful!"

"But what about Lida?"

"Lida got in, too."

"She did? So it's true what they said about special party quotas . . . To get in with such poor grades! Mother, did you hear? Lida got in, too!"

"Thank God! Tania, congratulations to you! All your worries are behind you!"

"Nina Ivanovna!" said Tania. "Take a good look at us! We must look different now! We are college students!"

THAT night Tania and I went to the park that belonged to the railroad workers' club—or the railway park, as we called it. It was a place where the town's young people would meet. When Tania and I arrived, everyone we wanted to see was already there. All the new college students were beaming. Going off to college was a huge event, and we were treated with respect. Valentin congratulated me. He had known me since childhood, but he had never paid any attention to me before because he was two years older.

My good friend, Sasha Grachev, had not been admitted. He was a very good student and dreamed of becoming a doctor, but his father's social origin had ruined his chances. His grandfather, and then his father, had owned a mill. After the revolution the mill had been taken away from them, and now his father was working as a foreman at what had been his own mill. As a former member of the bourgeoisie, he was "disenfranchised," which meant that he was not allowed to vote. Sasha had been unable to hide that fact from the admissions committee because all applicants were required to bring a letter from their town soviet stating whether their parents had the right to vote.

I STARTED to prepare for my new life in the city. The next morning I went to the hairdresser's and had my hair cut short. I had wanted to have my braids cut off for a while, but Mother would not let me. Now I had done it. Mother was horrified, but I said I would be better off not having to waste a lot of time taking care of my long hair. What really convinced her was the argument that short hair would be easier to dry in the winter—otherwise, I might have to leave home with wet hair and then catch a cold. It did not take me long to get my wardrobe together, but we had long discussions trying to figure out how much money Father was going to send me. Tuition was free, but I needed money for a place to live, for food, and for textbooks. Finally we decided that fifteen rubles would be enough, not counting the cost of clothing and shoes. My older sister, Shura, also promised to help out.

WE were lucky finding a place to live in Krasnodar. The very first house we went to had a room that was right for us. The landlady, who lived by herself, had two rooms: a front room, which also served as a kitchen and dining room, and another large room, which was her bedroom. She agreed to take all three of us. The best part was that the landlady worked at a restaurant. She always left for work after lunch and came back after the restaurant closed, at about one in the morning. She told us that she usually slept until ten o'clock, which meant we would be leaving for the institute while she was still asleep and coming back after she had already left. The rent—ten rubles—was quite reasonable.

The landlady, Domna Tarasovna, turned out to be a very nice, kind woman. When she saw how little we ate, she started bringing us food from the restaurant, leftovers from what the restaurant employees received for free: sliced sausage, cheese, fish—sometimes even sturgeon—and meat in jelly. Sometimes in the morning we would find our breakfast waiting for us. The only problem was that on weekend mornings, if we were at home, she would tell us her dreams. Her dreams were always long and gory and full of all sorts of horrors, which she described in excruciating detail. Tania and Lida often had Komsomol meetings on

Sunday mornings, so I had to listen to Domna Tarasovna's dreams all by myself. One morning, when the girls were gone, she told me her whole life story instead of the usual dream. She was Polish by birth. Toward the end of the Great War[2] she married a Russian officer, whose unit was stationed in Poland. He soon left for the front and then, after the revolution, joined the White Army. She followed her husband and spent most of the civil war working as a nurse in his regiment's field hospital. While they were in Krasnodar her husband was seriously wounded in battle, and they had to stay behind when the White Army retreated. They lived peacefully until 1926, when he was suddenly arrested and executed. For a long time Domna Tarasovna could not find a job, and was desperately poor. Finally she got a job as a waitress and started working under her maiden name. They must have felt lucky to get her: she was attractive and friendly.

When she had finished her story, she said:

"Valia, please don't talk about this to your friends. They are good girls but they are Komsomol members, and it would be better if they did not know that my husband was shot and that I worked in a White Army hospital."

I assured her I would not, thinking it was no wonder she dreamed of blood and horrors.

ONE evening Lida came home and announced: "Guess what? They've posted the names of all the freshmen who got scholarships. Tania and I both got one, but you didn't."

"Why not?"

"I have no idea. They didn't give any reasons. And it is a large scholarship, too: thirty rubles a month!"

"Was it just for Komsomol members?"

"No, almost two-thirds of the students got it."

Tania and I went to find out what we could.

"That's strange," said Tania. "Why did Lida get one, and not you? Their family is better off materially than yours: both her father and older sister work, so that Lida and her mother are the only dependents, whereas your father is supporting your mother and three children."

We found Grisha and asked him if he would try to find out what the reason could be for such an injustice.

"You bet," he said. "I have a friend on the committee. You wait here, while I look for him."

Soon Grisha came back.

"Does your father have a brick house?"

"Yes, but we don't get any profit out of it."

"That doesn't matter. You didn't get the scholarship because your father owns real estate—private property. Besides, the committee received a report from one of the students that your father's house is large—six or seven rooms—and that it has an orchard that must be profitable."

[2] That is, the First World War.

"We never sell anything from our orchard. It's a small orchard: we have only one of each kind of tree. And anyway, Kropotkin is a Cossack village, not really a town. Almost everybody has a house with a small garden and an orchard. We've got to live somewhere."

"But Tania here doesn't own a house, do you, Tania?"

"We live in a state apartment. My father moved to the Kuban right before the revolution and did not have time to buy a house. We like our apartment, and we are a small family, so it does not make sense to refuse ourselves everything in order to save enough money to build a house—the way Valia's father did many years ago."

I was upset and thought I had been treated unfairly. Everybody knew that it cost more to live in your own house than in a state apartment because the real estate tax was higher than the annual rent, not to mention that a house needed maintenance and constant repairs. Of course it was a lot nicer to live in your own house with an orchard, so we never even considered selling the house where we had all grown up to move to a state apartment. And we would certainly never have received a six-room apartment.

WE used to have frequent student meetings at the institute. They were held in the evenings and took up a lot of time. Most of the meetings were devoted to politics: we were expected to familiarize ourselves with all the latest resolutions adopted by the party, government, and trade union congresses and conferences. All speeches by our leaders had to be "studied" and applied to the local conditions. Also, there were obligatory meetings to mark such occasions as May Day, Revolution Day on November 7, Paris Commune Day, Lenin's birthday, International Women's Day on March 8, Antiwar Day on August 1, and Red Army Day. In addition to these, there were many organizational meetings: to elect representatives to the so-called voluntary associations, to elect delegates to various conferences, and so on. On average, we had one or two meetings a week, and party and Komsomol members had even more. Some of the party and Komsomol meetings were open, others were closed. We were forced to go to the open meetings; the closed meetings were secret, so those of us who were not members were not allowed to attend.

No wonder, then, that at these meetings—particularly the large, institute-wide ones—the students usually did their own work or tried to entertain themselves in inconspicuous ways. This was possible because only a small group of student activists actually took part in what was going on. They would make speeches, propose resolutions, and compose telegrams of congratulations, while the other students used the occasion to see friends, meet new people, or read books.

Not all meetings were boring, though. Indeed some were very interesting, for example, the open party meetings where the city's "purge" commission would purge our students and professors.[3] They were exciting not only because they

---

[3] That is, interrogate party members and reprimand or expel those deemed unworthy.

were, in effect, trials but also because they clarified what actions the party considered sinful—and thus enabled us to make the necessary adjustments. The members of the purge commission collected extremely detailed information on the lives of all party members. They analyzed their papers, sent queries to their hometowns and former employers, and questioned their friends and colleagues. We had a special mailbox at our institute, where information—that is, denunciations—about party members could be placed. The anonymous letters were just as welcome as the signed ones. At any given purge meeting, it would become immediately obvious from the nature of the questions who the party wanted to get rid of. The most important questions had to do with political activism, political literacy, and links to "ideologically alien elements." We often made bets before a meeting: would they keep him or purge him?

The five members of the commission always sat on the stage in our assembly hall. The purge candidates would be called up one at a time and interrogated in front of a huge crowd of students.

I, along with many others, never felt at all sorry for those who used to squirm on that stage under the commission's questions. Very few people had joined the party against their will, under pressure from the party committee, and, in any case, such people were rarely purged. Most of the people who used to squirm on that stage were careerists who had failed to memorize party dogma, had deviated from the party line, or, having become party members, had decided that "anything was allowed."

One particularly memorable event was the purge of Comrade Sokol, an assistant professor who had graduated from our institute the year before. Everyone in the hall realized that things were turning nasty when the chair of the commission asked:

"Tell us, Comrade Sokol, do you have any ties with socially alien elements?"

"Not personally."

"Then tell us about your wife's social origin."

"We got married when we were both juniors. She is the daughter of a prosperous Cossack: he used to own a creamery. Last year his creamery was taken away from him, and he himself was sent to Siberia. But, Comrade Chairman, at the time of our marriage he had not yet been arrested, and, anyway, the important thing is that we fell in love."

"Has your wife stayed in touch with her parents? Does she send them food?"

"Yes."

"Does she pay for the parcels with your money?"

"She also has a job, and in our family we do not keep our incomes separate."

"In other words, not only do you maintain ties with an enemy of the people— you are actually supporting him in exile?"

"My wife is not supporting an enemy of the people. She is supporting her father. He has been punished in accordance with the law for having been a kulak. My wife considers it her duty to help her own father."

"I see. Let us picture the following situation: your father-in-law escapes from exile, comes back, and asks your wife to hide him. You agree: you are not going to throw your father-in-law into the street, let alone hand him over to the militia because, as you put it, you will not be hiding an enemy of the people—you will be hiding your wife's father. In fact, however, the only point of his escape is to take revenge on the Soviet state. Do you see where your family affection might lead you? A Communist, a man in whom the party has total trust, could end up aiding and abetting an enemy of the people."

"Your conclusion is incorrect: I would never agree to hide an enemy of the people. In fact, he himself, knowing I am a Communist, would not ask me for help."

Sokol, realizing he might actually be expelled from the party, became frightened and tried to justify himself. Finally, seeing that his explanations were not having the desired effect, he exclaimed: "But Comrades, you can't choose who you fall in love with!"

"A Communist must know how to control his emotions," snapped the chairman.

Many of the students thought it would be wrong to expel Sokol. Lida was particularly upset.

"It's not right," she said. "Why can't she help her old father? Communists have hearts, too."

"You don't understand," I said. "He joined the party voluntarily. He gets special benefits for being a member, and in return he must do as he is told."

"What benefits? There are only duties! It's all meetings and volunteer work!"

"What do you mean, what benefits? We all know that many people were admitted with bad grades just because they were Komsomol members. We also know that all Komsomol members received scholarships. I'd be willing to bet that Sokol got his research position at the expense of somebody who was more talented but wasn't a party member. If you want the benefits, you have to pay for them, and everybody knows the price: the total subordination of your will to the party. If you don't like it, don't get involved."

To get expelled from the party was a real tragedy. The expelled person would be persecuted not just as a Communist but as a human being. The party did not trust such people. This meant that Sokol had to be expelled from the institute, too. The nonparty people were untested, as it were: nobody knew if they were worthy of trust. After all, not all reliable people were in the party. Some were too involved in their work or study, others were afraid of the strict party discipline, and still others did not want the extra work. There were a lot of anti-Soviets, too, but how could one distinguish them from the loyal ones?

ONCE, when I was in the physics lab, I ran into one of our most well-known students: Maksim Chumak. We had been given the same problem to solve. Maksim was what we called our "official speaker." He used to speak at meetings and take part in all discussions. He was always asked to "set the right tone" at the beginning of meetings and to "wrap things up" at the end. I knew he was a candidate member of the party and a member of the institute-wide Komsomol committee, and I wanted to get to know him better. He was not good-looking: short and very thin, with light reddish hair and a pale, sallow complexion. He dressed badly, too, always wearing the same cheap, faded, shapeless suit; his shirts, which he sometimes wore without a tie, were badly ironed; and he obviously never shined his shoes. Not only did he not have any good clothes—he didn't even pay attention to the clothes he had. What made his face attractive, though, were his eyes, which sparkled with unusual intelligence. During a conversation he always looked you directly in the eyes.

He was as active in the classroom as at meetings. He used to ask lots of questions, some only indicating how poor his high school preparation had been. Our problem was not difficult, and it did not take us long to solve it.

"There's another way to solve this problem," I said. "Let's try it."

"Why bother? We solved it, didn't we?"

I expected him to say, "Let's read some Lenin instead," but he didn't.

"What high school did you go to?" I asked.

"I graduated from the rabfak.[4] I dropped out of school when my father died, during the civil war. I was the oldest child and had to help my mother around the house. A couple of years later, after my sisters had grown up, I joined the rabfak."

We had several rabfak graduates. They were all older than the regular high school graduates. They were very active politically, but they were not as well prepared academically as the rest of us.

At about that time a new category of students was created; the so-called party thousanders. They arrived in the middle of the school year and were all put in the same class. They belonged to that famous group of a thousand Communist officials who had been sent to college by the Central Committee. They were being trained for top administrative jobs in industry and agriculture, such as factory manager, state farm director, and so on. Their academic level varied tremendously: some had dropped out of elementary school; others had spent some time at a gymnasium or a polytechnic. At first they attended the lectures but not the labs. Most of them were being tutored by professors or other faculty members. The idea was to help them catch up by the end of the year. They worked very hard—up to ten hours a day, somebody told me—and they were released from volunteer work. They were well looked after: they were still being paid the same wages they had been making before leaving for college.

AT the end of the year Tania and Lida left for Siberia, and I stayed behind to do my internship at our institute's butter and oil plant. I was assigned to the group headed by Professor Butov, who was researching the impact of temperature changes on the process of obtaining oil from sunflower seeds. Besides the permanent staff from the plant, the professor had two assistants: Alesha Krasnov and Vera Wolf. Alesha had graduated from our institute three years earlier, and Vera

[4] Rabfak—workers' faculty, established at many Soviet institutions of higher education to offer remedial preparation to workers and peasants who had not completed their secondary education.

had been out for only a year. Another freshman from our institute, Fedia Zorin, joined the group at the same time I did.

Once, after work, Professor Butov invited Vera and me to his house. When we arrived the table was already set for three: there was cold chicken, a salad, cheese, lots of fruit, and white wine. We were very impressed, but he kept apologizing, saying he was a single man and could not serve us a proper meal: "Poor girls," he said, "I have been working you to death. You look like you may have lost weight. Please don't say no if I invite you over for a filling meal every once in a while." We both promised not to say no.

"Wonderful, wonderful. I believe I owe whatever success I have in my work to my assistants. I am very happy that you regard your work not as a simple obligation but as a matter of personal satisfaction . . ."

The professor talked at great length about his work and his accomplishments while Vera and I ate. We left fairly early because Vera needed to get back to her child. On our way home Vera told me that Professor Butov was a widower and that he had an eleven-year-old daughter who lived with his mother in the village.

At the end of the summer I received a huge bouquet of roses, with a note from the professor. He wrote that he was leaving town, and because we were not going to see each other for a long time he wanted to say good-bye by sending me flowers.

I was quite upset. The flowers gave a certain romantic flavor to our relationship, and that bothered me. My landlady added to my discomfort by saying: "Oh, what beautiful roses! And so many! Who sent them to you?"

"A professor I have been working with. We finished an important project, and now he is sending presents to all those who helped him."

"A real gentleman! Is he handsome?"

"Not at all. He's not very young. He's bald, and he's a widower, on top of everything else."

It was unpleasant to think of an old professor as my "admirer."

ONCE, when I got home, the landlady was already there. She was very excited.

"What's the matter, Domna Tarasovna?"

"Something very good has happened, my dear Valia. I'm getting married."

"Congratulations! Who is he?"

"He's the manager of a cannery—a Communist, but a very nice person. I met him at our restaurant a long time ago. He was always very friendly and polite. When there weren't many customers, he would often ask me to join him at his table. That's how we got to know each other."

"Is he a widower or is he divorced?"

"Divorced. He got divorced five years ago. He told me that he got married as a very young village boy. Later he fought in the civil war, joined the party, and enrolled in a party course. After he graduated and returned home, he and his wife realized that they had nothing in common. She was a simple peasant woman, and he was a cultured person now. So they divorced."

"Does he know that you used to be married?"

"Yes. I told him the whole truth. He says that I'm not responsible for my husband: I was very young when I got married and knew nothing about politics. I just liked the man and married him."

"So you told him that you worked as a nurse in the White Army?"

"No, I didn't. I just told him that when I heard that my husband had been wounded, I came to the city to look after him. He knows that my husband was later executed."

At the end of the summer I did not see much of Tania and Lida in Kropotkin; they spent most of their time at party and Komsomol meetings and seminars. But I often went to see my old high school friend, Lena. Lena's fiancé, Tolia, played the flute in the railroad club band, and sometimes he and his friends from the band would give little concerts at Lena's place. One of the regular guests was Lena's older brother, Serezha, a Moscow University student who was spending his vacation at home. He did not play any instrument, but he was very clever, talked a lot, and was so funny that his one-man show was as good as any musical concert. His friends would play along as best they could.

Lena lived on the edge of town, very far from our house. There was no public transport in Kropotkin. It was dangerous to walk back late at night past the dark gardens and vacant lots, so Serezha always brought a revolver whenever he walked me home. I had an artificial pearl necklace, which Shura's husband had brought me from Moscow. Such a necklace was a novelty in Kropotkin, and Serezha assured me that it was my necklace, not me, that he was protecting from the bad guys. The revolver belonged to his neighbor, a Communist.

During the summer Serezha and I became good friends, and hardly a day went by without our seeing each other. Before leaving, we promised each other that we would write often.

In 1930 we were assigned to various departments, and, to my great joy, I was enrolled in the Department of Mechanical Engineering—my first choice. Besides Tania, Lida, and me, there was only one other woman there; the other twenty-six people were men, including three party thousanders, who were now supposed to study with the rest of us.

After the very first Komsomol meeting of the year, Tania and Lida came back with the news: "They're introducing a new way of studying: the brigade method."

"What does that mean?"

"All the students will be divided into brigades, with three to five people in each. The members of a brigade will study and take oral exams together. Each brigade will be given a collective grade, so that if one member fails, everyone has to take a make-up exam."

"But that's terrible! Everyone studies differently. One person may find one subject difficult, another may find a different subject difficult, and a third may find everything difficult. So the whole brigade will be no better than the worst student in it, with all the others having to explain things to him. I'm not going to join a brigade; I'd rather study by myself."

"Don't be silly," said Lida, "this decision has been handed down by the Commissariat of Enlightenment. You have to obey if you want stay in college. If I were you, I would not speak out against the brigade method at the meeting; all you'll accomplish will be to get the party committee mad at you. Our Komsomol cell supports the decision, too. You can join any brigade you like."

"What's supposed to be the advantage?"

"They say that this will even out the academic level. The better students will have to help the weaker ones and whip the lazy ones into shape."

"So the good students won't be able to study anything in depth?"

"I don't know. They say it is a temporary measure. But what are you so excited about?" asked Tania. "We study together most of the time anyway and help each other, so nothing will really change as far as we are concerned. I already told the Komsomol secretary that we wanted to be in the same brigade."

"You just said that people could choose any brigade they liked, and now it turns out that the composition of the brigades has already been discussed at the Komsomol meeting."

"Only Komsomol members were discussed. Also, because there are only three of us so far, we were asked to accept one more person, Degtiarenko."

"Which Degtiarenko? You mean that bald-headed party thousander? But he doesn't know anything at all! With him, we won't pass a single test on time. I remember him well: he likes to ask the professors questions, and you can tell from his questions that he doesn't know the most elementary things."

"If he didn't know the most elementary things, he would not have been admitted. He graduated from a village school and spent all last year studying with special tutors. At this point all the party thousanders are considered ready for college. In any case, every brigade is going to have both strong and weak students. Otherwise, what would be the point of the brigades? And this Degtiarenko is not too bad—I think he's kind of nice, actually. He works awfully hard— literally, day and night—and seems to be a friendly, cheerful sort of person, unlike that other party thousander, Serova. Now there's a real piece of work. Before coming here she was the head of the Rostov Women's Department, so she considers all the institute girls her subordinates. She's a real monster."

As Tania had predicted, Ivan Platonovich Degtiarenko did end up in our brigade. It became clear right away that he was going to take up a lot of our time. Almost every day, following eight hours of lectures and labs, Ivan Platonovich would ask: "Girls, what time is the brigade meeting tonight?"

"Ivan Platonovich, we can't get together every day. We have volunteer work, too, not to mention that we have to do our wash or take a bath every once in a while."

"But I don't need the whole brigade to get together. Maybe just Valia could stop by and explain one little thing I don't seem to understand."

Ivan Platonovich had been a Red partisan during the civil war, and his manners and clothes were still those of a partisan. He always wore boots, a Russian peasant blouse, and, in fall and winter, a leather jacket and tall mountaineer's hat. All he needed was a rifle slung over his back. He was quite a dandy: his boots were so well polished they looked like mirrors, and his blouse and pants were always neatly ironed. (He told us once that the reason his pants looked so good was because he put them under his mattress every night.) Most of his shirts were embroidered—probably by the loving hand of his wife. He walked with his back ramrod straight and his arms swinging briskly at his sides.

A NEW student named Olga Nikolaeva joined us that year. She had transferred from the math department of the Pedagogical Institute and quickly became quite visible. She did extremely well in class, was full of confidence, and always volunteered to go to the board when the professor wanted someone to repeat a particularly difficult point. There were other students, myself included, who could analyze tricky problems, but we were too shy to volunteer. She also smoked, wore her hair very short, and dressed like a man. She was quite pretty, but looked unkempt—probably because she had cigarette ashes all over her clothes. She made no attempt to be friendly with anyone, and when our union representative asked her, "Which brigade are you going to join?" she said: "I would prefer not to join any, but if that's not possible, put me wherever you like, I don't care." She was paired with one of the party thousanders, and they became the only two-person brigade we had.

Once, at a lecture on dialectical materialism, Olga Nikolaeva attracted everyone's attention. The professor was talking about the role of the individual in history. He said, for example, that France had fought all those wars not because a genius named Napoleon had appeared but because at that stage in its development France needed to wage colonial wars. To do that, it needed a military leader. When the historical preconditions for a certain action were ripe, he argued, the right individual always emerged.

Suddenly, Olga said: "If that is the case, why does the party extol Stalin so much, making him out to be the guiding force behind the successful construction of socialism in our country? Isn't that a deviation from dialectical materialism?"

All the students pricked up their ears.

"The party does not extol Stalin," said the professor. "Stalin was elected secretary of the Central Committee, the highest post in the party, and this shows that he is an outstanding politician. Stalin is being extolled by the people, who buy his portraits and praise him in print."

"That is not quite true," said Olga. "Take any speech by a party official, and you will find praise of Stalin. His portrait hangs in every government office. This is clearly the party line."

"The party does not extol Stalin; it considers his work worthy of praise," repeated the professor.

Olga did not say anything, but made it clear that she was not persuaded.

"What was the point of asking him about Stalin?" said Tania as we were walking home after class. "She knew perfectly well what the professor would say."

"She just wanted to show off," said Lida.

"That kind of attention isn't such a great thing. 'You know who' will find out that she has been criticizing party policy, and they'll watch her every move until she gets caught."

"Still, it was very brave of her. A lot of people have noticed the discrepancy between theory and practice, but she's the only one with enough guts to point it out."

ONE morning we were supposed to have a lecture on heating engineering. We waited for the professor for a long time, but he never came. Finally, our union representative called the office, and they told him that the lecture had been canceled. When we arrived in the main building, we learned that a lot of scientists had been arrested the night before, among them our heating engineering professor and Professor Butov, for whom I had worked as an intern in the summer. We were stunned. The place was buzzing with excitement.

Nothing had prepared me for this. That very night Professor Butov and I were supposed to go to the theater together. He had invited me several days before and was very happy when I accepted. The famous Bluhmenthal-Tamarin was on the program, and the ticket prices were so steep that I could not have dreamed of going on my own.

I saw Maksim coming out of the party committee room.

"Would you please tell me what's going on?"

"I have no idea. We were as surprised as anybody else. All I know is that our institute and the College of Agriculture are the only ones that have been affected. There have been no arrests at either the Medical School or the Pedagogical Institute."

"Have any of the students been arrested?"

"No, just professors."

A few minutes later Fedia called me aside and asked nervously: "Did you tell your friends about our visits to Professor Butov's place?"

"Yes, but they didn't seem interested and didn't ask me anything about them."

"I've been trying to remember: did he ever say anything anti-Soviet? Do you recall anything suspicious?"

"I've been thinking about that, too, but I can't remember anything unusual. We talked about Pushkin and about patriotism, and once he delivered a whole lecture on the virtues of wines from the Don region."

"I'm afraid we may get dragged into this. Let's find a quiet place and try to remember exactly what we talked about."

"Why don't you come over tonight. We can go to the movies and talk on the way."

"We have an emergency Komsomol meeting tonight, so I'll only be able to make it to the second showing."

Fedia's fears added to my own nervousness, and although I did not believe that anything anti-Soviet had been said, I was quite worried. Not only did Tania and

Lida know about my meetings with Professor Butov, they also knew that I was supposed to go to the theater with him later that day. They did not mention anything about it, however, pretending that they had completely forgotten.

ALL second-year students were being sent to the countryside for a week to help with the sowing. It was almost the end of spring but the collectivized Cossacks did not want to work, so large tracts of land remained fallow.

Before our departure, the party secretary made a speech, saying that the Cossacks, egged on by the kulaks, were sabotaging the sowing campaign and that the party and the government needed the help of all good citizens, especially students. If the fields were left unsown, we would all starve.

Maksim, who had spent the previous week in one of the villages, was appointed to be the leader of the second-year brigade.

We arrived in the Cossack settlement the day after Easter. To my surprise, however, nobody was out celebrating. We were housed in the school building, and soon after our arrival a large crowd of villagers—mostly young people— gathered outside the building. One girl asked us: "Is it true that you intend to start working in the fields tomorrow?'

"Yes, it is."

"But tomorrow is the second day of the Holy Week!"

"Then why haven't you prepared for the holidays by sowing the fields the way you were supposed to?"

"Easter always comes at sowing time, and we have always celebrated it. Nobody has ever starved because of Easter."

"They are godless! They are the Antichrists!" somebody yelled from the crowd.

"Talk about ingratitude," said Ivan Platonovich, getting very angry. "Because some lazy bastards did nothing all spring long, we had to quit studying and come here to help."

"We don't need a lecture from you. We didn't invite you here. Who needs workers like you? You'll eat more bread than you'll ever sow."

"And you'll starve to death if we don't help you now."

"No, you are the ones who'll starve to death; we'll do fine with what we've sown."

The conversation turned into a shouting match and would probably have ended in a fight had our activists, who had been discussing the next day's work with the kolkhoz leadership, not interfered.

It was too early to go to bed, so, at Ivan Platonovich's suggestion, we sat down in a circle and started singing. At first we sang student songs, but then somebody started, "Oh Kuban, our Land."[5] I saw Maksim tug several people by the sleeve, and the song was cut short in midsentence.

Later that night he told me: "I don't understand what's wrong with our people. First they start a fight with the locals, and then they sing the Cossack anthem.

[5] "Oh Kuban, Our Land"—the Kuban Cossack anthem.

Some people simply do not understand the seriousness of the situation. The villagers are extremely agitated. I've been hanging around here for a week now. We're trying to attract the young people to our side, trying to pull them away from the older people who resist collectivization, but it is really hard to do. It looks like there will be no collectivization until the kulaks and old people are removed from the village."

"What do you mean, removed? Where would they go?"

"Stalin said that the kulaks would be eliminated, and they will be eliminated."

"But he meant the economic elimination of a class, the confiscation of their property, and you're talking about their physical elimination. It frightens me just to hear you talk about it!"

"I'm not talking about their physical elimination, although some of them deserve it. I think that the kulaks should be removed from the villages and deported to Siberia, for example. Let them start from scratch over there. By now it is as clear as day that they will never be turned into collective farmers. They will remain property owners for the rest of their lives."

ONE morning, in huge letters on the front pages of all the newspapers, it was announced that the organs of state security had uncovered a plot against the party and the Soviet government. They went on to say that the Industrial Party (that was the name of the secret organization) included some of the most well-known engineers and agronomists in Russia: the engineer L. Ramzin, the agronomists A. V. Chaianov and N. D. Kondratiev, and many others.

It was difficult to believe that these scientists, who had been admired by the whole country, were in fact wreckers who had been accepting bribes from capitalists and planning acts of sabotage that would result in countless deaths. On the other hand, we knew that if they had not done anything wrong, they would not have been arrested.

I was afraid to talk about it even with my best friends, Tania and Fedia. Finally, I decided that the people from the Industrial Party had actually conspired against the Communists, but that the authorities were exaggerating their crimes in order to make them look as bad as possible before the trial.

The following day an institute-wide meeting was convened, and the party secretary made a speech, repeating what had been said in Pravda. Another Communist offered a resolution stating that the professors and students of the institute were demanding the death penalty for the conspirators. No one dared vote against it, and the resolution was passed unanimously.

The students adopted the resolution by raising their hands at the meeting (or not raising them—for who would have noticed?), but members of the faculty and staff were asked to sign the resolution as individuals. Some had probably heard what was coming and had left for home right after the meeting, in some cases skipping their afternoon lectures. Many people signed, but three professors—who had not been warned in advance and had therefore not hidden in time—refused to sign.

"It is the job of the prosecutor to prosecute, and the job of the court to render a verdict. I cannot take upon myself the responsibility of recommending the death penalty without knowing the details of the case," said one of the professors who had refused to sign the resolution.

After the meeting I said to Fedia: "Now we know why Professor Butov was arrested."

"That's right. He had been corresponding with Chaianov, and incriminating materials were found in those letters."

"How do you know?"

"The people from the party committee told me."

At the end of the semester we were told that this time we would be doing our factory internship in groups of two or three. Each group had to include at least one party or Komsomol member, all of whom were assigned to particular factories; nonparty people could choose where they wanted to go. I decided to join Fedia's group. We had worked together the previous summer and had become good friends. Also, I liked the fact that he did not show any enthusiasm for his party work, doing only what was absolutely necessary—perhaps because he was preoccupied with his health, trying to cure himself of tuberculosis.

Tania and Lida were going to the Far East. I also wanted to go there and get to know that remote region, but when I found out that Maksim was going to be the party supervisor of the whole Far Eastern contingent, I decided not to go. His attentions made me feel uncomfortable, and his political fanaticism frightened me.

At the end of the summer I received an extraordinary letter from Maksim. After the usual words of greetings he wrote:

"Valia, something happened during the summer, and I would rather you heard about it directly from me. It is easier for me to write about it than to tell you in person. This is what happened. When we were being assigned to our places of internship, Olga volunteered to go with me, and I had no reason to say no. After we arrived at the factory, Olga, to my great surprise, started showering me with all sorts of attentions, trying to become intimate with me. You probably know she is what they call a 'free spirit.' The combination of her efforts, our isolation, and the beautiful summer weather had their effect, and, against my will, I found myself in an intimate relationship with her. I must tell you that as soon as I realized what her intentions were, I let her know in no uncertain terms that I would never consider marrying her. Even now, after what has happened, I do not consider myself bound by any obligation. Now that she has left, I am sure that our relationship is over for good. Besides, Olga has obviously had experiences like this before. I am not planning to tell anyone about this adventure, but I knew people would find out and I wanted you to hear it from me, not from some gossipmonger."

I was surprised and angered by his letter. I could not imagine why he would want to involve me in his dirty affairs. If he was not planning on talking, and assuming that Olga was not either, what was the point? And why was he so sure

that any gossip about them would reach me? It was disgusting, the way he painted
himself as a helpless victim. He probably already knew what was going to happen
when he and Olga set out for the Far East. How obnoxious he must have looked
when he told her that he did not consider himself bound by any obligation! And
she was not much better! I had no trouble believing that she had started it all. It
was so much like her!

THEN disaster struck: my father was arrested. The day before, he had come home
very upset.

"I may be in serious trouble," he said to my mother. "I had a fight with a GPU
agent in Gulkevichi."

"Oh, my God! What happened?"

"He told me to work overtime, and I refused. Why should I disregard my orders
for him? Only two weeks ago we received an order from the depot manager,
forbidding all overtime unless it had been approved by him personally."

"What power does your manager have? They're all just pawns in the hands of
the GPU. But what was the rush, and what were you doing there?"

"I had been moving trains loaded with wheat—I'm talking about the grain that
they take from the Cossacks and then send some place north as quickly as they
can. It's no longer stored in the railway elevators—which makes sense, to be
honest with you, because the Cossacks may very well burn those elevators down.
The Cossacks are mad as hell these days: their entire harvest is being confiscated,
including the seed grain. Anyway, I'd just finished for the day and was about to
head home when a GPU man came up to me and said: 'You've got to stay for the
next shift; the brigade that's supposed to replace you hasn't arrived.' I told him:
'I can't, Comrade Representative. We have an order from the depot manager not
to do overtime without his personal approval. Contact the depot, and they'll send
over a new brigade.' 'I have called them, but who knows how long it will take
them to get here, and I cannot allow any stoppages. The state assignment must be
fulfilled without delay.' 'All our assignments come from the state, Comrade Representative. My order not to work overtime also comes from the state," I said, and
then I got on my locomotive and left. I didn't want to obey him. He's not my boss,
is he?"

"What an awful mess," Mother said. "Nobody goes to jail for disobeying a
depot manager, but the GPU can do whatever they want to you."

The next morning, when Father arrived at work, he was summoned by the GPU
and did not come back.

Our family was terribly frightened. We knew, of course, that Father was not a
wrecker or a saboteur and that everything had happened exactly the way he described it, but we also knew that people who had been arrested by the GPU did not
come back soon—or did not come back at all. At that time a lot of people were
being arrested—mostly Cossacks and mostly because of grain.

Mother went down to the GPU office every day, trying to get information.
Finally, she was told that the investigation had been completed and that Father
would soon be transferred to the Armavir Prison, where she would be allowed to

see him. She came back very depressed. During the short period he had spent in jail Father had grown older and lost a lot of weight. He looked scared, and Mother got the impression that he was not counting on an early release. However, many of our friends were saying that the fact that the investigation had been so quick was a good sign.

Besides worrying about our parents, Volodia and I could not help wondering about our own fate. If Father were to be found guilty of wrecking and sabotage, we would be expelled from college. I talked to Tania and Lida, and they advised me to go back to school. They promised not to tell anybody for the time being.

MEANWHILE, Tania had become a member of the Komsomol bureau. One day she came home after a meeting and said that Maksim had proposed that the Komsomol cell ask the administration to expel Olga from the institute. He had said that Olga, while undeniably talented, pretended not to understand political subjects, deliberately emphasized alleged contradictions in theory, tried to sway other students in the same direction, and, as a result, seriously hindered the work of the entire class. Furthermore, she was an extreme individualist: having read a lot of Dostoevsky, she was trying to imitate his pathological heroes.

"In what way is she imitating Dostoevsky's heroes?" asked the bureau secretary.

"When we were interns at a factory together she started an affair with me—to find out how a Communist behaved in conditions of intimacy, as she later explained to me. Also, proletarian life is completely alien to her. When I asked why she didn't have any friends among the workers of our factory, she said: 'We have nothing in common.' I told her that if she tried to get to know them better, she might find something in common with them, but her answer was: 'It's not worth the effort.' We cannot tolerate such a contemptuous attitude toward the workers on the part of a Soviet student. Finally, she is completely uninterested in volunteer work, and we know that a bad student volunteer will turn into a bad Soviet engineer."

Maksim was backed up by Serova. She described how at a political seminar, when the instructor had said that in Italy all the press was controlled by the Fascist party, Olga had asked: "Why do you consider this abnormal? Our press is also controlled by one party. I guess that's the way it is: whoever is in power controls the press." "She absolutely refuses to understand," said Serova, "that the Fascists are just a small pack of raving capitalist lapdogs, while the Communists represent all the people, so that that there can be absolutely no comparison between the two."

Kosenko, the party thousander who was in a brigade with her, came to her defense. "We shouldn't forget," he said, "that Olga is still in school, and that the task of any school is to teach and reeducate. We have done a lot of studying together. Her volunteer assignment was to help me, and she has carried it out willingly and very well, so it is wrong to say that she always avoids volunteer work. I have never noticed any anti-Soviet proclivities on her part, and as for her perversions in intimate relations, I have not had a chance to get to know her as well as Maksim has."

"Can you imagine," continued Tania, "she fooled around with Maksim last summer, and all for what? To explore new sensations! Had I heard about it under different circumstances, I would never have believed it! At least if she had loved him, it wouldn't be so disgusting."

"I think she does love him, but doesn't want him to know it. She must know that he does not love her."

"She shouldn't have complicated things. She should have told him how she felt. You know, I said something in her defense, even though I don't like her very much. I said: 'Maksim, you yourself said that you knew she was ideologically unsound, but instead of trying to reeducate her, the way a Communist should, you sank to her level and engaged in debauchery with her, even though we all know that she is not from a socially alien family and could therefore be reeducated. You are both at fault.'"

"What did he say to that?"

"He agreed that he was at fault, too. 'I gave in to a provocation,' he said. In the end, the bureau decided to hand the case over to the Proletarian Students Association and let them reeducate her in the proletarian spirit."

MY father was released from prison but not exonerated. He had been sentenced to six months of forced labor at his place of employment. This meant that he would keep his old job but would not get paid for it. We all knew that it would be very hard for us to spend half a year without any income, but we were very happy that Father's "misconduct" had not qualified as a political crime. Dad had grown a lot older and thinner, and it was very moving to see his joy at being back at home.

"Now I have experienced everything in life," he said jokingly, "including a GPU prison. If I get to fly an airplane, I'll die a happy man."

"What was prison like?" we asked.

"You can't even imagine what it's like. They have arrested so many Cossacks that the cells are packed to overflowing. People are sleeping not only on bunks but also on the floor and on top of one another. Most of them are older Cossacks, heads of their households. They were all taken during night raids, for not wanting to join the kolkhoz. They haven't even been interrogated: there will be some kind of 'general decision,' they say. They are suffering so much . . . But, children, I've got to tell you that never in my life have I heard such a beautiful rendition of 'Oh Kuban, Our Land.' One cell started singing, and then the whole prison joined in—the very walls were trembling!"

Father was worried about not being able to support the family and wanted to talk about it, but Mother stopped him very coolly, by saying: "Don't worry, Father, God will take care of us. Zina and Shura will help Valia; Volodia has his scholarship; and as for us, we won't starve: our garden will help us last through the winter. The important thing is that you are back home, all the rest we can deal with."

She was trying to make Father feel better, but, actually, she used to lay awake at night trying to think of ways to survive the winter. There was no money for bread, milk, shoe repairs, or a thousand other needs a family might have.

When I got back to the institute, Tania, Lida, and I had a long discussion about how we were going to live now. I decided not to ask for a scholarship until the end of Father's term. We were certain that the daughter of a convict would never get a scholarship. The girls promised to buy lunch coupons for me for as long as my father was not getting paid. The other meals would have to come from the food parcels that our parents were sending us. I was deeply moved by their generosity. I had known that they would help me, of course, but I had never expected that much help . . .

ONE night, when we were about to go to bed, Olga knocked on our door and said that she wanted to talk to me. We went to the library, which was empty at that hour.

"I just got back from the Proletarian Students Association," she said. "It's pretty bad. I have been expelled from the institute for a year."

"That's terrible! What are you going to do for a whole year?"

"They've decided that I need to be reeducated in the proletarian spirit. For that purpose, I am being sent to a large factory, to work as a rank-and-file worker for a year. If, a year from now, the factory leadership gives me a good recommendation, I will be readmitted."

SEVERAL party and Komsomol members were about to be sent to the countryside to help look for grain that was being hidden by the farmers. All those caught hiding grain were to be arrested. Among the ones being sent were Maksim and Fedia. The night they came over to say good-bye, they both looked depressed. They knew what awaited them in the Cossack villages, and besides, they did not want to fall behind in their studies. I asked Fedia how he was going to manage. He said he had no idea.

When Maxim left, Fedia stayed behind. He looked so miserable that we didn't have the heart to send him away. Lida had gone out to the bathroom to wash up before bedtime, while Tania and I sat around exchanging an occasional word with him. Finally, I said:

"Well, Fedia, it's probably time to call it a night."

"Oh, yes, I really should get going. Sorry for overstaying my welcome. If you girls only knew how much I dreaded the idea of going out there, you would cry out of sheer pity for me."

"We do understand. Who would want to miss so many classes? But they say you'll be back soon."

Lida was surprised to see Fedia when she returned from the bathroom.

"You're still here? You look like you've fallen apart completely! Pull yourself together. The party needs your help in the countryside, so stop whining. You are a Communist, aren't you?"

Fedia left. I thought about how he used to talk about the "romance of the revolution" at Professor Butov's parties. It may have looked romantic from a distance, but there was little romance in being forced to carry out party decisions with a gun in hand. Fedia was too soft-hearted to be a good Communist!

THE next night Lida came back from the institute completely furious. Muttering under her breath, she rummaged through her suitcase and tossed her things around. Finally, I asked:

"What's wrong, Lida?"

"Nothing's wrong. Leave me alone." And she continued pointlessly shifting her things around.

Finally, Tania, too, lost patience.

"You might as well tell us what happened. It doesn't help to be angry, and you'll feel much better if you share whatever it is with us."

"I'm mad at Ivan Platonovich. We were walking home together, when he suddenly said to me: 'Lida, you are a very good girl and I like you. Why don't you move into my room? We could live together.' I was completely shocked. 'Have you lost your mind, Ivan Platonovich?'—'What's the problem? You are a healthy young woman. You must be lonely without a man. I'm lonely, too. Why can't we live together if we like each other?'—'I'm not lonely. I don't even have time to be lonely. And, in any case, I don't love you. Who do you think I am, to even offer such a shameful thing to me? How dare you? I'll complain to the party secretary!'—'Wait a minute, just wait a minute, will you? Don't get yourself all worked up. I'm not offering you anything shameful. We can get registered and live as husband and wife. What's so shameful about that?' But I wouldn't listen to him. I just ran away."

Tania and I sat there, speechless, as if struck by lightening.

Tania was the first to recover. "What a bastard! We treat him nicely, like a friend, and look what he gets up to! I don't want to see him here in our room ever again! You went to the movies and to parks with him, and now see what has happened!"

"But what does he mean by offering to marry you? He has a wife and three children back in the village," I said.

"I don't believe he was thinking about marriage; he thought of it when I threatened to complain to the party bureau."

"Maybe he did mean to get married," said Tania. "It's not too hard to get divorced. You just go to the registry office, fill out an application form, and a week later you're divorced. That's not the problem. The problem is that he could imagine that you might like an ugly old fool like him. To be honest, I've never even thought of him as a man."

WE started hearing rumors about our boys who had been sent to help with collectivization. Something had happened to Fedia. It seemed to me that the girls knew but didn't want to tell me, so I decided to ask Ivan Platonovich. Although we had made it obvious that we no longer wanted to be friends with him, he continued to act in a friendly, natural manner.

When the right moment came, I called him aside and asked: "Ivan Platonovich, please tell me what happened to Fedia. I keep hearing that something is wrong, but no one will tell me exactly what it is."

"OK, I'll tell you, but don't go around talking about it. He shot himself."

"What? You mean, accidentally?"

"No, deliberately. It was a suicide. His nerves failed him. They were working on dekulakization: conducting searches, deporting the kulaks—in other words, helping the GPU. One case was particularly unpleasant, apparently: they evicted a large family with several children from their house and then found grain under the floor. They resisted and tried to take some of their things with them, so they were beaten, and the father was arrested on the spot. After that Fedia returned home and shot himself . . . It's a real shame. I feel sorry for the kid. When he was assigned to that detachment, I told the bureau: 'Don't send him; he doesn't have the guts for it.' But they said: 'Exactly, let him learn some toughness.' So he got to learn all right—all the way to heaven. But there's more. Maksim is not doing well either."

"What happened to him?"

"There was an attempt on his life, and he was wounded. Nothing major: they simply bandaged him up and didn't even call a doctor; but still, it's nothing to celebrate. He should be back any day now."

"Oh, how awful! I feel so sorry for Fedia!"

"There's nothing we can do about it. You know the saying: 'War is war.'"

I barely managed to sit through my lectures that day. I kept picturing Fedia. When I got home, I burst into tears.

"Why are you crying?" asked Lida.

"I found out about Fedia."

"Who told you?"

"Ivan Platonovich. Why didn't you tell me?"

"We only found out yesterday, at the Komsomol meeting. We meant to tell you, but we couldn't. You were such good friends."

"Poor, poor Fedia! He was so afraid of dying—always worrying about his health, trying to treat his TB. And then he goes and kills himself. What kind of horrible things did he see there, to make him do that?"

In January 1933 Serezha got a few days of vacation and came to see me in Krasnodar. While there, he found out that a job for an assistant professor in his field was available at the Krasnodar College of Agriculture. He had always wanted to work in his native Kuban, so he applied and was hired. This was especially lucky because now we could get married and live together during my last year in college. It was important to get married before graduating because, according to a new law, college diplomas were no longer to be given to the graduates themselves but instead sent directly to their first place of employment chosen by the commissariat. There, the graduate had to work for at least three years. Those who refused to go would not get their diplomas. Husbands and wives were supposed to be sent to the same place. We decided to get married in a week's time—as soon as I came back to Kropotkin for the winter break.

I told no one of our decision. I was superstitious, afraid that if I told people in advance, something might interfere with our plans.

When we arrived in Kropotkin and told my parents everything, they were very happy. They had always liked Serezha.

"There's one thing, though, children," said Mother. "As far as your father and I are concerned, your marriage will not be legitimate unless you have a church wedding. There can be no marriage without a proper wedding."

"How can we have a church wedding if all the priests have been arrested, and all the churches closed? Who is going to marry us and where?"

"I will take care of that. We have a priest here. He is homeless and penniless. He sleeps at a different house every night, and during the day he goes around begging, so as to avoid suspicion and not endanger the people who let him stay at their houses. He often travels to other towns, but fortunately he is here now. All the things that are necessary for the sacrament are kept by private individuals. A church can also be found. The church by the cemetery, for example, has been closed, but it has not been desecrated or vandalized yet. The cemetery guard has the key. Of course, we'll have to do it secretly, preferably at night, or all our religious life that we have managed to rebuild will be completely destroyed: the priest will be arrested, and everyone else will get into trouble. For you, too, it will be dangerous, of course. So if you think it would be more convenient or less risky, we could have the wedding at home."

"No," said Serezha. "If we are going to have a wedding, we might as well do it in a real church. Actually, I am glad that we can do it. It's much better to get married according to the real Russian custom, the same way our parents did."

"Only please, not a word to anyone. The fewer people who know about it, the better. Don't even tell your younger sister, Serezha: children cannot keep a secret."

"Mother, will you be able to arrange it soon? Serezha is leaving for Moscow next week."

"Why delay?" said Father. "Today the priest is here; tomorrow he may be arrested."

"I'll see if we can do it in a day or two," said Mother.

"But where am I going to get the rings? It's virtually impossible to buy them these days, especially at such short notice."

"If you can't find any, you can bring your parents' rings. That's also done, sometimes."

After Serezha left, Mother said: "What a good and brave person our Serezha is. He never even mentioned how dangerous it was for him. He will be in serious trouble if they find out."

"What kind of trouble?" asked my father.

"I'm not sure," I said. "We haven't had a case like this. I would probably be expelled as a socially alien element. For Serezha, as a college professor, the consequences would be more serious. He might even be put on trial for corrupting students with an alien ideology."

"No one will find out anything, and no one will be put on trial," said Mother. "Ask the Lord for protection, and He will protect you. Lots of people have secret church weddings these days. Don't worry about anything, but pray to God, asking Him to bless your marriage and give you happiness."

The next day Mother left in the morning and did not come back until late at night.

"Everything has been arranged, thank God. The day after tomorrow the priest will be waiting for you in front of the church between eleven P.M. and midnight. Savva (the husband of my older sister Zina) has agreed to go with you; he'll assist the priest during the wedding."

The next day we went to the town soviet to register our marriage in accordance with the law. Tania and Savva went with us, but it turned out that the presence of witnesses was not required. All they needed was the bride and groom, and their birth certificates. The whole ceremony took no more than ten minutes. After that, we all went to our place for dinner. Serezha's parents and sister joined us there. Those were hard and hungry times, but on that occasion my mother had cooked a goose and bought a bottle of wine.

For my wedding day I had been planning to wear the pretty dress that Shura had given me, but suddenly I decided that I wanted to wear a completely new dress on such a solemn day. It was impossible to buy cloth, but Mother happened to have a length of gray fustian she had been planning to use to make herself a night shirt, so we decided to make my wedding dress out of that. During the course of that evening and the following morning, a dressmaker we knew made a beautiful dress and even sewed some of her own large mother-of-pearl buttons on it.

The guests left soon after dinner, but later that night Serezha's parents and Zina and Savva returned.

We tried to put my thirteen-year-old brother, Alesha, to bed early, but he could probably sense that something important was about to happen and took forever to go to sleep.

I showed Serezha the ring I had chosen. It was my grandmother's ring: gold with three small rubies. I was afraid the priest might find it inappropriate because of the rubies. Mother said that the priest was not going to pay attention to the stones but suggested I take Zina's just in case. She could not pull her own ring off her finger.

Zina did not seem to want to part with her ring, and I did not really want to borrow someone else's wedding ring. Mother had several other rings, but they did not look like wedding rings because they all had stones, one in the shape of a little snake with emerald eyes. Grandmother's ring seemed the best.

In the evening it started snowing, and by eleven there were huge snowdrifts everywhere.

It was still snowing when we left the house. The paths that had been cleared during the day had disappeared, and we were forced to walk in single file. Savva, who was wearing high boots, walked in front, followed by me, and then Serezha.

As is usually the case after a snowstorm, it was exceptionally quiet and serene. We were all in a wonderful mood, and Savva and Serezha kept making jokes. The streets were deserted; we didn't see a single person.

The priest and the guard were waiting for us. It was dark inside the church: only one altar candle was burning. The priest was a very tall old man, who looked very thin and emaciated. All his movements were unhurried and solemn. He did not have all his vestments—only his cassock and stole. He greeted us kindly and blessed us. It would not have occurred to me to ask for his blessing because I had not been in church in a very long time and had forgotten all the rituals, but Savva went up first and showed us how to do it. Serezha showed the priest my ring with the stones, and the priest said it was fine.

He began immediately, reciting all the prayers slowly and with feeling. When the time for the crowns came, he put them directly on our heads, and I realized it was not the first time he had conducted a wedding under such circumstances. Traditionally the crowns were not put on but were held by the best men over the heads of the bride and groom during the whole ceremony.

At this point the church was lit up with three candles in addition to the one on the altar: two were held by Serezha and me, and the third by the priest himself, who used it to read his book. I remembered Zina's wedding six years before— then the church had been brightly lit with many candles and chandeliers; the choir had sung; the priest had worn a brocade chasuble; and the bride had worn a white dress and held a bouquet. There had been a lot of people, well-dressed and happy. At my wedding, we did not even take our coats off because it was so cold inside the church.

But I did not think our wedding was the worse for it. On the contrary, I believed it was closer to the sacrament that it was supposed to be in the Orthodox Church.

20 □ ALLA KIPARENKO

Building the City of Youth

□ Alla Vladimirovna Kiparenko was born in 1907 and joined the party in 1930. After leaving Komsomolsk she became a member of the Propaganda Section of the Komsomol Central Committee and then a professional party official. The city of Komsomolsk in the Far East was built primarily by convict labor,[1] but the (relatively minor) part played by Komsomol volunteers in its construction was much publicized at the time and subsequently. This volume belongs to the Soviet genre, particularly popular in the 1960s and 1970s, of celebration of Soviet achievements through the memoirs and oral histories of participants.

TODAY'S schoolchildren all learn in their geography classes that Komsomolsk-on-Amur is one of the largest industrial centers of the Soviet Far East. It is located on the Lower Amur, extending for almost fifteen kilometers along the left bank of that great river. It has a river port, a railway station, several large factories, various colleges, and numerous high schools, libraries, stadiums, and parks. There are also music and art schools. However, the information given about the city in geography textbooks and the *Great Soviet Encyclopedia* no longer corresponds to reality. This information simply cannot keep up with the reality.

Every once in a while *Ogonek*[2] publishes photographs of the city's handsome high-rises, wide avenues, shady parks, and streets. I pore over these photographs and reminisce . . . Once this was the village of Permskoe, which consisted of about a dozen soot-covered log cabins and a tiny wooden church deep in the taiga. The people living there fit their surroundings: they were sullen, suspicious, and tough, with only their eyes showing above their overgrown beards. They lived off hunting and fishing.

. . . In early May 1932 a curious convoy approached the landing at Permskoe—two old steamers with the proud-sounding names of Comintern[3] and Columbus were towing loaded barges behind them. This was the first detachment of Komsomol volunteers, the builders of the future city. Quite unexpectedly, sixteen young women were discovered to be among them—quite unexpectedly, because

From *Uchastnitsy velikogo sozidaniia* (Moscow: Gospolitizdat, 1962), 145–56 (abridged).
[1] For a thoroughly documented historical account of the events described in Kiparenko's memoir, see Jonathan A. Bone, "A La Recherche d'un Komsomol perdu: Who really built Komsomol'sk-na-Amure, and why," *Revue des études slaves* 71, no. 1 (1999).
[2] A popular illustrated magazine.
[3] Short for Communist International, the organization of Communist parties (1919–43) headquartered in Moscow.

not only had they not been invited but they had actually traveled without the knowledge of the Khabarovsk Territory Komsomol Committee or even the chief of construction, who had come on the same steamer. This is how it happened.

The person in charge of transporting the first party of volunteers was Comrade Zangiev, a Komsomol activist from North Ossetia who was a bright, energetic young man and a good administrator. According to the decision of the Khabarovsk Committee, women were not to be included—at least not until temporary barracks had been built. On this occasion, however, Zangiev's talents were of no avail. When he arrived at the volunteers' barracks on the Krasnaia River on the eve of the scheduled departure for Permskoe, he had a very angry crowd to deal with. "What do you mean, we are not going? Who do you think you are, anyway? Who gave you the right? We'll complain to the Central Committee! We knew what we were doing when we joined up! We can manage as well as you!"

Hoarse and disheveled, Zangiev appealed to our political consciousness and Komsomol discipline and called on the boys for support. But most of them were on the girls' side. All that consciousness-raising on the subject of women's equality had not been in vain! There were other reasons, of course, that were understood by all the young people . . . Finally Zangiev gave in, but on one condition: nobody in Khabarovsk would be told anything, and no girls would show up at the pier before dark. Once on the ship, they were to behave like "very special cargo" and come nowhere near the deck. At first this proposed compromise was also met with shouts of indignation: "We are not going to hide from anybody! We are going there to build socialism!" But Zangiev would not budge. He was risking a serious reprimand, so the girls had no choice but to agree.

When the first party arrived in Permskoe, the chief of construction was stunned to see women unloading the barges, but when he saw how well they were working, keeping up with the men in every way, he . . . thanked them on behalf of the administration.

The question of a women's dorm was solved to everyone's complete satisfaction: a bearded native turned over a shed where he had been storing his fishing nets.

In a recent letter to me, Zangiev reminisces about those difficult times: "The girls' first contribution was to organize the feeding of the workers. We will never forget that first bowl of steaming millet gruel, prepared for us by our dear female comrades." The same is true of the first loaf of bread, which was baked in a primitive oven built in the now empty church ("with 'opium for the people' as a starter," as the girls used to say).

The cauldrons in which the food was prepared were never idle. Work started very early, so preparations for breakfast had to begin the night before, right after dinner. The women would take turns carrying heavy lunches out to where the men were clearing the forest. Few of the women ever slept in the shed; most simply went to sleep wherever sleep caught up with them. One could often see a "chef" or two stretched out next to the warm cauldron. In the evenings they would hastily rinse out the lumberjacks' sweat-drenched shirts in the Amur and then try to bandage up the men's bloody palms.

Some women grumbled that if they were only going to cook dinners and wash clothes, they might as well have stayed home; but others would reason with them, explaining that the construction site had to be prepared. Even skilled mechanics were grubbing up roots! Nobody promised that everything would be ready for us, and what about that first conversation with Zangiev?

Meanwhile, strong, durable friendships were developing—friendships and love. Soon the first married couples began to appear. That is the way it should be. Those young people were working hard and living full lives, with a tremendous faith in their future. It was for the sake of that future that they endured privations and overcame difficulties.

Owing to the lack of vegetables and fat, cases of scurvy and night blindness began to appear. Once again, the women took charge. One of the best local remedies was a foul-tasting herbal brew. All the wives simply forced their husbands to drink it. The other women were given white jackets to wear at meal times and in the makeshift drug dispensaries in order to make them look more convincing. Soon after the women took over, things began to improve. As the men later said, "even that brew started tasting better."

Some of the women volunteered to become guides for the men who were suffering from night blindness. (For some reason women were not affected). They would take their charges gently by the arm and lead them to the barracks. Several of the bachelors started complaining: "Why can't I ever come down with this night disease?"

It takes hard work to win a victory. This axiom entered the consciousness of every builder, so that no one individual could conceive of a life outside the collective, outside the specific tasks that the group was trying to accomplish. None of the married women quit working. Not a single one even asked for a lighter assignment because of pregnancy or sickness, although they had the right to do so. Doctors and even Komsomol committees had to be vigilant because women were extremely reluctant to leave their work sites.

In this way, human beings of a new kind were being formed. This was true spiritual growth, a real aspiration to be better and to attain genuine culture in everything, from attitudes toward work to personal relationships. Even at that time the socialist pledges of the Komsomolsk shock-worker brigades often included resolutions that dealt with everyday life. I remember the speeches by female laborers that demanded the inclusion of such slogans as "Keep your workplace and your work clothes clean!" and "No cursing at work or at home—especially in the presence of women!" The men grumbled, but the girls insisted: "Don't worry, you'll get used to it. You'll even thank us for it later."

By 1934 Komsomolsk already had its own city soviet. It was housed in one of the tiny log cabins left over from Permskoe. The position of vice chair, secretary, and instructor—and just about every other position as well—was held by a Komsomol member named Anna Rumiantseva. The daughter of an old Communist, she had come to Komsomolsk as a volunteer, having left behind a position in a town on the Black Sea coast of the Caucasus. Small, feisty, and cheerful, she ran the place virtually single-handedly.

Once I stopped by on business. A dog sled was parked outside the door. Inside, in the chairman's "office," seated behind a desk covered with red cloth and beneath a large portrait of Lenin, Anna Rumiantseva was speaking angrily to someone on the telephone: "No, we won't allow you to destroy the forest in that way. There are magnificent birch trees there. That's right . . . That's right . . . We won't allow it . . . We are the Soviet government!"

On a stool by the door sat a young Nanai[4] girl wearing a beautifully embroidered fur coat and hat, and fur boots. She was listening very closely, trying not to miss a single word. When Anna put down the receiver, the Nanai girl smiled broadly. Her dark hand pointed to the portrait of Lenin, then to Anna, and then to the huge carcass of a new plant being built outside.

"Soviet gov'ment good . . . Komsomol good . . . Lenin good . . . Saksa also Komsomol . . ."

Rumiantseva hugged Saksa and patted her gently on the cheek:

"That's right, Saksa. Of course you are!"

Several months later I saw Saksa working at the construction site. She was singing along with everyone else:

> We're building, we're building, we're building . . .
> In place of old marshes and woods
> Our country will see a new city
> A city of smokestacks and schools!

ONE day the secretary of the city Komsomol committee, Minkin, told me: "The concrete worker Kotsar is planning to marry Menis. Do you think anything good will possibly come of it?" Menis, an Ossetian by nationality, was unbalanced and extremely hot-tempered. He was not very serious about his work; he preferred to drink and have a good time. He had been admonished, shamed, punished, and criticized at meetings, but nothing did any good. Kotsar was one of our best shock workers, a Komsomol activist, and a nice, pleasant girl. More than one builder of Komsomolsk had been hoping to call her his wife . . . And now, Menis!

The intelligent and very experienced committee secretary realized that the situation was a delicate one and that outside interference would probably do more harm than good. The newlyweds were given a room and a lot of good wishes, but a decision was made not to let them out of sight. Then a miracle occurred! Nobody could recognize the former hooligan; he tried his best to catch up with his wife, and soon his productivity results began to approach hers. He also became calmer and more cool-headed. After about a year the names of Kotsar and Menis were always mentioned together as the names of our best shock workers, our best Komsomol activists.

"How did you do it? How did you turn him around like that?" the other concrete workers kept asking.

----

[4] A Manchu-speaking indigenous group traditionally engaged in hunting and fishing.

To which Kotsar would reply: "Oh, one way and another. Sometimes by asking him, sometimes by teasing, but mostly by my own example. He just couldn't live with the fact that I was being praised while he was being criticized and that I was earning twice as much as he was. He has a lot of pride. But I have my pride, too. And it looks like my pride won out!"

Soon afterward, a lot of women arrived in Komsomolsk in response to V. S. Khetagurova's appeal. "Young women," she wrote, "come to the Soviet Far East. It is a rich and beautiful region, and there is work enough for everyone."[5]

. . . By 1936 there were more than two thousand "Khetagurovites" in Komsomolsk.[6] They received a warm welcome from the construction workers. A special dorm was built in time for their arrival. Each one received a job according to her wishes and qualifications. The best of the old-timers were asked to meet them and show them around the city. There were some amusing episodes, too. The young hosts could not wait to meet the new girls, but since they needed at least one day to rest up, settle in, and get their bearings, specially assigned old-timers were posted as guards by the entrances to the dorm. Imagine the astonishment of the guards in the evening when dressed-up "Khetagurovites" began emerging from the building arm in arm with beaming young builders! Secretary Minkin remains puzzled to this day. "I have no idea how they got in there!" he says.

The builders of Komsomolsk lived interesting, varied lives. Socialist competition in labor productivity and quality of output as well as the questions of how to organize everyday life and how to deal with the new morality, personal relationships, and personal happiness—all these elements filled their lives to the brim. And in that hard, busy, but magnificent and truly meaningful life, women were among the most active participants.

---

[5] The publication of Valentina Khetagurova's appeal in *Komsomol'skaia pravda*, February 5, 1937, signaled the beginning of a massive government campaign to attract young single women to the Far East. The first four hundred women recruited in Moscow were sent to Komsomolsk.

[6] The date is incorrect. The Khetagurova movement was not launched until 1937.

21 □ ANNA IANKOVSKAIA

A Belomor Confession

□ This interview comes from a four-hundred-page tribute to the construction of the Stalin White Sea–Baltic Canal, compiled by a group of leading Soviet writers including Maxim Gorky, Vsevolod Ivanov, Valentin Kataev, Aleksei Tolstoy, Viktor Shklovsky, and Mikhail Zoshchenko. The canal was built entirely by convicts, whose rehabilitation through labor was celebrated in this volume. Anna Iankovskaia was one of the prisoners interviewed by the authors.

I HAVE BEEN mistreated since I was eight years old. Once my stepmother told me: "Go fetch some water, and I'll give you tea with jam." I brought the water, but then she said: "I'll see you in hell before I give you any of my jam." She gave preserves to all the others, and I ran out of the room in tears.

Once, at the Jewish market, I met a man and woman. The man said: "Come stay with us. You'll be our babysitter. We'll provide you with clothes." So I went with them. The apartment looked all right, but there was no baby to be seen. When I asked, "Where's the baby?" they answered: "Grandma's going to bring him from Dnepropetrovsk."

But there never was any baby.

Once I woke up in the middle of the night and saw piles of money and glossy playing cards on the table. Wine, too. My master and mistress were talking to their guests in a strange kind of Russian.

In the morning I asked the mistress about it, and she gave me the whole story. Slowly but surely I learned their thieves' jargon and a couple of months later started asking them to take me along. At first the master was reluctant, but then he got me a boy's suit of clothes, cut my hair, and took me out on a job with him.

That night we were "doing" a jeweler's store. During the day we made wax molds (they had this special forge where they made burglars' tools), but then it turned out that we could not enter through the door because the guards could see us. So they pushed in a small panel, and I crawled in there with a flashlight. Inside, I found everything they wanted and passed it out to them. I was really scared that I would get stuck and wouldn't be able to get back out. I got out just fine, though.

The next time I wasn't a bit scared. This went on for five years. Finally, my master got caught and was sentenced to exile in a remote district. During the trial

From M. Gor'kii, L. L. Averbakh, S. G. Firin, eds., *Belomorsko-Baltiiskii kanal imeni Stalina: Istoriia stroitel'stva* (Moscow: Gosudarstvennoe izdatel'stvo "Istoriia fabrik i zavodov," 1934), 252–56.

his wife was unfaithful to him. He came down with tuberculosis and died three months later.

All alone and broke, I became a thief in my own right. I used to break into apartments. I had a whole set of lock picks that I would test on my own doors first.

About four months later I got caught, but instead of sending me to jail they sent me to a reform school for juvenile offenders. There were no bars there, no nothing, except for two teachers and a director—it was what they called the "trust" treatment.

I soon ran away from there, but first I robbed one of the teachers.

I spent a month and a half at large before I ended up at that school again. They forgave me and let me back in. I stayed there for two weeks, watching to see where the teacher kept her things and all her money, and then took everything and left. Soon I was back again. The teachers were new, but the kids were the same: they recognized me and told the director all about me.

At that point they added up my offenses and sent me to jail.

In jail I was put in a juvenile cell. I was there for a month and a half waiting for my trial. On the way to the courthouse some friends of mine distracted the guard and I got away. I left Kiev and started "touring" Briansk, Konotop, Dnepropetrovsk, Mariupol, and Krivoi Rog. I dressed nicely—like a "momma's girl": a little hat, a small suitcase, and a pretty summer dress. Some people would even say: "Would you please keep an eye on our things—there are so many thieves around these days."

I lived well at that time—I had money and a nice apartment—but I kept having these strange chills, and I wasn't sleeping well.

I got caught in Poltava. I always used to get terribly depressed when I got caught. Within three days my skin would turn sallow, and I wouldn't be able to eat anything.

From the Poltava Prison I was sent to a juvenile facility where I started doing good work at a stocking factory. I was allowed to go into town, but still I didn't run away. I kept thinking about how, when I got released, I would do this kind of clean work and give up my old ways: enough is enough! The head warden gave me his word of honor that I'd be sent to a state factory, and, bad as I was, I always took someone's word of honor seriously.

When I was released, he said there were no openings and that I would have to wait. In the meantime I was to go there to shovel snow for a month, which I did. I worked for one ruble, ten kopeks, a day, and still I resisted the urge to steal. A month later I reported to the head warden, and he asked me: "Iankovskaia, what did you do before your arrest?" I told him I used to steal from people. "Well then, go back to stealing," he said.

I could not believe my ears. I cursed him up and down, threw an inkwell at him, and yelled: "I was killing myself working for you! Like a fool I believed you, and now you're sending me back to steal!"

I left there as much a thief as when I first arrived, and I resumed my old ways knowing there was no justice in this world and no need to change anything. Six months later I heard from "our people" that the head warden had been arrested as a former White Guardist[1]—but as far as I was concerned, it was too late. I was already living my old life.

The thing that's wrong with the Criminal Police is that they don't have the right approach; they don't know how to find the right chord. It's as if they were looking at people through a sieve, without seeing the face properly. Everybody's different, and each person requires a special approach.

I started living with another apartment thief. He was polite but very strong. After his arrest I was left with a little baby, so I started "touring" again, leaving the baby with an old woman I had hired. The baby got to drink hot chocolate and generally didn't lack for anything, but eventually I became estranged from him.

Before then I used to dream about a normal life, but after that conversation with the warden I got to like my life as a thief much better.

Around 1924 the famous Kiev thieves' den had three different names: "Grand Hotel," "Crystal Palace," and "A Quiet House but a Very Jolly Family." It was a two-storied stone building, with every room, corner, and hallway occupied by criminals.

In the middle of the courtyard, under a special awning, four accordion players took turns playing twenty-four hours a day. Everybody wanted to hear them, and everybody contributed to their pay. Before I got used to it I thought I'd lose my mind—especially if you consider all the gambling, drinking, swearing, and fornicating that used to go on in there.

All sorts of things used to happen there. For example, some criminal would suddenly get jealous of the prostitute he was living with and start accusing her of cheating on him. She would proclaim her innocence, but he would refuse to listen. Then he would pull out his knife, and the slaughter would begin.

At one end of the house people would be dividing up stolen goods and getting drunk; at the other, a woman, all cut up, would be bleeding to death. And at the same time, drowning out all the other noises and completely oblivious to everything, the musicians would be playing away. In that place nobody ever joked around with women, entertained them, or showed them any affection. If a woman went to the theater, it meant that she was planning on finding herself a straight guy and moving out of there. But very few managed to do that. Most would just sit around naked because all their clothes had been gambled away. And in the winter nobody went anywhere anyway. Even if somebody did get a woman some nice clothes, within three days, at the very most, they would all be stripped off and lost at cards. It's hard to believe the things that went on there.

In 1932, when I was arrested and sentenced to be deported by the GPU, I got really scared. I thought I'd be punished without mercy. I thought I'd be tortured. I kept thinking that never again would I see my home or my baby—that I would waste away completely.

In March 1932 we arrived at Camp No. 2, Section 6, in Tunguda.

They took us to the assembly room, where some Cheka boss made a speech

---

[1] Officer in the White Armies that fought the Bolsheviks during the civil war.

about how they would try to reeducate us—how they were trying not to punish us but to reform us through labor and thus transform socially harmful elements into useful human beings.

"Just keep on talking," I said to myself. "You're all sewn up inside that uniform. It's easy for you."

That night they took us to a pine bathhouse. As I was washing myself with that bitter soap, I realized that it wasn't easy to wash away a person's past life . . . After a three-day quarantine we were sent out to work.

We were given sleds and told to clear the rocks and snow out of the pit. Some people dug, and we dragged the stuff out. The sled wouldn't obey me. I wasn't pulling it—it was pulling me. You had to dig in your heels, but then your legs would hurt terribly above your knees. I never worked so hard in all my life. When I got back to the barracks, I felt completely broken. So I decided that anything—a punishment cell, a malingering offense, transportation—was better than work.

At that moment the educator Kucheriavina came up to me and said: "So, Iankovskaia, how do you feel?"

I swore at her and said: "I don't care what you do; I refuse to work anymore."

That night she summoned me to the Red Corner[2] and said: "Look at me, Iankovskaia. What do I look like?"

"You look like what you are: a boss in a purple shawl. Congratulations."

"Believe it or not, I am an inmate, just like you. When I first arrived at the canal I also refused to work, and an educator came to see me, too. Tell me, Iankovskaia, what is it about your old life that you miss the most: your Ivan, your arrests, or your bottle?"

Kucheriavina conducted that conversation with me for at least four hours. She cited various examples from our lives and brought me to tears.

This was not the Criminal Police, where they treated everybody the same way. Here they tried to find the right approach to each individual and to understand what that person needed. That was the main reason why I started working.

[2] Red Corner—Originally a place for icons in a peasant hut; after the revolution, a special room where sacred objects such as red banners, honorary diplomas, portraits of party leaders, and revolutionary memorabilia were kept.

22 □ Lidia Libedinskaia

The Green Lamp

□ The fiction writer and literary historian Lidia Libedinskaia (Tolstaia) started her memoir in 1959 at the age of thirty-eight, several months after the death of her husband, the "proletarian" writer and civil war veteran Yuri Libedinsky. She finished it in the spring of 1964, when the "Khrushchev Thaw," which had made its conception and publication possible, was drawing to a close.

My MOTHER wore a checkered cap and hung out with the futurists, and later with the LEF crowd.[1]

My father would get misty-eyed reciting Bunin:[2]

The cheerful summer sun comes seeping through the shutters,
Through dusty curtains, heavy glass, a dry bouquet,
To pour golden crystals over the candle cutters,
The harpsichords, the ancient carpets and the dull parquet.

I do not know what these lines reminded him of. Perhaps his blue Tolstoyan blood still retained some memory of old manor houses, overgrown ponds, and hundred-year-old lindens, although he himself could not possibly remember any of that because my grandfather left Tambov Province for Baku, where he opened a notary office, right after the birth of his eldest son (who happened to have been my father).

That piece of property was less poetic than Bunin's cold rooms, but it turned out to be much more profitable, allowing my grandfather to live in a very large, comfortable apartment. After the fall of the autocracy, he tossed several thick bundles of crisp white bills into the green waves of the Caspian Sea. The bills carried the image of Tsar Peter, who had granted the Tolstoys their title.

My father had kept some cards that had gold trim, a picture of a small crown, and an intricate inscription written in a fancy spidery hand: "Count Boris Dmitrievich Tolstoy." Underneath, my father had added in purple ink: "An Employee of the RSFSR State Planning Commission."

To my mother's and grandmother's horror, he used to leave these cards at his friends' and acquaintances' apartments when he did not find them at home. According to him, just as only a scoundrel would have been ashamed of his proletar-

From Lidia Libedinskaia, *Zelenaia lampa* (Moscow: Sovetskii pisatel', 1966), 9–92 (abridged).
[1] LEF (Levyi front iskusstv)—Left Front of Art, 1923–28; group of avant-garde writers and theorists led by V. V. Mayakovsky, N. N. Aseev, and A. M. Rodchenko.
[2] I. A. Bunin (1870–1953)—Russian writer, some of whose early work is concerned with the decline of the gentry; emigrated to France in 1920; 1933 Nobel Prize winner.

ian origin before the revolution, so it did not become a decent person to deny his gentry background after the revolution.

Perhaps the most free-thinking member of our family was Grandma, my mother's mother. In her youth she worshipped Chernyshevsky,[3] slept on bare wooden boards to imitate Rakhmetov,[4] and, in the year 88 of the previous century, composed the following poem:

> If I could become a man,
> I would go to college
> And learn a little decadence
> Along with useful knowledge.

She never made it as a decadent and was quite indifferent to so-called decadent poetry. All her life she loved Nekrasov, and whenever my parents went out she would recite "Red-nosed Frost" and "Russian Women."

Our whole family lived in one room. We could not afford a maid, so Grandma took charge of the housework. Tall and statuesque, in a loose clean blouse with a black velvet bow and a very long skirt that touched the floor, she was constantly thinking about something she was reading, and, her pince-nez glistening, she would bemoan the defeat of the Decembrist uprising or, rolling her *r*'s in the French manner and occasionally employing a French word, she would relate the plot of *Faust* to me. There would hardly be any time left to cook dinner and no time at all to clean up. We would have to combine our efforts to finish the dishes and sweep the floor before my parents got home from work.

Another example of Grandma's influence was the game that the girls from our building loved to play; it consisted of spending whole days sitting on the roof amid bags full of toys and sacks filled with sand and pebbles. This signified a trip to Siberia to join our exiled husbands. The Decembrists! In our house that word was always uttered with particular reverence. My mother used to write historical novels about Bestuzhev-Marlinsky and Ryleev.[5]

Still, Bunin's dreamy lines had made a tremendous impression on me. My very first poem, which I wrote at the age of ten, began in the following manner:

> A hazy melancholy wrapped my heart
> In the soft silk of ancient recollections.

I cannot for the life of me explain what the terrible burden of those recollections was all about because my childhood was unusually peaceful and happy.

Probably the only real burden was having to go to the theater every Sunday. I was very shy and could not imagine how anyone could perform on stage. I suffered for the actors; I felt desperately sorry for them. I was overcome with guilt

[3] N. G. Chernyshevsky (1828–1889)—radical writer whose novel *What Is to Be Done?* (written in prison in 1863) became the gospel of Russian socialists.

[4] Rakhmetov—an ascetic revolutionary in Chernyshevsky's novel *What Is to Be Done?*.

[5] A. A. Bestuzhev-Marlinsky (1797–1837)—writer, member of the Decembrist movement; reduced to ranks and killed in action in the Caucasus; K. F. Ryleev (1795–1826)—poet, member of the Decembrist movement; executed along with four other leaders of the December 14 uprising.

for having to participate in their torture. My parents could not understand why I kept asking them what time it was. I used to count every minute, waiting anxiously for the end of the show.

However, my mother and father considered going to the theater a necessary element of a proper education and continued to press on relentlessly, even though I would often arrive at the theater with my eyes red from crying.

There was one more "heavy recollection" that did not manage to cloud the happiness of my childhood. In pursuit of the same goal of raising a "well-rounded human being," as my father used to put it, they decided to teach me ballet.

I have to admit that I am completely tone deaf and cannot sing even the simplest melody. Nevertheless, I was taken to the ballet studio at the Bolshoi, where some sensible people suggested that my mother sign me up for an art class at the local Pioneer Club. Why art, I have no idea because I am as bad at drawing as I am at singing. My parents refused to give up, however, and sent me to a private ballet school where they used the "Isadora Duncan method." I do not remember what the method consisted of, but I do remember endlessly jumping up and down, clumsy in our bare feet on the fluffy carpet, to the accompaniment of an out-of-tune piano. The classes were held in a spacious apartment (a "NEPman" apartment, as we used to say in those days). I was totally incapable of moving to the rhythm of the music, which drove our quietly irritable teacher with her sorrowful eyes to despair.

That just about completes the list of recollections that wrapped my nine-year-old heart in "soft silk."

I should probably have been told in no uncertain terms that such attempts at versification had to stop once and for all, but that would have gone against the humane spirit that reigned in our family.

Grandma said that the poem had a Nadsonian ring to it;[6] Mother was too busy to notice my literary efforts (she was working as a reporter for *Ogonek*); and Father delivered a long lecture on the history of Russian poetry, at the conclusion of which he told me that my work was imitative, which was pardonable at such an early stage of one's creative development. He was probably right: at that time my creative development was indeed at an early stage.

WE lived in an old, yellow house the color of autumn leaves. It stood at the intersection of two quiet streets in the very center of Moscow. A short distance away, Tverskaia and Malaia Dmitrovka Streets buzzed with the noise of rattling streetcars, honking automobiles, banging doors, and bustling pedestrians. But here, in Vorotnikovsky Alley, everything was quiet. The pink and yellow gentry townhouses dozed behind their wooden fences and the dusty greenery of overgrown gardens; the Pimenovsky Monastery rose silently behind its white walls. The former monastery, that is: now it was used as a place for weekly Saturday auctions at which pawned goods were sold. Sold cheaply enough, so that every once in a while a gorgeous velvet chair, a copper desk lamp, an inlaid table, or a

[6] S. Ia. Nadson (1862–1887)—Russian poet.

pair of silver spoons would show up in our one-room apartment. Arrivals from some strange, unknown world, these things were certainly not vital necessities, but Grandma always claimed that she could not "let them get away." Actually, our family was rather indifferent to material objects. The new purchase would be proudly shown to all our friends and neighbors and would have its origins investigated, to be completely forgotten within three days. The inlaid table would be used as a stand for the kerosene lamp; the velvet chair would become a bed for a neutered cat by the name of Planchik; and the silver spoons would become tarnished as they peacefully lived out their lives among their stainless-steel brethren.

I liked to hear the story of how, in the cold, frosty December of 1917, when leaving Petersburg for the warm and fertile Caucasus, Grandma had taken only two things from her well-furnished four-room apartment: a brass mortar and pestle and a huge, life-sized portrait of my admiral grandfather in a heavy bronze frame. The mortar is now in Tbilisi, at my aunt's place, and the portrait of my admiral grandfather was thrown off the train by revolutionary sailors.

A former monastery, former townhouses . . . I used to hear the word *former* at every turn. We got our bread at the former Filippov store, bought meat at the former Eliseev, purchased galoshes at the former Muir & Merrilies and received medical treatment at the former Catherine Hospital. There were "former people," as well. Professor Ivanov, who lived in our house, was known as the former palace doctor; the driver Toropov, as a former landless peasant; and Grandma, simply as a "former person."

Former things, former people . . . When were these former times, and what had they been like?

I often asked Grandma these questions, and it turned out that it had all ended very recently—some ten or twelve years before. And yet it was so unlike everything that surrounded me! It seemed to me that it was as far back as the Tatar Yoke,[7] about which Grandma had told me so many colorful stories—she had a wonderful memory and a fertile imagination.

I HAD a dream. A fairly ordinary dream: to have a bear. Not a live bear, brown or polar, of the kind I had often seen at the zoo, but a red, flannel bear like the one my friend Lidka Toropova had recently received as a present. The problem was that such bears could be found in only one Moscow store—the closed warehouse for the employees of the GPU. Lidka's father worked at the GPU as a driver, but none of my relatives had anything to do with that institution.

I told Grandma about my dream, and she set about making it a reality.

"Tania," she asked my mother when she got home from work, "is it true that you cannot manage to get a bear for your only child?"

My mother tried to protest, but Grandma was not to be deterred.

"Get your newspaper to give you an assignment to write a story about that store. I doubt you need a special ration card to buy a bear—surely they'll sell it to you for cash."

[7] Tatar yoke—term used to refer to the period of Mongol rule over Russia.

I do not know what kind of assignment my mother managed to get at her paper, but several days later she and I were cheerfully walking toward a large store just off Lubianka Square.

Indeed, one did not need ration cards to buy bears.

When we got home the bear received some calico pants and a blue Tolstoyan shirt embroidered with white and red flowers. My dream had come true. Everybody knows, however, that the fulfillment of a final dream signifies the end of life. My life, on the other hand, was only beginning, and desires followed one after another. My next dream was to get the bear some shoes. A long time ago, I had noticed that the Rubbertrust store on Tverskaia, which for some reason sold baby things, had some brown leather shoes of the kind children wear when they are learning to walk. I could not think of a better pair of shoes for my bear. But those particular ones cost one ruble, which was a lot of money. For one ruble you could buy two tickets to the only show at the Children's Theater, *A Negro Boy and a Monkey*, two "Napoleons" at the bakery, or two "Teddy Bear" and ten "Transparent" candies at the corner kiosk. All for one ruble. That is how expensive those shoes were!

Still, Grandma told me that as soon as she received her pension (twenty rubles), she would buy the shoes. Grandma always got her pension on the 15th of each month at ten in the morning, so by eleven A.M. on July 15, 1928, the bear was already sporting his new shoes.

Once again, one satisfied desire led to another. It was important for the bear to see the world and be seen himself. So Lidka and I grabbed him by his hard, sawdust-filled front paws and took him for a walk around the neighborhood.

On Tverskaia we stopped next to a bakery. It was one of the last NEPman bakeries, and the owner was trying to show his loyalty to the Soviet order by staging a kind of news show in his shop window. In those days the most dramatic event was the disappearance of Amundsen, who had flown to the North Pole on a hydroplane to rescue the Italian Nobile expedition and had vanished without trace, along with his whole crew.[8] The world was agitated over his disappearance, and in the shop window of the bakery, sugar icebergs floated next to sugar ice floes. A chocolate tent was sprinkled with powdered sugar, and small sugar people with pink candy faces stretched out their tiny sugar hands in a desperate plea for help. In front of them, right by the glass, stood a shaggy dog with its chocolate mouth wide open and its bright-red marzipan tongue hanging out.

After that we showed our bear the lions that guarded the entrance to the Museum of the Revolution: after all, he was a bear and they were lions, so perhaps he would find it easier to communicate with them. Then we decided to extend our itinerary and, in violation of a strict parental prohibition, we crossed Tverskaia, which was full of clanging streetcars. We walked under the museum arch, past the iron cannons and neat piles of cannonballs, and into the shady linden garden of

[8] Roald Amundsen, the Norwegian Polar explorer (b. 1872), never returned from that expedition; Umberto Nobile (1885–1978) was rescued on June 23, 1928, six days after Amundsen's disappearance.

the former English Club. Grandma used to take me there to talk about the Napoleonic invasion, Natasha Rostova, and Pierre Bezukhov.[9]

We walked along the wide linden alleys, sat on benches in the transparent shade of trembling leaves, and looked at the tall museum windows. Behind the windows, in the same rooms in which Moscow had welcomed Bagration,[10] an endless line of visitors was filing through. We could hear a ringing voice pronouncing the words that seemed to fill the air in those years: "dictatorship of the proletariat . . ."; "revolutionary underground . . ."; "class struggle . . ."; "storming of the Winter Palace . . . "

I WAS not accepted by the Young Pioneers. There were three of us: Irka Maleeva, Vovka Iakovlev, and I. I do not remember why they were not accepted, but in my case it was social origin.

At the meeting John Kuriatov said that his mother had known our family back in Baku.

"They used to receive the bourgeois poet Khlebnikov.[11] Tolstaia (that was me!) had the émigré Viacheslav Ivanov as her godfather.[12] And her grandmother speaks French!"

"Tolstaia, is that true?" asked our Pioneer leader, Fatia Gurari, a dark-skinned, curly-haired boy. He looked confused.

What could I say? Khlebnikov had been a frequent guest at my parents' place in Baku in 1920–21. He and my mother had worked in the Caucasus Telegraph Agency together. The memory of those encounters, as well as some yellow sheets covered with Khlebnikov's tiny, intricate handwriting, were being proudly and carefully preserved by my family. Viacheslav Ivanov was indeed my godfather, having named me after his favorite actress, Lidia Borisovna Iavorskaia. The small bouquet of violets he had given my mother on that occasion was kept in a special album. Grandma spoke fluent French and had even translated Verlaine.[13] All this was true, although I had not realized that it was bad.

"Yes," I said softly but firmly, "it is true."

"Well, her (that is Grandma's!) speaking French is no problem," said Fatia thoughtfully. "All knowledge can be used in the service of the revolutionary class. Now this Khlebnikov thing is more serious. From what I know, he was a friend of Mayakovsky's.[14] And Mayakovsky committed suicide, which is against Communist morality. Maybe he was under Khlebnikov's influence."

"But Khlebnikov died a long time ago," I said timidly. "From an illness. He did not shoot himself . . ."

[9] Natasha Rostova, Pierre Bezukhov—characters from Leo Tolstoy's novel *War and Peace* (1863–69).

[10] Prince P. I. Bagration (1765–1812)—Russian general, hero of the 1812 war with Napoleon, killed at the battle of Borodino.

[11] Velimir Khlebnikov (1885–1922)—avant-garde poet, one of the founders of Russian futurism.

[12] Viacheslav Ivanov (1866–1949)—symbolist poet and philosopher; emigrated from Russia in 1924.

[13] Paul Verlaine (1844–1896)—French poet.

[14] V. V. Mayakovsky (1893–1930)—Russian poet.

Fatia coughed.

"All this needs to be clarified," he said sadly. "I've never heard anything at all about this Viacheslav Ivanov. In any case, you were baptized without your consent, and chances are, Tolstaia, you would have disassociated yourself from your parent's incorrect action. Isn't that right, Tolstaia?

I was silent. There was no way in the world I was ever going to disassociate myself from my family, especially Grandma. Fatia realized he had said something wrong, and hastened to add: "Well, never mind, Tolstaia, we'll have it all cleared up, and everything will be all right!"

It usually took me three minutes to walk home from school. On that day it took about an hour. The cold autumn sun was shining down from the sky. The first patches of ice glistened between the cobblestones, and gusts of wind kept swirling up dirt, scraps of paper, and the last yellow leaves.

I had to decide what to do next. But when you have just celebrated your eleventh birthday the month before, such decisions are not easy to make. I did not have anyone I could talk to.

I sat down on a stone hitching post at the corner of Pimenovsky and Vorotnikovsky, took a new notebook and pencil out of my satchel, and, holding the pencil tightly in my freezing fingers, resolutely wrote on the cover: "Diary." I then turned the page and wrote down on the snow-white paper:

"October 26, 1932
I was not accepted by the Young Pioneers. I am terribly ashamed. What I ought to do:
    1. Not say anything to Father, Mother, or Grandma.
    2. Or Liuska or Galka. Nurakhmet is OK.
    3. Never go to school again. Ever."

I still have that page. "Nurakhmet is OK" meant that I could tell the oldest son of our janitor, a little Tatar boy by the name of Nurakhmet, about what had happened. Why he deserved such confidence I do not know; we had not been friends before then. He always used to do what I told him, though. Nurakhmet was a year and a half younger than I was and did not like to read.

I returned the notebook to my satchel and went to the janitor's room. It was dark as usual: thick smoke rose from the stove; diapers hung drying on the line; shiny black roaches brought specially from Kazan for good luck scurried up and down the walls; and a mountain of down pillows in bright pink pillowcases with large green roses rested solemnly on the bed. I really coveted those pillowcases and could not understand why we had to sleep on boring white pillows, thereby depriving ourselves of such pink happiness.

"Nurakhmet," I said in a peremptory tone, "starting tomorrow I will not be going to school anymore. But I will leave home every morning as if I were. Do you understand?" Nurakhmet nodded. "Tomorrow at a quarter past eight I want you to be waiting for me by the "Goldfish" kindergarten. Do you know where we are going?"

"No," said Nurakhmet sadly.

"You'll find out tomorrow, OK?"

"OK."

I had no idea where we were going to go.

The next morning was a gray one, with low clouds that seemed pregnant with the last rain or the first snow. The wind had subsided, and the world had become a little warmer and cozier. At a quarter past eight, I ran out the front door as usual, hid the hated galoshes under the porch, crossed the street, and opened the kindergarten gate. Nurakhmet was standing and waiting meekly under a naked pear tree.

"Let's go, young man!"

"Where? To the movies?" His eyes glistened with greed.

"It's not that simple." I was indignant at his mercenary attitude. "We've got to get some money first."

"How are we going to get it?"

"We'll look for it."

"Look for it?" Nurakhmet's face fell. "Where?"

"Don't you understand? In stores, on sidewalks ... You see, people lose money: sometimes five kopeks, sometimes ten. And we'll pick it up. Maybe we'll even find a wallet with a hundred rubles in it. Then we'll return it to the person who lost it, and he'll give us a reward . . ."

"What kind of reward?"

"I don't know—maybe even a bicycle."

"But whose will it be—yours or mine?"

"Both . . ."

Nurakhmet shook his head:

"No, mine, but I'll let you ride it."

"All right, you can have it," I consented generously.

We were in a large orchard; the dry, slightly frostbitten yellow leaves exuded a fermented, spicy aroma and crunched loudly underfoot. At the other end there was a hole in the fence. We climbed through and found ourselves in a courtyard that led out onto Tverskaia.

Our journey began with a visit to the store "Communard." We got lucky right away. We found a three-kopek coin, a black button from a man's pair of trousers, and a piece of hard candy. Nurakhmet took it all. I suggested that we take turns licking the candy, but he said that it would be better to find another one.

In the waiting room of the eye hospital we went through a trash basket and found an empty matchbox with a bright label. Nurakhmet already had that label in his collection, but I didn't, so he let me have it. "But the button is mine!" he added quickly.

Luck is capricious, and soon it had abandoned us completely. Cigarette butts, candy wrappings, and empty cigarette boxes were all we could find. We walked around the Strastnoi Monastery, which housed the antireligious museum, and hung out by the ticket window. Unfortunately, very few people were around, and we did not discover anything valuable on the floor. Next we went to the Eliseev

Department Store, but it was for foreigners, and simple mortals, especially minors, were not allowed inside.

By the time we made it to the Central Telegraph building, it was almost eleven and Nurakhmet was complaining that he was hungry. I had twenty kopeks in school-lunch money, but those were the days of ration cards, and we could not buy anything with them. Nurakhmet continued to whine. What could we do?

Keeping our eyes on the floor, we walked all around the huge room hoping to find something of value. But in the twentieth century people were less absentminded than in the good old days of Dickens. Besides, right in front of us, a cleaning lady had poured muddy water from a rusty bucket onto the floor and was quickly wiping it with a rag. The room was warm and quiet; it was still early in the day and very few people were there. We had no reason to hurry. I suggested that we read the signs on all the windows. But that is when his dislike of reading entered the picture. No sooner had we read "Telegrams" and "General Delivery" than he started saying he was hungry and wanted to go to the movies . . . When I did not respond, he demanded that I take him home immediately. That was a lot easier. The school day was almost over, and I had to get back, too.

We were heading for the door, when suddenly a huge figure loomed over us.

"Where are you going, my youthful friend?" I heard a soft but thick voice ask.

A large, warm hand took me under the chin. I raised my eyes and saw Artem Vesely.[15]

"Pray, to whom was your excellency pleased to mail a telegram?" he went on. "Or perhaps you were here to claim your poste restante correspondence?"

I just stood there frowning, watching Nurakhmet out of the corner of my eye. I was afraid he would burst into tears at any moment.

"What news have you received?" Artem Ivanovich continued joking.

"We haven't received anything," I muttered. "We were looking for money . . ."

"Found much?" asked Artem earnestly.

"Three kopeks, a button, a piece of candy, and a label," said Nurakhmet quickly, and then added: "The candy and the button are mine; the label is hers . . ."

"What about the three kopeks?" asked Artem sternly.

"It belongs to both of us, but it's in my pocket!"

"I see you don't forget your pocket, Sonny. But whatever made Vecherka's daughter set out in search of money?"

"Oh, Mother doesn't know anything," I said in alarm. "Nobody knows anything. I was not accepted into the Pioneers, so I am not going to school anymore, but I leave in the morning as if I were . . ."

"Now I understand," Artem Ivanovich interrupted my muttering. It is called playing hookey!"

"But I am never ever going back there."

"We'll decide about that later. But right now I am going to send my telegram,

---

[15] Artem Vesely (real name Nikolai Ivanovich Kochkurov, 1899–1939)—"proletarian" writer, civil war veteran, friend of the Tolstoy family; perished during the Great Terror.

and then we will all go home on the bus, is that clear? And do not even think about running away, your excellency . . ."

Nurakhmet jumped up and down in delight: on the bus!

Bus No. 1, with its black stripes and long yellow nose, did not make us wait. We sat down on the cool, bouncy seats covered with oilcloth, and Artem Ivanovich asked me seriously:

"So you were rejected because of your social origin?" And added just as seriously: "Everyone must share the fate of his social class . . ."

The bus growled as it climbed up Tverskaia. We had already passed Sovetskaia Square and the white columns of the Moscow Soviet building.

"Now listen to me, child," said Artem Ivanovich. "I don't know what should be done about the Pioneers. Now, as far as looking for money is concerned, it is an interesting but, I would say, rather uncertain occupation. Betting on absent-minded people is not a sensible thing to do. I can see that you are a child with initiative. You know what I'd like to suggest? Would you like to help me?"

My heart began beating with pride, and my already flushed cheeks must have turned beet red. I nodded silently.

"Do you know what a *chastushka* is?"[16]

"My nanny Sulatskaia sings them."

"Excellent! Write down a hundred *chastushki* for me. Is it a deal?"

He stretched out his large meaty palm, and, with great dignity, I put my round callused hand on top of it.

The bus was approaching the eye hospital. We had to get off.

Artem Ivanovich helped us out of the bus (not long before, his own little boy had been run over by a streetcar, and his kind heart was forever aching for all children).

"And now run along home! And make sure you tell your parents all about it! I'm going to check up on you! Now off you go!" He clapped his hands loudly, the way people do to scare chickens in villages.

We held hands as we ran. The timid autumn sun was peeking through the pale breaks in the clouds; gray shadows lay over the roofs, sidewalks, cobblestones . . .

That night we held a family council. My father absolutely refused to go to the school and talk to the teachers.

"I spent ten years in a gymnasium, and that was enough. Let them (he probably meant the teachers) educate her however they want . . ."

My mother did not refuse, but she was too busy, as usual. So it had to be Grandma.

The next morning, at exactly a quarter past eight, we set off for school. This time I had to wear my galoshes.

Occasional snowflakes fell from the overcast sky and melted before they reached the ground.

"I'll tell them," said Grandma belligerently, "that I speak not only French but also Latin and Greek!"

---

[16] *Chastushka*—a humorous four-lined folk ditty.

I knew my case had been won.

I do not know what Grandma told our assistant principal Aleksandr Semenovich Tolstov, but by the eve of Revolution Day I had a scarlet satin scarf tied solemnly around my neck, and Grandma had been elected to the parents' committee.

I wrote down considerably more than a hundred *chastushki* for Artem Vesely. All my friends from school and all the kids from the courtyard got involved. When the book came out, Artem Ivanovich thanked everyone who had helped him collect the *chastushki* in the acknowledgments. Among others, he mentioned . . . no, not my name (Tolstaia), but my mother's . . . Such was life!

MY father was not easily surprised. But one morning at breakfast, when Grandma handed him his cup of coffee, I heard him mutter softly but with unconcealed amazement: "My God, what is this? Where did you find it?"

On his normally expressionless, dark, Buddha-like face, with its high cheekbones, was an expression of extreme puzzlement. Grandma, who, like most mothers-in-law, was not overly fond of her daughter's husband, looked at my father condescendingly through her pince-nez.

"Are you so divorced from reality, Boris, that you did not know that this country had embarked on the path of industrialization?"

My father worked in Gosplan[17] and, of course, knew better than the rest of us what path the country had embarked on. However, he chose not to argue with Grandma (peace in the family was more important), but instead, having silently finished his coffee, he picked up his briefcase, kissed me on the forehead, and left for work.

My father's amazement had been provoked by the cups that Grandma had picked up at a manufactured goods warehouse the night before. Tall and wide, with small uneven bottoms, they teetered back and forth like little rocking horses, spilling their contents and burning one's hands. To make up for this, they were decorated with pictures of tractors, cranes, cogwheels, and wrenches. Those cups, the children of the First Five-Year Plan, filled me with patriotic fervor.

The country had embarked on the path of industrialization, and one could see signs of it everywhere: in small, trivial things and in works of art. Perhaps the greatest consequence, however, was the changed landscape of Moscow. Everything in the city seemed to have been set into motion: buildings, streets, squares, parks, even monuments. Ancient little churches, monasteries, and old buildings were being blown up, to be replaced by construction sites surrounded by gray wooden fences. The round heads of the belfries that had supported the Moscow sky for centuries began giving way to the camel-like necks of tall cranes that appeared to be munching on the low, peaceful, furry clouds as they floated by.

The streets resembled trenches: new gas and water pipes and endless cables were being laid. The newly turned earth gave birth to a new kind of people. In canvas overalls and wide-brimmed hats, with jackhammers and spades over their

[17] The State Planning Committee.

shoulders, talking loudly and clanking in their heavy boots, they walked around the city with a proprietary look: these were the subway builders.[18]

During a remodeling, move, or spring cleaning the most active participants tend to be the children. Their efforts are not always constructive, and the grown-ups occasionally have to restrain their enthusiasm. As a rule, however, they do not get their feelings hurt but continue to scurry in and out of rooms and up and down the halls and stairways, interfering with everything and trying desperately to be useful and to take part in the life of the adults.

The great Soviet house was being remodeled and thoroughly cleaned: the new political system was settling in for perpetual residency. And we children eagerly inhaled the free air mixed with construction dust. Our greatest desire was to march shoulder to shoulder with the grown-ups.

Every day after school we would run to construction sites to dig trenches, carry boards and logs, and help unload truckfuls of sand, bricks, or cement. We helped cut down hundred-year-old lindens on the Garden Ring Road and plant rickety poplar saplings in new parks. We collected books for kolkhoz libraries.

The Dnieper Hydroelectric Dam and Magnitogorsk,[19] industrialization and collectivization, five-year plans, and more five-year plans—these were the words of our adolescence, the words we repeated in a million different ways, wrote on posters and in wall newspapers, rhymed in poems and songs. *The Tale of a Great Plan* was one of our favorite books. And if someone among the adults complained of the lack of necessities or the long lines in the stores, we would respond with all the fervor and faith of an eleven-year-old:

"As soon as we complete the five-year plan, everything will be different!"

But then, more and more often, a sinister word began appearing in adult (and hence our own) conversations, a word whose terrible meaning we were destined to come to know many years later: *fascism*. On Staropimenovsky Street, an old monastery was blown up, and in its place a new high-rise was built. We heard that its future residents were to be German revolutionaries who had been forced to leave Germany because of the fascist takeover of power. There was a new movie called *The Worn-Out Shoes* that we went to see over and over again: the sad fate of the curly-haired German boy affected us as if it were our own. Even now, thirty years later, I can picture the last scene in the film with perfect clarity: the murdered boy in his checkered shirt is lying on the pavement; beside him lies his children's bugle, silenced forever because its little master has been silenced.

"The Reichstag fire," "the huge fascist provocation," Georgi Dimitrov, the Leipzig Trial . . .[20]

---

[18] That is, the workers constructing the Moscow metro.

[19] Magnitogorsk—large urban center at the southern tip of the Urals located near massive iron ore deposits; built up by the regime during the First Five-Year Plan, it became an important symbol of the industrialization drive.

[20] Georgi Dimitrov (1882–1949)—Bulgarian Communist accused by the Nazis of starting the Reichstag Fire (February 27, 1933) but acquitted at the Leipzig Trial (September 21–December 23, 1933); received a hero's welcome in the Soviet Union, where he became a member of the Supreme Soviet and the nominal head of the Communist International; prime minister of Bulgaria from 1946 to 1949.

For my own children, all these words represent the past. They are street names, monuments, and movies; a white mausoleum in the center of sun-drenched Sofia; just another question on a history exam. But for me they stand for the living and fiery epic of my childhood, for our dream of a World Union of Socialist Republics, for the pioneer rallies at which children's hot little hands used to soar upward in a common demand for freedom for the Bulgarian Communists.

THE open Komsomol meeting of the eighth through the tenth grades was about to begin. "Agenda: The expulsion of J. Kuriatov in connection with his anti-Komsomol behavior."

J. Kuriatov was the very same John Kuriatov (named after John Reed),[21] who had voted against my induction into the young pioneers several years earlier. All that had become ancient history, however. Since then he had sent me a love letter with the following less than felicitous paraphrase of the Pushkin poem:

> I love you with such tenderness, such passion,
> That I hope someone else will love you, too.[22]

Obviously this became known to the whole class the very next day, and John had become the butt of all sorts of jokes, which no doubt had helped cure him of his hopeless passion. But this, too, was ancient history. John and I were now in the habit of taking walks on the much quieter Moscow streets, going to the movies together, and even talking about affairs of the heart. For a long time (about six months), John had been in love (once again, hopelessly) with my friend, Masha . . .

I knew that John was being expelled from the Komsomol because he had refused to renounce his father, an old Bolshevik and an employee of a large ministry, who had been arrested the month before. After his father's arrest John had been avoiding his friends, and even I had not seen much of him. To Masha's credit, she had been giving John much encouragement in those difficult days. But even that had not distracted him from his grief. He had been disappearing after classes, only to reappear on time the next morning and get another "A." Masha and I had decided that even though we were "nonunion youth," that is, we were not Komsomol members, we would go to the meeting: perhaps John would derive some satisfaction from our being there.

But when we ran into him in the hall, he asked with uncharacteristic rudeness: "What the hell are you doing here? Just satisfying your curiosity?"

"You don't understand, we—"

"Get lost. I don't need anyone's pity."

"Masha, you go on home: he's embarrassed in front of you. I'll call you if you're needed," I said. "I'll go ahead and go to the meeting. Who knows . . ."

---

[21] John Reed (1887–1920)—U.S. Communist; author of *Ten Days That Shook the World* (1919), an eyewitness account of the October Revolution sympathetic to the Bolsheviks.

[22] In fact, the final lines of A. S. Pushkin's "I Loved You Once" are these:

> I loved you with such tenderness, such passion,
> As, God grant, you are someday loved again.

The children were quiet and morose; no one was laughing or joking. The representative of the Komsomol district committee walked in, and the meeting got under way. Let my children and grandchildren never experience anything like that. Let it never happen again on this Planet Earth.

John was standing. He was sweating profusely, and his face was beet red; only his dark blue myopic eyes remained firm behind his glasses.

"So, Kuriatov, do you persist in refusing to recognize your father's mistakes?"

"I am in no position to recognize mistakes that I did not commit," answered John woodenly, as if reciting by rote.

"But they have been recognized by the Soviet people."

John was silent.

"Do you renounce your father and the wrecking activity he directed against the Soviet people?"

"I know nothing about his activity, but I will never renounce my father no matter what! Even Lenin knew him and valued him!" The boy's resonant voice suddenly cracked.

"We want a straight answer, Kuriatov. Do you renounce your father, or do you not?"

"No, I do not," said John in a barely audible whisper that sounded like a sigh of relief.

"Turn in your Komsomol card."

"No, I won't. I will never part with it! I haven't done anything wrong . . ."

"What kind of discipline is this?"

John was not listening. Suddenly, he turned around and headed resolutely for the door. Pausing for a second, he said gloomily: "Let someone from Stalin's office call, and then I'll give it to you."

"Cut out the nonsense, Kuriatov," said the district committee representative. "As if Comrade Stalin had nothing better to do than deal with young whelps like you."

"We are not whelps, we are human beings," said John quietly. "And human beings are the party's main resource. The cadres decide everything,[23] Comrade Representative. Remember who said that? And anyway, I don't have my card with me . . ."

Realizing they could do nothing with the stubborn boy, the chair held a vote to have J. Kuriatov expelled from the Komsomol and then declared the meeting closed.

We walked out silently, and I caught up with John in the hall.

"Let's go for a walk," I said. "The weather is great."

"Why not?" said John with a defiant and guilty smile, as if to say: I don't want your pity.

AND then summer came, the dry, hot summer of 1937. The sun bore down mercilessly. Some sheets of paper that had been left outside withered, turned yellow, and crumbled.

---

[23] A Stalin quote and a major slogan of the day.

Red Spanish oranges, neatly wrapped in bright pieces of paper, were being sold on the street. Spanish revolutionary songs were being played on the radio. Somewhere far away, the valiant Spanish Revolution was struggling and bleeding, but refusing to surrender.

We dreamed of going there, to the mountains of Spain.

But it was only a dream, and we thought we had been born too late.

The Maksim trilogy was playing in all the movie theaters.[24] The silly song about the blue globe that "keeps turning, trying to fall down" had acquired a new meaning on the streets of Moscow. We could not take part in the exploits of Maksim and his friends, and, once again, we thought we had been born too late.

My mother sent me to a Pioneer camp in Koktebel, in the Crimea. For the first time I saw the blue expanse of the sea, the gray cliffs, and Voloshin's[25] white house standing all alone on the hill. For the first time I breathed in the Koktebel air flavored with thyme, mint, and wormwood, collected bright-colored rocks, and sat at night on the wet sand listening to the murmur of the waves and gazing at the reflection of the moon stretching to the horizon.

Mountain hikes, bugle reveille at dawn, kayaking in the sea, heart-to-heart conversations with friends, long hours in Voloshin's studio. Time spent over the poetry of Blok and Bely, Balmont and Voloshin, Severianin and Akhmatova, Mandelstam and Gumilev . . . The tattered volumes of Dickens and Thackeray, Goncharov and Tolstoy, Stendhal and Mérimée. Awkward attempts to write my own poems. This is how I remember the summer of the now infamous year 1937.

I left Koktebel in the middle of August. My friend Maika's mother had died, and Maika had to return to Moscow. We did not want to part, so I asked to be sent back with her.

Life at home was sad. My mother told me that my father had been arrested in Alma-Ata, where he had been working for the last two years. As a result my mother began having difficulties at work, and finally she was forced to leave the editorial office of *The History of Factories*. We had no money, so my mother took a course in proofreading that enabled her to receive a small but regular salary. Grandma continued to run the household. Now she had to save on everything in order to make ends meet, but she did not despair. In her free time Grandma used to read Lavisse and Rambaud,[26] talk a great deal and at great length about the reasons for the defeat of the French Revolution, and tell me all about Robespierre and Marat.

My friends had not yet returned from their summer vacations. Maika and I, suntanned, healthy, and still smelling of salt water and sunny breezes, wandered all around the city, not knowing what to do with ourselves. She would cry softly, grieving over her mother's death, while I tried to console her. I told her about my father.

---

[24] *The Maksim Trilogy* (1935–38)—popular adventure film about the revolution.

[25] M. A. Voloshin (1877–1932)—Russian poet and painter.

[26] The eight-volume *History of the Nineteenth Century*, by Ernest Lavisse and Alfred Rambaud, was issued in 1937 and 1938 in two different Russian translations and enjoyed great popularity in the Soviet Union.

Finally, the first of September arrived. What a happy, carefree day! No grades or homework yet, just the joy of seeing my friends and teachers and our good old school building. Everyone had grown and changed so much! Some boys had down on their upper lips, and some even had cuts from clumsy and premature attempts at shaving. The girls had new haircuts and fancy dresses. What a noisy, colorful, fun-loving crowd! How could we not forget our sadness?

PART III

☐ ## "Life Has Become Merrier"
(THE 1930s)

"Life has become merrier" was Stalin's 1935 slogan, suggesting that the end of bread rationing would bring with it a more relaxed and comfortable existence. More consumer goods did appear in urban shops, albeit at a higher price than in the early 1930s, and state pressure on collective farms was lifted somewhat. The mid-1930s brought many changes in social and cultural policy. Family values were stressed more than in the past (the Central Committee's Women's Department, linked with the old emancipatory approach to the family, was abolished in 1930); abortion was outlawed in 1936; the nineteenth-century literary and musical classics returned to favor; the experimental education methods of the 1920s were abandoned. The privileges of the administrative and professional elites—Milovan Djilas's "New Class"—increased and became more visible. The Russian émigré sociologist N. S. Timasheff was later to label this "the great retreat" from the values of the revolution.

"Retreat" was only relative and partial, of course: collectivization remained in place and rapid industrialization remained the state's main priority. As a result, the urban working class expanded greatly, mainly via recruitment of peasants; at the same time the trade unions ceased to function effectively as the protector of labor interests, and the old idea of collective class solidarity gave way to a new emphasis on individual achievement. From the late 1920s, high-achieving "shock workers" were given special rations and rewarded in other ways. The Stakhanovite movement, encouraging individual workers to break records and overfulfill norms, was born in the mid-1930s.

Politically, the promised relaxation never materialized. The assassination in December 1934 of Sergei Kirov, Leningrad party boss and Politburo member, revived political tensions, leading to mass arrests and deportations of "social aliens" and past oppositionists. Even before this, the Communist Party, which had expanded rapidly during the First Five-Year Plan, was in the throes of self-examination: the party *chistka* (purge or membership review) of 1933–34 was followed by a second *chistka* in 1935 and a third in 1936. With each *chistka*, the process became more vicious, as an increasing number of those expelled from the party (though still a comparatively small percentage) were arrested as "spies" and "counterrevolutionaries."

The external situation was becoming more threatening: having cried "Wolf!" about the capitalist threat for more than a decade, the Soviet Union now faced real possibilities of attack from foreign enemies, notably Nazi Germany and Japan, actively intruding on Soviet borders in the East. This danger, which culminated in June 1941 with Hitler's attack on the Soviet Union and Soviet entry into the Second World War, intensified a fear of foreign spies that merged with the fears of internal subversion stimulated by Kirov's assassination. A new category of threat emerged, that of "enemies of the people" who had allegedly masked their hostility to the Soviet state the better to sabotage it.

The unmasking of such enemies, many of them members of the Communist Party leadership with high government, industrial, and military posts, was the centerpiece of the Great Purges of 1937–38, a terror conducted by the NKVD under Stalin's oversight. Among targeted categories were the "wives of traitors to the motherland," who were sent to special labor camps under this rubric. Running parallel to the political Purge, but independent of it, was a mass round-up of marginal and criminal elements. Although estimates of the total number of victims of the Great Purges are still disputed, it is clear that several million people were executed or sent to Gulag. Few of the Gulag "political" contingent returned before the amnesties and rehabilitations of the 1950s after Stalin's death.

23 □ PASHA ANGELINA

The Most Important Thing

□ Praskovia Nikitichna ("Pasha") Angelina (1912–1959), an arche-
typal Stakhanovite, was the founder of the first Soviet all-female
(and originally ethnic Greek) tractor brigade and the most celebrated
and highly decorated female labor hero in Soviet history. She is the
author of several autobiographies describing both her labor achievements and her upward mobility (she became a deputy to the Supreme Soviet in the late 1930s and later graduated from college as an
agronomist).

NOT LONG AGO I received a letter from America. A teacher I know translated it for
me. The letter said that a publishing house in New York City, on 296 Broadway,
was going to publish a *Biographical Encyclopedia of the World* containing the
biographies of prominent people from all the countries of the world.

Among other things, the letter explained who was meant by "prominent people." They included, first, the leaders of the United Nations; second, the creators
of the atom bomb; and only then, other scientists as well as artists, writers, and
industrialists. On stationery that depicted a thick open book over a map of the
world, the editor informed me that the name of the Supreme Soviet deputy,[1]
Praskovia Angelina, had been included in the *Biographical Encyclopedia of the
World* and asked me to fill out the enclosed questionnaire.

Besides the usual questions (first name, last name, place and date of birth, etc.),
the questionnaire requested a list of all my occupations "from beginning of career
to the present," a list of titles and awards, home and work addresses, names of
parents and children, military distinctions, publications, and much, much more.

Here is what I wrote:

"Praskovia Nikitichna Angelina.

Born: 1912.

Place of birth (which also happens to be my "home and work address"): village
of Staro-Beshevo, Stalin Province, Ukrainian SSR.

Father: Nikita Vasilievich Angelin, kolkhoz member, formerly field laborer.

Mother: Efimia Fedorovna Angelina, kolkhoz member, formerly field laborer.

"Beginning of career": 1920, worked with parents for a kulak.

1921–22: coal carrier at Alekseevo-Rasnianskaia Mine.

1923–27: field worker for hire again.

1927–30: stable girl at cultivators' cooperative (later Lenin kolkhoz).

From P. Angelina, *O samom glavnom* (Moscow: Pravda, 1948), 3–29, 46.
[1] Supreme Soviet deputy—elected member of the Soviet parliament.

1930–present (except 1939–40: student at Timiriazev Agricultural Academy, Moscow): tractor driver.

Three children: Svetlana, Valery, and Stalina.

Since 1937, member of All-Union Communist (Bolshevik) Party.

Member of Union of Employees of Rural Organizations.

Publications: a little book entitled *My Brigade*, published in 1938 in Kiev, as well as magazine and newspaper articles and lectures, in which I discussed and tried to analyze my work on the organization of tractor brigades.

As for military distinctions, I include among them the title "guardsman," conferred on me by a front-line artillery brigade for good work in the rear under difficult wartime conditions.

USSR Supreme Soviet deputy from the 474th electoral district.

Awards and honorary titles: Hero of Socialist Labor, winner of the Stalin Prize, gold-medal winner at All-Union Agricultural Exhibit, two Lenin Orders, one Order of the Red Banner of Labor, medals . . ."

The questionnaire is so detailed, it even asks for my wedding date and my mother's maiden name. However, it does not ask the most important question: how did I, a simple field laborer, become an important state official and a Supreme Soviet delegate?

This question was asked in a different letter from America, which arrived shortly before the questionnaire. The letter had been written by a farmer from Alabama by the name of Benjamin Marten.

About his own affairs, he had only two words to say: "very bad." I could understand that without a translator . . .

He did not want to know the date of my wedding. Marten wanted to know how a biography such as mine—from field laborer to tractor driver to statesman—was possible in the Soviet Union.

I subscribe to the magazines *America* and *The British Ally*. They tend to embellish reality quite a bit, in my opinion, and often make claims that are at odds with what Marten complains about. But I am digressing . . .

In these foreign magazines one frequently finds descriptions of "dizzying careers" and "exceptional" biographies.

I remember, for instance, an enthusiastic account of the life of one important man who, in the words of the magazine, "came from the people." He used to be a simple newspaper boy but then made a lot of money, became the owner of many newspapers, and received the title of lord.

And so I thought to myself: let's say they print both our biographies, mine and the lord's, in their encyclopedia: mine under "A," his under "B" (I am referring to Lord Beaverbrook). His biography would go: last name, first name, date of birth, date of wedding, poor parents, newspaper boy to lord. And mine would go: last name, first name, date of birth, date of wedding, poor parents, field laborer to Supreme Soviet delegate."

"What's the difference?" my American friend Benjamin Marten and thousands like him will ask.

Indeed, without asking "how" it is impossible to understand and appreciate the life story of a Soviet person, and therefore my own life story. It is not my particular case that is important—it is the fact that my rise is not exceptional. For if that gentleman, as the magazine rightly puts it, "rose *from* the people," I rose *together with the people*, I became a hero along with the people. That is the important thing.

Therefore I will allow myself to go beyond the questionnaire of the *Biographical Encyclopedia of the World* and, addressing myself not so much to the esteemed editorial board as to the thousands of American farmers, talk about the important issue. At the same time I would like to answer the question I am always asked in the thousands of letters I receive from my comrades throughout our vast Union: "How did you get to be where you are now?"

Today, thirty years after the revolution, it is particularly appropriate to look back at the road we have traveled and remember the exciting biography of our country, which is also the biography of each and every Soviet citizen. Our lives are so inextricably linked to the lives of our state and party that, when we talk about our personal labors, achievements, sorrows, and joys, we cannot help talking about something that is a hundred times larger than our own biography.

Whatever good we have within us, whatever knowledge, wealth, strength, and happiness we enjoy—all this is the consequence of one great event: the triumph of Soviet power.

I have been working on a tractor for many years now. It is much more than a "job" for me—it is my place in the struggle for five-year plans and on the battlefields of the Patriotic War,[2] the source of my happiness, prosperity, and fame.

I will never forget how, thirteen years ago, after a reception at the Commissariat of Education, Nadezhda Konstantinovna Krupskaia[3] took us, simple country girls, to the Lenin Mausoleum.

Holding our breath, we walked by Lenin's casket . . . And when we reemerged onto Red Square, Nadezhda Konstantinovna said quietly: "He dreamed of a hundred thousand tractors for Russia . . ."

When I got behind the wheel of a tractor for the first time in the spring of 1930 I did not know about that dream of Lenin's or about the thousands of other tractors already out there. Of the sixty thousand tractor drivers in 1930 I was the only woman. I did not know that, either.

It was with my heart rather than my mind that I had apprehended the grandeur of what Stalin and the party were doing in the countryside.

IT was 1930, the year of the victorious struggles for collectivization, the year of the triumph of the great transformation in the life of the village.

New construction sites were popping up all over the enormous Soviet Union, and everywhere young people were in the forefront.

[2] That is, the Second World War (1941–45).
[3] Lenin's widow.

Every evening we, the young people of Staro-Beshevo, would gather in our club around a map of five-year-plan projects and talk about the future of our country and our own future. They were bright and limitless, and they were inseparable.

None of us was going to wait for that future with folded arms. We Komsomol members were activists playing a far from unimportant part in the tumultuous life of our village.

It seemed to me, however, that it was outside our Staro-Beshevo that the most significant and difficult battles were being waged. I was determined to go to some construction site, not just any construction site but one of the five-year plan's shock locations. Each day I avidly perused the ads that filled our newspapers that year: "Workers needed."

One day I would decide to go halfway across the world to Siberia in order to build Kuznetsk, the garden city of the future; the next day I would be getting ready to work at the Dnieper Hydroelectric Station. Or perhaps I did not have to go halfway across the world, after all: our village was smack in the middle of the Donbass region, so no matter which way you walked, you would come to a preeminent construction site: the Gorlovka or Kramatorsk heavy machinery plants, the famous Rutchenkov mines, the Azov Steel Plant . . .

My brother, Ivan, kept trying to convince me that the five-year plan was being decided in our Staro-Beshevo, too. I did not agree and persisted in my desire to go elsewhere.

Suddenly Ivan—our district's first tractor driver and the secretary of our party cell—was sent off for further education. So I decided to take his place.

At first people just laughed at me, but as the district administration did not send anybody to replace him and the tractor was sitting idle, I was allowed to give it a try. My brother had taught me a few things about the tractor's engine, and after doing some extra preparation, I passed the test.

"Okay," they told me, "go ahead and work. But please be careful!"

The next morning, very, very early, I drove out to the field for the first time. The air was so crisp, my cheeks burned. My tractor was rattling away. I kept looking back to see the black trail of my very first furrow. Light steam was rising over it . . . I felt like singing, like shouting at the top of my lungs . . .

I decided to become a tractor driver. And that is what I became.

Now it is easy to say, "decided and became," but back then, in the spring of 1930, it was very hard. It cost me so much strength and so many tears!

But I was not afraid of hardship and had plenty of strength. I had just turned eighteen, but was already a "Komsomol veteran." We Komsomol members were used to hardship: there were many behind us and quite a few still ahead . . .

By 1930 the same thing that had happened in many other villages around the country had happened in Staro-Beshevo. The kulaks (in Ukraine we called them "kurkuls") had been beaten and kicked out. Our Lenin Kolkhoz had been created. The tractor was plowing a common field.

All this had been achieved with great difficulty and was still weak and not fully formed.

I remember how my father used to refer to himself, only half-jokingly, as "the chair of the family party cell." He and my brothers—Vasily, Nikolai, and Ivan—were Communists, and my brother, Kostia, my sister, Lelia, and I were in the Komsomol. Along with the party and Komsomol cells, our family was in the forefront of kolkhoz construction, dekulakization, and propaganda work. It was wonderful to have such a family!

In 1927 we started a cultivators' cooperative in our village. The kulaks were still strong and powerful, while we were only learning how to run things ourselves. The cooperative was forced to use the equipment and draft animals that belonged to the kulaks. Also, the harvested grain was supposed to be distributed not only according to the work performed but also according to one's share of the animals and equipment.

So it was that our old enemy, the kulak Naum Nikolaevich Savin, who used to pay us next to nothing for our work, was still living better than we were. He did not work himself: he would just lend the cooperative his horses, oxen, and reaper, and then collect several times as much grain as the seven Angelins, who had spent the whole summer doing back-breaking work in the field.

We were not the only ones dreaming of a different, more just order. All the peasants were hoping for a new way, whereby the workers, and not their blood-suckers, would own the harvest. That is why the party, which was looking far ahead, moved the countryside in the direction of the kolkhozy. It was exactly what we had been waiting for.

I will never forget that village meeting on the square in front of the church. My father, a stern, silent man, made the first speech of his life. I remember every word of it:

"Look at this pile of rocks right here. It's a huge pile, but you don't even need to use your hands to level it." As proof of his words, my father kicked an enormous rock that was sitting on top of the pile, and the whole thing came crashing down with a loud noise. "See, these aren't smooth, polished rocks. But what if we were to build a wall out of these rocks? What if we were to sort them out by size and shape and then place them one upon the other, bump to groove, very tightly? With these silent rocks, we could build a wall so strong that five men could not break it. That's what we peasants should do: not sit by ourselves, like rocks in a pile, but get together in a kolkhoz—soul to soul, like rocks in a wall. It would be a stronghold that no one could ever break!"

My father finished his speech and climbed down from the church steps. A deathly silence was all the response he got. Peasant meetings tended to be very noisy—even a penny's contribution to the building of a fence somewhere usually provoked a long and loud discussion—but now, when they were talking about their entire future life, when they were being offered the light—now they were silent . . .

Why were the peasants of Staro-Beshevo silent?

At that time the situation in our village was very difficult (the same was apparently true of many other villages). The middle peasants were hesitating and dragging their feet, waiting to see what would happen and hoping not to end up on the losing side. The kulaks—all those Lefterovs, Savins, Antonovs, and Paniotovs—had all the agricultural equipment and all the power. So most of the villagers, while perhaps not respecting the kulaks, at least feared them.[4]

We were not afraid, however. We went after the "kurkuls," who were strong and ruthless in their hatred of everything new.

Vasily Angelin, the chairman of the poor peasants' committee, used to receive notes saying, "Get out of this village, chairman, before we slice you up."

The Communist Vasily did not "get out"—he continued to do his work even though these were not empty threats: the kulaks had been known to kill village activists.

In the summer of 1929, when my brother, Kostia, my sister, Lelia, and I were walking to a Komsomol meeting in the neighboring village of Novo-Beshevo, somebody shot at us with a sawed-off shotgun (we were still quite young: Lelia was fourteen, and I was seventeen). I will never forget how we ran, barefoot, through the prickly grass, our hearts beating wildly with fear. Even so, once we had passed the dangerous spot and caught our breath, we did not return home but forged ahead to Novo-Beshevo, to the Komsomol meeting . . .

My elderly mother, Efimia Fedorovna, was beaten by the "kurkuls" to within an inch of her life simply because she was our mother, the mother of Communists.

Our family, and many families like ours, had been working for the kulaks for many generations. We realized that it was impossible for us to live on the same earth with those bloodsuckers. The kulaks stood between us and the good life, and no amount of persuasion, constraint, or extraordinary taxation was sufficient to move them out of the way.

Once again, the party understood our needs and showed us the solution. Through Comrade Stalin, the party told us: "Move from limiting the kulaks to the liquidation of the kulaks as a class . . ."

These were the words that my older brother, Vasily, the head of agitation and propaganda at the district party committee, repeated to my brother, Ivan Angelin, the secretary of the village party cell, when he ran in to see him late one night. Ivan had brought bad news from the village meeting on the kolkhoz question . . .

At the meeting my father was followed by the kulak Paniotov, who said that the Angelins wanted to lay their hands on other people's property and that they wanted to be like the well-off households even though they did not own anything. When the vote was called, only seven poor peasants raised their hands for the kolkhoz, with twelve kulaks voting against. The overwhelming majority of the villagers (the middle peasants and some intimidated poor ones) abstained. "Let's wait and see," was their attitude, "there's no need to rush things."

Under pressure from the "kurkuls," the meeting decided to expel the Angelins and the other six families from the cooperative and let them form a kolkhoz as they saw fit.

We were very poor; we had only five cows and two goats among the seven households—and yet, in response to Ivan's question about what to do next, Vasily

---

[4] On class differentiation in the village, see selection 16, note 1, in this volume.

said, in the name of the party: "Dekulakize the rich. Take their land and implements away from them. Use those things to start the kolkhoz. Start the kolkhoz come what may, even if there are only seven of you!"

That is exactly how we started: there were seven of us—seven households.

I also took part in the dekulakization campaign. Those were difficult days, filled with tension and fierce class struggle. It was only after defeating the kulaks and chasing them off the land that we, the poor, felt truly in charge.

It was not easy to get the kolkhoz started. We worked day and night, all the while feeling the villagers' eyes upon us. We knew that the decision of the majority, those middle peasants and some poor ones who had abstained at the meeting, would ultimately depend on the success of our efforts.

It was then that the party and state came to the assistance of the first kolkhozy. Our new agronomist, Nikolai Angelin (who was called a "red agronomist" to distinguish him from the old experts bent on sabotage), was told by the district party committee to start introducing new technology. The kolkhoz received a loan from the district executive committee, but, even more important, it received a tractor. That is what helped make up all the doubters' minds.

The unaffiliated farmers would come and stand for hours, watching our first tractor driver, Ivan Angelin, plow the kolkhoz field. Meanwhile, at every kolkhoz board meeting more and more membership applications needed to be considered.

It seems to have worked the same way in most other places, as well.

We named our kolkhoz after Lenin.

Oh, those first kolkhozy! Their very names expressed so much faith, so much hope: "Forward toward Communism," "Ilich's Testament," "The Struggle for Culture," "A Happy Life."

Our life was not yet happy in those days. We, the ordinary people, did not yet realize to what pinnacles of wealth and joy our government, with its collectivization and industrialization, would lead us. But the party and Stalin could already perceive those pinnacles behind the mountains of hardship that stood in our way.

We trusted the party and the Soviet government. We were all following Stalin.

In the early thirties the country was on its way up—and going up is always more difficult . . .

Like all the neighboring kolkhozy, like the kolkhoz movement as a whole, our Lenin Kolkhoz withstood the early difficulties and grew stronger. When I first got behind that tractor wheel in the spring of 1930, the members of our kolkhoz may not yet have seen the fruits of the new life, but they believed in it firmly and irreversibly.

MY first tractor was a Fordson. It was an awkward and complicated machine, with a flywheel, belts, and so forth. The Americans must have sent those things over to us because they did not want them anymore themselves. They were considered obsolete even then. If a tiny hair got stuck to the flywheel or if the spark plugs got just a little bit damp, the whole thing would be out of commission for twenty-four hours.

It usually took five people to start the engine, and even that was not always enough. Also, they were incredible gluttons: it took sixty kilos of fuel for each hectare of deep tillage—as opposed to twenty or twenty-five these days.

When, two years later, we received some brand new "Kharkovs"[5]—the first fruits of industrialization—we all fell in love with them: not only because they were Soviet-made but also because they were a lot more reliable, simpler, and more economical than the Fordsons. Later I got to know a lot of different brands of tractors, and the more I worked, the more I realized that I had started with the most difficult and the most capricious of them all.

But back in 1930 I was in love with my awkward and complicated machine and was terribly worried that I might not be able to manage it, that I might—God forbid—ruin it somehow.

Anyway, I coddled my Fordson as if it were a baby. I worked around the clock, but in spite of all my efforts I was not really trusted, even by my own friends. As for my enemies, somebody kept spreading vile rumors about me, and "God-fearing" old women, egged on by the priest, would spit whenever they saw that "shameless Pasha" in her overalls behind the wheel of a tractor.

Once, on a Sunday, when I was loading grain, there was a thunderstorm. I was struck by lightening and thrown off the cart. (Fortunately some friends were nearby. They covered me with earth and I came to.) But according to the village rumor, "that was God's punishment for Pasha."

Even my fellow drivers from the Machine Tractor Station used to tease me.

"What else would you expect from a woman," they would say as they watched me shine my tractor with a little rag.

Still, I continued to look after my machine and check over every detail a thousand times in order to make the tractor more reliable.

Finally, I succeeded. My Fordson no longer broke down much at all, and I overtook some of my comrades in productivity. I was given my first shock-worker certificate, a badge for excellent work, and . . . transferred to the warehouse. I was told that it was a "promotion." Need I say how hurt I felt?

At first I was going to get together all my Komsomol friends and protest to the authorities, but then I decided on a different strategy.

"I've been working as a tractor driver for a year now," I said to myself. "I have even become a shock worker, and yet I haven't been able to overcome the distrust of my fellow villagers. Even my friends say: 'Pasha may be doing okay because she's so spunky, but basically a woman doesn't belong on a tractor.' This means that my example is not enough. I need to organize an all-female tractor brigade. We'll all become shock workers, and then we'll see if they dare say that a woman doesn't belong on a tractor."

I knew that in any just cause I could count on the support of the party, so I took my idea of an all-female tractor brigade directly to Ivan Mikhailovich Kurov, the head of the political department of the Machine Tractor Station.

I will always be grateful to this good person and intelligent and sensitive Bolshevik. Before the party sent him to the countryside to head the political depart-

---

[5] That is, tractors produced by the Kharkov Tractor Plant.

ment, Ivan Mikhailovich had been a worker in Petrograd and the commissar of a Red Army regiment in Turkistan.

Kurov became very excited about my new project. He could see more in it than even I had envisioned: the opportunity to transform a peasant woman into an even more active participant in the construction of a new life.

I cannot say that I was simply "lucky to have found the right person at the right time." Kurov was indeed very understanding, but first and foremost he was a Bolshevik. By supporting my idea of an all-female tractor brigade, *he was carrying out party policy*. After all, it was in that same February of 1933 that Comrade Stalin told a collective-farmer assembly in the Kremlin that kolkhoz women were a great force and that they needed to be promoted.

Ivan Mikhailovich Kurov's assistant for Komsomol affairs and I spent several nights in the poster-covered room of the political department trying to figure out which girls to invite, which machines to get, and how to organize technical instruction.

When the director of the Machine Tractor Station saw the list of future drivers, he flatly refused to let them use the machines. He had a point, of course: except for me, none of the girls had ever held a steering wheel or had a chance to learn anything about an engine. He had a point, all right—but Kurov said: "Let them have the tractors. I'll accept responsibility . . ."

In January 1933 we started a crash course for female tractor drivers, with me as the instructor.

Finally, that spring, our all-female brigade—the first in the Soviet Union—left the territory of the Machine Tractor Station.[6]

We were in a buoyant mood. All the way to the Red Plowman kolkhoz we sang Ukrainian songs and kept laughing at the slightest excuse.

Of course, we did not think that everything would go smoothly right away—we just did not want to think about anything bad at that beautiful moment. We had spent so much time getting ready for our first outing, scrubbing our machines, and checking over every little thing.

Suddenly something terrifying occurred. At the entrance to the village we were met by a crowd of agitated women. They were standing in the middle of the road and shouting all together: "Get out of here! We're not going to allow women's machines on our field! You'll ruin our crops!"

We Komsomol members were used to kulak hatred and resistance, but these were our own women, our fellow collective farmers! Later we became friends, of course, but that first encounter was terrible.

You can imagine what a state we were in: we had been expecting a triumphant entry, and now this . . . My girls were on the brink of tears, and even I, normally quite feisty, did not know what to do. The women surrounded us in a tight circle, yelling: "One inch more, and we'll tear your hair out by the braids and kick you out of here!"

---

[6] Machine Tractor Stations—state-owned depots of agricultural machinery for use by nearby collective farms.

We knew they meant it. If we made one move, there would be a fight.

Finally, I had to leave the girls by their machines and run several kilometers through the mud to Staro-Beshevo. Trudging through the puddles in my heavy army boots, I felt hurt and betrayed: there we were trying to help them, and they wanted to beat us up!

Fortunately Kurov was at his desk in the political department. When he heard what I had to say, he turned grim . . . We got into his jeep and sped toward the Red Plowman kolkhoz.

It had almost come to blows. The crowd had been joined by some men, who were screaming and cursing at the girls. When they saw Kurov they grew quieter but did not disperse.

"Get to work, Comrade Brigade Leader," ordered Ivan Mikhailovich . . .

We went over to start our Fordsons, but they refused to start (as I said, they were terrible machines). People in the crowd started laughing: "Looks like it's the machines that have been riding the girls, not the other way round!" Kurov was biting his lips, and his face was pale. It took us about ten minutes to start the engines . . .

Finally we got on our way, with the crowd behind us. Kurov kept up, too. When we reached the field, we got into formation and started working . . .

The festive mood was gone, of course. The girls' faces were sweaty and angry. We felt like we were on a battlefield: one mistake and you're dead.

We had been working for one hour, two hours, three, and still the crowd would not disperse. Finally, the women whispered among themselves and then walked away. Ivan Mikhailovich came up to me, shook my hand, and said: "Nothing can be accomplished without a fight, Pasha!"

That was certainly true. Our difficulties did not end there. The same thing happened at the next kolkhoz: we almost got beaten up by the local women, and two of my girls were locked up in a cellar.

But the main difficulty was that my women could barely drive and knew nothing about the engines. I was not too sure myself about many technical matters. Still, most important was that we all knew how to work hard.

We spent hours fooling with our machines, painstakingly repairing them and trying to understand the reason for each breakdown. We spent long nights with a Komsomol mechanic poring over tractor manuals.

But new professional knowledge did not come easily. When things were going well, the girls would be fine, but as soon as an engine would die, for example, they would come running back to me;

"Pasha, come see what's wrong!"

So I would have to stop my own tractor and walk to the other end of the field to take care of the problem. To be honest, I ended up losing a large part of my wages because of "other people's problems." In my first year as a group leader I received a lot fewer labor days[7] than when I used to be a rank-and-file driver.

But did I or any other Komsomol fighter for the First Five-Year Plan think

[7] Labor day—the unit of remuneration for kolkhoz work.

about my own selfish interest?! Our generation had been taught not to look for personal profit, for easy solutions . . .

In the end, all the members of our brigade became excellent tractor drivers! In the spring Takhtamyshev's brigade—the best in the district—refused to compete with us, saying: "We don't beat up on women." In the fall of that same year we finished first and took the championship red flag away from them.

ALTHOUGH we did not think much about our personal interest, we began to be rewarded for our honest labor—in accordance with the just kolkhoz laws—with a lot of bread. From then on our families had plenty to eat every day, and we started glancing at the shelves of our village store: "What can we buy with the money we've earned?"

We thought even less, as we asserted our right to be tractor drivers, of becoming famous some day. But, in accordance with the just Soviet custom, our hard and ardent work did not go unnoticed. We did become famous. We did not look for fame—it came looking for us . . .

When I was young we often argued about the meaning of fame (the young people of today probably do the same). So please allow me to say a few words on what I think about this subject.

Sometimes I hear the words *celebrated* and *famous* attached to my name. Indeed, the government has honored me with prestigious awards and high titles. There is even a Pasha Angelina Street in the city of Stalino, and a Pasha Angelina ship on the Moscow Canal. I treasure and appreciate all this very much. To be famous in our country means that your work has received the highest recognition from our people. This kind of fame brings great happiness and uplifts the soul!

I would like, however, to emphasize the following: whatever is being said about me is, first and foremost, praise for my country.

One Komsomol member from Voroshilovgrad Province writes in his letter to me:

"Comrade Angelina, for seventeen years now you have been doing excellent work behind the wheel of a tractor. I was wondering why you have not been promoted to a higher position?"

What a funny question! What does a position have to do with it?

More than once I have been offered important administrative posts (among them the directorship of a machine tractor station and the chairmanship of a district executive committee). It even seems to me (especially now, having studied at the academy) that I could probably do a decent job. In fact, many members of my generation have moved on to administrative work. Ten years ago my comrade, Petr Krivonos, was a train engineer, and now he is head of a huge railway district. Or take the coal miner Sasha Stepanenko, who is now the secretary of a city party committee in the Kuzbass. My older brother, Vasily, started out in the army as a private and is now a colonel. But I have remained a tractor driver, and I am proud to be one because in our country every position is a high position, as long as you put your heart into what you do.

In Stalin's *Short Course*[8] of the history of our party my name is mentioned among the leading Stakhanovites and shock workers in industry and agriculture.

How did we ordinary people—workers and collective farmers—make it into the history of the Bolshevik Party? How did we manage to start nationwide movements?

In the spring of 1933, when my friends and I were on our way toward the inhospitable fields of the Red Plowman kolkhoz, we did not know we were inaugurating a huge movement that would involve hundreds of thousands of Soviet women. Most pioneer Stakhanovites in industry, transport, and collective farms did not realize where their personal success would lead them, but the signs of a new life were everywhere.

Here I would like to say a few words about a man who raised my whole generation, a man whose name is associated with everything that is good in your lives and mine, with all our hopes for the future—about Stalin.

I had the happiness of seeing Comrade Stalin and talking to him. Every such encounter invigorated, inspired, and, I would even say, exalted me.

I remember the magnificent hall of the Kremlin Palace in March 1935. It was the Second Nationwide Congress of Shock-Worker Collective Farmers. Comrade Stalin was taking part in the work of the congress . . .

Suddenly the chairman announced: "The next speaker is the leader of the first all-female tractor brigade, Pasha Angelina."

I walked to the podium feeling totally numb. There was a lump in my throat, and I could not utter a sound. I just stood there silently, looking at Stalin.

He understood my nervousness and said softly, so that only I could hear: "Be brave, Pasha, be brave . . ."

Those words became the guiding light of my whole life. Whenever things get tough or I have to start something new and risky, I always remember Stalin's words—"Be brave, Pasha, be brave."

After a moment's pause, I started speaking. From that high Kremlin platform I talked about the simplest things: our brigade, proper work culture (not knowing the right terms yet, I expressed myself in a convoluted and, I am afraid, not very grammatical way), and even the little verses we sang . . .

The congress elected me to the committee responsible for the preparation of the "Model Statute of the Agricultural Cooperative."[9] The committee was to be chaired by Iosif Vissarionovich[10] . . .

For the first time in my life I got to see the way important affairs of state were being conducted in our country—the way the fate of our people was being decided.

In the Small Assembly Hall there were statesmen, scientists, party officials, and ordinary collective farmers like me. I was very young then and quite certain that I would not be able to contribute anything to that high assembly.

---

[8] Stalin's *Short Course*—official history of the Communist Party, written in 1938.

[9] The Kolkhoz Charter of 1935.

[10] Iosif Vissarionovich—respectful but somewhat informal way of referring to Stalin.

So I sat in a far corner and started following avidly what was being said.

The leader and ordinary people from various parts of the country were jointly deciding the future fate of kolkhoz agriculture. I could see how happy Comrade Stalin was whenever one of the collective farmers made a sensible suggestion and how attentively he listened to their advice.

Suddenly I was asked for my views on the size of household garden plots. I thought of my village and the needs of my people, and then said what size I considered most appropriate. One of the scientists objected in a kind of self-assured and patronizing way, as if to say that Comrade Angelina had bitten off more than she could chew. I just sat there, afraid to look up. "Who am I to offer my opinions about matters of state?" I thought.

At that moment Comrade Stalin got up and recommended the same size I had mentioned. The leader's support meant a lot to me and the other collective farmers on the committee. It was our first lesson in statesmanship.

During the break I saw Comrade Stalin in the hall. He asked me about my plans for the future and about the work of our brigade. I was so nervous that I could not answer coherently, but finally I summoned up all my courage and said:

"I give you my promise, Comrade Stalin, that we will reach the mark of twelve hundred hectares per tractor!"

On my way home I thought about my promise and suddenly got scared: Could it be that I had overreached myself? After all, there was the official norm approved by the People's Commissariat of Agriculture: three hundred hectares. Twelve hundred—that was unheard of . . .

But, as they say, "in for a penny, in for a pound!" "I'll work twenty hours a day if I have to, but I will keep my promise," I decided.

Ultimately, however, it all depended on my friends—the eight cheerful girls in identical green berets known as "bruins" because of their thick overalls. Would they support me? What if the "bruins" said that I had made an empty boast?

My friends already knew from the newspapers about my promise to Comrade Stalin. They were full of enthusiasm and did not even want to hear about the Commissariat norms. At the same time everyone realized that our "heroic" determination to work twenty hours a day simply would not do. Grit and zeal alone were not enough to beat the norm. We needed to find new solutions.

We started looking for those new solutions, and found them. We carried out a radical reorganization of our work; introduced prophylactic checkups (which saved us a lot of repair hours); and eliminated "smoking breaks" (known among the nonsmoking girls as "chit-chat breaks"). Our tow operators tightened their procedures as well, and our fuel supplies were successfully streamlined. In other words, we took care of our rear . . .

As for sleepless nights—well, at the height of the season, that, too, was part of the equation.

The whole village was following our progress. The new district committee secretary, Ivan Mikhailovich Kurov, asked us every day: "How are things going,

Angelinites? Do you need any help?" Collective farmers would stop us in the street to ask the same question: "How are things going?"

IT is such a great feeling to know that people need your work and that they wish you well! This was very different from 1933, when we first started out. People had been transformed. They had found faith in the future and had become its steadfast supporters.

But we still had enemies—the kulak remnants, or "leftovers," as they were called in the village. They had been waging a fierce struggle against anything new, trying to slow down our kolkhoz's march forward. Finally, their hatred caught up with me . . .

Once I was on my bike heading toward the field. Suddenly I heard the rattling noise of a cart behind me. I moved off the road—and so did the cart; I swerved to the right—and the cart swerved, too. I was being chased. The next second I was knocked down by huge horses and run over by a heavy cart . . .

For several hours I lay bleeding in a broken-up furrow. By the time I was found and taken to the hospital, I had lost consciousness.

The people who ran me over were caught. It came out at the trial that they were kulak sons who had been stalking me for a while. I guess I really was standing in the enemy's way . . .[11]

I was in the hospital, in great pain and unable to move, but it was the fate of my brigade, not the pain, that concerned me most. The harvesting was about to start any day: would they be able to manage without me? That night the doctor handed me a note, saying that it had been brought by some very persistent young women. They had even tried to break into my ward, despite his strict prohibition.

It was a remarkable note, and it spoke directly to my greatest worry: "In response to the vile deed perpetrated by the class enemy," wrote my friends, "the all-female tractor brigade pledges to reach the mark of 1,230 hectares per tractor, thus exceeding its previous pledge." All eight signatures followed.

There I was, worried about whether they could manage without me, and in the meantime they had decided to add to my original promise! My dear, dear friends!

The weather was particularly bad that fall. It rained day and night. Consumed with worry, I kept looking out my hospital window. Finally, I could stand it no longer. As soon as I could walk I lied to my doctors about how I felt and left for Staro-Beshevo.

I received a very nice welcome—neighbors kept coming with all kinds of gifts—but I simply could not stay at home. Somehow I hobbled over to the kolkhoz office and asked to be taken out to the field (I would have run all the way if I could have!).

When I got there all the girls rushed toward me and started hugging and kissing me, while the accountant kept pointing to the books: "Look at this productivity!"

---

[11] This episode is missing from the revised and expanded version of Angelina's memoirs published four years later; see P. Angelina, *Liudi kolkhoznykh polei* (Moscow: Detgiz, 1952).

I set to work immediately and got so involved that I no longer remembered that I was sick and that the doctors had forbidden me to move.

The last days of the season were especially difficult. The first freeze hit in early November, and we lost all sleep, worrying that we would not be able to reach the promised target. Finally, one morning, the accountant ran up to me and said: "You've made it—1,230 hectares!"

I rushed to the village store, bought some sausage, gingerbread, and red wine, and, right there on the field, we celebrated our first victory.

In December all eight of us went to Moscow to the All-Union Conference of the Best Agricultural Workers.

I reported to Comrade Stalin on the fulfillment of our pledge and, of course, made a new one: to do sixteen hundred hectares.

I was very nervous—you cannot help being nervous when you are speaking in the Kremlin in front of Stalin—but I felt more sure of myself than I had before. This time I had a fulfilled pledge under my belt.

In my speech I said that now that we had overturned the old norm, many other brigades should also be able to attain better productivity and that we would be happy if they achieved even better results.

At this point Comrade Stalin interjected: "Cadres, Pasha, cadres!"

This was a new, major assignment for us, the next stage in our development. From then on, we needed not only to reach high marks ourselves but also to teach others how to do it.

We talked about this all the way back to the Donbass, and eventually we decided to start ten all-female tractor brigades in our district.

Of course it would have been a lot easier to repeat last year's success by keeping our old brigade. We had gotten used to one another, learned our machines, and were well-disciplined. If we did it this new way, we would have to accept new girls unfamiliar with our work.

But, of course, such considerations could not deter us. Comrade Stalin's assignment had to be fulfilled at any cost . . .

The party had taught me, and now I would be teaching the young. My brigade would become a real school.

LIKE many other ordinary winners of socialist competitions, I was more and more frequently asked by the party to take part in governing our country, in deciding important affairs of state. I was a delegate to the Eighth Extraordinary Congress of Soviets, which ratified the Stalin Constitution; a deputy at various Komsomol and Ukrainian Communist Party congresses; and a member of numerous Commissariat of Agriculture committees.

In December 1937 my fellow countrymen elected me to the Supreme Soviet of the USSR. Before then I had been an ordinary comrade—a famous and decorated one perhaps, but still an ordinary one. Now I was to be entrusted with the task of governance.

I was not a bad tractor driver and was, apparently, a fairly successful brigade leader. But this work carried a lot more responsibility, and I was afraid I would not be able to live up to my comrades' expectations. "We are sending you to the Supreme Soviet," wrote my voters, "in the hope that you will continue to work the Stalin way, for the good of the people and Soviet power." And then I heard Comrade Stalin's election speech, in which he talked so well about the huge responsibility facing our deputies . . .

I remember my first batch of mail. One voter needed my advice; another wanted his invention recognized; a third was asking for my help in securing a building for a village club; a fourth was complaining about some district office . . . As a deputy, I was responsible for the outcome of every one of those requests and complaints, yet I was a collective farmer just like my voters.

Now I can only smile when I remember how lost I felt during my first week as a deputy. I even sat down to write a letter to the Supreme Soviet Presidium, asking for instructions or some kind of written manual.

However, it was not for nothing that the party had been raising us up, training us, and involving us in decision making. Eventually, like all the other deputies, I overcame my timidity and got down to business.

In newspapers we often see quotations from speeches by foreign politicians, in which they attack what they call the "Soviet ruling circles." Such an expression (quite appropriate in the West, with its "Wall Street," "City," and "Two Hundred Families") can only annoy a Soviet citizen. Because our ruling circle is not two hundred families but two hundred million Soviet people—all our people. This is evident from the composition of the supreme organ of Soviet power and from countless other examples.

Take our family, for instance, an ordinary rural family. Would it not be correct to say that the children of the poor peasant Nikita Vasilievich Angelin are the ruling circle of the USSR?

My brother, Vasily, is a colonel, decorated eight times by the government. During the war he was head of the political department of the Railway Corps at the front. My other brother, Konstantin, is a chairman of a kolkhoz. My third brother, Nikolai, is a Ministry of Supplies representative and holder of the Order of the Great Patriotic War. My younger sister, Nadia, a former tractor driver decorated with the Order of Lenin, is in her last year at the Interregional Party School, preparing to become a Soviet official. My other sister, Lelia, is the secretary of the village party organization. My third sister, Kharitina, is an ordinary collective farmer. I am a Supreme Soviet deputy.

All of us—the colonel Vasily and the demobilized soldier Konstantin; the party secretary Lelia and the nonparty collective farmer Kharitina—are one happy family. Indeed, all Soviet people have become one happy family, no matter what race or nationality they may be, whether they live in the city or in the country, whether they happen to be ordinary citizens or "high officials." They are all Soviet people.

In March 1939 the Eighteenth Congress of our party was convened in Moscow. A new Communist, I was sent to the congress as a delegate from the Moscow party organization.

The report to the congress was given by Comrade Stalin. Referring to the state of our country, Iosif Vissarionovich used the most appropriate word possible: *prosperity*.

As he talked about the affluent, cultured life of Soviet people, I thought of the many recent events in our village that could illustrate his words. One collective farmer was building a brick house with a metal roof; another had gone to Stalino to buy a motorcycle; a third was planning a trip to a resort in Sochi; and a fourth was all set on sending his daughter to a music school. The stars from the Moscow Art Theater had visited Staro-Beshevo, and new movies were being shown in our village club. All this had become so familiar . . .

MY five-year-old daughter, Stalina, is playing by my side. She was born to the sound of bombs exploding in Saratov [the city on the Volga to which Angelina had been evacuated], in the frightening year of 1942.

My faith, and the faith of all our people, was not in vain. Stalin saved my little daughter and millions of other children in the USSR—and, believe me, not just in the USSR but in America, too—from the vicious enemy of humanity.

Because Stalin is with us, we can look into the future with confidence. We will be able to build and, if necessary, defend our happy tomorrow. The biography of our country and the two hundred million biographies of ordinary Soviet people, including my own, are a guarantee of that.

THIS is what I wanted to tell the friends of the USSR and the people abroad about what I consider the most important thing in the life of every Soviet citizen, including my own.

If the editors of the *Biographical Encyclopedia of the World* are still interested in publishing my biography, here it is . . .

Village of Staro-Beshevo, Stalin Province, 1947

24 □ Efrosinia Kislova et al.

Peasant Narratives (2)

□ See selection 17 in this volume.

Efrosinia Vasilievna Kislova (b. 1909)
Recorded in 1972 in the village of Riabtsevo,
Usvitatsky district, Pskov Province

I had more sorrows than anybody else. Writing the story of my life would be like writing the Bible. You know, there's a song written about me—they sing it in the spring, during Lent, when the cuckoos start calling:

> I was young and full of sorrow,
> Shedding tears into the Danube.

> Shedding tears into the Danube,
> And reproaching my beloved:

> "Oh, my one and only darling,
> Please don't beat me without reason.
> Don't keep beating me unjustly,
> Or I won't hold back my tears,
> I will cry and cry forever.

They say that the bottle will cure any sorrow. Take me, for instance: when I've had a drink, I can sing even when I'm crying:

> I can run and I can hide,
> Still my sorrow's by my side.

> When I'm sure that it won't find me,
> I look back—and it's behind me.

> It is dancing, it is prancing,
> It is singing little songs.

Before the war my old man was taken away in a black raven. You want to know why? Because he went to the Latvian theater. The old folks say that the Latvians arrived here in 1907. They came down here, bought swampy land, and built their houses. They did everything themselves: they were really hard-working. They lived well. They gave their villages numbers. There were ten of them here. In

From E. N. Razumovskaia, ed., "60 let kolkhoznoi zhizni glazami krest'ian," in *Zven'ia: Istoricheskii Al'manakh* I (Moscow: Progress Feniks Ateneum, 1991), 125–28, 149–50.

1928, when the kolkhozy got started, the black raven kept going there. It took three hundred people away, maybe more. They were all executed. Only Number 2 and Number 5 were left standing, just a few households each. Well, anyway, right before the war the Latvian theater came down here. They gave one concert, and the next day all the guys who went to it were taken away in a black raven. They said it was politics, but I don't have any idea what kind of politics they were talking about. That was the last we ever saw of our men . . . During the war there was nothing to eat . . . After the Germans got chased way, the kolkhozy came back, and we were still starving. The government got all the grain, and we got the ashes. What could you get for those labor days? Pig feed, that's all. One night I stole a sack of flax, and went to prison for ten years. My son was sent to an orphanage.

EFROSINIA TIMOFEEVNA STEPANOVA (B. 1917)

Recorded in 1984 in Uste Village, Kuninsky District

Around here one rooster sings for three provinces: our village is located on this side of the West Dvina, while on the other side, where the Mezha flows into the Dvina, there is Dorozhkino, Kalinin Province, on the left bank, and Serteia, Smolensk Province, on the right, so that whenever a rooster crows or a dog barks in one village, you can always hear them in the other two. In the old days the bell also used to ring for all three provinces, only they were called governorships then. We belonged to the Serteia parish. There were two churches in Serteia, both of them wooden: the big one, called the Assumption, stood on the mountain, and the little one, the "Friday," was by the cemetery. My grandfather built the Friday all by himself, to fulfill a vow. In 1930 both churches were destroyed, and this dekulakization mess began. Anyone who refused to join the kolkhoz or who could not pay the fixed tax was taken away in a black raven.

First they tried to start a commune. The Forty-third Rifle Division came and forced two villages, Zhiguli and Pankovo, to move together—with all their things. Ten soldiers stayed behind, and the rest of them left to start communes in other places. They forced us into that commune with pitchforks and shotguns. We took with us everything we had: the cattle, bacon, bread, and eggs. Everything was fine, until we had eaten all our stuff. Then we all went back home. The commune became the Forty-third Rifle Division kolkhoz.

After 1932 there were kolkhozy all over the place. They had the 2 percent fund: everyone had to give grain to the kolkhoz in case there was a bad harvest. One neighbor said: "Why do we have to take it to the kolkhoz? If the harvest is bad, we'll give it to the needy folks for free anyway." He got five years for that . . . In those years girls were forced to clear the land for planting. For three- to four-hundredths of a hectare you got three to four meters of calico for thirty-five kopeks a meter (you couldn't get it any other way) . . . My dad told me that he used to mow "half-and-half" in the old days: half for the landowner and half for himself. But now you have to mow enough for ten kolkhoz cows before they let you mow for an eleventh, your own.

25 □ Fruma Treivas

We Were Fighting for an Idea!

□ Fruma Efimovna Treivas recorded this oral narrative for Narodnyi arkhiv in her Moscow apartment in 1993, when she was eighty-eight years old.[1]

I WAS BORN in 1905 in a picturesque Jewish shtetl, on the road from Sebezh to Polotsk. I had three brothers and three sisters. I was the youngest and the most spoiled. My father taught Hebrew, and I learned how to speak it when I was little.

My brother, Boris, and I went to my father's school together. We started with the Bible, and the boys went on to the Talmud. The girls were not allowed to study the Talmud. My parents were very religious and tried to raise us accordingly. Every Saturday we went to the synagogue. At home we followed all the traditions. Meat and dairy dishes were kept apart. Even the towels were different.

My father was a *reznik*, that is, a person who cuts up chicken, beef, or veal. According to tradition, meat could be eaten only if it had been prepared by a *reznik*.

We read a lot of fiction, too. We subscribed to *Niva*, [a popular illustrated weekly magazine] which included various literary supplements with works by Chekhov, Kuprin, Nadson[2] . . . I particularly liked Nadson and Nekrasov. I still remember a lot by heart. Later I went to Polotsk, entered a private gymnasium, and studied there until the revolution.

In 1914 my brother left for Petersburg. He had a very hard time there; he did not have a residence permit. After the 1917 revolution he became a Komsomol official.

Our dad was very much against the revolution. He wrote to my brother that it would bring nothing but blood and destruction. I decided to join my brother. A woman I knew was about to leave for Petrograd, and she agreed to take me with her. We lived on Gorokhovaia Street. The woman called up the Petrograd Komsomol committee. They told her that Boris was at the front.

One fine day Boris came back. The Petrograd Komsomol Committee offices were located on the fifth floor of the Astoria. My brother and I moved into Room 523. It was a big room, with good blankets, down pillows, and a beautiful wardrobe with a mirror. I still remember it well.

From *Zhenskaia sud'ba v Rossii. Dokumenty i vospominaniia*, ed. B. S. Ilizarov, comp. T. M. Goriaeva (Moscow: Rossiia Molodaia, 1994), 87–98; text prepared by N. A. Landysheva.

[1] The transcript is in Tsentr dokumentatsii "Narodnyi arkhiv" (TsDNA), OAVD.FD no. 2/21.

[2] A. P. Chekhov (1860–1904) and A. I. Kuprin were the most popular realist writers of the period; S. Ia. Nadson was a lyric poet.

I enrolled in the rabfak[3] at Pokrovsky University. None of my fellow students ever got enough to eat. Boris was receiving a special ration as secretary of the organizational department, so I always shared with my friends. At the Astoria we used to get free lunches. Streetcars and theaters were also free. At the Mariinsky we always sat at the very top, so we could only see the legs of the dancers.

I went to school during the day. I did not have a scholarship. Sometimes we would get herring and some awful-tasting watery soup. Kolia Vikhrev, the secretary of our Komsomol cell, helped me out sometimes. He was in love with me. In the morning he would wait for me at the door and hand me a small paper bag with sugar the color of chocolate in it (they were getting rations). I lived in Petrograd until 1922, when I moved to Moscow. My brother had been transferred to the Moscow Komsomol committee.

I moved in with my brother, who was living in what is now the Red Army Theater. In those days it was called the Center for the Communist Education of Working Youth. My brother had a room there. He was still a rabfak student. He felt strongly about protecting my virtue. Kolia Vikhrev was still courting me. I met his family: his mother and sister were also rabfak students. He used to call me his "little Jerusalemite" and thought it sounded tender, but I did not really like it.

I enrolled in the Moscow rabfak, too. I went to their personnel department and said that I wanted to transfer from Petrograd to Moscow and that I had only one year left. They admitted me in spite of my nonworker background[4] because of my brother's work.

I often walked home at night. Before Trubnaia there was enough light and it was not scary, but on Tsvetnoi Boulevard there were always a lot of prostitutes. Once Efim, Tosia Kuznetsova, and I were walking from Commune Square to Tsvetnoi, when some boys assaulted us. Efim tried to defend us and got stabbed in the back.

I started working. You had to live somehow. I got a job at the *Iunosheskaia Pravda* newspaper, the predecessor of today's *Moskovskii komsomolets*. The editor was Grishka Waltenberg (Vasilkovsky). I was in charge of subscriptions. Later Vasilkovsky became my husband. We did not get married officially, but I moved to his place on Polianka and considered myself his wife.

In 1923 he was sent to Warsaw to work in the underground (he knew some Comintern workers).[5] At that time we got registered, and I became Treivas-Waltenberg. That was in 1923, and in 1924 I gave birth to my son. Everybody from our editorial offices came to see me at Hospital No. 1. They asked me to name my son Engel, in honor of the Polish Komsomol member Engel, who had been hanged for killing an *agent provocateur*.

In 1925 I started working at the *Molodaia Gvardiia* press. I was living on Polianka. I got a nanny for my son. Every once in a while I would receive some

[3] Rabfak—workers' faculty, preparatory to a university.

[4] Workers and their children had preferential admission to higher education under Soviet affirmative action programs.

[5] Comintern—the Communist International, the organization of Communist parties (1919–43) headquartered in Moscow.

money from the Polish Section. I moonlighted a little. It was hard living by my-self. I did not have much education—just the rabfak diploma.

My husband was in prison in Poland. I received letters from him only rarely. He'd gotten eight years.

In 1928 Vasilkovsky came back. He started working at [the newspaper] *Komsomolskaia pravda*. At that time I was working for *Pionerskaia pravda*, in the "young correspondent" department. Of course, the task of our newspaper was to instill in our young readers a love for the motherland, the party, and Stalin.

I remember 1930. I was a student at the Lenin Pedagogical Institute. We were on our way to work in the countryside in Cheliabinsk Province. The railway stations looked horrible: sick, hungry people everywhere; dekulakized families, looted houses. We took it all for granted. Now we know better, but in those days . . . It was terrible to see, but they were kulaks, exploiters, anti-Soviets. Now Pavlik Morozov[6]—there was a hero: he denounced his own father . . . And those idlers, the "poor peasants," were an example to everybody. It was only in prison that I saw the light.

By 1932 my husband had become the head of the Economics Section at *Pravda*. Ordzhonikidze[7] valued my husband and always invited him along when-ever he was touring a factory. "Section head" sounds fancy, but he had only one suit. I wasn't exactly a dream wife myself—I didn't know how to look after him properly.

We enjoyed what are now called privileges. The place to go for special food packages was on Kirov Street, where the bookstore is now. We were so far re-moved from the lives of ordinary people that we thought this was the way it should be. The way I looked at it, Vasilkovsky was killing himself working long hours at an important job, all for the glory of the motherland and Stalin. He was driven to work by a chauffeur, of course. We lived on Sretenka [a street in central Moscow], in a building for foreign experts. Our apartment had large rooms, a library, and free furniture from a warehouse. Everything we had be-longed to the state. We also had a maid, who kept house for us. I was a terrible housekeeper.

When I graduated, I started teaching Russian language and literature in high school. Grishka [Vasilkovsky] was getting his "party maximum wage"[8]—1,200 rubles, I think. He used to send whatever he could to the Polish Section, for his friends who were in prison. I was making 560 rubles. I can't really say we were living in luxury.

While Vasilkovsky was working at *Pravda*, we had parties all the time. I re-member that most *Pravda* people hated Mekhlis.[9] At *Za industrializatsiiu*, [the

---

[6] Pavlik Morozov—a fourteen year old held up by the regime as a hero for denouncing his father to the authorities as a kulak in 1932; killed that same year, allegedly by his father's relatives.

[7] G. K. "Sergo" Ordzhonikidze (1886–1937)—member of the Politburo of the Central Committee (1930–37), people's commissar of heavy industry (1932–38).

[8] In the 1920s, in the interests of egalitarianism, Communists were not allowed to earn more than the "party maximum."

[9] L. Z. Mekhlis (1889–1953)—official of the Central Committee responsible for the press and editor of *Pravda* from 1930 to 1937.

newspaper] where Grishka later worked, relations among colleagues weren't as friendly and relaxed.

Then came 1937. We normally received a special pass to Red Square for the May 1 celebrations, but that year, when I went to pick it up, I was told we were no longer on the list. That was our first warning. Then, at the end of May, Vasilkovsky was expelled from the party. My brother, Boris, who was the secretary of the Kaluga party committee, had been arrested in April. My husband wrote lots of letters, and asked Lazar Kaganovich,[10] whom he knew personally, for help, but no answer ever came. Vasilkovsky sat at home all day, unemployed and suffering terribly. From our balcony we could see all the other balconies in the courtyard. If no one appeared for a while, and the balcony was sealed, it meant that those people had been taken away. What a state we were in! At night, when the vans would arrive, you would think: "Oh, God, are they coming for us or someone else?" On the night of July 17, they came for us. There was a search, with janitors as witnesses. Four agents turned everything upside down. My son was not at home at the time. I had sent him off to Polotsk, to my mother's. Thank God he was not present at the arrest. Grishka did not even have time to get dressed. I was in my robe, four months pregnant. We had Hitler's *Mein Kampf*: they took that, too. Why not, it constituted proof of our ties to Hitler! They sealed two of our rooms, leaving the bedroom for me.

I started going to Petrovka and Kuznetsky Most,[11] trying to find my husband. All in vain. You see, I should have given him some of his things and some food, but it hadn't occurred to me—all I had given him were several handkerchiefs, fool that I was. They had said he did not need to take anything with him. I thought he would come right back because, after all, he was not guilty of anything, so it had to be a mistake.

Somebody told me to take some money to Lefortovo Prison. I took thirty rubles, and they accepted them, which meant he was there and alive. That way he, too, would realize I knew where he was. It never occurred to me that he might be lying there, beaten and tortured. That was in August.

One day they called me from Lefortovo and told me to come down. I decided it must be the end. But I was pregnant. What should I do? I went to see a friend of ours. Our families were very close. He was an interesting man, very smart, even wise. He used to own a pharmacy in Bobruisk where he would prepare the most amazing concoctions. He said not to have an abortion but to go there as I had been told to do. If anything happened to me, he would look after my son, Engel.

I was received by some boss. I asked him: "How is my husband? Has he been reading a lot?" I had even brought his glasses with me. I could not have asked a dumber question. And all because I was convinced that it was some kind of misunderstanding. I told him I was four months pregnant. That time they let me go.

On the night of September 5, they finally came for me . . . "Get dressed!" I left

[10] L. M. Kaganovich (1893–1991)—member of the Politburo of the Central Committee (1930–57), deputy chairman of the Council of People's Commissars (1938–57), people's commissar for transport of the USSR (1935–37, 1938–42, 1943–44).

[11] Kuznetsky Most—street where NKVD offices were located in Moscow.

my son sleeping there, idiot that I was! I should have at least called my sister. But I did not have time: I had to hurry and go to prison!"

They took me to the Malaia Lubianka Prison. There they undressed and searched me. It was terribly humiliating. You knew right away that you were not a human being to them. My stockings kept sliding down because they had cut through the elastic. I would pull them up, and they would slide back down again. My shoes were loose, too: all the buttons and fasteners had been cut off. Later I got used to these inconveniences.

I had brought a little suitcase with me, where I had put my night shirt and a few handkerchiefs—plus, of course, the skirt I had on. But my stomach kept growing. After a little while I could barely pull the skirt up—it was funny, really—and a month later it just tore down the seam. It was quite a sight . . .

Then they took me to some kind of basement—me and another woman, a tiny, slender, pretty little woman in a gabardine suit. She was the wife of Goldenberg, from Bukharin's circle.[12] We sat there looking at each other suspiciously, each one convinced of her own innocence.

Then they took me to Butyrskaia Prison. I heard the names of some of the people around me and could not believe my ears. My God, what was I doing there, among such people? I kept thinking: they, of course, were guilty, but I was not. That's how foolish I was.

Then I was transferred to a large room, where there were already three other women. Some bread and gruel were handed in, and one of the women started eating. We were shocked: how could she eat that stuff? At first there were four of us—Milia, Sonia, Zhenia, and I—but later it became so crowded! As the original residents of the cell, we got to remain on our bunks, away from the toilet bucket. We could only change positions on cue, all at once. There was no room to turn by yourself.

Several days later I was taken for interrogation. I still remember the investigator's name; it was Gordeev. I told him that my husband was an honest and loyal Communist and that I wanted to raise his son the same way. He did not tell me anything about my husband's fate. He just said that he had tried to assassinate Comrade Stalin. I was supposed to tell him about Vasilkovsky's counterrevolutionary activities. I wrote that I could not do that. They never asked me anything again.

After that I was transferred to a special place for sick and pregnant women. When it was time, they came with stretchers, but I told them I could walk by myself. So I started walking down the corridor, and there was a mirror there, the first I had seen since the day of my arrest. I looked into it and saw a gray-haired woman. I looked behind me, but there was no one else around. Only then did I realize that it was me. My hair had turned completely white . . .

After I had my baby I was sent to another cell. There were no politicals there, just thieves and prostitutes. They kept yelling at one another—screaming and cursing—it was just awful! On the second day they brought my baby to me. He

---

[12] N. I. Bukharin (1888–1938)—leading Bolshevik, member of the Politburo from 1923 to 1929; one of the main opponents of Stalin's collectivization policy.

had terrible sores; his armpits and groin looked like raw meat! I asked for rags and water, and washed him. He seemed okay. Finally, I was transferred to Pugachevskaia Tower. Before I left they undressed and searched me, and unwrapped the baby to see if I had hidden anything. God, what could I have smuggled out of the prison hospital?

The Pugachevskia Tower was a prison within a prison. The cell had a toilet and a sink, but it was crawling with bedbugs. I asked the guard for a bowl of water and spent the whole night picking bedbugs off my son and throwing them in the water. I complained. For some reason, it worked, and I was taken to another scary cell, but this time without any bedbugs. Two days later they transferred me back to the first one, but it had been whitewashed, and there were no bedbugs anymore. There were other women with children there, but I was the only one who had had her baby in prison. There were about ten of us. Among them was the mother of Maia Plisetskaia,[13] Rakhil, with her six-month-old son, Azarik.

The conditions were decent. We all had our own bunks, with mattresses and blankets. The sheets were old and torn, but clean. There were little basins and even disinfectant. They brought hot water, and we bathed our children every day. Our meals consisted of gruel and cereal made of shredded grain, and sometimes boiled fish. We nursed our children. Those who had money were allowed to order things from the prison shop. It turned out that I had fifty rubles in my account. My sister had found me and sent me some money.

I was sentenced to eight years without the right to correspond. They never told me anything about my husband. Only later did I realize that he had probably been shot. They kept me in prison while he was alive, and after he died, I was sent off to a camp. The other women were in the same position. On April 28, 1938, they led me and my baby out of the cell, put us into a black raven, and drove us somewhere across the whole city. Through the window, I could see springtime Moscow, with May Day posters everywhere. I felt so terribly sad . . .

Finally, we arrived at some railway station on the outskirts of town. I was the only one with a baby. When the others saw me, they all started crying. We arrived at the Potma Station, four hundred kilometers from Riazan. We got out of the train; they counted us, put me—the only one—in a little cart called a Cuckoo Bird; and took us over to our camp. When we got there some women surrounded us: "What's new on the outside? Where are you from? Have you seen our husbands?"

They were wearing padded jackets and black dresses, which looked awful. On their heads they had tiny caps made out of fustian, which reminded me of the "little mamas," which were fashionable in those days. We called them "camp mamas." I thought that all these women were criminals, but it turned out that they had all been arrested because of their husbands. At the camp I saw my old cellmates—Sonia Romanovskaia, Milia, and Zhenia—and felt less lonely. That was in the summer of 1938.

The camp was surrounded by observation towers, where armed guards stood. In front of the gate was a little path, which was covered with new sand every day.

---

[13] Maia Plisetskaia (b. 1925)—famous Soviet ballerina.

A footprint in the sand meant that somebody had tried to escape. There was barbed wire everywhere, and five wooden cell buildings, each one divided into two rooms. The rooms were pretty clean—we did our best to keep them in decent shape. Beyond the barbed wire was the Mordovian Forest, with its billions of mosquitoes. They kept biting us like mad. We would scratch till we bled, and our eyes, arms, and legs would become swollen. Then the sores would get infected, and sometimes we ended up with a high fever.

Our children were kept in a nursery. I became friendly with Nina Mdivani from Tbilisi. We still write to each other. She had a little baby—a two month old—that she had had in the camp. My Seva was already six months old. As long as we were breast-feeding, we worked in the nursery. It was very clean, and no wonder: we were the ones doing the cleaning. The doctors and teachers were inmates, too, so the children were well treated.

The way we worked was like this. We had a textile factory and some seamstress shops, all of them designed and equipped by our own women engineers. We would make those awful black camp dresses and blouses, as well as pants and shirts for the guards.

Our diet consisted of lentils and salt cod. There was not enough water, however, and we were always thirsty. There was plenty of bread, though: whole basketfuls at the entrance to the dining hall. We even used to receive parcels.

In 1939 my sister came and got Seva. He was just over a year old. The children had started dying, and we had been given permission to send our children away to our relatives if we wanted to. I really wanted for my sister to come and get Seva, but I knew she was very badly off. She already had my older boy, in addition to her own two kids, and they were all living in a communal apartment. It was very difficult to go ahead and write, but I simply had to: my baby was dying.

Our camp was located in a much better area than most. The climate was moderate, and it never got very cold. Even when it did, we could make ourselves coats and padded pants out of leftover material. We had our own laundry room, and once a week we got to go to the bathhouse. In the summer we could swim in the river. We kept ourselves clean.

The camp commander, Shapochkin, treated us well. He used to call us "my wives." He was good to us. Then there was the head of the guards. We used to call him Violet, because he always smelled of "Violet" cologne. He was supposed to count us every night before bedtime, but he always got mixed up. We used to tease him about this. Once he made a whole speech. "We didn't go to no universities," he said, "but the party knows who it can trust."

☐ F. E. Treivas was released in 1945. Forbidden to return to Moscow, she settled in Malyi Iaroslavets, where she taught Russian in a high school. Fired as an ex-convict in 1949, she moved to Unecha, Briansk province, where she worked as a janitor. In 1955 she was permitted to return to Moscow. She retired in 1956.

26 ☐ N. I. SLAVNIKOVA ET AL.

Speeches by Stakhanovites

☐ The Stakhanovite movement, named for the miner Aleksei Stakhanov, started in 1935 and rapidly spread throughout the country. Stakhanovites—workers and peasants who exceeded their production quotas—were rewarded, honored, and, above all, publicized for breaking production records. At regional and national Stakhanovite meetings, Stakhanovites were encouraged to report on their work achievements and the rewards they had received and to give brief formulaic life stories. These speeches by worker and peasant women are taken from national Stakhanovite meetings; interjections by Stalin and other Politburo members, who often attended the meetings, are included in the minutes.

SLAVNIKOVA, N. I.
(MACHINIST, DEFENSE FACTORY)

Comrades! On behalf of our plant, please allow me to extend to you my warmest Bolshevik greetings, as well as greetings to our beloved Comrade Stalin. [*Applause*]

Long live our beloved Comrade Stalin! Hurray! [*With shouts of "Hurray," members of the audience stand up to greet Comrade Stalin.*]

Comrades, the Stakhanovite movement is leading our country to new victories. Comrades, we know very well that the founder of our movement, Stakhanov, has raised our production targets to a great height. The targets that were set before have now been overturned.

How did our Stakhanovite movement originate? We had a meeting of the management and the best shock workers.[1] I was a good shock worker, but I had exceeded the norm by only one and a half times and was still a long way from what I am today. At our factory, two Komsomol members had become very famous. I felt hurt and upset: how could these two comrades exceed the norm by so much, when I couldn't? Was it possible that I could not achieve the same speed? I began to look into this more closely. I began to produce 300–350 percent of the norm, but I was still not satisfied. Then a new, totally untested machine arrived at our factory from the Kharkov plant. After the machine was installed, I examined it from top to bottom and inspected its gears and transmission. You see, I had done really well on the technology test, and I knew a thing or two. The machinist

From *Geroini Sotsialisticheskogo Truda* (Moscow: Partizdat TsK VKP(b), 1936), 4–108 (extracts).

[1] The shock worker movement, begun in the early 1930s, had many resemblances to the Stakhanovite movement, though the latter was supposed to stress innovations rationalizing production as well as sheer output.

Makarova had finished thirty-nine pieces instead of the assigned seventeen. So I came up to the technologist and said: "Comrade Gubarev, I want to challenge Makarova to a competition."

He said: "Are you serious? There is no way you could beat Makarova: you have never worked on this machine, it's brand new . . ."

But I replied: "I am a fearless parachutist,[2] and this norm doesn't scare me. I will overturn it."

He said that it was a serious matter. I answered: "Of course it is a serious matter, but if you will just create the right conditions,[3] I'll be ready to compete."

So the technologist reported to the section head that I wanted to have a competition, and the head promised to create the right conditions for me to try—perhaps something would come of it.

Makarova accepted my challenge on October 23. The 24th was a holiday, but I didn't take the holiday. I went to the factory, looked over the machine, set out the parts, and started testing it. Sometime earlier I had asked Marusia Makarova what gear she was using and where she had placed the parts. She told me everything. The very next day she found out that I was going to compete against her, and said, "You're a fine one, Nina. First you ask me about everything [*Laughter*], and then you start competing."

We arrived early on the morning of the 25th. I came forty minutes before the beginning of the shift, but Marusia had gotten there even earlier. They did not let us start before the whistle, however. We prepared everything, and, as soon as the whistle sounded, we turned on our engines. I had my parts on my left, and my tools on my right. Hundreds of comrades came by, stopped, and watched us as we worked. They all said, "That's great!"

My machine was new and heavy—five times my size. They had given us fifty units, but we did thirty each in less than half the shift. They realized there weren't enough units and started bringing more, so we would not have to sit and wait. That day we fulfilled 500 percent of the plan! At four o'clock there was a meeting, and they gave us flowers for our good work. That day we made 175 rubles each. [*Applause*]

At that meeting I, of course, declared to my comrades that I would help everybody work like a Stakhanovite.

The Stakhanov method allows us to improve our performance to a considerable degree. I promise Comrade Ordzhonikidze that within a month I will overturn the present norms and raise them twofold.

I don't know of a single delegate at this conference who has achieved the same results as Makarova and me. I think we won't stop at these records, but will go even further.

---

[2] Parachute jumping was enormously popular in the Soviet Union in the 1930s, both recreationally and in connection with military training. For another parachute jumping Stakhanovite, see Misostish-khova, below.

[3] Stakhanovite record breaking required extensive organization so that the Stakhanovite would be regularly supplied with the necessary technical support, supply of parts, raw materials, and so on. The whole shop was involved.

Our base salary is 158 rubles a month. In September I made 462 rubles. In October I made 886 rubles. I could have made more, of course, but there were days when we were prevented from working.

MIKOIAN:[4] And how much did your friend make?

SLAVNIKOVA: In October my friend made 1,336 rubles.

MIKOIAN: Is she a Komsomol member, too?

SLAVNIKOVA: No, she is nonparty.

MIKOIAN: What does she do with the money?

SLAVNIKOVA: I also wanted to know what to do with the money. I asked my friend, "Marusia, what are we going to do with all this money?" She said, "I'm going to buy myself some cream-colored shoes for 180 rubles, a crêpe-de-chine dress for 200 rubles, and an overcoat for 700 rubles."

We help people work faster. Our workers used to manufacture seventeen parts at the most. They couldn't do any more. One worker, who has been working in our factory for seven years, was producing a lot of defective parts. So she told me, "You're a Komsomol member, why don't you help me?" I put the gig on her machine and showed her how to drill, and also recommended that she use more power. And what do you think happened? She started producing forty parts.

Now we have special tutors who help us raise our political level and master technology.[5]

Our practice has overturned the norms set for us by the engineers. In the future we will work with even greater enthusiasm and turn our whole plant into a Stakhanovite, norm-breaking enterprise.

STALIN: Do you have enough machines?

SLAVNIKOVA: Yes, we do. Now we must put those machines to better use. We told our director: "If you provide us with more parts, we'll be able to produce even more." The director has promised to do this.

STALIN: Do you have enough workers?

SLAVNIKOVA: Yes, we do now because some workers are producing six times their norm.

I assure my party, my beloved leader, Comrade Stalin, and the people's commissar, Comrade Sergo [Ordzhonikidze], that we will supply our country and our beloved Red Army and its leader, Klim Voroshilov, with hundreds and thousands of top-quality tanks and armored cars! [*Prolonged applause*]

Comrades, I hope our dear Stakhanov, who started this whole thing, does not hold it against us, but we would very much like to overtake him. [*Prolonged applause*]

Long live our unwavering leader, our beloved Comrade Stalin, and our beloved Red Army chief, Klim Voroshilov! [*Applause*]

Long live our Leninist Komsomol and its leader, Comrade Kosarev![6] Hurray! [*Prolonged applause, shouts of "Hurray"*]

[4] A. I. Mikoian (1895–1978)—member of the Politburo of the Central Committee (1945–66), people's commissar of the food industry (1934–38).

[5] "Mastering technology" was one of Stalin's much-quoted injunctions of the mid-1930s.

[6] A. V. Kosarev (1903–1939)—general secretary of the Komsomol (1929–38).

VINOGRADOVA, A. N.
(WEAVER, BOLSHAIA DMITROVSKAIA
FACTORY, IVANOVO)

Comrades! Before I begin my speech, let me suggest that we honor the memory of Comrades Lenin, Frunze,[7] and Kirov[8] by standing up. [*Everyone stands*]

Let me speak from this exalted platform. It is so unexpected and incredible for me to be here. Comrades, I am forty-five years old, but I have been truly alive for only eighteen years. [*Applause*]

Under the guidance of our great and wise leader who works great miracles, we are going to continue conquering such achievements.

There is not a single country where a person can live as well as we live now. I know it from my own experience. I had been working since I was fifteen, but I didn't know what Communists were like, although I was active in public life. But then I met Comrade Frunze.

We will walk the great path shown to us by our leaders, under the red banner of Communism, and under the leadership of Comrade Stalin, and we will overfulfill our plan, and overfulfill it with honor!

The Stakhanovite movement means new methods of work. The work front is more difficult than the war front, but we'll uproot everything that gets in our way. We won't allow anybody to get in our way! We are not afraid of any obstacles! We are strong! We are invincible!

Let me say, Comrades, that in spite of my forty-five years, I'm not in the least tired of working because I eat well and am satisfied with my family life and with the conditions that make me healthier and put me in a better mood.

As soon as I got back from the sanatorium in June, Comrades, I talked to the management and asked to be given more machines.

But our management refused me. So when I read the article about Dusia Vinogradova[9] and about how her initiative had been carried out, I once again demanded more machines. From the 12th to the 28th I worked on ten machines and made sixty extra rubles.

I remember how we used to live before the revolution. I used to work on two or three machines. I didn't have any desire to work. The cloth we produced wasn't for me because my salary was small, and I couldn't buy it.

I remember my childhood. I lived in a tiny apartment. There was one bed where Mother and Father slept and a cradle for the baby, while my brother and I slept under the bed. But now I have received a good apartment, with good furniture. So my heart is rejoicing.

If I work on twenty machines, I'll be making 360 meters of cloth a day. I

[7] M. V. Frunze (1885–1925)—civil war hero, people's commissar for military and naval affairs (1924–25).

[8] S. M. Kirov (1886–1934)—member of the Politburo of the Central Committee (1930–34), first secretary of the Leningrad Regional Party Committee (1926–34).

[9] E. V. ("Dusia") Vinogradova (1914–1962)—the first Stakhanovite in the textile industry, member of the Supreme Soviet between 1937 and 1946.

guarantee that I'll be producing the best items in the world because there is a demand on the part of the kolkhozniks. We are linked by unbreakable ties: we give them industrial goods; they give us food. So it's quite understandable that we're full of fighting zeal, energy, and Bolshevik enthusiasm for our work.

Why am I saying this? I'm saying this because I'm not just marking time—I fly over with the speed of an airplane whenever I see that a machine has stopped.

Comrades, we should love our work with all our heart; we should put our entire proletarian soul into it. We will never give our achievements to anybody. It's not just me who works according to the new intensive schedule—on our floor, all the workers have had theirs intensified.

After this conference I will try to get everyone on our floor and the whole factory to work the way they should.

Comrade Stalin has raised the question of mastering technology. I have worked for thirty years and haven't mastered technology because I didn't have the right kind of education; in other words, I've had the practice, but not the theory.

Comrades, we used to be completely illiterate and confused by the priests. It should be mentioned that some peasants suffer from this even now, though not many .

I am sure that we can now liquidate not only our lack of basic education but also our technological illiteracy. At our factory almost everybody got "excellent" on the technology test, while just a few got "good."

We are now in the process of retraining. We want everybody to pass the test with excellence. We want the factory to produce only high-quality material and to fulfill the industrial and financial plan.

I give my promise to our leaders, headed by Comrade Stalin, that we are going to acquire more knowledge because Comrade Stalin has said that the cadres decide everything.

Long live our party and our Soviet government! [*Tumultuous applause*]

BUDAGIAN, Z. S.
(BRIGADE LEADER, ARSHALUIS KOLKHOZ,
VAGARSHAPAT DISTRICT, ARMENIAN SSR)

[*Comrade Budagian's appearance on the platform is greeted with applause that turns into an ovation, with shouts of "Hurray." Comrade Budagian speaks in Armenian.*]

My first thought and my first word is to pass on the heartfelt greetings of the Armenian kolkhozniks to the great leader of the working people, Comrade Stalin. [*Tumultuous applause*]

Recently we, in Soviet Armenia, celebrated the fifteenth anniversary of our liberation from the yoke of tsarist officials, imperialists, and their lackeys, the dashnaks.[10]

[10] Dashnaks—members of Dashnaktsutiun, the ruling party in the independent Armenian republic of 1918–20. In the 1930s the term *dashnak* was used pejoratively to mean an "Armenian bourgeois nationalist."

Fifteen years ago Armenia was a land of ruins, wars, and starvation. But now, thanks to the correct policy of our party and our great Stalin, Armenia has become a land of prosperous living, fun, and happiness. Fifteen years ago Armenia was a country of orphans. I also became an orphan at that time, but Soviet power, the party, and Comrade Stalin took the place of my father; the kolkhoz became my home; and now I am in charge of a whole brigade. [*Applause*]

I have the honor to be present at this conference together with members of the government and to see with my own eyes the greatest man in the world, Comrade Stalin. I was awarded this great honor because my brigade was successful in its fight for a good harvest.

We have different kinds of soil. I regarded each piece of land separately and applied the specific type of fertilizer that a given piece of land required. I treated and fertilized the wheat-growing area with particular care. I did it with ashes. I also made a special effort in the fight against the scourge of our fields—weeds. This year I weeded the fields three times.

I was just as particular with the cotton and used one hundred cartloads of manure for every hectare.

I carefully tended every grapevine by fertilizing the roots and treating each one with blue vitriol three times.

Thanks to all this, my brigade produced an average of 162 puds of first-class winter wheat per hectare this year, compared to 61 puds last year. I succeeded in delivering 570 puds of grapes, compared to 420 last year. I harvested 111 puds of cotton, compared to last year's 51 puds.

Thanks to this harvest, our kolkhoz has become prosperous. For every labor day we distributed 8.5 kilos of wheat, 15 rubles in cash, half a kilo of grapes, and a liter of wine. Every kolkhoznik received between 12 and 15 pailfuls of sweet wine, to make his joyful life even more joyful. [*Laughter, applause*]

Next year my brigade promises to produce more than 200 puds of wheat, 600 puds of grapes, and 150 puds of cotton of the best quality from every hectare.

Our kolkhozniks have built 27 new houses and bought 250 new beds, 100 sewing machines, 60 gramophones, and 30 radio sets.

The houses of the kolkhozniks now have electricity.

Our kolkhoz met its obligations to the state completely and ahead of schedule and, in particular, carried out the directive of Comrade Stalin concerning the liquidation of cowlessness. We do not have a single cowless kolkhoznik left.

Comrade Stalin has said quite correctly that women were exploited in the old days. This was especially obvious in our Armenian villages, where women were virtual slaves. Now our female kolkhozniks have become free. Now they sometimes make more money than their husbands. How can your husband exploit you when you make more money than he does? That usually shuts him up.

The female kolkhozniks have asked me to say a big thank you to Comrade Stalin for the article that he introduced into the statute of the agricultural cooperative[11]—the article according to which a pregnant female kolkhoznik gets a paid

[11] The Kolkhoz Charter of 1935. Stalin's initiative in changing the original draft to provide maternity leave was much publicized.

vacation. This year twenty-three women took pregnancy leave, and I was asked to say a very special thank you to Comrade Stalin on their behalf. [*Applause*]

Finally, we now have something that we in Armenia did not have for hundreds of years—an opportunity to work in peace. For fifteen years now, our villages have not seen interethnic wars. Fifteen years ago our land was covered with trenches. Now those trenches have been replaced by irrigation ditches filled with water, given to us by the Bolsheviks. Where there used to be ruins, flowers now bloom. This peace is the result of the correct party policy—the correct, Leninist-Stalinist, nationality policy. The friendship of all Transcaucasian peoples has been cemented by the Transcaucasian Federation, headed by the steadfast Bolshevik, Comrade Beria.[12] [*Applause*]

Thank you, Comrade Stalin, for your correct nationality policy! Thank you for sending us such a good and firm Bolshevik as Comrade Beria!

Our peaceful labor and our borders are being protected by our beloved Red Army and its chief, Comrade Voroshilov!

Long live our great Communist Party and the greatest leader of nations, Comrade Stalin! [*Applause*]

GADILIAEVA, SH. IA.
(MILKMAID, KUIURGAZIN STATE FARM,
BASHKIR ASSR)

[*Speaks in Bashkir. The speech is translated into Russian.*]

Comrades! On behalf of the Stakhanovite socialist cattle breeders from the Kuiurgazin meat farm, as well as on behalf of the kolkhozniks of the decorated Bashkir Autonomous Republic,[13] I send my warmest greetings to the great and beloved leader of the Communist Party and the working people, Comrade Stalin. [*Applause*]

Let me tell you what I used to be and how I found the good life. When I was one and a half, I became a fatherless orphan. Till the age of eleven I was supported by my brother. In 1922 my brother died, and I became a day laborer. I worked as a day laborer till I was sixteen. At that time I was married off against my will, according to the old custom that was still in force then.

Having lived with my husband for a year and a half, I divorced him and began working in the kolkhoz on my own. In 1930 I became a milkmaid at the Kuiurgazin meat state farm. During the first three years I was in charge of fourteen cows. At that time my cows gave, on average, no more than 1,500 liters a year. In 1935 I was in charge of eight cows, but my cows gave, on average, 4,370 liters of milk. I was so successful because I treated my cows with affection, fed them correctly, and took good care of them.

I give my promise to obtain an average of no fewer than 5,000 liters of milk

---

[12] L. P. Beria (1899–1953)—first secretary of the Transcaucasus Communist Party from 1932 to 1938, when he became head of the NKVD.

[13] Republics and cities, as well as individuals and organizations, could receive decorations (honors, awards, and titles) in the Soviet Union.

from every cow, no fewer than 6,000 liters from the cow named Shock worker, and no fewer than 8,000 liters from the record-holding cow, Prudent.

Our state farm has pledged to produce, in 1936, twice as much milk, butter, and meat as in 1935. I assure you that this pledge, too, is going to be fulfilled.

We are grateful to our leader, Comrade Stalin, for the good and bright life he has given us. Before Soviet power we Bashkir women and Bashkir girls didn't have any rights at all. Only thanks to the leadership of the Communist Party and Comrade Stalin did we Bashkir girls and women become active participants and conscious builders of the new life.

Before, we couldn't even dream of what we can see now. Here I am, speaking in the Kremlin before our leaders. Our parents couldn't have imagined anything like that. Thanks again to Comrade Stalin and all the Communist Party that gave us this wonderful and joyful life. [*Applause*]

Long live our great Stalin! [*Applause*]

Long live our Communist Party! [*Applause*]

[*Comrade Gadiliaeva walks up to the presidium and shakes hands with the leaders of the party and state. The audience is on its feet, applauding continuously.*]

RAZINA, M. K.
(MILKMAID FROM STATE FARM #54,
OMSK DISTRICT, OMSK PROVINCE)

Comrades, please allow me to greet our dear teacher and leader, Comrade Stalin. [*Applause*]

Also, please allow me to greet our government. [*Applause*]

We collective farmers and state farm employees are happy to report to our party and government that the state plan for the development of animal husbandry in Omsk Province has been fulfilled, even overfulfilled.

The kolkhozniks and state farm employees have asked me to thank Comrade Stalin for our prosperous, cultured, and joyful lives. [*Applause*]

I will tell you about my life and about how I used to live. I was born in Penza Province. When I was eleven I lost my mother and became an orphan. When I was twelve I was given as a nanny to the village kulaks, and then, when I was fourteen, to the manor house, to look after their children. By the age of sixteen I was already married. They thought that my husband was going to be a good one because he was an only child and that meant he wouldn't be drafted into the army. In those days people thought your life would be good if your husband wasn't going to be drafted.

I couldn't read or write. My life was very bad, and I didn't know that there was a different, better life.

I joined state farm No. 54, in Omsk Province. That was in 1930. At first it was difficult for me. I was made a milkmaid, and I didn't know the job. They gave me eighteen cows, but I couldn't read and didn't even know the numbers of my cows.

I worked for a while and, although it was hard, I got used to it. In 1935 they opened an adult literacy course in our sovkhoz. I did well on the test, learned to read and write, and it became easier for me to do my work. As a good worker, I was transferred to the shed with the calves. I worked there from 1933 to 1934. Our livestock expert, Comrade Karelin, taught us how to take care of the calves. After I learned the calf-feeding norms, it became easy for me to work. But at that time I was going through a difficult period. My husband died, and I was left with three children. I had a really hard time with them. At that time the director of farm No. 3 surrounded himself with kulaks, and I was deprived of my party candidate status and kicked out of the state farm.

So I moved to the city of Omsk. I thought about the state farm often and felt homesick, so I sent an application to the head of the state farm political department. Soon afterward a party purge began, and all the alien elements who had surrounded the farm director were purged from the party. I was reinstated as a party candidate member and returned to the state farm. I started working as a milkmaid at the head farm. But those who were left over after the purge continued to persecute me for my good work. So I'm really grateful to the political department: it has protected me and has always helped me in my work. In 1934 I passed the technology test and became a Class-One milkmaid. I work well and live well. I have my own apartment with electric lighting, a gramophone, and a radio set. My daughter is in the sixth grade.

Having studied Comrade Stalin's speech at the conference for leading harvester operators, all our milkmaids joined the Stakhanovite movement in order to obtain more milk and turn more cows into record-holding producers.

I pledge to obtain an average of 5000 liters of milk per cow in 1936: 6000 liters from the cow Steel, 7000 liters from the cow Freedom, 6500 liters from the cow Construction Site, and 6500 liters from the cow Zaza. [*Applause*]

When Comrade Kaganovich[14] was in Omsk, he said that our milk yields were low and had to be improved. It is true. We will meet the demands of our party and government and produce as much milk and butter as necessary. We challenge Cheliabinsk Province to a socialist competition. [*Applause*]

We live very well! We are happy people, Comrades, because we are working with our beloved leader and teacher, Comrade Stalin. [*Applause*]

Long live our leader and teacher, Comrade Stalin! [*Applause*]

Long live our government! [*Applause*]

Long live our great Red Army! [*Applause*]

Long live our conference! [*Applause*]

Allow me to shake hands with our leaders.

[*Tumultuous applause, shouts of "Hurray." The audience is on its feet. Comrade Razina goes up to the presidium and shakes hands with the leaders of the party and government.*]

---

[14] L. M. Kaganovich (1893–1991)—member of the Politburo of the Central Committee (1930–57), deputy chairman of the Council of People's Commissars (1938–57), people's commissar of transport of the USSR (1935–37, 1938–42, 1943–44).

MISOSTISHKHOVA, B. SH.
(TEAM LEADER, PSYGANSU KOLKHOZ, URVAN DISTRICT,
KABARDINO-BALKAR AUTONOMOUS REGION)

[*Comrade Misostishkhova speaks in Kabardian.*]

On behalf of the collective farmers of the Kabardino-Balkar Autonomous Region, please allow me to extend my heartfelt greetings to the leader of nations, our beloved Comrade Stalin. [*Applause*]

Our collective farm includes eight hundred households and fourteen field brigades. Our kolkhoz is one of the best in the region, and my team is the best in our kolkhoz. [*Applause*]

Bearing in mind Comrade Stalin's words that a kolkhoz woman is a great force,[15] we worked very well in 1935.

But whatever we accomplished in 1935, we consider to be insufficient.

I am hereby making my firm commitment to our beloved Comrade Stalin, to all the other leaders of the party and state gathered here today, and to the conference as a whole that in 1936 my team will harvest one hundred centners[16] of corn and forty centners of wheat from each hectare of land. [*Applause*] We have reached the point where we can force the earth to yield as much grain as we may possibly need. [*Applause*]

I challenge everyone present to harvest one hundred centners of corn and forty centners of wheat from each hectare. I challenge Maria Demchenko, who unfortunately is not here today, to enter into a socialist competition with me.[17] I will accept as a referee between Maria Demchenko and myself any party organization or party member that Comrade Stalin may appoint to that role. [*Tumultuous applause*] And let them report to Comrade Stalin whether it is Maria Demchenko or me who becomes number one. [*Tumultuous applause*]

Our success in 1935 is not only the result of our use of agricultural technology, but, most of all, it is the result of Stalin's concern for real people. We worked heroically, but we were no less heroic in our concern for each and every kolkhoznik.

Our kolkhoz, our brigade, and my team live a cultured and prosperous life. We have everything necessary for civilized work and leisure: a radio, a telephone, electricity, a club, a school, a movie theater, and a newspaper. We have everything in abundance. We live cultured lives. [*Applause*]

Now let me say a few words about myself. In my kolkhoz I am a record-holding worker of the kolkhoz fields. But in addition to that, I am also ready for labor and defense. [*Points to her "Ready for Labor and Defense" and "Voroshilov's Marksman" badges.*]

---

[15] Stalin told the First All-Union Congress of Kolkhoz Shock Workers in February 1933 that "women in the kolkhozy are a great force."

[16] Centner—a unit of weight equivalent to one hundred kilograms.

[17] At the Second All-Union Congress of Kolkhoz Shock Workers, the Ukrainian combine operator Maria Demchenko formally initiated the "500'er movement," a campaign to grow more than five hundred centners of sugar beets per hectare.

STALIN: How old are you?

MISOSTISHKHOVA: Seventeen. I am also a record-holding mountain climber. I was the first, together with Comrade Kalmykov, to climb the highest mountain in Europe, Elbrus. [*Tumultuous applause, turning into an ovation. Shouts of "Hurray."*] When I reached the highest point of Mount Elbrus, my first words were "Long live our beloved leader, our dear Comrade Stalin! May he live a thousand years!" [*Tumultuous applause, turning into an ovation. All rise. Shouts of "Hurray."*]

Everything I am wearing I received as a reward for my good work in the kolkhoz. Besides the dress and the shoes, I received a sewing machine in Nalchik.

Now I'm preparing myself for parachute jumping. I haven't done it yet because I didn't have enough time after storming Mount Elbrus. But, Comrades, I give my word to Comrade Voroshilov that in parachute jumping I am also going to be ahead of the men. [*Tumultuous applause, turning into an ovation.*]

Everything we have, all our achievements have only become possible under the Soviet regime, as a result of the victory of socialism. In the old days our people were abused. Our people were backward and illiterate. But now I study Russian; I study literature.

Rest assured, Comrade Stalin, that, if need be, I and all the female kolkhozniks of Kabardino-Balkaria will beat back the enemies of the revolution and the enemies of socialism with the same success we are achieving in the kolkhoz. [*Applause*]

We have been brought up and are still being brought up by our glorious, great Communist Party.

We are being guided by Comrade Stalin—that's why we are invincible! [*Prolonged ovation by everyone in the audience.*]

Long live the great Communist Party!

Long live our friend, our teacher, the beloved leader of the world proletariat, Comrade Stalin! [*Tumultuous applause, turning into an ovation. Shouts of "Hurray."*]

Long live the leader of our dear Red Army, Comrade Voroshilov! [*Ovation. Shouts of "Hurray for Comrade Voroshilov!"*]

[*Upon the conclusion of her speech, Comrade Misostishkhova goes up to the presidium and shakes hands with Comrade Stalin and all the other members of the presidium. The audience is on its feet, applauding tumultuously. The ovation lasts several minutes.*]

27 □ Ulianova

A Cross-Examination

□ It was customary for candidates standing for election for public office to make a speech giving a short account of their lives, which was then open to discussion and questions. At times of high political tension, this could become a process of challenge and "working over" similar in tone to that of a purge (*chistka*) or self-criticism session. That was what happened to Ulianova (no first name or patronymic recorded) when she stood for election to the Central Committee of the trade union of workers in state institutions in January 1938, at the height of the Great Purges.

CHAIRMAN: The next candidate is Ulianova from Odessa.

ULIANOVA: I was born in 1898 in the Jewish settlement of Bogachevka. Most of the people there were poor, though.[1] It is down in Odessa Province, formerly Kamenets-Podolskaia Province. My father died when I was four years old. He left behind two desiatinas[2] of land and a run-down hut. We lived with our mother. I had one brother and three sisters. We all worked as hired hands. When I was ten I moved to the city, where I worked for three years as a servant, but then my mother got sick, and I went back home. In the summer I worked in the fields, but in the winter I had no income, so I became a Yiddish teacher (although I probably did more harm than good).

At the beginning of 1920, when the Reds entered Pervomaisk, I moved there and started working in the revolutionary committee. Later, through Komsomol channels, I was transferred to the Cheka, where I worked for two years in a responsible position. Then I was recalled by the district party committee. That move was a matter of party discipline. I did not want to leave, and the Cheka people did not want to let me go.

I spent two years working in the district party committee, until both my husband and I were transferred to the party committee of Odessa Province. I have been working in Odessa since 1924.

After a few months of working in the provincial committee, I asked to be transferred to one of the districts. I worked in a district committee for about a year, and then asked for the opportunity to study. For the first time in my life, I went to school (a rabfak). I graduated from the rabfak in two years.

I wanted to continue my studies, but I was transferred to the Stalin district committee. I worked there for about two years.

From Gosudarstvennyi arkhiv Rossiiskoi Federatsii (GARF), f. 7709, op. 8, d. 2, ll. 269–82 (II Vsesoiuznyi s"ezd Soiuza rabotnikov gosuchrezhdenii. Ian. 1938 g. Stenogramma, chap. 2).

[1] *Bogachevka* means "rich" in Russian.
[2] 1 desiatina = 2.7 acres.

After that I worked as a party secretary at the Odessa Housing Union. Then I was made party secretary of the Odessa Candy Factory, and, after that, head of the organizational department in the Ilichevsky district party committee. Six months later I was transferred to the provincial committee of the Government Employees' Union, where I am still working.

I joined the party in September 1920, in Pervomaisk. I was a Komsomol member between April 1920 and 1923. I have never been reprimanded by the party. I have never deviated from the party line.

My volunteer assignment is to be a party investigator in the provincial party committee. During the purge I worked on the provincial appeals commission. When documents were being verified I was on the verification commission.

I have one son. My husband has been a party member since 1917, but we are separated now. My sisters live abroad. Two of my sisters emigrated before the war. I have only a vague recollection of them. My third sister went abroad in 1924 as a Soviet citizen. Her husband had left before the war. In 1924 he sent her a passport, and she went to join him.

I am not in contact with my sisters. The older ones I don't know at all. The third one used to write at first, but it has been five years since I last heard from her.

The sister who left in 1924 was living in Argentina, and the other two, in America. I have no idea where they are now.

QUESTION: What education do you have?

ULIANOVA: As I said, the only time I was in school was when I was sent to the rabfak. Currently, though, I am a student at the Institute of Economic Managers.

QUESTION: You said you had never been to school before the rabfak, and yet you worked as a teacher?

ULIANOVA: I felt I had to mention that fact, just as I have always mentioned it at all verification meetings. I knew how to read and write in Yiddish, and in the wretched place where I lived, that meant I could teach children. I made only fifty kopeks a season.

QUESTION: In your autobiography you stated: "I became a Yiddish teacher (although I probably did more harm than good)." What does that mean?

ULIANOVA: I said that because I taught them incorrectly. I did not know the language very well myself.

QUESTION: When did your correspondence with your sister stop?

ULIANOVA: Around 1932. I don't know anything about my other sisters. I don't even know if they are still alive. As for the one who left in 1924, I did receive a letter from her in 1932.

QUESTION: Comrade Ulianova said that she never went to school. I would like to know where and how she learned Yiddish.

ULIANOVA: I went to the cheder.[3]

QUESTION: What did your sisters do before they left?

ULIANOVA: Their husbands were workers. Here in Russia they were workers, but I have no way of knowing what they are doing in America because I have no contact with them. The husband of the sister who left in 1924 used to be a farmer.

---

[3] Cheder—a Jewish religious school.

QUESTION: What was the reason for your sisters' emigration?

ULIANOVA: Two of the sisters left before the war. They had been in a pogrom, their husbands were workers, and they decided to emigrate. The husband of the sister who left in 1924 was a worker. He went abroad several months before the war. After the war started, he couldn't return.

QUESTION: You have been a party member since 1920. Your sister emigrated in 1924. What was your reaction?

ULIANOVA: My reaction was very negative. I did everything I could to talk her into staying. She had a little child, and no matter how much I argued, she was set on going. You know the Jewish way: How can I stay here without my husband? What am I going to do? I consulted various party officials, but they said: "If she wants to join her husband, there's nothing that can be done about it. If she gets a passport, she can go."

QUESTION: If your reaction was negative, why did you correspond with her?

ULIANOVA: I didn't see why I couldn't correspond with her.

QUESTION: Then why did you stop corresponding?

ULIANOVA: Even when we were still corresponding, I rarely wrote because I was always very busy. I didn't write because I didn't have time, not because I was afraid I was writing something counterrevolutionary.

QUESTION: When did your sister's husband leave?

ULIANOVA: In 1913 or 1914, I don't remember exactly.

QUESTION: How long have you been separated from your husband, and why?

ULIANOVA: We have been separated for several years now. He has been a party member since 1917. We have a son. My husband works as a prosecutor. We are on friendly terms. Actually, he was here at the congress, and I introduced him to many of the comrades here. Why did we separate? That's not the kind of thing that can be discussed at a congress.

QUESTION: Is Ulianova your husband's name?

ULIANOVA: My family name is Buber. When I started working for the Cheka, my boss said: "Get yourself a pseudonym." So I chose the name of Ulianova, and for a while I was Ulianova-Buber. During the last exchange of party documents, "Buber" was crossed out, and I became Ulianova.

QUESTION: When you were asked the reason for your sister's emigration, you said, "You know the Jewish way." What is this "Jewish way"?

ULIANOVA: My sister grew up in a rural settlement. She had never been to a city. The way she looked at it, if she was married, she was supposed to live with her husband. Her husband was living abroad, and so she had to join him, and that was all there was to it.

CHAIRMAN: It seems to me that it probably does not make sense to talk about the sisters who left Russia before the revolution. As for the sister who left after the revolution, that's a different matter, and the congress has every right to concern itself with that.

QUESTION: How did your party organization react to your sister's emigration?

ULIANOVA: The party organization knew about it. At that time I was working in the provincial party committee, and I told them that my sister was leaving the country in order to join her husband. She got her Soviet passport from the NKVD and left.

VOICE FROM THE AUDIENCE: I don't understand. I also worked in the Cheka. What do you mean, you got yourself a new name? I don't understand.

ULIANOVA: Long-time Cheka employees know that in 1920 you could take a pseudonym. I got a pseudonym and have lived with it for eighteen years now. During the exchange of party documents they crossed out "Buber" and left only "Ulianova."

VOICE FROM THE AUDIENCE: What does your party organization think about your ties with your sister?

ULIANOVA: I don't have any ties. When I received those letters in 1932, the NKVD knew about them.

VOICE FROM THE AUDIENCE: Did you help your sister obtain the papers she needed in order to leave?

ULIANOVA: I never petitioned on her behalf or vouched for her. I did not even go to the NKVD to pick up her passport. She did everything herself. I did not help her because I was against her leaving. I didn't think that she should leave.

VOICE FROM THE AUDIENCE: What is your husband's nationality?

ULIANOVA: He is Jewish.

VOICE FROM THE AUDIENCE: In what year did you and your husband get divorced?

CHAIRMAN: She already said, several years ago. Her husband is a party member and is working. If he had been expelled from the party or were politically compromised in some fashion, we would be justified in pursuing this. Her husband is a party member. He works as a prosecutor. Perhaps they just weren't compatible or something, and here we are asking her about it at the congress.

ULIANOVA: I can answer that. Comrades, my husband and I never got officially divorced. I don't think it's a good idea to go into this. All I can say is that he comes to visit sometimes, but we don't live together. He might come, and then leave again. That's just the way he is ... I don't know how to judge ... We haven't been living together for three or four years.

VOICE FROM THE AUDIENCE: Does the party organization in which you are registered know that, up until 1932, you were in contact with your sister who lives abroad?

ULIANOVA: During the purge I was questioned individually because I was a party investigator on the provincial appeals commission. I wrote down everything in my questionnaire. I have never hidden the fact that my sisters live abroad. I mentioned it to the commission. I have no contact with them, and I don't have anything in common with them.

VOICE FROM THE AUDIENCE: Still, I would have to ask in what year she and her husband got divorced. Maybe they got divorced in 1924, when her sister was getting ready to leave.

CHAIRMAN: Comrade Ulianova, give us the exact year.

ULIANOVA: But we never got officially divorced.

CHAIRMAN: Tell us, were there any party-related or political reasons for your divorce?

ULIANOVA: Absolutely none.

CHAIRMAN: Is that clear?

VOICES: Yes, it is.

CHAIRMAN: Let us then consider this issue settled.

VOICE FROM THE AUDIENCE: The majority of the delegates are asking the right questions. We don't insist that the comrade tell us why she does not live with her husband. But we do insist that she tell us exactly when they stopped living together.

CHAIRMAN: The congress has agreed to consider the husband issue closed. I do not believe it would be correct for the congress to concern itself with such matters. I will ask one more time: Comrade Ulianova, are there any party-related or political reasons why you do not live with your husband?

ULIANOVA: There are no such reasons. We got separated . . . You know, all sorts of things happen . . . He left in 1926—he simply got transferred to another town. He worked there for a year and then came back. We lived together for a while, but then he left again, to work in Novosibirsk. He married somebody else. They had a child, but he does not live with her either. He has been living alone for several years now. He works as a prosecutor in Tula.

CHAIRMAN: Has the husband issue been clarified now?

VOICES: Yes, it has.

CHAIRMAN: And has been for quite some time, if you ask me.

VOICE FROM THE AUDIENCE: Would you tell us why you stopped writing to the sister who left in 1924? And where is she: in Spain or in America?

ULIANOVA: She is in Argentina. I stopped writing because she stopped writing. I heard that she was very sick, so I don't even know if she is still alive.

VOICE FROM THE AUDIENCE: Have you tried to find out?

ULIANOVA: How can I try if I don't even know where she is?

MEMBER OF THE PRESIDIUM: Did you and your sister try to get her husband to come to the Soviet Union—given that our life was already Soviet and life abroad was capitalist?

ULIANOVA: No, I did not try to get him to come here. I had nothing to do with any of that. I told her what I thought—that I was against her going—but she did not listen to me and went anyway. Before she got married, she had been a factory worker and a maid.

CHAIRMAN: I move that we conclude the question period.

[*By majority vote, the question period is concluded.*]

CHAIRMAN: Would anyone like to speak against Comrade Ulianova's candidacy?

BADAEV: I don't agree with the way Comrade Zelenko [the chairman] is handling this. He wants to rush it through, but I think it is a very serious matter.

I must remind you (one citizen has mentioned it, and as a long-time NKVD employee I know what I am talking about) what it means to be a Chekist and allow your sister to go abroad rather than detaining her. I am more than certain, and I state this before the congress, that for her to get a passport, somebody had to vouch for her. The way I look at it is this: can you be a Chekist and a party member and not be able to influence your sister's political actions? It seems to me that, based on what we've heard, there's something fishy about the whole thing, and so we should reject the comrade's candidacy and have this matter looked into. Having ties with foreign countries is a serious matter these days, Comrades. We need to look into this matter.

KAZARINOV: I don't know, Comrades, but I find the whole thing very strange. We have our Soviet law. Before 1935 all name changes had to be approved by the court, and since 1935, by the All-Union Central Executive Committee [of the Congress of Soviets], with notification in the press. We need to look at this very carefully. Maybe she deliberately changed her name because she had something to hide. Therefore I believe she should be removed from the list of candidates for the Central Committee Plenum.

NESTERENKO: There is another odd thing here, Comrades. When the delegates correctly asked her in what year she and her husband got divorced, she seemed to hesitate, for some reason or another. She couldn't tell us. When Comrade Ulianova said that they had gotten divorced in 1926, I thought (I don't know about the other delegates, but I personally thought) that maybe, because her husband had been a party member since 1918 or 1917, maybe her sister's emigration and her continuing contact with her sister had resulted in the kind of family discord that ultimately led to a divorce. This could have happened, but Comrade Ulianova didn't say for sure. Therefore I also support the previous speaker's proposal that her candidacy be removed from the ballot for secret voting and that this matter be carefully looked into.

CHAIRMAN: There are more delegates wishing to speak against the candidacy. Would anybody like to speak in her favor?

KORSHUNOV: I would like to speak. Comrades, we have nothing incriminating against Comrade Ulianova. Comrade Ulianova has been working in party organizations for a long time. She spent a long time working in the NKVD. Everybody in Odessa knows her extremely well, yet nobody has accused her of anything or shown any interest in trivial matters.

[*Noise*]

KORSHUNOV: We need to be cautious, but in this case there is no reason to play it safe. It doesn't make sense to—

VOICE FROM THE AUDIENCE: You can't be serious.

KORSHUNOV: I am being very serious. I am not trying to be funny here. It seems to me that what's going on here is not serious. I have stated my reasons: this person has been in the public eye and has been properly checked. If you have your doubts, let individual party members, individual citizens of the Soviet Union, look into this, but I don't see why it should prevent her from running as a candidate.

CHAIRMAN: It seems to me that the comrade's statement to the effect that this congress is dealing with trivial matters is incorrect. The congress has shown some interest in Comrade Ulianova's family situation. I don't think it is right to present the congress's activity in that kind of light.

Second, rejecting this or that candidate is not the same as incriminating that candidate. It seems to me that we ought to be discussing the substance of Comrade Ulianova's work as a party member and as chair of her union's provincial committee.

Would anyone like to speak on Comrade Ulianova's behalf?

LIUBIMOVA: I have known Comrade Ulianova since 1934, when she was promoted from secretary to chair of the provincial Government Employees' Union. I was in Odessa Province at the time, checking the work of the Service Employees' Section.

Last August—when, as you know, the situation was delicate and all appointees were being checked very thoroughly—I was in the provincial party committee again, and I talked with Comrade Ivanchenko. Comrade Ulianova's candidacy had been approved; there had been no objections and nothing incriminating had been found. In fact, she had been recommended by the provincial party committee.

For a long time now, Comrade Ulianova has been working as a party investigator. She has been involved in verification work. At the provincial conference the delegates expressed their total confidence in Comrade Ulianova. It seems to me that Comrade Ulianova's candidacy should not be rejected, and that her name should be kept on the ballot.

VOICE FROM THE AUDIENCE: Did she mention any of this during the elections at the Odessa conference?

LIUBIMOVA: Not during the elections, but she mentioned it to me personally.

CHAIRMAN: Let's have a vote. Who is for rejecting Comrade Ulianova's candidacy? [*261 votes*]

Who is for keeping Comrade Ulianova's name on the ballot? [*4 votes*]

[*Comrade Ulianova's name is removed from the list for secret ballot*]

VOICE FROM THE AUDIENCE: I think that the congress's vote of political no confidence in Comrade Ulianova leads to a logical conclusion. As Odessa Province borders on Romania, the question arises: Can Ulianova continue to be chair of the provincial committee?

CHAIRMAN: I don't believe that this was a vote of political no confidence. The point is that the congress was not entirely clear on Comrade Ulianova's biographical data, and so it removed her from the ballot. I don't think there were grounds for a vote of political no confidence, especially because Comrade Ulianova is not a bad chair of the provincial committee. As for the specific matters that have not been cleared up, they will be looked into.

Would this be a correct formulation?

VOICES: Yes, it would.

VOICE FROM THE AUDIENCE: As we have rejected her candidacy, I think we should make the following notation: "The new presidium of the Central Committee is directed to look into this matter."

CHAIRMAN: I don't think it makes sense to do that. The Central Committee presidium will handle this, and besides, the Odessa organization will investigate Comrade Ulianova.

☐ At a later session, the chairman—obviously sympathetic to Ulianova—reported that he had called her former husband and received assurances from him that their separation had nothing to do with politics. As a result, the meeting voted by an "overwhelming majority" to return her name to the list of candidates, and she was duly elected.[4] Her later fate is unknown.

[4] For a detailed account of the Ulianova story, see Sheila Fitzpatrick, "Lives under Fire: Autobiographical Narratives and Their Challenges in Stalin's Russia," in *De Russie et d'ailleurs. Feux croisés sur l'histoire. Pour Marc Ferro* (Paris, 1995).

28 □ Anna Shchetinina

A Sea Captain's Story

□ *Obshchestvennitsa* was the journal of the wives' movement, a voluntary organization that provided an outlet for nonworking elite women—wives of Soviet industrial managers, government officials, and military officers—in the second half of the 1930s. The journal often publicized the achievements of women who had entered male professions, such as aviation, as well as celebrating domestic virtues and voluntarism. Anna Ivanovna Shchetinina, a sea captain, was interviewed in 1937 as a female trailblazer.

My name is Anna Ivanovna Shchetinina.

Why did I become a sailor?

It is very simple: I love the sea. I do not want you to imagine that it was because of sentimentalism, romanticism, or exaltation. Not at all. I am a practical person with a mathematical mind. How old am I? Twenty-eight.

There was another journalist here before you, who was all excited: "A female sea captain! A woman in charge of sailors!"

I was furious. That interview never did take place. It would have been impossible: I don't like these "Ohs" and "Ahs." I don't like sentimental ballads. That's just the kind of person I am.

So, as you can see, I'm not a romantic.

I was sixteen when I entered the Naval College in Vladivostok. It was in the spring of 1925. I went to the president of the college and said: "I want to enroll!"

"You can't be serious," he said. "Even some of the men drop out after practical training, so there's no point in your even trying."

"What nonsense! I won't drop out, and you can bet on that!"

He looked at me and said: "Listen, why don't you just run along home and bake some pies. Who ever heard of a thing like this: a woman wanting to be a navigator! Has it ever happened before? Never—for as long as people have been at sea. [Captain] Cook never heard of it, and neither did Magellan."

"All kinds of things have never happened before," I said.

So then he tried to scare me. He said that it was very hard work at sea, that I'd have to do a sailor's job, and that there had never ever been any women sailors before.

Well, it isn't easy to make me change my mind. I knew there was no rule against women being admitted. And if there was no such rule, I wasn't going to be intimidated by Magellan or anybody else!

E. Gabrilovich, "Razgovor s kapitanom [A. I. Shchetininoi]," *Obshchestvennitsa*, no. 12 (June 1937): 16–17.

To make a long story short, he let me take the entrance exam. I did very well on it—better than the men. Then the classes began.

There were three of us girls at the college. Of course, at first everyone was skeptical. That's understandable: after all, when it comes right down to it, the female nature is somewhat softer than the male nature . . .

At first they made fun of us, but then they realized we weren't paying any attention to them so they stopped bothering us.

In the summer we had our first training voyage.

I was a cadet first, and then a sailor. It's not easy work, but I did well. To begin with, I never refused any work, no matter how difficult. You refuse just once—and you'll never be an equal with the sailors; you'll always remain a passenger.

Of course it was hard. It's manual work. But I'm a strong, healthy person.

In those days I used to get a lot of help from boatswain Matchenko. I'll be grateful to him for the rest of my life. He's the one who taught me how to be a sailor. He was a rough old man: he used to get real mad when I made mistakes and would grumble all the time. He was never happy with anything.

He taught me how to do the rigging, and he taught me how to tie knots.

Tying knots is very difficult work. Once I even burst into tears. I just sat there crying and thinking of my mother and father. "Why did I ever decide to become a sailor?" I thought. "Now just go ahead and try to figure out these damn knots and destroy your hands while you're at it." It was late at night. The moon was up, and it was very quiet. And the tears just kept flowing.

Suddenly I heard Matchenko's footsteps. "Another dressing down," I thought. He came up to me and patted me on the head.

"You're having a hard time, aren't you, girl? That's okay. You'll manage. At first it's really tough, I tell you. I remember how I cried once, just like you. Don't fool yourself: men just pretend to be cool, but when it gets tough, they cry just like any woman. It was hard for me at first, but then I got used to it. You'll get used to it, too. We'll help you—we're all Soviet people, after all."

We became friends. He was a good, thoughtful teacher, although he could get very angry sometimes.

I lived in the crew's quarters with ten men.

They treated me well, with respect. There was some courting, of course. One comrade kept giving me flowers. I obviously couldn't accept them, or there'd be no end to the gossip and rumors. So I'd tell him: "You'd better give these flowers to Misha Panfilov: he also scrubs the decks, on the same shift as I do!"

The men would laugh. They laughed once, twice, and then he stopped doing it. The next thing you knew, he was giving flowers to girls on land. He'd simply forgotten that I was a woman.

That's the most important thing—to make them forget that you are a woman; to make them accept you as a buddy, as one of them.

I GRADUATED at the top of my class. We studied more than thirty different subjects at the college: astronomy, sea training, steam engines, mechanics—all kinds of things. There were two departments: mechanics and navigation. I was a navigator.

After graduation we did two years of internship. Without it you couldn't get your navigator's license. I worked on launches and barges in the port, and also went to sea as a sailor.

After my internship, in 1930, I started working as a first mate.

Was it hard work? Of course, it was not easy. It was a great test—a test of courage, determination, thoughtfulness, and precision. I had moments of hesitation and uncertainty, but I knew my job and did it conscientiously. I never received any reprimands.

Of course, a woman on the bridge is an unusual sight. Not every boatswain likes to receive orders from a captain who is wearing a skirt. At difficult moments, when a quick decision is needed, many subordinates will look at you expectantly and somewhat distrustfully. At these moments you can't show any hesitation; you've got to prove that you're a real sailor, a professional, and an expert seafarer. As soon as a seaman realizes that he is not dealing with a helpless female but with a determined, self-assured person who knows her job and has a loud voice, his respect and obedience will be guaranteed.

Of the two mates, I was the one the sailors respected and listened to. The other mate, a man, was a dandy and a weakling, and often made mistakes. He wore a flower in his lapel.

In 1931 I was sent to Hamburg to inspect a trawler we had bought. I was third mate then, in charge of the navigational section. My job was to inspect the navigational equipment.

The Germans were naturally surprised to see a woman. They kept saying that it was not for real, that it must be a poster of sorts. They kept whispering and winking at one another.

I straightened them out pretty soon, though. I inspected the equipment so thoroughly that it immediately put a stop to their whispering. I knew my job and examined every detail, forcing the German builders to break into a sweat. I looked at every little screw, checked every part.

"Don't bring this 'Mädchen'[1] with you the next time," the Germans told our captain. In 1934 I received my sea captain's certificate.

In the winter of 1935 the Commissariat of the Food Industry bought several foreign steamers. I was appointed captain of one of those ships, the *Chavycha*.

I went to Hamburg to take my command.

When the crew caught sight of me, they looked puzzled. The sailors and officers ran to get spiffed up: they shaved and put on new collars and uniforms.

When I came on board I was greeted politely, but with excessive gallantry. Many of the men were staring at me in amazement. I could hear them saying:

"She's real young!"

"She'll get seasick! Run get the lemons, guys!"

---

[1] *Mädchen*—the German for "girl."

I set to work immediately. I inspected the vessel so thoroughly that the whole crew became convinced of my skill and experience. When, on the day of our departure, I put on my uniform and came out onto the deck, the first mate rose to greet me and clicked to attention. He did this to show his respect for me and his recognition of my authority.

In each of the foreign ports on the way home I was besieged on all sides by reporters, photographers, and cameramen. The newspaper people made a complete sensation out of my voyage, covering page after page with descriptions of my appearance, my uniform, and my relationship with the crew.

I have been a sea captain ever since. My ship is on the Kamchatka line.

I have a good relationship with the crew. Discipline is good.

We have a drama group on board. I am the leader. We are quite isolated. We spend five months at a time in Kamchatka and naturally need some distraction. So we perform dances and stage plays.

You ask if we've been in dangerous situations: yes, we have. The sea doesn't like to fool around. Dangers await you at every turn. But a person can get used to anything. After a while you stop seeing anything unusual in this.

I understand that you'd like to hear some "sea stories"—with gales and thunder and high wind. But I don't have any stories like that. Nothing special has ever happened to me. Everything has been quite ordinary. No adventures. So what can I tell you?

For example, this summer we were on our way from Petropavlovsk to the western coast of Kamchatka. We didn't have any cargo. Then a storm blew up.

A ship with no cargo is very light: it bobs around like a cork. Every time the propeller comes out of the water, the ship becomes ungovernable. For four days we struggled against the winds that kept pushing us toward the coast. We'd break away for a while, and then be forced back toward the coast.

During those four days I never left the bridge. There were times when shipwreck seemed inevitable, but every time we managed to find the right maneuver and slip away.

On the fourth night the wind started pushing us toward the cliffs with incredible force. There was no way out.

We let down the life boats. Everything was ready for the crew to abandon ship, but at the very last moment the wind abated somewhat. I caught that moment and slipped out of the trap.

That's it. As you can see, it's nothing special. Or romantic.

Soon new female captains will join our ranks. I know several women who will be graduating soon.

We will travel on the high seas. We will work hard, so as to maintain the reputation of Soviet women captains.

And when the time comes, we women captains, engineers, mechanics, and scientists will fight the enemy shoulder to shoulder with the men.[2]

---

[2] Such references to the imminence of war, when women would have to take over men's jobs, became very common in *Obshchestvennitsa* toward the end of the 1930s.

29 □ KH. KHUTTONEN

Farewell to the Komsomol

□ Kh. Khuttonen, a young Leningrad worker, wrote this cri de coeur as a letter resigning her membership in the Komsomol in 1934. While the language of the letter is so inflated as to suggest the possibility of parody, an investigation by the Leningrad Komsomol (whose report is appended to Khuttonen's letter in the archival file) found that the author had been deeply hurt by a series of unhappy love affairs with Communist men (hence her disillusionment with Communism) and suffered from "neurasthenia." As a result of this investigation, Khuttonen was reinstated in the Komsomol with the recommendation that she be sent to a resort to recover her health.

TO COMRADE Golubev, Komsomol Cell Secretary:

You have asked me why I ever joined the Komsomol. I will tell you: I was full of energy and the desire to work and study. I was hungry for a vibrant and exciting life. I wanted to give all of myself to my work, to forget my individuality, to lose track of time, to live solely for the joys and worries of the collective. I thought that the Komsomol community was the one place where I could find this. From the very beginning, however, I felt disappointed.

When the time came to discuss my application, the chair asked indifferently if anyone had anything to say, and one member, who had not been paying any attention to the proceedings and was obviously still thinking about the previous application, yelled, "accept her," and I was accepted. They gave me my Komsomol card and then forgot all about my existence, and I was too shy to demand work.

I never did anything during my two years in trade school. At the factory it was no different: the same stagnation and the same rot of idleness. Uninspired by anybody or anything, I gradually lost interest and started avoiding what little work there was. I wanted to live within the Komsomol, but there was no life there, and I began to look for it outside the Komsomol.

Now I am not looking for anything and do not want anything. I have no faith, no energy, no fire. I do not know if it is my own fault that I never became a true Komsomol member. I only know that I am capable of work—good work, but not among the dead and for the dead.

Farewell, Komsomol. Farewell, hope. You will go on; you will continue to

From Tsentral'nyi gosudarstvennyi arkhiv istoriko-partiinoi dokumentatsii (TsGAIPD), f. 24, op. 2v, d. 772, ll. 23–24.

struggle for a new life, for the victory of the dictatorship of the proletariat all over the world, while I—a miserable, slimy frog—will go on croaking in my stinking pond until I go belly up.

[signed]
Kh. Khuttonen
17. VI. 1934

30 □ Anastasia Plotnikova

Autobiography

□ All Soviet citizens had to write short narrative "Autobiographies" (*Avtobiografii*) for their personnel files. This "Autobiography," written in 1936 and found in the archives of the Leningrad party committee, was probably part of Anna Mironovna Plotnikova's party dossier. Such "Autobiographies" were expected to give an account of their authors' social origins, political involvement, and activities during the revolution and civil war, indicating any blots on the record such as kulak or émigré relatives or past connections with an opposition group in the party.

AUTOBIOGRAPHY: PLOTNIKOVA, ANASTASIA MIRONOVNA, VKP(B)[1] MEMBER SINCE MAY 20, 1920, MEMBERSHIP CARD NO. 3011671

I was born in 1893 in the village of Ponizovie, Leontievskaia township, Ustiuzhensky District, Novgorod Province.

My father was a worker from the time he was twelve. My mother was a hired laborer. We were landless. My father shared a hut with his brother. Sometimes he would have a cow. As far back as I can remember, my father worked as a carpenter. For about twelve years he worked as a stevedore in Rybinsk.

In 1911 or 1910 he worked in Leningrad as a carpenter and joiner: at the former Ganskevich lumber yard in Staraia Derevnia, in the Botkin barracks, etc.

In 1917 he caught tuberculosis, and in 1918 he died in his native village.

My closest relatives were my two brothers and two sisters. Both brothers worked as carpenters from the time they were ten; my older brother, Fedor Mironovich Khorev, is currently employed at the Port of Leningrad.

My younger brother also worked in Leningrad as a carpenter. In 1917 he was a Red Army volunteer. In 1932 he died when he was accidentally electrocuted while working as a carpenter at the Red Banner Factory.

At present, one of my sisters is a kolkhoz member in our native village.

My other sister, Matrena Mironovna Astafurova, is a kolkhoz member in the village of Kakui, Tapkigsky District, West Siberian Province.

My two half-brothers on my mother's side are both carpenters. One works on a state farm in the town of Ustiuzhny, and the other one in the Erisman Hospital.

From 1904 to 1905 I worked as a maid and lived at home in the winter.

From 1906 through 1912 I worked as a field hand.

From Tsentral'nyi gosudarstvennyi arkhiv istoriko-politicheskoi dokumentatsii Sankt-Peterburga (TsGAIPD), f. 24, op. 2v, d. 1833, ll. 87–88.
[1] VKP(b)—All-Union Communist Party (Bolsheviks).

In 1913 I arrived in Leningrad, got married, and, until June–July 1916, worked in private shops: Weiss's, on former Karavannaia Street; Zubkov's, in the village of Isakovka; and Osinkin's, in the former Gostiny Dvor.

During the summer I used to work at the peat factory or at the lumber yard in Staraia Derevnia because there were no jobs in the boot-making shops in the summer.

In 1915 my husband was arrested, sent to a reserve unit in Medved township, former Novgorod Province, and then straight to the front.

In 1916 it became easier for soldiers' wives to find jobs, thanks to the "assistance" program. I was hired by the Treugolnik Factory, but got only as far as the shop floor because the foreman refused to admit me. He said that I could not be considered a soldier's wife because my husband had been arrested, not drafted, and so in August I returned to my village, where I stayed and worked as a field hand until 1917.

In 1917 my husband was brought from the front and placed in a hospital on Mir Street in Leningrad. I left my village in September and came back and went to work in Grigorev's shop, on former Simeonovskaia Street, as a women's shoemaker.

In early May 1918 my whole family left for Siberia. Our reasons were the following: my husband had scurvy and could not walk; we had two small children; and my sister, Matrena Mironovna Khoreva, had become unemployed owing to the closure of the Treugolnik Factory. Therefore we all moved to the village of Katkovo, Shcheglovsky District, Tomsk Province, joining our fellow villagers, who had moved there in 1908.

As a result of the Kolchak takeover, we did not get properly registered, but both my husband and I worked as field hands in the villages of Katkovo, Berezovo, and Kozlovo. I also worked as an unskilled laborer on the Kemerovo Railway Line.

At that time we came into contact with some miners from Kemerovo: Comrade Kornev, a member of the VKP(b); Loskutov; and others. On their instructions, we mobilized the poor peasants for the struggle against Kolchak and located firearms on the territory of the former Shcheglovsky District. My husband and I were both members of the Shevelev-Lubkov partisan unit and took part in the liquidation of the local bandits.

In 1920 my husband and I formed a sixty-person party cell in the villages of Katkovo and Berezovo.

On May 20, 1920, I was admitted to the party as a member of the Katkovo cell of the Shcheglovsky party organization, and I became the chair of the Katkovo cell as well as a volunteer women's organizer at the Torsminsky township party committee.

In 1920 we organized a commune in the village of Katkovo, where I worked (and resided permanently) and where all my family lived.

In January 1923 the Shcheglovsky district party committee sent us to Leningrad.

The Leningrad provincial party committee requested permission from the Shcheglovsky district committee to keep us in Leningrad—which permission, along with my personal file, was received, and I was officially registered in the Leningrad organization. I already had my party membership card with me.

From 1923 to 1924 I worked as a machine operator at the Petrograd District sawmill.

From 1924 to 1928 I worked at the Red Sail Factory as a women's organizer, deputy head of the cultural activities section, and party secretary.

In late 1928 I served as chair of the organizational department at the Petrograd district soviet.

From May 1930 to 1935 I worked as the secretary of the party committee of the Red Banner Factory.

Since 1935 I have been working in the Petrograd district soviet.

My husband has been a member of the VKP(b) since 1920. From the age of seventeen, when his mother died, he has been living on his own, studying and working in various boot-making shops as well as at the peat factory. In Siberia we worked together. After the defeat of Kolchak he served as the chairman of the Katkovo village soviet, chairman of the commune council, and as an official of the Workers' and Peasants' Inspectorate at the Shcheglovsky district committee of the VKP(b). In 1921–22 (for a year and a half) he was the secretary of the Torsminsky township party committee. Since our arrival in Leningrad he has spent most of his time working at various factories in the Vyborg District.

I have two sons, both Komsomol members. Both are currently serving in the Red Army.

(Signed) 22.V.1936

☐ Unfortunately for Plotnikova, her file contained not only her "Autobiography" but also "compromising materials" gathered by the Leningrad NKVD that cast doubt on Plotnikova's own version of her life, particularly her claim to poor-peasant and proletarian origins. According to these materials, Plotnikova was really the adopted daughter of a kulak and had protected dekulakized relatives. After an investigation in 1936, the Leningrad party committee recommended that Plotnikova be demoted from her senior administrative position in Leningrad but not expelled from the party. Plotnikova continued to defend her "Autobiography": in the wake of the verdict, she submitted a certificate from her home district attesting to her poor-peasant origins and stating that she had been a hired hand, not an adopted daughter, of a kulak.[2] Her subsequent fate is unknown.

[2] For a detailed analysis of this case, see Sheila Fitzpatrick, "The Two Faces of Anastasia: Narratives and Counter-Narratives of Identity in Stalinist Everyday Life," in Eric Naiman and Christina Kiaer, eds., *Everyday Subjects: Formations of Identity in Early Soviet Culture* (Ithaca, N.Y.: Cornell University Press, forthcoming).

31 □ A. V. Vlasovskaia et al.

Speeches by Stakhanovites' Wives

□ These autobiographical statements come from a meeting of wives of Stakhanovite workers with regional party leaders held in Arkhangelsk in 1936. The model was the "Obshchestvennitsa" wives' movement (see selections 28 and 35 in this volume), with the interesting difference that the Arkhangelsk women were working-class, not elite, wives. In their speeches they described how they created a supportive and "cultured" domestic environment and encouraged their husbands to increase productivity.

SPEECH BY A. V. VLASOVSKAIA
(WIFE OF A TRAIN ENGINEER FROM THE
NIANDOMA RAILROAD TERMINAL)

Comrade women, please accept heartfelt Bolshevik greetings from the Niandoma District. [*Applause*]

Please forgive me: this is the first time I've ever spoken in public, so maybe it'll come out all wrong.

KHOROSHKO: That's okay, go right on talking!

VLASOVSKAIA: Comrades, I'll just tell you a little bit about myself and my husband, and how I helped him become a Stakhanovite.

My husband has been working in transport since 1911. He started off as a fitter's apprentice and then moved up to become an engineer. Comrade women, at first my husband was a shock worker. He even has an honorary diploma for good work. But then he kind of let himself go and couldn't become a Stakhanovite for a long time. I was very upset because my husband wasn't a Stakhanovite. In a way, I felt separated from my comrades and friends. Their husbands were all Stakhanovites, and mine wasn't. I was really angry at my husband, and there were times when I would yell at him because of this. I felt hurt. I thought: "He used to be the best worker, and now he isn't making the grade. This is really terrible!"

So I started talking to him. I kept asking him why he couldn't become a Stakhanovite, and so on and so forth. My husband is very serious. He doesn't talk much. "You don't understand anything," he would say. "There's no point in talking to you."

The locomotive he'd been given was pretty bad. He got it into really good shape, though, and made a couple of trips on it, but then it was put in reserve. After that, he started riding on different locomotives again. He told me: "I'm not

From *Zhenshchina—bol'shaia sila. Severnoe kraevoe soveshchanie zhen stakhanovtsev* (Arkhangelsk, 1936), 36–94 (abridged).

a Stakhanovite because they give me a different locomotive every time, and this way you can't keep up the speed or do anything else."

On February 29 there was going to be a meeting of Stakhanovites in Niandoma. I had been invited, but I was too embarrassed to go. How could I, the wife of a non-Stakhanovite, go to the meeting? I talked it over with my husband, and we decided that I ought to go. I learned a lot of new things at that meeting, and when I got home I told my husband all about it.

Several days later my husband found out that his old locomotive had been taken off reserve. I was hoping that my husband would get it back, so that he would be able to become a Stakhanovite, but as it turned out, that locomotive was going to be given to another driver. My husband also found out about this and came home really angry. "What's the matter," I asked him, "was there an accident or something?" "No," he said, "but they've given my locomotive to another driver." That's when I really blew my top. I told him: "You have to fight for your locomotive! Go down there and demand it!" [*Applause. Voices from the audience: Right!*] "If you can't do it, I'll run down to the trade union office myself."

VL. IVANOV:[1] He wasn't able to do it himself?

VLASOVSKAIA: He ran right down there himself without even finishing his dinner.

VL. IVANOV: Did you threaten him?

VLASOVSKAIA: I wasn't trying to scare him, but I told him that if he couldn't do it, I would go over there myself and ask for it. So he dropped everything and ran over there. Some time later he came back and said, without even sitting down to eat, "Get my things together, fast. I'm going in my locomotive."

I got his things together very quickly and thought to myself: "I ought to follow him and see which locomotive he's really going to take."

KHOROSHKO: Do you know his engine?

VLASOVSKAIA: Yes, I do. I have a daughter who is a sharp little thing. I told her: "Run down there and see, dear."

VL. IVANOV: Was your daughter nervous, too?

VLASOVSKAIA: Of course she was. But she ran down there and then came back and told me: "Mama, Papa left in his own locomotive." So I started counting the hours, waiting for him to return. After a while, I began to get worried. But I was ashamed to go down and ask myself. Twenty-four hours went by, and there was still no word of him. I was afraid there might have been an accident. So I sent my daughter to find out. She found out that he had gone to the very end of the line. "That's okay," I thought. "He's got some money. He won't go hungry there." That is how my husband got his own locomotive. He started traveling to the end of the line. The first two trips didn't go very smoothly, but I was happy that he had his own locomotive now. "Well," I thought, "now he will be a Stakhanovite." He started coming home in a happy, cheerful mood, and it made me feel great. He liked everything—his work and his locomotive. After a while he started carrying

---

[1] V. I. Ivanov (1893–1938)—first secretary of the Northern Regional party organization from 1932 to 1936.

heavy loads of sixteen hundred tons or more, and saying: "I'm going to ask for even heavier loads." My daughter was also interested in her father's progress.

KHOROSHKO: Is she a big girl? Does she go to school?

VLASOVSKAIA: Yes, she's in fifth grade. She's eleven years old. She used to always run to look at the board where her father's name was. Then she would come home and say: "Papa is on a 'snail' again." But these days she comes home and says: "Papa is number one on the honor board." Yes, our daughter is also interested. I keep telling her: "Papa is going to be a Stakhanovite, and you should also study like a Stakhanovite . . ."

KHOROSHKO: Did Papa buy a present for his daughter?

VLASOVSKAIA: Yes, he promised to. He made 980 rubles and promised to buy her a bicycle. Last month he made 600 rubles, and before that he was making between 300 and 400 rubles. When he finally made 980 rubles, he set 300 aside to buy a bicycle for our daughter—it's just that we don't know where to get it yet.

VOICE FROM THE PRESIDIUM: Do you keep the apartment clean? Can your husband relax there?

VLASOVSKAIA: The apartment is no problem at all. My husband is not at home very often, but when he does come back, I have everything ready. Before, he used to help me around the house—bring the firewood and things like that. But now it's all ready for him. When he gets home at night, I put the samovar on. Sometimes he says: "Oh, that's okay, don't worry about it." But I still cook for him, wait on him, and talk to him for a couple hours before his train leaves. I can rest when he's gone.

Our dinners are always good. We eat well. There are only three of us, but we have a little house of our own, a cow, some chickens, and some geese. Everything is in order. My husband doesn't have to worry or get upset about household chores—his work is the only thing he knows. When the locomotive is resting, he gets to rest, too—in a special room, where he can read and study. And when they're cleaning the locomotive, I tell my husband: "Go down there yourself. Don't trust anybody. Check every little screw, so they don't let you down." So he goes at night to watch the cleaning. This, Comrade Women, is how I helped my husband become a Stakhanovite.

VOICE FROM THE PRESIDIUM: You helped him all right, and you did a good job of it, too.

VLASOVSKAIA: I create all the right conditions at home, so he doesn't need to worry about anything.

Now I'll tell you about myself. I'm involved in volunteer work. Our women's brigade checks over the locomotives. Once I had to take part in the cleaning of my husband's locomotive. Did I ever try! I worked so hard my hands bled. I told my husband that I would always check to see if his locomotive was all right. So I used to go there as if to see my husband, but actually to see the locomotive—to make sure it was all right. That's all I have to say.

VOICE FROM THE PRESIDIUM: You said it well. [*Applause*]

VLASOVSKAIA: Comrade Women whose husbands are still lagging behind: I am asking you to help your husbands become Stakhanovites. [*Applause*]

SPEECH BY A. M. POLIAKOVA
(WIFE OF A BLACKSMITH FROM TIMBER MILL #25)

Let me tell you about myself. After the National Conference of Stakhanovites I set the following task for myself: to work so that my husband would become a Stakhanovite. He was a shock worker, but he wasn't a Stakhanovite. I applied myself to this task and did my very best until I finally succeeded—my husband received the honorary title of Stakhanovite. It must be said that a wife plays a very important role in her husband's success at work.

KHOROSHKO: She is a great force!

POLIAKOVA: Right. For example, if a husband comes home and his wife doesn't pay any attention to him—

VL. IVANOV: Are there such wives?

POLIAKOVA: Yes, very often. If a wife doesn't pay any attention to her husband, if she isn't nice to him—he gets upset.

Before the Stakhanovite movement began, I was working in an office and doing a lot of volunteer work. My husband used to come home for dinner only. I would always gave him a good dinner, of course, but the general conditions just weren't the same as the ones I've created for him now. That was my mistake. Other women make the same kind of mistake. Meanwhile, everybody knows that if a husband has a fight with his wife or if their apartment is always dirty, he will probably be thinking while he's at work: "At home my wife nags me all the time and the apartment is always dirty. It's dirty here, too—even my overalls are dirty." Now if a wife welcomes her husband home with love and tenderness, if she respects him and talks to him, then the husband will go back to work in a good mood and think only about his work. It is obvious that in this case his labor productivity will increase. I repeat that our husbands' labor productivity greatly depends on how we treat them and on whether we are their friends and helpers.

Now I work in production and also take care of my husband. In my free time I try to do all I can for him. My husband didn't have a lot of education—he taught himself how to read. He used to read only newspapers, and even then with great difficulty. He never read books—not only did he not read them himself, but he did not even like to listen to other people reading. Every time I tried reading out loud to him, he would say: "Leave me alone. I'd rather go to bed." However, I wanted him to be a cultured person. I didn't want him to lag behind other men.

STROGANOV:[2] Right!

POLIAKOVA: I began to look for books that would interest him. After learning that he was interested in war stories, I got the book *How the Steel Was Tempered*[3]

---

[2] A. Stroganov (1888–1941)—chairman of the Executive Committee of Soviets of the Northern Region at the time.

[3] *How the Steel was Tempered*—1932 autobiographical novel by N. A. Ostrovsky that became a canonical text of socialist-realist literature.

and read it out loud to him. I read slowly and with feeling, rather than rushing through the whole thing without stopping, the way some people do. I discussed it with him bit by bit. We would talk and argue. Afterward my husband told me: "You're right, a book is a good thing. Bring me another one."

I got in touch with the district library and, with the help of the director of the library, Comrade Lobanova, I began selecting books for him. Lobanova still sends us books—I just need to tell her which ones we want. First I read every book myself—I read fast—then I read it to my husband, and afterward we discuss it. Sometimes our daughter reads to us. Now my husband always listens attentively. I've trained him to the point where he brings home books himself and always asks me which ones are the most interesting. I give him my advice: this one is interesting, that one . . . In this way, he read *Virgin Soil Upturned* by Sholokhov,[4] *Without Catching a Breath*,[5] and so on. Now we are reading works by Vera Figner.[6]

We go to the theater and to the movies quite often—we almost never miss a show. To tell you the truth, in the beginning he used to sleep in the theater. It was the same at the movies—he would sit there watching for a while and then fall asleep. I started warning him: "If you're sleepy, then you'd better sleep at home beforehand because I'm not going to let you go to sleep there." After the movies I started asking him, "Well, what did you see? Did you see this or that?" I would make things up, and if he said there had been no such thing in the movie, I would know he had been paying attention. [*Applause*]

Speech by A. N. Zinovieva
(wife of a carpenter from Sulfatstroi)

Let me tell you about my life. I was born in 1905. I didn't see much of the old regime, of course, but I had to work for the kulaks, too. We were badly off. When my father died, I was ten years old and the oldest child. There were six of us—five children and my mother. So I had to work for other people.

How did I work? During the day I looked after the children, and at night I weeded the garden and fetched hay for the animals. Early in the morning I had to be back at work. Once, by accident, I dropped a bucket into the well. The master grabbed me by the feet and held me head first over the well. "You're going to have to go down in there after it," he said—but then, for some reason, didn't let go. Three years later my mother sent me to work for some other people. They were very rich. I started baby-sitting again, and doing the wash. I was thirteen at the time.

---

[4] *Virgin Soil Upturned*—novel by M. A. Sholokhov that became the canonical socialist-realist representation of collectivization.

[5] *Without Catching a Breath*—1935 novel by I. E. Ehrenburg (1891–1967) on the changes in Soviet society resulting from industrialization.

[6] Vera Figner (1852–1947)—prominent leader of revolutionary terrorists in the 1870s and 1880s; author of popular memoirs.

Once they heated up the bathhouse for Easter. While the mistress was taking her bath, I stayed with the children. At midnight she let me into the bathhouse but didn't give me the kerosene lamp: "You haven't earned any kerosene," she said. I was too scared to go into the bathhouse without a light. Instead, I stayed outside and rubbed my face with snow—so it would look hot—and then went back into the house. On Easter Sunday the mistress made me mend the children's stockings. While I was sitting there crying with anger, I somehow lost the needle. When the mistress found out about it, she started beating me, saying: "That needle wasn't made in Russia. It was brought from overseas. Go find it!" I put on my coat and ran home to my mother. I told her: "Give me a needle. My mistress is beating me because I've lost her needle." When I turned eighteen, I got married. This is where I finish the story of my old life and begin the story of my new life.

When I married, life became good. My husband respected me, and I loved and respected him, too. But life was hard, and my husband had to go off to a remote area. In 1931 I had to come here, to the Molotov Factory. Although bread was rationed, I liked factory life. My husband became a shock worker. It's been four years since he became a brigade leader and a shock worker. In all this time he's never made less than four hundred or five hundred rubles a month. And when the Stakhanovite movement began, he started making seven hundred to eight hundred rubles. Now we live well and have decent clothes to wear. In his five years at the factory he has received eleven prizes. This year we spent one thousand rubles on coats alone—for us and for the children.

I do a bit of volunteer work—I check the consumer goods that we get for the workers. Now they've given me another job: as the wife of a Stakhanovite, I'm supposed to help the wives of non-Stakhanovites. The wives of non-Stakhanovites often come to me to borrow money. Once the wife of a worker came to me to ask for money. "I'm not going to give you any money," I said. "Make your husband work like a Stakhanovite, and you won't ever need to borrow money." She went home and had a fight with her husband. After a while her husband started making a lot of money. Some time later she came by and thanked me for the good advice, saying: "We live well now. We have lots of money."

IVANOV: Good for you! [*Applause*]

ZINOVIEVA: I have two daughters in high school. One is an A-student, and the other, a B-student. I dress them neatly. I received a prize from the school for doing such a good job raising them and for keeping their room clean and cozy.

KHOROSHKO: Do they have a room of their own?

ZINOVIEVA: Yes, and separate beds, too.

VL. IVANOV: Do they brush their teeth?

ZINOVIEVA: They brush their teeth. They have their own towels, skates, and skis—they have everything.

VL. IVANOV: Do they live better than you used to live?

ZINOVIEVA: You bet—nobody ever humiliates them or beats them up.

Speech by M. I. Nesgorova
(wife of a VTsIK[7] member,
a foreman at the Molotov Timber Mill)

Greetings to the wives of Stakhanovites, our best people. [*Applause*] My husband and I got married when he was seventeen and I was nineteen. His parents had died, leaving four children. He had to get married. A year later I had a baby girl, so we had five children.

Then my husband was drafted into the Red Army. My life was hard. My children were often sick, but my parents used to help me out. Eighteen years have passed since then. I have only two children left.

[*Vl. Ivanov appears in the presidium. The delegates rise and greet him with tumultuous applause.*]

I used to worry a lot.

They took my children to an orphanage, but when my husband came back from the Red Army, we got them back. My husband went to work at Factory No. 23. I wanted to go with him, but he said: "Let me go live there by myself first—so I can get used to it." Later he was transferred to Permilovsky Factory, where he lived for six years. Meanwhile, I stayed in the village all by myself.

I managed all right around the house: I had one cow and a horse. At that time, my husband was living in a dormitory, and I heard rumors that he had started drinking. I didn't like that, so I went to see him. After I got there, we lived in a laundry room for a while. Then we, along with two other families, got transferred to a one-room apartment. Those were hard times.

After I arrived, he started behaving himself. Other people even started saying: now that Nesgorova is here, her husband is finally behaving himself. I've always protected him from bad influences. He managed to pull himself together and start working better. There are women here who were living with me at the time—they know I'm telling the truth.

Gradually he began to move up. He started working as a sorter, then they moved him to trimming, and, finally, he became a shift foreman. He received a lot of prizes for good work. He became a shock worker and received an honorary diploma.

Then one day they changed managers. My husband didn't like the new manager, and he said: "I'm going to move to another factory." So one day I came home from the cafeteria and saw that he was already packing. I asked him: "What's the matter?" and he answered: "We're moving to another factory."

So we arrived at the Molotov Factory. They made him a shift foreman there. Things got better, although we lived in a small apartment at first. Now we have two rooms and a kitchen. My husband makes 1,250 rubles a month and receives prizes. His shift is in first place now. I helped my husband become a Stakhanovite,

---

[7] VTsIK—All-Russian Central Executive Committee, the legislature of the RSFSR between 1918 and 1936.

and now he's become a model worker. He is a VTsIK member now, and that makes me extremely happy. We both go to school, and so do our children. I go to literacy classes and to a sewing circle.

When the production figures are good, my husband comes home in a good mood. I know right away that everything is okay. If something is going wrong, that shows, too. I ask him: "What's wrong?" and he tells me what it is, and we discuss it. I cook his dinner on time, and try to let him rest. If you greet him calmly and say good-bye calmly, he is also calm, and then he works better.

Now we are preparing for May 1, and our whole family is going to go to the demonstration.

Long live our dear Comrade Stalin! [*Applause*]

32 □ INNA SHIKHEEVA-GAISTER

A Family Chronicle

□ Inna Aronovna Shikheeva-Gaister tape-recorded her "family chronicle" for her daughters and grandchildren in 1988–90. The text was
transcribed and published by her husband, V. N. Shikheev. A complete English translation is currently in preparation.

THE HOUSE OF GOVERNMENT: I lived there for six years. It is located on Serafimovich Street, between the Bolshoi Kamenny and Maly Kamenny bridges, not
far from the Kremlin. It was built in 1931. A long time ago it used to be the site
of the Royal Gardens; then Peter had the *streltsy* hanged there; and later Catherine
had Pugachev drawn and quartered there.[1] Nowadays this house is mostly known
as the "House on the Embankment." It has also been called the "House of Pretrial
Detention" and the "House of the Dead."

I was not born there, however. I was born in a dormitory at the Institute of Red
Professors. I was my mother's third baby. The two previous ones had died at
birth. Everyone was anxiously awaiting my arrival. As if that were not enough,
my father had just recovered from a severe case of consumption. Nobody thought
he was going to survive. Those were hard times. There was not enough food. It
was a difficult pregnancy, and my mother was completely emaciated. My father
did all he could to make sure things went well this time. He even managed to
secure the services of the famous Moscow doctor, Professor Arkhangelsky.

Finally I was born—a big baby with lots of hair. I weighed five kilograms.[2] It
was August 30, 1925. Where was I born? No, not in any hospital, but right there
in the dorm. Later they put the Foreign Relations Institute in that building—the
one by the Krymsky Bridge. My father had just graduated from the Institute of
Red Professors and been hired there as an instructor.[3] My mother was a student
in the rabfak of the Plekhanov Institute.[4]

Two weeks after I was born someone found us a maid, Natasha Ovchinnikova.
She and my parents agreed on the terms, and then she went back to her village to
finish up some things. Two weeks later, when my mother went back to school,

From Inna Shikheeva-Gaister *Semeinaia khronika vremen kul'ta lichnosti, 1925–1953 gg.* (Moscow: N'iudiamed-AO, 1998), 5–55 (abridged).

[1] *Streltsy* (musketeers)—regular infantry regiments in Muscovite Russia. In 1698 several Moscow
streltsy units staged an unsuccessful rebellion against Peter I (the Great). More than a thousand streltsy
were executed, and their bodies were exposed to the public. E. I. Pugachev was the leader of a large
rebellion against Catherine II's rule.

[2] 5 kilograms = 11 pounds.

[3] The Institute of Red Professors was founded in Moscow in 1921 to train Communist scholars,
lecturers, and party and government officials.

[4] The G. V. Plekhanov Institute of Economics, founded in 1906 as the Superior Commercial
Courses.

Natasha moved in and started working. She was twenty-six years old. I do not know what would have happened to me if it had not been for her. After my mother and father, she was the person closest to me. She shared all my losses and all my joys. She raised not only me but also my daughters, and lived to see my grandchildren, who became her great grandchildren. She died in my arms in my home at the age of eighty-seven.

My father and mother met in Gomel. My mother came for a provincial conference of textile workers in 1919, when my father was working there as the editor of *Polesskaia Pravda*. The following year my father moved to Moscow and enrolled in the history department of the Institute of Red Professors. He also started working at the *Trud* newspaper.[5] My mother got a job in the central committee of the textile workers' union. That's when they started living together.

UNTIL my little sister Natalka was born, I used to spend summers with my kindergarten at camps in Akulovka and Zvenigorod. Natalka was sick a lot, so after she was born we started renting a dacha. We spent the summer of 1932 at a dacha in Kraskovo. My father was already working at Gosplan as Kuibyshev's deputy for agriculture.[6] Kuibyshev had been given a state dacha in Kraskovo, so my father rented a dacha nearby so he could go over there to work. He sometimes took me with him.

In the fall we moved straight from the dacha to the famous House of Government, which had been built especially for the upper echelons of the party and state leadership. We were given an apartment on the ninth floor, in Entryway No. 8, Apartment No. 162. It had four rooms, two of them quite small. One of these, around six to eight square meters in size, was mine. It had a bed with a bedstand and a desk. There was no room for a bookcase. The other small room—around twelve square meters—was my parents' bedroom. Natalka's bed was also in there. The large rooms served as my father's study and the dining room. Natasha's bed was in the kitchen. That's where she lived. We never ate in the kitchen—that's what the dining room was for—except for my lunch, which Natasha used to serve to me there after I got home from school.

My father managed to keep one of the rooms in our old apartment on Palikha Street for his parents: the one on the sunny side, where Natalka and I used to sleep. At that time Grandpa Srul and Grandma Sofia were occupying a corner in a communal apartment somewhere on Sadovo-Triumfalnaia. My father's youngest brother Izia was still living with them then. He was eighteen years old. All three of them moved to Palikha.

My father had brought them to Moscow from Elizavetgrad some time in the 1920s. He had been born not far from there, in a shtetl called Zlatopol, in 1899. My grandfather had been an artisan, a leather cutter. As he used to say proudly, a "leather cutter of the ninth rank." I do not think there really was such a category, but that is what he called it. It was a large family. Besides my father and Izia, there

---

[5] *Trud*—newspaper of the Soviet Trade Union Federation.
[6] V. V. Kuibyshev (1888–1935)—member of the Central Committee's Politburo (1927–35), deputy chairman of the Council of People's Commissars (1930–35), chairman of Gosplan (1930–34).

were two more sons, Siunia and Yura, and two daughters, Fania and Batia. Six children altogether. They were poor, but my father, as the eldest, had been given an education. He had gone to a trade school because it was easier for a Jew to get admitted there. After graduating he had left for Petrograd. At the time of the October Revolution he was a second-year law student at the Iuriev (Tartu) University. My father quit school and plunged into revolutionary activity. In 1919 he joined the party.

My father's brother, Siunia, with his wife, Faina Saulovna, and son, Igor, moved into the House of Government at the same time we did. Igor was exactly two months older than I was. Siunia was in charge of the freight section in Kaganovich's[7] Transportation Commissariat.

In the fall of 1933 I was to start school. The question was, which school? There were several schools nearby. One of them was on Ostozhenka, which meant that you had to cross the Moscow River on the Bolshoi Kamenny Bridge to get there. This was the famous Moscow Exemplary School—the one Anatoly Rybakov describes in his novel *Children of the Arbat*. It was considered the best in Moscow and was extremely difficult to get into. All the well-placed parents tried to send their children there. From among my friends and neighbors in the house, Marina Miliutina, Svetlana Tukhachevskaia, and Alina, Svetlana, Oksana, and Timur Broido[8] all went there.

My parents said they did not need such a prestigious school and that I would go to School No. 19. It was nearby and would be easier for Natasha to take me to. It was located on the Sofiiskaia Embankment, right across from the Kremlin. All you had to do was to cross the streetcar track by the Bolshoi Kamenny Bridge. It was considered the worst in the area, but it turned out to be the best in the world!

Before the revolution our school had been a gymnasium. It had large classrooms and large recess halls, two on each floor. There was also an assembly hall. In the middle of our class's hall was an enormous aquarium and two palm trees. We were supposed to march around them during recess. Most of the children came from three neighboring houses: our House of Government, the huge house No. 26 on the Sofiiskaia Embankment—also known as 4 Faleevsky Alley, and house No. 34 on the Sofiiskaia Embankment (the one next to the belfry), which was a dorm for army officers and their families. Since we all lived close to the school, we could stay there until late in the evening. Even those who used to run home for lunch would come back in the afternoon. There were a lot of afterschool classes and all sorts of special events. It was interesting to be in school, and I was absolutely devoted to it. I remember how once, when I was in third grade

---

[7] L. M. Kaganovich (1893–1991)—member of the Central Committee's Politburo (1930–57), deputy chairman of the Council of People's Commissars (1938–57), people's commissar of transport (1935–19, 1938–42, 1943–44).

[8] Daughters of high-ranking party officials V. P. Miliutin (1884–1937), head of the State Statistical Administration (1928–34) and chairman of the Committee for Scholars of the Soviet Parliament (1934–37); M. I. Tukhachevsky (1893–1937), civil war hero, deputy commissar of defense (1931–37); and G. I. Broido (1885–1956), first secretary of the Communist Party of Tajikistan (1934–35), deputy commissar of enlightenment of the RSFSR (1934–41), and director of several publishing houses. Miliutin and Tukhachevsky were executed; Broido spent fourteen years in camps and in exile.

and we were putting our class newspaper together, Natasha, absolutely furious, burst in screaming at our teacher, Galina Vladimirovna, "How dare you keep children without any lunch until five o'clock!" and then grabbed me and dragged me home. I had to apologize for her the next day.

The school was not the only place that kept me busy. There was a children's club in our house. In those days such clubs were called "outposts." I took drama there, and later dance. My mother wanted me to lose weight. I can only imagine what I looked like in that dance class! But that was not enough to satisfy my mother, so she arranged for me to take dance in the Tukhachevskys' apartment as well. Svetlana Tukhachevskaia's mother had started a private class there. It was sheer torture for me, but I always went dutifully nonetheless. It had no effect on my weight, however. Then finally, what Jewish family can exist without its own musical prodigy? So, prompted by our neighbor, Zina, my mother decided I should be taught music. She must have been thinking about her own father, who had played the trumpet while he was in the army, except that I was to take up the piano. Zina was teaching at the Gnesin Music College. With her help, my mother bought a very good piano. Then Zina said that if we were going to do this, we might as well get the best teacher around. So we got Abrasha Diakov himself! He had graduated from the Conservatory with distinction and was a very well-known performer at that time. I remember how I used to run away from Abrasha and hide in our courtyard. Natasha would look for me everywhere, but my friends would warn me: "She's coming, she's coming," so she could not always find me. Finally, Natasha got tired of this and announced to my mother that she was not going to go searching for me anymore: let the "mistress" do it herself. Whenever Natasha was angry, she would always call my mother the "mistress." She had quite a temper. The upshot of it all was that my mother ended up apologizing profusely to Diakov and canceling the remaining classes. That was the end of my musical education. They also taught me one foreign language (German).

I used to read a lot—at home, in school, anywhere I could. I read voraciously and indiscriminately: Turgenev, Gogol, Pushkin, Balzac, Zola, Pushkin's prose (but not his poetry). I read not only the classics, however, but all kinds of trash as well. I remember one Soviet novel about boxers that was terribly popular in our class. It was complete rubbish, but we could not wait to get our hands on it. We all loved to read.

Whenever my father had a Sunday off, he would say, "Let's go to the Tretiakov"—or the Fine Arts Museum.[9] They were both close to our house. But generally my father had little to do with my education. He understood, of course, that our education required some effort on his part, but he was simply too busy. By the time he got home from work, I would usually be fast asleep. After all, our leader and teacher suffered from insomnia, so everybody had to work at night. This meant that our education was in my mother's hands. It was her job. She knew all about my school life.

---

[9] Tretiakov—Moscow museum of Russian art; Pushkin Fine Arts Museum—Moscow museum of Western European art.

My parents and I used to go to the theater, too, but very rarely. My father had a pass to the royal box at the Bolshoi.[10] I remember going there with him to see *The Little Humpbacked Horse*.[11] It was a personal pass, so my mother could not use it. Sometimes it was Natasha Kerzhentseva who would take me to the theater. Her father was the head of the Committee for the Arts, so she could go to the theater any time she wanted. Very often she would take me with her.[12]

But mostly we went to the movies. There were two movie theaters next to the House of Government: the *Shock Worker* and the *Children's*. We never missed a movie and used to see many of them several times—*Chapaev*,[13] for example. In those days there were not many new movies coming out: no more than one a month.

I never had any problem finding money for the tickets. Natasha always gave me enough. Natasha had all the money. My mother used to give it to her, and then she would run the household. But of course I never went to the movies with Natasha. I used to go with the girls from our courtyard: Svetlana Khalatova, Tania Samsonova, Marisha Usievich, Ramsa Filler.[14] There were three separate courtyards in our house where we used to play—there and by a little church behind the house. It was a pretty little church but, like all other churches at the time, it was no longer a working one.

Next to the little church was an alley leading to the houses where the workers from the Red October Candy Factory lived. They were two-story buildings, with lots of tiny rooms overflowing with people—real slums. The contrast between those houses and ours was striking. I noticed it, of course, but never thought much about it. I was only ten, after all. In one such tiny room lived the family of my classmate and friend, Toma Kuzina. I visited her often, but much more often she would visit me. Natasha singled her out among my friends and always made sure she got enough to eat. Natasha's sister Masha and her family lived fairly close by—next to the dam where the Moscow River forks. They had moved from their village to Moscow some time in the twenties, most likely to escape collectivization. According to Natasha, they had had a prosperous farm back home. Aunt Masha's husband was a guard at the dam. He used to drink a lot. Aunt Masha did not work outside the home. They had a large family: two grown sons, the eldest daughter with her family, and two more daughters, one of whom was my age. Aunt Masha and her daughters used to come over quite often to visit Natasha, and sometimes I would run over to their place. They were not so badly off—they had two rooms, I think. Generally the girls from the House of Government and

[10] Bolshoi—opera and ballet theater in Moscow.

[11] A popular Russian children's story (1834) by P. P. Ershov.

[12] P. M. Kerzhentsev (1882–1940)—high-ranking party and government official, chairman of the Central Committee's Committee for the Arts (1936–38).

[13] *Chapaev*—popular Soviet film (1934) about a civil war hero.

[14] Daughters of Artemy Bagratovich Khalatov (1896–1938), chairman of the State Publishing House (1927–32), executed during the Great Terror; T. P. Samsonov (1888–1955), head of the Central Committee's Housekeeping Department (1929–34); Elena Feliksovna Usievich (1893–1968), well-known Soviet literary critic (daughter of the prominent Old Bolshevik Feliks Kon and the wife of the Bolshevik revolutionary hero G. A. Usievich); and S. I. Filler (1882–1952), member of the party's Central Control Commission.

from the tenement buildings got along just fine, but the boys often ganged up on each other.

Whenever my parents went on vacation, they would take me with them. In the summers we always went to the south. At first we went to the Crimea. We used to live in a resort in Foros where my father and I would catch crabs. For some reason, I can remember an important military man named Kulik and his young wife. At that time it was fashionable for high officials to leave their wives for young secretaries. There were lots of these secretary-wives in the House of Government. Later we went to Kislovodsk, where I ruined my parents' vacation by coming down with an attack of appendicitis. I spent two weeks in bed, and then, after another attack the following winter, had an operation. When my parents got some time off in the winter, they would go somewhere outside Moscow—usually to a resort in Astafievo, Viazemsky's old estate. I enjoyed accompanying my parents, and I still love to travel.

In 1935 we started spending our summers at a dacha in Nikolina Gora. Some time in the late twenties O. Iu. Shmidt[15] had selected this place for the construction of summer homes for scholars and artists. The settlement was located in a beautiful pine forest, on a high hill above a bend in the Moscow River. It was a magnificent place, one of the finest in the Moscow area. To get there you had to take a train to Perkhushkovo and then try to get a ride. Or you could go by car straight from Moscow.

By that time my father already had a car assigned to him personally. In 1935 he had become the deputy commissar of agriculture of the USSR and vice president of the Agricultural Academy. He had joined the dacha cooperative in 1932 but was not able to buy a dacha until 1934. Our plot was right above the river, on a high bank. The dacha itself was a large two-storied house, which my mother's brother, Veniamin, not without jealousy, used to call the "villa." It really was a villa. It had three large rooms upstairs and three downstairs. They were always full. Some of my parents' numerous relatives—mostly my cousins—were always staying there. On weekends my mother's and father's friends would come from Moscow. Our neighbors from the nearby dachas used to come over, too. We often saw the poet Bezymensky,[16] who was a good friend of my father's. I had my own friends from the nearby dachas. We used to spend most of our time on the Moscow River. My father had built a stairway from our dacha down to the river, to make it easier for my grandmother to get down to the water. It was a winding stairway and had at least a hundred steps—the slope was so steep. It was still being called the Gaister Stairway long after we left. In front of each dacha was a little wooden pier for swimming. The water around our pier was very deep, so I was only allowed to swim there with my father. My friends and I liked spending time on the pier below the Kerzhentsev dacha. The water there was shallow and good for swimming.

[15] O. Iu. Shmidt (1891–1956)—Soviet mathematician, astronomer, and Arctic explorer, member of the Soviet Academy of Sciences, editor of the *Great Soviet Encyclopedia* (1924–41), professor at Moscow State University (1923–56).

[16] A. I. Bezymensky (1898–1973)—Soviet poet, mostly known as the poet laureate of the Komsomol.

In the summer of 1936 my father decided to transfer me to the Moscow Exemplary School. I do not know what his motives were, but that was his decision. I loved my School No. 19 and kept saying no, but my father insisted, so on September 1, I went off, sobbing, to the wretched "Exemplary." I hated it right away, but what really made up my mind for me was an unpleasant little episode that took place on the stairs when I stopped to pull up one of my stockings. A huge woman—I think it must have been Sveta Kaminskaia's mother[17] from our house—came up to me and said in a very loud voice (and this shows how bright she was): "Young lady, your stocking should be adjusted in the bathroom, not on the stairs." That was the last straw. I sat through all the classes that day, but I do not even remember where the classroom was or how it looked, or what the kids were like. I only remember that I sat next to my friend Sveta Broido. The next morning I said that I could not go to school because my legs were hurting. We had just arrived from the dacha, and my knees were all covered with scratches and bruises. My father had already left for work, and my mother, who immediately understood what was up, allowed me to stay at home.

My parents were planning to leave for Kislovodsk in two days with baby Valiushka, Natalka, and Natasha. Valiushka was my new sister. Natasha had informed me of her expected arrival back in the winter.

"We're going to have a new baby soon," she said.

"How do you know?"

"I just know."

"But how? My mother doesn't have a big stomach. Where is the new baby going to come from?"

"I'm telling you, we're going to have a baby soon!"

Valiushka was born on May 27, 1936. The tradition of giving birth at home had had to be broken: Professor Arkhangelsky had grown too old, so my mother had had Valiushka at the hospital. Anyway, on September 1 they were to leave for Kislovodsk. Some friend of my father's was going off to the coast and had left him his house in Kislovodsk. In their absence I was to live with my grandparents. So I went with my grandparents to the railway station to say good-bye. At the railway station I began throwing a fit: "I am not going to go to that new school anymore!" The train was about to leave, but I continued to sob: "I am never, ever going to go to that school again!" My mother, who was already inside, just nodded helplessly and said: "Okay, Sweetie, just go to whatever school you want." But my father, who was standing behind her, said: "You will do as I say. You are going to stay at the new school!" I spent a week sitting around and thinking about what to do. In the end I went back to No. 19—the one I loved.

My mother and father had many friends and acquaintances. We used to have lots of people over when we were living on Palikha. After we moved to the House of Government we had even more. Natasha was forever grumbling that she never knew how many people to expect for dinner: two or ten. There was always some-

---

[17] The wife of G. N. Kaminsky (1895–1938), the people's commissar of health, executed during the Great Terror.

body: Mikhail and Zina Mikhailov, a very nice colleague of my father's by the name of Boris Troitsky, or my mother's dearest friend, Natasha Kuznetsova. Her son, Garik, and I were great friends, too. There were many more, but in those days grown-ups did not interest me very much, so I do not remember them all. Kuibyshev used to come over, too. My father loved and respected him very much. And this wasn't just because he was my father's boss. My sister Valiushka was born after Kuibyshev's death, and her real name was Valeria—after Valerian Vladimirovich Kuibyshev. I remember being very sleepy when my father first introduced me to him. My parents' brothers and sisters with their husbands and wives and all my countless cousins were permanent guests as well. Uncle Veniamin even had his wedding at our place. My father also brought new friends home after each business trip.

It was Natasha who suffered most from all this. Every once in a while she would lose her patience and complain to my mother. Once, when I was ten years old, she walked out on us, saying "I can't stand this anymore. There are people coming and going at all hours. I never know how many mouths I have to feed or how many people I need to put up for the night. And why did the master go to the store himself to buy sausages?"

The problem was that the master loved going to the store to buy soy sausages, or soy candy, or some other novelty that nobody would ever eat. He would bring these sausages home and say: "In China they eat nothing but soy products." My father loved buying things like that.

"He was spying on me!"

"Oh come on, Natasha, you know what he's like," my mother would plead. Natasha liked my father and had a lot of respect for him, but my mother's attempts to defend him would get Natasha even more worked up. In such cases it was useless to argue with her. She had quite a temper:

"I don't know; I just can't take it anymore. That Natasha Kuznetsova of yours, for example, never eats a single meal at home—and why should she, when she gets full board here. I've simply had it. I'm going to go work for the Alksnis. They have only one child, and just look at this place! The mistress leaves early in the morning without a care for her children, and the master is never around before 3:00 A.M. I have to do everything around here, everything! That's it, I'm going to the Alksnis."

So she left us for General Alksnis, the head of aviation.[18] One month later, however, Natasha was back. She, not my mother, was the head of our household. Probably the most important thing, though, was that we were more Natasha's children than my mother's. I was just two weeks old when she came to work for us.

At this point I would like to mention one very special family. When my father was in Odessa in 1918 doing underground work, he had hidden out at the house of a certain Miron Ilich Lopshits, who taught calligraphy in a Jewish orphanage.

---

[18] Ia. I. Alksnis (1897–1938)—commander of Soviet aviation (1931–37), executed during the Great Terror.

It was a large and very close-knit family. The children went on to become teachers, doctors, and musicians—a typical intelligentsia family. They were not revolutionaries, but they must have been sympathizers since they agreed to hide my father in their house. While he was there, my father had become great friends with the Lopshits kids who were around his age: Ida, Sarra, and Abram. According to the family legend, my father and Sarra had just started courting when my father suddenly disappeared. The party probably had sent him somewhere else. They resumed their friendship in the early twenties, when Ida, Sarra, and Abram arrived in Moscow. By then, they all had their own families. Sarra was married to Nikolai Aleksandrovich Shikheev. He was a turner at the Moscow Automobile Plant, and Sarra worked as a dentist at the factory polyclinic. They had a son who was half a year older than I was: Volodia, my future husband. I do not remember him as a boy, nor does he remember me. I guess we didn't find each other very interesting. All I remember is that during one of their visits to our house he broke my favorite doll. We did not meet again until 1953. In the late 1920s and early 1930s, however, our parents saw a lot of each other. I remember, we used to celebrate May Day at Ida's. But by the mid-1930s our friendship had begun to fade. First, the Shikheevs stopped coming over. Nikolai Aleksandrovich did not approve of my father's eager acceptance of Stalin's little gifts, such as the beautiful apartment in the House of Government, the dacha, or the car that my mother did not mind using herself. Nikolai Aleksandrovich was a steadfast Stalinist, an unwavering enthusiast of the five-year plans, the destruction of the monasteries, and the struggle against the enemies of the people. He was a wonderful person, however, forthright and honest to a fault. For example, he always refused to accept the so-called money envelope—the party salary bonus. In the mid-1930s he also had a service car, but my mother-in-law could not remember ever getting a single ride in it. They lived right next to the plant, in a one-story barracklike building with about 150 rooms opening onto an interminable corridor and several communal kitchens—for twenty families each. The building itself was made of stone and had high ceilings (it used to be a tannery), but there were no amenities inside, so in all weather people had to run a hundred meters to a wooden outhouse. In the early 1930s the plant manager, Likhachev, ordered the construction of several dozen five-storied buildings and offered Nikolai Aleksandrovich a nice apartment in one of them. At the time Nikolai Aleksandrovich was a member of the plant's party committee and the editor of the plant's newspaper with the catchy title *Catch Up and Overtake*.[19] Nikolai Aleksandrovich refused to move, telling Likhachev that he would not be able to look his old neighbors in the eye since more than half of them were living two or three families to a room. He died in that house in late 1954. When he died, the whole population of the house came out to say farewell. Five years after his death, the plant gave Sarra two rooms in a communal apartment. Volodia and I and our two daughters were living with her at the time.

[19] "Catch Up and Overtake"—official slogan of the 1930s urging Soviet people to work toward overtaking the West in industrial production.

In any case, the friendship between my father and Nikolai Aleksandrovich began to disintegrate after we moved to the House of Government. They were both orthodox Communists, but their views differed on party benefits. Here, I must defend my father from Nikolai Aleksandrovich's reproaches. My father did accept those benefits, but he did not work in order to receive them. For example, our apartment in the House of Government did not contain any fancy furniture. All the pieces, except perhaps the bookshelves, had brass tags with inventory numbers on them. They all belonged to the state, not to us, and they were all quite ordinary. There were probably only two objects of any value in our apartment: the concert piano that my mother had bought for me and the refrigerator that Aunt Lipa's husband had brought from America. So there was no cult of things in our household.

As for Abram, he stopped seeing my father around 1936. Abram's best friend, Osia Roitershtein, had been arrested, and Abram came to my father asking him to intercede on Osia's behalf. My father refused to help. I think he was moved not simply by fear but also by the realization of just how hopeless such attempts were.

Meanwhile, around 1936–37, the atmosphere became quite tense. There was the trial of the "Anti-Soviet Left-Trotskyite Alliance" and the trial of the "Parallel Anti-Soviet Trotskyite Alliance." Kamenev, Zinoviev, Piatakov, and Sokolnikov were shot. I remember paying attention to these things. I was already eleven years old, but I believed everything I heard. Only Tukhachevsky's arrest puzzled me. After all, I had seen him so many times when I was still going to their apartment for my dance classes. His daughter Sveta and I were friends. How could it be possible? How could one of the first marshals, the legendary Red Army commander and such an important person, turn out to be a spy and an enemy of the people? My mother's explanations did not really make sense; "He himself probably didn't do anything wrong . . . But he created a certain mood among his people . . . And maybe because of that mood they did something wrong . . ." I could not understand anything: "What mood? A shooting mood?" "Well, you know, when lots of people, particularly in the army, get affected by such a mood, it's a bad thing." In other words, my mother got tangled up in her own explanation, and I never understood anything.

In May 1937 my maternal grandmother, Gita, arrived from Poland where she was living with her youngest daughter in the small town of Zelva. She came by herself, to see her other children. She had quite a few: seven sons and daughters. My grandfather was not around any more; he died in 1931. They were very poor. According to family history, my grandfather was an impractical man. Before his marriage he had been in the army and had played the trumpet in the regimental band. In civilian life trumpet playing proved much less useful. On the other hand, my grandfather never learned how to trade either. So he became a hired laborer. Before the First World War he worked as a weigher at a mill, for sixteen rubles a month. As a bonus, the miller allowed him to collect the flour dust that accumulated on the walls of the mill. The Kaplan family remembered those years as the golden age of childhood. The garden and the cow were the main sources of their livelihood. Grandma Gita was in charge of everything. Potatoes, vegetables, and curdled milk were the children's staples. Butter was sold at the market. Grandma Gita baked rye bread mixed half and half with potatoes. Once a week she treated her children to pancakes made from ground raw potatoes fried in sunflower oil.

My mother was the eldest child. She was born on New Year's Eve, December 31, 1897. As a teenager, she went to Warsaw to work in a textile factory. Her job was to spin the wheel of a sewing machine fourteen to sixteen hours a day, making straw hats. When she would come home for Passover, she would always bring twenty-five rubles for my grandfather. It must have been a lot of money if her little brother still remembers the sum after seventy years. During the First World War, when the Germans were advancing toward Warsaw, my mother was evacuated to the east along with the factory. After the October Revolution she found herself in Moscow and went to work in a textile factory. In 1918 she joined the party. Now she was working as an economist at the Commissariat of Heavy Industry.

All her brothers and sisters ended up following my mother to Moscow. Not all at once, of course. Khaim was one year younger. He started out as a manual laborer. During the civil war he joined the Red Army as a volunteer, and then after the war he graduated from the Chemical Defense Academy. For several years he worked as Iakir's[20] deputy for chemical defense in the Kiev military district. In 1937 he became the assistant head of the Chemical Defense Academy in Moscow. He had three stripes on his collar, which meant that he was what we would call a colonel. He was married to Fekla Ignatievna Gondzhuro. We changed her name to Fena, to make it sound more Jewish. They had three children: Nina, Nella, and Lenia.

My mother's second brother, Veniamin, had his share of hardships, too. At the age of sixteen, after several years of sawing lumber and laying railroad tracks, he decided to run away to America. However, in 1918, before Zelva became Polish, my mother went there and talked him into coming to Moscow with her. In Moscow he graduated from the rabfak and then college, was drafted and then demobilized, and finally became a staff scholar at the Institute of World Economy and International Politics. By 1937 he already had a Ph.D. in history. I have already mentioned that he had his wedding in our apartment. His wife, Sarra Iosifovna, was a wonderful singer. They had a daughter named Nina.

All the Kaplan women were good-looking, but it was Lipa who was the prettiest and smartest of them all. She was cheerful, good-natured, and rosy-cheeked. She was married to a Hungarian Communist, Bela Lander, whom she had met in our apartment. They had a little girl. In 1926 Lander was sent to Hungary to do underground work. Soon after he arrived, he was arrested and sentenced to five years in prison. At the end of his term he received an additional sentence, and it became clear that he would never return to Russia. Lipa had plenty of admirers, among them my father's graduate student, our future éminence grise, Misha

---

[20] I. E. Iakir (1896–1937)—Soviet general, commander of the Ukrainian military district (1925–37), executed during the Great Terror.

Suslov.[21] Finally Lipa married an engineer from the Moscow Automobile Plant, Naum Iakovlevich Rabinovich (Niuma). She herself worked at a small tannery. In 1932 their son Alik was born.

The most remarkable of my mother's brothers was Pinia. All the other brothers were short, rather plain, and reserved, and Khaim could be downright sullen. Pinia was different: tall, slender, and broad-shouldered, he wore a handsome aviator's uniform that looked great on him. He always had a smile on his face. He was also extremely kind, just like Lipa and my mother. His wife, Musia, was worthy of him. She was a true Russian beauty. Whenever she would see the two of them together, our Natasha would always shake her head and say, "What a couple, what a couple!" Having graduated from the rabfak in 1923, Pinia was admitted to Moscow University. After his freshman year Komsomol members were being mobilized for service in the navy, and Pinia ended up at the Naval College. There he became a navy pilot and soon distinguished himself in a rescue operation. By 1937 he was already a colonel, like Khaim, and was studying at the Naval Academy. Chkalov[22] and Kamanin[23], the first heroes of the Soviet Union, were among his friends. When Pinia's son was born, he named him Valery—after Valery Pavlovich Chkalov.

In 1923 my mother's sister, Adassa, and several of her friends crossed the Polish-Russian border illegally and made their way to Moscow. In due time she graduated from college and started working as a chemical engineer. She was married to Kostia Vorobiev. They had a little boy named Vitia. In 1929 the youngest Kaplans—Tania and Leva—were allowed to visit us. Leva got a job at the Automobile Plant and enrolled in the Bauman Institute of Technology as a correspondence student, but Tania said she could not leave Grandma Gita by herself, so she went back to Poland.

Grandma Gita did not speak Russian, so Adassa met her at the border town of Negoreloe. From the Belorussky Railway Station she was taken to Lipa's in my father's car. That night all seven children and their spouses came to see her. Many years had gone by since they, as young people, had left the family home. We can only guess what her hopes for them may have been back then. What kind of fate had she asked God to grant her uneducated children from a miserable Jewish shtetl? And now here she was, surrounded by prosperous people with all kinds of degrees: engineers, colonels, Ph.D.s. As far as she was concerned, my mother, for example, was "Madame Minister's Wife"! She had a lot of grandchildren, too. All her life she had been tied to her garden and her cow. My great-great grandfather, Grandma Gita's grandfather, had been a rabbi who had written famous Talmudic commentaries called "Elijah's View." Her own literacy was limited to reading Hebrew prayers and painstakingly composing letters in her own shtetl dialect.

[21] M. A. Suslov (1902–1982)—secretary of the Central Committee (1946–82), member of the Central Committee's Politburo (1955–82), responsible for ideology and known for his conservatism.

[22] V. P. Chkalov (1904–1938)—popular Soviet aviator, acclaimed for his flight across the North Pole from Moscow to Portland, Oregon, in 1936.

[23] N. P. Kamanin (b. 1908)—popular Soviet aviator, took part in the widely publicized 1934 rescue of the crew of a Soviet ship stranded in the Arctic Sea.

I was there that night. According to the Jewish custom, Grandma was wearing a wig. It was red. I was also surprised that she was eating off special plates that she had brought with her from Poland. She sat proudly at the head of the table in the place of honor. I also remember her full dark skirts that reached the ground. That night must have been the first time in her life that she was truly happy. As Veniamin said later, none of her children had ever seen her in such a good mood. Having spent some time at Lipa's, she moved to Veniamin's dacha. At the end of June she went back to Lipa's before joining us at our dacha in Nikolina Gora.

In Nikolina Gora Natalka, Valiushka, our cousin, Nina, and I were living with Natasha. Nina was two years older than I was, but we were great friends. We used to walk along the river, swim, or just lie around on blankets in our garden. We read out loud to each other. Nina loved staying with us at our dacha. The weather was beautiful.

In the evenings my father and mother would come down from Moscow. They lived on the first floor, and we occupied the second. Nina and I had separate rooms. When we knew my parents were not coming for the night, Nina would come to my room, and we would squeeze into bed together and read or talk until midnight. Nina knew and loved a lot of poetry and even tried to write some herself. Life was wonderful.

On the morning of June 27, 1937, my parents were both at the dacha. Before they left my father took a splinter out of my foot (he was an expert at that) and put iodine on the spot. While climbing into the car, he said: "Natasha, keep an eye on Valiushka!" Valiushka was indeed tiny and kept falling and getting bruises. She had two huge bumps on her forehead. They said they would be back in the evening, and my father repeated: "Natasha, be sure to look after Valiushka!" Natasha got a little angry and said, "What do you think I've been doing?"

She often recalled that sentence of my father's. Valiushka was exactly a year and one month, Natalka was seven, and I was about to turn twelve in two months.

SINCE my parents had said that they would be back in the evening, Nina and I went to sleep in our separate rooms. In the middle of the night I was awakened by my mother's voice, saying, "I don't have the keys to this desk. This is a child's desk. I don't know where she put the key." I realized that the "she" was me and that the desk she was talking about was my desk. I do not remember why I had locked my desk—probably because the key came with the desk and so had to be used. Two men in uniform were standing by the desk. I thought they were Khaim and Pinia since they were both in the military. I lay quietly watching while pretending to sleep, the way children do. Suddenly Khaim and Pinia started breaking into the desk. For some reason I decided they must be looking for soap in order to wash their hands. Then I realized they were not Khaim and Pinia, and decided they must be friends who had come along with my parents. When they were about to leave the room, I called out to my mother. She came up to me, and I saw that she was crying: "Father has been arrested!" She started telling me that my father was completely innocent; that everything would be all right; that I should not get upset; and that the two military men were strangers who were conducting a search. I was in my room the whole time the search was going on, so I did not see any of it. Nina, Natalka, and Valiushka slept through the whole thing. Natasha kept following my mother from one room to another. By the time they finished the search, I was already fully dressed. I came out of my room looking for my mother. It was six o'clock in the morning. Natasha was crying, and my mother was getting into the car with the military men. "What about me?" I asked. "Take me with you." "I have to be at work in the morning, Sweetie. Don't worry. I'll get a car and come get you all tonight and take you home."—"No, take me with you. Take me with you!" So she did. My mother and I left with the military men.

What followed is a total blank. I do not remember the trip itself or where we were let off or where we ended up that day. It is a complete blank. I do not remember if we went home to the House of Government or to a relative's place. Later, Natasha came and brought the children. Where she brought them exactly, I also cannot remember. Then Khaim, or maybe Fena, came to pick up Nina. I think they took Natalka, too. I have a total memory lapse.

That morning some people had come to the dacha, kicked out Natasha and the kids, and sealed the building. Natasha tried to find a ride to Moscow. In those days few people in Nikolina Gora had cars. Knowing that Bezymensky was a good friend of my father's, she went to his place. Bezymensky was at home. He started the car, took Natasha and the children to Perkhushkovo, and put them on a train to Moscow. We never saw him again, but his wife Rakhil—they lived on Palikha in my grandmother's building—always asked me about my parents whenever we ran into each other in the courtyard. She always did it secretly, in a whisper, but even that required a great deal of courage. You had to overcome your fear for your own child.

My father's arrest was, of course, totally unexpected for me. I loved him very much. I did not believe he was an "enemy of the people." My father was innocent—he had simply been slandered. Very soon the truth would be revealed, and he would come back home. Other people could be "enemies of the people," but not my father. It just did not make any sense. After all, I knew him so well. I never doubted for a second that it was a mistake. Not once. I am absolutely certain of that.

Right after my father's arrest, Lipa was also arrested. Sometime before, the director of personnel at her factory had made a pass at her, and she had told him to get lost. The director of personnel! So he had forced some worker to write a denunciation saying that Lipa had told her at the solemn meeting held on the day of Kirov's murder that if more of them got killed off, the rest of us would not have to work so hard and that Kirov's successor, Zhdanov,[24] should also be killed. Or something of the sort. The denunciation had been too absurd: on the day of Kirov's murder nobody had known who would become his successor, so the investigator had let Lipa go. But the day after my father's arrest, they came for her. Grandma Gita was staying with her at the time. No sooner had she learned of

[24] A. A. Zhdanov (1896–1948)—secretary of the Central Committee (1934–48), member of the Central Committee's Politburo (1939–48), succeeded Kirov as first secretary of the Leningrad provincial and city party committees (1934–44).

the arrest of her son-in-law than her daughter was taken away. Her happiness turned out to be short-lived. Yet this was only the beginning. In Lipa's case there was a trial, even a lawyer. It was the lawyer who told Niuma, who was not allowed to attend, that Lipa had been sentenced to ten years—for terrorism.

Several days after my father's arrest we were evicted from our apartment. Rather, my mother was evicted because we were living at Grandma Sofa's dacha. We were moved into the Karpovs' apartment on the fourth floor. A couple of years before, they had returned from Germany, where Karpov had been working at the trade mission.[25] Before his arrest he had been my father's colleague at the Soviet Control Commission. He was arrested at almost the same time as my father. He had a wife, Natalia (I do not remember her patronymic), and three children. The eldest, Ia, had just graduated from high school; Yura was a year older than I was; and Vova was a year older than Natalka. They also had a four-room apartment. They were allowed to keep two rooms, and we were told to move into the other two. At first not all our things were confiscated. For example, we got to keep the refrigerator that we had bought from Niuma. Niuma had brought it from America, where he had spent a year as an intern at a Ford plant. The plant director, Likhachev, had sent him there. The piano was gone. My father's library—several thousand volumes—had been sealed in his office, but my mother managed to smuggle out a few. I think they were children's books. She also managed to salvage some clothes and sheets.

According to my mother, all our friends and relatives disappeared without a trace after my father's arrest. They simply vanished. Uncle Veniamin, for example, whose dacha was next to Grandma Sofa's, never visited us there. Everyone was gripped with fear. On the basis of past show trials and party meetings, people knew that even a casual encounter with an "enemy of the people" could make an "enemy of the people" out of you. Fear—especially fear for one's children—made people look the other way or cross the street whenever they saw their "marked" friends. Fear, fear, and more fear. Before I knew it, it started creeping into my own soul—where it was to remain for a long, long time. Some of it is still with me to this day.

My mother kept going to the Lubianka[26] to try to get information about my father. In the middle of August an investigator called her at work and said she could bring some warm things and some garlic for my father. My mother put together a parcel and took it to the prison. That day, instead of staying in Moscow, she came to the dacha to give us the good news. Since they had accepted a parcel with warm clothes, that must mean my father was going to be exiled—and therefore not shot. In exile he would certainly need warm clothes. She even found fur boots for him. But when she arrived at work the next morning, Natalia Karpova called and told her not to come home that night. It turned out that they had come to arrest her the night before. After that, my mother spent her nights at the dacha.

---

[25] At the time of his arrest, V. Z. Karpov (1895–1937) was working in the Soviet Control Commission; he was shot on November 27, 1937.

[26] Lubianka—secret police headquarters in Moscow.

It would soon be September 1, and I would have to start school. On August 30, my birthday, we moved back to Moscow, to the Karpovs' apartment. I remember seeing Vova Karpov in the hall. One of our rooms was filled with books. There was also a table and the refrigerator. My mother set up her bed in there and put us to sleep in the other room. They came for her that night. I woke up right away, and so did Natasha and Valiushka. Only Natalka stayed asleep. My mother kept walking back and forth, from one room to the other. I followed after her in my nightshirt, and Natasha, with Valiushka in her arms, followed behind me. Thus, in single file, we paced in my mother's wake. At one point she had to go to the bathroom. In the Karpovs' apartment the bathroom door had a glass window with a curtain over it. When my mother entered the bathroom, the NKVD agent ordered her to open the curtain and stood there watching. Natasha, with Valiushka in her arms, and I were standing by the door. My mother came out, and we resumed our trek in single file from one room to the other. I was sobbing the whole time, but my mother kept saying: "Don't worry, Sweetie. We haven't done anything wrong. Father and I are completely innocent. I'll be back soon." At about five in the morning they took her away. Both before and after she had gone, I kept hearing the sound of people walking up and down the stairs. My mother was probably not the only person arrested that night.

Some of the NKVD agents stayed behind to continue the search. Then they moved the refrigerator and something else into the back room and were about to seal it when Natalka woke up and asked where our mother was. The agents told Natasha to prepare the children for the orphanage. Natasha said firmly that we were staying with her. They demanded to see her passport, but she did not have it because she kept it at her sister's. So they said that we would have to go with them. I have already mentioned Natasha's temper. She started screaming at them that she was not going to let anyone take the children, that she was not going to let us go anywhere. I was running back and forth, crying at the top of my lungs. Natalka and Valiushka were crying, too.

This roused the Karpovs. They had been awake the whole time, of course, listening to what was going on, but when we started screaming, Natalia Karpova could not stand it any more and came out of her room. Those scoundrels told her that if she showed them her passport, they would let us stay. She brought her passport, and we were left in Natasha's charge. Before they left, they said that if no relatives formally applied to become our guardians, we would be sent to an orphanage. In the morning Natasha left Natalka and Valiushka with me and rushed off to the dacha to get Grandma Sofa. They returned together, and Grandma filled out the guardianship papers. Natalka and I remained in our room in the Karpovs' apartment. That is how Natasha and Natalia Karpova saved us from the orphanage.

Several days later they came for Natalia Karpova. Since Ia already had a passport, she was able to become her brothers' guardian. Unlike us, they were immediately kicked out onto the street. Just like that. So Ia took her brothers and left for Kharkov where they had relatives. I do not know for sure what happened to them. From what I have heard, Ia managed to graduate from the Nonferrous Metals

Institute, but the boys' fate was tragic: Yura died in the war, and Vova joined a gang of homeless children and died somewhere in the north.

Meanwhile we were moved down to the first floor, to the Korytnys' apartment.[27] Korytny's wife had been arrested at about the same time as my mother and Natalia Karpova, and their son and their daughter, Sveta, had been taken to an orphanage. I think it was a two-room apartment. One room was occupied by what was left of the Knorin family,[28] and we moved into the other one. It was a long, narrow room. Natalka and I slept together on a couch, and Valiushka slept in her crib. Natasha had a cot that she would pull out each night. We also had a table, but very little else. After each move we were left with fewer possessions. Natasha had managed to take some things to her sister's and was selling them off one by one. Also, Grandma Sofa had given Natasha about a hundred rubles. It was not enough for four people, but Natasha managed to keep us well fed.

On September 6 Nadia, Uncle Siunia's maid, came to see us. She told us that Siunia had been arrested the night before and that Faina, Igor, and she had been moved to another apartment. After my father's arrest, Siunia had been fired from his job and expelled from the party. Then he sat at home waiting to be arrested. Later, some kids from the house told me that they heard him screaming as he was being dragged down the stairs: "Lazar Moiseevich! Lazar Moiseevich, don't you know what's happening? Lazar Moiseevich, help me!"[29] No help came from Lazar Moiseevich. Siunia was shot in February 1938.

My parents' arrest had marked the end of my childhood—my happy and peaceful childhood. On September 1 Natasha sent me off to school. She was busy looking after Valiushka and procuring food for all of us. Natalka still had a year left before starting school, so she used to stay at home or play in the courtyard with her friends. I was going to school. I loved school. I knew I had to do well. I never thought about why I had to do well—I just knew it was so. I had it in my blood. Perhaps those were my Jewish survival genes.

Igor and I continued going to school. We had to report that our parents had been arrested. The children in our class all knew, of course, but the principal had to be told. That is the way we both felt about it. I had no doubt it had to be done, but I was terribly scared and kept postponing the inevitable. Two weeks had passed since my mother's arrest. Finally, Igor could stand it no longer. "Inka," he said, "let's go ahead and do it." We were only twelve years old at the time. So we went to the teachers' room, found our class supervisor, Inna Fedorovna Grekova, and told her everything. She gave us a funny look and said: "So? Why are you telling me this? Go back to your classrooms." That was the end of it. We were puzzled. We could not quite understand why Inna Fedorovna had reacted the way she did—as if nothing had happened. Many years later, my mother liked to repeat: "How lucky it was that you did not go to the Exemplary!" There, children were

---

[27] S. Z. Korytny (1900–1939)—secretary of the Moscow party committee, executed on September 1, 1939.

[28] V. G. Knorin (1890–1938)—worked in the Comintern secretariat (1928–35), served as deputy head of the propaganda department of the Central Committee (1935–38), executed on July 29, 1938.

[29] Refers to L. M. Kaganovich (see footnote 7, above), his boss at the Transport Commissariat.

forced to renounce and curse their parents in a huge assembly hall in front of the
whole school.[30]

On November 13 my mother's sister, Adassa, was arrested. She got ten years
for being a Polish spy—presumably because she and her friends had crossed the
Polish border illegally in 1922, in order to enter the workers' paradise. Her husband, Kostia Vorobiev, was left with their three-year-old son, Vitia.

After the arrests of Lipa and my mother, Grandma Gita had been living with
Adassa. After Adassa was taken to prison, Grandma moved in with Veniamin. In
early December Elochka, Lipa's daughter, came home from school one day and
found Grandma Gita sitting on the stairs in front of their apartment. Veniamin,
without warning Niuma or Leva, had brought her there and left her by the locked
door. Grandma moved in with Niuma. I would often see her there. She was no
longer the same proud and happy Grandma I had seen arrive from Poland. I can
still picture her with her red wig all twisted round and her bun hanging over her
ear. She could not understand why her children had been imprisoned. She kept
pacing up and down the apartment, intoning; "It's all my fault. I have brought
grief to my children. I must return home immediately. As soon as I leave, things
will get better again." She said all this in Yiddish. Of course, Elochka and I could
not understand a word of what she was saying, so Leva had to translate for us. She
could not leave, however, because her visa had expired. With great difficulty,
Leva managed to get an exit visa for her. Right before New Year's, he put her on
a train to Warsaw. She never found out what happened to her children. All contact
between us was broken off. Grandma Gita, her youngest daughter Tania, and her
four grandchildren were all shot by the Nazis in a Jewish ghetto somewhere.

On December 31, 1937, Fena Ignatievna received a message from Kineshma
saying that Khaim had been arrested. In January came the turn of Faina Saulovna,
Siunia's wife. Igor was taken in by Grandma Sofa, but soon Grandma Sofa left for
Krasnoiarsk to see Aunt Fania, whose husband had also been arrested. He had
been the rector of a forestry college. Fania remained in Krasnoiarsk in order to
take parcels to the prison for her husband, while Grandma Sofa brought nine-
year-old Galka and one-year-old Slava back to Moscow with her. Now there were
eight of them in Grandma's room on Palikha. Grandma's family kept growing.

On March 4, 1938, the Bukharin trial began.[31] Among the accused was my
father's boss, Chernov, the commissar of agriculture. He had been arrested after
my father. My father was not among the accused, but on the fifth or sixth day
Maksimov, Kuibyshev's secretary, mentioned my father's name in his testimony.
According to the accusation, Maksimov had organized the murder of Kuibyshev
on my father's orders. This came as a total shock. I was absolutely devastated.
How could my father have plotted Kuibyshev's murder when our Valiushka was
named after Kuibyshev! When Valerian Vladimirovich Kuibyshev died, one of
the first people his widow had called with the news was my father. My father had
immediately rushed over to their house. He had absolutely adored Kuibyshev. He

[30] See selection 22, in this volume.
[31] N. I. Bukharin (1888–1938)—leading Bolshevik, member of the Politburo (1923–29), one of the
main opponents of Stalin's collectivization policy, executed after a show trial.

could not possibly be Kuibyshev's murderer. It was a mistake. It was slander. I was sure that sooner or later the misunderstanding would be cleared up.

In late March we had to move again. The apartment where we lived was to become a dorm for the guards. We were put into a beautiful apartment on the tenth floor, where the Stetskys used to live.[32] The huge, sunlit room was quite a contrast to our previous abode. The Knorins moved into another room in the same apartment. Natasha said: "We aren't going to get to stay here very long. This apartment is going to catch someone's fancy pretty soon." That is exactly what happened. Soon after our move Nina Aleksandrovna Knorina was arrested, and on April 7 we were kicked out of the House of Government. The Knorin children left for Dnepropetrovsk, and we went to Grandma's. By then, Fania had come back from Krasnoiarsk. Her husband had received ten years without the right to correspond. We did not know then that this meant a death sentence. There were thirteen of us on Palikha: too many for one room. Natasha said that she did not want to live with Grandma, so Grandma rented a house three kilometers from the Udelnaia station on the Kazan Railway line. Natasha, Natalka, and Valiushka moved there, and I went to live with Niuma.

On May 13, 1938, Fena Ignatievna was arrested. She went to the prosecutor's office to ask about Khaim and never came back. The next day Nina, Nella, and Lenia were taken to the Danilovsky Children's Home. It was also known as a facility for juvenile delinquents—or simply a children's prison. They did not stay there long. On May 21 they were put into a prison van, taken to a railway station, and eventually sent to the Brailov Orphanage for children of prisoners outside Zhitomir, in Ukraine. They had a very hard life there. I know that from Nina. She was fourteen then, Nella was twelve, and Lenia, only nine. They all suffered a great deal during the war. After the eighth grade Nina went to Leningrad to study. She barely survived the siege. Lenia was picked up by our soldiers as they were passing through Zhmerinka in 1941 and remained with them as a "son of the regiment." Nella got the roughest deal. The orphanage was on occupied territory. Nella did not look Jewish—after all, Fena Ignatievna was Russian—but one of the teachers denounced her to the Nazis. However, she was hidden by some good people. Later, she was sent with the local girls from Brailov to Germany to work. After the war she married a Pole, had a daughter, and settled in Poland. She was afraid to go back home—and, anyway, there was no home to go back to. She never told anyone she was from Russia. Only after Stalin's death did she start cautiously looking for Nina and Lenia. In 1960 she came to the Soviet Union. She was met by her sister, her brother, and her mother, whom she had not seen in more than twenty years. It was both a happy and sad occasion. Nella returned to Poland. Now she is raising her grandchildren and occasionally comes to visit us.

In the summer of 1938 Grandma came to live with us in Udelnaia. As soon as Grandma arrived, Natasha left. She had not been paid since my father's arrest. Grandma simply did not have any money for her. She had to earn a living

---

[32] A. I. Stetsky (1896–1938)—head of the propaganda department of the Central Committee (1930–38), executed on August 1, 1938.

somehow. So she went to work at a textile factory and rented a corner in Kali-novka on the Paveletskaia Railway line. I often went there to visit her. As Natasha was leaving, she told me to take good care of Valiushka and to wash her bottom every day. She was only two, after all, and it was summer, so she would run around naked. I was horrified, but every day I did a conscientious job of washing her and her dresses. Natalka also required attention. I was the oldest. I did not learn right away—I was not even thirteen myself. Natasha did not abandon us. She came regularly to see Natalka and Valiushka, especially in the fall when we returned to Moscow.

Sometime in May the principal, Valentin Ivanovich, stuck his head in the door and said: "Gaister, there's a telephone call for you!" I was amazed. Nobody had ever called me at school before. As I walked out of the classroom, Valentin Iva-novich said: "It's your grandmother." I was even more shocked. What could it be? I ran to the principal's office to pick up the phone. Grandma said that we had received a telegram from my mother and read it to me. The telegram had arrived from Akmolinsk, in Kazakhstan. It had a return address, where we could send letters and parcels. This was the first time we had heard from my mother since her arrest. When Grandma received the telegram, she had looked up the telephone number at the school and called the principal. She told him about the telegram, and he came to get me himself. I can imagine what I must have looked like when I got off the phone! Valentin Ivanovich only asked: "Are you going to go back to the classroom or do you want to go home?" I went back to class. So there were always good things happening.

I started sending parcels to my mother. To do this I needed money, but Grandma did not have any, so I started tutoring. I was in sixth grade the first time I tried, and then I continued tutoring regularly until ninth grade. I taught kids from our school—those who were not doing well in certain subjects. For example, we had a girl named Tamara Orekhova in our class. She lived in the House of Gov-ernment and was even a friend of mine. After school I would go over to her place, and we would study together. It wasn't much money, but it was a substantial addition to our little budget.

I do not remember exactly how often I sent those parcels, but I know I was thrilled if I managed to do it once a month. Camp parcels were only accepted on certain days. You could not just go to a post office and send them. They could tell by the address the kind of parcel it was. There were special post offices for camp parcels—or rather, on a certain day a certain post office would accept camp par-cels. Nothing was ever announced, of course, but usually someone working at that post office would have friends or relatives in a camp, so they would send word to their friends in prison lines; in this way everybody would quickly find out where to take the parcels.

At first they accepted parcels in Moscow, but that soon ended because on those days the post office lines would be longer than those in the grocery stores. After that, we had to go to Aleksandrov or Mozhaisk—that is, about one hundred kilo-meters outside Moscow. I remember well those trips to Mozhaisk. I used to leave from the Belorussky Railway Station. Fortunately, it was not far from Palikha, so

I could get there on foot before the streetcars started up, and make it to the first train. They would accept only a limited number of parcels, so if you got there late, they might close the window before your turn came. The trip to Mozhaisk took two hours. The post office was not far from the station, but to get there you had to cross a very long pedestrian bridge over the tracks. So to get to the post office quickly and take your place in line, you had to get into a particular car—the one that stopped right in front of the bridge. That whole car would be filled with parcels in plywood boxes. Also, if you wanted to be by the right door, you had to be the first one to enter. The idea was to be the first one to get off the train in Mozhaisk. Everything had to be calculated. Not a second could be lost. You had to stand by the right door. Then, when the train arrived in Mozhaisk, there would be a terrible stampede. Everyone would try to be the first to get off. Finally, you would squeeze out of there and rush for the bridge as fast as you could. Then you would run on and on and on over that bridge, with your box in your arms—not to mention the hammer and nails. Everyone would be running like crazy, pushing and shoving, trying to get ahead. In the beginning I was frightened, but then I got used to it.

The parcel had to weigh exactly eight kilos—no more, no less. Imagine standing in that line and then having your parcel rejected because of an extra two hundred grams. Every post office had its own unique scales. If it was too heavy you had to open your box and take something out. In the meantime, you might miss your turn: then you would try to push your way back through to the window, with the people in line acting like wild animals, growling and pouncing on one another. That's what the hammer and nails were for: you would nail the lid back on right there in front of the clerk. If you finally had it accepted, you would walk back to the station in a state of utter bliss—as if you had just come out of the bathhouse after a good steam.

After my mother's telegram, we started receiving letters. She was in the Akmolinsk Camp for traitors' wives. She wrote that the trip to the camp had lasted more than a month. One of her letters contained a note for Veniamin. I do not remember exactly what it said, but it went something like this: "Dear Nema![33] I am the only person in our camp of many thousands who never receives any letters from her brother. I am not asking you to write, but I am asking you to please take care of my children." After the episode with Grandma Gita, I did not want to see Veniamin, but Niuma and Leva talked me into taking the note to him. Leva and I went to his place. Both Veniamin and Sarra were at home. They asked us to come in, took my mother's note, and went into the study. Then Sarra came out and said: "Don't ever come here again." Veniamin never came out. Leva and I left without saying a word. This did not save Veniamin from prison, however.

Sometime in early 1939 Pinia was arrested. He got five years and was sent to the north. It was an amazingly mild sentence for those days. In the spring of 1939, when they stopped accepting Musia's parcels for Pinia, she and Valerik returned to Moscow. Musia immediately rushed to see Pinia's friend, Kamanin. Kamanin

[33] Short for Veniamin.

was one of the first Heroes of the Soviet Union. He was one of the pilots who had rescued the members of the *Cheliuskin* expedition. That had been a heroic page in our history. The whole country followed the rescue epic. At our school we drew maps of the Arctic Ocean, and each day we marked the location of the drifting, ice-bound *Cheliuskin*. But how could Kamanin help Musia? She and Valerik ran all over Moscow and finally came knocking on Niuma's door. Niuma and Leva let them stay. For Niuma, that was not a problem. But I decided to move back to Grandma's and live with Natalka and Valiushka.

After my return, there were twelve people living in one room. How did we manage? Well, we found ways. In the center of the room was a dinner table. There was also a small desk by the window. Natalka, Valiushka, and I all slept together on a narrow bed made from a couch with three chairs propped against it. It is interesting that when Natalka came down with diphtheria and had to be taken to the hospital, Valiushka and I were fine. We were lucky, I guess. Grandma and Grandpa slept on a metal-frame bed with knobs. Slavka's crib stood beside their bed. Aunt Fania slept on the couch. Izia and his family occupied the double bed behind the wardrobe. Igor and Fania's daughter, Galka, would set up their cots at night. There was also a china cabinet, but Grandma's family china was gone.

On the very first day after I moved back in, Grandma gave me the job of washing all the sheets. I had never done any washing before, so I just swished them around a little and hung them up to dry. When Fania saw them, she yelled at me for hanging up dirty linen. Later, I got used to washing all the sheets and pillow cases. I did it all by hand—we did not have washing machines in those days.

Before my father's arrest our family had been very close. On holidays Grandma used to have family dinners, and everybody loved to come. Now things had turned sour. We were treated as unwanted outcasts who only got in the way. Family ties were disintegrating. Natalka and Igor were the worst off. They really were pretty spoiled and had a very hard time adjusting to the new conditions. Natalka was persecuted mercilessly: everybody from Grandma to Galka was constantly yelling at her. The only relief came from Natasha, who used to come at least once a week to comfort Natalka and Valiushka. Soon after I had moved in, I understood that I was now the head of the family and had to take care of Natalka and Valiushka and defend them when needed. I was not treated very well myself, but Igor and I would talk back. They were afraid of me and my sharp tongue. I never raised my voice, though—I would just look at them with contempt. Fania, especially, was scared of me.

It was, of course, a very hard life. There was not enough money for such a crowd. The fear of new arrests hung over the family. The grown-ups could not stand the strain and often took it out on us. At that time we did not understand this. The only person who never yelled at us was Grandpa. He treated all his grandchildren the same, but did not talk to us much. Grandpa was a taciturn, quiet man, and Grandma could order him around all she wanted. When my father was arrested, Grandpa, at the age of seventy, went to work at a little cooperative. His job was to glue envelopes together. His fingers were all crooked from having worked with leather for so long. Gluing the envelopes did not pay much, so Grandpa found a job at a leather-making cooperative, making purses and gloves. He said that it was practically his specialty because he used to make fancy made-to-order shoes. We all lived on his earnings. I remember taking his lunch to him at that cooperative. His salary was not enough, of course. Whatever I made tutoring was spent on parcels to my mother.

In other words, it was a difficult life. We did not eat well at all. Igor suffered the most. Boys grow fast at that age, and his ration was obviously too small for him. I was okay because I was still pretty fat, but Natalka and Valiushka were doing poorly. Grandma used to feed Fania's children at our expense. It was a fact, and we knew it. We did not starve, but we were never full.

I remember those solemn tea parties. Grandma must have decided that Fania's husband would never come back. Or maybe they already knew he had been shot. Fania used to tell people that her husband had left her and that she had gotten a divorce. She was still a young, good-looking woman. Anyway, Grandma decided to find her a new husband. It was completely hopeless for a woman with two children, of course, but some men did come over every once in a while. Or one of Grandma's relatives would come by for a visit. Those were the occasions for the solemn tea parties. Grandma would put a teapot on the table and lay out the preserves she had made during the summer. Sometimes Fania would bring home a cake or some cookies. I do not remember any other treats. Of the children, only Galka was invited, but whenever a guest arrived, Igor and I would be ready. Whatever we happened to be doing—homework or whatever else—we would signal to each other and, with all proper decorum, take our places at the table. Grandma would get absolutely furious but didn't dare send us away in front of the guest. Fania always remained silent, afraid of what I might say. We would push our cups toward Grandma, help ourselves to the preserves, and take our time enjoying the treat. We did not want to be too slow, though: having emptied our cups, we would innocently ask Grandma for a refill while helping ourselves to more preserves. Such tea parties were rare, of course, but Igor and I never missed a chance to be there. I tried to talk Natalka into joining us, but she was too scared and never took part. Fania would yell at me afterward: "These are all your tricks!" And I would snap back at her. But Fania had a point, too. Tiny as her hopes for marriage might be, they kept her going. Perhaps those tea parties for suitors were her salvation. It would have been so easy for a single woman with two children— not to mention the rest of us—to lose all interest in life and let herself go.

Finding a place to do homework was a problem, too. Four of us were in school. Igor and I were still going to No. 19, and Natalka and Galka were going to the neighborhood school. There was not enough room for all of us, so somebody had to study in the kitchen or in the bathroom. Grandma put a little table in the bathroom, and it became the best place to do homework. We always fought over the place in the bathroom. And we were not even the only ones in that apartment. When we had moved to the House of Government in 1932, the second room had been occupied by a Gosplan employee by the name of Ratner. Soon afterward he had married Galina Mikhailovna, the sister of Shepilov's wife (the very same

Shepilov who, under Khrushchev, would acquire the nation's longest name: "And-Shepilov-Who-Sided-With-Them").[34] Galina Mikhailovna was a kind and friendly woman. In 1938 both Ratner and Galina Mikhailovna were arrested, and their room occupied by a waiter from some restaurant. I can still see his bent figure. He had eight children. One daughter worked, the second one was my age, and so on and so forth. In other words, the density of the child population in our apartment exceeded all norms.

Igor and I went to school on the streetcar, but in the fall of 1940, Grandma refused to continue giving us transportation money. It cost her twenty-five rubles a month and was a considerable strain on her meager budget. Besides, tuition fees had just been introduced—two hundred rubles a year. We simply did not have the money for all that. So Igor went to a technical school, and I had to transfer to our neighborhood school. Fortunately, my favorite teacher, Anna Zinovievna, moved there at the same time (she lived not far from us on Novoslobodskaia). She was the one who paid the two hundred rubles for me. This shows what kind of teachers we had.

In my new school I joined the Komsomol. I was in the eighth grade then. I had tried to join earlier but hadn't been accepted because of my age. The fact of the matter is, I was a true believer. We believed all the slogans. They screwed our heads on any way they wanted. I believed everything—completely and sincerely. That is what good propaganda can do. I believed everything I was supposed to about the enemies of the people and about all the arrests. As for my father and mother—that was a mistake. You could not make an omelet without breaking eggs!

☐ During the war I. A. Shikheeva-Gaister's cousin, Igor, died of pel-
lagra, and her six-year-old sister, Valiushka, died of tuberculosis. In
1944 Shikheeva-Gaister was admitted to the physics department of
Moscow State University. On the day she was to defend her thesis,
she was arrested and sentenced to five years' exile as the daughter of
enemies of the people. Her sister, Natalka, arrested several weeks
later, received the same sentence. After Stalin's death, both were
released. In 1988 they were officially informed that their father had
been shot four months after his arrest and one day after being sentenced; their mother survived the camps. Of their uncles and aunts,
four were executed, six spent five or more years in labor camps, and
one (Aunt Lipa) committed suicide to avoid a second arrest. I. A.
Shikheeva-Gaister was allowed to graduate from the university in
1954; she is currently teaching physics in a Moscow school.

[34] D. T. Shepilov (1905–1995)—held various posts in the Central Committee bureaucracy in the 1940s, chief editor of *Pravda* (1952–56), minister of foreign affairs (1956–57), ousted by Khrushchev for siding with Khrushchev's opponents in a 1957 attempt to overthrow him.

33 □ Evdokia Maslennikova

The Story of My Life

□ Born in a poor peasant-worker family, Evdokia Vasilievna Maslennikova worked at the Trekhgorka Factory in Moscow and was one of the initiators of socialist competition there. Married to a Communist, she joined the party in 1931 and received many public honors including nomination as a deputy to the Supreme Soviet in 1938. This autobiographical statement, together with a large photograph showing a confident woman, bare-headed and smiling, was published in a Moscow evening newspaper during the 1938 election campaign.

UNEXPECTEDLY for me, yesterday became one of the happiest days of my life. I will never forget the moment when, sitting in the presidium of the general preelection meeting of workers, engineers, and employees of our plant, I heard Comrade Grigorieva, a worker from the spinning shop, propose my candidacy for deputy to the Supreme Soviet of the RSFSR.

It is hard to put into words the excitement I experienced at that meeting and the feelings still overflowing within me. Most of all, I am proud that the people showed me such great honor and trust.

There is nothing particularly remarkable about my biography. Like the biographies of many people who were once mistreated and without rights, it began in a squalid hovel, in the midst of poverty and human sorrow.

Now I look at my daughter Tamara, and my heart fills with joy. Like all the children in our wonderful country, she was born under the bright sun of socialism. She knows the true happiness of childhood. In my own, I saw nothing but grief and tears. And from my mother's stories, I know how hard the worker's lot used to be under the tsar, the landowners, and the capitalists.

My mother is sixty-seven years old, but she still remembers vividly the cruel punishment the landowner inflicted on her father—my grandfather. He was whipped almost to death for protesting against the inhuman work conditions.

I never knew my father. I was five years old when he died. All I know is that he worked in Ozeri, twenty kilometers from our village. My mother spent thirty-five years there at a weaver's loom in the Shcherbakov Factory. She used to travel forty kilometers round-trip on summer Sundays just to see us. She would spend a couple of hours with us and then be back on the road again.

After my father's death, my mother was left with five people on her hands. I had to go out to work as a nanny at the age of nine. I worked as a servant until I was fifteen.

E. Maslennikova, "Rasskaz o moei zhizni," *Vecherniaia Moskva*, May 16, 1938, 3.

In 1921 I went to Moscow. In December I went to work in the Trekhgorka Weaving Shop. That is when the second half of my biography begins. Times were hard. The economy was still in a state of collapse, but Soviet power was already firmly established. So I never had to hear the shouts of the overseer in the shop or suffer on narrow bunks in barracks. My mother and I were put in a dormitory in the house of the former Prince Shcherbachev on Novinsky Boulevard.

Seventeen years have passed since that time. Moscow has become unrecognizable. Much has changed in the factory, too. Beautiful tall buildings have sprung up everywhere, while the cursed Prokhorov flophouses have been converted into fine workers' apartments. I live with my family in one of them. The workers at our factory live a wonderful, full-blooded creative life.

There have been great changes in my life as well.

Soon after arriving in Moscow I got married. My husband has been a party member since 1918. And if I am now an active Bolshevik, it is to a great extent thanks to him, his conversations with me, and his friendly, comradely advice.

Following my husband's advice, I began to study. In 1925, together with two other weavers—Popugina and Balashova—I switched from two looms to three, then to four, six, and eight, and finally I became the first in the weaving shop to start working on twelve looms.

There was never a month when I fulfilled the norm by less than 105–107 percent.

But it is possible to work even better.

I pass on my experience of Stakhanovite work to others. Right now I am preparing to enter the Industrial Academy, and so I have been studying Russian and geography.

My eyes were opened here at the factory. In 1931 I joined the party and took up social work. I was a woman's organizer and editor of the wall newspaper. At the last district party conference I was elected a member of the Krasnaia Presnia district party committee; in addition, I am a member of the party committee of the weaving shop.

During the elections to the Supreme Soviet our workers did me the honor of nominating me to the republican electoral commission of the RSFSR for elections to the Soviet of Nationalities of the Supreme Soviet of the USSR. When I first began this responsible job, I was very anxious, afraid I might not be able to cope with it. But then I understood that you could master anything: you just had to have a love for it and to realize that the people who elected you to the post have enormous confidence in you.

The preelection meeting took place yesterday in the factory courtyard— the same courtyard where thirty-three years ago, in 1905, fourteen Prokhorov workers, who had fought heroically on the barricades of Presnia, were shot down by brutal tsarist butchers.

And I remembered the wise words of our great leader, Comrade Stalin: "It is pleasant and joyful to know that the blood that was so abundantly spilled by our people did not flow in vain, that it had its result."

We live in a happy time. Only in our country is the road wide open to each Soviet patriot, to each Soviet woman. Could a female or male worker in the capitalist countries even dream of being sent to the organs of state power?

Only in the Soviet Union are the people the masters of their own happiness, their own fate. We will never surrender that happiness to anyone.

The people's trust—that is what each party and nonparty Bolshevik must cherish. I have no other happiness than the happiness of our great motherland, the happiness of our socialist country, blossoming under the wise leadership of I. V. Stalin.

34 □ VALENTINA BOGDAN

Memoirs of an Engineer

□ Valentina Bogdan's *Mimicry in the USSR: Reminiscences of an Engineer* is a sequel to *Students of the First Five-Year Plan* (see selection 19 in this volume). After getting married and graduating from college, Valentina and her husband, Serezha, moved to Rostov, where Serezha was offered a job at the local university.

FINALLY we received the permit for our new apartment and went to see it right away. It was in a new, very large five-storied apartment building, right next to Nakhichevan's main street with its stores, offices, and buses. Nakhichevan used to be a separate Armenian town, and the majority of the population was still Armenian, but now it was, for all practical purposes, a part of Rostov. Our apartment was not finished yet—workers were still inside, painting doors and window frames, but they assured us that we would be able to move in that week. We liked the apartment very much. It had two large rooms, a tiny kitchen, a shower instead of a bathroom, a toilet, and a very spacious entry hall. The front door opened onto a stairway, from which five other doors could be seen. Our apartment was on the first floor. Coal was stored in the basement. I particularly liked the fact that over the kitchen stove, right under the ceiling, was a fairly large hot-water tank that was connected to both the kitchen and the shower. The windows were large, and the whole apartment looked bright and festive, partly because all the walls had a border about fifteen centimeters wide painted at the very top, with a pattern that was basically the same color as the rest of the wall but much brighter. Such borders had recently become popular. Where the old apartments had had molded stucco cornices, the new ones had stenciled borders.

The building was in the shape of an H, with courtyards on either side of the horizontal line. In the courtyards, workers were digging deep holes where trees would be planted in the spring.

The building had been built for the elite. All the apartments had been assigned to prominent engineers, party officials at the provincial level, and actors. Several apartments had been set aside for Stakhanovites. Some apartments were quite large—with three or four rooms.

The apartment building was not far from the largest factory in town, the Agricultural Machinery Plant, so I decided to apply for a job there. It would have been easier for me to get into one of Rostov's food-producing factories, but none of them was big enough to have its own research lab, and I was eager to do research.

From Valentina Bogdan, *Mimikriia v SSSR: Vospominaniia inzhenera 1935–1942 gody* (Frankfurt/Main: Polyglott-Druck GmbH, n.d.), 14–305 (abridged).

I was well received at the plant's personnel office, where I was told that the combine-harvester shop had an opening for a young engineer interested in research.

The shop manager agreed to take me on and explained what my job would entail. Recently they had opened a so-called Defective Parts Clearing House, which would receive some of the parts that had been rejected by quality control: for instance, if the cause of the defect could not be determined; if the shop responsible for the defect was not known; if the defect in question could be corrected manually; or if a defective part could be used elsewhere.

"This is a new idea," said the shop manager, "and we need a young engineer who could get it off the ground. Your background in research will come in handy."

I found the work interesting, accepted the offer, and started working the very next morning.

ON Sunday night I went to the railway station to meet [my daughter] Natasha and her nanny, Davydovna. The next day I went to the local trade union office to register the nanny. They asked me a lot of questions to determine whether I really needed her services. Then Davydovna and I were asked to sign a contract, which listed our mutual obligations. I was responsible for paying her salary (thirty rubles a month), providing her with housing and work clothes (one dress and one pair of shoes a year), giving her one day a week off, allowing her to attend trade union meetings, and guaranteeing her a two-week paid vacation every year, at my convenience. Her responsibilities included taking care of my child and cleaning the apartment. In fact, she did less than that. She was very slow, and soon the apartment got so dirty that I was forced to hire extra help to do the big weekly cleaning. We never did the wash at home: the laundress would pick it up and do it at her place.

THE manager and I had agreed that my main task would be to determine the cause of a particular defect and recommend a way to correct it. But when I started working, it turned out that I was also supposed to find out who was responsible for the defect and report my findings to the manager. This put me in a very unpleasant position. Workers were punished for producing defective parts, so they tried to cover them up or deny responsibility. Very soon it became clear to me that most of the defects were the result of haste. Workers were paid by the piece, like everywhere else, and young workers who were trying to become Stakhanovites were in an even greater hurry and so ruined even more parts.

I worked the day shift. Sometimes, when I arrived in the morning, I literally could not get to the door of my office because of all the defective parts piled up in front of it. At first I did not understand: how could there be so few defective pieces during the day and such huge mountains of them at night? Finally, one of my employees explained it to me: the workers were trying to avoid personal responsibility and, whenever possible, they would hand over the defective parts to their night-shift counterparts, asking them to dump them in front of my door.

I was sure the shift foremen knew about this and found it quite convenient. Before my arrival they had been responsible for their own defective production, but now everybody was happy to get rid of it. They all tried to, at any rate. I found myself in the role of prosecutor. I was not supposed to register a piece without indicating where it had been produced, but the night pile did not come with any of the required forms from the shift foreman. It did not take me long to figure out that whenever a defect was the result of bad material or the fault of another shop, I would be asked to register it or would receive it with the appropriate form attached. Whenever a worker himself was responsible, the defective item would get dumped by my door at night.

After two weeks of this, I reported the situation to the shop manager.

"Comrade Manager, I have been made into a spy! All I do is try to find the guilty parties. I have no time for analyzing the causes of the defects or thinking of ways to correct them. Why not go back to the old system, where the shift foremen reported on defective production?"

"The foremen do that already when they send you the parts with the appropriate forms. Your job is to catch those who try to avoid responsibility."

"But this is not what you hired me for! You need a spy, not an engineer!"

"You were hired to curtail defective production. That's exactly what you are doing."

The shop manager, the shift foremen, and I understood that the main causes of the defects were Stakhanovism and piecework, but we could not talk about it. According to the official rhetoric, Stakhanovism was the highest form of socialist labor!"

SEREZHA's older brother, Dima, was arrested. He had been living with his family in Piatigorsk and working as a soil scientist in the agricultural department of the North Caucasus Province. Then one day he went to Stavropol on business and disappeared. Weeks passed, but we heard nothing from him. His wife became quite worried and wrote to his supervisors requesting information, but they said that they did not know anything. However, when several of his colleagues from the department were arrested, she rushed to the GPU, and, sure enough—he, too, had been arrested.

It was no secret as to why he had been arrested. Before his disappearance he had been very worried and talked a lot about the troubles he was having at work, so all the members of his family knew what had happened. The previous fall, each district had been told by the center to increase its overall tillage. In the mountainous district where Dima worked, there was very little land fit for cultivation. Most people engaged in animal husbandry, letting their cows and sheep graze on the mountain slopes, and grew barley and corn wherever possible. When Dima received his order to place hundreds of hectares under cultivation, he argued that in his district it was impossible because it was dangerous to plow up sandy soil on mountain slopes. He was told that the order had to be carried out come what may and that any failure to fulfill the state plan would be punished severely. Having written one more report warning about the dangers, he determined which areas could be plowed up with the least amount of risk. In the spring, strong winds and torrential rains washed away the thin layer of fertile soil that used to be protected by grass. Many hectares of valuable pasture were turned into a wasteland.

There was a big scandal, and the GPU launched an investigation. They did not question those who had issued the order to plow up the slopes "come what may"; they questioned only those who had carried out the order, having first resisted it.

AFTER six months at the Agricultural Machinery Plant, I realized I couldn't take it anymore. In order to catch workers responsible for defects, I had to go home very late or arrive at work very early, when the night-shift workers were still there. Those I managed to catch would usually come to my office, argue, and curse up a storm. Shop managers tried to convince me that their defects were of no importance in the final shape of the product. But we had strict norms about what could and could not be passed, and I would not let myself be moved by their arguments. Then they would become angry with me and hint that I was incompetent and did not know what I was doing. I used to come home in a bad mood almost every day. Every month, the shop would have tens of thousands of rubles worth of losses because of defective production, and my success at catching those responsible never seemed to reduce that number.

In six months of work I managed to lose five kilograms of weight. I had never been fat—now I looked like a skeleton! Besides, I had absolutely no time left over for Natasha. She did spend time with Serezha, but I felt bad that it was her father she would call whenever she woke up at night. I decided to leave the plant and find a more peaceful job close to home.

I went to see the shop manager and told him I wanted to leave because I had a small child and could not afford to work so many hours.

"It's up to you to organize your work in such a way that you get everything done by closing time."

"I haven't been able to do it, and I'm asking you to let me go."

The more he tried to talk me into staying, the more I wanted to leave that industrial Sodom and Gomorrah.

The shop manager sympathized with me and would have simply let me go without any fuss, but, by law, employees could only be fired if their enterprise no longer needed them, so another two weeks passed before he was able to move people around and finally discharge me as part of a personnel reduction scheme.

Before looking for a new job, I needed a good rest. Through Serezha's Teachers' Union, I bought a one-month vacation at a resort in Khost. On my way I dropped Natasha off at my mother's, as Rostov was very hot and dusty in midsummer.

As soon as I got off the bus in front of the resort's main building, I saw, standing on the veranda, my high school math teacher, Ekaterina Vasilievna.

"So this is where we finally meet," she said, obviously pleased to see me. "I have been here for days and have not seen a single familiar face. Let's talk to the manager and ask him to put you in the room where I am staying. There is still one free bed left."

The manager did not mind, so my things were taken to E.V.'s room. Besides my former teacher and me, there were two other women in the room. It was a large, clean room, but, to my horror, a bat was hanging from the ceiling in the corner, right over my bed. I said I would be too afraid to sleep there, but E. V. explained that as soon as it got dark, the bat would fly off to hunt and would not return until morning—probably to a different corner.

An incredible amount of flirting went on at that resort. Flirtation seemed to be the main form of entertainment there. Every night, before the curfew bell rang, the only people left in the main building were the old folks: all the rest had broken up into couples and were scattered around the grounds or the nearby woods. As for me, it was impossible to get even a tiny flirtation started because E. V. followed me around wherever I went and would not leave me alone for a second.

There were beautiful moonlit nights, and once she and I decided to go for a walk by the sea. As soon as we started down the path leading to the beach, however, someone shouted "Halt!" We stopped, of course. A man in a border-guard uniform came up to us.

"What are you doing here, Comrades?"

"We wanted to see the sea by moonlight."

"Who are you?"

"We are staying at the teachers' union resort up there."

"Didn't they tell you that it was forbidden to walk on the beach after dark?"

"No, they didn't. Why is it forbidden?"

"Don't be naive. Don't you know that the sea forms part of the border zone? Follow me, I will take you back to your resort."

WHEN I returned home from the resort, I rushed off to see if there was a job for me at the pasta factory—the factory nearest to where we lived. It was just one block from our building—about a three- to four-minute walk—and I had always thought of it as my number-one choice for a new job. I knew that managers tended to be busy in the morning with problems that had accumulated during the previous evening and night shifts, so I went to see the chief engineer after lunch. To my delight, he was in his office and agreed to receive me right away.

He was a small, frail-looking man with a Chekhovian goatee and an exhausted, unshaven face. Having heard who I was and what I wanted, he said:

"You have come at the best possible time. The trust[1] wants us to expand production and add to our selection. That will require the installation of new machinery and perhaps some structural changes, so we have been thinking about hiring someone with your background. Besides, I badly need an assistant: our factory is fairly large—we produce fifteen tons of pasta a day and our mill turns out one hundred tons of flour, and that's before the expansion—but I am the whole technology department. I have neither a deputy nor an assistant."

"Do you have a chief mechanic?"

[1] Trusts—autonomous management units with authority over several industrial enterprises and subordinate to the Supreme Council of the National Economy.

"We have just one mechanic, who also happens to be in charge of the mechanics shop, the steam power plant, and general maintenance. We have a rather complicated system here: both the mill and the pasta dryer are powered by steam from the same boiler. Our mechanic, Comrade Iusupov, is an extraordinarily gifted individual, but he is entirely self-taught. He is a good helper, but he cannot make any designs or calculations, and even if he could, he doesn't have the time. Today or tomorrow morning I will tell the trust headquarters about you, so please come back tomorrow afternoon, and we will agree on terms."

The next day I went back to the factory and learned that the trust had authorized the factory to hire me as a designer engineer. The chief engineer suggested I start immediately.

It was an incredible stroke of luck. First of all, I loved designing; second, I had no administrative responsibilities—in other words, I did not have to be responsible for other people's work; and, finally, the factory was very close to my house. This meant I would not be spending hours waiting for streetcars or buses, that I could go home for lunch, and that in case of an emergency Davydovna would have no difficulty finding me.

FINALLY the new theater was built, and the well-known Moscow director Zavadsky and several of his actors, including the "Distinguished Actress of the Republic," Maretskaia, arrived in Rostov for the year (having been forced to do so by their union, as I later found out).

Soon our local paper published the season's program, which provoked a great deal of enthusiasm among our theater lovers. The program included several plays that had not been seen in the city for many years: several by Chekhov, Gorky's *The Lower Depths*, some Shakespeare, and a few tired old plays about revolutionary heroes. We bought season tickets.

The season's premier was *Liubov Iarovaia*,[2] which was about revolutionary heroes, but because Maretskaia was in the title role, we decided to go. In the foyer, in front of the billboard listing the program for the next several weeks, we saw a large crowd of agitated people. We came closer and saw something that made us extremely angry. The program had nothing to do with the one we had been given when we bought our season tickets. Three-fourths of the total were plays by Soviet authors devoted to the "majesty of socialist construction" and the "heroism of the revolution." Everyone around us looked dismayed, and we could hear people whispering as they walked away.

SIGNS of the approaching New Year's Eve were everywhere. Christmas tree ornaments had appeared in the stores, and even though the most beautiful and interesting ones were quite expensive, people were in a hurry to buy them. Almost every evening, after work, I would take Natasha shopping for new and interesting toys and decorations. That year we bought a large silvery glass star to go on top of the tree, and a whole family of brightly colored birds. They were no longer selling

[2] A 1926 play by K. A. Trenev (1876–1945).

angels, but one could buy fairies in sparkling dresses with wings. Once, when we walked into our local grocery store, we spotted that traditional Christmas treat and decoration: oranges. Oranges had become a rarity; they had to be imported from abroad, and because precious hard currency could not be spent on such things, we had been doing without them for many years.

"Where do these beauties come from?"

"From Spain. We are helping our Spanish friends, so it's a sweet deal all around," laughed the clerk.

"At least we're getting something in return," I said to myself as I bought a whole crate of oranges—fifty of them altogether!

There was one problem with the tree. Serezha and I had wanted to wait and set it up for Christmas, on January 7, the way we did when we were children, but the new official, government-supported holiday was celebrated one week earlier, and that is when the magnificently decorated trees on city squares and in schools were lit up, and children's parties in offices and factories were organized. Seeing that the time for the trees had arrived, the children did not want to wait an extra week before they could start decorating their own, so we agreed on the following compromise: we would decorate and light up the tree before New Year's Eve, and on January 7 we would have a special "undressing of the tree" celebration: invite lots of kids, move the tree to the center of the room, have them sing and dance traditional dances around it, and, at the end, take off all the decorations. Everything edible—gingerbread cookies, candy, and fruit—would be given away, and the ornaments would be put away until the following year. Even so, I felt I was short-changing the real holiday when I lit up the tree before Christmas.

It was inconvenient to keep a Christmas tree in a small room for seven days. It took up a lot of room and quickly began to shed its needles, but those who wanted to have a tree for Christmas had no choice because no trees were sold after New Year's. The city soviet also tried to interfere by publishing special newspaper ads about the fire hazard posed by dry trees being kept in homes after the New Year's celebrations. Many people worried that, under the pretext of fire safety, the authorities would ban the keeping of trees for more than one or two days. In fact, there was no reason to be concerned about fires because virtually everybody was now using electric lights rather than candles.

DIMA and his supervisors were tried by a "troika"—that is, by three people appointed by the GPU. They considered cases and pronounced verdicts without following normal legal procedures, and their decisions could not be appealed.

Before the trial Dima had undergone lengthy interrogations by GPU agents, whose job had been to make him confess that he had conspired with wreckers.[3] Dima had refused to do so, and this ended up saving his life. All those who had been forced to confess were shot. During the troika proceedings (which were not even referred to as a "trial"), Dima explained that, before issuing the order to plow

---

[3] Wrecker—an individual accused of sabotaging the economy.

up the pastures, he had submitted written warnings about the possible dangers to the agriculture department and had even gone there in person in an attempt to have the plan assignment reduced. To this, one of the members of the troika said that, as a Soviet citizen, he should have exposed this wrecking by complaining to the provincial party committee, to the GPU, to the Central Committee in Moscow, or even to Comrade Stalin himself!

Why should a nonparty specialist complain about his nonparty supervisor to the Central Committee of the party—especially if he knew that the order had been given by the party in the first place?

The troika sentenced all the "conspirators" to death, but some sentences, including Dima's, were later commuted to ten years of labor in a camp.

My father told me that when he went to visit Dima in prison, he could not recognize him at first. Standing before him was not the healthy thirty-five year old he had known but a gray-haired, bent old man.

The arrest and sentencing of Serezha's brother had an immediate effect on my life. Once, when I was at work, our secretary came to announce that the head of the special section wanted to see me. He was the only person in the section but was always referred to as the "head," probably because he had informers reporting to him. I had never been to see him and was afraid that he either had an informer's report on me or wanted to ask me about one of my colleagues. It was not a secret to anybody that the special section was part of the GPU. Every factory and every office had its own special section. Its job was to keep an eye on the employees, mostly through secret informers, and to keep personnel files that included reports on political reliability from former employers and even from residential apartment managers.

It was not a good idea to keep the special section head waiting, so I drank a glass of cold water to calm my nerves and immediately went to see him.

His office was located at the very end of the hall and had a special soundproof door. I entered and looked around. Much of the office was taken up by a safe, which probably contained the personnel files. In the corner was a desk, and behind the desk, with his back to the wall, sat the "head." You could not reach him across the desk. Above him was a portrait of Stalin. In front of him lay an open file, and I could see the form I had had to fill out when I applied for a job there.

Pointing to the chair across the desk from him, he said: "Sit down, Comrade Engineer."

"You wanted to see me?"

"We have received information that one of your relatives has been convicted under Article 58, yet you failed to indicate it in the form you filled out when you were hired."

"I haven't heard anything about any relative of mine having been arrested. Who are you talking about?"

"Your husband's brother has been sentenced to ten years for wrecking."

"Oh, you mean him! I do not consider my husband's family as being my relatives."

"What do you mean?" he asked, sounding surprised.

"It's very simple. Some women marry four or five times. Today you have one husband, tomorrow another . . . Before you know it, you'll have too many relatives to be responsible for."

He burst out laughing.

"Well, if that's your attitude toward marriage, then of course your husband's brother is not your relative!"

"I think a lot of people have the same attitude."

"That's one way of looking at it," he said, indicating that I could go.

That night I told Serezha about it: "That son of a bitch wanted me to renounce Dima. So that's what I did, just like St. Peter. But what choice did I have? The last thing I need is a note in my file, stating that I am not trustworthy."

"You did the right thing," said Serezha.

THE same "volunteer work," which I had hated so much when I was in college, caught up with me at work, too. One day I was asked to go see our trade union representative. Besides Comrade Svetlov, who was one of the shift foremen at the mill, the secretary of our party cell, Comrade Khubiev, was also there. Khubiev was our only full-time activist.

"Comrade Bogdan," said Svetlov, "the party and the trade union have a little commission for you. You have been assigned to the city soviet, to help them with the election campaign. Your job will be to conduct several educational meetings at the polling station, explain the constitution to the toiling masses, and do some campaigning on behalf of our candidate, Comrade Evdokimov."

"Comrade Svetlov, that would be very difficult for me to do. I work all day long, and I have a small child who needs my attention. Couldn't you get one of the workers to do it? I simply cannot do it!"

"You mustn't refuse, Comrade," said Khubiev. He was a Tatar and spoke Russian with a fairly strong accent. "We have considered all the eligible members of the union and have concluded that you are the only person we can entrust with such an important task. You won't be there all by yourself: we will also be sending the head of the lab and one of the shift managers. You must understand that this particular assignment can only be carried out by educated people who understand the constitution and will be able to answer any questions the voters may have. Bear in mind that some voters, especially women, like to ask trick questions, and it is important that they be answered correctly."

"But Comrade Khubiev, the constitution was written by Comrade Stalin for ordinary Soviet people. Everything in it is clear and unambiguous. All one needs to do is read it! If you want to make sure the voters have read it, send any literate Komsomol member to the polling station, and he can read it to them."

"It is not as simple as you may think!" laughed Khubiev. "You say that everything in the constitution is completely clear, but I have taught a few classes on the constitution to the party members of our factory, and I assure you that lots of people have difficulty understanding and require explanations."

"You may be right, but that doesn't change the fact that I am terribly busy.

When I'm not at work, I have to keep up with the professional literature—especially now that we are retooling the factory. I simply cannot afford to accept any additional responsibilities."

"You will be required to conduct only three classes: two on the constitution, and one, on our candidate, Comrade Evdokimov. You have read about him in the *Molot*,[4] of course, and we have a special campaign booklet as well. You can bring your child, if you like: child care will be available at the polling station to which you have been assigned."

Finally I gave in because to go on refusing would have led to a conflict with our party and trade union cells, and that would have been a risky proposition.

The people at the polling station turned out to be a lot less active than Khubiev had predicted. As always in such cases, most of them had been forced to come by their district representative, who had gone door to door trying to persuade every single resident to come. They sat through my lecture, thinking their own thoughts.

At the end of my presentation on Comrade Evdokimov, I asked if there were any questions. No one had anything to say . . .

Rostov had its own "Scholars' House," a fairly nice club for the city's academics. It had a library; a small hall for concerts, lectures, and various meetings; a good tennis court; and a gym with boxing, fencing, and gymnastic equipment. Serezha often played tennis, and even though I did not like sports, I took it up, too, so as not to be left out. I found the game boring though, both as player and spectator, and was soon sick of bouncing the ball against the wall. Only once, when a French champion came to Rostov, did I enjoy watching tennis. He had come straight from France, and I went to see a real Frenchman, not a tennis player, but it turned out that his game was worth seeing, too.

When I tired of tennis drills, I joined a dancing class to learn the fox-trot, tango, and other recently permitted dances. The class was very popular among assistant professors and the children of older scholars. We danced to the piano, but because our piano player knew very few good tunes, we always began with the fox-trot "Me and My Masha at the Samovar" and ended with the "Rhumba." Someone had written very obscene lyrics to go with the "Rhumba" tune, and it was unpleasant when your partner would sing that filth under his breath while dancing with you.

Once we asked the piano player:

"Why do you always play the same songs? We're tired of dancing to 'Masha'!"

"What choice do I have? I don't know any other songs. Haven't you noticed that I have been playing from memory? Get me some new songbooks, and I'll play a new song every time."

"But where can we get them?"

"You can copy them, if anyone you know has any."

A couple of weeks later one of the students brought in some handwritten music.

---

[4] *Molot*—Rostov's main daily newspaper.

"One of my friends, a student at the conservatory, jotted this down while listening to Radio Budapest," he explained. "If it doesn't sound quite right, feel free to change it however you like."

So that is what she did. Then somebody else brought in more handwritten music, and soon she could afford to drop "Rhumba" from her repertoire.

ONE day I received a letter from my college friend, Olga. She would be passing through Rostov and wanted to come by to see me. I was curious to see her again. I heard from someone that she had graduated from one of the institutes in Leningrad and gone to work in a very remote part of the Soviet Union.

Olga arrived Sunday morning and said she had to leave that same evening. She had not changed in the four years since I had last seen her. She still looked striking, and she was still wearing severe, somewhat masculine clothes: a rough raglan coat, a dark narrow skirt, and a blouse with a tie-like collar. Her short, curly hair also looked the same.

Serezha started asking her questions: "Is your work interesting? Are you happy there?"

"It's interesting, but hard. We're building a hydroelectric station with prisoner labor. I am one of the very few free employees there. I chose the place myself when I graduated. Everybody at the institute was happy: few people wanted to go to the Far North. They respect me up there and trust me with the kinds of jobs that very few recent college graduates get to do. Before I got there, I hadn't realized I'd be working with prisoners. Perhaps I wouldn't have gone if I had known. But now I know it's good for me. I have seen how Communism is actually being built."

"Serezha's brother is one of those builders in the Lake Baikal area."

"Even from a purely professional point of view, it's a terrible waste of human energy. With free people living in decent conditions, we could have built two power stations by now. And the country desperately needs such stations! But the party has two goals: to build a power station, but at the same time to destroy anyone capable of resisting its will. That's the horror of it all."

"And what about you, do you also live pretty badly?"

"Not so badly. We live in huts in the woods, but I have a room of my own, and I've even been given some servants."

When we were by ourselves, I asked her: "Olga, what about your daughter? Where is she?"

"I left her with my parents. I'm glad I had a girl. I don't like boys."

"You're glad, but you still left her behind! Couldn't you have taken her with you?"

"No, it's not the right kind of place for a kid, and, in any case, I'm busy all day long."

"Does your daughter have a father?" I asked.

"Don't be ridiculous. Of course she has a father. It was not by immaculate conception, but if you mean to ask if I have a husband, the answer is no.

"You haven't changed at all."

"Tell me, Valia, what do I need a husband for? There are so many interesting things in life. There's so much to do! I just don't want to waste my energies on a family. I don't want to tie myself down. There are too many unavoidable burdens in life—why would I want to take one on voluntarily?"

"But if you love someone, having a family with that person is not a burden."

"I don't happen to love anybody."

"But what about your daughter, aren't you going to take her with you at some point?"

"Only when she's capable of taking care of herself and helping me. To tell you the truth, I had a baby because I wanted to have someone who would be really close to me for the rest of my life. As soon as I met the right man, I had her."

"What does her father think about all this?"

"Her father? He doesn't think anything. Do men ever think about babies under those circumstances?"

VASIA, my sister Shura's husband, was arrested. Nobody had expected it. Before his arrest, Vasia had been a very successful district manager at one of the biggest mines in the Donbass. He had received several awards for outstanding work; his district had been considered a Stakhanovite one; and shortly before his arrest he had written to say that he was going to a Stakhanovite conference in Moscow. One week before his departure, however, there was a gas explosion in his district. Seven miners were killed, and his assistant was badly wounded.

Mother went to stay with Shura and remained there until the end of the trial. There was nothing in the newspapers about either the accident or the trial, and we did not learn anything until Mother returned.

Vasia's mine was a "gas mine," which meant that it generated so much gas that the use of dynamite to reach the coal deposits was forbidden. But in order to meet the demands of the trust and the party organization on plan overfulfillment, Vasia had been setting off illegal dynamite explosions. That is why his mine had achieved such high results in coal output and become a "Stakhanovite" one. He had always taken serious precautions, however: having sent his workers to the main shaft as far from the explosion site as possible, he would—all by himself—set off small explosions during a time when the amount of gas in the mine was minimal. But that time he had gotten sick and spent two weeks in bed. In his absence the output had fallen, and the director of the mine had summoned Vasia's assistant and yelled at him for not knowing how to work the "Stakhanovite way." The next day the assistant had set off an explosion without having taken the usual precautions and, most important, without having sent the workers off to the main shaft. In the explosion all the workers had been killed, and the assistant himself had been badly wounded and had died in the hospital several days later.

Had the assistant not died, he would have been put on trial, and Vasia might have been left alone, but, as it was, somebody had to be punished for the deaths of the workers, so Vasia was arrested. He admitted right away that he had been violating the safety laws. In his defense he said that he had never risked anyone's life but his own, and that he had done so to "get as much coal as possible for our socialist motherland." During the trial he did not try to shift the blame onto somebody else—he did not say, in other words, that the director, the party organization, and the safety engineer, whose authorization was needed to receive dynamite from the warehouse, had all known about it. All the people who had been giving him awards for being a Stakhanovite had known how he was achieving his outstanding results.

The investigation did not take long; two weeks after the arrest he was put on trial. He was found guilty of safety violations and sentenced to three years of forced labor in a camp. When we heard the sentence, we all breathed a deep sigh of relief because if he had been found guilty of "wrecking," he would probably have been shot. But the court was not as strict with Stakhanovites as with ordinary people.

My parents were very upset not only because Vasia had been sent to a camp, but also because it turned out that he had been breaking records by risking his workers' lives. Like many workers, Father had always been suspicious of various Stakhanovite records, saying that they seemed "fishy" to him.

OUR nanny Davydovna loved all kinds of meetings and rallies, and, according to our contract, I had to let her attend them all. Her meetings took place in the evening, and she usually found out about them from our janitor, who belonged to the same union.

One day she returned from her meeting very excited and immediately told me everything that had been said there. I did not particularly encourage talk about these meetings—I had had enough of my own—but the following words made me sit up and pay attention:

"Today we had an especially important meeting. You know how many enemies of the people they've been discovering recently, so at today's meeting they told us how we maids and nannies could help the Soviet state fight its enemies."

"I don't think you can do much to help," I said, trying to provoke her into saying more. "Only the GPU can do that job."

"You're wrong. They told us that since we live in people's homes, we can see and hear things that others can't: What do our masters think about the Soviet state? What do they talk about when guests come over? If certain people come over regularly, it may be worth listening in on their conversations."

"Well, some of our friends come over on a regular basis to play cards. What's so suspicious about that?"

"There's nothing suspicious about that. You don't even close the door when you have people over, so I can always hear what you're saying. But there are others who always close their doors to make sure their maids can't hear them—it's in those cases that we were told to try to listen. If they say something suspicious or name names, we are supposed to write those names down on a piece of paper, so as not to forget."

"But, Davydovna, some people might want to talk about personal things, or just simply gossip, and not want strangers to hear. Who would want a maid who eavesdrops? That would be terrible!"

"I didn't mean eavesdropping all the time; only when the talk was about politics. And besides, it's not 'eavesdropping,' it's just paying attention."

I felt as if I were about to faint. They were teaching our maids how to spy on us! If she started "paying attention," she could interpret anything as a conspiracy!

"And you know what else?" continued Davydovna excitedly. "They told us about cases where maids had proved their usefulness to the Soviet state. You heard about the recent arrest of the Semenovs from our building? It turns out that it was their maid, Nastia, who helped unmask them. Their apartment is bigger than ours, and she noticed that when certain people came over they would always take them into the study and close the door behind them. Once she heard Trotsky's name mentioned. Everybody knows that Trotsky is our enemy, so she became suspicious and started listening in, trying to overhear their conversation. And once, when her mistress threw a bunch of letters into the fire and left, Nastia pulled them out and took them to the union. When they read those letters, they confirmed that her employers were Trotskyites and they were arrested."

"So, did Nastia get a reward?"

"You mean you haven't heard? After their arrest, Nastia got their whole apartment, with everything in it."

"And she is living by herself in that big apartment?"

"No, she exchanged it for a smaller one, but she kept all the things. And you probably don't know what happened to the Semenov children?"

"No, I don't."

"I feel sorry for them. They were taken to an orphanage the day after the arrest. Soon their grandmother came to take them home with her, but she couldn't find them. She spent several days looking for them (Nastia let her stay in her apartment during that time), but they had simply vanished. She looked for them in all the shelters and orphanages, but she never found them. People say that they must have been sent to another town or placed in an orphanage under a different name—the kids themselves were too little to know their own names."

"Listen, Davydovna, we also burn old letters, as you know. We have lots of relatives and friends, and there's no point in keeping all the letters we get. Are you going to start reading them now?"

"What are you saying, Valentina Alekseevna?! I know that you and Sergei Vasilievich are loyal Soviet citizens. You often don't even burn your old letters yourself—you give them to me, to start the fire with. You don't even lock anything. In fact, if I wanted to, I could read all the papers that Sergei Vasilievich keeps in his desk, only of course I wouldn't do such a thing."

When I told Serezha about it later that night, he did not look surprised.

"Did you really doubt that they would turn such people as Davydovna into spies? It's not even called spying anymore; it's "proletarian vigilance." I'm sure she feels proud that the state is asking her for help."

"But she is a mature woman and should know what it means."

"A lot of people do, but she used to be married to a policeman, so she doesn't find it strange. What is strange is that they were not warned not to say anything about it to their employers."

"Perhaps they were, but in her mind we are still 'one of us.'"

THAT year the North Caucasus military district planned to stage a huge holiday celebration. Voroshilov[5] and Budenny[6] were expected to attend. The preparations were begun long in advance. The main event was to be a horse race. I was dying to see it and was delighted when Serezha received an invitation to the race as well as to the solemn ceremony at the Red Army Club. Imagine my disappointment when, just a few days before the holiday, somebody from the district called Serezha and said that the celebrations had been canceled.

Immediately afterward, we heard rumors that there had been a plot to assassinate Voroshilov during the festivities, as well as the whole provincial party leadership, including First Secretary Sheboldaev.

Somewhat later, Sheboldaev himself was arrested, and from then on his name could only be mentioned when preceded by the words *traitor*, *murderer*, and the like.

Several years before, some trees had been planted next to the Agricultural Machinery Plant, and the place had been named Sheboldaev Park. It was a children's park. Once I heard one little boy ask another: "Where are you going?"

"To the Traitor Sheboldaev Park," was the answer.

Evdokimov, the Supreme Soviet delegate from our district, was also arrested. There was no official report to that effect, but the news spread quickly. That day I stayed late at work and overheard the following conversation between a guard and a cleaning woman:

"Have you heard? Evdokimov was arrested, and his wife hanged herself," said the guard. "What a terrible way to go."

"Who is Evdokimov?"

"Don't you know? He was a member of the Provincial Executive Committee and our delegate to the Supreme Soviet. His wife was a big Communist, too."

"Then she got what she deserved!" said the cleaning woman.

As was happening everywhere else in the country, the arrests of the top leadership, in this case Sheboldaev and Evdokimov, were followed by the arrests of their closest friends and collaborators. The director of the Agricultural Machinery Plant was arrested, too, as were many of the plant's engineers. The population of our own apartment building, which consisted mostly of engineers and government officials, was practically wiped out. Almost every night the GPU's black raven[7] came to take someone away.

---

[5] K. E. Voroshilov (1881–1969)—Bolshevik military leader during the civil war, and later a member of the Central Committee's Politburo (1926–60) and the people's commissar of military and naval affairs (1925–34) and of defense (1934–40).

[6] S. M. Budenny (1883–1973)—Bolshevik cavalry commander during the civil war.

[7] Black raven—police van.

I remember one horrible night in particular, when our upstairs neighbor was arrested and his apartment was searched. He was some kind of party bigwig by the name of Siuda. The search lasted a very long time, and we could hear men in heavy boots walking around and, for some reason, moving furniture back and forth, then the sound of a van leaving, and finally the loud wailing of his wife and children.

After that, several professors were arrested, including the physics professor from the university and all the employees in his radio lab. I was very lucky, as it turned out, to have been turned down by them!

My nerves began giving out, and I wrote to Mother, asking her to come and get Natasha and take her home with her for a while. I was afraid that if we were arrested, she would be sent to an orphanage and get lost there. I did not explain in my letter why we had decided to send Natasha to Kropotkin in the middle of the fall (we had never done that before), but Mother understood and came right away.

"Why do you think Serezha may be arrested?" she asked.

"Because we don't know why everybody else is being arrested, and because we do know that some of them have never committed any crimes. The simple fact that Serezha never praised Stalin in his lectures may be enough to get him arrested."

"But how can he praise Stalin in lectures on botany?"

"None of it matters anyway because, as you know very well, most people are arrested without being guilty of anything at all, but then, under torture, begin to slander their friends. The authorities want to make sure that people are too frightened to resist. I think the GPU has a production plan, like the rest of us. They are told how many people must be arrested in a given town. Anyway, Mother, I also want you to take all our valuables. I have told Davydovna that Father is going away on business and that you are taking Natasha back with you to keep you company."

There were so many arrests that it was impossible to keep completely silent about them, impossible not to say a few words to a trusted friend. When my friend, Vadim, came by, I, knowing that he lived with his mother and brother, a military engineer, asked him if everything was okay.

"My brother is fine, so far, but my mother really surprised and upset us the other day. We knew, of course, that she was concerned about us, but we certainly hadn't realized to what extent."

"All wives and mothers are concerned."

"Yes, but it manifests itself in different ways. You know what my mother dreamed up? A while back, I started noticing that she kept writing things down in a little school notebook. Several days ago, I walked into her room, and there she was, writing again. When she saw me, she looked embarrassed, perhaps even a little scared, and quickly closed her notebook and put it away. I asked her if she was writing poetry, by any chance, but she only said in an irritated way: 'When did you get home? I didn't realize you were back.'

"Later, over dinner, I said, jokingly, to my brother: 'Mother is writing poetry again (she used to write poetry when she was young), but she's being very secretive about it and doesn't want us to know.' My brother joined in the teasing, but suddenly she burst into tears, rushed out of the room, and then returned with two notebooks: 'Here, take a look at these poems.'

"And do you know what it was? It was her diary, except that she had interspersed everyday events with praise to Stalin. 'Today I bought delicious sausage: how right Comrade Stalin was when he said that our life had become happy and cheerful!' Or a nut cake recipe, with the following explanation: 'Now, thanks to the wise policies of Comrade Stalin, we can afford to make a nut cake!' Not too many of them—just a few here and there. My brother asked her: 'Why are you writing this? If I get arrested, they'll want to read my papers, not yours. And it's too obvious, anyway: the dates are old, but anyone can see that it was written recently.' But she said: 'No, look, I used different kinds of ink, and sometimes a pencil. When they come to arrest someone, they read everything, so when they read this, they will realize how loyal our family is.' Can you believe it?"

MY brother-in-law, Savva, died. He had been sick for a long time—more than a year, I think—but he had ignored the pain because of trouble at work. His boss at the railway department had been arrested, and Savva had been asked to replace him, so, as he used to say, he "had no time to be sick." When he could no longer stand the pain, he went to see the doctor, and from there went straight into the hospital. They said he had a case of badly neglected cancer of the stomach, and he didn't make it out of the hospital alive. While Savva was in the hospital, several more of his colleagues were arrested, and a GPU agent came a few times to interrogate him. He even asked the doctor if Savva was only pretending to be sick.

Mother went to stay with Zina the last two weeks before his death, and she told me afterward that he had been interrogated literally a few hours before his death. Savva already knew that he did not have long to live, and, as he said to Mother afterward, he told the agents the whole truth—that is, exactly what he thought of them.

When Savva died the union refused to help, and Zina had to pay for the funeral with what little money she had left. Normally the union would pay the full cost of a member's funeral; the higher the position, the more magnificent the funeral. Savva had been a division head at the Mineralvodsky railway district, and someone in his position should have been buried with all the division employees present and a brass band playing Chopin. As it was, none of his colleagues came to his funeral. Even his closest friends, to say nothing of his acquaintances, had been scared away by the GPU's interest in him during his illness, especially because several of the arrested engineers had been shot shortly before Savva's death.

ON our visit to Leningrad we stayed with my college friend, Maksim Chumak. He lived just outside Leningrad, in Detskoe Selo. He had a fairly large apartment, by Leningrad standards: two rooms, a kitchen, and a balcony. The apartment was in a former monastery, and right outside the walls was a park.

Maksim had not changed much. By the age of thirty, he had become an assistant professor in a Leningrad institute, started a family, and moved into a good apartment, so I expected to find him looking happy and healthy. But he was the same old Maksim, pale and skinny.

"How come you look so exhausted?" I asked him. "You must still be doing too much volunteer work!"

"Somebody has to," he said curtly.

He had a small family: a wife and daughter, and his wife's mother. His father-in-law had died recently, so his mother-in-law had moved in with them. This was very convenient: Lialia could keep her job without having to worry about her daughter.

It did not take me long to realize that they were not doing too well as a family. Once, when everyone else was gone, Maksim's mother-in-law asked me: "Valentina Alekseevna, you're an old friend of Maksim's. Tell me, has he always been a heavy drinker?"

I was shocked. "He would have a drink now and then, like all the men, but he was never a heavy drinker. I've never even seen him drunk!"

"Well, now he seems to be turning into an alcoholic. Have you noticed that we've been having drinks with every meal?"

"I thought the vodka was to celebrate our arrival."

"No, he's been drinking less since your arrival. He gets very angry when I mention his drinking. We have fights about it all the time."

"What about Lialia?"

"Lialia's under his thumb; she's afraid to say anything to him. But she's also worried that he won't last long on this kind of diet."

"You mean, he just gets drunk all by himself?"

"Yes, he has a few drinks with dinner, and at night he goes to bars. Lialia says he drinks at lunch, too."

When we were going home, I asked Serezha: "How did you like Maksim? Did you find him interesting?"

"It's hard to tell. I don't know him well enough."

"You'd seen him before, more than once, and you just spent a whole week in his house. You must have an opinion."

"Actually I found him a very dull, uninteresting person."

"Really?!"

"You say that he's very good at what he does; I can't judge, it's not my field. But, as a man, I thought he was narrow-minded and not very cultured."

"Because he's always talking about politics?"

"No, the problem is that he talks about politics in such a trite, official way that you can't help getting bored."

WE in Rostov were very proud of our symphony and its conductor, Paverman. He came in fifth in a nationwide competition—a not inconsiderable achievement at an event with several dozen participants. Many people thought that he should have gotten third or even second place (first place clearly belonged to Melik-

Pashaev). I went to several concerts of the Kharkov conductor, who was ranked above ours, and I did not think he was any better. He twitched and fidgeted, and waved his arms around so much that you had a hard time concentrating on the music!

ONCE I asked our mechanic: "Iusupov, I've always wanted to ask you: what were your father and brothers arrested for?"

"For nothing. Our family moved here from southern Armenia, in Turkey. In 1936 we were all asked to take Soviet citizenship, and they refused. Having seen enough of what was going on around him, my father decided that he would be better off as a foreigner."

"But why did you leave Turkey in the first place?"

"Because after the war the Turks started oppressing Christian Armenians—not oppressing them actually, but slaughtering them. My father had lived in Russia before the revolution, and he knew that Russia had always protected the Orthodox, so we came—right out of the frying pan into the fire!"

"Why weren't you arrested along with them?"

"Because I immediately agreed to take Soviet citizenship."

SOON afterward I went to the mechanic's shop to take a look at the new presses, but Iusupov looked terribly depressed and did not seem to be listening to what I was saying. Finally, he said: "Valentina Alekseevna, could you stop by my office for a second?"

In his small, brick-walled office one could talk without fear of being overheard. His friends among the workers would not have allowed anyone to eavesdrop at the door. They would have come in to ask a question, and then warned him.

"You know, Valentina Alekseevna, the GPU is on my case again. They called yesterday and told me to come by in the evening. And you know what they asked me to do? To give them a list of all the people I know in the technical division: this one and the one where I worked before. I asked them why, and they said they wanted to know who was friendly with whom."

"You mean, not just a list of your own friends, but a list of everyone you know and *their* friends?"

"That's the way I understood it. I asked them: 'Do you want just my buddies or casual acquaintances, too?' They said: 'Make up two lists, one of your close friends, another of casual acquaintances.' "

"Why did they choose you?"

"They know that my father and brothers are in a camp, and so they think that I'll be easy to scare. Their own party spies are not enough for those sons of bitches!"

"Well, it makes sense. People trust you more. What are you going to do?"

"I'm not going to write down anything for them. Let them go to hell. This morning I went to see the head of the secret section and told him what they wanted and what I thought about it. He comes down here all the time: he's building a country house for himself and keeps asking for locks, hinges, pipes, and so on. I never refuse him anything. Anyway, his advice was to wait and hope they forget . . . They don't even call it spying, the bastards—'just a list of who is friendly with whom!' You, for example, would be mentioned twice: as my friend and as the friend of Iakov Petrovich. I guess I'm supposed to write: 'She often goes to Iakov Petrovich's office and talks to him one on one.' I am not going to write down anything for them!"

"It sounds pretty bad . . . Should I warn Iakov Petrovich?"

"Don't tell him anything. He's a party member now, so they'll take care of him. And anyway, there won't be a list."

"Don't be so sure. They may force you to write it down right there, in their presence."

"Over there, I'd be in a rush, and would write such a work of art nobody would ever be able to read it. I'm barely literate, you know."

The GPU did not forget Iusupov. Two weeks later they called him in again. He told them he was terribly busy with the new presses and had no time to write down anything, what with the director pushing him so hard. The director did, indeed, come down every day to look at the presses. Having listened to all his complaints and explanations, they gave him three more weeks.

Then he got lucky. The purge of the Rostov GPU began, and the agent who had asked for the list was arrested. The head of the secret section himself told Iusupov about it.

MY old friend Tania came to see me, but unfortunately could not stay for more than a day. She and her husband, who was also an engineer, lived in Leningrad. They were on their way to Kropotkin to see her parents and had stopped in Rostov to see me.

I was very happy to see her. We had sat at the same desk for fourteen years. As a senior, she had gotten married and moved to Leningrad, and I had not seen much of her since. She told me about her life in Leningrad:

"We received a new apartment recently, within the city limits. We had been waiting for it for several years. Our chances weren't very good because Viktor's parents had a small house in Gatchina, and we could live there, even though the commute was terrible. Besides, I was sick of living with my in-laws! I had to ask his mother's permission to do anything, so I was dying to have a place of my own."

"Did you hire a nanny for Yura?"

"No, nannies are very expensive in Leningrad, so Yura spends most of his time with his grandmother, and comes to see us on Sundays, but soon he'll start going to kindergarten, and then grade school, and he'll move in with us."

"Is it a good apartment?"

"Yes, it is. We have two rooms, although the kitchen and bathroom are communal: we share them with two other families. But that's not too bad—I only cook on Sundays, and we never take baths. I take my showers at the factory after work or go to a bathhouse. Remember how good the Leningrad bathhouses are?"

"Of course I remember. Some even have swimming pools."

"We can't complain. Our apartment not only came fully furnished, it actually had dishes, linen, dresses, and even playing cards! The previous owners must have been some kind of old-regime people: in their trunk we found very old-fashioned dresses with spangles and lace, and lots of silverware—spoons, glass-holders, candlesticks, and so on. They had all been arrested and, I guess, sent to a camp, so we inherited the apartment the way they had left it on the day of their arrest."

"It can't be very pleasant to live in such an apartment. Everything around you must remind you of the previous residents, who, chances are, were taken away and shot."

"How absurd! I never even think about it. They weren't arrested because of us, after all! And, anyway, perhaps they'll be released soon. I've put away all the personal things in the trunk, just in case: photographs, letters, linen, and dresses. If they show up, they can have them, but the rest of it I've been using without worrying too much about it."

"So they don't even have any relatives who could pick up their personal things?"

"Our neighbors say that they did have some distant relatives, but they must be afraid to introduce themselves as relatives of convicted people. Parents or children wouldn't be afraid, I don't think. Also, if their sentence included the confiscation of property, then nobody from their family has the right to that property."

"Perhaps furniture and silverware are property, and linen and dresses are not?"

"I don't have the slightest idea. All I know is that no one has come to claim the things."

I WAS asked several times to send Natasha to our factory's kindergarten. The director of the kindergarten even came to see me and suggested that I go to see for myself how well the children were being looked after. The director had a special degree in preschool education, and her assistant was a certified nurse.

"It doesn't look good," the director told me. "We're trying to convince our working mothers that children in our kindergarten get the best possible food and care—and they really do—but we don't have any of the engineers' children. The workers may think that our educated people don't trust our kindergarten. Why don't you send your child there?"

"My daughter gets sick a lot, and I'm afraid that at the kindergarten she'll be exposed to contagious diseases more often."

"We examine all our children every morning, and if there are any signs of illness, we send them back home."

"Okay, I'll talk to my husband."

When I was elected to the trade union committee, the committee chair raised the issue again: "Why don't you send your daughter to our kindergarten, Comrade Bogdan? We have an excellent kindergarten, and there's no reason in the world why you should prefer to leave your child in the care of an illiterate old woman."

By then, I had been to see the kindergarten and found it impressive. It was impeccably clean; all the children had their own lockers; all the beds used for afternoon naps had fresh sheets; and there were lots of good and expensive toys and textbooks. As a member of the trade union committee, I knew that the director gave the kindergarten all the money they asked for. Besides, they had a big playground, where the children could play both in summer and winter.

"My nanny happens to be literate," I laughed, "but why do you care whether I send my child to the kindergarten or not?"

I knew why, of course. Not trusting the parents, the party wanted to take over the raising of children as early as possible.

"You see, if the engineers start sending their children to the kindergarten, they'll be more demanding than the workers, and the quality of the kindergarten will improve. We have very few specialists with small children, and, besides, as a union committee member, you'll be keeping an eye on them."

Serezha and I discussed it and decided to try it. It could turn out to be a lot better for us if it worked out. As an only child Natasha was bored. Of course, she played with other kids in the playground, but in bad weather she was stuck at home by herself. Also, I had noticed that she was doing a lot of reading. Davydovna had probably encouraged her in this because it must have been more convenient for her to have the child sitting in an armchair reading, but for Natasha it was a little early to spend hours bent over a book. Finally, there was one more consideration in favor of the kindergarten: we would no longer need a live-in nanny. Ever since Davydovna told me that she had been asked to spy on us and had found nothing strange about it, I was afraid to have her around the house. If I did not need a permanent nanny, I could hire a more reliable person to do the cleaning—this time all of it.

So we sent Natasha to the kindergarten, first for half the day, then for the whole day—because they had their nap time after lunch, and the director recommended that we leave Natasha there to rest.

Davydovna realized her services were no longer needed, and she came to me before I could work up the courage to talk to her. It was not easy for me to let Davydovna go: during the five years she had spent with us, she had become very attached to the child.

Natasha loved her kindergarten. Every time I came to pick her up, she would have important news for me: that two boys, for example, had gotten into a fight, and Aunt Tania (their teacher) had told them to make up, but that when they were about to shake hands, one had punched the other one in the nose; or that Natasha had torn her dress while sledding, and Aunt Tania had taught her how to mend it.

I was happy that she had lots of friends and was doing well, but sometimes her stories put doubts in my mind. One day, for example, she announced: "Mama, you told me that the people I was supposed to love the most were Papa, Grandma, Grandpa, and you, but Aunt Tania said that the person we must love more than anybody else is Comrade Stalin!"

It took me a while to figure out how I could safely and persuasively refute such an awful statement. Finally, I made up my mind: "You see, Sweetie, there are different kinds of love, so you can love Stalin in one way, and Grandpa, Grandma, and Papa, in another. Papa and I, Grandpa and Grandma—we are all very close relatives; we are one family. We are almost the same as you. We love our relatives even if they are bad, mean, or ugly; relatives defend one another, especially the small and the weak—that's the way life works. Now, we love our government, and Stalin as the head of that government, in a very different way: we love them only when they are good to us."

"Stalin is good to us."

"When he is good to us, we love him."

Could I really tell Natasha that Stalin was a monster in human form, as Mother called him, and that it was impossible to love him? She would probably have told her teacher the next morning, and I would have been in trouble!

I was lucky with my new maid. Soon I got a letter from Mother, saying that she knew a person who was just right for me: hardworking and absolutely honest, a former nun. She was looking for work in a family that would allow her to pray and would not make fun of her religion. I wrote to her asking her to come as soon as possible.

JUNE 22, 1941, was a Sunday, and, as on every other Sunday, I had gone to the farmers' market to do my shopping.

Above the fish counter was a loudspeaker, which usually played music, but this time there was no music. In the din and noise of the market place no one had noticed this, but suddenly a voice came over the radio: it was Molotov[8] saying that Germany had attacked our country.

At first no one paid attention to his speech, but when some of the people there realized what he was saying, they started listening and telling the others the news, until, like metal shavings attracted by a magnet, they had all gathered under the loudspeaker.

The first thought that came to my mind: "This is the beginning of the end of Soviet power!" Somehow, it did not occur to me that war was a terrible disaster and that my husband and brothers would be dragged into it; everything was overshadowed by one thought: the war would knock the Bolsheviks out of the saddle. I obviously was not the only one who felt that way: even though people were leaving quietly, most faces expressed excitement. The market place became deserted, as everybody rushed home to discuss the news with their families.

MY younger brother Alesha arrived unexpectedly. Mother had written to me that he had been drafted in spite of his bad eyesight, and I did not expect to see him so soon. There was a knock at the door, and a few seconds passed before I realized that the tall soldier standing on the doorstep was my little brother.

"Alesha! I'm so glad to see you! How did you manage to get here? How long can you stay?"

[8] V. M. Molotov (1890–1986)—member of the Central Committee's Politburo (1926–57), chairman (1930–41) and deputy chairman (1941–57) of the Council of People's Commissars, and Soviet foreign minister (1939–49; 1953–56). His was the first official Soviet announcement of Germany's attack.

"Till tomorrow morning. I'm working as a staff officer at regimental head-quarters—a desk soldier, you might say. So I went ahead and gave myself a day off—in my capacity as my own boss!"

"Are you based near here?"

"Not too far." He did not name the place, and I did not ask.

Alesha arrived after we had had our dinner, so we sat him down and, while he was eating, told him all our local and family news. The main piece of news concerned Vasia. After his period of exile was over, he had not been allowed to live in any industrial areas, but recently he had received an order from the Commissariat of Coal Production instructing him to leave immediately for the Urals, where he was to become the chief engineer in charge of several mines.

When Natasha had gone off to bed, Alesha turned serious and said: "I've come to warn you of the grave danger you may be in. Our commissar gave me special leave so I could come and talk to you. You see, it's possible that Rostov may be temporarily occupied by the Germans. If that happens, do not stay here under any circumstances. Leave as early as you can. The Germans are committing horrible atrocities in the towns they occupy. I myself saw a film showing the massacre of civilians. They are killing hundreds, even thousands of innocent people."

"You mean killing them for no reason at all? But why?"

"During a war there's always a reason to kill people. They want to murder as many people as they can in order to take over the land. They kill Communists and Komsomol members, and if, for example, the partisans kill one German soldier, they simply grab thirty Russian men and shoot them on the spot, in front of their families. When they enter a town, they check all the bomb shelters and cellars, and if they see a single Red Army man in uniform, they throw in a grenade, even if there are dozens of civilians there."

"That's impossible to believe! Are they deliberately trying to stir up resistance?"

"There already is resistance. Partisan units are popping up everywhere in Belorussia. I saw it myself on film, and I've been reading spy reports from the occupied territories."

"You can stage anything for a film. Do you really expect us to believe this? The Germans are a civilized people."

"Also, before entering a city, they bomb it ruthlessly. Rostov may very well be razed to the ground. Think about that, too."

"How can we leave? Evacuations are carried out at the last moment, and if you say one word about leaving earlier, they'll shoot you as a panic monger."

"Serezha can send you and Natasha off earlier, because children are already being evacuated; then, even if he stays until the last moment, it will be easier for him to leave by himself."

"We're not going anywhere without him."

"Please believe me, it's terribly dangerous to be captured by the Germans."

"This is all Soviet propaganda."

"Oh, my God! How can I convince you that there is much truth in it?"

He was terribly upset.

"I want to give you some advice, too, Alesha. Don't try to be a hero and don't be first in a fight. This war will be lost by the Bolsheviks. You know, of course, that people don't want to defend Communism and are surrendering by the thousands. Try to do it yourself if you can."

He looked at me in total disbelief.

"What are you telling me? To surrender to the enemy? To give up my country without a fight?! Is that what you're telling me, you . . .—he seemed at a loss for the right word—you, a Cossack woman?!"

"Your country! Your country has been in enemy hands for twenty-three years now, and it is them, not your country, that you will be defending! You're telling me about the horrors of German occupation, but we, who have seen the horrors of collectivization and the horrors of the Communist-inspired famine of 1931–32,[9] can no longer be horrified by anything!! You're telling me that the Germans are killing Russians by the thousands—well, the Bolsheviks have killed or jailed millions!! During collectivization, whole Cossack towns were deported to Siberia in the middle of winter. And how many innocent people were imprisoned or shot in 1937—just to make the rest of us more obedient. When is it going to end?!

"And you expect the Germans to grant you freedom for nothing, on a silver plate?"

"I don't expect anything. But back in high school I studied the history of the Russian Revolution and Lenin's revolutionary strategy, and I know that the Bolsheviks did everything they could to bring about Russia's defeat in the war, hoping that a defeat would provoke a revolution and result in a change of government. Lenin was a great strategist, and he won. I hope that some modern-day anticommunist politicians will follow the lead of the "great revolutionary leader" and take advantage of their country's defeat to topple his followers the way he toppled the tsar."

"For this kind of talk you could be shot without a trial."

"I'm not planning on saying it to anyone else. There's no need, anyway: everybody knows and remembers. I've never taken part in politics, and I never will. Life is short, and there are other, more interesting ways to live it. I believe that we should let the Germans beat the Bolsheviks and try to get out of this war with as few losses as we can. And then we'll see."

"And in the meantime, we should just let the Germans kill and humiliate us Russians? You know, they put Russian prisoners behind barbed wire and then starve and freeze them to death."

"I don't believe it. This is all Bolshevik propaganda designed to make people fight for them."

"But I've seen all this with my own eyes—not just on film, but in villages that have been liberated!"

Neither one of us could convince the other. Very upset, Alesha left early the next morning. As we were saying good-bye, I was filled with a terrible sadness and foreboding. I knew we would never see each other again.

---

[9] The famine was the result of excessive state procurements of grain following the collectivization of agriculture in 1929–30.

35 □ Frida Troib et al.

Engineers' Wives

□ The "Obshchestvennitsa" movement was nationally launched in the spring of 1936 at a meeting of wives of managers and engineers in heavy industry held in the Kremlin and attended by Stalin and other leaders. Its purpose was to involve nonworking wives in voluntary, unpaid activity—smartening up barracks, organizing cafeterias, planting gardens, teaching literacy, and so on—at their husbands' plants. Although some thought the movement smacked of "bourgeois charity work," it quickly became popular with wives of managers, army officers, and technical personnel. The statements published here came from women belonging to the core group of "Obshchestvennitsa" initiators, mainly wives of directors of big industrial plants in the provinces.

Frida Markovna Troib

Early in the morning, as my husband is leaving for work, I ask the usual question: "When will you be back?" "When I finish all my work," comes the expected reply. The day drags on, empty and boring. I lie down on the couch and read, and read, and read. Evening comes. It grows dark, and I get tired of reading. My husband has still not returned. He will probably come home at eight. Eight o'clock, nine o'clock . . . he is still not here. I press my face against the window and watch for car headlights. Here comes one. Let's see where it will turn. Maybe to our door. I try to listen harder—the horn sounds familiar. No, it just seemed that way. Cars keep passing by. I hear a horn, but not the one I'm waiting for.

The clock keeps ticking away. I grab the telephone receiver. But what number should I dial? He is never in the same place for very long. After many calls, a sleepy voice answers: "They were just here, but they've gone again."

All right, when he gets back, I won't talk to him, and tomorrow I won't wait for him at all. Let him look for me . . . Suddenly, there is the familiar ring at the door. I could never fail to recognize it. It is after midnight, but how fresh, how cheerful his voice is:

"You must be tired of waiting. Guess what, the 'Titan' crusher has let us down again!"

"I know that crusher means more to you than I do," I reply with tears in my voice as I run into my room.

I vent all of the day's frustration, and the tears come pouring down my cheeks.

From Z. N. Rogachevskaia, ed., *Zhena inzhenera (K Vsesoiuznomu soveshchaniiu zhen ITR tiazheloi promyshlennosti)* (Moscow-Leningrad: Ob"edinennoe nauchno-tekhnicheskoe izdatel'stvo NKTP, 1936), 16–23.

During the night something goes wrong with the clamshell crane. I can see him getting dressed—quietly, trying not to disturb me.

"Going to the factory again? I can't live like this anymore . . ."

"Please, try to understand, I must go . . ."

The door slams, and once again I am alone with my sad thoughts . . .

Why do the crusher and the crane fail to interest me?

The morning begins just as it did yesterday. It will begin the same way tomorrow.

I once read *Marx's Youth* by Galina Serebriakova. The book fascinated me.

Here is how Jenny Westphalen, Marx's wife, talks about him to a friend of hers:

"I want to be his helper, his equal friend, his companion. But for this I need to be his comrade and adviser as well as a kind and good mother to his children. I need to earn his respect as well as his trust."

I want to be his helper, his equal friend!

And I? Was I helping him in his work?—No.

What did I know about his work?—Nothing.

That is why we were speaking different languages.

I needed to work, to have my own place under the sun, rather than living in the reflection of someone else's light.

With these thoughts in mind, I took up volunteer work.

Now they call me an activist.

N. N. STAROSELETS

One of the remarkable features of our women's movement is that it involves so many different kinds of women. Among us, there are many wives of old engineers—women who have never worked anywhere, women who came out of the old intelligentsia. Among us, there are many wives of Stakhanovite workers, wives of young Soviet experts.

My biography is different from that of many of the other members of our movement. I have had a hard life, typical of thousands of others whose childhood coincided with the hard years of economic ruin, hunger, and civil war. In 1920 my parents and two little brothers died of typhus and starvation. Like thousands of others who were trying to avoid starvation, I used to hang around railway stations and climb into train cars. Now, when I remember those terrible times, I hug my little daughter very, very hard and am happy that she did not have—and will not have—such a hard childhood.

Once I was lying half-conscious in a dark corner of one of the southern railway stations, dying of hunger. Suddenly I saw the face of a Red Army soldier right above me. Later I kept seeing his face in my fleeting moments of consciousness. This unknown friend gave me tea and a bit of bread and then took me to the hospital. I remember feeling lonely and abandoned as I was recovering. But I was lucky again—a woman who was there visiting her sick daughter bolstered me up with her tenderness and sympathy.

I was brought up in a children's home. Once, when we were cleaning the Department of People's Education building, I became fascinated by a typewriter. Every day after I finished cleaning, I would sit at that typewriter, trying to learn how to type so that I could get a job. It was right there, at that typewriter, that I met another woman, a very good person. She must have taken an interest in the little girl who kept diligently pecking away at those typewriter keys with one finger. We talked. Then she gave me a note addressed to a friend of hers—an old Bolshevik, as I found out later—asking him to help me get a job. Not only did this man find me a job, but he also took me into his family, although it already consisted of seven people.

That is how I found my new mother and father.

The worst remained in the past. My life acquired meaning, and the wounds in my heart healed.

I grew up and got married. I worked hard. I took a course in preschool education and worked with children a great deal. Then, when my husband was transferred, I had to switch to trade union work. My new job was extremely exciting. I had to deal with real live people, and I knew every one of them—how they lived and what they needed.

It was with great sadness that I had to move again.

For a while in Zaporozhstal' I did not work. I was not used to the life of a housewife, and it depressed me. I wanted meaningful, creative work. I wanted to use all my energy and initiative.

Then came Sergo Ordzhonikidze's appeal to us, the wives of experts. Oh, how grateful I was to Comrade Ordzhonikidze, and with what joy I joined in the work!

I went out to the people, to workers' settlements. It must be said that we still have people who need a great deal of support, help, and attention—I'm talking about abandoned mothers with young children. Also, a lot of effort should be put into improving the workers' dormitories and into cultural work with the new workers who have just joined our ranks.

Those were the kind of people I wanted to reach out to.

Such work is very exciting to me, and I work a lot and with total abandon.

I cannot reconcile myself to the cold indifference of those bureaucrats who regard their duty to improve the living conditions of human beings as simply a formality.

What difficulties, what obstacles we have had to overcome—in the housekeeping office, for example—in order to get good beds, clean pillow cases, sheets, and flowers for the dormitories.

It is painful to think that if those same dorm managers loved their job and respected people's needs, we would not have had such bad and dirty rooms.

More than once I ran into a thick wall of indifference, lost heart, and did not know what to do. But the desire to accomplish what I had set out to do and the realization that my work was badly needed would make me forget my failures and persevere.

Now I am paying for all the good things that honest and generous Soviet people have done for me.

N. P. IVANOVA

I still have my student card from the gymnasium. Among other rules of behavior listed there is the following: "While on visits to places of amusement, at times prescribed by the authorities and in accordance with written permission given expressly for the purpose, it is strictly forbidden that schoolgirls from government-run gymnasia show any approval or disapproval of any performance." That is the way we lived, that is the way we were brought up. Any approval or disapproval was strictly forbidden. Many of us, mutilated by our families and our upbringing, have remained, for the rest of our lives, half-people and half-shadows unaware of real life and trying to escape from it.

I was lucky. Together with my husband, a prominent engineer, I emerged unscathed from the years of economic ruin, hunger, and civil war. My husband worked hard and with dedication. He was a well-known, well-paid expert. All the privations of the hard years of the civil war passed us by.

My husband continued to work. The more time he spent at the factory, the more he participated in construction, the larger grew the distance between us. He made new acquaintances. They were not just engineers—industrial administrators and party workers also began to frequent our house. My husband would talk to them not only about technology and his work. At first with surprise, then with indifference, I started hearing hundreds of new words and incomprehensible expressions.

Ever since childhood, I had been taught to entertain guests. I remember the time when I was still an expert at this art. Then it turned out that it was not enough to be able to make conversation; one had to know what to talk about. At first I tried to entertain our new guests, too. They would smile at me politely. But once, as I was trying to carry on a conversation, I looked over at my husband and stopped short. His eyes were full of anxiety and such terrible pity. I realized that I was not saying the right thing. Indeed, when I would hear the word horsepower, the only thing I could visualize was a horse-drawn carriage. I may be exaggerating a little, but, honestly, I never was interested in technology.

What was I to do? I put my old student card between myself and my husband's new words and new interests. Unwilling to learn about this new life that fascinated my husband, unwilling to understand what was going on in the country, I began to deliberately choose friends who were even less cultured than I was. Before meeting someone new, I would ask some of my old friends:

"Do you know if she is from an intelligentsia family?"

Oh, but I never had any doubt that I was an educated woman myself! I would read Zweig,[1] play the piano, and visit the select few with whom I would have charming three- or four-hour conversations.

Then I would return home.

At home once more there would be Zweig, the piano, and occasional letters from friends.

---

[1] Stefan Zweig (1881–1942)—an Austrian author of psychological short stories and fictionalized biographies.

My husband began to get on my nerves. I would ask him, "Read the newspaper to me." He would say, "No important events today." I would get upset and start screaming, "I don't need any events, just read the whole thing." My husband would start reading. I would be able to understand only half of what he was saying, but even that half I would interpret in the most primitive way.

I remember how difficult it was to pronounce some of the new words. Once I got the Control Commission and the Central Revision Commission mixed up.

It went on this way for a long time. During the first years of our married life my husband and I had had many passionate discussions.

Now we had nothing to talk about.

I was completely alone.

I began to gossip out of spite. It was I, for example, who started the rumor that our women activists who were working in the barracks had brought lice from there.

Once our maid got sick, so we had to get our lunch from the factory cafeteria. I went down there myself. I walked into the kitchen. The cook was making dry meat cutlets, the size of your palm. When he gave me those cutlets, I started yelling:

"You incompetent fools! You can't even cook. Such cutlets should be given to pigs, not to engineers."

The cook started yelling back at me.

Suddenly one of the women who was on kitchen duty that day intervened. She said: "Instead of screaming and cursing, N. P. (she called me by my first name and patronymic), why don't you show us how to make good cutlets."

I was taken aback by her presumption. Later they told me that I had turned red and then white.

I took off my coat.

My neighbor's maid took our lunch home.

I worked in the cafeteria till eight o'clock that night and, although they had just asked me to show them how to make the cutlets, I went on and made about one hundred of them myself.

My husband came home at about eleven.

I looked at him with barely concealed triumph.

He did not notice but just walked off to his room with a newspaper in his hand.

The next day I was at the cafeteria demonstrating how to make kissel.[2]

Gradually I became absorbed by the work.

This happened about a year ago.

Now I'm the one reading the newspaper to my husband.

[2] Kissel is a thick drink made of fruit juice and sugar, thickened with potato starch or corn starch.

36 □ EKATERINA OLITSKAIA

My Reminiscences (3)

□ Olitskaia ended up spending thirty years in prisons, in camps, and in exile. Her husband perished in prison. Her daughter died of croup at the age of five while Olitskaia, recently released, was living elsewhere under an assumed name, trying to print anti-regime leaflets. She was rearrested several weeks later.

ONE GRAY prison day, the door of our cell suddenly opened.

"Which one of you has a name that begins with *O*?"

I said that I did.

"The prison commander wants to see you."

What could he want? I stepped out of the cell. We walked for a long time. The commander's office was a huge, clean, light, beautifully furnished room: I saw curtains and rugs, couches and armchairs, a mahogany desk . . . Was I dreaming? The windows did not have bars . . .

"I wanted to let you know that in a couple of days you'll be transferred out of here."

"Where am I going?"

"You'll find out later. I wanted to let you know that your personal belongings will be sent directly from the prison warehouse to your place of destination. (This was a lie. We never did receive any of our things.)

"Is that all?"

"Yes, you may go now."

I returned to my cell and tried to listen to the sounds coming from the corridor. Cell doors were being opened one after another, and prisoners were being taken in and out.

What was going on? Were all the prisoners being sent away? We were puzzled and nervous. Where to? Why? Were things going to get better? Surely they could not get any worse.

The next day the cell door was opened.

"Leave your things behind and follow me. All noise is strictly forbidden."

Quietly, we left our cell. On my way down the stairs I saw a sight that was so unexpected in the usually deserted prison corridors that I stopped short.

All along the lower corridor, standing in two straight lines, were women dressed in prison uniforms: young and old, and all frightened and nervous. We were escorted down to the corridor and told to take our places at the end of the

From E. Olitskaia, *Moi vospominaniia* (Frankfurt/Main: Possev-Verlag, 1971), pp. 189–219 (abridged). For earlier selections from Olitskaia, see selections 1 and 13 in this volume.

lines. Then we saw two more prisoners appear on the stairs, and then two more . . . They came down and stood behind us. There were guards walking up and down between the lines.

I could not tell how many pairs there were. More and more new ones kept coming down the stairs. Then came the order: "There will be absolutely no talking, noise, or lagging behind. Let's go!"

Like a serpent, the file of women glided down the corridor, slipped out into the prison yard, slid around the exercise cages and the prison building, and crawled through a wide gate into another building. It was a bathhouse, but not the one where they usually took us. It was the one for large transport parties.

The next morning, right after the usual routine of toilet and breakfast, we were escorted out of our cells—with the same stern warning, but this time with our belongings. We had so few things, though: a small bundle with a pair of stockings, a couple of handkerchiefs, a scarf, a pair of gloves . . .

Pair after pair, we were taken to the yard and into the exercise cages—about forty people per cage. The yard was full of guards. Several female guards entered our cage and began the search.

It was a warm, almost hot, day. The guards on duty were in their observation posts on top of the cages. First the women were herded to one side of the cage. Then they were called up one by one, searched, and sent to the other side. The prisoners looked one another over and peered through the cracks at the neighboring cages where similar searches were going on.

After the search they were each called up—"last name, first name, patronymic, code article, sentence"—and then let out of the cage into the prison yard.

There were a lot of black vans standing in the yard. Each one was being filled to capacity. So many women were being squeezed in that it was utterly impossible to turn around or move an arm. We were suffocating inside, but the van just stood there. Apparently, we could not start until everyone had gotten in. Finally, we set off and rode for a very long time. When the doors of our van were opened, we could see a long red freight train. We were told to get out of the vans and onto the train. Our car was divided into two halves. In each half, facing each other, were four rows of wooden bunks. On the lowest bunk there was enough room to sit up—if you bent your head and shoulders; on the other ones, you could only lie down. The younger women were told to climb up on the higher bunks; the older ones took their places below.

The car was full, but the guards continued to bring in new prisoners. In the end, there were ten people per bunk. We lay on our sides, packed together so tightly that we could not bend our legs. In the middle of the car, in front of the huge sliding door, was an empty space with a toilet hole, covered with a heavy wooden lid.

I do not remember how many of us there were in that car. There were a lot, a whole lot. It was unbelievably dark and unbelievably hot. It must have been tolerable, though, because during the entire trip from Iaroslavl to Vladivostok, which lasted exactly one month, only three half-dead women were carried out of our car. One was a fragile, elderly woman who had asthma and obviously could not survive a trip like that. She started suffocating on the very first day. She told me that she had suffered from asthma ever since she had done hard labor time before the revolution, when she was an SR. After 1917 she had become a Communist and eventually had ended up in the Iaroslavl prison. Our train proved to be the end of her life's journey.

The other two were quite young. Prison life had destroyed their health. After one week on the train, their organisms could no longer tolerate the food we were being given.

It was on that train that I first got to know many of the women who had filled the Iaroslavl Special Prison. Liusia Orandzhanian and I were the only socialists. Liusia had been arrested in exile in 1936 and taken to Iaroslavl. Like me, she was desperate to see her comrades. She and I spoke the same language. But the rest? I looked at them with curiosity and interest. Judging by their sentences, they were all political prisoners. With very few exceptions, they had all been sentenced to ten years under the articles 58^{10}–58^{11} and 58^8: terror and complicity.

I looked at them, and could not believe my eyes or ears: it was a motley crowd that had nothing but the prison uniform in common. Some of them were extremely agitated, others silent and submissive. Some believed that their innocence had finally been established and that they were on their way to their place of exile; others thought that such a transfer of the whole prison population meant that there had been no review of the sentences and that this could only be a transfer to another prison or to a camp. Having spent years in tiny cells with only one other inmate or in solitary confinement, these women could not stop talking. Each one wanted to tell the others about her case, her interrogation, her unjust sentence. The most frightening thing was that they were all in prison for crimes they had not committed. I was amazed at the things they seemed to take for granted. Never before had I heard about beatings or torture during interrogations. I was also astonished to hear that all of them—or almost all—had signed fictitious confessions incriminating themselves and others. I could hear their conversations. Some of my bunkmates told me their own stories.

Two very young girls—Tamara and Nina—stood out in the crowd. They had become friends in Iaroslavl and were trying to stick together. They had climbed up onto the top bunk, from where they could look down on us. Their faces were puffy and sallow, like all prison faces, but their eyes were young and bright. They were happy to be out of solitary confinement, interested in what was going on around them, and full of hope for the future. They had both received ten-year sentences, but they did not believe for a moment that they would stay locked up for that long. "We are learning about life," they used to say.

Next to them was an Uzbek woman or perhaps a Tajik—or "a national minority," as the other women used to say.[1] "Don't you recognize her?" someone asked me. "Her portrait was in all the papers. She gave Stalin flowers, and he hugged

---

[1] *Natsmen*, an acronym for "national minority," was a new Soviet term that originally referred to any ethnic group residing on another ethnic group's territory but was increasingly used to describe members of non-European nationalities.

her. She was the first woman to discard her veil, the first to join the Komsomol. During her interrogation she had to stand for twenty-two hours straight in a hot room wearing her winter coat. She was not allowed to sleep for seven nights. But she is a true believer. She still thinks that we are all enemies of the people, and that she is the only victim of a terrible mistake."

Directly across from me, on the bottom bunk, was a huge, broad-shouldered woman. Her face was bloated and flabby, and her cheeks hung down like pouches. My neighbor told me her story:

"I met her in a cell for pregnant women. Before 1937 she used to be a camp commandant. A real animal, they say. She was arrested after Iagoda[2] was unmasked. She slandered everybody at her trial—she thought she would get off easily that way. When she first arrived in our cell, she was as broad as a house and full of self-importance. "You are all enemies of the people," she told us. "You should be shot." But then the beatings started, and she quickly got deflated. They kicked her and stomped all over her—so she had a miscarriage, of course, right there in the cell. The next day they came for her again.

"And what about your own child, where is he?" I asked.

"I spent eight months in a mother's camp with him. Then they took him away—literally tore him right out of my arms. I have three in all. At least the two older boys got to stay together after my arrest, but this one . . . I don't know if I'll ever be able to find him again. He was such a cute, chubby little thing." She began to cry.

"Why were you arrested?" I asked, trying to distract her.

"Both my father and brother were oppositionists.[3] My father joined the Bolsheviks before the revolution. They took him first, and then they arrested my brother. I kept taking parcels to them. I used to be a Komsomol member, but when my father was arrested, I was kicked out of the Komsomol and my husband was expelled from the party. In 1937 we were both arrested. My father is a wonderful, honest person, and they wanted me to denounce him. My two older boys are in an orphanage. Their teacher sent me news of them while I was still in prison, but the little one ended up in a camp nursery somewhere."

Some of the other prisoners heard us talking about children. Among them was Zinaida Tulub, a small elderly woman with amazingly bright eyes. Tulub did not try to join our conversation—she simply started speaking aloud. We could not tell if she was talking to herself or to everyone there.

"You may not agree with me, but I think my case is the worst. I have done nothing against our beloved Communist Party. I have never belonged to the party, but I have always been loyal to it. I am a loyal Soviet writer. I have been working on my book, a long historical novel. For ten years I have been living in a different age, totally engrossed in the story I was writing. My book was approved and accepted for publication. I'll stay in prison, if I have to. I am not complaining.

[2] G. G. Iagoda (1891–1938)—deputy chair of the GPU (1924–34) and head of the NKVD (1934–36). He was removed in 1936 and shot in 1938 after a show trial.

[3] That is, supporters of the internal party oppositions to Stalin's "general line."

Some people have children, I know that. It is hard on them, of course, but our party will take care of their children. They will be put in orphanages and brought up well. As for me, I had twelve cats in my apartment when I was arrested. Who will take care of them? Who will feed them?

This was met with shouts of indignation: "Cats! How dare she talk about cats!"

One of the women became hysterical. The mothers missed their children terribly. Most had very small children. The writer shrank and withdrew into herself, feeling misunderstood. Later she turned to me with a question. "Somebody told me that you were not a Communist. What are you?"

"I am an SR."

"An SR? I know about the SRs, but that was such a long time ago . . . What about now?"

"I have never renounced my party. I still think the same way."

"That's amazing," she said excitedly. "You are a true dinosaur! Please, don't feel offended. I am not judging you. But it is not every day that I meet such a fossil. A real dinosaur. I would love to talk to you, but not right now. Ever since my arrest, I have been feeling empty inside. You, of all people, should understand that I can think of nothing but those little creatures. What do they care about politics? But they will all die anyway."

I did not reply. Tulub did not seem to be insane. She would talk willingly and very sensibly about her literary work and her archival research. She knew Ukrainian history very well. And she . . . kept talking about cats. I never heard her mention politics, her interrogation, or prison.

Next to me on the bunk was a nice young woman of about thirty-two. She had the open, kind face of a Russian peasant woman. She spoke a rural dialect. Niura told me that she was not very literate and that she did not understand much about her case. Her sentence was ten years in prison and five years of exile. Niura did not have any children, but she did have a boyfriend. I was surprised to hear that his name was Waldemar. She mostly talked about him, about how happy she was that he had not been arrested. Niura said that at the interrogation his name had never been mentioned, and so she had not mentioned it either, even though this meant that she had had to keep silent about where she used to spend her evenings. Niura was extremely happy to be out of prison. She had no hopes for release; she was dreaming about life in the camp.

"In prison I withered away completely. I kept thinking about death. The cell was like a coffin! I wish I knew how to read. I can sign my name, but that's about it. If they are taking us to a camp, we'll have to work, and time will go by faster. If only they would let me do the job I am used to!"

"And what is that?"

"I worked in a kitchen for four years. I was even assistant chef for a while. Are you from the Moscow area? I'll tell you about my life, if you don't mind. I kept thinking about my life while I was in prison. I kept pacing back and forth, thinking and thinking . . .

"I grew up in a village. I dropped out of school after the fourth grade. Our whole village was collectivized before I turned sixteen. I was on sick leave, so I worked only when I wanted to. I dreamed of going back to school . . . And then I met Waldemar. He was a chauffeur, and he often passed by our house. There was a resort for high Moscow officials nearby. Waldemar's job was to drive them around. He is the one who got me a job as a dishwasher at the resort. He knew some people there . . . If only you could see my Waldemar! He doesn't smoke or drink, and he is both smart and handsome. I guess that's why they hired him to drive the leaders around. I saw all of them at the resort. I saw Kalinin,[4] too. Usually they would just come down for the evening, but sometimes they would stay for one or two days. Those were royal vacations they had; they could order any food they wanted. After three years I got promoted. They kept promising to send me to a cooking school. Waldemar and I were happy together. We were about to get married. In my cell I kept thinking about him. While I was still in Moscow, he visited me in prison. "I'll wait for you," he said. But how can he? When I heard "ten years," I knew right away he would not wait that long. They had arrested everyone who worked in the kitchen."

"Why were you all arrested?"

"I don't even want to think about it. I turned out to be a terrorist. We were planning to poison someone. We were murderers. They said I had been working with a murderer, helping him. At our last meeting I told Waldemar: "Forget about me. Live your own life. I am not guilty, but . . ."

"But why do you call him by a French name?"

"He liked it that way. He used to call me Nellie. 'We are the masters of the country now,' he would say, 'so our names should be noble, too.'"

Niura and I became good friends. A kind and simple woman, she had been terribly lonely in prison. She would listen with sympathy to the other women's stories and was always happy to talk about Waldemar. She was not at all interested in her own case. She had not signed the confession that the investigators had written for her. "How could I look Waldemar in the eye if I had signed something like that about myself?"

AT one of the stops the door opened, and the guard announced: "We have been authorized to buy some green onions for this car. If you have money in your account, put your name down on this piece of paper and indicate how much you want to spend."

There was a great deal of commotion. I, as a long-time inmate, was asked to make up the list. Everyone who had any money signed up: some for twenty kopeks, some for fifty. I took down the names, figured out the total, and handed the list to the guard on duty.

After a while we were brought a large pile of green onions.

"You made the list, so you should divide them up," the women told me.

I divided the onions into equal piles according to the number of bunks and asked that each bunk divide their pile among the occupants.

---

[4] M. I. Kalinin (1875–1946)—member of the Central Committee's Politburo (1926–46), head of the Soviet Parliament (i.e., titular head of state) (1919–46).

As I was distributing the onions, I heard some grumbling: first in a whisper, and then louder and louder. I had acted incorrectly, I was told. I should have divided the onions according to the size of the contribution, not into equal parts. Why were the onions being distributed among those who had not paid anything (to those, in other words, who did not have any money)?

"I am not going home. I have got to save money . . ."

"I am not in a position to feed the poor . . ."

"These are our last crumbs; we can't afford to give them away . . ."

At first I did not understand. Then I felt lost. I had known that I could expect almost anything from these women, but this was a shock. They were supposed to be Communists, after all! I think I even had tears in my eyes.

Prison had taken its toll on me as well. I was angry at myself for crying over those miserable onions. If only to fight back the tears, I started telling them about the way imprisoned socialists used to live: how they would share their last crumb, how they would not care who had contributed what, and how they would protect the sick and the weak. I do not remember what else I said, but the car grew silent. The onion issue was never raised again. I noticed, however, that the majority were not happy with me. Many of those who had wanted me to be their representative were now avoiding me. But some expressed their support for me. Tonia was one of them.

Tonia Bukina was my age. At the time of the 1917 revolution she had been a worker in a Leningrad factory. Her wages had barely been enough to get by on. On February 23 she and her fellow workers had attended a demonstration. There was no going back for her: the revolutionary wave had turned her whole life around. Tonia had begun to devote most of her time to volunteer work and soon afterward joined the Bolshevik Party. She had worked and gone to school at the same time. As an activist, she had been sent to a special training course. Then she had become a women's organizer. She fell in love with one of her party comrades, but she had no time to spend at home, no time to raise her son. She spent all her time traveling on party business. The year 1937 found her in Donetsk Province.

I asked Tonia about the show trials—she was still on the outside at the time. Tonia said:

"I can only tell you how they appeared to me. The first trial took place in 1936. I remember hating the enemies of the people and the party who had betrayed their motherland and the revolution and sold themselves to the capitalists. I had total trust in the Central Committee and the organs of state security. The arrests of more and more people both scared and pleased me. We were unmasking our enemies. But when our own provincial officials—our immediate bosses—were arrested, we became confused. How could it be that none of us had sensed or noticed this treason in our midst? Along with all the others, I demanded the death sentence. I spoke to factory women, explaining to them the desperate need for a ruthless struggle. But before we knew it, our comrades from the regional party headquarters had also been arrested. They were people who had worked by my side. I had close friends among them. We had been through the revolution together. We had been through the first trials together. I thought I was losing my mind. Everyone was turning out to have been a traitor . . . I did not know what or whom to believe. I could not go on living. I would have gone mad, but, fortunately, I was arrested.

At first I thought I had been slandered by traitors and was certain that the investigation would establish my innocence. But the investigator did not want to establish anything. He was not interested in anything. He just wanted me to sign some testimony that did not contain a single word of truth. He demanded that I lie about myself and others. I don't want to talk about the actual interrogation. I was treated the same way everyone else was treated. But in the end I was saved by the ordeal—saved because I understood that my friends were not traitors. Because I knew the truth about myself. I knew that in my own work I had always followed Central Committee guidelines."

"Did you sign the confession?" I asked.

"No," she shook her head.

"Did they beat you?"

"I don't want to talk about it. I do not understand how it could have happened, what all those horrors could possibly mean. And what could be more horrible than what I went through?!! The investigator told me that I was a Communist and that the party required my signature on the confession. I did not sign. My son, my family, and my friends consider me an enemy of the people. That is exactly what I used to think about others before I was arrested."

THE train moved slowly along. Every evening the guards would do roll call. They would warn us by banging on the door with a wooden hammer. Swearing, they would herd us all to one side of the car and then push us, one by one, into the other half.

Nobody ever told us where we were being taken, but we knew that the train was heading east. Once a day we would be given a revolting gruel. The door would open, and a vat filled with liquid that looked and smelled like slops would be brought in. In addition, each inmate would receive three hundred grams of bread. A water tank—enough for about half a liter per person—would also be brought in. We would be told to drink it or wash with it, whatever we preferred. To pass the time, the women would start reciting poetry. Zhenia Ginzburg[5] turned out to be a wonderful performer. A young, dark-haired woman who, I believe, had been a teacher at the University of Kazan, she possessed an amazing memory. With great skill, she recited all of *Eugene Onegin*, *Poltava*, *The Bronze Horseman*,[6] and *Woe from Wit*.[7] When the guard heard her reading, he climbed into the car and demanded that we surrender our books immediately. He absolutely refused to believe that there were no books there. Cursing furiously, he searched the whole car, but found nothing, of course.

Most of the women in our car were high-ranking Communists. Not a single one considered herself guilty, and not one ever protested or expressed any

---

[5] Evgenia Ginzburg (1906–1977)—author of the famous camp memoir *Into the Whirlwind*.
[6] Poems by A. S. Pushkin.
[7] Play by A. S. Griboedov (1822–24).

indignation. Each one was begging for her own case to be reviewed. Each one knew the truth about herself but did not believe any of the others.

Our train moved very slowly, often stopping at stations or crossings. As long as we were moving, we would be allowed to talk, but during stops the guards would demand total silence. A single word uttered aloud would result in the banging of a hammer against the wall.

About two weeks into our journey we stopped at a large station—I believe it was Novosibirsk—and were told to get out of the car and form into lines of five people each. The barking of the dogs made me shudder. Every guard was holding a dog on a leash.

"Take a look at that," said a woman standing next to me, pointing to the train with her eyes.

On each car had been scrawled, in chalk and in huge letters, the word *Cattle*.

There was a sign like this on our car, and on the one next to it, and the next . . . It was a large train. Was it possible that it was completely filled with prisoners?

So that is why the guards had beat on the walls with a hammer rather than yell at us! That is why we had not been allowed to talk when the train was stopped, or to come near the tiny openings under the roof that served as windows. Everything had been thought through. Train after train was heading north, transporting cattle.

I had not been particularly affected by the sign, but the other women looked depressed.

When we had all lined up, we heard a new order: "Take three steps forward. No talking. Keep your eyes straight ahead."

Even without turning our heads we could see the doors of the next car opening and women in prison uniforms coming out. The doors of the third car opened. More women came out.

When everybody had lined up, the roll-call began. We tried to listen, of course, but it was the same thing over and over again: the same sentences, the same criminal code articles. Finally, we were told to start moving.

The guards were having a lot of trouble with the women. Frightened as they were of the bayonets, dogs, and shouts, they were incapable of staying in formation. Every ten to fifteen minutes the line would waver. The guards kept stopping us and repeating: "One step to the left or right is considered an attempt to escape. We will open fire without warning."

With the guards screaming and dogs barking and constantly being forced to stop, we made our way to a tall fence. After another roll call they led us through a large yard into a huge empty building. Another roll call, another short march, and we found ourselves in an enormous bathhouse. "Take off your clothes and hand them over!"

In the presence of male guards, the women took off their clothes, marked them with special metal rings, and handed them over for delousing. Every woman received a tiny piece of soap. The guards—clean-shaven, well-trained, and dressed in neat uniforms—ordered the naked women to form into a line and step forward one at a time. A guard by the door pointed his finger at each one as he counted: "One, two, three . . ." Behind the door was a long corridor. All along the corridor, standing shoulder to shoulder, were guards. The women, one after another, filed past them. As if by design, there was a huge mirror on the wall. The entire scene was reflected in it: the line of guards and the file of naked women.

The women had their eyes lowered and were shrinking with humiliation. But who was being humiliated here? The naked prisoners or the men who were guarding them?

Still, most of the women were trembling from head to toe, their eyes filled with tears: "We are no longer human; we are worse than cattle."

Meanwhile, I kept looking at our bodyguards, thinking: "Are they truly human? And what about the ones who sent them here?"

The wonderful, luxurious bathhouse had been partitioned into countless little stalls. In each stall there was a shower, a basin, and a mirror attached to the door. How good the water felt after two weeks in a hot, crowded, smelly freight car! Did any greater happiness exist than to be able to soap oneself up and then get into a shower?

Suddenly the water was turned off. The five minutes allotted for bathing had run out. Our hair and bodies were covered with soap. But who cared about that? The order had been given. The water had been cut off. "Put your clothes on and get out."

We wiped the soap off with our towels. Our dirty hair stuck together in clumps. In the dressing room we got our clothes back. They were still hot from having been steamed. One woman's clothes had gotten lost; another's had fallen on the floor and been trampled on . . . One could hear shouting, cursing, threats . . .

We had been formed into a line again and eventually taken back to our car. I was on my bunk, lying completely straight and squeezed tightly on both sides, thinking . . .

SOME people had fallen ill, mostly because of malnutrition. Zhenia Ginzburg had recited *Mtsyri*,[8] and Marusia M. had recited Mayakovsky. We had been keeping quiet during stops, but once, when the train started moving again, the prisoners decided to try to cheer themselves up by singing. Somebody suggested the "Internationale," but others reacted indignantly: "How can we? We are prisoners; we don't have the right to sing it." Suddenly someone started singing "Wide Is My Beloved Country."[9] I shuddered and raised myself on my bunk. What was this? Was this a farce? A mockery? The chorus grew louder, and soon the freight car full of prisoners resonated with the words, "I don't know another country, where man breathes so gloriously free." I simply could not understand. I looked at the singing women, and said to myself: "They have just been forced to walk naked past a line of male guards. They are being transported like cattle, locked up in a prison car . . . "Wide Is My Beloved Country" . . . Was there no limit to human baseness and stupidity? I must truly be a dinosaur, after all, or some other prehistoric animal.

[8] Poem by M. Iu. Lermontov (1838–39).

[9] "Wide is my beloved country"—the first line of "Hymn to the Motherland" by I. O. Dunaevsky and V. I. Lebedev-Kumach (1936).

From the next bunk R. glanced over at me. She had an intelligent face and bright, mocking eyes. I could hear her whisper to Zina: "It would be sad if it were not so funny."

On the top bunk somebody was having a hysterical fit. I hated hysterics, but at least this time it put an end to the song.

Who was I surrounded by? Who were these unfortunate women? Were they the best daughters of the party or the refuse, the ballast? Why were they here? Who had prepared this fate for them, and for what reason?

GLOSSARY

Black ravens — colloquial term for vans used by the secret police.

Bolsheviks — the radical wing of the Russian Social Democratic Party. Under V. I. Lenin's leadership, the Bolsheviks took power in the name of the soviets in the October 1917 Revolution; renamed the Communist Party in 1919.

Central Committee — nominally the main governing body of the Communist Party, elected at party congresses. In fact, all important political decisions were made by the Central Committee's Politburo.

Central Executive Committee — the legislature of the Soviet Union from 1924 to 1936.

Cheka — the Extraordinary Commission for Combating Counterrevolution, Sabotage, and Speculation; the name of the Soviet secret police from 1918 to 1922.

Constituent Assembly — the body that was to determine the constitutional future of Russia after the February Revolution; elected in November 1917, it was dissolved by the Bolsheviks on its first meeting (in January 1918).

Cossacks — armed farmers organized into autonomous "armies" (eleven in all at the time of the revolution) that received grants of land in the imperial borderlands in exchange for military service; in the last decades of the Russian Empire Cossack units were often used to suppress strikes and demonstrations.

Decembrists — military officers who staged an unsuccessful liberal-constitutionalist coup against autocracy in December 1825, during a succession crisis following the death of Alexander I. Five coup leaders were executed, and more than a hundred were banished to Siberia.

Desiatina — Russian measurement equivalent to 2.7 acres.

Duma — Russian word for parliament; the State Duma was created by Tsar Nicholas II following the 1905 revolution.

February Revolution — the overthrow of Tsar Nicholas II in February 1917 and his replacement by the Provisional Government.

GPU — State Political Directorate, the name for the Soviet secret police from 1922 to 1923 (renamed OGPU, 1923–34).

Gymnasium — elite high school with emphasis on classical studies and the humanities.

Kadets — the Constitutional Democratic Party, the main liberal party in Russia before the October Revolution.

Kolkhoz — collective farm; kolkhoznik—collective farm member (peasant).

Kolkhoz Charter (1935) — an official document regulating conditions of kolkhoz work and making some concessions to peasants, such as private plots and maternity leave.

Komsomol — the Communist Youth League.

Kulak — in official Soviet terminology, a rich peasant; ultimately a term of political opprobrium rather than an economic category.

Mensheviks — the moderate wing of the Russian Social Democratic Party that subscribed to the "orthodox" Marxist view that Russia must pass through the capitalist stage of development before reaching socialism.

NEP — the New Economic Policy (1921–28) that permitted small-scale private trade and manufacturing as well as some foreign economic investment.

NKVD — the name of the Soviet secret police (formerly Cheka, GPU, OGPU) from 1934 to the Second World War.

Party cell — the smallest organizational unit of the Communist Party, consisting of several party members.

Pravda — the daily newspaper of the Communist Party Central Committee; the Russian word for "truth."

Provisional Government — the government formed in February 1917 after the fall of tsarism, originally composed of Kadets and other liberals, and later of Socialist Revolutionaries and Mensheviks; overthrown by the Bolsheviks in October 1917.

Pud — Russian measure of weight equivalent to approximately 36 pounds.

Rabfak — worker faculty, established at many Soviet institutions of higher education to offer remedial preparation to workers and peasants who lacked complete secondary education.

Shock work — campaign launched during the First Five-Year Plan (1928–31) to increase industrial output through formalized competition among work brigades; the term *shock worker* was sometimes used more broadly to describe outstanding workers in the factory or kolkhoz.

Socialist Revolutionary (SR) Party — the main pro-peasant party in Russia and heir to the tradition of nineteenth-century populism; it received the largest number of votes in the elections to the Constituent Assembly in the fall of 1917.

Soviets — councils of workers', peasants', and soldiers' representatives during the Russian Revolution; in the Soviet Union, legislative bodies on the local and national level culminating in the Central Executive Committee (later Supreme Soviet).

Stakhanovites — workers who increased their productivity by using new methods of their own invention; named after the coal miner Aleksei Stakhanov, who set a productivity record in August 1935.

Troikas — three-person boards that conducted extrajudicial trials.

Trotskyites — supporters of Trotsky's Left Opposition in the Communist Party in the 1920s; later a term of political approbrium.

Verst — Russian measurement equivalent to 3,500 feet.

Volunteer Army — an anti-Bolshevik army formed in the North Caucuses in 1918.

War Communism — a set of measures adopted by the Bolsheviks between 1918 and 1921 that involved strict administrative centralization; the nationalization of banking, transport, foreign trade, and large-scale industry; the expropriation of peasant produce; and the rationing of basic goods and services.

White Guards — Officers in the White Armies that fought the Reds during the civil war.

Women's Section — a Central Committee department with branches in local party units, formed in 1918 to conduct propaganda and educational work among women; dissolved in 1930.

INDEX

Abortion, 216, 327; laws permitting, viii, 167; prohibition of, viii, 213, 303
Agranov, Ia. S., 67, 67n
Alekseev, M. V., 89, 89n.6, 90
Alksnis, Ia. I., 374, 374n
Altai, 219, 220
America (U.S. periodical), 306
Amundsen, Roald, 290, 290n
anarchists, 43, 43n.17, 65; in exile, 211
Andersen, Hans Christian, 144
Andzhievsky, Grigory, 73, 74, 75, 76, 80; arrest of, 80–81; execution of, 81
Anna Karenina. See Tolstoy, Leo
Anti-Bolshevik Alliance for the Rebirth of Russia, 66
Armenia, 102, 105, 335–336, 337, 394

Bagaeva Architecture School, 130–131, 132
Bagration, P. I., 291, 291n.10
Baku, 286, 291
Balzac, Honoré de, 30, 370
Bashkir Autonomous Republic, 337, 338
Bashkir Brigade, 145, 145n.5
Bath, 140–141
Beria, L. P., 337, 337n.13
Bestuzhev-Marlinsky, A. A., 287, 287n.5
Bestuzhev Women's Institute of Higher Learning, 66, 113, 113n, 114, 116
Bezymensky, A. I., 372, 372n.16, 380
black markets, 32
black raven, 241–242, 241n.1, 322, 435
Bolsheviks, 5, 7, 9, 13, 16, 19, 22, 23, 24, 25, 28, 38, 41, 44, 53, 58, 79, 85, 86, 114, 180, 214, 246, 430, 435, 436; becoming a member of, 53, 181; during Civil War, 45, 47–48, 75, 86, 88, 91, 94, 96, 98, 99, 100, 104, 119; during collectivization, 41, 313; and corruption, 75, 86, 88; corruption among leadership of, 41–42, 213, 215; and the defense of workers, 55; and drunkenness, 75, 86, 87; and the February Revolution, 7, 52, 73–74; and looting, 75, 145–146; as Marxists, 12, 13; and the October Revolution, vii, 31–32, 39, 54–55, 57, 59, 63, 74; and the Provisional Government, 74; and religion, 86, 113, 115; and searches, 104, 105, 134, 221; and social class, 12–13, 32, 53; and victimization of women, 10; women as, 57–58, 64–65, 74, 75, 114–115, 119; and women's equality, 113. *See also* Communist Party *and* communists
Bolshoi, 50, 50n, 288, 371, 371n.10
Bourget, Paul, 134
Britain, 80–81, 80n
British Ally (British periodical), 306

Budenny, S. M., 119–120, 119n.3, 122, 408
Bukharin, N. I., 328, 328n, 384, 384n.31
Bunin, I. A., 286, 286n, 287

censorship, 4–5, 40, 42
Central Committee for the Assistance to the Starving, 42
Chaianov, A. V., 266
Chapaev (film), 371, 371n.13
Charskaia, Lidia, 19
Cheka, 7, 31–32, 66, 66n, 66–72, 114–115, 116, 142, 148, 149, 152, 156, 158, 164, 216, 342, 344, 345, 346, 435; arrests by, 66, 67, 70, 148, 241, 284; escape from, 114–115; executions by, 113, 408; searches by, 68–72, 155–156. *See also* GPU, KGB, *and* NKVD
Chekhov, A. P., 324, 324n.2, 398, 399
Chernyshevsky, N. G., 287, 287n.3
Chesterton, G.K., 18, 18n.1
childbirth, 19, 77, 171, 250, 325, 373; death during, 171
childhood, 10, 18–19, 30, 241, 243, 282–283, 334, 337, 338, 342, 368, 372–373, 383, 391, 420; during industrialization, 297–298; in a kolkhoz, 223–224; and labor, 51, 232, 234, 244, 245–246, 337, 338, 356, 363; in an orphanage, 182–184, 232; physical abuse during, 174, 232; before the Russian Revolution, 8, 111, 123–125, 126–129, 169–171, 219, 286–294, 369; under socialism, 391; and Stalin, 415–416
Children of the Arbat. See Rybakov, Anatoly
Chinese, 116–117
chistka. See purges, Great Purges, *and* Great Terror
Chkalov, V. P., 378, 378n.22
Chopin, Frederic, 128, 410
Christianity. *See* religion
Christmas, 18, 30, 124–125, 136, 177, 400
Civil War, vii, 4, 7, 21, 27, 31–32, 74, 76–80, 87, 89–90, 91, 95, 96–99, 100–101, 118–119, 131, 220; and the anti-Bolsheviks, 79, 87, 94; arrests during, 80–81, 88; choosing sides in, 47; in Ekaterinodar, 102–103; in Ekaterinoslav, 118, 119; and families, 31, 44, 45, 48, 78–79, 99, 131, 132; immediate aftermath of, 103–104; in Korenovskaia, 3, 89, 92–93, 101–102; in Kursk, 43–45, 46, 47; looting during, 90, 91–92; peasants and, 118, 119; preparations for, 58; rape during, 75, 86; in Rostov, 120–121; searches during, 14, 45–46, 48, 80–81, 86, 88, 91; in Vladikavkaz, 78–80; women's roles in, 75–76, 77, 97, 119, 120–121, 122, 196

collectivization, vii, 4, 6, 7, 21, 27–28, 168, 219, 220, 222, 235, 237–238, 303, 307, 418; deportation during, 6; escape from, 371; exile during, 228; and food rationing, 230, 303; resistance to, 27, 239–240, 265–266, 272–273; suicide during, 7, 273; and women, 27–28, 27n. See also kolkhoz

Comintern, 277, 277n.3, 325, 325n.5

Committee of Public Safety, 59, 59n.12, 64

committees of the poor, 13, 39, 241–242, 241n.2

communism, 14, 316, 393, 404; disillusionment with, 354; and families, 37, 156; hopes for, 57, 59, 83, 84–85, 87, 205–206, 308, 354; and peasants, 40. See also War Communism and Communist Party

Communist Party, 31, 40, 167, 303, 356, 356n, 357–358, 435; becoming a member of, 213, 249, 343; bureaucracy of, 116, 197, 204; and censorship, 42; corruption among leadership of, 41–42, 135, 375–376; drunkenness among leadership of, 203, 205; expulsion from, 258, 327, 427; and peasants, 85–87, 309; privilege among leadership of, 15, 109, 153, 156, 326, 368, 372, 375, 376, 394, 429; propaganda of, 192, 213, 309; recruitment for, 187; and "reeducation," 270, 271, 285; and religion, 86, 187–188, 196, 200, 238–239; and religious baptism, 188–189; and volunteer work, 115–116, 154–155, 198, 249, 402–403; women's sections of, 192, 196, 198–199, 201–202, 203, 205, 214; women's work in, 41, 182, 185, 187, 195–196, 197–198, 200, 277, 307. See also Bolsheviks

communists, 14, 15, 430

Constituent Assembly, 39, 39n.10, 435, 436

Cossacks, 13, 30, 34, 34n, 78, 82, 102, 268, 435; arrests of, 268, 270; and civil war, 77, 78, 85, 86, 89, 90, 91, 96, 101–102; collectivization of, 86, 265; and the February Revolution, 34, 49, 83–84; hospitality of, 78; and the October Revolution, 85; and resistance to the Bolsheviks, 87; in World War I, 103

Cross of St. George, 120, 120n

Decembrists, 19, 22, 98, 98n.9, 140, 287, 435

dekulakization, 6, 7, 9, 13, 24, 28, 39, 39n.13, 40, 168, 222, 224, 231, 238–239, 241, 242, 266, 310, 311, 323, 358; confiscation of goods during, 40, 226–227, 238, 241. See also collectivization and kulaks

Denikin, A. A., 43–44, 43n.19, 89, 89n.7, 119; in Kursk, 43, 46

Dickens, Charles, 30, 294, 300

Dimitrov, Georgi, 297, 297n.20

"Discovery of America" (operetta), 130

divorce, 126, 130, 192, 206, 207, 209, 216, 234, 260–261, 337, 344, 345–346; and abandonment, 208; availability of, 167; and child custody, 207, 208; frequency of, 402

Dnepropetrovsk. See Ekaterinoslav and Civil War and Ekaterinoslav

Dnieper Hydroelectric Dam, 297, 308

Dorpat University, 123

Dostoevsky, Fedor, 269

Dzerzhinsky, F. E., 157, 157n.31, 158

education, 10, 111, 123, 341, 389, 390; brigade method of, 261–263, 269; in college, 253–254, 305; experimental methods of, 261–263, 303; in gymnasium, 10, 57, 111, 128–129, 130, 207, 214, 422, 435; in high school, 364; in kindergarten, 414–415; in rabfak, 259, 259n, 325, 325n.3, 342, 367, 435; and religion, 128; of women, 33, 82, 111, 113, 125–126, 128–129, 130, 133, 171–172, 213, 233, 244, 245, 246, 253, 261, 342, 343, 351–352

Ehrenburg, I. E., 363n.5

Ekaterinodar, 104, 106, 254, 255. See also Civil War and Ekaterinodar

Ekaterinoslav, 118, 119, 121. See also Civil War and Ekaterinoslav

Elpatievsky, S. Ia., 40, 40n.14

emigration, 4, 18, 20–21, 30, 141, 161, 162, 344; and the Communist Party, 344; to the Crimea, 106; to England, 46; to Finland, 135–139, 140; forced, 66; to Latvia, 113; from Nikolaev, 118; to Turkey, 412

Engels, Friedrich, 56

Erfurt Program, 56–57, 56n

Estonia, 157

Eugene Onegin. See Pushkin, A. S.

exile, 112, 140; anarchists in, 211; Cossacks in, 257; during the Great Terror, 381, 386, 390, 428; SRs in, 209, 211; Zionists in, 211

family, 11, 19, 30, 41, 51, 54, 124, 145–146, 160, 161, 162, 163, 164,169–171, 172, 176, 178–179, 186–187, 207, 209–212, 220, 286–287, 292, 296, 411, 421; and arrests, 300, 388; in the Communist Party, 309, 320; and nannies, 10, 19, 30, 33, 104, 123–125, 368, 395, 406–407, 413; and revolution, 167; and stepmothers, 171, 172–173, 178, 282. See also husbands; Civil War and; October Revolution and; and February Revolution and

fascism, 269, 297

Faust, 287

February Revolution, 7, 28, 33–36, 49–50, 73, 82, 83, 179, 245, 430, 435; in Korenovskaia, 82–83; peasants and, 84, 245; and the Russian provinces, 37; and the secret police, 34; strikes and demonstrations during, 33–34, 73, 179–180, 430; women's role in, 35, 73. See also October Revolution and Russian Revolution

Figner, Vera, 363, 363n.6

Finnish Civil War, 131, 131n

First Five-Year Plan, 26, 30, 168, 252–253, 296, 303, 436

First World War. *See* World War I
"former people," 13, 20, 24, 132, 132n.5, 289
France, Anatole, 134
Free Education (journal), 112
Frunze, M. V., 334, 334n.8
futurists, 286

Gamaiun, Ia., 219
Gandhi, Mahatma, 154, 154n
Genghiz Khan, 152, 152n.25
Georgia, 104, 104n, 105
Ginzburg, Evgenia, 7, 431, 431n.5, 433
glasnost, 219
Gogol, N. V., 51, 252, 370
Golovin, V. E., 127, 127n, 132, 132n.4
Gorky, Maxim, 5, 22, 23, 42n, 51, 147, 282;
    Among the People, 22; *Childhood*, 22; "History of Factories and Plants," 5, 8; and the intellectuals, 147, 147n.15, 149; *Lower Depths*, 399; *Mother*, 57; *Novaia zhizn'*, 42; *Song of the Stormy Petrel*, 57
Gosplan, 296, 296n, 368
GPU, 109, 109n, 110, 167, 400–401, 406, 408, 409–410, 435; arrests by, 268, 273, 284, 396–397, 401; prison of, 270; privilege among members of, 289; purges of, 413; and searches, 109–110, 273, 412–413; and troikas, 400–401, 436. *See also* Cheka, KGB, *and* NKVD
Great Purges, 4, 5, 7–8, 10, 15, 16, 28, 304, 327, 342, 379–381, 384, 408–410, 427, 430–431; sending packages during, 386–387; suicide during, 8, 390. *See also* Great Terror *and* purges
Great Terror, vii, 376, 384–385, 388, 418. *See also* Great Purges *and* purges
Griboedov, A. S., 252, 252n. 431n.7; *Woe from Wit*, 252, 431
Gromova (Samoilova), K. N., 25, 113, 114, 115n; as a Bolshevik, 114; death of, 114; as an executioner, 115
Gulag, 7, 17, 168, 304
GUS, 112, 112n.7

Hitler, Adolf, 327; and the attack on the Soviet Union, 304; *Mein Kampf*, 327
household labor. *See* women, domestic role of
housework. *See* women, domestic role of
husbands, 11, 19, 25, 93–94, 95, 359; abuse by, 51; abandonment by, 250; devotion to, 104, 150–151; and devotion to wives, 95, 96; infidelity of, 214, 215, 217; women on, 405. *See also* divorce, family, marriage *and* wives

Iagoda, G.G., 427, 427n.2
Iakir, I. E., 377, 377n
illiteracy, 10, 169, 196, 338; liquidation of, 191, 192, 200, 205, 339
industrialization, 27, 168, 303; Moscow during, 296–297

Iskra (periodical), 112, 112n.4, 112n.5
Italy, 269
Iudenich, N. N., 43, 43n.18
Ivanov, V. I., 360, 360n, 365, 365n.8
Ivanov, Viacheslav, 291, 291n.12, 292
Ivanov, Vsevolod, 282

Jews, 7, 13, 159, 324, 342–344, 345, 374, 383, 385; and childhood, 324; during the Civil War, 45; and education, 324, 343, 369; and family, 344, 369–370; and music, 370; and Passover, 377; and the pogroms, 43–44, 47, 344; and shtetl life, 7, 324, 368, 378; and Yiddish, 342, 343, 384. *See also* religion
July Massacre, 58, 58n

Kaganovich, Lazar, 327, 327n.10, 339, 369, 369n.7, 383
Kalabukhov, A. I., 104, 104n
Kaliaev, I. P., 98, 98n.11
Kalinin, M. I., 429, 429n
Kamanin, N. P., 378, 378n.23
Karamzin, N. M., 40, 40n.14
Karpov, V. Z., 381, 381n.25
Kataev, Valentin, 282
Kerensky, A. F., 31, 36, 36n.5
Kerzhentsev, P. M., 371, 371n.12
KGB, 167. *See also* Cheka, GPU, *and* NKVD
Khetagurova, V. S., 281, 281n
Khlebnikov, Velimir, 291, 291n.11
Kholodnaia, Vera, 102, 102n.14
Kirov, Sergei, 303, 334, 334n; death of, 303, 304, 380
Kliuchevsky, V. O., 40, 40n.14
Knorin, V. G., 383, 383n.28
Kochkurov, N. I. *See* Vesely, Artem
Kogan, F. A., 243
Kolchak, A. V., 43, 43n.17
kolkhoz, 23, 221, 223, 236, 323, 335, 336, 340, 435; Charter of 1935, 316n, 336, 336n, 435; expulsion from, 224, 225–228, 323; formation of, 221, 310–311; resistance to, 221, 270, 318; reward structure in, 11, 221, 232, 237–238, 315, 436; work in, 221, 225. *See also* collectivization
Kollontai, A. M., 117, 117n
Kommunarka Ukrainy (journal), 215, 215n.1
Komsomol (Communist Youth League), 6, 194, 213–214, 216, 217, 221, 233, 235, 237–238, 258, 277, 278, 280, 298, 308, 324, 333, 354, 390, 426, 435; Central Committee of, 277; expulsion from, 298–299, 427; resignation from, 354–355
Komsomol Easter, 194, 194n
Komsomolsk-on-Amur, 277, 277n.1, 281; construction of, 277, 278–280
Kondratiev, N. D., 266
Korenovskaia. *See* Civil War and
Kornilov, L. G., 89, 89n.5, 90, 91, 92, 93, 103
Korytny, S. Z., 383, 383n.27

Kosarev, A. V., 333, 333n.7
Krasnaia Presnia, 49, 49n
Krasnodar. *See* Ekaterinodar *and* Civil War and
    Ekaterinodar
Krasnodar College of Agriculture, 273
Krasnodar Institute of Food Industry, 252, 256
Kremlin, 50, 59, 316, 367
Krest'ianskaia gazeta (newspaper), 192
Krupskaia, N. K., 111–112, 306, 307
Kuban, 82, 85, 85n.3, 87, 89, 90, 92, 102
Kuibyshev, V. V., 368, 368n.6
kulaks, 167, 220, 221, 235, 308, 309, 310, 435;
    during Civil War, 77; suspicion of, 236;
    threats by, 310. *See also* collectivization *and*
    dekulakization
Kuprin, A. I., 324, 324n.2
Kursk, 33, 37, 38, 43–45, 47; during the Octo-
    ber Revolution, 39–40; during collectiviza-
    tion, 41
Kursk District Tanning Commission, 40, 44
Kuznetsk, 308

labor days, 221, 221n
Latvians, 322–323
Lavisse, Ernest, 300, 300n.26
League for Women's Equality, 180–181
LEF (Left Front of Art), 286, 286n.1
Leipzig Trial, 297, 297n.20
Lenin, V.I., 21, 25, 58, 66, 74, 76, 111, 112,
    149, 216, 217, 218, 280, 311, 334, 435; death
    of, 167; and lice epidemic, 154; reverence
    for, 189, 251, 259, 299, 307
Leningrad, 410–411, 413. *See also* Petrograd
Lenin Kolkhoz, 305, 308
Lenin Levy, 187, 187n
Lenin Pedagogical Institute, 326
Lermontov, M. Iu., 433n.8; *Mtsyri*, 433
Leuchtweiss Cave. See Reder, V. A.
Libedinsky, Yuri, 286
lice, 153–154, 160, 184
Little Hunchbacked Horse (children's story),
    371
Liubov Iarovaia (play), 399, 399n
London, 144, 148
Lunacharsky, A. V., 182, 182n

Magnitogorsk, 297, 297n.19
Madame Butterfly (opera), 130
Makhno, Nestor, 119, 119n.2
Maksimov, Vladimir, 102, 102n.14
Maksim Trilogy (film), 300, 300n.24
malnutrition, 233, 279, 357, 433
Manchuria, 110
Marat, Jean, 300
Mariinsky Theater, 126, 126n, 325
marriage, 12, 16, 19, 25, 27, 74, 134, 171 173–
    174, 192, 207, 209, 220, 234, 241, 243, 249,
    260–261, 267, 272, 338, 357, 364, 365, 389,
    392; arranged, 175–176, 241, 337; under com-
    munism, 58, 216, 279, 280; and dowries,

171, 173; frequency of, 402; and love, 176;
    and religion, 176, 274–296; unofficial, 325.
    See also divorce, family, husbands, *and*
    weddings
Marx, Karl, 16, 56
Marxism, 111
Marx's Youth (book), 420
Mashonkin, Fedia, 236, 238
mastitis, 79
Mayakovsky, V. V., 291, 291n.14, 433
May Day celebrations, 38, 48, 181–182, 194,
    327, 329
Mekhlis, L. Z., 326, 326n.9
Melgunov, S. P., 66, 68
Mensheviks, 31, 52–53, 57, 75, 246, 435, 436;
    and the October Revolution, 60, 73, 74–75
Mikoian, A.I., 333, 333n.5
Military Medical Academy, 35
Minin, Kuzma, 59, 59n.11
Molot (newspaper), 403, 403n
Molotov, V. M., 416, 416n
Morozov, Pavlik, 326, 326n.6
Moscow, 7, 16, 36, 40, 41, 66, 76, 82, 106, 113,
    145, 149, 212, 219, 245, 288, 325, 370–371,
    392; during the October Revolution, 59;
    under War Communism, 106–109, 152–153
Moscow Exemplary School, 369, 373
Moscow University, 152, 261, 390
Moscow Women's Institute for Higher Learn-
    ing, 82
motherhood, 51, 78, 79–80, 81, 82, 212, 330,
    364, 397, 404; and death of child, 81; during
    Civil War, 78, 79–80, 81; in prison, 328–330,
    427; by single women, 207–208, 284, 250,
    339, 391
Mozzhukhin, Ivan, 102, 102n.14
Mtsyri. See Lermontov, M. Iu.
Muslim, 81
My Brigade (book), 306

Nadson, S. Ia., 288, 288n, 324
nannies. *See* family
nationalization, 39, 41, 64–65, 104–105, 221–
    222, 436
Nazis, 384
Negro Boy and a Monkey (play), 290
Nekrasov, N.A., 19, 20, 57, 57n.9, 158, 287,
    324
New Economic Policy (NEP), vii, 25, 32, 148,
    148n, 167, 435
New Life (periodical), 38
New York City, 305
Nice, 165
Nicholas I, 20. *See also* Romanovs
Nicholas I Orphanage for Noble Girls, 82
Nicholas II, 36, 435; abdication of, 36, 82, 436.
    See also Romanovs
Niva (magazine), 324
Nizheviasov affair, 75
NKVD, 167, 304, 327, 345, 346, 347, 358, 382,

435; arrests by, 328; and searches, 327, 382.
   See also Cheka, GPU, and KGB
Nobile, Umberto, 290, 290n

Obolensky, Anna, 159, 159n
Obshchestvennitsa (magazine), 350, 353n
Obshchestvennitsa Movement, 359, 419, 419
October Coup. See October Revolution
October Revolution, vii, 7, 23–24, 28, 31,
   33n.2, 39, 59–64, 74, 85, 131, 169, 190, 196,
   213, 435, 436; celebrations of, 106; choosing
   sides in, 52–55, 180, 246–247; immediate
   aftermath of, 64; in Moscow, 59–63; and
   peasants, 39, 54, 85; and restrictions on
   religion, 39; and searches, 14, 24; youth
   leadership in, 39, 59; women in, 61, 62–63.
   See also February Revolution and Russian
   Revolution
Odessa, 342–343, 347
Ogonek (magazine), 219, 277, 277n.2, 288
Ordzhonikidze, G. K. "Sergo," 326, 326n.7,
   332, 421
Orel, 43, 46
Osoaviakhim (voluntary society), 249, 249n
Ostrovsky, Nikolai, 22, 26, 362n.3; How the
   Steel Was Tempered, 22, 362
Overseas League of Russian Social Democrats,
   112

Paris, 113, 134, 153, 160, 165
Paris Treaty, 104
Patriotic War. See World War II
People's Cause (periodical), 38
People's Commissariat (Ministry) of Enlighten-
   ment, 111
People's Voice (periodical), 38
perestroika, 5, 7, 9, 27
Perovskaia, S. L., 98, 98n.10
Petliura, S. V., 118, 118n
Petrograd, 8, 33, 33n.1, 111, 113, 123, 127,
   135, 141, 149, 207, 324, 410–411, 413; dur-
   ing Civil War, 131–133, 134, 143, 144;
   during the February Revolution, 33, 35–36,
   37; during the October Revolution, 59, 74;
   during War Communism, 132. See also
   Leningrad
Petrograd Pedagogical Institute, 113
Petrograd Polytechnic, 47
Petrovsk, 81
Piatigorsk, 73, 75, 81, 396; abandonment of,
   78; during Civil War, 77
Pinkerton, Nat, 13, 51, 54
Pisarevka, 84
Platonov, S. F., 40, 40n.14
Plevitskaia, N. V., 102n.12
Plisetskaia, Maia, 329, 329n
pogroms. See Jews
Pokrovsky, M. N., 40, 40n.15
Pokrovsky University, 325
Polonsky, Vitold, 102, 102n.14

Popular Astronomy (book), 198
Pozharsky, Dmitry, 59, 59n.11
Pravda (newspaper), 38, 114, 266, 326, 436
pregnancy, 24, 27, 30, 76, 77, 229, 327, 367,
   427; during Civil War, 76, 77; in a kolkhoz,
   336–337; and miscarriage, 427; in prison,
   328, 427; and Stalin, 9–10, 337; work and,
   279. See also motherhood and abortion
prison, 145, 145n.4, 150, 151, 158, 270, 283,
   284–285, 327, 328–330, 424–425, 428, 430,
   432–433; for children, 385
Provisional Government, 31, 52, 52n, 54, 57,
   58, 82, 436; and the October Revolution, 59,
   74
"purge" commission, 256–258, 256n
purges, 257–258, 264–265, 266–267, 303–304,
   342; of Communist Party officials, 303–304;
   and families, 257, 268–269, 322–323; of the
   GPU, 413. See also Great Purges and Great
   Terror
Pushkin, Aleksandr, 19, 93, 264, 298, 298n.22,
   370, 431n.6; The Bronze Horseman, 431;
   Eugene Onegin, 431; Poltava, 431

Quakers, 114

rabfak. See education
Rambaud, Alfred, 300, 300n.26
Ramzin, L. K., 266
rape, 75, 86, 177. See also women, sexual exploitation of
Raskolnikov, F. F., 160, 160n.37
Razumovskaia, E. N., 241
reading hut, 185, 185n, 187, 190, 193, 195. See
   also education and illiteracy
Red Cavalryman (periodical), 121
Red Cross, 113
Reder, V. A., 51n.3; Leuchtweiss Cave, 51,
   51n.3
Reed, John, 298, 298n.21
"reeducation." See Communist Party
Reisner, L. M., 160, 160n.36
religion, 30, 71, 83, 124, 164, 170, 187–188,
   190, 230, 270, 312, 416; and baptism, 188–
   189, 210, 292; during Civil War, 86, 96; and
   communism, 86, 115, 168, 312, 323, 335,
   412; and weddings, 274–276. See also Jews
revolution. See February Revolution, October
   Revolution, and Russian Revolution
Revolutionary Dictionary (book), 179
Ridder, 229, 230
Rights of the Peasant Woman (book), 192
Robespierre, Maximilien, 300
Rodzianko, M. V., 36, 36n.6
Romanov, Mikhail Aleksandrovich (Grand
   Duke), 36; abdication of, 36
Romanovs, 31, 36, 82, 215, 215n.2. See also
   Nicholas I and Nicholas II
Rosen, L. R. (Baron), 125
Rostov, 21, 120, 394, 403, 411, 417

Rozhkova, M. K., 243
RSFSR, 365, 369n.8, 391, 392
Russian Revolution, vii, 4, 7, 16, 18, 20, 21, 23,
    24, 27, 207–208, 324, 436. *See also* February
    Revolution *and* October Revolution
Russian Social Democratic Labor Party. *See*
    Social Democrats
Rybakov, Anatoly, 369; *Children of the Arbat*,
    369
Ryleev, K. F., 287, 287n.5

St. Petersburg. *See* Leningrad *and* Petrograd
Samoilova, K. M. *See* Gromova, K. M.
Second World War. *See* World War II
Serebriakova, Galina, 420
sexual liberation. *See* women, liberation of
Shakespeare, William, 399
Shepilov, D. T., 390, 390n.34
Shikheev, V. N., 367
Shklovsky, Viktor, 282
Shkuro, A. G., 76, 76n.5, 80
Shmidt, O. Iu., 372, 372n.15
shock worker, 206, 206n, 221, 243, 279, 303,
    312, 331, 331n, 359, 364, 436
Sholokhov, M. A., 363, 363n.4; *Virgin Soil Up-
    turned*, 363, 364n.4
*Short Course of the History of the Communist
    Party*. *See* Stalin
shtetl. *See* Jews
Siberia, 7, 19, 20, 22, 30, 43, 114, 140, 287,
    357, 418, 435
Sibirskaia gazeta, 69
Skoblin, Nikolai, 102n.12
Smirnov, V. D., 123
Socialist Democrats (SDs), 38, 38n, 43, 44, 46,
    52, 210; in exile, 211
Socialist Revolutionaries (SRs), 7, 31, 37, 37n,
    38, 39, 43, 46, 54, 57, 74n, 83, 180, 246,
    426, 428, 436; banishment of, 39; in exile,
    209, 211; promises of, 52; during October
    Revolution, 60, 73, 74, 74n
Society for the Assistance to the Army and Avi-
    ation, 236
Some Advice for Mothers (book), 192
Song of the Stormy Petrel. *See* Gorky, Maxim
Sorokin affair, 77, 88, 103
Sosnovsky, Lev, 207
Sovnarkom, 75–76, 76n.2
Spanish Revolution, 300, 400
Spiders and Flies (pamphlet), 13, 54
Stakhanovites, 5, 8, 9, 10, 11, 13, 14, 15, 16,
    24, 29–30, 303, 332, 331, 334, 337, 392,
    436; problems associated with, 395–396,
    397, 405–406; wives of, 11–12, 359–361,
    362–363, 364, 365–366; women as, 305, 316,
    333, 339
Stalin, Joseph, 5, 7, 10, 15, 24, 29–30, 167,
    168, 234, 263–264, 266, 299, 303, 317, 319,
    321, 341, 392, 417–418; reverence for, 24,
    28, 29–30, 307, 311, 316, 321, 331, 336, 337,

338, 340–341, 393; *Short Course of the His-
    tory of the Communist Party*, 24, 316,
    316n.8; and the Stakhanovites, 333; and
    women, 9–10, 313, 340. *See also* Stalinism
Stalingrad, 223
Stalinism, 30, 223. *See also* Stalin
Stalin White Sea–Baltic Canal, 282
Staro-Beshevo, 305, 308, 309, 321
starvation, 228–229, 230, 231–234, 420–421
State Economic Council, 247, 247n
Stebut Agricultural Institute for Women, 33, 35
Stetsky, A. I., 385, 385n
Stroganov, A., 362, 362n.2
suicide, 7, 174, 234, 273, 291; contemplation
    of, 79, 177. *See also* Communist Party
Suslov, M. A., 377–378, 378n.21
syphilis, 187

Tale of the Great Plan (book), 297
Tauride Palace, 35, 35n, 36
Terek Republic, 76, 76n.2
Thackeray, William Makepeace, 30, 300
Timasheff, N. S., 303
Timiriazev Agricultural Academy, 306
Tolstoy, Aleksei, 282
Tolstoy, Boris, 286
Tolstoy, Leo, 18, 19, 30, 40, 111, 111n.1,
    291n.9, 300; *Resurrection*, 40; *War and
    Peace*, 40, 291n.9
Tolstoyan, 111, 111n.1, 286
Torquemada, Thomas, 152, 152n.24
*Trial of the Worker Potekhin Who Subjected
    His Wife to Beatings* (play), 190
troikas. *See* GPU
Trotsky, Leon, 5, 15, 15n, 155, 167, 407
Trotskyites, 250, 250n, 407, 436
Trud (newspaper), 368, 368n.5
Tula, 46
Turgenev, I. S.,51, 370

Ukraine, 49
Union for the Liberation of the Working Class,
    111, 111n.2
Union of Employees of Rural Organizations,
    306
Union of Writers, 169
University of Geneva, 82
urbanization, 167–168, 303

Verlaine, Paul, 291, 291n.13
Vertinsky, Aleksandr, 102, 102n.13
Vesely, Artem, 294–296, 294n
Vinogradova, E. V., 334, 334n.10
Vladikavkaz, 76, 76n.2
Volkonskaia, Princess Maria, 19, 140, 158,
    158n.33
Volkonsky, Prince Petr Petrovich, 140, 145
Volkonsky, Serge, 140, 149
Voloshin, M. A., 300, 300n.25
volunteer labor. *See* Communist Party

Voroshilov, K. E., 121, 122, 121n.5, 408
VKP(b). *See* Communist Party
VTsIK, 365, 365n.7, 366

War Communism, 32, 39, 39n.12, 113, 117,
208, 436. *See also* Moscow *and* St.
Petersburg
War and Peace. See Tolstoy, Leo
weddings, 44, 172, 176, 275–276; during the
Russian Revolution, 58; in secrecy, 275–276
Wells, H. G., 150, 150n.21
What Are Soviets (book), 179, 180
What Is a Republic? (book), 179
Without Catching a Breath (book), 363, 363n.5
wives, 41, 357, 420, 422–423; infidelity of,
283. *See also* Obshchestvennitsa Movement
Woe from Wit. See Griboedov, A. S.
Woman's Benefit (play), 189
Woman's Gain (book), 192
womanhood, 129–130
women, vii, viii, 27, 129–130, 191; and autobiography, 3–4, 5, 6, 7, 8, 9, 15–16, 17, 18–
19, 21–23, 27, 28–29, 198, 321, 356; in the
Communist Party, 49, 57–58, 64–65, 111–
112, 121, 133, 167, 196, 200, 206, 235–240,
248–249, 319–321, 391–393; and cross dressing, vii, 25, 27, 120; domestic role of, 19, 25,
109, 167, 201, 206, 208, 209, 287, 350, 361,
362; and hopes for communism, 308, 354–
355; as leaders of the Communist Party, 49,
57–58, 64–65, 111–112, 133, 189–190, 235–
240, 319–321, 358, 391–393; liberation of,
viii, 9, 27, 167, 191, 192, 196, 201–202,
207–208, 213–218, 278, 312–313, 338, 350,
402; and life expectations, 26, 50–51, 207,
253; occupations of, 10–11, 41, 51, 66, 82,
113, 118, 130, 169, 178, 179, 182–183, 191,
222, 243, 247–248, 250–251, 311–312,
313–315, 317–319, 326, 337, 350–353, 357,
395, 404, 421; oppression of, 8, 10, 178; sexual exploitation of, 9, 27, 167, 354. *See also*
education
World War I, 31, 73, 82, 102–103, 131, 219,
241, 255
World War II, vii, 4, 223, 223n.3, 234, 304,
307, 416–418
Worn-Out Shoes (movie), 297
Wrangel, P. N., 121, 121n.6

Yiddish. *See* Jews
Young Pioneers, 12, 112, 188, 291, 292, 294–
296

Zarkenau, M. E., 147, 147n.14
Zhdanov, A. A., 380, 380n
Zola, Émile, 370
Zoshchenko, Mikhail, 282
Zweig, Stefan, 422, 422n